Suzuki Burgman Scooters
Service and Repair Manual

by Phil Mather

(4909 - 7AO1 - 336)

Models covered

AN250	249 cc	1998 to 2002
AN400	385 cc	1999 to 2006
AN400	400 cc	2007 to 2015

ABCDE
FGHIJK
LMNOP

© Haynes Publishing 2015

A book in the **Haynes Service and Repair Manual Series**

ISBN 978 1 78521 285 7

British Library Cataloguing in Publication Data
A catalogue record for this book is available from the British Library

Printed in the UK

Haynes Publishing
Sparkford, Yeovil, Somerset BA22 7JJ, England

Haynes North America, Inc
859 Lawrence Drive, Newbury Park, California 91320, USA

Contents

LIVING WITH YOUR SUZUKI

MAINTENANCE

Contents

REPAIRS AND OVERHAUL

The Suzuki Story

by Julian Ryder

From Textile Machinery to Motorcycles

Suzuki were the second of Japan's Big Four motorcycle manufacturers to enter the business, and like Honda they started by bolting small two-stroke motors to bicycles. Unlike Honda, they had manufactured other products before turning to transportation in the aftermath of World War II. In fact Suzuki has been in business since the first decade of the 20th-Century when Michio Suzuki manufactured textile machinery.

The desperate need for transport in post-war Japan saw Suzuki make their first motorised bicycle in 1952, and the fact that by 1954 the company had changed its name to Suzuki Motor Company shows how quickly the sideline took over the whole company's activities. In their first full manufacturing year, Suzuki made nearly 4500 bikes and rapidly expanded into the world markets with a range of two-strokes.

Suzuki didn't make a four-stroke until 1977 when the GS750 double-overhead-cam across-the-frame four arrived. This was several years after Honda and Kawasaki had

established the air-cooled four as the industry standard, but no motorcycle epitomises the era of what came to be known as the Universal Japanese motorcycle better than the GS. So well engineered were the original fours that you can clearly see their genes in the GS500 twins that are still going strong in the mid-1990s. Suzuki's ability to prolong the life of their products this way means that they are often thought of as a conservative company. This is hardly fair if you look at some of their landmark designs, most of which have been commercial as well as critical successes.

The T500 two-stroke twin

the first of a series of 500 cc twins which were good looking, robust and versatile marked the start of mainstream success.

So confident were Suzuki of their two-stroke expertise that they even applied it to the burgeoning Superbike sector. The GT750 water-cooled triple arrived in 1972. It was big, fast and comfortable although the handling and stopping power did draw some comment. Whatever the drawbacks of the road bike, the engine was immensely successful in Superbike and Formula 750 racing. The roadster has its devotees, though, and is now a sought-after bike on the classic Japanese scene. Do not refer to it as the Water Buffalo in such company. Joking aside, the later disc-braked versions were quite civilised, but the audacious idea of using a big two-stroke motor in what was essentially a touring bike was a surprising success until the fuel crisis of the mid-'70s effectively killed off big strokers.

The same could be said of Suzuki's only real lemon, the RE5. This is still the only mass-produced bike to use the rotary (or Wankel) engine but never sold well. Fuel consumption in the mid-teens allied to frightening complexity and excess weight meant the RE5 was a non-starter in the sales race.

Development of the Four-stroke range

When Suzuki got round to building a four-stroke they did a very good job of it. The GS fours were built in 550, 650, 750, 850, 1000 and 1100 cc sizes in sports, custom, roadster and even shaft-driven touring forms over many years. The GS1000 was in on the start of Superbike

One of the later GT750 'kettle' models with front disc brakes

Two-stroke Success

Early racing efforts were bolstered by the arrival of Ernst Degner who defected from the East German MZ team at the Swedish GP of 1961, bringing with him the rotary-valve secrets of design genius Walter Kaaden. The new Suzuki 50 cc racer won its first GP on the Isle of Man the following year and winning the title easily. Only Honda and Ralph Bryans interrupted Suzuki's run of 50 cc titles from 1962 to 1968.

The arrival of the twin-cylinder 125 racer in 1963 enabled Hugh Anderson to win both 50 and 125 world titles. You may not think 50 cc racing would be exciting - until you learn that the final incarnation of the thing had 14 gears and could do well over 100 mph on fast circuits. Before pulling out of GPs in 1967 the 50 cc racer won six of the eight world titles chalked up by Suzuki during the 1960s as well as providing Mitsuo Itoh with the distinction of being the only Japanese rider to win an Isle of Man TT. Mr Itoh still works for Suzuki, he's in charge of their racing program.

Europe got the benefit of Suzuki's two-stroke expertise in a succession of air-cooled twins, the six-speed 250 cc Super Six being the most memorable, but the arrival in 1968 of

Suzuki's GT250X7 was an instant hit in the popular 250 cc 'learner' sector

The GS400 was the first in a line of four-stroke twins

racing in the early 1970s and the GS850 shaft-driven tourer was around nearly 15 years later. The fours spawned a line of 400, 425, 450 and 500 cc GS twins that were essentially the middle half of the four with all their reliability. If there was ever a criticism of the GS models it was that with the exception of the GS1000S of 1980, colloquially known as

the ice-cream van, the range was visually uninspiring.

They nearly made the same mistake when they launched the four-valve-head GSX750 in 1979. Fortunately, the original twin-shock version was soon replaced by the 'E'-model with Full-Floater rear suspension and a full set of all the gadgets the Japanese industry was then

keen on and has since forgotten about, like 16-inch front wheels and anti-dive forks. The air-cooled GSX was like the GS built in 550, 750 and 1100 cc versions with a variety of half, full and touring fairings, but the GSX that is best remembered is the Katana that first appeared in 1981. The power was provided by an 1000 or 1100 cc GSX motor, but wrapped around it was the most outrageous styling package to come out of Japan. Designed by Hans Muth of Target Design, the Katana looked like nothing seen before or since. At the time there was as much anti feeling as praise, but now it is rightly regarded as a classic, a true milestone in motorcycle design. The factory have even started making 250 and 400 cc fours for the home market with the same styling as the 1981 bike.

Just to remind us that they'd still been building two-strokes for the likes of Barry Sheene, in 1986 Suzuki marketed a road-going version of their RG500 square-four racer which had put an end to the era of the four-stroke in 500 GPs when it appeared in 1974. In 1976 Suzuki not only won their first 500 title with Sheene, they sold RG500s over the counter and won every GP with them - with the exception of the Isle of Man TT which the works riders boycotted. Ten years on, the RG500 Gamma gave road riders the nearest experience they'd ever get to riding a GP bike. The fearsome beast could top 140 mph and only weighed 340 lb - the other alleged GP replicas were pussy cats compared to the Gamma's man-eating tiger.

The RG only lasted a few years and is already firmly in the category of collector's item; its four-stroke equivalent, the GSX-R, is still with us and looks like being so for many years. You have to look back to 1985 and its launch to realise just what a revolutionary step the GSX-R750 was: quite simply it was the

The GS750 led the way for a series of four cylinder models

Later four-stroke models, like this GSX1100, were fitted with 16v engines

first race replica. Not a bike dressed up to look like a race bike, but a genuine racer with lights on, a bike that could be taken straight to the track and win.

The first GSX-R, the 750, had a completely new motor cooled by oil rather than water and an aluminium cradle frame. It was sparse, a little twitchy and very, very fast. This time Suzuki got the looks right, blue and white bodywork based on the factory's racing colours and endurance-racer lookalike twin headlights. And then came the 1100 - the big GSX-R got progressively more brutal as it chased the Yamaha EXUP for the heavyweight championship.

And alongside all these mould-breaking designs, Suzuki were also making the best looking custom bikes to come out of Japan, the Intruders; the first race replica trail bike, the DR350; the sharpest 250 Supersports, the RGV250; and a bargain-basement 600, the Bandit. The Bandit proved so popular they went on to build 1200 and 750 cc versions of it. I suppose that's predictable, a range of four-stroke fours just like the GS and GSXs.

Suzuki Burgman

Ever since the motorcycle stopped being a primary means of transport in developed countries manufacturers have been looking for a vehicle they could market to people who aren't necessarily motorcycle enthusiasts. Before the advent of the affordable family car every maker had a range of ride-to-work bikes designed down to a price. Manufacturers like Velocette even produced radical designs like the LE, a fully enclosed flat twin with a monocoque chassis as they tried to find the Holy Grail of a bike they could sell to car drivers. It didn't work, British factory carparks were full of Villiers two-stroke powered lightweights, or they were until Soichiro Honda came up with the most successful motorcycle ever, the Cub. As usual, he had it right. Here was a bike that obviously wasn't a motorcycle but neither was it a scooter. Crucially, it didn't have the engine built in unit with the swinging arm and it had big wheels, so it felt and handled like a motorcycle but had the step-through layout of a scooter. It also had decent weather protection, a vital selling point for anyone you're trying to entice out of the comfort of a car.

Honda kept trying. The first 'big scooter', the Helix arrived in the 1980s. It was too soon. The twist-and-go scooter market hadn't yet boomed and motorcyclists weren't really interested. An attempt to attack the problem from the other direction, the PC800 didn't work either. This was a fully-enclosed softly-tuned V-twin with integral luggage space accessed by raising the pillion seat. Too much like a motorcycle but not enough like one to sell to motorcycle enthusiasts.

In the end it was the scooter boom that started in the late 1990s that laid the foundations for what would become the 'super scooter' or 'maxi scooter.' Big cities all over the world were having trouble coping with the volume of car traffic. In some places,

The 2000 AN400Y

commuting on four wheels became almost impossible. What to do if public transport didn't work for you? The answer was the scooter, a modern automatic-transmission electric-start twist-and-go scooter. Most of them were Italian, with makers like Aprilia and Italjet producing some very stylish examples that went down well with the fashion conscious. But they were still scooters.

The company that got it right was Suzuki. The most conservative of the Japanese factories launched the first models in the Burgman range in the late nineties, a 125, 250 and 400. Against expectations, it was the 400cc version that was the hit. Commuters who had taken to the twist-and-go scooter were ready to spend more money for a higher specification: it was big enough for two adults to travel in comfort, had massive storage space, linked disc brakes front and rear, good lights and brisk performance thanks to

an SOHC 385cc water-cooled motor. Details like the lockable storage boxes on the dash, faired-in indicators and a pillion backrest went down well with the target market and the Burgman was soon a common sight on the streets of cities like Madrid and Milan. Suzuki added more refinement and features, like a 12V power take-off for powering accessories such as a sat-nav. In 2003 the 400 motor got fuel injection and a 650cc version was launched, which could be specced-up with ABS and electric screen and mirrors.

As well as the commuter market, where it was aimed at the urban professional, the Burgman also found success with older enthusiasts and it was quite usual to see maxi scooters in the bike parks at MotoGP events in Spain and Italy. Of course other manufacturers joined in the race for sales but it was Suzuki with the Burgman who had the right product at the right time.

The 2004 AN400K4

0•8 Acknowledgements

Our thanks are due to Bridge Motorcycles of Exeter and Fowlers Motorcycles of Bristol who supplied the models featured in the photographs throughout this manual. We would also like to thank NGK Spark Plugs (UK) Ltd for supplying the colour spark plug condition photos and Draper Tools for some of the tools shown. Julian Ryder wrote the introduction 'The Suzuki Story'.

About this Manual

The aim of this manual is to help you get the best value from your scooter. It can do so in several ways. It can help you decide what work must be done, even if you choose to have it done by a dealer; it provides information and procedures for routine maintenance and servicing; and it offers diagnostic and repair procedures to follow when trouble occurs.

We hope you use the manual to tackle the work yourself. For many simpler jobs, doing it yourself may be quicker than arranging an appointment to get the scooter into a dealer and making the trips to leave it and pick it up. More importantly, a lot of money can be saved by avoiding the expense the shop must pass on to you to cover its labour and overhead costs. An added benefit is the sense of satisfaction and accomplishment that you feel after doing the job yourself.

References to the left or right side of the scooter assume you are sitting on the seat, facing forward.

We take great pride in the accuracy of information given in this manual, but manufacturers make alterations and design changes during the production run of a particular machine of which they do not inform us. No liability can be accepted by the authors or publishers for loss, damage or injury caused by any errors in, or omissions from, the information given.

Buying spare parts

When ordering replacement parts, it is essential to identify exactly the machine for which the parts are required. While in some cases it is sufficient to identify the machine by its title eg 'Burgman 250', any modifications made to components mean that it is usually essential to identify the scooter by its year of production, or better still by its frame or engine number.

To identify your own scooter, refer to the engine and frame numbers as detailed below.

To be absolutely certain of receiving the correct part, not only is it essential to have the scooter engine or frame number to hand, but it is also useful to take the old part for comparison (where possible). Note that where a modified component has superseded the original, a careful check must be made that there are no related parts which have also been modified and must be used to enable the replacement to be correctly refitted; where such a situation is found, purchase all the necessary parts and fit them, even if this means replacing apparently unworn items.

Purchase replacement parts from an authorised Suzuki dealer or someone who specialises in scooter parts; they are more likely to have the parts in stock or can order them quickly from the importer. Pattern parts are available for certain components; if used, ensure these are of recognised quality brands which will perform as well as the original.

Expendable items such as lubricants, spark plugs, some electrical components, bearings, bulbs and tyres can usually be obtained at lower prices from accessory shops, motor factors or from specialists advertising in the national motorcycle press.

Frame and engine numbers

The frame serial number, or VIN (Vehicle Identification Number) as it is often known, is stamped into the right-hand side of the frame, and also appears on an identification plate. The engine number is stamped into the top of the drive belt housing on the left-hand side of the scooter. Both of these numbers should be recorded and kept in a safe place so they can be furnished to law enforcement officials in the event of a theft.

The frame and engine numbers should also be kept in a handy place (such as with your driving licence) so they are always available when purchasing or ordering parts for your scooter.

The frame number is stamped into the frame

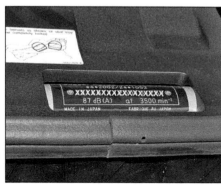

The frame number also appears on the VIN plate

Production year codes

Production years are identified by the model code suffix (e.g. AN250W or AN400K6).

Model code	Production year
AN250W	1998
AN250X	1999
AN250Y	2000
AN250K1	2001
AN250K2/RK2	2002
AN400X	1999
AN400Y	2000
AN400K1	2001
AN400K2/RK2	2002
AN400K3	2003
AN400K4	2004
AN400K5	2005
AN400K6	2006
AN400K7	2007
AN400K8	2008
AN400K9/ZAK9	2009
AN400L0/ZAL0	2010
AN400L1/ZAL1	2011
AN400L2/ZAL2	2012
AN400L3/ZAL3	2013
AN400L4/ZXL4	2014
AN400L5/ZAL5	2015

The engine number is stamped into the drive belt housing

AN250W to Y models

Introduced in 1998, it is powered by a liquid-cooled, single-cylinder four-stroke engine with one overhead camshaft. The engine/transmission unit is constructed from aluminium alloy with the crankcase divided vertically. The left-hand half incorporates the drive belt housing, a variable size drive pulley (variator), and an automatic centrifugal clutch.

The camshaft is driven by a chain from the right-hand side of the crankshaft and the valves are operated by rocker arms. The crankcase incorporates a wet sump, pressure-fed lubrication system with a chain-driven oil pump. A gear-driven balancer shaft is located on the right-hand side of the crankcase and the alternator rotor is mounted on the right-hand end of the crankshaft.

A single 30 mm CV carburettor supplies the fuel and air mixture to the engine and a fully transistorised electronic system ignites the mixture.

An all-steel, twin downtube, cradle frame houses the engine/transmission unit which is pivoted at the front as an integral part of the rear suspension. Rear suspension movement is controlled by a single horizontal shock absorber and rising rate linkage. Front suspension is by conventional, oil-damped telescopic forks.

The front and rear brakes are single, hydraulically operated discs. The front brake is actuated by the right-hand handlebar lever and both front and rear brakes are actuated by the left-hand lever. A cable operated parking brake is linked to the rear brake caliper.

Both front and rear wheels are cast aluminium with tubeless tyres.

AN250K1 and K2 models

A number of modifications were introduced in 2001, most notably to the rear bodywork, tail light unit and passenger handles. The one-piece floor panel was replaced by a three-piece assembly and the original two-piece upper engine mounting was replaced by a single unit.

A catalytic converter was incorporated in the silencer.

AN400X to K2 models

Introduced in 1999 and similar in most respects to the AN250 with the obvious exception of larger engine capacity and carburettor size.

The appearance of the AN400 was updated in 2001 in line with the 250 cc model.

AN400K3 to K6 models

The AN400 was revised in 2003. The new model featured fuel injection with an all-new engine management system. The fuel pump was located in the fuel tank and an oxygen sensor was mounted in the exhaust header pipe.

The bodywork was restyled with a new, twin bulb fox-eye headlight and brake/tail light unit.

AN400K7 model onward

The AN400 was further revised in 2007. The new model featured an all-new dohc engine with cam follower-and-shim valve adjustment. The oil pump was located inside the crankcases.

The instrument cluster featured LED illumination.

The front brake featured twin, hydraulically operated discs. The combined braking system, linking the front and rear brakes, was discontinued. ABS was available from 2009.

Scooter spec

Dimensions and weight

Wheelbase
AN250 models and AN400X to K6 models	1590 mm
AN400K7 model onward	1585 mm

Overall length
AN250 models and AN400X to K6 models	2260 mm
AN400K7 model onward	2270 mm

Overall height
AN250W and X models	1360 mm
AN250Y to K2 and AN400X to K2 models	1365 mm
AN400K3 to K6 models	1375 mm
AN400K7 model onward	1385 mm

Overall width
AN250 models and AN400X to K2 models	765 mm
AN400K3 model onward	760 mm

Seat height
AN250 models and AN400X to K6 models	695 mm
AN400K7 model onward	710 mm

Ground clearance
AN250W and X models	125 mm
AN250Y to K2 and AN400X to K2 models	120 mm
AN400K3 model onward	125 mm

Dry weight
AN250W and X models	159 kg
AN250Y to K2 models	166 kg
AN400X to K2 models	174 kg
AN400K3 to K6 models	184 kg
AN400K7 model onward	199 kg

Engine

Type	Liquid-cooled, 4-stroke single cylinder
Capacity	
AN250W to K2 models	249 cc
AN400X to K6 models	385 cc
AN400K7 model onward	400 cc
Bore x stroke	
AN250W to K2 models	73.0 x 59.6 mm
AN400X to K6 models	83.0 x 71.2 mm
AN400K7 model onward	81.0 x 77.6 mm
Compression ratio	
AN250W to K2 models	10.5:1
AN400X to K6 models	10.2:1
AN400K7 model	11.2:1
Camshaft	
AN250W to K2 models	SOHC, chain driven
AN400X to K6 models	SOHC, chain driven
AN400K7 model onward	DOHC, chain driven
Lubrication	Wet sump
Ignition	Transistorised electronic ignition
Fuel system	
AN250W to K2 models	Keihin CVK30 carburettor
AN400X to K2 models	Keihin CVK36 carburettor
AN400K3 model onward	Fuel injection
Clutch	Centrifugal, fully automatic
Transmission	Variator and drive belt

Chassis

Type	Duplex steel tube cradle
Rake	
AN250W to K2 models	27.0°
AN400X to K2 models	26.57°
AN400K3 to K6 models	27.0°
AN400K7 model onward	25.20°
Trail	
AN250 models and AN400X to K6 models	106 mm
AN400K7 model onward	102 mm
Front suspension	
Type	Telescopic forks
Travel	
AN250 models and AN400X to K6 models	100 mm
AN400K7 model onward	110 mm
Adjustments	None
Rear suspension	
Type	Rising rate linkage with single shock
Wheel travel	100 mm
Adjustments	Spring pre-load
Tyre sizes	
Front	
AN250 models and AN400X to K6 models	110/90 13M/C 55P
AN400K7 model onward	120/80 14M/C 58S
Rear	
AN250 models and AN400X to K6 models	130/70 13M/C 63P
AN400K7 model onward	150/70 13M/C 64S
Brakes	
Front	
AN250 models and AN400X to K6 models	Single disc with two-piston sliding caliper
AN400K7 model onward	Twin discs with two-piston sliding calipers
Rear – all models	Single disc with two-piston sliding caliper

Professional mechanics are trained in safe working procedures. However enthusiastic you may be about getting on with the job at hand, take the time to ensure that your safety is not put at risk. A moment's lack of attention can result in an accident, as can failure to observe simple precautions.

There will always be new ways of having accidents, and the following is not a comprehensive list of all dangers; it is intended rather to make you aware of the risks and to encourage a safe approach to all work you carry out on your bike.

Asbestos

● Certain friction, insulating, sealing and other products - such as brake pads, clutch linings, gaskets, etc. - contain asbestos. Extreme care must be taken to avoid inhalation of dust from such products since it is hazardous to health. If in doubt, assume that they do contain asbestos.

Fire

● Remember at all times that petrol is highly flammable. Never smoke or have any kind of naked flame around, when working on the vehicle. But the risk does not end there - a spark caused by an electrical short-circuit, by two metal surfaces contacting each other, by careless use of tools, or even by static electricity built up in your body under certain conditions, can ignite petrol vapour, which in a confined space is highly explosive. Never use petrol as a cleaning solvent. Use an approved safety solvent.

● Always disconnect the battery earth terminal before working on any part of the fuel or electrical system, and never risk spilling fuel on to a hot engine or exhaust.

● It is recommended that a fire extinguisher of a type suitable for fuel and electrical fires is kept handy in the garage or workplace at all times. Never try to extinguish a fuel or electrical fire with water.

Fumes

● Certain fumes are highly toxic and can quickly cause unconsciousness and even death if inhaled to any extent. Petrol vapour comes into this category, as do the vapours from certain solvents such as trichloro-ethylene. Any draining or pouring of such volatile fluids should be done in a well ventilated area.

● When using cleaning fluids and solvents, read the instructions carefully. Never use materials from unmarked containers - they may give off poisonous vapours.

● Never run the engine of a motor vehicle in an enclosed space such as a garage. Exhaust fumes contain carbon monoxide which is extremely poisonous; if you need to run the engine, always do so in the open air or at least have the rear of the vehicle outside the workplace.

The battery

● Never cause a spark, or allow a naked light near the vehicle's battery. It will normally be giving off a certain amount of hydrogen gas, which is highly explosive.

● Always disconnect the battery ground (earth) terminal before working on the fuel or electrical systems (except where noted).

● If possible, loosen the filler plugs or cover when charging the battery from an external source. Do not charge at an excessive rate or the battery may burst.

● Take care when topping up, cleaning or carrying the battery. The acid electrolyte, evenwhen diluted, is very corrosive and should not be allowed to contact the eyes or skin. Always wear rubber gloves and goggles or a face shield. If you ever need to prepare electrolyte yourself, always add the acid slowly to the water; never add the water to the acid.

Electricity

● When using an electric power tool, inspection light etc., always ensure that the appliance is correctly connected to its plug and that, where necessary, it is properly grounded (earthed). Do not use such appliances in damp conditions and, again, beware of creating a spark or applying excessive heat in the vicinity of fuel or fuel vapour. Also ensure that the appliances meet national safety standards.

● A severe electric shock can result from touching certain parts of the electrical system, such as the spark plug wires (HT leads), when the engine is running or being cranked, particularly if components are damp or the insulation is defective. Where an electronic ignition system is used, the secondary (HT) voltage is much higher and could prove fatal.

Remember...

✗ **Don't** start the engine without first ascertaining that the transmission is in neutral.

✗ **Don't** suddenly remove the pressure cap from a hot cooling system - cover it with a cloth and release the pressure gradually first, or you may get scalded by escaping coolant.

✗ **Don't** attempt to drain oil until you are sure it has cooled sufficiently to avoid scalding you.

✗ **Don't** grasp any part of the engine or exhaust system without first ascertaining that it is cool enough not to burn you.

✗ **Don't** allow brake fluid or antifreeze to contact the machine's paintwork or plastic components.

✗ **Don't** siphon toxic liquids such as fuel, hydraulic fluid or antifreeze by mouth, or allow them to remain on your skin.

✗ **Don't** inhale dust - it may be injurious to health (see Asbestos heading).

✗ **Don't** allow any spilled oil or grease to remain on the floor - wipe it up right away, before someone slips on it.

✗ **Don't** use ill-fitting spanners or other tools which may slip and cause injury.

✗ **Don't** lift a heavy component which may be beyond your capability - get assistance.

✗ **Don't** rush to finish a job or take unverified short cuts.

✗ **Don't** allow children or animals in or around an unattended vehicle.

✗ **Don't** inflate a tyre above the recommended pressure. Apart from overstressing the carcass, in extreme cases the tyre may blow off forcibly.

✔ **Do** ensure that the machine is supported securely at all times. This is especially important when the machine is blocked up to aid wheel or fork removal.

✔ **Do** take care when attempting to loosen a stubborn nut or bolt. It is generally better to pull on a spanner, rather than push, so that if you slip, you fall away from the machine rather than onto it.

✔ **Do** wear eye protection when using power tools such as drill, sander, bench grinder etc.

✔ **Do** use a barrier cream on your hands prior to undertaking dirty jobs - it will protect your skin from infection as well as making the dirt easier to remove afterwards; but make sure your hands aren't left slippery. Note that long-term contact with used engine oil can be a health hazard.

✔ **Do** keep loose clothing (cuffs, ties etc. and long hair) well out of the way of moving mechanical parts.

✔ **Do** remove rings, wristwatch etc., before working on the vehicle - especially the electrical system.

✔ **Do** keep your work area tidy - it is only too easy to fall over articles left lying around.

✔ **Do** exercise caution when compressing springs for removal or installation. Ensure that the tension is applied and released in a controlled manner, using suitable tools which preclude the possibility of the spring escaping violently.

✔ **Do** ensure that any lifting tackle used has a safe working load rating adequate for the job.

✔ **Do** get someone to check periodically that all is well, when working alone on the vehicle.

✔ **Do** carry out work in a logical sequence and check that everything is correctly assembled and tightened afterwards.

✔ **Do** remember that your vehicle's safety affects that of yourself and others. If in doubt on any point, get professional advice.

● If in spite of following these precautions, you are unfortunate enough to injure yourself, seek medical attention as soon as possible.

Engine oil level

✔ Make sure you have a supply of the correct oil available.
✔ Support the scooter in an upright position on level ground.
✔ Check the oil level when the engine is cold, otherwise wait about 3 minutes after the engine has been run to allow the oil level to stabilise.

The correct oil

☐ Modern, high-revving engines place great demands on their oil. It is very important that the correct oil for your scooter is used.
☐ Always top up with a good quality 4-stroke motorcycle oil of the specified type and viscosity and do not overfill the engine. A different viscosity oil can be used if required (see oil viscosity chart).

Oil type	API grade SG, SH or SJ, to JASO MA standard
Oil viscosity	SAE 10W-40

Scooter care

● If you have to add oil frequently, you should check whether you have any oil leaks. If there is no sign of oil leakage from the joints and gaskets the engine could be burning oil due to worn piston rings or failed valve stem seals (see *Fault Finding*).

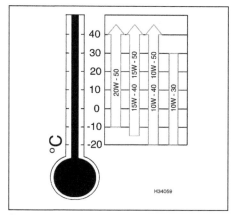

Select the oil best suited to the conditions

AN250W to K2 models and AN400X to K6 models

1 The engine has a dipstick on the oil filler cap (arrowed). Unscrew the cap and wipe the dipstick on clean rag.

2 Insert the dipstick into its hole, but do not screw it in. Withdraw the dipstick – the oil level should lie between the 'F' and 'L' lines on the dipstick.

3 If the level is on or below the 'L' line, top-up to the 'F' line with the recommended grade and type of oil. Do not overfill. If necessary, drain off any excess (see Chapter 1).

AN400K7 models onward

1 Clean the oil level window in the lower right-hand side of the engine. With the scooter held upright, the oil level should lie between the 'F' and 'L' lines.

2 If the level is on or below the 'L' line, remove the filler cap.

3 Top the engine up to the 'F' line with the recommended grade and type of oil. Do not overfill. If necessary, drain off any excess (see Chapter 1).

Suspension and steering

● Check that the front and rear suspension operates smoothly without binding.

● Check that the rear suspension is adjusted as required.
● Check that the steering moves smoothly from lock-to-lock.

Coolant level

> **Warning: DO NOT leave open containers of coolant about, as it is poisonous.**

Before you start:

✔ Make sure you have a supply of coolant available (use either an ethylene glycol based pre-mixed coolant, or prepare a mix of 50% distilled water and 50% corrosion inhibited ethylene glycol anti-freeze).

✔ Support the scooter in an upright position on level ground.

✔ Always check the coolant level when the engine is cold.

Scooter care:

● Use only the specified coolant mixture. It is important that anti-freeze is used in the system all year round, and not just in the winter. Do not top the system up using only water, as the system will become too diluted.

● Do not overfill the reservoir tank. If the coolant is significantly above the upper 'F' line at any time, the surplus should be siphoned or drained off to prevent the possibility of it being expelled under pressure.

● If the coolant level falls steadily, check the system for leaks (see Chapter 1). If no leaks are found and the level continues to fall, it is recommended that the machine is taken to a Suzuki dealer for a pressure test.

1 On AN250 and AN400X to K6 models, open the centre cockpit panel in the kick panel to access the reservoir tank.

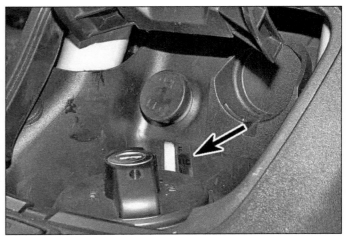

2 On AN400K7 models onward, open the fuel filler flap. Note the coolant level indicator.

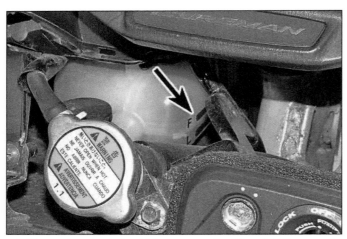

3 The coolant level should lie between the 'F' and 'L' lines on the reservoir.

4 If topping up is required, remove the reservoir filler cap. Top the coolant level up with the recommended coolant mixture, using a funnel to avoid spillage. Fit the cap securely, then close the panel or filler flap.

Brake fluid levels

> **Warning: Brake fluid can harm your eyes and damage painted surfaces, so use extreme caution when handling and pouring it and cover surrounding surfaces with rag. Do not use brake fluid that has been standing open for some time, as it absorbs moisture from the air which can cause a dangerous loss of braking effectiveness.**

Before you start:

✔ Make sure you have a supply of fresh DOT 4 brake fluid.
✔ Support the scooter in an upright position.
✔ Position the handlebars so the reservoir you are checking is as level as possible.
✔ Wrap a rag around the reservoir to ensure that any spillage does not come into contact with painted or plastic surfaces.

Scooter care:

● On AN250 models and AN400X to K6 models, the right-hand handlebar lever operates the front brake; the left-hand lever operates the combined front and rear brakes.

● The fluid in the brake master cylinder reservoirs will drop slightly as the brake pads wear down.
● If either fluid reservoir requires repeated topping-up this is an indication of a leak somewhere in the system, which should be investigated immediately.
● Check for signs of fluid leakage from the brake hoses, unions and components – if found, rectify immediately.
● Check the operation of the brakes before riding the scooter; if there is evidence of air in the system (spongy feel to lever), it must be bled as described in Chapter 7.

1 The brake fluid level is visible through the window in the rear of the reservoir.

2 If the level is below the LOWER level line, undo the two reservoir cover screws and remove the cover, diaphragm plate and diaphragm.

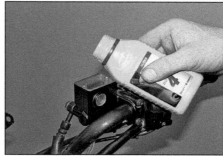

3 Top-up with fresh DOT 4 brake fluid.

4 The fluid level should be just below the line inside the reservoir. Take care to avoid spills (see Warning above).

5 Wipe any moisture out of the diaphragm using a paper towel.

6 Ensure that the diaphragm is correctly seated, then install the diaphragm plate and cover. Tighten the cover screws securely.

Legal and safety checks

Lighting and signalling:

● Take a minute to check that the headlight, tail light, brake light, instrument lights and turn signals all work correctly.
● Check that the horn sounds when the switch is operated.
● A working speedometer graduated in mph is a statutory requirement in the UK.

Safety:

● Check that the throttle grip rotates smoothly and snaps shut when released, in all steering positions. Also check for the correct amount of freeplay (see Chapter 1).

● Check that stand return spring holds the stand securely up when retracted.
● Check that both brakes work correctly when applied and free off when released.

Fuel:

● This may seem obvious, but check that you have enough fuel, to complete your journey. If you notice signs of leakage – rectify the cause immediately.
● Ensure you use the correct grade unleaded petrol (gasoline), minimum 91 octane.

Tyres

The correct pressures:

● The tyres must be checked when **cold**, not immediately after riding. Note that incorrect tyre pressures will cause abnormal tread wear and unsafe handling. Low tyre pressures may cause the tyre to slip on the rim or come off.

● Use an accurate pressure gauge. Many forecourt gauges are wildly inaccurate. If you buy your own, spend as much as you can justify on a quality gauge.

● Correct air pressure will increase tyre life and provide maximum stability and ride comfort.

Tyre care:

● Check the tyres carefully for cuts, tears, embedded nails or other sharp objects and excessive wear. Operation of the scooter with excessively worn tyres is extremely hazardous, as traction and handling are directly affected.

● Check the condition of the tyre valve and ensure the dust cap is in place.

AN250W to K2 models and AN400X to K6 models

Loading	Front	Rear
Rider only	25 psi (1.75 Bar)	29 psi (2.0 Bar)
Rider with passenger	25 psi (1.75 Bar)	41 psi (2.8 Bar)

AN400K7 models onward

Loading	Front	Rear
Rider only	25 psi (1.75 Bar)	29 psi (2.0 Bar)
Rider with passenger	25 psi (1.75 Bar)	36 psi (2.5 Bar)

● Pick out any stones or nails which may have become embedded in the tyre tread. If left, they will eventually penetrate through the casing and cause a puncture.

● If tyre damage is apparent, or unexplained loss of pressure is experienced, seek the advice of a tyre fitting specialist without delay.

Tyre tread depth:

● At the time of writing UK law requires that tread depth on machines over 50 cc must be at least 1 mm over 3/4 of the tread breadth all the way around the tyre, with no bald patches (see *MOT Test Checks* in the *Reference* section). Many riders, however, consider 2 mm tread depth minimum to be a safer limit.

● Tyres incorporate wear indicators in the tread. Identify the triangular pointer on the tyre sidewall to locate the indicator bar and replace the tyre if the tread has worn down to the bar.

1 Check the tyre pressures when the tyres are cold and keep them properly inflated.

2 Measure tread depth at the centre of the tyre using a tread depth gauge or ruler.

3 Tyre tread wear indicator bar (arrowed) and its location marking (usually an arrow, a triangle or the letters TWI) on the sidewall.

Chapter 1
Routine maintenance and servicing

Contents

Degrees of difficulty

Easy, suitable for novice with little experience	**Fairly easy,** suitable for beginner with some experience	**Fairly difficult,** suitable for competent DIY mechanic	**Difficult,** suitable for experienced DIY mechanic	**Very difficult,** suitable for expert DIY or professional 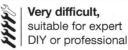

Introduction

1 This Chapter is designed to help the home mechanic maintain his/her scooter for safety, economy, long life and peak performance.

2 Deciding where to start or plug into a service schedule depends on several factors. If the warranty period on your scooter has just expired, and if it has been maintained according to the warranty standards, you will want to pick up routine maintenance as it coincides with the next mileage or calendar interval. If you have owned the machine for some time but have never performed any maintenance on it, then you may want to start at the nearest interval and include some additional procedures to ensure that nothing important is overlooked. If you have just had a major engine overhaul, then you will want to start the maintenance routine from the beginning as with a new machine. If you have a used scooter and have no knowledge of its history or maintenance record, you may desire to combine all the checks into one large service initially and then settle into the maintenance schedule prescribed.

3 Before beginning any maintenance or repair, clean your scooter thoroughly, especially around the suspension, brakes, engine and transmission covers. Cleaning will help ensure that dirt does not contaminate the working parts and will allow you to detect wear and damage that could otherwise easily go unnoticed.

4 Certain maintenance information is sometimes printed on decals attached to the scooter. If the information on the decals differs from that included here, use the information on the decal.

Note 1: *The Pre-ride checks detailed at the beginning of this manual cover those items which should be inspected on a daily basis. Always perform the pre-ride inspection at every maintenance interval (in addition to the procedures listed).*

The intervals listed below are the intervals recommended by the manufacturer for each particular operation during the model years covered in this manual. Your owner's manual may have different intervals for your model.

Note 2: *An initial (one-off) service will be performed by a Suzuki dealer after the first 600 miles (1000 km) from new. Thereafter, the scooter should be serviced according to the intervals specified in the service schedules which follow.*

AN250 models

Servicing specifications, lubricants and torque settings

Drive belt minimum width
    AN250W to Y . . . . 21.7 mm
    AN250K1 and K2 . . . . 21.6 mm
Idle speed. . . . . 1500 rpm
Spark plug type
    Standard. . . . . NGK CR8EK/ND U24ETR
    Stop-start riding . . . . NGK CR7EK/ND U22ETR
    Continuous high speed riding . . . . NGK CR9EK/ND U27ETR
Spark plug electrode gap. . . . . 0.6 to 0.7 mm
Tyre pressures . . . . see Pre-ride checks
Throttle twistgrip freeplay . . . . 2 to 4 mm
Valve clearance
    Intake . . . . 0.08 to 0.13 mm
    Exhaust. . . . . 0.17 to 0.22 mm
Air filter oil. . . . . Dedicated filter oil or engine oil
Engine oil . . . . SAE 10W-40, API grade SG, SH or SJ, to JASO MA standard
Engine oil capacity . . . . 2.0 litres
Gearbox oil. . . . . SAE 10W-40, API grade SG
Gearbox oil capacity . . . . 190 ml
Brake fluid . . . . DOT 4
Coolant capacity . . . . 1.5 litres
Torque settings
    Cooling system bleed bolt . . . . 10 Nm
    Engine oil drain plug. . . . . 23 Nm
    Gearbox oil filler plug . . . . 23 Nm
    Gearbox oil level and drain plugs. . . . . 12 Nm
    Spark plug . . . . 11 Nm

Service intervals – AN250 models

Note: *Always perform the Pre-ride checks before every service interval – see the beginning of this Manual.*

	Text section in this Chapter	Every 3000 miles (5000 km)	Every 6000 miles (10,000 km)	Further intervals
Engine air filter – clean*	1	1800 miles (3000 km)		
Drive belt cooling fan filter – clean*	2	1800 miles (3000 km)		
Valve clearances – check and adjust	3	✓		
Spark plug	4	check	change	
Exhaust system bolts – check	5	✓		
Throttle cable – check and adjust	6	✓		
Fuel hose – check	7	✓		renew every 4 years
Idle speed – check and adjust	8	✓		
Engine oil – change	9	✓		
Engine oil filter – change	9		✓	
Cooling system hoses – check	10	✓		renew every 4 years
Coolant	10			change every 2 years
Brake pads – check	11	✓		
Brake fluid – check	11	✓		change every 2 years
Brake hoses – check	11	✓		renew every 4 years
Wheels and tyres – check	12	✓		
Steering head bearings – check	13	✓		
Nuts and bolts – tightness check	14	✓		
Gearbox oil – check	15		✓	
Suspension – check	16		✓	
Drive belt	17			check every 7500 miles (12,000 km)
Secondary air system	18		✓	renew hoses every 4 years

* *Clean the filters more often if the scooter is ridden in dusty conditions.*

AN400X to K2 models

Servicing specifications and lubricants

Drive belt minimum width	22.0 mm
Idle speed	1300 to 1500 rpm
Spark plug type	
Standard	NGK CR7E/ND U22ESR-N
Continuous high speed riding	NGK CR9E, CR8E/ND U27ESR-N, U24ESR-N
Spark plug electrode gap	0.7 to 0.8 mm
Tyre pressures	see Pre-ride checks
Throttle twistgrip freeplay	2 to 4 mm
Valve clearance	
Intake	0.08 to 0.13 mm
Exhaust	0.17 to 0.22 mm
Air filter oil	Dedicated filter oil or engine oil
Engine oil	SAE 10W-40, API grade SG, SH or SJ, to JASO MA standard
Engine oil capacity	2.0 litres
Gearbox oil	SAE 10W-40, API grade SG, SH or SJ
Gearbox oil capacity	190 ml
Brake fluid	DOT 4
Coolant capacity	1.5 litres
Torque settings	
Cooling system bleed bolt	10 Nm
Engine oil drain plug	23 Nm
Exhaust system bolts	23 Nm
Gearbox oil filler plug	23 Nm
Gearbox oil level and drain plugs	12 Nm
Spark plug	11 Nm

Service intervals – AN400X to K2 models

Note: *Always perform the Pre-ride checks before every service interval – see the beginning of this Manual.*

	Text section in this Chapter	Every 4000 miles (6000 km)	Every 7500 miles (12,000 km)	Further intervals
Engine air filter – clean*	1	1800 miles (3000 km)		
Drive belt cooling fan filter – clean*	2	1800 miles (3000 km)		
Valve clearances – check and adjust	3		✓	
Spark plug	4	check	change	
Exhaust system bolts – check	5		✓	
Throttle cable – check and adjust	6	✓		
Fuel hose – check	7	✓		renew every 4 years
Idle speed – check and adjust	8	✓		
Engine oil – change	9	✓		
Engine oil filter	9			change every 11,000 miles (18,000 km)
Cooling system hoses – check	10	✓		renew every 4 years
Coolant	10			change every 2 years
Brake pads – check	11	✓		
Brake fluid – check	11	✓		change every 2 years
Brake hoses – check	11	✓		renew every 4 years
Wheels and tyres – check	12	✓		
Steering head bearings – check	13		✓	
Nuts and bolts – tightness check	14	✓		
Gearbox oil – check	15		✓	
Suspension – check	16		✓	
Drive belt – check	17		✓	
Secondary air system	18		✓	renew hoses every 4 years

Clean the filters more often if the scooter is ridden in dusty conditions.

AN400K3 to K6 models

Servicing specifications and lubricants

Drive belt minimum width	20.85 mm
Idle speed	1300 to 1500 rpm
Spark plug type	
Standard	NGK CR7E/ND U22ESR-N
Stop-start riding	NGK CR6E/ND U20ESR-N
Continuous high speed riding	NGK CR8E/ND U24ESR-N
Spark plug electrode gap	0.7 to 0.8 mm
Tyre pressures	see Pre-ride checks
Throttle twistgrip freeplay	2 to 4 mm
Valve clearance	
Intake	0.08 to 0.13 mm
Exhaust	0.17 to 0.22 mm
Air filter oil	Dedicated filter oil or engine oil
Engine oil	SAE 10W-40, API grade SG, SH or SJ, to JASO MA standard
Engine oil capacity	2.0 litres
Gearbox oil	SAE 10W-40, API grade SG, SH or SJ
Gearbox oil capacity	190 ml
Brake fluid	DOT 4
Coolant capacity	1.3 litres
Torque settings	
Cooling system bleed bolt	6 Nm
Engine oil drain plug	23 Nm
Exhaust flange bolts	23 Nm
Exhaust pipe joint nuts	30 Nm
Oil filter cover bolt	10 Nm
Silencer mounting nut	23 Nm
Gearbox oil level, filler and drain plugs	12 Nm
Spark plug	11 Nm

Service intervals – AN400K3 to K6 models

Note: *Always perform the Pre-ride checks before every service interval – see the beginning of this Manual.*

	Text section in this Chapter	Every 4000 miles (6000 km)	Every 7500 miles (12,000 km)	Further intervals
Engine air filter – clean*	1	1800 miles (3000 km)		
Drive belt cooling fan filter – clean*	2	1800 miles (3000 km)		
Valve clearances – check and adjust	3	✓		
Spark plug	4	check	change	
Exhaust system bolts – check	5	✓		
Throttle cable – check and adjust	6	✓		
Fuel hose – check	7	✓		renew every 4 years
Idle speed – check and adjust	8	✓		
Engine oil – change	9	✓		
Engine oil filter	9			change every 11,000 miles (18,000 km)
Cooling system hoses – check	10	✓		renew every 4 years
Coolant	10			change every 2 years
Brake pads – check	11	✓		
Brake fluid – check	11	✓		change every 2 years
Brake hoses – check	11	✓		renew every 4 years
Wheels and tyres – check	12	✓		
Steering head bearings – check	13		✓	
Nuts and bolts – tightness check	14	✓		
Gearbox oil	15		change	
Suspension – check	16		✓	
Drive belt – check	17		✓	renew every 15,000 miles (24,000 km)
Secondary air system	18		✓	renew hoses every 4 years

* *Clean the filters more often if the scooter is ridden in dusty conditions.*

AN400K7 model onward

Servicing specifications and lubricants

Drive belt minimum width	24.1 mm
Spark plug type	
Standard	NGK CR7E/ND U22ESR-N
Continuous high speed riding	NGK CR8E/ND U24ESR-N
Spark plug electrode gap	0.7 to 0.8 mm
Tyre pressures	see Pre-ride checks
Throttle twistgrip freeplay	2 to 4 mm
Valve clearance	
Intake	0.10 to 0.20 mm
Exhaust	0.20 to 0.30 mm
Engine oil	SAE 10W-40, API grade SG, SH or SJ, to JASO MA standard
Engine oil capacity	1.3 litres
Gearbox oil	SAE 10W-40, API grade SG, SH or SJ
Gearbox oil capacity	180 ml
Brake fluid	DOT 4
Coolant capacity	
Radiator and engine	1.7 litres
Coolant reservoir	250 ml
Torque settings	
Cooling system bleed bolt	6 Nm
Engine oil drain plug	23 Nm
Exhaust flange bolts	23 Nm
Exhaust pipe joint bolt	23 Nm
Oil filter cover bolt	10 Nm
Silencer mounting bolt	23 Nm
Gearbox oil drain plug	12 Nm
Gearbox oil level plug	16 Nm
Spark plug	11 Nm

Service intervals – AN400K7 model onward

Note: *Always perform the Pre-ride checks before every service interval – see the beginning of this Manual.*

	Text section in this Chapter	Every 4000 miles (6000 km)	Every 7500 miles (12,000 km)	Further intervals
Engine air filter – clean*	1	1800 miles (3000 km)		renew every 11,000 miles (18,000 km)
Drive belt cooling fan filter – clean*	2	1800 miles (3000 km)		
Valve clearances – check and adjust	3			every 14,500 miles (24,000 km)
Spark plug	4	check	change	
Exhaust system bolts – check	5		✓	
Throttle cable – check and adjust	6	✓		
Fuel hose – check	7	✓		
Engine oil – change	9	✓		
Engine oil filter	9			change every 11,000 miles (18,000 km)
Cooling system hoses – check	10	✓		
Coolant	10			change every 2 years
Brake pads – check	11	✓		
Brake fluid – check	11	✓		change every 2 years
Brake hoses – check	11	✓		renew every 4 years
Wheels and tyres – check	12	✓		
Steering head bearings – check	13		✓	
Nuts and bolts – tightness check	14	✓		
Gearbox oil	15		change	
Suspension – check	16		✓	
Drive belt – check	17		✓	renew every 14,500 miles (24,000 km)

* *Clean the filters more often if the scooter is ridden in dusty conditions.*

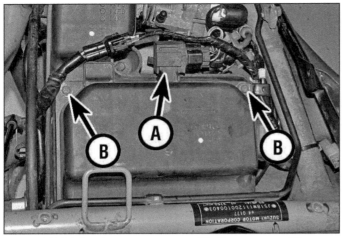

1.2 Intake air pressure sensor (A). Cover screws (B)

1.3 Draw the cover forwards

1.4a Lift out the frame . . .

1.4b . . . and the filter element

Note: *Refer to the model specifications at the beginning of this Chapter for service intervals*

1 Engine air filter

Caution: If the machine is continually ridden in continuously wet or dusty conditions, the filter should be checked more frequently.

AN250 models and AN400X to K6 models

1 Lift up the seat and remove the underseat cover (see Chapter 8).
2 On AN400K3 to K6 models, unclip the intake air pressure sensor from the front edge on the filter housing cover **(see illustration)**.
3 Undo the screws securing the filter cover and remove the cover **(see illustration)**.
4 Lift out the filter frame and filter element **(see illustrations)**. Note which way round the element fits.

5 Fill a suitable container with cleaning solvent, immerse the filter element and wash it **(see illustration)**.
6 Dry the filter element by pressing it inside a folded towel. Never wring the filter dry as it may tear. If the filter is excessively dirty and cannot be cleaned properly, or is torn or damaged in any way, fit a new one.
7 When completely dry, soak the filter element

1.5 Wash the filter element thoroughly

in engine oil or dedicated air filter oil, then squeeze out the excess oil, making sure you do not damage the filter by twisting it.
8 Ensure the inside of the air filter housing is clean. If necessary, remove the underseat panel and left-hand side panel (see Chapter 8), then remove the filter housing drain plug **(see illustration)**.
9 Fit the filter element back into the housing,

1.8 Air filter housing drain plug

1.12 Displace the wiring guide

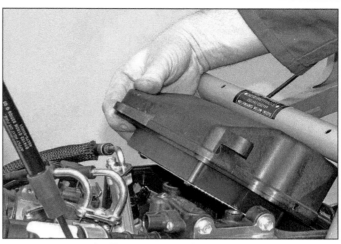

1.13a Remove the air filter cover . . .

1.13b . . . and the filter element

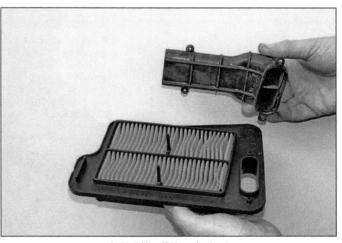

1.14 Lift off the air duct

ensuring it is correctly seated. Install the frame and filter cover and tighten the cover screws securely.

10 Install the remaining components in the reverse order of removal.

AN400K7 model onward

11 Lift up the seat and remove the underseat cover (see Chapter 8).

12 Undo the screw securing the wiring guide to the front, left-hand edge of the air filter housing and displace the wiring **(see illustration)**.

13 Undo the screws securing the filter cover and remove the cover and filter element **(see illustrations)**.

14 Remove the air duct and inspect the filter element **(see illustration)**.

15 If the filter element is excessively dirty, clogged or damaged, fit a new one. **Note:** *A new filter should always be fitted at the specified service interval.*

16 Ensure the inside of the air filter housing

is clean. If necessary, remove the underseat panel and left-hand side panel (see Chapter 8), then remove the filter housing drain plug.

17 Once the inside of the filter housing is clean and dry, install the drain plug and bodywork panels.

18 Fit the filter element into the cover, then install the air duct.

2.2 Remove the cooling fan cover

19 Fit the cover onto the housing and tighten the cover screws securely.

20 Install the wiring guide and the underseat cover.

2 Drive belt cooling fan filter

Caution: If the machine is continually ridden in continuously wet or dusty conditions, the filter should be checked more frequently.

AN250 models and AN400X to K2 models

1 Remove the left-hand belly panel for access (see Chapter 8).

2 Undo the screws securing the fan cover and remove the cover **(see illustration)**.

3 Lift the filter assembly and ease the filter element off its frame, noting how it fits.

4 Follow the procedure in Section 1, Steps 4

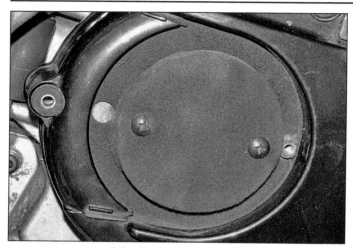

2.7a Undo the screws . . .

2.7b . . . and remove the air filter

and 5, to wash and dry the filter element or, if necessary, replace it with a new one.

5 Installation is the reverse of removal. Ensure the element is completely dry before installation. Do not apply oil to the element.

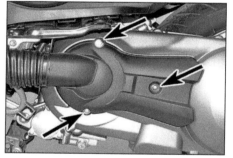

2.8a Undo the screws . . .

AN400K3 model onward

6 Remove the left-hand belly panel for access (see Chapter 8).

7 On AN400K3 to K6 models, undo the screws securing the fan cover and remove the cover **(see illustration 2.2)**. Undo the screws securing the filter assembly and lift it out **(see illustrations)**. Ease the filter element off its frame, noting how it fits.

8 On AN400K7 and later models, undo the screws securing the fan cover and displace the cover **(see illustrations)**. Undo the screws securing the filter and lift it out **(see illustration)**.

9 On AN400K3 to K6 models, follow the procedure in Section 1, Steps 5 and 6, to wash and dry the filter element or, if necessary, replace it with a new one.

10 On AN400K7 and later models, inspect the filter element – if it is excessively dirty, clogged or damaged, fit a new one

11 Installation is the reverse of removal. Do not apply oil to the element.

3 Valve clearances

Special tool: *A set of feeler gauges is necessary for this job (see Step 8).*

1 The engine must be completely cool for this maintenance procedure, so let the scooter stand overnight before beginning.

AN250 models and AN400X to K6 models

2 On AN250 models and AN400X to K2 models, remove the underseat cover, front frame cover, left-hand floor panel and storage compartment (see Chapter 8). Remove the air filter housing and the carburettor (see Chapter 4A).

2.8b . . . and displace the cover

2.8c Remove the air filter

3.5 Unscrew the timing inspection cap

3.8 Turn the crankshaft, not the variator nut

3 On AN400K3 to K6 models, remove the left-hand floor panel and storage compartment (see Chapter 8). Remove the air filter housing and the throttle body assembly (see Chapter 4B).

4 On all models, remove the drive belt cooling fan filter element (see Section 2).

5 Unscrew the timing inspection cap from the alternator cover **(see illustration)**. Discard the sealing washer as a new one must be fitted.

6 Remove the spark plug (see Section 4).

7 Remove the valve cover (see Chapter 2A or 2B as appropriate).

8 To check the valve clearances the engine must be turned to position the piston at top dead centre (TDC) on its compression stroke – at this point all the valves will be closed. The engine can be turned using a suitable spanner on the flats on the end of the crankshaft **(see illustration)**.

9 Turn the engine anti-clockwise until the line next to the T mark on the alternator rotor

aligns with the static timing mark – the arrow next to the inspection hole **(see illustration)**. Ensure the line on the end of the camshaft is parallel with the valve cover mating surface **(see illustration)**. With the piston at TDC on its compression stroke there should be a small amount of freeplay between the rocker arms and the valve stems i.e. they should not be in direct contact with each other **(see illustration)**. **Note:** *If there is no freeplay in the rocker arms it is likely the piston is at TDC on its exhaust stroke. Rock the crankshaft backwards and forwards to check – if the rocker arms depress the exhaust valves and the intake valves alternately the engine is in the wrong position.* Turn the engine one complete rotation anti-clockwise until the line next to the T mark on the alternator rotor again aligns with the static timing mark and the line on the end of the camshaft is parallel with the valve cover mating surface **(see illustrations 3.9a and b)**. Check for a small amount of freeplay

between the rocker arms and the valve stems **(see illustration 3.9c)**.

10 Check the clearance of each valve by inserting a feeler gauge of the same thickness as the correct valve clearance (see *Specifications* at the beginning of this

3.9a Static timing mark and line on alternator rotor

3.9b Check position of line on camshaft

3.9c Check for freeplay in the rocker arms

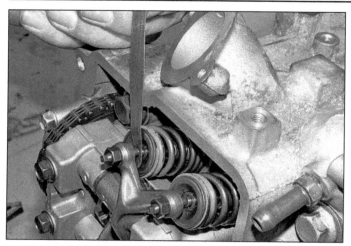

3.10 Check clearance with a feeler gauge

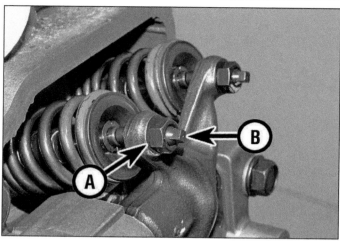

3.11 Locknut (A) and adjuster (B)

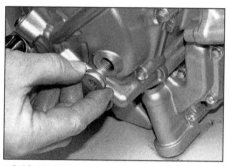

3.18 Unscrew the timing inspection cap

Chapter) in the gap between the rocker arm and the valve stem **(see illustration)**. The exhaust valves are on the front of the cylinder head and the intake valves are on the back. If the clearance is correct, the gauge should be a firm sliding fit – you should feel a slight drag when you pull the gauge out. **Note:** *The intake and exhaust valve clearances are different.*

11 If the clearance is either too large or too small, slacken the locknut on the adjuster in the rocker arm **(see illustration)**. Using a small spanner, turn the adjuster until the gap is as specified, then hold the adjuster still and tighten the locknut. Recheck the clearance after tightening the locknut.

12 When the clearances are correct install the valve cover (see Chapter 2A or 2B as appropriate).

13 Install the timing inspection cap using a new washer **(see illustration 3.5)**.

14 Install the remaining components in the reverse order of removal.

15 On completion, on models fitted with carburettors, check and adjust the idle speed (see Section 8).

AN400K7 model onward

16 Remove the underseat cover, front frame cover, left-hand floor panel and storage compartment (see Chapter 8). Remove the air filter housing and the throttle body assembly (see Chapter 4B).

17 Remove the cooling fan filter element (see Section 2).

18 Unscrew the timing inspection cap from the alternator cover **(see illustration)**. Discard the sealing washer as a new one must be fitted.

19 Remove the spark plug (see Section 4).

20 Remove the valve cover (see Chapter 2B).

21 To check the valve clearances the engine must be turned to position the piston at top dead centre (TDC) on its compression stroke – at this point all the valves will be closed. The engine can be turned using a suitable spanner on the flats on the end of the crankshaft **(see illustration 3.8)**.

22 Turn the engine anti-clockwise until the line on the alternator rotor aligns with the static timing mark – the notch in the inspection hole **(see illustration)**. Ensure the lines on the ends of the camshafts are parallel with the valve cover mating surface and the lines No. 2 (exhaust camshaft sprocket) and No. 3 (intake camshaft sprocket) are at 90° to the mating surface **(see illustration)**.

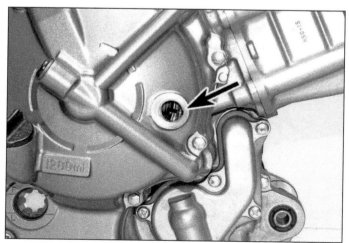

3.22a Line on alternator rotor and static timing mark (arrowed)

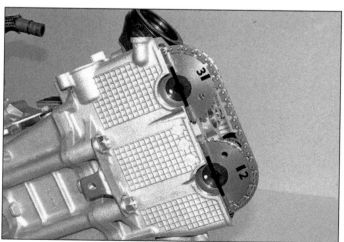

3.22b Timing marks on camshafts and sprockets

3.23 Camshaft holder identification

3.24 Check clearance with a feeler gauge

23 Make a chart or sketch of all valve positions so that a note of each clearance can be made against the relevant valve. The exhaust valves are on the front of the cylinder head and the intake valves are on the back – note the markings on the camshaft holder **(see illustration)**.

24 Check the clearance of each valve by inserting a feeler gauge of the same thickness as the correct valve clearance (see *Specifications* at the beginning of this Chapter) in the gap between the camshaft lobe and the cam follower. The gauge should be a firm sliding fit – you should feel a slight drag when you pull the gauge out **(see illustration)**. If not, use the feeler gauges to obtain the exact clearance. Record the measured clearances on your chart. **Note:** *The intake and exhaust valve clearances are different.*

25 When all clearances have been measured

and recorded, identify whether the clearance on any valve falls outside that specified. If it does, the shim between the follower and the valve must be replaced with one of a thickness which will restore the correct clearance.

26 Changing the shims requires removal of the camshafts (see Chapter 2B). There is no need to remove both camshafts if shims from only intake or exhaust valves need changing. Place rag over the spark plug hole and the cam chain tunnel to prevent a shim dropping into the engine on removal.

27 With the camshaft removed, lift out the cam follower of the valve in question using a magnet or suction tool such as a valve lapping tool **(see illustration)**. Retrieve the shim from either the inside of the follower or pick it out of the top of the valve using a magnet or a small screwdriver with a dab of grease on it – the shim will stick to the grease **(see illustrations)**.

Do not allow the shim to fall into the engine.

28 The shim size should be marked on its upper face – a shim marked 170 is 1.70 mm thick – but the shim should be measured

3.27a Lift out the cam follower

3.27b Shim will be inside follower . . .

3.27c . . . or on top of the valve

3.28 Measure shim with a micrometer

with a micrometer to check that it has not worn **(see illustration)**. If the shim has worn undersize, this must be taken into account and the valve clearance adjusted accordingly.

29 Using the appropriate shim selection chart, find where the measured valve clearance and existing shim thickness values intersect and read off the shim size required **(see illustrations)**.

Note: *If an exact match to a shim thickness cannot be found on the chart, use the nearest size to it e.g. existing shim measures 1.68 mm, nearest thickness on chart 1.70 mm.*

30 New shims are available in 0.05 mm increments from 1.20 to 2.20 mm and can be obtained from a Suzuki dealer. **Note:** *If the required replacement shim is greater than 2.20 mm (the largest available), the valve is probably not seating correctly due to a build-up of carbon deposits or valve damage. Remove the valve for checking (see Chapter 2).*

31 When replacing a shim, lubricate it with engine oil and fit it into its recess in the top of the valve with the size marking facing up **(see illustration)**. Check that the shim is correctly seated, then lubricate the follower and install it over the valve **(see illustration)**. Repeat the process for any other valves as required, then install the camshafts (see Chapter 2B).

32 Rotate the crankshaft several turns to seat

MEASURED TAPPET CLEARANCE (mm)	PRESENT SHIM SIZE (mm)																				
	1.20	1.25	1.30	1.35	1.40	1.45	1.50	1.55	1.60	1.65	1.70	1.75	1.80	1.85	1.90	1.95	2.00	2.05	2.10	2.15	2.20
0.00-0.04			1.20	1.25	1.30	1.35	1.40	1.45	1.50	1.55	1.60	1.65	1.70	1.75	1.80	1.85	1.90	1.95	2.00	2.05	2.10
0.05-0.09		1.20	1.25	1.30	1.35	1.40	1.45	1.50	1.55	1.60	1.65	1.70	1.75	1.80	1.85	1.90	1.95	2.00	2.05	2.10	2.15
0.10-0.20	SPECIFIED CLEARANCE/NO ADJUSTMENT REQUIRED																				
0.21-0.25	1.30	1.35	1.40	1.45	1.50	1.55	1.60	1.65	1.70	1.75	1.80	1.85	1.90	1.95	2.00	2.05	2.10	2.15	2.20		
0.26-0.30	1.35	1.40	1.45	1.50	1.55	1.60	1.65	1.70	1.75	1.80	1.85	1.90	1.95	2.00	2.05	2.10	2.15	2.20			
0.31-0.35	1.40	1.45	1.50	1.55	1.60	1.65	1.70	1.75	1.80	1.85	1.90	1.95	2.00	2.05	2.10	2.15	2.20				
0.36-0.40	1.45	1.50	1.55	1.60	1.65	1.70	1.75	1.80	1.85	1.90	1.95	2.00	2.05	2.10	2.15	2.20					
0.41-0.45	1.50	1.55	1.60	1.65	1.70	1.75	1.80	1.85	1.90	1.95	2.00	2.05	2.10	2.15	2.20						
0.46-0.50	1.55	1.60	1.65	1.70	1.75	1.80	1.85	1.90	1.95	2.00	2.05	2.10	2.15	2.20							
0.51-0.55	1.60	1.65	1.70	1.75	1.80	1.85	1.90	1.95	2.00	2.05	2.10	2.15	2.20								
0.56-0.60	1.65	1.70	1.75	1.80	1.85	1.90	1.95	2.00	2.05	2.10	2.15	2.20									
0.61-0.65	1.70	1.75	1.80	1.85	1.90	1.95	2.00	2.05	2.10	2.15	2.20										
0.66-0.70	1.75	1.80	1.85	1.90	1.95	2.00	2.05	2.10	2.15	2.20											
0.71-0.75	1.80	1.85	1.90	1.95	2.00	2.05	2.10	2.15	2.20												
0.76-0.80	1.85	1.90	1.95	2.00	2.05	2.10	2.15	2.20													
0.81-0.85	1.90	1.95	2.00	2.05	2.10	2.15	2.20														
0.86-0.90	1.95	2.00	2.05	2.10	2.15	2.20															
0.91-0.95	2.00	2.05	2.10	2.15	2.20																
0.96-1.00	2.05	2.10	2.15	2.20																	
1.01-1.05	2.10	2.15	2.20																		
1.06-1.10	2.15	2.20																			
1.11-1.15	2.20																				

H31236

3.29a Shim selection chart – intake valves

MEASURED TAPPET CLEARANCE (mm)	PRESENT SHIM SIZE (mm)																				
	1.20	1.25	1.30	1.35	1.40	1.45	1.50	1.55	1.60	1.65	1.70	1.75	1.80	1.85	1.90	1.95	2.00	2.05	2.10	2.15	2.20
0.05-0.09			1.20	1.25	1.30	1.35	1.40	1.45	1.50	1.55	1.60	1.65	1.70	1.75	1.80	1.85	1.90	1.95	2.00	2.05	
0.10-0.14		1.20	1.25	1.30	1.35	1.40	1.45	1.50	1.55	1.60	1.65	1.70	1.75	1.80	1.85	1.90	1.95	2.00	2.05	2.10	
0.15-0.19	1.20	1.25	1.30	1.35	1.40	1.45	1.50	1.55	1.60	1.65	1.70	1.75	1.80	1.85	1.90	1.95	2.00	2.05	2.10	2.15	
0.20-0.30	SPECIFIED CLEARANCE/NO ADJUSTMENT REQUIRED																				
0.31-0.35	1.30	1.35	1.40	1.45	1.50	1.55	1.60	1.65	1.70	1.75	1.80	1.85	1.90	1.95	2.00	2.05	2.10	2.15	2.20		
0.36-0.40	1.35	1.40	1.45	1.50	1.55	1.60	1.65	1.70	1.75	1.80	1.85	1.90	1.95	2.00	2.05	2.10	2.15	2.20			
0.41-0.45	1.40	1.45	1.50	1.55	1.60	1.65	1.70	1.75	1.80	1.85	1.90	1.95	2.00	2.05	2.10	2.15	2.20				
0.46-0.50	1.45	1.50	1.55	1.60	1.65	1.70	1.75	1.80	1.85	1.90	1.95	2.00	2.05	2.10	2.15	2.20					
0.51-0.55	1.50	1.55	1.60	1.65	1.70	1.75	1.80	1.85	1.90	1.95	2.00	2.05	2.10	2.15	2.20						
0.56-0.60	1.55	1.60	1.65	1.70	1.75	1.80	1.85	1.90	1.95	2.00	2.05	2.10	2.15	2.20							
0.61-0.65	1.60	1.65	1.70	1.75	1.80	1.85	1.90	1.95	2.00	2.05	2.10	2.15	2.20								
0.66-0.70	1.65	1.70	1.75	1.80	1.85	1.90	1.95	2.00	2.05	2.10	2.15	2.20									
0.71-0.75	1.70	1.75	1.80	1.85	1.90	1.95	2.00	2.05	2.10	2.15	2.20										
0.76-0.80	1.75	1.80	1.85	1.90	1.95	2.00	2.05	2.10	2.15	2.20											
0.81-0.85	1.80	1.85	1.90	1.95	2.00	2.05	2.10	2.15	2.20												
0.86-0.90	1.85	1.90	1.95	2.00	2.05	2.10	2.15	2.20													
0.91-0.95	1.90	1.95	2.00	2.05	2.10	2.15	2.20														
0.96-1.00	1.95	2.00	2.05	2.10	2.15	2.20															
1.01-1.05	2.00	2.05	2.10	2.15	2.20																
1.06-1.10	2.05	2.10	2.15	2.20																	
1.11-1.15	2.10	2.15	2.20																		
1.16-1.20	2.15	2.20																			
1.21-1.25	2.20																				

H31237

3.29b Shim selection chart – exhaust valves

3.31a Install shim on top of the valve

3.31b Lubricate the followers on installation

4.3 Pull off the spark plug cap

4.4a Unscrew the spark plug . . .

the new shim(s), then check the clearances again (Steps 22 to 24).

33 When the clearances are correct install the valve cover (see Chapter 2B).

34 Install the timing inspection cap using a new washer **(see illustration 3.18)**.

35 Install the remaining components in the reverse order of removal.

4 Spark plug

Check and adjustment

1 Make sure your spark plug socket is the correct size (16 mm) before attempting to remove the plug.

2 Remove the front frame cover and, on AN400K3 to K6 models, the left-hand side panel for access (see Chapter 8).

3 Pull off the spark plug cap **(see illustration)**. **Note:** *Pull on the cap, not the HT lead – the cap is screwed into the lead and may become disconnected.*

4 Ensure the spark plug socket is located correctly over the plug and unscrew the plug from the cylinder head **(see illustrations)**.

Note: *On AN400K7 and later models, the plug is deeply recessed.*

5 Compare your spark plug to the colour spark plug reading chart on the inside rear cover. Look for excessive deposits and evidence of a cracked or chipped insulator around the centre electrode.

6 Inspect the electrodes for wear. Both the centre and side electrode should have square edges and the side electrode should be of uniform thickness.

7 Check the condition of the threads and washer, and the ceramic insulator body for cracks and other damage.

8 If the electrodes are not excessively worn, and if the deposits can be easily removed with a wire brush, the plug can be re-gapped and re-used (if no cracks or chips are visible in the insulator). If in doubt concerning the condition of the plug, replace it with a new one, as the expense is minimal.

9 Before installing the plug, make sure it is the correct type and heat range and check the gap between the electrodes **(see illustrations)**. Compare the gap to that specified and adjust as necessary. If the gap must be adjusted, bend the side electrode only and be very careful not to chip or crack the insulator nose **(see illustration)**. Make sure the washer is in place before installing the plug.

4.4b . . . and lift it out of the cylinder head

10 Since the cylinder head is made of aluminium, which is soft and easily damaged, first thread the plug into the head by hand. Once the plug is finger-tight, tighten it securely with the spark plug socket, then reconnect the plug cap.

 HAYNES HiNT *A stripped plug thread in the cylinder head can be repaired with a thread insert.*

11 Fit a new spark plug at the specified service interval.

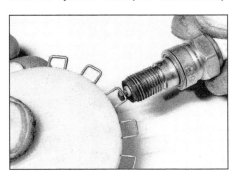

4.9a Using a wire type gauge to measure the spark plug electrode gap

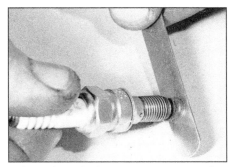

4.9b Using a feeler gauge to measure the spark plug electrode gap

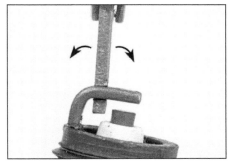

4.9c Adjust the electrode gap by bending the side electrode only

5 Exhaust system check

1 Remove the right-hand belly panel (see Chapter 8).
2 Check that all the exhaust system fixings are tightened to the torque settings specified at the beginning of Chapter 4A or 4B as appropriate. Note that on AN400K7 and later models the silencer front pipe is secured to the exhaust header pipe by a clamp.
3 If there is evidence of leakage at any of the joints, including the header pipe to the cylinder head, but the fixings are tightened correctly, it is likely that the gasket has failed. Do not over-tighten the fixings. Disassemble the exhaust system and renew the gasket (see Chapter 4A or 4B as appropriate).

4 Where fitted, check that the oxygen sensor is tightened correctly.
Note: *The nuts securing the silencer front pipe to the header pipe flange are prone to corrode on their studs. To ensure easy disassembly, as when removing the rear wheel, unscrew each nut in turn and apply copper or nickel based grease to the threads. The grease will also ensure that the nuts can be tightened to the correct torque setting.*

6 Throttle cables

1 Ensure the throttle twistgrip rotates easily from fully closed to fully open with the handlebars turned at various angles, and that the twistgrip returns automatically to the fully closed position released.

2 If the throttle sticks, this is probably due to a cable fault. Follow the procedure in Chapter 4A or 4B, as appropriate, and disconnect the opening and closing cables at the twistgrip end, then lubricate them using a pressure adapter and aerosol cable lubricant **(see illustrations)**.
3 If the throttle action is still stiff, remove the body panels as appropriate to access the cables and check for a trapped or damaged section. If required, follow the procedure in Chapter 4A or 4B and install new cables.
4 With the throttle operating smoothly, check for a small amount of freeplay in the opening cable, measured in terms of the amount of twistgrip rotation before the throttle opens, and compare the amount to the specification at the beginning of this Chapter **(see illustration)**.
5 If there is insufficient or excessive freeplay,

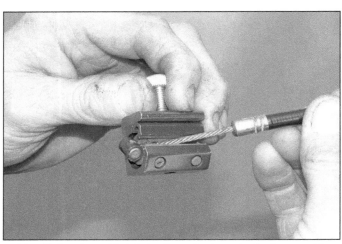

6.2a Fitting the cable lubricating adapter onto the inner cable

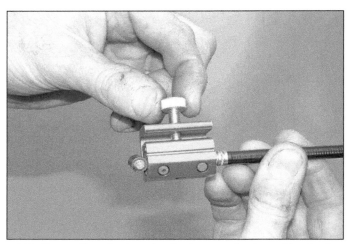

6.2b Ensure the adapter grips the inner and outer cables firmly

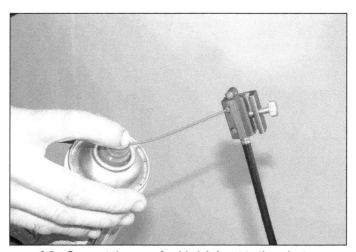

6.2c Connect the can of cable lubricant to the adapter

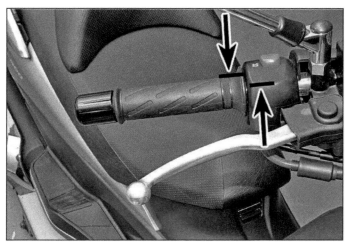

6.4 Throttle cable freeplay is measured in terms of twistgrip rotation

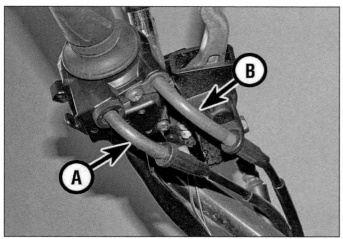

6.5 Closing cable (A) and opening cable (B)

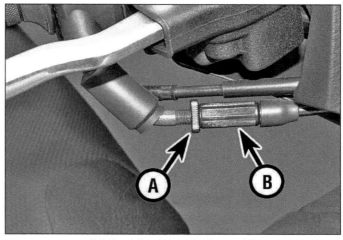

6.6 Lockring (A) and adjuster (B)

on all except AN400K7 and later models, first loosen the lockring on the closing cable adjuster and turn the adjuster all the way in **(see illustration)**.

6 On all models, now loosen the lockring on the opening cable adjuster and turn the adjuster in or out until the specified amount of freeplay is evident at the twistgrip **(see illustration 6.5)**. Tighten the lockring **(see illustration)**.

7 If the adjuster has reached its limit of adjustment, replace the cable with a new one (see Chapter 4A or 4B).

8 If applicable, turn the adjuster on the closing cable out until all freeplay in the cable has been removed, then tighten the lockring.

9 Check that the twistgrip freeplay is still correct and readjust if necessary.

10 Start the engine and check the idle speed. If the idle speed is too high, this could be due to incorrect adjustment of the opening cable. Loosen the locknut and turn the adjuster in – if the idle speed falls as you do, there is insufficient freeplay in the cable. Reset the adjuster (see Step 6). **Note:** *The idle speed should not change as the handlebars are turned. If it does, the throttle cable is routed incorrectly. Rectify the problem before riding the scooter.*

7 Fuel system

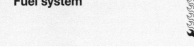

⚠ **Warning: Petrol is extremely flammable, so take extra precautions when you work on any part of the fuel system. Don't smoke or allow open flames or bare light bulbs near the work area, and don't work in a garage where a natural gas-type appliance is present. If you spill any fuel**

on your skin, rinse it off immediately with soap and water. When you perform any kind of work on the fuel system, wear safety glasses and have a fire extinguisher suitable for a Class B type fire (flammable liquids) on hand.

1 Remove the front frame cover, the left, right-hand and the centre floor panel for access to the fuel tank and carburettor or throttle body assembly (see Chapter 8).

2 On AN250 and AN400X to K2 models, check the fuel tank, fuel filter, pump, carburettor and fuel hose for signs of leakage (see Chapter 4A)

3 On AN400K3 and later models, check the fuel tank, throttle body and fuel hose for signs of leakage (see Chapter4B).

4 In particular check that there is no leakage from the fuel hose or the hose unions. Renew the fuel hose if it is cracked or deteriorated. Ensure the hose clips are secure and fit new ones if they are corroded or sprained.

5 On AN250 and AN400X to K2 models, inspect the fuel filter for accumulations of sediment and fit a new filter if necessary (see Chapter 4A).

6 On AN400K3 and later models, the fuel filter system is incorporated in the fuel pump assembly located inside the fuel tank. If fuel starvation is suspected, carry-out fuel pressure and delivery checks (see Chapter 4B). Alternatively, follow the procedure in Chapter 4B to remove the fuel pump assembly and inspect the fuel strainer on the bottom of the pump.

7 All models are fitted with a fuel tank pressure control valve which allows air into the tank as fuel is used by the engine, but restricts the outlet of fuel vapour into the atmosphere. A fuel cut-off valve prevents fuel leaking through the pressure control valve in the event of the scooter falling over. If either

of the valves ceases to work normally, of if the hose between them becomes blocked or trapped, fuel starvation will occur. See Chapter 4A or 4B as applicable for details.

8 Idle speed

⚠ *Warning: Do not allow exhaust gases to build up in the work area; either perform the check outside or use an exhaust gas extraction system*

AN250 models and AN400X to K2 models

1 The idle speed (engine running with the throttle twistgrip closed) should be checked and adjusted when it is obviously too high or too low. Before adjusting the idle speed, make sure the throttle cable is correctly adjusted (see Section 6) and check the spark plug gap (see Section 4).

2 The engine should be at normal operating temperature.

3 Support the machine on its centre stand and make sure the rear wheel is clear of the ground. Lift up the seat and remove the underseat cover to access the carburettor (see Chapter 8).

4 These scooters are not fitted with a tachometer – if a test tachometer is not available to check the idle speed, it is sufficient to ensure that at idle the engine speed is steady and does not falter, and that it is not so high that the automatic transmission engages. Otherwise, connect the test tachometer according to the manufacturer's instructions.

5 The idle speed adjuster screw is located

8.5 Location of the idle speed adjuster screw – carburettor models

8.12 Location of the idle speed adjuster screw – AN400K3 to K6 models

on the carburettor (see illustration). With the engine running, turn the screw clockwise to increase idle speed, and anti-clockwise to decrease it. If a tachometer is available, set the idle speed to match the specification at the beginning of this Chapter.

6 Snap the throttle open and shut a few times, then recheck the idle speed. If necessary, repeat the adjustment procedure.

7 If a smooth, steady idle can't be achieved, the fuel/air mixture may be incorrect (see Chapter 4A) or the engine air filter may need cleaning (see Section 1). Check the valve clearances (see Section 3).

8 With the idle speed correctly adjusted, recheck the throttle cable freeplay (see Section 6).

AN400K3 to K6 models

9 Refer to Steps 1 and 2, then support the machine on its centre stand and make sure the rear wheel is clear of the ground.

10 Remove the underseat cover and the left-hand side panel to access the throttle body assembly (see Chapter 8).

11 If available, connect a test tachometer according to the manufacturer's instructions,

otherwise check the engine speed against the tachometer in the instrument cluster.

12 The idle speed adjuster is located on the throttle body (see illustration). With the engine running, turn the adjuster clockwise to decrease idle speed, and anti-clockwise to increase it. Set the idle speed to match the specification at the beginning of this Chapter.

13 Snap the throttle open and shut a few times, then recheck the idle speed. If necessary, repeat the adjustment procedure.

14 If a smooth, steady idle can't be achieved, reset the idle speed adjuster to the standard setting (see Chapter 4B).

15 Check the engine air filter (see Section 1). Check the valve clearances (see Section 3).

16 If all the components are good, check the IAP sensor vacuum hose and the IAC valve – note that faults with either of these components should normally be indicated by the fuel injection system warning light (see Chapter 4B).

AN400K7 model onward

17 On these scooters the idle speed is governed electronically by the ECM and is not adjustable. However, if the idle speed is erratic, follow the procedure in Chapter 4B,

Section 12, to remove the valve and clean it. On installation, set the valve to its pre-set position using the Suzuki mode select switch as described.

9 Engine oil and filters

 Warning: Be careful when draining the oil, as the exhaust pipe, the engine, and the oil itself can cause severe burns.

Oil change

1 Regular oil changes are the single most important maintenance procedure you can perform. The oil not only lubricates the internal parts of the engine, transmission and clutch, but it also acts as a coolant, a cleaner, a sealant, and a protector. Because of these demands, the oil takes a terrific amount of abuse and should be replaced as specified with new oil of the recommended grade and type.

> **HAYNES HINT** Saving a little money on the difference in cost between a good oil and a cheap oil won't pay off if the engine is damaged.

2 Before changing the oil, warm up the engine so the oil will drain easily. Support the bike on its centrestand on level ground.

3 Position a drain tray below the engine – the oil drain plug is on the underside of the engine on the left-hand side (see illustrations).

4 Unscrew the oil filler cap to vent the crankcase and to act as a reminder that there is no oil in the engine (see Pre-ride checks).

9.3a Location of the oil drain plug – AN250 and AN400X to K6 models

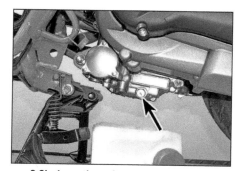

9.3b Location of the oil drain plug – AN400K7-on models

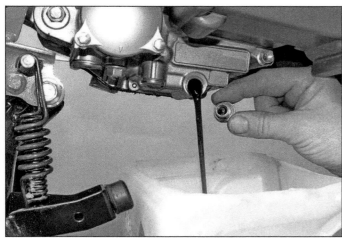

9.5a Drain the oil into a suitable container

9.5b Use tin snips to cut the old washer off

5 Unscrew the drain plug and allow the oil to drain into the tray **(see illustration)**. Note the location of the sealing washer on the drain plug and discard it as a new one must be fitted – you may have to cut the old one off **(see illustration)**.

> **HAYNES HiNT** *To help determine whether any abnormal or excessive engine wear is occurring, place a strainer between the engine and the drain tray so that any debris in the oil is filtered out and can be examined. If there are flakes or chips of metal in the oil, then something is drastically wrong internally and the engine will have to be disassembled for inspection and repair.*

6 When the oil has completely drained, install the drain plug using a new sealing washer and tighten it to the torque setting specified at the beginning of this Chapter **(see illustration)**. Do not overtighten it as the threads in the crankcase are easily damaged.

7 Refill the engine to the correct level using the specified grade and type of oil (see *Pre-ride checks*). Check the condition of the O-ring on the filler cap and renew it if necessary. Install the filler cap securely.
8 Start the engine and let it run for two or three minutes. Shut it off, wait a few minutes, then check the oil level. If necessary, add more oil to bring it up to the correct level.
9 Check around the drain plug for leaks.
10 The old oil drained from the engine cannot be re-used and should be disposed of properly. Check with your local refuse disposal company, disposal facility or environmental agency to see whether they will accept the used oil for recycling. Don't pour used oil into drains or onto the ground.

Note: It is antisocial and illegal to dump oil down the drain. To find the location of your local oil recycling bank in the UK, call 08708 506 506 or visit www.oilbankline.org.uk

9.6 Fit a new sealing washer on the drain plug

Filter change

11 Follow the procedure in Steps 2 to 5 to drain the engine oil.
12 Position the drain tray below the oil filter cover **(see illustrations)**. Note the position of the arrow on the cover. Undo the bolts securing the cover and remove it, noting the location of the spring inside the cover **(see illustration)**. Discard the cover O-ring as a new one must be fitted.

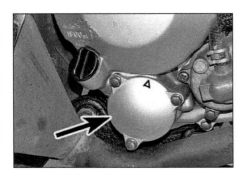

9.12a Location of the oil filter cover – AN250 and AN400X to K6 models

9.12b Location of the oil filter cover – AN400K7-onmodels

9.12c Note the spring inside the cover

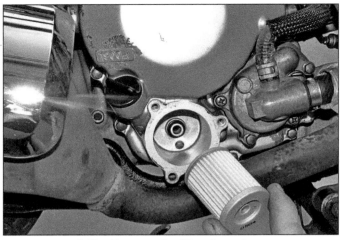

9.13a Draw out the filter element . . .

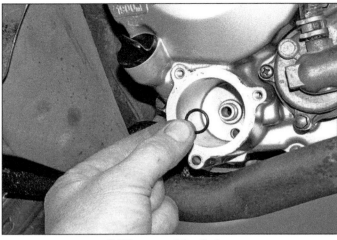

9.13b . . . and the O-ring

9.15 Fit a new O-ring in the cover groove

9.17 Remove the oil strainer cover

13 Draw out the filter element, noting how it fits, and the O-ring **(see illustrations)**. Discard the O-ring as a new one must be fitted.

14 Wipe any residual oil out of the filter housing with a clean cloth, then install a new O-ring and filter element, making sure it is the correct way round.

15 Install a new O-ring on the filter cover, ensuring it is located in its groove **(see illustration)**. Lubricate the O-ring with a smear of engine oil.

16 Install the cover as noted on removal **(see illustration 9.12a and b)** and tighten the bolts securely. On AN400K7 and later models, now go to Step 23.

Oil strainer

17 On AN250 models and AN400X to K6 models, position the drain tray below the oil strainer cover on the left-hand side of the engine, then undo the bolts securing the cover and remove it **(see illustration)**. Discard the cover O-ring as a new one must be fitted.

18 Draw out the strainer element, noting how it fits **(see illustration)**.

19 Wash the element carefully in a suitable solvent and inspect the mesh for damage. If the element is damaged fit a new one. If there are flakes or chips of metal in the strainer, then something is drastically wrong internally and the engine will have to be disassembled for inspection and repair.

20 Wipe any residual oil out of the strainer housing with a clean cloth, then install the strainer narrow edge first, with the outside lip facing down **(see illustration)**.

21 Install a new O-ring on the strainer cover, ensuring it is located in its groove **(see**

9.18 Location of the oil strainer

9.20 Ensure the strainer is fitted correctly

9.21 Fit a new O-ring in the cover groove

illustration). Lubricate the O-ring with a smear of engine oil.

22 Install the cover and tighten the bolts securely **(see illustration 9.17)**.

23 Follow the procedure in Steps 7 to 10 to fill the engine with oil.

24 Check around the drain plug, filter and strainer covers for leaks.

10 Cooling system

System check

1 Support the machine on its centre stand. Remove the left and right-hand belly panels, headlight panel and radiator panel to access the coolant hoses, radiator and coolant header tank (see Chapter 8).

2 The coolant hoses will deteriorate with age – examine each hose along its length, looking for cracks, abrasions and other damage. Squeeze each hose at various points. They should feel firm, yet pliable, and return to their original shape when released. If they are cracked or hard, fit new ones (see Chapter 3). **Note:** *The coolant hoses should be renewed at the specified service interval.*

3 Check for evidence of leaks at each cooling system joint. Ensure that the hoses are pushed fully onto their unions and that the hose clips are tight **(see illustrations)**. **Note:** *Check the tension of the hose spring clips and replace them with new ones if they are loose.*

4 Check the radiator for leaks and other damage. Leaks in the radiator leave tell-tale scale deposits or coolant stains on the outside of the core below the leak. If leaks are noted, remove the radiator (see Chapter 3) and have it repaired or replace it with a new one.

Caution: Do not use a liquid leak stopping compound to try to repair leaks.

5 Inspect the radiator fins for mud, dirt and insects which will impede the flow of air through the radiator. If the fins are dirty, remove the radiator (see Chapter 3) and clean it using water or low pressure compressed air directed through the fins from the back. If the fins are bent or distorted, straighten them carefully with a screwdriver **(see illustration)**. If the air flow is restricted by bent or damaged fins over more than 30% of the radiator's surface area, fit a new radiator.

6 Check the seal on the radiator pressure cap for cracks and other damage **(see illustration)**.

10.3a Check the coolant unions for leaks . . .

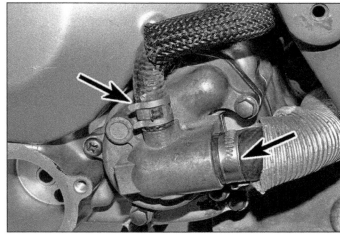

10.3b . . . and ensure the coolant hose clips are tight

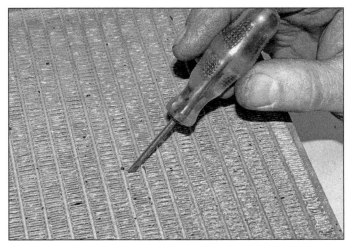

10.5 Straighten damaged fins carefully

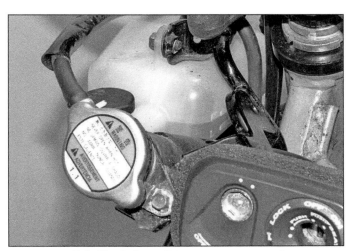

10.6 Check the radiator pressure cap seal

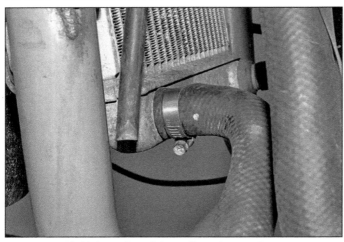

10.14 Location of the radiator bottom hose

10.15 Radiator bottom hose – AN400K7 model onward

If in doubt about the pressure cap's condition, have it tested by a Suzuki dealer or fit a new one.

7 Check the antifreeze content of the coolant with an antifreeze hydrometer. If the system has not been topped-up with the correct coolant mixture (see *Pre-ride checks*) the coolant will be too weak to offer adequate protection. If the hydrometer indicates a weak mixture, drain, flush and refill the system (see below).

8 Install the pressure cap – align the tabs on the cap with the cut-outs in the filler neck, then press the cap down and turn it clockwise until it is tight.

9 Start the engine and let it reach normal operating temperature, then check that here are no leaks. As the coolant temperature increases, the fan should come on automatically and the temperature should begin to drop. If it does not, refer to Chapter 3 and check the fan, the fan switch and fan circuit carefully. Also, if necessary, check the operation of the thermostat.

10 If the coolant level is consistently low, and no evidence of leaks can be found, have the entire system pressure checked by a Suzuki dealer.

Coolant change

⚠️ *Warning: Allow the engine to cool completely before performing this maintenance operation. Also, don't allow anti-freeze to come into contact with your skin or the painted surfaces of the motorcycle. Rinse off spills immediately with plenty of water. Anti-freeze is highly toxic if ingested. Never leave anti-freeze lying around in an open container or in puddles on the floor; children and pets are attracted by its sweet smell and may drink it. Check with local authorities (councils) about disposing of anti-freeze. Many communities have collection centres which will see that anti-freeze is disposed of safely. Anti-freeze is also combustible, so don't store it near open flames.*

11 Remove the body panels as described in Step 1. Remove the radiator panel.

12 Remove the radiator filler cap **(see illustration 10.6)**.

13 On AN250 and AN400X to K2 models, position a suitable container beneath the left-hand side of the radiator. Loosen the clips securing the flexible hoses to the coolant pipes, disconnect the hoses and allow the coolant to drain completely from the system. Next, position the container beneath the water pump on the right-hand side of the scooter. Disconnect the coolant hose and drain the coolant.

14 On AN400K3 to K6 models, position a suitable container beneath the left-hand side of the radiator. Loosen the clip securing the radiator bottom hose, disconnect the hose and allow the coolant to drain completely from the system **(see illustration)**. Next, position the container beneath the water pump on the right-hand side of the scooter **(see illustration 10.3b)**. Disconnect the large diameter coolant hose and drain the coolant.

15 On AN400K7 and later models, position a suitable container beneath the left-hand side

10.16 Drain the coolant header tank

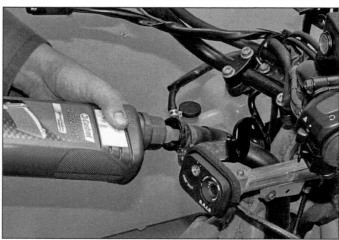

10.19a Add coolant slowly to minimise air locks

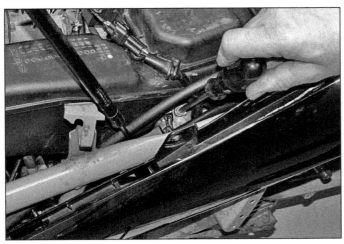

10.19b Release trapped air via the bleed screw

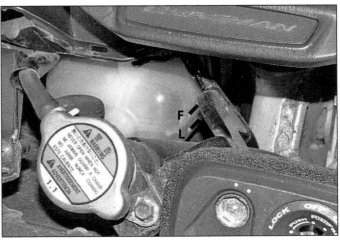

10.20 Fill the reservoir to the F level line

of the radiator. Loosen the clip securing the radiator bottom hose, disconnect the hose and allow the coolant to drain completely from the system **(see illustration)**.

16 On all models, remove the reservoir tank cap, then detach the hose from the bottom of the tank and drain the coolant **(see illustration)**. Rinse the inside of the reservoir with clean water, then reconnect the hose and secure it with the clip.

17 Flush the radiator with clean water by inserting a garden hose in the filler neck. Allow the water to run through until it is clear. If there is a lot of rust in the water, remove the radiator and have it cleaned professionally (see Chapter 3).

18 Reconnect the hoses to the radiator and, if appropriate, the water pump, and tighten the clips securely.

19 Fill the system via the radiator filler neck with the correct coolant mixture (see *Pre-ride checks*). Pour the coolant in slowly to minimise the amount of air entering the system **(see illustration)**. Rock the machine from side to

side to bleed out any trapped air and top-up as necessary. Loosen the bleed screw on the thermostat housing to release any trapped air, then tighten the screw **(see illustration)**.

20 Fill the coolant reservoir to the F level line with coolant mixture and fit the cap **(see illustration)**.

21 Start the engine and allow it to idle for 2 to 3 minutes. Flick the throttle twistgrip part open 3 or 4 times, so that the engine speed rises and falls. Any air trapped in the system should bleed out through the radiator filler neck. Loosen the bleed screw on the thermostat housing to release any trapped air, then tighten the screw.

22 Check the coolant level in the filler neck and top-up as necessary, then fit the radiator filler cap.

23 Do not dispose of the old coolant by pouring it down the drain. Instead pour it into a heavy plastic container, cap it tightly and take it into an authorised disposal site or service station – see *Warning* at the beginning of this sub-Section.

11 Brake system

1 A routine check of the brake system will ensure that any problems are discovered and remedied before the rider's safety is jeopardised.

2 Make sure all brake fasteners, including the reservoir cover screws, brake hose banjo bolts and caliper mounting bolts are tight (refer to *Specifications* in Chapter 7 for torque settings).

3 Make sure the brake light operates when each brake lever is pulled in. The brake light switches are not adjustable. If they fail to operate properly, check their operation (see Chapter 9).

Brake pads

4 To check the condition of the brake pads, look carefully into the caliper either side of the brake disc **(see illustrations)**. Remove the

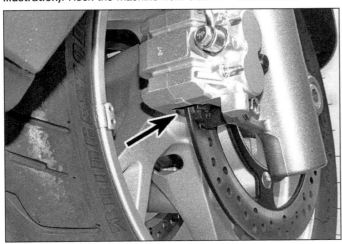

11.4a Check the front brake pads

11.4b Check the rear brake pads – AN400K7-on models

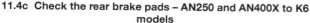

11.4c Check the rear brake pads – AN250 and AN400X to K6 models

11.12 Inspect the brake hoses and connections

rear brake caliper cover, where fitted, and on AN250 and AN400X to K6 models, if necessary, remove the rear wheel (see Chapter 7) to check the rear brake pads **(see illustration)**.

5 The friction material on the original Suzuki pads has wear indicators on the edge next to the backing plate – if the pads are worn down to the indicators (approximately 1.5 mm of friction material remaining) new ones must be fitted. If the pads are dirty or if you are in doubt as to their condition, follow the procedure in Chapter 7 and remove them.

Note: *On AN250 and AN400X to K6 models, two pairs of brake pads are fitted in the front caliper. The upper pair is actuated by the right-hand brake lever and the lower pair is actuated by the left-hand combined front and rear brake lever.*

⚠ **Warning: Brake pads often wear at different rates. If there is any doubt about the condition of either of the pads in a pair, renew them both. Brake failure will result if the friction material wears away completely.**

6 Some aftermarket pads may not have wear indicators – if necessary, remove the pads and measure the thickness of the friction material. If it has worn down to the service limit (approximately 1.5 mm), fit new brake pads.

7 Refer to Chapter 7 for full details of pad removal, inspection and installation.

Brake levers

8 Check the brake levers for looseness, rough action, excessive play and other damage. Replace any worn or damaged parts with new ones (see Chapter 7).

9 The lever pivots should be lubricated periodically to reduce wear and ensure safe and trouble-free operation.

10 In order for the lubricant to be applied where it will do the most good, the lever should be removed (see Chapter 7). However, if chain and cable lubricant is being used, it can be applied to the pivot joint gaps and will usually work its way into the areas where friction occurs. If motor oil or light grease is being used, apply it sparingly as it may attract

dirt (which could cause the controls to bind or wear at an accelerated rate). **Note:** *One of the best lubricants for the control lever pivots is a dry-film lubricant.*

11 If the lever action is spongy, bleed the brakes (see Chapter 7).

Brake hoses

12 Look for leaks at the hose connections. Twist and flex the hose while looking for cracks, bulges and seeping fluid. Check extra carefully where the hose connects to the banjo fittings as this is a common area for hose failure **(see illustration)**.

13 Inspect the banjo fittings; if they are rusted, cracked or damaged, fit new hoses.

14 Inspect the banjo union connections for leaking fluid **(see illustration)**. If they leak when tightened securely, unscrew the banjo bolt and fit new washers (see Chapter 7).

15 Flexible brake hose will deteriorate with age and should be renewed at the specified service interval (see Chapter 7).

11.14 Inspect the banjo union connections for leaking fluid

11.18a Inspect the brake master cylinders . . .

11.18b . . . and the front . . .

11.18c . . . and rear brake calipers

Brake fluid

16 The fluid level in the master cylinder reservoirs should be checked before riding the machine (see *Pre-ride checks*).

17 Brake fluid will degrade over a period of time. Suzuki recommends that it should be changed every 2 years, or whenever a new master cylinder or caliper is fitted. Refer to the brake bleeding and fluid change section in Chapter 7.

Brake caliper and master cylinder seals

18 Check the front and rear brake master cylinders and calipers for signs of leaking fluid **(see illustrations)**.

19 Brake system seals will deteriorate over a period of time and lose their effectiveness. Old master cylinder seals will cause sticky operation of the brake lever; old caliper seals will cause the pistons to stick or fluid to leak out. The seals should be renewed immediately any defects are evident.

20 Replace all the seals in each caliper as a set – a rebuild kit for each caliper is available. Front and rear master cylinder seals are supplied as a kit along with a new piston and spring assembly (see Chapter 7).

Parking brake

21 The parking brake lever operates the rear piston in the rear brake caliper via a cable **(see illustration)**. Pull the brake lever once to engage the brake, and once again to disengage the ratchet and release the brake. If the brake lever will not stay in the ON position it is likely the lever ratchet is damaged (see Chapter 7).

22 If the rear wheel can be turned when the brake is ON, support the machine on its centre stand and adjust the brake as follows.

23 Pull the brake lever ON by one notch on the ratchet. Where fitted, remove the rear brake caliper cover.

24 Loosen the brake adjuster locknut, then turn the adjuster clockwise until resistance is felt and the brake pad is pressing lightly

against the disc **(see illustration)**. Hold the adjuster to prevent it turning and tighten the locknut securely.

25 Check the operation of the parking brake.

26 The wheel should spin freely when the brake is not activated. If the brake is binding, disconnect the cable from the actuating arm on the rear caliper (see Chapter 7). Check that the inner cable slides smoothly in the outer cable. If the action is stiff, inspect along the length of the outer cable for splits and kinks, and the ends of the inner cable for frays, and replace it with a new one if necessary (see Chapter 7).

27 If there are no signs of damage, lubricate the cable using a pressure adapter as described in Section 6. If the cable is still stiff after lubrication, replace it with a new one (see Chapter 7).

28 If the brake cable is in good condition, check the operation of the actuating arm (see Chapter 7).

11.21 Parking brake lever – AN400K3 to K6 models

11.24 Location of the parking brake adjuster

12.2 Checking for play in the front wheel bearings

12.4 Checking for play at the rear wheel

12 Wheels and tyres

Wheels

1 Cast wheels are virtually maintenance free, but they should be kept clean and checked periodically for cracks and other damage. Also check the wheel runout and alignment (see Chapter 7). Never attempt to repair damaged cast wheels; they must be replaced with new ones.
2 The front wheel bearings will wear over a period of time and result in handling problems. Support the scooter on its centre stand and check for any play in the bearings by pushing and pulling the wheel against the hub **(see illustration)**. Also rotate the wheel and check that it turns smoothly.
3 If any play is detected in the hub, or if the wheel does not rotate smoothly (and this is

not due to brake drag), the wheel bearings must be inspected for wear or damage (see Chapter 7).
4 Follow the same procedure to check for play at the rear wheel. There are no rear wheel bearings as such. The wheel is mounted on the rear axle/gearbox output shaft which turns on bearings located inside the gearbox **(see illustration)**. If any play is detected, refer to Chapter 2C to check the gearbox. Also check that play is not due to a fault or wear in the rear suspension (see Section 16).

Tyres

5 Check the tyre condition and tread depth thoroughly – see *Pre-ride checks*.
6 Check that the directional arrow on the tyre sidewall is pointing in the normal direction of wheel rotation.
7 Check the valve stem rubber for signs of damage or deterioration and have it replaced if necessary by a tyre specialist **(see illustration)**.

8 Make sure the valve stem cap is in place and tight. If a tyre looses pressure, and this is not due to damage to the tyre itself, check that the valve is tightened securely – valve keys are available in automotive accessory shops.
9 A smear of soapy water will indicate if the valve is leaking – the leak will show as bubbles in the water. If required, use a valve key to unscrew the old valve and install a new one.
10 If fitted, check that the wheel weights are firmly attached to the rim **(see illustration)**.

13 Steering head bearings

1 The steering head bearings consist of ball or tapered roller bearings which run in races at the top and bottom of the steering head. The races can become dented or rough

12.7 Check the valve stem and cap

12.10 Check the wheel weights are secure

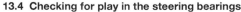

13.4 Checking for play in the steering bearings

15.4 Unscrew the oil level plug

during normal use and the balls will gradually wear. In extreme cases, worn or loose steering head bearings can cause steering wobble – a condition that is potentially dangerous.

2 Support the scooter on its centre stand with the front wheel off the ground. **Note:** *Do not rest the weight of the scooter on the bodywork – have an assistant push down on the rear or place a support under the frame once any bodywork has been removed.*

3 Point the front wheel straight-ahead and slowly turn the handlebars from side-to-side. Any dents or roughness in the bearing races will be felt and the bars will not move smoothly and freely. If the bearings are damaged they must be renewed (see Chapter 6).

4 Next, grasp the front suspension and try to move it forwards and backwards **(see illustration)**. Any freeplay in the steering head bearings will be felt as front-to-rear movement of the steering stem. If play is felt in the bearings, follow the procedure described in Chapter 6 to adjust them.

5 Over a period of time the grease in the bearings will harden or may be washed out. Follow the procedure in Chapter 6 to disassemble the steering stem and re-grease the bearings.

14 Nuts and bolts

1 Since vibration tends to loosen fasteners, all nuts, bolts, screws, etc. should be periodically checked for proper tightness.

2 In addition to the exhaust system (see Section 5), pay particular attention to the following:
- *Spark plug*
- *Carburettor/throttle body clamps*
- *Engine oil drain plug*
- *Gearbox oil drain plug*

- *Stand pivot bolts*
- *Engine mounting bolts*
- *Suspension bolts*
- *Wheel bolts*
- *Brake caliper mounting bolts*
- *Brake hose banjo bolts*
- *Handlebar levers*

3 If a torque wrench is available, use it along with the torque specifications given in this manual.

15 Gearbox oil

Level check – AN250 models and AN400X to K2 models only

1 Support the machine on its centre stand on level ground.

2 Remove the left-hand floor panel and support bracket for access (see Chapter 8). Remove the drive belt cooling fan filter (see Section 2).

3 Remove the outer drive belt cover (see Chapter 2C).

4 Clean the area around the oil level plug, then unscrew the plug **(see illustration)**. Discard the sealing washer as a new one must be fitted.

5 The gearbox oil should be level with the threads of the level hole – to check, add a small amount of the specified grade and type of oil (see *Specifications* at the beginning of this Chapter) using a pump-type oil can. The level is correct when the oil runs out the level hole **(see illustration)**.

 Warning: If the oil level is very low, or oil is leaking from the gearbox, refer to Chapter 2C and inspect the condition of the seals and gaskets and replace them with new ones as necessary.

6 Install the level plug using a new sealing washer and tighten it to the torque setting specified at the beginning of this Chapter. Do not overtighten it as the threads in the case are easily damaged.

7 Install the outer drive belt cover, then install the remaining components in the reverse order of removal.

Note: *On AN250 models and AN400X to K2 models, Suzuki suggests changing the gearbox oil after a 'long period'. To ensure the long life of the gearbox pinions and bearings it is good practice to change the oil on these models at every other service interval, following the procedure below.*

Oil change – All models

8 Support the machine on its centre stand on level ground.

9 Remove the left-hand floor panel and support bracket for access (see Chapter 8). Remove the drive belt cooling fan filter (see Section 2).

10 On AN250 and AN400X to K6 models, undo the screws securing the outer drive belt cover, noting the location of the screws, and remove the cover (see Chapter 2C).

11 On AN400K7 and later models, remove the outer and inner drive belt covers (see Chapter 2C).

15.5 Oil should be level with hole

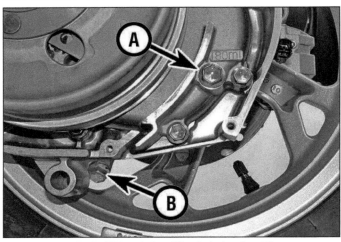
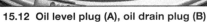

15.12 Oil level plug (A), oil drain plug (B)

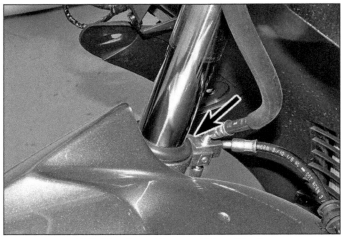

16.3 Check seal (arrowed) for oil leaks

12 Clean the area around the oil level and drain plugs **(see illustration)**.

13 Position a drain tray below the drain plug, then unscrew the filler and drain plugs and drain the oil into the tray. Allow the oil to drain thoroughly. Discard the plug sealing washers as new ones must be fitted.

 To help determine whether any abnormal or excessive geabox wear is occurring, place a strainer below the drain hole so that any debris in the oil is filtered out and can be examined. If there are flakes or chips of metal in the oil, then something is drastically wrong internally and the gearbox will have to be disassembled for inspection and repair.

14 When all the oil has drained, install the drain plug with a new sealing washer and tighten it to the torque setting specified at the beginning of this Chapter. Do not overtighten it as the threads in the case are easily damaged.

15 Refill the gearbox with the correct amount of the specified grade and type of oil – the

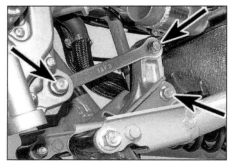

16.11 Ensure pivot assembly bolts are tight

level is correct when the oil runs out the level hole **(see illustration 15.5)**. **Note:** *If the oil is not available in a bottle with a spout, use a pump-type oil can.*

16 Install the level plug using a new sealing washer and tighten it to the torque setting specified at the beginning of this Chapter. Do not overtighten it as the threads in the case are easily damaged.

17 Install the drive belt cover(s), then install the remaining components in the reverse order of removal.

16 Suspension

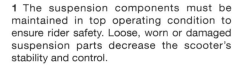

1 The suspension components must be maintained in top operating condition to ensure rider safety. Loose, worn or damaged suspension parts decrease the scooter's stability and control.

Front suspension

2 While standing alongside the scooter, apply the front brake and push on the handlebars to compress the suspension several times. See if it moves up-and-down smoothly without binding. If binding is felt, the suspension should be disassembled and inspected (see Chapter 6).

3 Inspect the area around the dust seal for signs of oil leaks, then carefully lever up the seal using a flat-bladed screwdriver and inspect the area below it **(see illustration)**. If corrosion due to the ingress of water is evident, the seals must be renewed (see Chapter 6).

4 If oil is leaking from the forks, the oil seal has failed and the fork leg must be dismantled and a new seal fitted (see Chapter 6).

5 The chromed finish on the fork inner tubes is prone to corrosion and pitting, so it is advisable to keep them as clean as possible and to spray them regularly with a rust inhibitor.

If corrosion and pitting is evident, tackle it as early as possible to prevent it getting worse and damaging the seals.

6 Check the tightness of all suspension nuts and bolts to ensure none have worked loose. Refer to the torque settings specified at the beginning of Chapter 6.

Rear suspension

7 Follow the procedure in Chapter 8 and remove the belly panel to inspect the full length of the rear shock absorber. Check for fluid leaks and corrosion on the damper rod. If a shock is faulty it should be renewed (see Chapter 6). Check that the upper and lower shock mounting bolts and the suspension linkage bolts are tight.

8 On AN250 models and AN400K7 models onward, ensure that the spring pre-load adjuster is clean and free from corrosion. Using the C-spanner from the toolkit, check that the adjuster moves freely – there are seven pre-load settings (see Chapter 6).

9 On AN400X to K6 models, ensure that the remote spring pre-load adjuster turns freely. Refer to the procedure in Chapter 6 to reset the pre-load.

10 With the aid of an assistant to support the scooter, compress the rear suspension several times. It should move up and down freely without binding. If any binding is felt, the worn or faulty component must be identified and renewed. The problem could be caused by the shock absorber, the linkage bearings or the engine mounting/pivot assembly (see Chapter 6).

11 Support the scooter on its centre stand so that the rear wheel is off the ground. Grip the engine/transmission unit at the rear and attempt to rock it from side to side – there should be no discernible freeplay felt between the engine and frame. If there is movement, check the tightness of the bolts securing the engine pivot assembly **(see illustration)**.

12 Re-check for movement. If freeplay is felt, inspect the bearings and bushes in the pivot

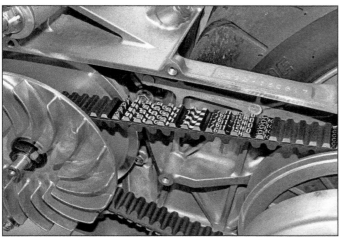

17.3 Inspect drive belt and measure width

17.6 Renew a cracked, frayed or greasy belt

mounting and the bushes in the front of the crankcase for wear (see Chapter 6).

13 Grasp the top of the rear wheel and pull it upwards – there should be no discernible freeplay before the shock begins to compress. Any freeplay indicates a worn shock or shock mountings. The worn components must be renewed (see Chapter 6).

17 Drive belt

1 Remove the left-hand belly panel for access (see Chapter 8). Remove the drive belt cooling fan filter (see Section 2).

2 Remove the outer and inner drive belt covers (see Chapter 2C).

3 The edges of the belt will gradually wear away – black dust inside the casing is evidence of belt wear. Measure the width of the belt and compare the result with the specifications at the beginning of this Chapter **(see illustration)**. If the belt has worn to the specified minimum width a new one must be fitted (see Chapter 2C).

4 On AN400K3 and later models, the drive belt must be renewed at the specified service interval, irrespective of its apparent condition (see Chapter 2C).

5 In the event of premature belt wear, the cause should be investigated (see Chapter 2C).

6 If the belt shows signs of fraying or cracking, or if it is contaminated with oil or grease, it should be renewed **(see illustration)**. Oil or grease inside the casing is evidence that a crankshaft, transmission shaft or clutch assembly seal has failed. Trace the source of the leak and renew the seal.

Note: *If there is any doubt about the condition of the drive belt, replace it with a new one. A broken belt could cause severe damage to engine or transmission components.*

7 Clean any dust from inside the casing before installing the inner drive belt covers.

8 Install the remaining components in the reverse order of removal.

18 Secondary air system

1 On AN250 models and AN400X to K6 models, to reduce the amount of unburned hydrocarbons released in the exhaust gases, a secondary air system is fitted. The system consists of the control valve and the air intake and outlet hoses. In addition, on AN400K3

to K6 models, the air enters the exhaust system through a reed valve located on the valve cover (see Chapter 2A) – the reed valve prevents exhaust gasses passing back though the system into the control valve.

2 Negative pressure pulses in the exhaust system draw filtered air through the control valve into the exhaust port. The air mixes with the exhaust gases, causing any unburned particles of fuel to be burnt in the exhaust port/pipe. This process changes a considerable amount of hydrocarbons and carbon monoxide into relatively harmless carbon dioxide and water.

3 On AN250 models and AN400X to K2 models, the control valve is actuated by vacuum in the intake manifold via a small bore hose. On AN400K3 to K6 models. the control valve is actuated electronically by the ECM.

4 During engine deceleration, when the throttle is closed, the valve shuts off the air supply to the exhaust port, preventing backfiring in the exhaust system.

5 The system requires no maintenance other than to check the condition of the hoses and their unions.

6 On AN250 models and AN400X to K2 models, the control valve is located on the right-hand side of the engine **(see illustration)**. Remove the underseat cover, front frame cover and right-hand floor panel for access (see Chapter 8).

7 On AN400K3 to K6 models, the control valve is located below the throttle body **(see illustration)**. Remove the underseat cover, front frame cover and right-hand floor panel (see Chapter 8), then remove the air filter housing (see Chapter 4B).

8 Check that the hoses are not kinked or pinched, are in good condition and are securely connected at each end. Renew any hoses that are cracked, split or generally deteriorated.

9 If the control valve is thought to be faulty, check its operation as described in Chapter 4A or 4B as applicable.

18.6 Location of the control valve – AN250 and AN400X to K2 models

18.7 Location of the control valve – AN400K3 to K6 models

Chapter 2A
Engine – AN250 and AN400X to K6

Contents

Degrees of difficulty

| **Easy,** suitable for novice with little experience | | **Fairly easy,** suitable for beginner with some experience | | **Fairly difficult,** suitable for competent DIY mechanic | | **Difficult,** suitable for experienced DIY mechanic | | **Very difficult,** suitable for expert DIY or professional | |

Specifications

Cylinder compression

AN250 models
- Standard . . . . 215 psi (14.8 Bar)
- Minimum . . . . 149 psi (10.3 Bar)

AN400 models
- Standard . . . . 128 psi (8.8 Bar)
- Minimum . . . . 90 psi (6.2 Bar)

Lubrication system

Oil pressure . . . . 11 to 23 psi (0.8 to 1.6 Bar) at 3000 rpm, engine warm

Camshaft

Intake lobe height
    Standard.. 33.43 to 33.47 mm
    Service limit (min)... 33.13 mm
Exhaust lobe height
    Standard.. 33.50 to 33.54 mm
    Service limit (min)... 33.20 mm
Journal diameter
    Nominal 22 mm.. 21.959 to 21.980 mm
    Nominal 17.5 mm... 17.466 to 17.484 mm
Camshaft holder journal diameter
    Nominal 22 mm.. 24.012 to 24.025 mm
    Nominal 17.5 mm... 17.512 to 17.525 mm

Journal oil clearance	Standard	Service limit (max)
Nominal 22 mm	0.032 to 0.066 mm	0.15 mm
Nominal 17.5 mm	0.028 to 0.059 mm	0.15 mm

Runout (max)
    AN250... 0.08 mm
    AN400... 0.10 mm

Rocker arms

Shaft diameter... 11.973 to 11.984 mm
Arm internal diameter.. 12.000 to 12.018 mm

Cylinder head

Warpage (max)... 0.05 mm

Valves, guides and springs

Valve clearances.. see Chapter 1
Intake valves
    Head diameter
        AN250 models... 28.3 mm
        AN400 models... 30.5 to 30.7 mm
    Margin thickness (min)..................................... 0.5 mm
    Stem diameter.. 4.975 to 4.990 mm
    Guide bore diameter....................................... 5.000 to 5.012 mm
    Stem-to-guide clearance.................................. 0.010 to 0.037 mm
    Stem deflection (max)...................................... 0.35 mm
    Stem runout (max).. 0.05 mm
    Head runout (max)... 0.03 mm
    Stem end length (min)
        AN250 and AN400X to K2 models..................... 1.8 mm
        AN400K3 to K6 models................................. 1.7 mm
    Seat width.. 0.9 to 1.1 mm
Exhaust valves
    Head diameter
        AN250 models... 25.0 mm
        AN400 models... 26.9 to 27.1 mm
    Margin thickness (min)..................................... 0.5 mm
    Stem diameter.. 4.955 to 4.970 mm
    Guide bore diameter....................................... 5.000 to 5.012 mm
    Stem-to-guide clearance.................................. 0.030 to 0.057 mm
    Stem deflection (max)...................................... 0.35 mm
    Stem runout (max).. 0.05 mm
    Stem end length (min)
        AN250 and AN400X to K2 models..................... 1.8 mm
        AN400K3 to K6 models................................. 1.7 mm
    Head runout (max)... 0.03 mm
    Seat width.. 0.9 to 1.1 mm
Valve spring free length (min)
    AN250 models and AN400X to K2 models
        Inner... 34.9 mm
        Outer.. 38.2 mm
    AN400K3 to K6 models.................................... 38.8 mm
Spring tension
    AN250 models and AN400X to K2 models
        Inner... 28.0 mm with 5.3 to 6.5 kg load
        Outer.. 31.5 mm with 13.1 to 15.1 kg load
    AN400K3 to K6 models.................................... 31.5 mm with 18.2 to 21.0 kg load

Cylinder

Bore diameter
  AN250 models
    Standard . . . . 73.000 to 73.015 mm
    Service limit (max). . . . . 73.090 mm
  AN400 models
    Standard . . . . 83.000 to 83.015 mm
    Service limit (max). . . . . 83.085 mm
Cylinder distortion (max) . . . . 0.05 mm

Piston

Piston diameter (measured 15 mm up from bottom of skirt, at 90° to piston pin axis)
  AN250 models
    Standard . . . . 65.465 to 65.480 mm
    Service limit (min) . . . . 65.380 mm
  AN400 models
    Standard . . . . 82.950 to 82.965 mm
    Service limit (min) . . . . 82.880 mm
Piston-to-bore clearance
  AN250 models
    Standard . . . . 0.040 to 0.050 mm
  AN400 models
    Standard . . . . 0.035 to 0.065 mm
  Service limit (max) . . . . 0.120 mm
Piston pin diameter
  AN250 models
    Standard . . . . 18.996 to 19.000 mm
    Service limit (min) . . . . 18.980 mm
  AN400 models
    Standard . . . . 19.996 to 20.000 mm
    Service limit (min) . . . . 19.980 mm
Piston pin bore diameter in piston
  AN250 models
    Standard . . . . 19.002 to 19.008 mm
    Service limit (max). . . . . 19.030 mm
  AN400 models
    Standard . . . . 20.002 to 20.008 mm
    Service limit (max). . . . . 20.030 mm

Piston rings

Ring end gap (free) – AN250 models
  Top ring
    Standard . . . . 9.3 mm (approx.)
    Service limit (min) . . . . 7.4 mm
  Second ring
    Standard . . . . 7.2 mm
    Service limit (min) . . . . 5.7 mm
Ring end gap (free) – AN400 models
  Top ring
    Standard . . . . 11.3 mm (approx.)
    Service limit (min) . . . . 9.0 mm
  Second ring
    Standard . . . . 7.7 mm
    Service limit (min) . . . . 6.2 mm
Ring end gap (installed) – AN250 models
  Top ring
    Standard . . . . 0.10 to 0.30 mm
    Service limit (max). . . . . 0.50 mm
  Second ring
    Standard . . . . 0.35 to 0.50 mm
    Service limit (max). . . . . 1.0 mm
Ring end gap (installed) – AN400 models
  Top and second rings
    Standard . . . . 0.20 to 0.35 mm
    Service limit (max). . . . . 0.70 mm
Ring thickness – top and second rings . . . . 0.97 to 0.99 mm

Piston rings (continued)

Ring groove width in piston
  AN250 models
    Top and second ring grooves . . . . 1.01 to 1.04 mm
    Oil ring groove . . . . 2.01 to 2.03 mm
  AN400 models
    Top and second ring grooves . . . . 1.01 to 1.03 mm
    Oil ring groove . . . . 2.01 to 2.03 mm
Ring-to-groove clearance
  Top ring (max) . . . . 0.18 mm
  Second ring (max) . . . . 0.15 mm

Connecting rod

Small-end internal diameter
  AN250 models
    Standard . . . . 19.006 to 19.014 mm
    Service limit (max) . . . . 19.040 mm
  AN400 models
    Standard . . . . 20.006 to 20.014 mm
    Service limit (max) . . . . 20.040 mm
Big-end side clearance
  AN250 models and AN400X to K2 models
    Standard . . . . 0.10 to 0.65 mm
    Service limit (max) . . . . 1.0 mm
  AN400K3 to K6 models
    Standard . . . . 0.10 to 0.75 mm
    Service limit (max) . . . . 1.0 mm
Big-end width . . . . 21.95 to 22.00 mm
Deflection . . . . 3.0 mm

Crankshaft

Runout (max) . . . . 0.08 mm
Web outside width . . . . 59.9 to 60.1 mm

Torque wrench settings

Alternator rotor nut . . . . 160 Nm
Alternator cover bolts . . . . 11 Nm
Balancer driven gear nut . . . . 50 Nm
Cam chain tensioner blade bolt . . . . 10 Nm
Cam chain tensioner cap bolt . . . . 8 Nm
Cam chain tensioner mounting bolts . . . . 10 Nm
Camshaft holder bolts . . . . 10 Nm
Camshaft sprocket bolts . . . . 15 Nm
Crankcase bolts
  8 mm bolts
    Initial setting . . . . 13 Nm
    Final setting . . . . 22 Nm
  6 mm bolts . . . . 11 Nm
Crankshaft gear nut . . . . 150 Nm
Cylinder nuts . . . . 6 Nm
Cylinder head 6 mm nuts . . . . 10 Nm
Cylinder head 8 mm nuts . . . . 25 Nm
Cylinder head bolts
  Initial setting . . . . 20 Nm
  Final setting . . . . 42 Nm
Engine mountings
  Lower mounting bolt . . . . 50 Nm
  Upper mounting bolt . . . . 93 Nm
Exhaust manifold bolts . . . . 23 Nm
Oil gallery plugs . . . . 21 Nm
Oil pressure take-off plug . . . . 35 Nm
Oil pump mounting bolts . . . . 10 Nm
Starter clutch housing bolts . . . . 25 Nm
Valve cover bolts . . . . 14 Nm

1 General information

The engine unit is a liquid-cooled, single cylinder 4-stroke. The engine/transmission unit is constructed from aluminium alloy with the crankcase divided vertically into two halves. The left-hand half incorporates the drive belt housing.

The crankcase incorporates a wet sump, pressure-fed lubrication system with a chain-driven oil pump.

The crankshaft assembly is pressed together, the connecting rod big-end running on a caged roller bearing. A gear-driven balancer shaft is located on the right-hand side of the crankcase and the alternator rotor is mounted on the right-hand end of the crankshaft.

The valves are operated by rocker arms and a single overhead camshaft which is chain driven off the crankshaft. Valve clearances are adjusted by screw and locknut adjusters on the rocker arms (see Chapter 1).

Power from the crankshaft is transferred to the rear wheel via a variable size drive pulley (variator), drive belt, automatic centrifugal clutch and reduction gearbox (see Chapter 2C).

2 Component access

Operations possible with the engine in the frame

The components and assemblies listed below can be removed without having to remove the engine/transmission assembly from the frame. If however, a number of areas require attention at the same time, removal of the engine is recommended.

Note that to gain access to engine components it is first necessary to remove the appropriate body panels. Refer to Chapter 8 for full details of panel removal and installation.

- *Valve cover*
- *Cam chain tensioner*
- *Camshaft*
- *Cylinder head*
- *Cylinder*
- *Piston*
- *Starter motor and alternator (see Chapter 9)*
- *Starter clutch and gears*
- *Oil pump*
- *Water pump (see Chapter 3)*
- *Transmission shafts and gears (see Chapter 2C).*

Operations requiring engine removal

It is necessary to remove the engine/transmission assembly from the frame to gain access to the following components.

- *Connecting rod*
- *Crankshaft and bearings*
- *Balancer shaft*

3 Engine wear assessment

Cylinder compression check

Special tool: *A compression gauge with a 10 mm thread size adaptor is required for this test.*

1 Poor engine performance, exhaust smoke, heavy oil consumption and poor starting are indications of low compression. This may be caused by leaking valve stem seals, incorrect valve clearances, a leaking head gasket, or worn piston, rings and/or cylinder wall.

2 Make sure the valve clearances are correctly set (see Chapter 1) and that the cylinder head bolts are tightened to the specified torque setting (see Section 9).

3 Run the engine until it reaches normal operating temperature. Stop the engine and remove the spark plug (see Chapter 1), taking care not to burn your hands on the hot components.

4 Install the adaptor in the spark plug hole, ensuring it is a tight fit, and connect the compression gauge.

5 Turn the ignition ON, open the throttle twistgrip fully and crank the engine over on the starter motor for a few seconds until the gauge reading stabilises. Take a note of the gauge reading, then turn the ignition OFF.

6 Compare the reading obtained with the appropriate specification at the beginning of this Chapter. If it is close to or below the minimum limit, further investigation is required.

7 To distinguish between cylinder/piston wear and valve leakage, use a pump-type oil can to inject a small quantity (teaspoonful) of oil into the cylinder via the spark plug hole – this will serve to temporarily seal the piston rings. Repeat the compression test. If the result shows a noticeable increase in pressure this confirms that the cylinder bore, piston or rings are worn. If there is no change in the reading, the cylinder head gasket or valves are leaking.

8 Although unlikely with the use of modern fuels, a higher than normal compression reading indicates excessive carbon deposits in the combustion chamber.

Engine oil pressure check

Special tool: *A pressure gauge with a suitable hose and adapter and a test tachometer are required for this test.*

9 An oil pressure check will provide useful information about the condition of the engine's lubrication system.

10 To check the oil pressure, a suitable gauge, hose and adapter (which screws into the crankcase) will be needed. Suzuki produces service tools for this purpose. For AN250 and AN400X to K2 models the gauge and adapter are Part Nos. 09915-74510 and 09915-74540. For AN400K3 to K6 models the gauge and adapter are Part Nos. 09915-74511 and 09915-74521.

11 Clean the area around the main oil gallery

3.11 Location of the main oil gallery plug

plug on the underside of the crankcase **(see illustration)**.

12 Position a drain tray underneath the crankcase to catch any residual oil, then unscrew the plug. Discard the sealing washer as a new one must be fitted.

13 Install the adapter and pressure gauge. Connect the test tachometer according to the manufacturer's instructions.

14 Warm the engine up to normal operating temperature (between 10 and 20 minutes running at 2000 rpm) then increase the engine speed to 3000 rpm whilst watching the gauge reading. The oil pressure should be similar to that given in *Specifications* at the beginning of this Chapter.

15 If the pressure is significantly lower than the standard, either the oil pump is faulty, the oil filter is blocked, or there is critical engine wear or damage. Begin diagnosis by checking the oil filter, then the oil pump (see Section 15). If these items are good, it is likely the bearing oil clearances are excessive and the engine needs to be overhauled.

16 If the pressure is too high, either an oil passage is clogged or the wrong grade of oil is being used.

17 Turn the engine OFF. Disconnect the gauge and adapter from the crankcase.

 Warning: Be careful when removing the pressure gauge and adapter as the engine and hot oil can cause severe burns.

18 Install the oil gallery plug using a new sealing washer and tighten it to the torque setting specified at the beginning of this Chapter. Do not overtighten it as the threads in the crankcase are easily damaged.

19 Check the engine oil level (see *Pre-ride checks*).

4 Engine removal and installation

 Warning: The engine is heavy. Removal and installation should be carried out with the aid of an assistant; personal injury or damage could occur if the engine falls or is dropped. If available, an hydraulic or mechanical floor jack should be used to support and lower or raise the engine.

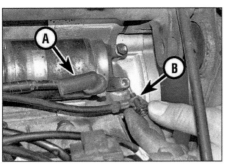

4.8 Starter motor terminal (A) and earth lead (B)

4.9 Engine coolant temperature sensor wiring connector

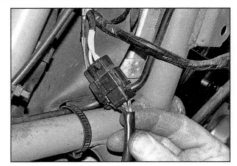

4.11 Alternator and ignition pulse generator/CKP sensor connectors

Removal

1 Support the scooter securely in an upright position using the centerstand. Work can be made easier by raising the machine to a suitable working height on an hydraulic ramp or a suitable platform.

2 Remove the seat, storage compartment and appropriate body panels to gain access to the engine and upper and lower engine mountings (see Chapter 8).

3 Disconnect the negative (-) lead from the battery (see Chapter 8).

4 Drain the engine oil and the coolant (see Chapter 1). Disconnect the coolant hoses from the water pump and the thermostat housing (see Chapter 3).

5 On AN250 and AN400X to K2 models, remove the air filter housing and, if applicable, the secondary air system valve and mounting

bracket (see Chapter 4A). Remove the carburettor (see Chapter 4A).

6 On AN400K3 to K6 models, remove the air filter housing and support bracket, and the throttle body assembly (see Chapter 4B).

7 Plug the engine intake manifold with clean rag to prevent debris falling into the engine.

8 Disconnect the lead from the starter motor terminal, then undo the starter motor mounting bolt securing the starter motor earth (ground) lead and disconnect the lead **(see illustration)**.

9 Disconnect the engine coolant temperature sensor wiring connector **(see illustration)**.

10 Remove the ignition coil (see Chapter 4B or 5 as applicable).

11 Trace the alternator wiring from the cover on the right-hand side of the engine and disconnect it at the connector **(see illustration)**. On AN250 and AN400X to K2 models, disconnect the ignition pulse

generator wiring connector. On AN400K3 to K6 models, disconnect the CKP sensor wiring connector.

12 Remove the silencer and exhaust system, and the silencer mounting bracket (see Chapter 4A).

13 Remove the rear wheel (see Chapter 7). Displace the rear brake caliper and secure it to the machine with a cable-tie to avoid straining the brake hose, then remove the brake disc. On AN400K3 to K6 models, slide the hub off the transmission output shaft.

14 At this point, position an hydraulic or mechanical jack under the engine with a block of wood between the jack head and crankcase. Make sure the jack is centrally positioned so the engine will not topple in any direction when the mounting bolts are removed. Take the weight of the engine on the jack **(see illustration)**.

15 Check that all wiring, cables and hoses are disconnected and clear of the engine.

16 Undo the nut on the lower engine mounting bolt and remove the washer, then withdraw the bolt from the right-hand side **(see illustrations)**. Position the suspension linkage rod assembly clear of the engine mounting lugs.

17 Undo the nut on the upper engine mounting bolt and remove the washer **(see illustration)**.

18 Make sure the engine is properly supported on the jack and have an assistant support it as well. Withdraw the upper mounting bolt from the right-hand side **(see illustration)**.

4.14 Support the engine on a jack

4.16a Undo the nut (arrowed) . . .

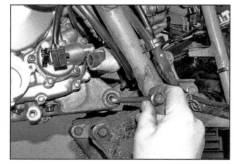

4.16b . . . and withdraw the lower engine mounting bolt

4.17 Upper engine mounting bolt nut and washer

4.18 Withdraw the upper engine mounting bolt

19 Carefully lower the engine and draw it back and out of the frame.
20 If the engine is dirty, particularly around the intake manifold, cylinder and starter motor, wash it thoroughly before starting any dismantling. This will make work much easier and rule out the possibility of dirt falling into some vital component (see Section 5).

Installation

Note: *The mounting bolt nuts are self-locking – it is good practice to renew the nuts when installing the engine.*
21 Clean the threads of the engine mounting bolts.
22 Ensure the sleeves are pressed fully into the needle bearings in the (upper) pivot mounting – if not already done, check the condition of the bearings and lubricate them with fresh grease (see Chapter 6).
23 With the aid of an assistant place the engine unit on top of the jack and block of wood and carefully manoeuvre it into position in the frame **(see illustration 4.14)**. Ensure no wires, cables or hoses become trapped between the engine and the frame.
24 Align the upper mounting bolt holes and slide the bolt through from the right-hand side **(see illustration 4.18)**. Install the washer and nut finger-tight.
25 Position the end of the suspension linkage rod between the lower engine mounting lugs and slide the bolt through from the right-hand side **(see illustration 4.16b)**. Install the washer and nut finger-tight.
26 Counter-hold the lower engine mounting bolt and tighten the nut to the torque setting specified at the beginning of this Chapter **(see illustrations 4.16a)**.
27 Counter-hold the upper engine mounting bolt and tighten the nut to the specified torque setting.
28 Ensure the scooter is supported securely on the centre stand, then lower the jack and remove it.
29 The remainder of the installation procedure is the reverse of removal, noting the following points.
• *Make sure all wires, cables and hoses are correctly routed and connected, and secured by the relevant clips or ties.*

• *Tighten all bolts to the specified torque settings where given.*
• *Adjust the throttle cable freeplay (see Chapter 1).*
• *Refill the engine with oil and coolant (see Chapter 1 and Pre-ride checks).*
• *Start the engine and check that there is no coolant or oil leakage. Check the engine idle speed (see Chapter 1).*

5 Engine overhaul – general information

Disassembly

1 Before disassembling the engine, the external surfaces of the unit should be thoroughly cleaned and degreased. This will prevent contamination of the engine internals, and will also make working a lot easier and cleaner. A high flash-point solvent, such as paraffin (kerosene) can be used, or better still, a proprietary engine cleaner such as Gunk. Use a paraffin brush or old paintbrush to work the solvent into the recesses of the engine casings. Take care to exclude solvent or water from the electrical components and intake and exhaust ports.

 Warning: The use of petrol (gasoline) as a cleaning agent should be avoided because of the risk of fire.

2 When clean and dry, clear a suitable area for working – a workbench is desirable for all operations once a component has been removed from a machine. Gather a selection of small containers and plastic bags so that parts can be grouped together in an easily identifiable manner. Some paper and a pen should be at hand so that notes can be made and labels attached where necessary. A supply of clean rag is also required. If the engine has been removed from the scooter (see Section 4), have an assistant help you lift it onto the workbench.
3 Before commencing work, read through the appropriate section so that some idea of the necessary procedure can be gained. When removing components it should be noted that

great force is seldom required. In many cases, a component's reluctance to be removed is indicative of an incorrect approach or removal method – if in any doubt, re-check with the text. In cases where fasteners have corroded, apply penetrating fluid before disassembly.
4 When disassembling the engine, keep 'mated' parts that have been in contact with each other during engine operation together (e.g. rocker arms and shafts). These 'mated' parts must be reused or renewed as assemblies.
5 A complete engine/transmission disassembly should be done in the following general order with reference to the appropriate Sections.
• *Remove the valve cover*
• *Remove the cam chain tensioner*
• *Remove the camshaft*
• *Remove the cylinder head*
• *Remove the cam chain tensioner blade*
• *Remove the cylinder*
• *Remove the piston*
• *Remove the water pump (see Chapter 3)*
• *Remove the variator assembly (see Chapter 2C)*
• *Remove the alternator and starter motor (see Chapter 9)*
• *Remove the starter clutch and idler gear*
• *Remove the oil pump*
• *Remove the cam chain and guide blade*
• *Remove the balancer shaft driven gear*
• *Separate the crankcase halves*
• *Remove the crankshaft and connecting rod assembly*
• *Remove the transmission shafts and gears (see Chapter 2C)*

Reassembly

6 Reassembly is accomplished by reversing the general disassembly sequence.

6 Valve cover and secondary air system reed valve

Note: *This procedure can be carried out with the engine in the frame. If the engine has been removed, ignore the steps which do not apply.*

Removal

1 Remove the air filter housing (see Chapter 4A or 4B as applicable).
2 On AN250 and AN400X to K2 models, remove the carburettor (see Chapter 4A). On AN400K3 to K6 models, remove the throttle body assembly (see Chapter 4B).
3 On AN400K3 to K6 models, partially drain the cooling system and remove the coolant hose between the thermostat housing and the water pump (see Chapter 3).
4 Pull off the spark plug cap.
5 Undo the valve cover screws and remove them – note the location of the washer on the left-hand screw **(see illustrations)**.
6 Lift the valve cover off the cylinder head

6.5a Undo the valve cover screws . . .   **6.5b . . . noting the location of the washer**

6.6 Lift off the valve cover

6.7a Undo the bolts . . .

6.7b . . . and remove the reed valve cover

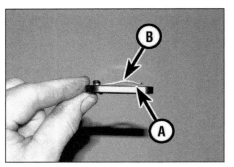

6.7c Reed (A) and stopper plate (B)

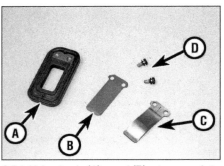

6.7d Valve body (A), reed (B), stopper plate (C) and fixing screws (D)

6.9 Install the valve reed side down

(see illustration). If it is stuck, tap around the joint with a soft-faced mallet to dislodge it – don't not try to lever it off with a screwdriver as the sealing surfaces will be damaged. Discard the cover gasket as a new one must be fitted on reassembly.

7 On AN400K3 to K6 models, if required, remove the secondary air system reed valve cover (see illustrations). Lift out the reed valve and inspect it for damage and gum and carbon deposits. The reed should lay flat against the valve body (see illustration) – if the reed has become distorted, fit a new valve assembly. For cleaning purposes, undo the screws securing the stopper plate and reed and separate the components (see illustration). Note the washers on the screws. Remove any gum or carbon deposits carefully with a soft cloth and a suitable solvent. Install

the reed and stopper plate in the correct order and tighten the screws securely (see illustration 6.7c).

Installation

8 Clean the mating surfaces of the cylinder head and valve cover with a suitable solvent to remove all traces of old sealant and gasket. If a scraper is used, take care not to scratch or gouge the soft aluminium. Ensure none of the old gasket material falls into the engine.

9 On AN400K3 to K6 models, if removed, install the secondary air system reed valve reed side down (see illustration). Clean the threads of the cover screws and apply a suitable non-permanent thread-locking compound, then install the cover and tighten the bolts securely.

10 Press the new gasket onto the valve cover, making sure it locates correctly in its

groove (see illustration). Apply a suitable, non-permanent sealant to the camshaft cut-out in the cylinder head (see illustration).

11 Position the cover on the cylinder head carefully, making sure the gasket stays in place, and install the cover screws. Don't forget to fit the washer to the left-hand screw (see illustration 6.5b). Tighten the screws evenly to the torque setting specified at the beginning of this Chapter.

12 Install the remaining components in the reverse order of removal.

7 Cam chain tensioner

Note: *This procedure can be carried out with the engine in the frame. If the engine has been removed, ignore the steps which do not apply.*

Removal

1 Remove the valve cover (see Section 6). Remove the spark plug (see Chapter 1).

2 Remove the drive belt cooling fan filter element (see Chapter 1, Section 2).

3 The engine must be turned to position the piston at top dead centre (TDC) on its compression stroke. The engine can be turned using a suitable spanner on the flats on the end of the crankshaft as when checking the valve clearance (see Chapter 1, Section 3).

4 Unscrew the tensioner cap bolt and

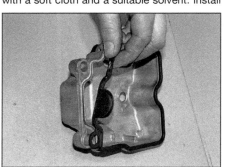

6.10a Press the gasket into its groove

6.10b Apply sealant to the cut-out

7.4a Unscrew the tensioner cap bolt . . .

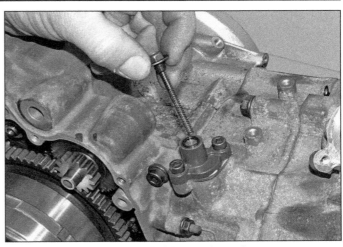

7.4b . . . and withdraw the spring

withdraw the spring from the tensioner **(see illustrations)**. Discard the O-ring as a new one must be used.

5 Undo the tensioner mounting bolts and withdraw the tensioner body from the back of the cylinder **(see illustrations)**. Discard the gasket as a new one must be fitted on reassembly.

Caution: Do not rotate the engine with the cam chain tensioner removed.

Inspection

6 Examine the cam chain tensioner and spring for signs of wear or damage. If the

spring appears compressed, replace it with a new one.

7 Release the catch and ensure that the pushrod slides smoothly in the tensioner body **(see illustrations)**. Check that the teeth on the pushrod are not worn. If necessary, fit a new cam chain tensioner.

Installation

8 Check that the piston is still at top dead centre (TDC) on its compression stroke (see Step 3).

9 Ensure the push rod is pushed fully into the tensioner body **(see illustration)**. Fit a

new gasket onto the body and install it on the cylinder **(see illustration 7.5b)**. Tighten the mounting bolts to the torque setting specified at the beginning of this Chapter.

10 Install the spring and the cap bolt with a new O-ring and tighten the bolt to the specified torque **(see illustrations 7.4c, b and a)**. Note that a clicking noise will be heard as the cap bolt is installed and the pushrod is extended against the tensioner blade under spring pressure.

11 Turn the engine in the normal direction of rotation to ensure the camshaft and rocker arms operate correctly and the camchain is fully tensioned.

7.4c Note the location of the O-ring

7.5a Undo the tensioner mounting bolts . . .

7.5b . . . and withdraw the tensioner body

7.7a Release the catch . . .

7.7b . . . and ensure that the pushrod slides smoothly

7.9 Compress the pushrod fully

8.2a Undo the bolts . . .

8.2b . . . and remove the camshaft end holder

8.2c Note the location of the dowels

8.3 Loosen the sprocket bolts as described

12 Install the drive belt cooling fan filter element, then install the remaining components in the reverse order of removal.

8 Camshaft and rocker arms

Removal

1 Remove the valve cover (see Section 6).
2 Undo the bolts securing the camshaft end holder and lift it off (see illustrations). Note the location of the dowels and remove them for safekeeping if they are loose (see illustration).
3 Bend down the tabs locking the camshaft sprocket bolts and loosen the bolts (see illustration).
4 Remove the cam chain tensioner (see Section 7).
5 Undo the bolts securing the camshaft holder and lift it off (see illustrations). Note the location of the dowels and remove them for safekeeping if they are loose (see illustration).
6 Unscrew the upper camshaft sprocket bolt (see illustration). Rotate the engine carefully to access the second sprocket bolt. Secure the locking piece to prevent it falling into the engine, then unscrew the second bolt and remove the locking piece (see illustration).

8.5a Undo the camshaft holder bolts . . .

8.5b . . . and lift it off

8.5c Note the location of the dowels

8.6a Unscrew the upper camshaft sprocket bolt

8.6b Remove the locking piece

8.7 Remove the camshaft and sprocket

8.8 Remove the half-ring retainer

8.10a Inspect the bearing surfaces of the head . . .

Discard the locking piece as a new one must be fitted.

7 Displace the camshaft sprocket from its seat on the camshaft, lift the chain off the sprocket and remove the camshaft and sprocket **(see illustration)**. **Note:** *Secure the cam chain to some convenient point with wire or a cable-tie to prevent it falling into the engine.*

8 Remove the half-ring retainer from the lower half of the middle camshaft journal **(see illustration)**.

9 Cover the cylinder head to prevent anything falling into the engine.

8.10b . . . and the holder . . .

8.10c . . . and the corresponding camshaft journals

Inspection

10 Inspect the bearing surfaces of the head and the holders and the corresponding journals on the camshaft – look for score marks, deep scratches and evidence of spalling (a pitted appearance) **(see illustrations)**.

11 Inspect the camshaft lobes for heat discoloration (blue appearance), score marks, chipped areas, flat spots and spalling. Measure the height of each lobe with a micrometer and compare the results to the *Specifications* at the beginning of this Chapter **(see illustration)**. If damage is noted or wear is excessive, the camshaft must be replaced with a new one.

12 Check camshaft runout by supporting each end of the camshaft on V-blocks, and measuring any runout at the centre journal using a dial gauge (see *Tools and Workshop Tips* in the *Reference* section). If the runout

exceeds the specified limit the camshaft must be replaced with a new one.

13 On AN400 models, check the operation of the centrifugal decompressor cam on the exhaust camshaft, noting the location of the return spring on the back of the cam mechanism **(see illustrations)**. If the mechanism is stuck or broken a new camshaft will have to be fitted.

 HAYNES HiNT *Refer to Tools and Workshop Tips in the Reference section for details of how to read a micrometer and dial gauge.*

14 The camshaft journal oil clearance should now be checked. There are two

possible ways of doing this, either by direct measurement (see Steps 15 to 18) or by the use of a product known as Plastigauge (see Steps 19 to 22). If Plastigauge is used and the oil clearance is excessive, use direct measurement to determine whether it is the camshaft or the holder that is worn.

15 If direct measurement is to be used, make a sketch of the cylinder head so that a note of each measurement can be made against the appropriate bearing surface.

16 Make sure the camshaft holder dowels are in position then fit the holder and tighten the holder bolts evenly to the specified torque setting. Using telescoping gauges and a micrometer (see *Tools and Workshop Tips*), measure the internal diameter of both holder journals and record them on the sketch

8.11 Measuring camshaft lobe height

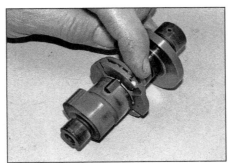

8.13a Check the operation of the centrifugal decompressor cam

8.13b Note location of the return spring (arrowed)

8.16a Measuring the internal diameter of the camshaft holder journals

8.16b Ensure the end holder is fitted correctly

8.16c Measuring the internal diameter of the end holder journal

(see illustration). Next, fit the end holder, ensuring it is the right way round, and tighten the bolts to the specified torque setting **(see illustration)**. Measure and record the internal diameter of the end holder journal **(see illustration)**.

17 Now measure the diameter of the corresponding camshaft journals with a micrometer and record them on the sketch **(see illustration)**.

18 To determine the journal oil clearance, subtract the camshaft journal diameter from the internal holder journal diameter. Compare the result with the specifications at the beginning of this Chapter. If any oil clearance is greater than specified, compare the individual measurements of the camshaft and holder journals to the *Specifications* and replace whichever component is worn beyond its service limit with a new one. **Note:** *If a*

holder journal is worn beyond its service limit a new cylinder head will have to be fitted.

19 If the Plastigauge method is to be used, clean the camshaft and the bearing surfaces in the cylinder head and camshaft holders with a clean, lint-free cloth, then install the camshaft, not forgetting to install the half-ring retainer **(see illustrations)**.

20 Cut strips of Plastigauge and lay one piece on each camshaft journal, along the camshaft centreline **(see illustration)**. Make sure the camshaft holder dowels are in position, then fit the holders and tighten the holder bolts evenly to the specified torque setting. **Note:** *The camshaft must not rotate during this procedure.*

21 Now unscrew the bolts evenly and carefully lift off the camshaft holders.

22 To determine the oil clearance, compare the crushed Plastigauge (at its widest point)

on each journal to the scale printed on the Plastigauge card **(see illustration)**.

23 Compare the results to this Chapter's *Specifications*. If any oil clearance is greater than specified, follow Steps 15 and 17 to determine which component is worn beyond its service limit and replace that component with a new one. **Note:** *If a holder journal is worn beyond its service limit a new cylinder head will have to be fitted.*

24 Check the camshaft sprocket for wear, chipped teeth and other damage. If the sprocket is worn, the cam chain and the drive sprocket on the crankshaft are probably worn as well and should be checked (see Section 16).

25 Check for freeplay between each rocker arm and its shaft. Mark one arm, shaft and the holder to aid reassembly, then pull out the shafts and remove the arms, noting how they fit **(see illustration)**. Measure the

8.17 Measuring camshaft journal diameter

8.19a Install the half-ring retainer . . .

8.19b . . . and lay the camshaft in the head

8.20 Lay Plastigauge on each camshaft journal

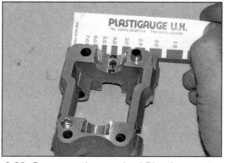

8.22 Compare the crushed Plastigauge to the printed scale

8.25a Remove the rocker shafts and arms

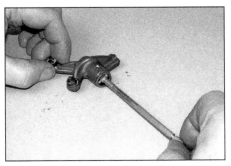

8.25b Measuring the arm bore . . .

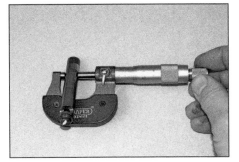

8.25c . . . and the shaft diameter

8.26 Inspect the rocker arms for wear and damage

internal diameter of each arm bore and the corresponding diameter of the shaft and compare the results with the specifications **(see illustrations)**. Renew any component that is worn beyond its service limit.

26 Inspect the rocker arms for heat discoloration, score marks, chipped areas, flat spots and pitting where they contact the camshaft lobes **(see illustration)**. Similarly check the bottom of each valve clearance adjuster and the top of each valve stem. If damage is noted or wear is excessive, the rocker arms, adjusters and valves must be renewed as required.

Installation

27 Lubricate each rocker shaft and arm with engine oil, then position the arms in the

holder and slide in the shafts – ensure the cut-out in both shafts aligns with the hole for the right-hand mounting bolt **(see illustration 8.25a)**.

28 Make sure the bearing surfaces in the cylinder head, on the camshaft and in the holders are clean, then lubricate them with engine oil.

29 Ensure that the line next to the T mark on the alternator rotor aligns with the static timing mark on the alternator cover (see Chapter 1, Section 3). Note that if the alternator cover has been removed, a line is cast in the crankcase for the purpose of timing the engine **(see illustration)**. If it is necessary to turn the crankshaft to restore the alignment, hold the cam chain up to prevent it jamming between the crankcase and the crankshaft sprocket.

30 Fit the sprocket onto the camshaft, marked face out **(see illustration)**, then position the camshaft in the cylinder head and lift the chain onto the sprocket **(see illustration 8.7)**. Ensure that the line on the end of the camshaft is parallel with the valve cover mating surface and the camshaft lobes are facing towards the cylinder head **(see illustrations)**.

31 Ensure the sprocket is seated correctly on the camshaft, then install the new locking piece and camshaft sprocket bolts **(see illustrations 8.6b and a)**. Hold the camshaft in position and tighten the sprocket bolts to the torque setting specified at the beginning of this Chapter. Bend the tabs on both ends of the locking piece to secure the bolts **(see illustrations)**.

32 Fit the half-ring retainer into the groove in the camshaft and slide in round to the

8.29 Using the crankcase timing mark and a straight edge

8.30a Fit the sprocket onto the camshaft

8.30b Check the camshaft position . . .

8.30c . . . with both cam lobes facing the cylinder head

8.31a Bend the tabs on the locking piece . . .

8.31b . . . to secure the camshaft sprocket bolts

underside of the camshaft **(see illustrations)**. If removed, install the camshaft holder dowels **(see illustration 8.5c)**.

33 Lubricate the camshaft lobes with molybdenum grease, then install the holders ensuring they are pressed down firmly over the camshaft and onto the dowels. Install the holder bolts and tighten them evenly to the specified torque setting

34 Install the cam chain tensioner (see Section 7). Rotate the engine to check the timing marks and ensure that the camshaft and rockers are operating correctly.

35 Check the valve clearances and adjust them if necessary (see Chapter 1). Install the remaining components in the reverse order of removal.

8.32a Fit the half-ring retainer . . .

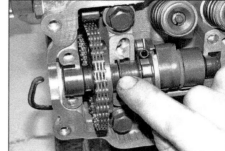

8.32b . . . and slide into the underside of the camshaft

9 Cylinder head removal and installation

Note: *This procedure can be carried out with the engine in the frame. If the engine has been removed, ignore the steps which do not apply.*

Removal

1 Drain the cooling system (see Chapter 1) and remove the thermostat housing (see Chapter 3).

2 Remove the exhaust system (see Chapter 4A or 4B as applicable).

3 Remove the valve cover (see Section 6). Remove the front support bracket for the air filter housing. On AN250 and AN400X to K2 models, remove the intake manifold if required.

4 Remove the camshaft and rocker arms (see Section 8).

5 Undo the bolt securing the cam chain tensioner blade and lift out the blade **(see illustrations 16.3a and b)**. Note the location of the sealing washer and discard it as a new one must be fitted.

6 The cylinder head is secured by two 6 mm nuts, two 8 mm nuts and four 10 mm bolts **(see illustrations)**.

7 First undo the 6 mm nuts on the right-hand side of the head, noting the location of the guide. Next, undo the 8 mm nuts on the rear and front of the head. Finally, working in a

criss-cross pattern, loosen the 10 mm bolts evenly and a little at a time, then remove the bolts and their copper washers **(see illustration)**. Discard the washers as new ones must be fitted

8 Lift the head off the cylinder, passing the cam chain down through the tunnel as you do **(see illustration)**. If the head is stuck, tap around the joint with a soft-faced mallet to free it. Do not attempt to free the head by levering it off – you'll damage the sealing surfaces.

9 Remove the cylinder head gasket **(see illustration)**.

10 Secure the cam chain to prevent it falling into the engine and stuff a clean rag into the cam chain tunnel to prevent any debris falling in.

11 If they are loose, remove the two dowels from the top of the cylinder for safekeeping

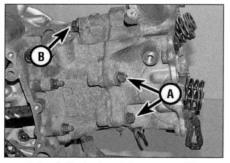

9.6a Cylinder head 6 mm nuts (A), rear 8 mm nut (B) . . .

9.6b . . . front 8 mm nut (arrowed) . . .

9.6c . . . and 10 mm bolts

9.7 Note the location of the copper washers

9.8 Lift off the cylinder head . . .

9.9 . . . and remove the gasket

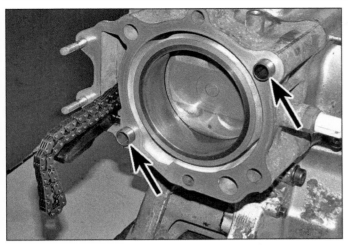

9.11 Location of the cylinder dowels

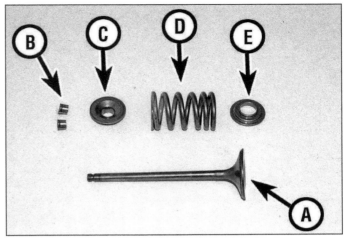

10.5 Valve components – valve (A), collets (B), spring retainer (C), spring (D) and spring seat (E)

(see illustration).If either appears to be missing it is probably stuck in the underside of the cylinder head.

12 Inspect the cylinder head gasket and the mating surfaces on the cylinder head and cylinder for signs of leakage, which could indicate that the head is distorted. If necessary, check the cylinder head with a straight-edge (see Section 10). Discard the old head gasket as a new one must be fitted on reassembly.

13 If required, remove the exhaust header pipe (see Chapter 4A).

Installation

14 Clean the mating surfaces of the cylinder head and cylinder with a suitable solvent to remove all traces of old gasket. If a scraper is used, take care not to scratch or gouge the soft aluminium. Ensure none of the old gasket material falls into the cylinder bore or the oil and coolant passages.

Refer to Tools and Workshop Tips for details of gasket removal methods.

15 If removed, install the exhaust header pipe with a new gasket (see Chapter 4A).

16 If removed, install the two dowels in the top of the cylinder and fit the new head gasket **(see illustrations 9.11 and 9)**. Check that the gasket locates over the dowels and that all the holes are correctly aligned.

17 Remove any rag from the cam chain tunnel and check that the lower end of the cam chain guide blade is properly located. Align the front and rear cylinder head mounting studs with the appropriate holes in the cylinder **(see illustration 9.8)**. Keep the cam chain taut and pass it up through the tunnel in the head while the head is lowered onto the cylinder. Secure the cam chain.

18 Fit new copper washers on the cylinder head bolts, then install the bolts and tighten them finger-tight **(see illustration 9.7)**. Working in a criss-cross pattern, tighten the bolts evenly and a little at a time to the initial torque setting specified at the beginning of this Chapter, then tighten them in the same sequence to the final torque setting.

19 Install the 8 mm nuts and tighten them to the specified torque setting **(see illustrations 9.6a and b)**.

20 Install the 6 mm nuts and tighten them to the specified torque setting – don't forget to fit the guide under the lower nut **(see illustration 9.6a)**.

21 Install the cam chain tensioner blade, fit a new sealing washer on the mounting bolt, then tighten the bolt to the specified torque setting **(see illustration 16.3b and a)**.

22 Install the remaining components in the reverse order of removal.

10 Cylinder head and valve overhaul

1 Because of the complex nature of this job and the special tools and equipment required, most owners leave servicing of the valves, valve seats and valve guides to a professional. However, you can make an initial assessment of whether the valves are seating correctly, and therefore sealing, by pouring a small amount of solvent into each of the valve ports. If the solvent leaks past any valve into the combustion chamber area the valve is not seating correctly and sealing.

2 With the correct tools (a valve spring compressor is essential – make sure it is suitable for motorcycle work), you can also remove the valves and associated components from the cylinder head, clean them and check

them for wear to assess the extent of the work needed.

3 A dealer service department or engine specialist can replace the guides and re-cut the valve seats if required.

4 After a valve service has been performed, be sure to clean the head very thoroughly before installation to remove any metal particles or abrasive grit that may still be present from the service operations. Use compressed air, if available, to blow out all the holes and passages.

Disassembly

Special tool: *A valve spring compressor suitable for motorcycle work is essential for this procedure (see Step 6).*

5 Before proceeding, arrange to label and store the valves along with their related components in such a way that they can be returned to their original locations without getting mixed up **(see illustration)**. A container with four compartments is ideal. Alternatively, labelled plastic bags will do just as well.

6 Install the spring compressor on the first valve to be removed **(see illustration)**. Ensure there is sufficient room to remove the collets from inside the spring retainer **(see**

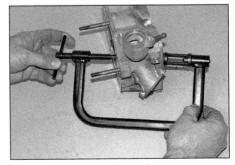

10.6a Install the valve spring compressor

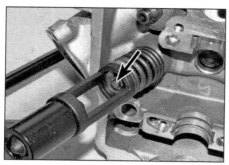

10.6b Ensure the collets (arrowed) are accessible

10.6c Compressor must not contact the cylinder head

10.7a Remove the valve collets

10.7b Remove the spring retainer . . .

10.7c . . . and valve spring

10.8a Remove the valve

illustration). On the underside of the head make sure the compressor only contacts the valve and not the soft aluminium of the head (see illustration). If the compressor is too big for the valve, use a spacer between them.

7 Compress the spring(s) just enough to allow the collets to be removed, using either tweezers or a magnetic wand (see illustration). Carefully release the valve spring compressor and remove the spring retainer and the spring(s), noting which way up each component fits (see illustrations). Note: On AN250 models and AN400X to K2 models, two springs per valve are fitted; on AN400K3 to K6 models there is only one spring per valve.

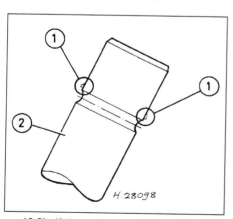

10.8b If the valve stem (2) won't pull through the guide, deburr the area (1) above the collet groove

8 Pull the valve out from the underside of the head (see illustration). If the valve binds in the guide and won't pull through, push it back into the head and deburr the area around the collet groove with a very fine file (see illustration).

9 Pull the valve stem seal off the top of the valve guide with pliers and discard it (see illustration) – never reuse the old seals. Remove the spring seat, noting which way up it fits (see illustration).

10 Repeat the procedure for the remaining valves. Remember to keep the parts for each valve together so they can be reinstalled in the same locations.

11 Clean the cylinder head with solvent and dry it thoroughly. Compressed air will speed the drying process and ensure that all holes and recessed areas are clean. Note: Do not

10.9a Remove the valve stem seal . . .

use a wire brush mounted in a drill motor to clean the combustion chambers as the head material is soft and may be scratched or eroded away by the wire brush.

12 Clean all the valve springs, collets, retainers and spring seats with solvent and dry them thoroughly. Do the parts from one valve at a time so that no mixing of parts between valves occurs.

13 Remove any carbon deposits that may have formed on the valve heads using a scraper or a motorised wire brush. Again, make sure the valves do not get mixed-up.

Inspection

14 Inspect the cylinder head very carefully for cracks and other damage, especially around the valve seats and spark plug hole (see

10.9b . . . and the spring seat

10.14 Inspect the cylinder head for cracks

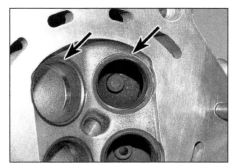

10.16 Measure the width of each valve seat

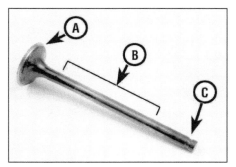

10.17a Check the valve head (A), stem (B) and collet groove (C)

10.17b Check the width of the valve face

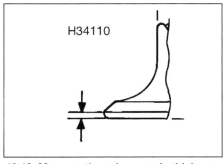

H34110

10.18 Measure the valve margin thickness

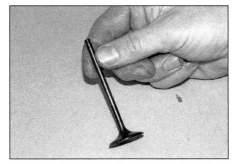

10.19 Make sure the valve isn't bent

illustration). If cracks are found, a new head will be required.

15 Using a precision straight-edge and a feeler gauge, check the head gasket mating surface for warpage **(see illustration 11.2)**. Refer to *Tools and Workshop Tips* in the Reference section for details of how to use the straight-edge. If the head is warped beyond the limit specified at the beginning of this Chapter, consult a Suzuki dealer or take it to a specialist repair shop for rectification.

16 Examine the valve seats in the combustion chamber. If they are pitted, cracked or burned, the head will require work beyond the scope of the home mechanic. Measure the valve seat width and compare it to this Chapter's *Specifications* **(see illustration)**. If it exceeds the service limit, or if it varies around its circumference, overhaul is required.

17 Examine the head of each valve for cracks, pits and burned spots **(see illustration)**. The valve face should be a uniform width all the way round **(see illustration)**.

18 Measure the valve margin thickness and compare it to this Chapter's *Specifications* **(see illustration)**. If it exceeds the service limit, or if it varies around its circumference, replace the valve with a new one.

19 Rotate the valve and check for any obvious indication that it is bent **(see illustration)**. If available, use V-blocks and a dial gauge to measure the valve stem and valve head runout and compare the results to the *Specifications*. If either measurement exceeds the service limit, a new valve must be fitted.

20 Check the valve stem and the collet groove area for wear and damage **(see illustration 10.17a)**. Measure the valve stem diameter and compare it to the *Specifications* **(see illustration)**. Measure the valve stem

end length from the top of the stem to the top of the collet groove and compare it to the *Specifications.*

21 Clean the valve guides to remove any carbon build-up, then install each valve in its guide in turn so that its face is 10 mm above the seat and check the amount of side clearance (wobble) between the valve stem and its guide in two directions **(see illustration)**. If available, mount a dial gauge against the side of the valve face and measure the deflection. If the deflection exceeds the service limit and the valve stems are not worn, new valve guides will have to be fitted.

22 Check the end of each valve spring for wear. Measure the spring free length and compare it to that listed in the specifications **(see illustration)**. If any spring is shorter than specified it has sagged and must be renewed. Place each spring upright on a flat surface

10.20 Measure the valve stem diameter

10.21 Check the valve deflection

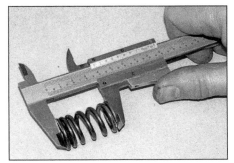

10.22a Measure the valve spring free length

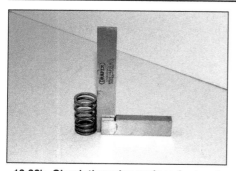

10.22b Check the valve springs for bend

10.30 Tap each valve stem to set the collets

and check it for bend with a set square **(see illustration)**. If the bend in any spring is excessive, it must be replaced with a new one. **Note:** *It is good practice to fit new valve springs when an engine is being overhauled.*
23 Check the spring retainers and collets for wear and damage. Any questionable parts should not be reused, as extensive damage will occur in the event of failure during engine operation.
24 If the inspection indicates that no overhaul work is required, the valve components can be reinstalled in the head.

Reassembly

25 Working on one valve at a time, lay the spring seat in place in the cylinder head with its shouldered side facing up **(see illustration 10.9b)**. Lubricate the new valve stem seal with molybdenum disulphide oil (a mixture of engine oil and molybdenum grease) and press

it squarely over the end of the guide until it is felt to clip into place **(see illustration 10.9a)**.
26 Coat the valve stem with molybdenum disulphide oil, then insert it into its guide, rotating it slowly to avoid damaging the seal **(see illustration 10.8a)**. Check that the valve moves up and down freely in the guide.
27 Install the valve spring(s), with the closer-wound coils facing down into the cylinder head **(see illustration 10.7c)**. **Note:** *On the original equipment valve springs the upper ends are painted blue.* Install the spring retainer with its shouldered side facing down into the top of the spring **(see illustrations 10.7b)**.
28 Apply a small amount of grease to the collets to help hold them in place. Compress the spring with the valve spring compressor and install the collets **(see illustrations 10.6a and 7a)**. When compressing the spring, depress it only as far as is absolutely

necessary to slip the collets into place. Make certain that the collets are securely located in the collet groove, then carefully release the spring compressor.
29 Repeat the procedure for the remaining valves. Remember to keep the parts for each valve together and separate from the other valves so they can be reinstalled in the same location.
30 Support the cylinder head on wooden blocks so the valves can't contact the work surface, then tap the end of each valve stem lightly to seat the collets in their grooves **(see illustration)**.

11 Cylinder

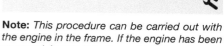

Note: *This procedure can be carried out with the engine in the frame. If the engine has been removed, ignore the steps which do not apply.*

Removal

1 Remove the cylinder head (see Section 9).
2 Remove the rear support bracket for the air filter housing **(see illustration)**.
3 On AN400K3 to K6 models, disconnect the engine coolant temperature sensor wiring connector **(see illustration)**.
4 Lift out the cam chain guide blade **(see illustration 16.4)**.
5 Undo the nuts securing the cylinder on the right-hand side **(see illustration)**.
6 Ease the cylinder up off the crankcase. If it is stuck, tap around the joint face between the cylinder and the crankcase with a soft-faced mallet to free it. Do not attempt to free the cylinder by levering with a screwdriver between the cylinder and crankcase – you'll damage the sealing surfaces.
7 Once the cylinder has separated from the crankcase, secure the cam chain so that the cylinder can be lifted off completely. Support the piston to prevent the connecting rod or piston skirt hitting the crankcase **(see illustration)**. Once the cylinder has been removed, stuff clean rag around the connecting rod to protect it and to prevent anything falling into the crankcase.
8 Remove the cylinder base gasket **(see illustration)**.

11.2 Remove the air filter housing support bracket

11.3 Engine coolant temperature sensor wiring connector – AN400K3 to K6 models

11.5 Undo the cylinder base nuts

11.7 Support the piston as the cylinder is removed

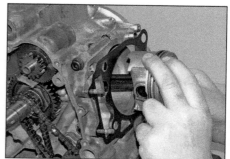

11.8 Remove the cylinder base gasket

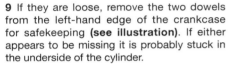

11.9 Remove the dowels (arrowed) if they are loose

11.10 Location of the ECT sensor

11.12 Checking the head gasket mating surface for warpage

9 If they are loose, remove the two dowels from the left-hand edge of the crankcase for safekeeping **(see illustration)**. If either appears to be missing it is probably stuck in the underside of the cylinder.

10 On AN400K3 to K6 models, if required, unscrew the engine coolant temperature sensor and discard the O-ring as a new one must be fitted **(see illustration)**.

11 Clean any traces of old gasket material from the cylinder and crankcase mating surfaces. If a scraper is used, take care not to scratch or gouge the soft aluminium. Be careful not to let any debris fall into the crankcase.

Inspection

12 Using a precision straight-edge and a feeler gauge, check the head gasket mating surface for warpage **(see illustration)**. Refer to *Tools and Workshop Tips* in the Reference section for details of how to use the straight-edge. If the cylinder is warped beyond the limit specified at the beginning of this Chapter, consult your Suzuki dealer or take it to a specialist repair shop for rectification.

13 Check the cylinder wall carefully for scratches and score marks **(see illustration)**. If it is badly scratched, scuffed or scored, a new cylinder and piston will have to be fitted. **Note:** *Because of its special coating the cylinder bore should not be honed.*

14 Use a telescoping gauge and micrometer (see *Tools and Workshop Tips*) to check the dimensions of the bore to assess the amount

of wear, taper and ovality **(see illustration)**. Measure near the top (but below the level of the top piston ring at TDC), centre and bottom (but above the level of the oil ring at BDC) of the bore, both parallel to and across the crankshaft axis **(see illustration)**. Compare the results to the specifications at the beginning of this Chapter. If the bore is oval, tapered or worn beyond the service limit a new cylinder and piston will have to be fitted.

15 If the precision measuring tools are not available, take the cylinder to a Suzuki dealer or specialist motorcycle repair shop for assessment.

Installation

16 If removed, fit a new O-ring onto the engine coolant temperature sensor, then install the sensor and tighten it to the specified torque setting (see Chapter 3).

11.13 Examine the cylinder wall for damage

11.14a Measure the cylinder bore . . .

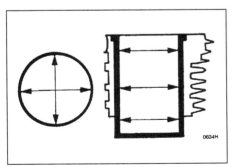

11.14b . . . in the directions shown

11.22a Fit the piston into the cylinder . . .

11.22b . . . feeding the rings in carefully . . .

17 Remove any rag from around the connecting rod.

18 If removed, install the two dowels in the crankcase **(see illustration 11.9)**.

19 Fit a new cylinder base gasket.

20 Ensure that the piston ring end gaps are correctly staggered (see Section 13) then lubricate the piston, rings and cylinder bore with clean engine oil.

21 Release the cam chain so that the cylinder can be lowered down over the chain.

22 Support the piston and fit the top edge into the bottom of the cylinder bore **(see illustration)**. Working on one piston ring at a time, carefully compress and feed it into the bore as the cylinder is pressed down – use your finger-tips and a small screwdriver to do this **(see illustration)**. Don't press the cylinder down too hard as this will only cause the rings to snag and take care not to score the surface of the piston skirt with the screwdriver.

11.23a . . . until the piston is in the bore completely

11.23b Press the cylinder down onto the crankcase

12.2 Indent (arrowed) on top of piston

23 Gradually slide the cylinder over the piston until all the rings are inside **(see illustration)**. Pull the cam chain up through the tunnel, then align the base of the cylinder with the mounting studs and dowels and press if firmly down onto the crankcase **(see illustration)**.
24 Install the cylinder nuts but only tighten them finger-tight at this stage **(see illustration 11.5)**.
25 Install the cam chain guide blade and secure the cam chain **(see illustration 16.4)**. Note the location of the lower end of the guide blade (see Section 16).
26 Once the cylinder head has been installed and the head bolts and nuts have been fully tightened, tighten the cylinder nuts to the specified torque setting. Don't forget to install the rear support bracket for the air filter housing **(see illustration 11.2)**.

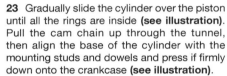

12 Piston

Note: *This procedure can be carried out with the engine in the frame. If the engine has been removed, ignore the steps which do not apply.*

Removal

1 Remove the cylinder (see Section 11). Once the cylinder has been removed, don't forget to stuff clean rag around the connecting rod to protect it and to prevent anything falling into the crankcase.
2 Before removing the piston, note the indent

on the top which faces the exhaust side of the engine **(see illustration)**. If this is not visible, mark the piston accordingly so that it can be installed the correct way round.
3 Carefully prise out the circlip on one side of the piston using needle-nose pliers or a small flat-bladed screwdriver inserted into the notch **(see illustration)**. Push the piston pin out from the other side with a suitably sized socket to free the piston from the connecting rod **(see illustration)**. Remove the other circlip and discard them both as new ones must be used. When the piston has been removed, install its pin back into its bore so that it can be installed the same way round.

HAYNES HINT *If the piston pin is a tight fit in the piston bosses, heat the piston gently with a hot air gun – this will expand the alloy piston sufficiently to release its grip on the pin. If the piston pin is particularly stubborn, extract it using a drawbolt tool, but be careful to protect the piston's working surfaces – see Tools and Workshop Tips in the Reference section.*

4 Using your thumbs or a thin blade, carefully remove the rings from the piston **(see illustration)**. Do not nick or gouge the piston in the process. Note which way up each ring fits and in which groove as they must be installed in their original positions if being re-used (see Section 13). The oil control ring

(lowest on the piston) is composed of three separate components – the expander and the upper and lower side rails (see Section 13). **Note:** *It is good practice to fit new piston rings when an engine is being overhauled.*
5 Clean all traces of carbon from the top of the piston. A hand-held wire brush or a piece of fine emery cloth can be used once most of the deposits have been scraped away. Do not, under any circumstances, use a wire brush mounted in a drill motor; the piston material is soft and will be eroded away by the wire brush.
6 Use a piston ring groove cleaning tool to remove any carbon deposits from the ring grooves. If a tool is not available, a piece broken off an old ring will do the job. Be very careful to remove only the carbon deposits. Do not remove any metal and do not nick or gouge the sides of the ring grooves.
7 Once the carbon has been removed, clean the piston with a suitable solvent and dry it thoroughly. Make sure the oil return holes at the back of the oil ring groove are clear.

Inspection

8 Carefully inspect the piston for cracks around the skirt, at the pin bosses and at the ring lands. Normal piston wear appears as even, vertical wear on the thrust surfaces of the piston and slight looseness of the top ring in its groove. If the skirt is scored or scuffed, the engine may have been suffering from overheating and/or abnormal combustion, which caused excessively high operating temperatures. The oil pump should be checked thoroughly.

12.3a Remove the circlip . . .

12.3b . . . and push out the piston pin

12.4 Remove the piston rings carefully

12.10 Measuring the piston diameter

12.11a Measure the piston pin . . .

12.11b . . . and the pin bore

9 In extreme cases, a hole in the top of the piston or burned areas around the edge of the piston crown indicate that pre-ignition or knocking under load have occurred, although on fuel injected models the engine control module should detect problems with the fuel or ignition systems long before serious damage takes place. Check the symptoms of poor running in *Fault Finding* in the *Reference* section and refer to Chapter 4B for full details of the engine management system fault codes.

10 Check the piston-to-bore clearance by measuring the bore (see Section 11) and the piston diameter. Measure the piston 15 mm up from the bottom of the skirt and at 90° to the piston pin axis **(see illustration)**. Subtract the piston diameter from the bore diameter to obtain the clearance. If it is greater than the figure specified at the beginning of this Chapter, check whether it is the bore or piston that is worn. If the piston diameter is less that the service limit, a new piston and ring set should be fitted. Note that the bore is unlikely to show signs of wear unless a very high mileage has been covered.

11 Measure the piston pin external diameter and the pin bore in the piston and compare the results to the *Specifications* at the beginning of this Chapter **(see illustrations)**. Repeat the measurements between the pin and the connecting rod small-end **(see illustrations)**. Renew components that are worn beyond the specified limits. **Note:** *If the connecting rod small-end is worn a new crankshaft assembly will have to be fitted (see Section 19).*

12.11c Measure the piston pin in the centre . . .

12 Measure the piston ring-to-groove clearance of the top two rings by fitting the rings into their grooves and slipping a feeler gauge in beside them **(see illustration)**. Make sure you have the correct ring for the groove (see Step 4). Check the clearance at three or four locations around the groove. If the clearance is greater than specified, check whether it is the piston or rings that are worn. Remove the rings and measure the groove width with a feeler gauge, then measure the ring thickness with a micrometer **(see illustration)**. Compare the results with the *Specifications* and renew whichever parts are worn. If new rings are being fitted, measure the clearance using the new rings.

Installation

13 Inspect and install the piston rings (see Section 13).

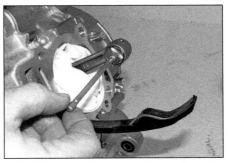

12.11d . . . and the connecting rod small end bore

14 Install a **new** circlip into one side of the piston – never re-use old circlips. When installing the circlips, compress them only just enough to fit them in the piston, and make sure they are properly seated in their grooves with the open end away from the removal notch **(see illustration)**.

15 Lubricate the piston pin, the piston pin bore and the connecting rod small-end bore with clean engine oil, then install the piston on its connecting rod **(see illustration 12.3b)**. Ensure the indent on the top of the piston faces the exhaust side of the engine **(see illustration 12.2)**.

16 Insert the piston pin from the side without the circlip and push it all the way in. Secure the pin with the other **new** circlip (see Step 15).

17 Remove the rag from around the connecting rod and install the cylinder (see Section 11).

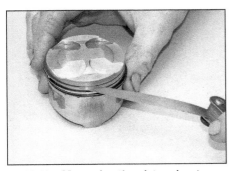

12.12a Measuring the piston ring-to-groove clearance

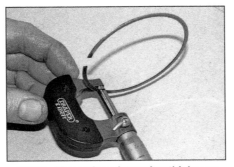

12.12b Measuring piston ring thickness

12.14 Piston circlip removal notch (arrowed)

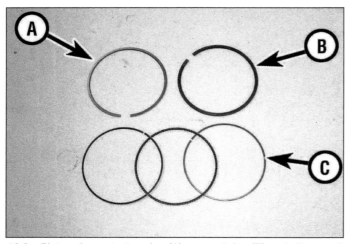

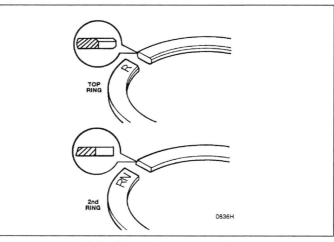

13.2a Piston ring set – top ring (A), second ring (B) and oil control side rails and spacer (C)

13.2b Piston ring cross-sections

13 Piston rings

Inspection

1 It is good practice to fit new piston rings when an engine is being overhauled. Before installing the new rings, measure the end gaps of the top two rings as follows.

2 Lay out the ring set so the rings can be checked in order **(see illustration)**. The upper surface of the top two rings should have a manufacturer's mark at one end – the marks on each ring are different, so note which mark is for the top ring and which is for the second. On the machine used to illustrate this procedure the top ring was marked 'O' and the second ring was marked 'RN'. Also note that the rings can be identified by their different cross-sections **(see illustration)**.

3 To measure the free end gap, lay each ring on a flat surface and measure the gap between the ends using a Vernier caliper **(see illustration)**. Note the results.

4 To measure the installed end gap, insert each ring into the top of the cylinder and square it up with the cylinder walls by pushing it in with the top of the piston. The ring should be about 20 mm below the top edge of the cylinder. Slip a feeler gauge between the ends of the ring to measure the gap **(see illustration)**.

5 Compare the results to the *Specifications* at the beginning of this Chapter. If the gaps are larger or smaller than specified, check that you have the correct rings before proceeding. Excess end gap is not critical unless it exceeds the service limit.

Installation

6 The oil control ring (lowest on the piston) is installed first. It is composed of three separate components – the expander and the upper and lower side rails **(see illustration 13.2a)**.

13.3 Measuring piston ring free end gap

Slip the expander into the groove, positioning its ends so that they touch but do not overlap **(see illustration)**.

7 Install the lower side rail. Do not use a piston ring installation tool on the oil ring side rails as they may be damaged. Instead, place one end of the side rail into the groove between the expander and the ring land. Hold it firmly in place and slide a finger or thin blade around the piston while pushing the rail into the groove **(see illustration)**. Next, install the upper side rail in the same manner.

13.6 Installing the oil control ring expander

13.4 Measuring piston ring installed end gap

8 After the oil control ring been installed, check that both its upper and lower side rails can be turned smoothly in the ring groove.

9 Fit the second ring into the middle groove in the piston with its mark facing up (see Step 2). Do not expand the ring any more than is necessary to slide it into place **(see illustration 12.4)**.

10 Follow the same procedure to install the top ring into the top groove in the piston

11 Once the rings are correctly installed,

13.7 Installing the lower side rail

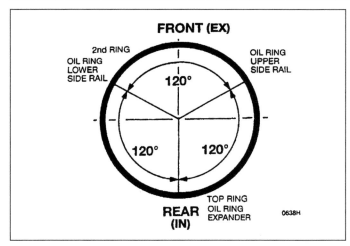

13.11 Position the piston ring end gaps – second ring and lower side rail (A), upper side rail (B), top ring and expander (C)

14.5a Alternator cover bolts – note sealing washers (A)

check they move freely without snagging and stagger their end gaps as shown **(see illustration)**.

14 Starter clutch and gears

Note: *This procedure can be carried out with the engine in the frame. If the engine has been removed, ignore the steps which do not apply.* **Special tool:** *A puller will be required to draw the alternator rotor off the crankshaft (see Chapter 9).*

Check

1 The operation of the starter clutch can be checked while it is in situ. First remove the starter motor (see Chapter 9). Check that the reduction gear, located inside the starter motor aperture, rotates freely anti-clockwise (as you look at it from the left-hand side), but locks when rotated clockwise. If not, the starter

clutch or one of the intermediate gears is faulty and should be removed for inspection.

Removal

2 Drain the coolant and remove the water pump (see Chapter 3).
3 Drain the engine oil and remove the oil filter (see Chapter 1). Position a suitable tray underneath the alternator cover to catch any residual oil when the cover is removed.
4 Disconnect the alternator wiring connector **(see illustration 4.11)**. On AN250 and AN400X to K2 models, disconnect the ignition pulse generator coil wiring connector. On AN400K3 to K6 models, disconnect the CKP sensor wiring connector. Release the wiring from any ties and feed it back to the cover.
5 Undo the alternator cover bolts, noting the location of the sealing washers, and draw off the cover **(see illustration)**. Remove the cover gasket and discard it; note the position of the cover dowels and remove them for safe-keeping if they are loose **(see illustrations)**.

14.5b Remove the cover gasket

6 Note how the smaller pinion on the reduction gear engages with the driven gear on the starter clutch **(see illustration)**. Check the operation of the starter clutch – the driven gear should rotate freely anti-clockwise as you look at it, but should lock when rotated clockwise. If not the starter clutch is faulty and should be removed for inspection.

14.5c Location of cover dowels (arrowed)

14.6 Pinion (A) engages with starter clutch driven gear (B)

14.8 Remove the key from the crankshaft

14.9 Remove the starter driven gear

14.10a Remove the reduction gear . . .

7 Remove the alternator rotor – the starter clutch is mounted on the back of it (see Chapter 9). **Note:** *Before removing the alternator rotor, slacken the six starter clutch bolts while holding the rotor centre bolt.*

14.10b . . . and the gear shaft

8 Note the location of the key in the slot on the crankshaft, then carefully tap it out using a small chisel **(see illustration)**.
9 Draw the starter driven gear off the crankshaft, noting how it fits **(see illustration)**.

14.11a Unscrew the starter clutch bolts . . .

10 Remove the reduction gear and its shaft, noting how the larger pinion engages with the starter motor pinion **(see illustrations)**.

Inspection

11 Unscrew the starter clutch bolts and lift the alternator rotor off the clutch housing **(see illustrations)**. Separate the clutch assembly from the housing **(see illustration)**. On AN250 and AN400X to K2 models, depress the spring lock on the outside edge of the clutch assembly and withdraw it from the housing.
12 Inspect the condition of the sprags and the sprag cage **(see illustration)**. Clean the assembly with a suitable solvent, dry it thoroughly, then lubricate it with clean engine oil. The sprags should turn freely inside the cage – if they are damaged or worn, the corresponding surfaces of the housing and the driven gear are likely to be worn also **(see illustration)**. **Note:** *The sprag clutch and the driven gear are supplied as a matched assembly.*
13 If the clutch assembly is good, press it squarely into the housing with the flange uppermost **(see illustration)**. On AN250 and AN400X to K2 models, the assembly should 'click' into place. Position the alternator rotor on top of the housing and align the bolt holes **(see illustration 14.11b)**. Clean the threads of the starter clutch bolts and apply a suitable non-permanent thread-locking compound, then install the bolts and tighten them to the torque setting specified at the beginning of this Chapter.
14 Inspect the internal bearing surface of the

14.11b . . . and lift the alternator rotor off the clutch housing

14.11c Separate the clutch assembly from the housing

14.12a Inspect the sprags and the sprag cage

14.12b Inspect the clutch surface (A). Note bearing surface (B)

14.13 Install the clutch assembly, flange uppermost

14.15 Inspect the reduction gear and gear shaft

14.17 Ensure gear rotates freely clockwise

14.21 Apply sealant across the wiring grommet

driven gear for signs of wear and scoring **(see illustration 14.12b)**. If the bearing surface show signs of excessive wear, replace the gear assembly with a new one and inspect the surface of the crankshaft for damage.

15 Inspect the teeth of the driven gear and the reduction gear for wear and damage. The reduction gear should be a sliding fit on its shaft – renew any components that are worn or damaged **(see illustration)**.

16 Check the teeth on the starter motor shaft (see Chapter 9).

Installation

17 Prior to installation, lay the rotor face down and lubricate the clutch assembly with clean engine oil, then fit the driven gear, rotating it clockwise to spread the sprags and allow the

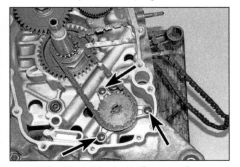

15.2a Undo the bolts (arrowed) . . .

gear hub to enter. Ensure that the driven gear rotates freely in an clockwise direction and locks against the rotor in an anti-clockwise direction **(see illustration)**. Withdraw the driven gear – if it appears stuck, rotate it clockwise to free it from the clutch sprags.

18 Lubricate the reduction gear shaft with clean engine oil, then install the shaft and gear **(see illustrations 14.10b and a)**.

19 Slide the driven gear onto the crankshaft, then install the key, ensuring it is squarely located in its slot **(see illustrations 14.9 and 8)**.

20 Clean the tapered section of the crankshaft and inside of the alternator rotor with suitable solvent, then install the rotor (see Chapter 9).

21 Clean all old gasket and sealant from the alternator cover and crankcase. If removed, install the cover dowels, then fit the new cover

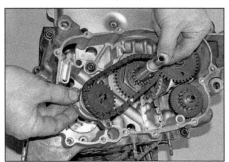

15.2b . . . and lift off the pump and drive chain

gasket, making sure it locates correctly onto the dowels **(see illustrations 14.5c and b)**. Apply a smear of suitable sealant across the wiring grommet **(see illustration)**.

22 Install the cover and cover bolts with new sealing washers as noted on removal **(see illustration 14.5a)**. Tighten the bolts evenly in a criss-cross pattern to the specified torque setting.

23 Install the remaining components in the reverse order of removal.

15 Oil pump

Note: *This procedure can be carried out with the engine in the frame. If the engine has been removed, ignore the steps which do not apply.*

Removal

1 Remove the alternator cover (see Section 14), then remove the alternator rotor (see Chapter 9).

2 Mark the oil pump drive chain so that it can be fitted the same way around, then undo the bolts securing the pump and lift it off together with the chain **(see illustrations)**.

3 Remove the circlip and lift off the sprocket **(see illustration)**.

4 Withdraw the drive pin from the pump shaft and remove the thrust washer **(see illustration)**.

15.3 Remove the circlip and sprocket

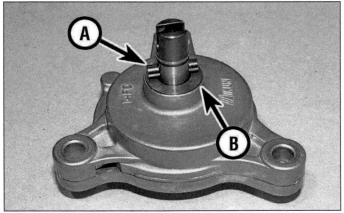

15.4 Remove the drive pin (A) and thrust washer (B)

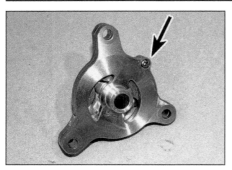

15.7a Undo the screw . . .

15.7b . . . and remove the cover

15.8a Withdraw the drive pin . . .

15.8b . . . and slide the rotor off the shaft

15.9a Remove the pump shaft . . .

15.9b . . . and the outer rotor

Inspection

5 Inspect the pump body for any obvious damage such as cracks or distortion, and check that the shaft rotates freely, without any side-to-side play, excessive endfloat or binding.
6 Individual components are not available for the pump, but the rotors can be removed for cleaning and a general check for wear or damage if there is a problem with low oil pressure (see Section 3).
7 Undo the screw on the back of the pump and remove the pump cover **(see illustrations)**.
8 Withdraw the drive pin from the inner rotor and slide the rotor off the shaft, noting the register mark on the front face of the rotor **(see illustrations)**.
9 Draw out the pump shaft and lift the outer rotor out from the pump body, noting the register mark on the front face of the rotor **(see illustrations)**.
10 Clean all the components in a suitable

solvent, then inspect the pump body and rotors for scoring and wear. If any damage is evident, a new pump will have to be fitted.
11 Check the pump sprocket and the drive chain for wear or damage, and renew them as a set if necessary.

Installation

12 Install the outer rotor, shaft, inner rotor and drive pin in the pump body as noted on removal **(see illustration 15.8a)**. Don't forget that the register marks on the rotors should face into the pump body.
13 Fit the cover and tighten the cover screw securely **(see illustrations 15.7b and a)**.
14 Lubricate the pump with clean engine oil and check that the shaft rotates freely.
15 Fit the thrust washer and drive pin, then install the sprocket and secure it with a new circlip **(see illustrations 15.4 and 3)**. Ensure the circlip is correctly located in its groove.
16 Assemble the chain on the pump sprocket,

then hook the chain around the pump drive sprocket on the crankshaft **(see illustration 15.2b)**.
17 Install the pump mounting bolts and tighten them to the torque setting specified at the beginning of this Chapter.
18 Install the remaining components in the reverse order of removal.

16 Cam chain, chain guide and tensioner blade

Note: *This procedure can be carried out with the engine in the frame. If the engine has been removed, ignore the steps which do not apply.*
1 Except in cases of oil starvation, the cam chain wears very little. If the chain has stretched excessively and can no longer be correctly tensioned by the cam chain tensioner, it is likely that the chain guide and tensioner blades will be worn and in need of renewal as well. Also check the condition of the camshaft sprocket (see Section 8) and crankshaft sprocket (see Step 9). **Note:** *Check the operation of the cam chain tensioner if the chain is slack but appears to be in good condition (see Section 7).*

Removal

2 To remove the cam chain tensioner blade, first follow the procedure in Section 8 and remove the camshaft and rocker arm assembly.
3 Undo the bolt securing the cam chain tensioner blade and lift out the blade **(see illustrations)**. Note the location of the sealing

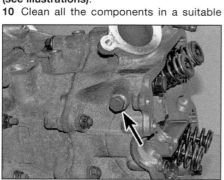

16.3a Undo the bolt (arrowed) . . .

16.3b . . . and lift out the cam chain tensioner blade

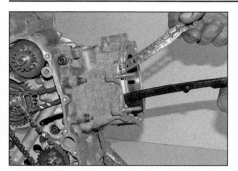

16.4 Lift out the cam chain guide blade

16.6 Remove the cam chain through the crankcase

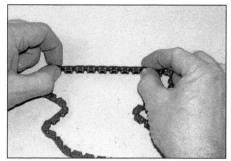

16.8 Check the chain for freeplay between the links

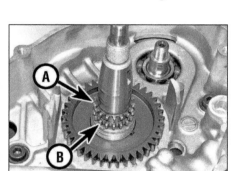

16.9 Oil pump drive sprocket (A), camshaft drive sprocket (B)

washer and discard it as a new one must be fitted.

4 To remove the cam chain guide blade, follow the procedure in Section 9 and remove the cylinder head, then lift out the guide blade **(see illustration)**.

5 To remove the cam chain, first remove the cylinder head, the alternator rotor (see Chapter 9) and the oil pump (see Section 15).

6 Mark the cam chain so that it can be fitted the same way around, then feed it down into the crankcase and remove it **(see illustration)**.

Inspection

7 Examine the sliding surface of the guide and tensioner blades for signs of wear or damage. Check them carefully for cracks in the surface and along the edges. Install new components if necessary.

8 Lay the chain on the work surface and

16.12 Installed position (arrowed) of cam chain guide blade

pull it taut **(see illustration)**. Check all round the chain – if there is any discernible slack between the links, or if there is any doubt about its condition, fit a new chain.

9 Inspect the teeth of the crankshaft sprocket **(see illustration)**. If there are any signs of wear or damage, a new crankshaft will have to be fitted.

10 Inspect the teeth on the camshaft sprocket and renew the sprocket if necessary (see Section 8).

Installation

11 Fit the cam chain onto the inner crankshaft sprocket, then feed the chain up through the aperture in the crankcase and secure it **(see illustration 16.6)**. Install the oil pump (see Section 15).

12 If required, the guide blade can be fitted now – note the location of the lower end of the blade in the recess in the crankcase **(see**

illustration). Alternatively, install the guide blade once the cylinder has been fitted (see Section 11).

13 Install the tensioner blade once the cylinder head has been fitted (see Section 9). Don't forget to use a new sealing washer on the tensioner blade bolt.

14 Install the remaining components in the reverse order of removal.

17 Balancer shaft driven gear

1 The balancer shaft is located inside the crankcases (see Section 18). However, before the crankcase halves can be separated, the balancer shaft driven gear must be removed. The gear is a two-piece, spring loaded assembly designed to eliminate backlash between the crankshaft and the balancer shaft.

Removal

2 Remove the alternator cover (see Section 14), then remove the alternator rotor (see Chapter 9).

3 To prevent the crankshaft from turning while the driven gear nut is loosened, position the crankshaft so that a suitable 12 mm bolt or steel bar can be inserted through the right-hand crankcase half and the crankshaft webs into the recess in the left-hand crankcase half **(see illustrations)**.

4 Undo the driven gear nut and remove the washer **(see illustration)**.

17.3a Insert the bar through the right-hand side . . .

17.3b . . . into the recess (arrowed) on the left-hand side

17.4 Remove the nut and washer

17.5 Align the gears with bolt (arrowed) then pull the assembly off

17.6 Remove the key from the balancer shaft

17.7a Remove the circlip . . .

17.7b . . . and the washer(s)

17.8 Lift off the rear gear with springs

5 Insert a suitable bolt into the hole in the two halves of the driven gear to hold them in alignment, then pull the gear off the balancer shaft **(see illustration)**.

6 Note the location of the key in the slot on the shaft, then carefully tap it out using a small chisel **(see illustration)**.

Inspection

7 Remove the circlip securing the two halves of the driven gear **(see illustration)**. On AN250 models and AN400X to K3 models, remove the shim, spring washer and plain washer. On AN400K4 to K6 models, remove the plain washer **(see illustration)**.

8 Mark the outer face of the rear gear to aid reassembly, then lift off the rear gear, noting the location of the springs **(see illustration)**.

9 The springs should be a secure fit in the rear gear – if they are loose or broken, install

a new set. Inspect the teeth of both gears and renew them if they are worn or damaged.

Installation

10 Fit the rear gear onto the front gear, ensuring it is the correct way round, and align the holes in the two gears. Fit the springs into the rear gear and press them into the recesses in the front gear.

11 Install plain washer, spring washer and shim, or plain washer only, according to model (see Step 7) and secure the assembly with a new circlip.

12 Install the key, ensuring it is squarely located in its slot in the balancer shaft **(see illustration 17.6)**.

13 Align the teeth on the two halves of the driven gear and insert a suitable bolt into the hole to hold them in position **(see illustration)**.

14 Align the keyway in the centre of the driven gear with the key in the balancer shaft, then align the register mark on the driven gear with the mark on the crankshaft gear and press the driven gear firmly onto its shaft **(see illustration 17.5)**. Remove the bolt. Ensure the balancer shaft driven gear and the crankshaft gear are aligned exactly **(see illustration)**.

15 Install the washer and driven gear nut finger-tight **(see illustration 17.4)**.

16 Lock the crankshaft to prevent it turning (see Step 3) and tighten the driven gear nut to the torque setting specified at the beginning of this Chapter. Remove the locking piece.

17 Install the remaining components in the reverse order of removal.

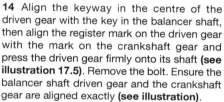

18 Crankcase separation and reassembly

Note: *To separate the crankcase halves, the engine must be removed from the frame.*
Special tools: *A 46 mm deep socket will be required to undo the nut securing the crankshaft gear (see Step 6). Pullers may be required to separate the crankcase halves (see Step 11), press the crankshaft out of the crankcase (see Step 16) and draw the crankshaft into the crankcase on reassembly (see Step 21).*

Separation

1 To gain access to the connecting rod, crankshaft and bearings, and balancer shaft, the crankcase must be split into two parts.

2 Remove the engine from the frame (see Section 4).

3 Before the crankcases can be separated the following components must be removed:
* Oil filter (Chapter 1)
* Cylinder head (Section 9)
* Cylinder (Section 11)
* Piston (Section 12)
* Water pump (Chapter 3)
* Alternator rotor and starter motor (Chapter 9)
* Oil pump (Section 15)
* Balancer shaft driven gear (Section 17).
* Variator and drive belt (Chapter 2C).

4 Pull out the crankcase breather gauze **(see**

17.13 Hold the gears in alignment with a bolt

17.14 Register marks (arrowed) must align exactly

18.4 Remove the crankcase breather gauze

Cut a 46 mm socket into two parts below the shoulder. Extend the socket with a length of tube so that the overall length below the shoulder measures 105 mm.

18.7a Install the deep socket . . .

18.7b . . . and undo the crankshaft gear nut

illustration). Wash the gauze in a suitable solvent and allow it to dry.

5 Lock the crankshaft to prevent it turning using a 12 mm bolt as described in Section 17.

6 A 46 mm deep socket is required to undo the nut securing the crankshaft gear. Suzuki produces a service tool (Part No. 09922-21410) to do this. Alternatively a suitable tool can be made from a socket and a length of tube (see **Tool Tip**).

7 Slide the socket over the end of the crankshaft and undo the nut **(see illustrations)**. Remove the locking piece.

8 Lift off the washer and the gear, noting how the gear locates over the pin in the crankshaft, then remove the pin **(see illustrations)**.

9 Support the crankcases on the work surface with the left-hand side uppermost. Undo the 6 mm crankcase bolts, then undo the

8 mm bolts, noting the position of the sealing washers **(see illustration)**. **Note:** As each bolt is removed, store it in its relative position in a cardboard template of the crankcases. This will ensure all bolts are installed in the correct location on reassembly. Also note the washers fitted with certain bolts, and keep them with their bolts as an aid to reassembly.

10 Turn the engine over so that the right-hand side is uppermost. On AN250 models, undo the 6 mm crankcase bolts, then undo the 8 mm bolts evenly in a criss-cross pattern, noting the position of the sealing washer. On

AN400 models, undo the 8 mm bolts evenly in a criss-cross pattern, noting the position of the sealing washer **(see illustration)**.

18.8a Remove the washer . . .

18.8b . . . and the gear . . .

18.8c . . . and pull out the pin

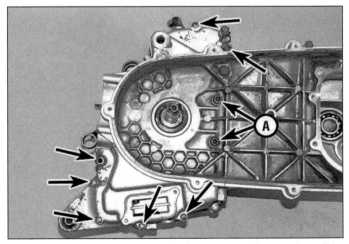

18.9 Left-hand side crankcase bolts – note sealing washers (A)

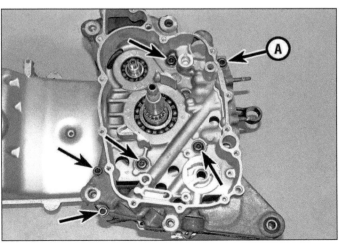

18.10 Right-hand side crankcase bolts – note sealing washer (A)

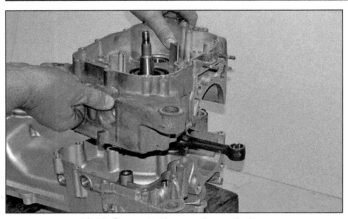

18.11 Separate the crankcase halves

18.12a Set-up for separating the crankcase halves – tighten the nuts (arrowed) . . .

11 Carefully lift the right-hand crankcase half off the left-hand half **(see illustration)**. If it is stuck, tap around the joint with a soft-faced mallet to dislodge it. If the halves do not separate easily, first make sure all fasteners have been removed. Do not try and separate the halves by levering between the sealing surfaces as they are easily damaged and will leak on reassembly. If required, Suzuki produces a service tool to help with crankcase separation (Part No. 09920-13120). Alternatively, a suitable puller can be made from a piece of steel bar and two lengths of threaded rod – drill two holes in the bar with the centres approximately 235 mm apart – check with the alternator cover bolt holes on your machine. Cut two 120 mm lengths of 6 mm threaded rod. You will also require two M6 nuts and washers.

12 To use the puller, screw the threaded rods fully into two alternator cover bolt holes on opposite sides of the crankshaft. Slide the bar down the rods until it rests over the end of the crankshaft. Fit the washers and nuts onto the rods, then tighten the nuts evenly to draw the crankcase off the crankshaft **(see illustrations)**.
13 The right-hand crankcase half will come away leaving the crankshaft and balancer shaft in the left-hand crankcase. Note the location of the oil gallery O-ring and discard it as a new one must be fitted; note the location of the crankcase dowels and remove them for safekeeping if they are loose **(see illustrations)**.
14 Lift out the balancer shaft **(see illustration)**. Inspect the shaft journals for wear and pitting, especially if the shaft bearings in the crankcase are worn or damaged (see Section

20). Ensure that the key slot in the shaft is not damaged **(see illustration)**.
15 On the machine used to illustrate this procedure the crankshaft was a firm sliding fit in the left-hand main bearing. Secure the crankcase upright and have an assistant support the right-hand end of the crankshaft to avoid it dropping when it comes free. Tap the left-hand end of the crankshaft gently to displace the crankshaft **(see illustration)**.
16 Alternatively, if the crankshaft is a tight fit in the bearing, fabricate a tool similar to the one used in Step 12 to press the crankshaft out of the crankcase. Support the crankcase on wooden blocks with sufficient space below the right-hand end of the crankshaft to allow it to come free and have an assistant support the crankshaft. Tighten the nuts evenly to

18.12b . . . and lift the right-hand case off

18.13a Location of O-ring

18.13b Location of crankcase dowels

18.14a Remove the balancer shaft . . .

18.14b . . . and inspect the journals and key slot

18.15 Free the crankshaft with a gentle tap

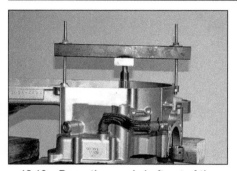

18.16a Press the crankshaft out of the main bearing . . .

18.16b . . . and lift the left-hand crankcase off

18.20 Heat the main bearing

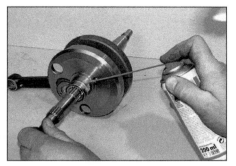

18.21a Apply freeze spray to the crankshaft

18.21b Check connecting rod alignment

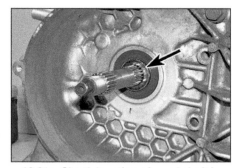

18.21c Check location of crankshaft in main bearing

press the crankshaft out (see illustrations). **Note:** *If either of the main bearings remains on the crankshaft during disassembly an external bearing puller will be required to remove it (see Section 19).*

17 Refer to Section 19 for details on the crankshaft and connecting rod and Section 20 for details on the crankcases and bearings.

18 If required, follow the procedure in Chapter 2C to remove the transmission components.

The lower end of the sleeve must be wide enough to bear on the crankcase seal housing. The M18 x 1.5 nut on the drawbolt assembly threads onto the crankshaft. The additional nuts welded onto the M18 nut provide internal clearance for the crankshaft tip. The nut assembly is secured on the threaded bar by the locknut.

Reassembly

19 Remove all traces of old sealant from the crankcase mating surfaces with a suitable solvent and clean the threads of all the crankcase bolts.

20 Support the left-hand crankcase half securely on the work surface with sufficient room below it for the left-hand end of the crankshaft when it is installed. Use a hot air gun to heat the main bearing (see illustration).

21 Apply a freeze spray to the left-hand crankshaft journal, then immediately drop the crankshaft into place, ensuring the connecting rod is aligned with the crankcase mouth (see illustrations). Ensure the crankshaft passes all the way through the main bearing (see illustration).

22 Alternatively, Suzuki produces service tools to draw the crankshaft into the crankcase (Part Nos. 09910-32812, 09910-32870 and

09913-70210). A similar tool can be made utilising the deep socket used to undo the crankshaft gear nut combined with a sleeved extension and a fabricated drawbolt (see **Tool Tip**).

23 Support the crankcase on wooden blocks and have an assistant support the crankshaft in position below it. Install the tool, ensuring the crankshaft is aligned with the crankcase (see illustration). Tighten the top nut on the drawbolt slowly to draw the crankshaft into position, ensuring it remains aligned exactly with the crankcase (see illustration). Ensure the crankshaft passes all the way through the main bearing (see illustration 18.20).

24 Install the balancer shaft (see illustration 18.14a).

25 Fit a new oil gallery O-ring (see illustration 18.13a). If removed, install the crankcase dowels (see illustration 18.13b).

18.23a Set-up for drawing the crankshaft into the crankcase

18.23b Draw the crankshaft into place slowly

18.26 Apply sealant to the right-hand crankcase half

18.28a Ensure crankcase halves are seated

26 Apply a thin coating of suitable sealant to the mating surface of the right-hand crankcase as shown **(see illustration)**.
Caution: Do not apply an excessive amount of sealant as it will ooze out when the case halves are assembled and may obstruct oil passages.
27 Use a hot air gun to heat the right-hand main bearing.
28 Apply a freeze spray to the right-hand crankshaft journal, then immediately install the crankcase half, ensuring the balancer shaft and the crankcase dowels align correctly. Ensure the crankshaft passes all the way through the main bearing and that the crankcase halves are correctly seated **(see illustration)**. If necessary, tap around the inner race of the main bearing with a flat-nosed punch to ensure the crankcase is seated **(see illustration)**. **Note:** *The crankcases should fit together without being forced. If the casings are not correctly seated, remove the right-hand half and investigate the problem. Do not attempt to pull the casings together using the crankcase bolts as they will crack and be ruined.*
29 Install the right-hand crankcase bolts with new a sealing washer as noted on removal **(see illustration 18.10)**. Secure all the bolts finger-tight, then tighten the 8 mm bolts evenly

in a criss-cross pattern to the initial torque setting specified at the beginning of this Chapter. Now tighten the bolts in the same sequence to the final torque setting specified. On AN250 models, tighten the 6 mm bolts to the torque setting specified.
30 Turn the engine over so that the left-hand side is uppermost. Install the crankcase bolts with new sealing washers as noted on removal **(see illustration 18.9)**. Secure all the bolts finger-tight, then tighten the 8 mm bolts evenly in a criss-cross pattern to the initial torque setting specified. Now tighten the bolts in the same sequence to the final torque setting specified. Finally, tighten the 6 mm bolts to the torque setting specified.
31 Support the engine the right way up. Lubricate the main bearings and connecting rod big-end bearing with clean engine oil. Hold the connecting rod to prevent it hitting the crankcase and check that the crankshaft rotates smoothly and easily. If there are any signs of undue stiffness, tight or rough spots, or of any other problem, the fault must be rectified before proceeding further.
32 Fit the crankshaft gear pin **(see illustration 18.8c)**. Install the gear and the washer – the outer rim of the washer should be placed against the gear **(see illustration 18.8b and a)**. Fit the gear nut finger-tight.

33 Lock the crankshaft to prevent it turning using a 12 mm bolt as on disassembly, then tighten the nut to the specified torque setting **(see illustration 18.7b)**.
34 Install the crankcase breather gauze **(see illustration 18.4)**.
35 Install the remaining components in the reverse order of removal.

19 Crankshaft and connecting rod

Note: *To remove the crankshaft assembly the engine must be removed from the frame and the crankcases separated.*
Special tool: *If necessary, an external bearing puller will be required to remove the main bearings from the crankshaft (see Step 3).*
1 The crankshaft assembly is a pressed-together unit for which a new connecting rod, crankpin and big-end bearing are available if required. However, because of the complex nature of the job and the special tools and equipment involved, rebuilding the crankshaft should only be undertaken by a dealer service department or engine specialist. Nevertheless, once the crankshaft has been removed (see Section 18) it can be checked for wear and the need for repair assessed.
2 If either of the main bearings has remained on the crankshaft, refer to *Tools and Workshop Tips* in the *Reference* section to assess its condition. Only remove a bearing if it is unserviceable. **Note:** *Ideally crankshaft runout should be checked with the bearings removed (see Step 9).*
3 To remove the old bearing, use a puller that clamps behind the bearing as shown **(see illustration)**.
Protect the end of the crankshaft by installing a suitable end cap. Apply steady pressure to draw the bearing off. Install the new bearing in the crankcase half (see Section 20).
4 If the connecting rod big-end bearing has

18.28b Tap around the bearing inner race

19.3 Set-up for removing a bearing from the crankshaft

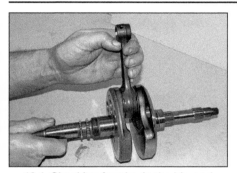

19.4 Checking for play in the big-end bearing

19.6 Measuring the connecting rod side clearance

19.7 Measuring the width of the crankshaft webs

failed, there will be a pronounced knocking noise when the engine is running, particularly under load and increasing with engine speed. Hold the crankshaft still and check for any radial (up and down) play in the big-end bearing by pushing and pulling the rod against the crankpin **(see illustration)**.
5 If a dial gauge and V-blocks are available, measure the amount of deflection at the top of the rod and compare the result with the service limit specified at the beginning of this Chapter; position the dial gauge tip against the side of the small-end aperture.
6 Measure the connecting rod side clearance (the gap between the connecting rod big-end and the crankshaft web) with a feeler gauge and compare the result with the service limit **(see illustration)**. Measure the width of the connecting rod big-end to determine if it is worn.
7 Measure the width between the crankshaft webs and compare the result with the specifications **(see illustration)**.
8 If any clearance is greater than the service limit the big-end bearing has failed. A new bearing and crankpin will have to be fitted or the crankshaft assembly will have to be replaced with a new one.
9 Place the crankshaft on V-blocks and check the runout at the outer end of the alternator rotor taper using a dial gauge. Compare the reading to the maximum specified and renew the crankshaft if the runout exceeds the limit.
10 Refer to Section 12 and check the connecting rod small-end and piston pin for wear.

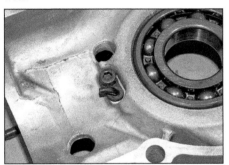

20.2a Location of piston oil jet

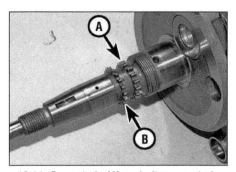

19.11 Cam chain (A) and oil pump chain (B) sprockets

11 Check the cam chain and oil pump chain sprockets for wear and damage **(see illustration)**. Refer to Section 16 to check the condition of the cam chain. Inspect the keyway and alternator rotor taper for wear and damage.
12 Inspect the variator splines **(see illustration)**. If they are worn, check the corresponding splines in the centre of the variator (see Chapter 2C).
13 Follow the procedure in Section 18 to install the crankshaft assembly.

20 Crankcases and bearings

Special tool: *A slide-hammer and knife-edged bearing puller attachment will be required to remove some bearings and seals .*

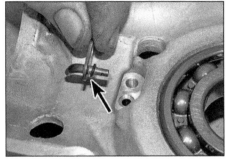

20.2b Note location of O-ring

19.12 Inspect the variator splines

Crankcase inspection

1 After the crankcase halves have been separated (see Section 18), remove all traces of old gasket from the sealing surfaces, taking care not to nick or gouge the soft aluminium if a scraper is used. Wash the components in a suitable solvent and dry them with compressed air, if available.
2 Undo the screw securing the piston oil jet and remove the jet – discard the O-ring as a new one must be fitted **(see illustrations)**. Use compressed air to blow through the oil galleries in the cases. On installation, lubricate the new O-ring with engine oil and tighten the screw securely. **Note:** *If new bearings are to be fitted, install the oil jet afterwards to avoid damaging the O-ring when heating the case.*
3 Check both crankcase halves very carefully for cracks and damaged threads. Small cracks or holes in aluminium castings may be repaired with an epoxy resin adhesive, or with one of the low temperature welding kits. Permanent repairs can be effected by welding, but only a specialist in this process is in a position to advise on the economy or practical aspect of such a repair. If any damage is found that can't be repaired, renew both crankcase halves as a set.
4 Damaged threads can be reclaimed using a thread insert of the Heli-Coil type, which is fitted after drilling and re-tapping the affected thread (see *Tools and Workshop Tips* in the *Reference* section). Most motorcycle dealers and small engineering firms offer a service of this kind. Sheared screws and studs can usually be removed with screw extractors

20.6 Note installed position of mounting bushes

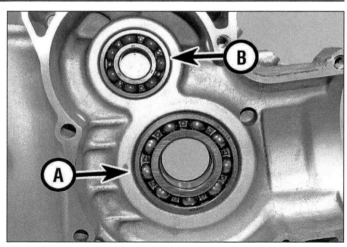

20.8a Main bearing (A) and balancer shaft bearing (B) – left-hand crankcase

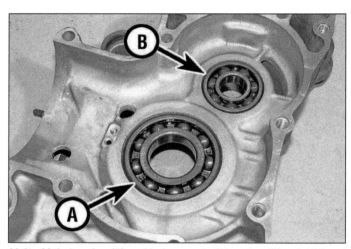

20.8b Main bearing (A) and balancer shaft bearing (B) – right-hand crankcase

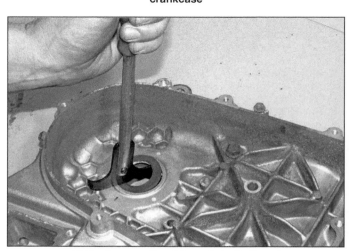

20.8c Remove the old crankshaft oil seal

which consist of a tapered, left thread screw of very hard steel. These are inserted into a pre-drilled hole in the broken fixing, and usually succeed in dislodging the most stubborn stud or screw (see *Tools and Workshop Tips* in the *Reference* section). If you are in any doubt about removing a sheared screw, consult a Suzuki dealer or automotive engineer.

20.9 Driving out the old main bearing

5 Always wash the crankcases thoroughly after any repair work to ensure no dirt or metal swarf is trapped inside when the engine is rebuilt.
6 Inspect the engine mounting bushes for wear and deterioration **(see illustration)**. To remove a bush, first support the case to avoid breaking the mounting lug. Heat the case with a hot air gun and drive the bush out using a suitably-sized socket. Ensure the bush housing is free from corrosion, then press the new bush in until it is level with the lug on both sides.

Crankcase bearings

7 If the crankshaft main bearings have failed, excessive rumbling and vibration will be felt when the engine is running. Check the condition of the bearings – they should spin freely and smoothly without any rough spots (see *Tools and Workshop Tips* in the *Reference* section). Renew the bearings if there is any doubt about their condition.
8 Before removing the bearings, note which

way round they are fitted **(see illustrations)**. Before removing the left-hand bearing, lever out the oil seal and discard it as a new one must be fitted **(see illustration)**.
9 Lay the casing inside face down, heat the bearing housing with a hot air gun and drive the bearing out with a suitably sized socket **(see illustration)**.

 Warning: Be careful when handling the crankcases and wear protective gloves – when heated, the cases could cause severe burns.

10 Also check the condition of the balancer shaft bearings **(see illustrations 20.8a and b)**. Note that the bearing in the left-hand casing is fitted in a blind hole and will require a slide-hammer and knife-edged bearing puller to remove it (see *Tools and Workshop Tips* in the *Reference* section).
11 Prior to installing the new bearing, check that the housing is clean and free from surface damage. If either of the main bearings was loose in its housing and stayed on the crankshaft during disassembly, or had seized

20.14a Install oil seal closed side uppermost

20.14b Press the seal in . . .

20.14c . . . until it is level with the housing

and damaged its housing, have the condition of the casing assessed by a Suzuki dealer. A loose bearing can often be secured using a suitable bearing lock compound.

12 Lay the casing inside face up and support it securely, then heat the housing. The bearing should be fitted with its marked side uppermost. Drive it in squarely until it seats – ensure pressure is only applied to the bearing's outer race.

13 If required, follow the same procedure to fit the new balancer shaft bearings.

14 Locate the new crankshaft oil seal in position in the left-hand casing, ensuring that it is the correct way round **(see illustration)**. Use a suitably-sized socket or driver to press the seal in until it is level with the edge of the housing **(see illustrations)**. Lubricate the inside of the seal with a smear of clean engine oil.

15 Note that there is an additional crankshaft bearing inside the alternator cover **(see illustration)**. To renew the bearing, first remove the circlip, then use a slide-hammer and knife-edged bearing puller to draw it out (see *Tools and Workshop Tips* in the *Reference* section). Use the bearing puller to remove the oil seal located underneath the bearing. This seal must be in good condition to maintain pressure in the oil feed to the crankshaft.

16 Install the new oil seal, ensuring that it is the correct way round, then install the new bearing and secure it with a new circlip. Ensure the circlip is located correctly in its groove. Lubricate the bearing and the inside of the seal with clean engine oil.

17 Reassemble the crankcase halves (see Section 18).

21 Start-up and running-in procedure

Initial start-up

1 Make sure the engine oil level and coolant level are correct (see *Pre-ride checks*). Make sure there is fuel in the tank.

2 Pull the cap off the spark plug, then turn the ignition switch ON and crank the engine over with the starter for a few seconds to prime the lubrication system. Turn the ignition OFF and reconnect the plug cap.

3 Start the engine and let it run at idle until it reaches normal operating temperature. Check carefully that there are no oil or coolant leaks. Do not be alarmed if there is a little smoke from the exhaust – this will be due to the oil used to lubricate the piston and bore during assembly and should subside after a while.

4 If the engine proves reluctant to start, remove the spark plug and check that it has not become wet and oily. If it has, clean it and try again. If the engine refuses to start, go through the fault finding charts at the end of this manual to identify the problem.

5 Make sure the controls, especially the throttle and brakes, function properly before road testing the machine.

Recommended running-in procedure

6 Treat the machine gently for the first few miles to make sure that the oil is circulating and any new parts have started to seat.

20.15 Location of alternator cover bearing

7 Even greater care is necessary if a major engine overhaul has been undertaken. In the case of a new crankshaft or piston and cylinder, the bike will have to be run in as when new. This means a restraining hand on the throttle until at least 500 miles (800 km) have been covered.

8 There's no point in keeping to any set speed limit – the main idea is to keep from labouring the engine and to gradually increase performance up to the 1000 mile (1600 km) mark. Make sure that the throttle position is varied, and use full throttle only for short bursts to start with. Experience is the best guide, since it's easy to tell when an engine is running freely.

9 Pay particular attention to the *Pre-ride checks* at the beginning of this manual. Check the tightness of all relevant nuts and bolts.

Notes

Chapter 2B
Engine – AN400K7 onwards

Contents

Degrees of difficulty

Easy, suitable for novice with little experience 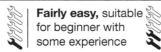	**Fairly easy,** suitable for beginner with some experience	**Fairly difficult,** suitable for competent DIY mechanic	**Difficult,** suitable for experienced DIY mechanic	**Very difficult,** suitable for expert DIY or professional

Specifications

Cylinder compression
Standard	150 to 162 psi (10.6 to 11.4 Bar)
Minimum	94 psi (6.6 Bar)

Lubrication system
Oil pressure	4.27 to 15.64 psi (0.3 to 1.1 Bar) at 3000 rpm, engine warm

Camshaft
Intake lobe height	
Standard	36.61 to 36.66 mm
Service limit (min)	36.31mm
Exhaust lobe height	
Standard	35.94 to 35.99 mm
Service limit (min)	35.64 mm
Journal diameter	21.972 to 21.993 mm
Camshaft holder journal diameter	22.012 to 22.025 mm
Journal oil clearance	
Standard	0.019 to 0.053 mm
Service limit (max)	0.15 mm
Runout	0.10 mm

Cylinder head
Warpage (max)	0.05 mm

Valves, guides and springs

Valve clearances	see Chapter 1
Intake valves	
Head diameter	31.0 mm
Margin thickness (min)	0.5 mm
Stem diameter	4.475 to 4.490 mm
Guide bore diameter	4.500 to 4.512 mm
Stem-to-guide clearance	0.010 to 0.037 mm
Stem deflection (max)	0.35 mm
Stem runout (max)	0.05 mm
Head runout (max)	0.03 mm
Seat width	0.9 to 1.1 mm
Exhaust valves	
Head diameter	27.0 mm
Margin thickness (min)	0.5 mm
Stem diameter	4.455 to 4.470 mm
Guide bore diameter	4.500 to 4.512 mm
Stem-to-guide clearance	0.030 to 0.057 mm
Stem deflection (max)	0.35 mm
Stem runout (max)	0.05 mm
Head runout (max)	0.03 mm
Seat width	0.9 to 1.1 mm
Valve spring free length (min)	38.6 mm
Spring tension	33.35 mm with 14.0 kg load

Cylinder

Bore diameter	81.000 to 81.015 mm
Cylinder distortion (max)	0.05 mm

Piston

Piston diameter (measured 15 mm up from bottom of skirt, at 90° to piston pin axis)	
Standard	80.970 to 80.985 mm
Service limit (min)	80.880 mm
Piston-to-bore clearance	
Standard	0.025 to 0.035 mm
Service limit (max)	0.120 mm
Piston pin diameter	
Standard	19.996 to 20.000 mm
Service limit (min)	19.980 mm
Piston pin bore diameter in piston	
Standard	20.002 to 20.008 mm
Service limit (max)	20.030 mm

Piston rings

Ring end gap (free)	
Top ring	
Standard	7.5 mm (approx.)
Service limit (min)	6.0 mm
2nd ring	
Standard	11.5 mm
Service limit (min)	9.2 mm
Ring end gap (installed)	
Top ring	
Standard	0.06 to 0.21 mm
Service limit (max)	0.50 mm
2nd ring	
Standard	0.06 to 0.18 mm
Service limit (max)	0.50 mm
Ring thickness	
Top ring	1.17 to 1.19 mm
2nd ring	0.97 to 0.99 mm
Ring groove width in piston	
Top ring	1.21 to 1.23 mm
2nd ring	1.01 to 1.03 mm
Oil ring	2.01 to 2.03 mm
Ring-to-groove clearance	
Top ring (max)	0.18 mm
2nd ring (max)	0.15 mm

Connecting rod

Small-end internal diameter
    Standard . . . . 20.006 to 20.014 mm
    Service limit (max) . . . . 20.040 mm
Big-end side clearance
    Standard . . . . 0.10 to 0.65 mm
    Service limit (max) . . . . 1.00 mm
Big-end width . . . . 21.95 to 22.00 mm
Deflection . . . . 3.0 mm

Crankshaft

Runout (max) . . . . 0.08 mm
Web outside width . . . . 59.9 to 60.1 mm

Torque wrench settings

Alternator rotor nut . . . . 160 Nm
Alternator cover bolts . . . . 11 Nm
Balancer driven gear nut . . . . 50 Nm
Cam chain guide bolt . . . . 23 Nm
Cam chain tensioner blade bolt . . . . 23 Nm
Cam chain tensioner cap bolt . . . . 23 Nm
Cam chain tensioner mounting bolts . . . . 10 Nm
Camshaft holder bolts . . . . 10 Nm
Camshaft sprocket bolts . . . . 15 Nm
Coolant union bolts . . . . 10 Nm
Crankcase bolts
    8 mm bolts . . . . 22 Nm
    6 mm bolts . . . . 11 Nm
Crankshaft gear . . . . 150 Nm
Cylinder head 8 mm bolts
    Initial setting . . . . 25 Nm
    Final setting . . . . 42 Nm
Cylinder head 6 mm bolts . . . . 25 Nm
Engine coolant temperature (ECT) sensor . . . . 12 Nm
Engine mountings
    Lower mounting bolt . . . . 85 Nm
    Upper mounting bolt . . . . 93 Nm
Intake manifold bolts . . . . 10 Nm
Oil gallery plugs . . . . 10 Nm
Oil pressure take-off plug . . . . 16 Nm
Oil pump driven gear nut . . . . 23 Nm
Oil pump mounting bolts . . . . 10 Nm
Valve cover screws . . . . 14 Nm

1 General information

The engine unit is a liquid-cooled, single cylinder 4-stroke. The engine/ transmission unit is constructed from aluminium alloy with the crankcase divided vertically into two halves. The left-hand half incorporates the drive belt housing.

The crankcase incorporates a wet sump, pressure-fed lubrication system which uses a chain-driven oil pump.

The crankshaft assembly is pressed together, the connecting rod big-end running on a caged roller bearing. A gear-driven balancer shaft is located on the right-hand side of the crankcase and the alternator rotor is mounted on the right-hand end of the crankshaft.

The valves are operated by double overhead camshafts which are chain driven off the crankshaft. Valve clearances are adjusted by screw adjusters (see Chapter 1).

Power from the crankshaft is transferred to the rear wheel via a variable size drive pulley and belt, automatic centrifugal clutch and reduction gerabox (see Chapter 2C).

2 Component access

Operations possible with the engine in the frame

The components and assemblies listed below can be removed without having to remove the engine/transmission assembly from the frame. If however, a number of areas require attention at the same time, removal of the engine is recommended.

Note that to gain access to engine components it is first necessary to remove the appropriate body panels. Refer to Chapter 8 for full details of panel removal and installation.
- Valve cover
- Cam chain tensioner
- Camshafts
- Cylinder head
- Cylinder
- Piston
- Starter motor and alternator (see Chapter 9)
- Starter clutch and gears
- Water pump (see Chapter 3)
- Transmission shafts and gears (see Chapter 2C)

Operations requiring engine removal

It is necessary to remove the engine/ transmission assembly from the frame to gain access to the following components.
- Connecting rod
- Crankshaft and bearings
- Balancer shaft
- Oil pump

3 Engine wear assessment

Cylinder compression check

Special tool: *A compression gauge with a suitable adaptor is required for this test.*

1 Poor engine performance, exhaust smoke, heavy oil consumption and poor starting are indications of low compression. This may be caused by leaking valve stem seals, incorrect valve clearances, a leaking head gasket, or worn piston, rings and/or cylinder wall.

2 Make sure the valve clearances are correctly set (see Chapter 1) and that the cylinder head bolts are tightened to the specified torque setting (see Section 9).

3 Run the engine until it reaches normal operating temperature. Stop the engine and remove the spark plug (see Chapter 1), taking care not to burn your hands on the hot components.

4 Install the adaptor in the spark plug hole, ensuring it is a tight fit, and connect the compression gauge.

5 Turn the ignition ON, open the throttle twistgrip fully and crank the engine over on the starter motor for a few seconds until the gauge reading stabilises. Take a note of the gauge reading, then turn the ignition OFF.

6 Compare the reading obtained with the appropriate specification at the beginning of this Chapter. If it is close to or below the minimum limit, further investigation is required.

7 To distinguish between cylinder/piston wear and valve leakage, use a pump type oil can to inject a small quantity (teaspoonful) of oil into the cylinder via the spark plug hole – this will serve to temporarily seal the piston rings. Repeat the compression test. If the result shows a noticeable increase in pressure this confirms that the cylinder bore, piston or rings are worn. If there is no change in the reading, the cylinder head gasket or valves are leaking.

8 Although unlikely with the use of modern fuels, a high compression reading indicates

excessive carbon deposits in the combustion chamber area.

Engine oil pressure check

Special tool: *A pressure gauge with a suitable hose and adapter are required for this test.*

9 An oil pressure check will provide useful information about the condition of the engine's lubrication system.

10 To check the oil pressure, a suitable gauge, hose and adapter (which screws into the crankcase) will be needed. Suzuki produces service tools for this purpose – the gauge, hose and adapter are Part Nos. 09915-77331, 09915-74521 and 09915-74570.

11 Clean the area around the main oil gallery plug on the underside of the crankcase **(see illustration)**.

12 Position a drain tray underneath the crankcase to catch any residual oil, then unscrew the plug. Discard the sealing washer as a new one must be fitted.

13 Install the adapter and pressure gauge. Connect the test tachometer according to the manufacturer's instructions.

14 Warm the engine up to normal operating temperature (between 10 and 20 minutes running at 2000 rpm) then increase the engine speed to 3000 rpm whilst watching the gauge reading. The oil pressure should be similar to that given in *Specifications* at the beginning of this Chapter.

15 If the pressure is significantly lower than the standard, either the oil filter is blocked, the oil pump is faulty or there is critical engine wear or damage. Begin diagnosis by checking the oil filter, then the oil pump (see Section 20). If these items are good, it is likely the bearing oil clearances are excessive and the engine needs to be overhauled.

16 If the pressure is too high, either an oil passage is clogged or the wrong grade of oil is being used.

17 Turn the engine OFF. Disconnect the gauge and adapter from the crankcase.

 Warning: Be careful when removing the pressure gauge and adapter as the engine and hot oil can cause severe burns.

18 Install the oil gallery plug using a new sealing washer and tighten it to the torque

setting specified at the beginning of this Chapter. Do not overtighten it as the threads in the crankcase are easily damaged.

19 Check the engine oil level (see *Pre-ride checks*).

4 Engine removal and installation

 Warning: The engine is heavy. Removal and installation should be carried out with the aid of an assistant; personal injury or damage could occur if the engine falls or is dropped. If available, an hydraulic or mechanical floor jack should be used to support and lower or raise the engine.

Removal

1 Support the scooter securely in an upright position using the centrestand. Work can be made easier by raising the machine to a suitable working height on an hydraulic ramp or a suitable platform.

2 Remove the seat, storage compartment and appropriate body panels to gain access to the engine and upper and lower engine mountings (see Chapter 8).

3 Disconnect the negative (-) lead from the battery (see Chapter 9).

4 Drain the engine oil and the coolant (see Chapter 1). Disconnect the coolant hoses from the thermostat housing and the union on the cylinder (see Chapter 3).

5 Remove the air filter housing and throttle body assembly (see Chapter 4B).

6 Plug the engine intake manifold with clean rag to prevent debris falling into the engine.

7 Disconnect the lead from the starter motor terminal, then undo the starter motor mounting bolt securing the engine earth (ground) lead and disconnect the lead **(see illustration)**.

8 Remove the outer drive belt cover (see Chapter 2C). Trace the wiring from the speed sensor at the rear of the transmission casing and disconnect it at the connector **(see illustration)**. Free the wiring from any clips or ties.

9 Disconnect the alternator wiring connector

3.11 Location of the main oil gallery plug

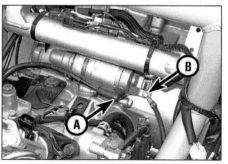

4.7 Starter motor terminal (A) and earth lead (B)

4.8 Speed sensor wiring connector

and the the CKP sensor wiring connector **(see illustration)**.

10 Loosen the clip securing the air intake tube to the drive belt cooling fan cover, then release the ties securing the tube and manoeuvre it out **(see illustrations)**.

11 Remove the exhaust silencer (see Chapter 4B).

12 Displace the rear brake caliper and secure it to the machine with a cable-tie to avoid straining the brake hose, then remove the rear wheel (see Chapter 7).

13 At this point, position an hydraulic or mechanical jack under the engine with a block of wood between the jack head and crankcase. Make sure the jack is centrally positioned so the engine will not topple in any direction when the mounting bolts are removed. Take the weight of the engine on the jack **(see illustration)**.

14 Check that all wiring, cables and hoses are disconnected and clear of the engine.

15 Undo the nut on the lower engine mounting bolt and remove the washer, then withdraw the bolt from the right-hand side **(see illustrations)**. Position the suspension linkage rod assembly clear of the engine mounting lugs.

16 Undo the nut on the upper engine mounting bolt and remove the washer **(see illustration)**.

17 Make sure the engine is properly supported on the jack and have an assistant support it as well. Withdraw the upper mounting bolt from the right-hand side **(see illustration)**.

18 Carefully lower the engine and draw it back and out of the frame.

4.9 Alternator and CKP sensor connectors

4.10b ... and remove the air intake tube

4.10a Loosen the clip ...

4.13 Support the engine on a jack

19 If the engine is dirty, particularly around the intake manifold, cylinder and starter motor, wash it thoroughly before starting any dismantling. This will make work much easier and rule out the possibility of dirt

falling into some vital component (see Section 5).

20 If required, undo the bolts securing the heat shield, noting the location of the washers, and lift it off **(see illustrations)**.

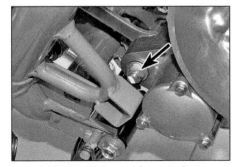

4.15a Undo the nut (arrowed) ...

4.15b ... and withdraw the lower engine mounting bolt

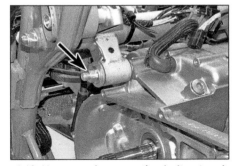

4.16 Upper engine mounting bolt nut and washer

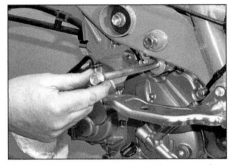

4.17 Withdraw the upper engine mounting bolt

4.20a Undo the heat shield bolts ...

4.20b ... note location of large washers

4.21a Remove the header pipe . . .

4.21b . . . and exhaust sealing washer

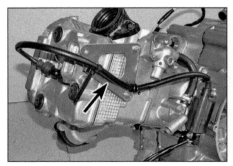

4.22a Remove the bracket

4.22b Disconnect the ECT sensor wiring connector

4.22c Undo the coil mounting bolts . . .

4.22d . . . and remove the assembly

21 Undo the bolts securing the exhaust header pipe and remove the pipe and sealing washer **(see illustrations)**.
22 Disconnect the spark plug cap and undo the bolts securing the bracket to the left-hand side of the cylinder head **(see illustration)**. Disconnect the ECT sensor wiring connector **(see illustration)**. Undo the bolts securing the ignition coil and remove the coil and wiring sub loom **(see illustrations)**.

Installation

Note: *The mounting bolt nuts are self-locking – it is good practice to renew the nuts when installing the engine.*
23 Clean the threads of the engine mounting bolts.
24 Ensure the sleeves are pressed fully into the needle bearings in the (upper) pivot mounting – if not already done, check the condition of the bearings and lubricate them with fresh grease (see Chapter 6).
25 With the aid of an assistant place the engine unit on top of the jack and block of wood and carefully manoeuvre it into position in the frame **(see illustration 4.13)**. Ensure no wires, cables or hoses become trapped between the engine and the frame.
26 Align the upper mounting bolt holes and slide the bolt through from the right-hand side **(see illustration 4.17)**. Install the washer and nut finger-tight.
27 Position the end of the suspension linkage rod between the lower engine mounting lugs and slide the bolt through from the right-hand

side **(see illustration 4.15b)**. Install the washer and nut finger-tight.
28 Counter-hold the lower engine mounting bolt and tighten the nut to the torque setting specified at the beginning of this Chapter **(see illustrations 4.15a)**.
29 Counter-hold the upper engine mounting bolt and tighten the nut to the specified torque setting.
30 Ensure the scooter is supported securely on the centrestand, then lower the jack and remove it.
31 The remainder of the installation procedure is the reverse of removal, noting the following:
• *Make sure all wires, cables and hoses are correctly routed and connected, and secured by the relevant clips or ties.*
• *Tighten all bolts to the specified torque settings where given.*
• *Adjust the throttle cable freeplay (see Chapter 1).*
• *Refill the engine with oil and coolant (see Chapter 1 and Pre-ride checks).*
• *Start the engine and check that there is no coolant or oil leakage.*

5 Engine overhaul –
general information

Disassembly

1 Before disassembling the engine, the external surfaces of the unit should be thoroughly cleaned and degreased. This will

prevent contamination of the engine internals, and will also make working a lot easier and cleaner. A high flash-point solvent, such as paraffin (kerosene) can be used, or better still, a proprietary engine cleaner such as Gunk. Use a paraffin brush or old paintbrush to work the solvent into the recesses of the engine casings. Take care to exclude solvent or water from the electrical components and intake and exhaust ports.

 Warning: The use of petrol (gasoline) as a cleaning agent should be avoided because of the risk of fire.

2 When clean and dry, clear a suitable area for working – a workbench is desirable for all operations once a component has been removed from a machine. Gather a selection of small containers and plastic bags so that parts can be grouped together in an easily identifiable manner. Some paper and a pen should be at hand so that notes can be made and labels attached where necessary. A supply of clean rag is alsp required. If the engine has been removed from the scooter (see Section 4), have an assistant help you lift it onto the workbench.
3 Before commencing work, read through the appropriate section so that some idea of the necessary procedure can be gained. When removing components it should be noted that great force is seldom required. In many cases, a component's reluctance to be removed is indicative of an incorrect approach or removal method – if in any doubt, re-check with the text. In cases where fasteners have corroded, apply penetrating fluid before disassembly.

6.3 Undo the valve cover screws

6.4a Remove the spark plug seal . . .

6.4b . . . and the cover gasket

6.6a Install the spark plug seal and gasket

6.6b Apply sealant in the cut-outs

6.7 Install the cover carefully

4 When disassembling the engine, keep 'mated' parts that have been in contact with each other during engine operation together (e.g. camshafts and followers, valve assemblies). These 'mated' parts must be reused or renewed as assemblies.

5 A complete engine/transmission disassembly should be done in the following general order with reference to the appropriate Sections.

• *Remove the valve cover*
• *Remove the cam chain tensioner*
• *Remove the camshafts*
• *Remove the cylinder head*
• *Remove the cam chain guide blade*
• *Remove the cylinder*
• *Remove the piston*
• *Remove the water pump (see Chapter 3)*
• *Remove the variator assembly (see Chapter 2C)*
• *Remove the alternator and starter motor (see Chapter 9)*
• *Remove the starter clutch and idler gear*
• *Remove the cam chain and tensioner blade*
• *Remove the balancer shaft driven gear*
• *Remove the oil pump driven gear*
• *Remove the transmission shafts and gears (see Chapter 2C)*
• *Separate the crankcase halves*
• *Remove the balancer shaft*
• *Remove the oil pump*
• *Remove the crankshaft and connecting rod assembly*

Reassembly

6 Reassembly is accomplished by reversing the general disassembly sequence.

6 Valve cover

Note: *This procedure can be carried out with the engine in the frame. If the engine has been removed, ignore the steps which do not apply.*

Removal

1 Remove the air filter housing and the throttle body assembly (see Chapter 4B).
2 Pull off the spark plug cap.
3 Undo the valve cover screws and remove them, noting the location of the sealing washers **(see illustration)**. Discard the washers as new ones must be fitted on reassembly.
4 Lift the valve cover off the cylinder head. If it is stuck, tap around the joint with a soft-faced mallet to dislodge it – don't not try to lever it off with a screwdriver as the sealing surfaces will be damaged. Discard the spark plug seal and cover gasket as new ones must be fitted on reassembly **(see illustrations)**.

Installation

5 Clean the mating surfaces of the cylinder head and valve cover with a suitable solvent to remove all traces of old sealant and gasket. If a scraper is used, take care not to scratch or gouge the soft aluminium. Ensure none of the old gasket material falls into the engine.
6 Lay the new spark plug seal and cover gasket onto the valve cover, making sure they locate correctly and using dabs of grease to

hold them in place **(see illustration)**. Apply a suitable, non-permanent sealant to the camshaft end cap cut-outs in the cylinder head **(see illustration)**.
7 Position the cover on the cylinder head carefully, making sure the gasket stays in place **(see illustration)**. Install the cover screws with new sealing washers – lubricate the washers with a smear of engine oil. Tighten the screws evenly to the torque setting specified at the beginning of this Chapter.
8 Install the remaining components in the reverse order of removal.

7 Cam chain tensioner

Note: *This procedure can be carried out with the engine in the frame. If the engine has been removed, ignore the steps which do not apply.*

Removal

1 Remove the valve cover (see Section 6). Remove the spark plug (see Chapter 1).
2 Remove the drive belt cooling fan filter element (see Chapter 1, Section 2).
3 The engine must be turned to position the piston at top dead centre (TDC) on its compression stroke. The engine can be turned using a suitable spanner on the end of the crankshaft as when checking the valve clearance (see Chapter 1, Section 3).
4 Unscrew the tensioner cap bolt and

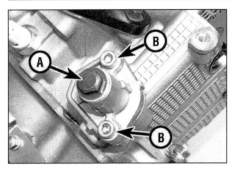

7.4a Tensioner cap bolt (A) and mounting bolts (B)

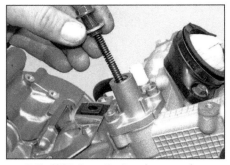

7.4b Withdraw the tensioner spring

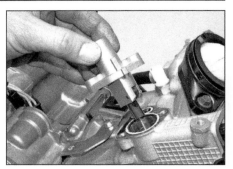

7.5 Withdraw the tensioner body

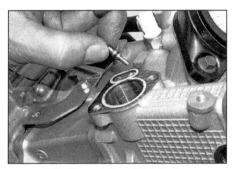

7.6 Discard the oil jet O-ring

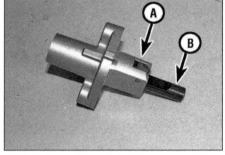

7.8 Release the catch (A) and check the pushrod (B)

withdraw the spring from the tensioner **(see illustrations)**. Discard the sealing washer as a new one must be used.

5 Undo the tensioner mounting bolts and withdraw the tensioner body from the back of the cylinder head **(see illustration)**. Discard the gasket as a new one must be fitted on reassembly.

6 Note the location of the oil jet and draw it out – discard the O-ring as a new one must be fitted **(see illustration)**.
Caution: Do not rotate the engine with the cam chain tensioner removed.

Inspection

7 Examine the cam chain tensioner and spring

for signs of wear or damage. If the spring appears compressed replace it with a new one.
8 Release the catch and ensure that the push rod slides smoothly in the tensioner body **(see illustration)**. Check that the teeth on the push rod are not worn. If necessary, fit a new cam chain tensioner.
9 Check that the oil jet is clear.

Installation

10 Check that the piston is still at top dead centre (TDC) on its compression stroke (see Step 3).
11 Lubricate the new oil jet O-ring with a smear of engine oil and install the oil jet **(see illustration 7.6)**.

12 Fit a new gasket onto the cylinder head **(see illustration)**.
13 Ensure the push rod is pushed fully into the tensioner body, install the tensioner and tighten the mounting bolts to the torque setting specified at the beginning of this Chapter.
14 Install the spring and the cap bolt with a new sealing washer and tighten the bolt to the specified torque. Note that a clicking noise will be heard as the cap bolt is installed and the push rod is extended against the tensioner blade under spring pressure.
15 Turn the engine in the normal direction of rotation to ensure the camshafts operate correctly and the camchain is fully tensioned.
16 Install the drive belt cooling fan filter element, then install the remaining components in the reverse order of removal.

8 Camshafts and followers

Removal

1 Remove the cam chain tensioner (see Section 7).
2 Unscrew the camshaft holder bolts evenly and a little at a time in the **reverse** of the numerical tightening sequence marked on the holder **(see illustration)**. While loosening

7.12 Fit a new gasket

8.2 Camshaft holder bolt tightening sequence

8.3 Remove the upper cam chain guide

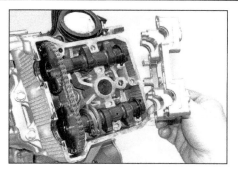

8.4a Remove the camshaft holder

8.4b Note location of the dowels

8.5a Centrifugal decompressor cam

8.5b Remove the intake . . .

8.5c . . . and exhaust camshafts

the bolts make sure that the holder is lifting squarely away from the cylinder head and is not sticking on the locating dowels.

3 Lift off the upper cam chain guide **(see illustration)**.

4 Lift off the camshaft holder and remove the dowels for safekeeping if they are loose **(see illustrations)**.

5 Note the centrifugal decompressor cam on the exhaust camshaft, then slip the cam chain off the intake and exhaust camshaft sprockets in turn and lift the camshafts out of the head **(see illustrations)**. **Note:** *Secure the cam chain to some convenient point with wire or a cable-tie to prevent it falling into the engine.*

6 If the cam followers and shims are being removed, obtain a container which is divided into four compartments, and label each compartment with the location of its corresponding valve in the cylinder head. If a container is not available, use labelled plastic

bags. **Note:** *It is essential that the followers and shims are stored according to their position in the head and fitted back on their original valves otherwise all the clearances will be wrong.*

7 Refer to the procedure in Chapter 1, Section 3, to remove the cam followers and shims

8 Cover the cylinder head to prevent anything falling into the engine.

Inspection

9 Inspect the bearing surfaces of the head and the holder and the corresponding journals on the camshaft – look for score marks, deep scratches and evidence of spalling (a pitted appearance) **(see illustrations)**.

10 Check the camshaft lobes for heat discoloration (blue appearance), score marks, chipped areas, flat spots and spalling **(see illustration)**. Measure the height of each lobe with a micrometer and compare the results to the *Specifications* at the beginning

of this Chapter. If damage is noted or wear is excessive, the camshaft must be replaced with a new one.

11 Check camshaft runout by supporting each end of the camshaft on V-blocks, and measuring any runout at the journals using a dial gauge (see *Tools and Workshop Tips* in the *Reference* section). If the runout exceeds the specified limit the camshaft must be replaced with a new one.

12 Inspect the outer surfaces of the cam followers for evidence of wear, scoring or other damage. If the surface of a follower is in poor condition, it is probable that the bore in which it works is also damaged. Remove the valve

 Refer to Tools and Workshop Tips in the Reference section for details of how to read a micrometer and dial gauge.

8.9a Inspect the bearing surfaces of the head and holder . . .

8.9b . . . and the corresponding camshaft journals

8.10 Inspect the camshaft lobes

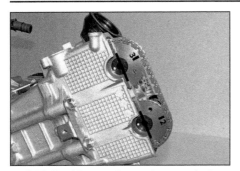

8.17 Position marks on the camshaft sprockets

8.22 Check the operation of the centrifugal decompressor cam

8.28 Locate the cam chain on the sprockets as described

(see Section 10) and check the follower bore – if it is seriously out-of-round the cylinder head will have to be replaced with a new one.

13 The camshaft journal oil clearance should now be checked. There are two possible ways of doing this, either by direct measurement (see Steps 14 to 16) or by the use of a product known as Plastigauge (see Steps 17 to 21). If Plastigauge is used and the oil clearance is excessive, use direct measurement to determine whether it is the camshaft or the holder that is worn. **Note:** *Illustrations of the measurement procedures can be found in Chapter 2A, Section 8.*

14 If direct measurement is to be used, make sure the camshaft holder dowels are in position then fit the holder. Tighten the holder bolts evenly to the specified torque setting.

15 Make a chart or sketch of the cylinder head so that a note of each measurement can be made against the appropriate bearing surfaces. Using telescoping gauges and a micrometer (see *Tools and Workshop Tips*), measure the internal diameter of each holder journal and record it on the chart. Now measure the diameter of the corresponding camshaft journals with a micrometer and record them on the chart.

16 To determine the journal oil clearance, subtract the camshaft journal diameter from the internal holder journal diameter. Compare the result with the specifications at the beginning of this Chapter. If any oil clearance is greater than specified, compare the individual measurements of the camshaft and holder journals to the *Specifications* and replace whichever component is beyond its service limit with a new one. **Note:** *If a holder journal is worn beyond its service limit a new cylinder head will have to be fitted.*

17 If the Plastigauge method is to be used, clean the camshafts and the bearing surfaces in the cylinder head and camshaft holder with a clean, lint-free cloth. Lay the camshafts in the cylinder head with the line on the end of the camshafts parallel with the valve cover mating surface and the lines 2 (exhaust camshaft sprocket) and 3 (intake camshaft sprocket) at 90° to the mating surface **(see illustration)**.

18 Cut strips of Plastigauge and lay one piece

on each camshaft journal, along the camshaft centreline. Make sure the camshaft holder dowels are in position then fit the holder. Tighten the holder bolts to the specified torque setting in the numerical sequence marked on the holder **(see illustration 8.2)**. Tighten the bolts evenly and a little at a time, ensuring that the holder comes down squarely onto the cylinder head and does not stick on the locating dowels. **Note:** *The camshafts must not rotate during this procedure.*

19 Now unscrew the bolts evenly and a little at a time in the reverse order and carefully lift off the camshaft holder.

20 To determine the oil clearance, compare the crushed Plastigauge (at its widest point) on each journal to the Plastigauge scale.

21 Compare the results to this Chapter's *Specifications*. If any oil clearance is greater than specified, follow Steps 14 and 15 to determine which component is worn beyond its service limit and replace that component with a new one. **Note:** *If a holder journal is worn beyond its service limit a new cylinder head will have to be fitted.*

22 Check the operation of the centrifugal decompressor cam on the exhaust camshaft, noting the location of the return spring on the back of the cam mechanism **(see illustration)**. If the mechanism is stuck or broken a new camshaft will have to be fitted.

23 Check the camshaft sprockets for wear, chipped teeth and other damage. If the sprockets are worn, the chain and the drive sprocket on the crankshaft are probably worn as well and should be checked (see Section 15).

Installation

24 Make sure the bearing surfaces in the cylinder head, on the camshafts and in the holders are clean, then lubricate them with molybdenum oil (a mixture of molybdenum grease and engine oil). Also apply oil to the camshaft lobes and the followers.

25 Refer to the procedure in Chapter 1, Section 3, to install the shims and cam followers. **Note:** *It is most important that the shims and followers are returned to their original valves otherwise the valve clearances will be inaccurate.*

26 Ensure that the line on the alternator rotor aligns with the static timing mark on the alternator cover (see Chapter 1, Section 3). If it is necessary to turn the crankshaft to restore the alignment, hold the cam chain up to prevent it jamming between the crankcase and the crankshaft sprocket.

27 Keeping the front run of the cam chain taut, lay the exhaust camshaft into the cylinder head – the line on the end of the camshaft must be parallel with the valve cover mating surface and the line No. 2 on the sprocket should be at 90° to the mating surface **(see illustration 8.17)**. Engage the chain on the sprocket, pulling up on the front run so there is no slack between the drive sprocket on the crankshaft and the sprocket on the camshaft.

28 Lay the intake camshaft into the cylinder head with the line on the end of the camshaft parallel with the valve cover mating surface and the line No. 3 on the sprocket at 90° to the mating surface **(see illustration 8.17)**. Starting with the cam chain pin that is directly above line No. 2 on the **exhaust** camshaft sprocket, count 15 pins along the chain towards the intake side and engage the chain on the **intake** camshaft sprocket so that the 15th pin is directly above line No. 3 **(see illustration)**. Ensure that the line on the alternator still aligns with the static timing mark.

29 Make sure the camshaft holder dowels are in position, then fit the holder **(see illustration 8.4b and a)**. Install the upper camchain guide.

30 Tighten the camshaft holder bolts to the specified torque setting in the numerical sequence marked on the holder **(see illustration 8.2)**. Tighten the bolts evenly and a little at a time, ensuring that the holder comes down squarely onto the cylinder head and does not stick on the locating dowels.

31 Install the cam chain tensioner (see Section 7). When rotating the engine to check the timing marks, ensure that the camshafts are not pinched by the holder.

32 Check the valve clearances and adjust them if necessary (see Chapter 1). Install the remaining components in the reverse order of removal.

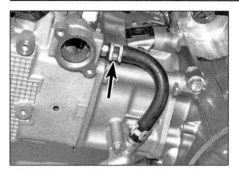

9.1 Disconnect the coolant bypass hose

9.6a Location of the cylinder head bolts – 6 mm bolts (A)

9.6b Note washers on 8 mm bolts

9 Cylinder head removal and installation

Note: *This procedure can be carried out with the engine in the frame. If the engine has been removed, ignore the steps which do not apply.*

Removal

1 Drain the cooling system (see Chapter 1) and remove the thermostat (see Chapter 3). Disconnect the coolant bypass hose from the thermostst housing **(see illustration)**.
2 Remove the exhaust system (see Chapter 4B).
3 Remove the heat shield (see Section 4).
4 Remove the valve cover (see Section 6).
5 Remove the cam chain tensioner (see Section 7), the camshafts, cam followers and shims (see Section 8).

6 Unscrew the cylinder head bolts evenly in a criss-cross pattern **(see illustration)**. Note the location of the washers on the 8 mm bolts **(see illustration)**.
7 Lift the head off the cylinder, passing the cam chain down through the tunnel as you do **(see illustration)**. If the head is stuck, tap around the joint with a soft-faced mallet to free it. Do not attempt to free the head by levering it off – you'll damage the sealing surfaces.
8 Secure the cam chain to prevent it falling into the engine and stuff a clean rag into the cam chain tunnel to prevent any debris falling in. Remove the cylinder head gasket **(see illustration)**.
9 If they are loose, remove the two dowels from the front and rear edge of the cylinder for safekeeping **(see illustration)**. If either appears to be missing it is probably stuck in the underside of the cylinder head.

10 Lift out the cam chain guide blade **(see illustration)**.
11 Inspect the cylinder head gasket and the mating surfaces on the cylinder head and cylinder for signs of leakage, which could indicate that the head is distorted. If necessary, check the cylinder head with a straight-edge (see Section 10). Discard the old head gasket as a new one must be fitted on reassembly.
12 If required, undo the bolts securing the intake manifold, noting how it fits **(see illustration)**. Discard the O-ring as a new one must be fitted on reassembly.
13 If required, unscrew the ECT sensor and discard the O-ring as a new one must be fitted on reassembly **(see illustration)**.

Installation

14 Clean the mating surfaces of the cylinder head and cylinder with a suitable solvent to remove all traces of old gasket. If a scraper

9.7 Lift off the cylinder head . . .

9.8 . . . and remove the gasket

9.9 Location of the cylinder dowels

9.10 Remove the cam chain guide blade

9.12 Note which way the intake manifold is fitted

9.13 Location of the ECT sensor

9.17 Note which way the cam chain guide blade is fitted

is used, take care not to scratch or gouge the soft aluminium. Ensure none of the old gasket material falls into the cylinder bore or the oil and coolant passages.

 Refer to Tools and Workshop Tips for details of gasket removal methods.

15 If removed, fit a new O-ring smeared with grease into the groove in the intake manifold. Clean the threads of the manifold bolts and apply a suitable non-permanent thread-locking compound, then install the manifold and tighten the bolts to the torque setting specified at the beginning of this Chapter.
16 Install the ECT sensor with a new O-ring lubricated with coolant and tighten it to the specified torque.
17 Install the cam chain guide blade (see illustration).
18 If removed, install the two dowels in the cylinder (see illustration 9.9). Fit the new head gasket ensuring the gasket locates over the dowels and that all the holes are correctly aligned.
19 Remove any rag from the cam chain tunnel and check that the lower end of the cam chain guide blade is properly located. With the help of an assistant, keep the cam chain taut and pass it up through the tunnel in the head while the head is lowered onto the cylinder (see illustration). Secure the cam chain.
20 Lubricate the underside of the cylinder head bolt heads, the washers and the bolt threads with clean engine oil, then install

9.19 Lower the cylinder head carefully

the bolts and tighten them finger-tight (see illustration 9.6b).
21 Working in a criss-cross pattern, tighten the 8 mm bolts evenly and a little at a time to the initial torque setting specified at the beginning of this Chapter, then tighten the 6 mm bolts to the specified torqe (see illustration 9.6a).
22 Tighten the 8 mm bolts in the same sequence to the final torque setting.
23 Install the remaining components in the reverse order of removal.

10 Cylinder head and valve overhaul

1 Because of the complex nature of this job and the special tools and equipment required, most owners leave servicing of the valves, valve seats and valve guides to a professional. However, you can make an initial assessment of whether the valves are seating correctly, and therefore sealing, by pouring a small amount of solvent into each of the valve ports. If the solvent leaks past any valve into the combustion chamber area the valve is not seating correctly and sealing.
2 With the correct tools (a valve spring compressor is essential – make sure it is suitable for motorcycle work), you can also remove the valves and associated components from the cylinder head, clean them and check them for wear to assess the extent of the work needed.
3 A dealer service department or engine specialist can replace the guides and re-cut the valve seats if required.

4 After a valve service has been performed, be sure to clean the head very thoroughly before installation to remove any metal particles or abrasive grit that may still be present from the service operations. Use compressed air, if available, to blow out all the holes and passages.

Disassembly, inspection and reasembly

5 Refer to the procedure in Chapter 2A, Section 10, noting the following:
• *Take great care not to mark the bore of the cam follower with the valve spring compressor. Suzuki recommends inserting a protective plastic sleeve around the valve spring to protect the surface of the follower bore. They produce a service tool (Part No. 09919-28610) to do this.*
• *Only one spring is fitted to each valve.*
• *When inspecting components for wear, refer to the Specifications at the beginning of this Chapter.*

11 Cylinder

Note: *This procedure can be carried out with the engine in the frame. If the engine has been removed, ignore the steps which do not apply.*

Removal

1 Remove the cylinder head and lift out the cam chain guide blade (see Section 9).
2 Ease the cylinder up off the crankcase. If it is stuck, tap around the joint face between the cylinder and the crankcase with a soft-faced mallet to free it. Do not attempt to free the cylinder by levering with a screwdriver between the cylinder and crankcase – you'll damage the sealing surfaces.
3 Once the cylinder has separated from the crankcase, secure the cam chain so that the cylinder can be lifted off completely. Support the piston to prevent the connecting rod or piston skirt hitting the crankcase (see illustrations). Once the cylinder has been removed, stuff clean rag around the connecting rod to protect it and to prevent anything falling into the crankcase.
4 Remove the cylinder base gasket (see illustration).

11.3a Support the piston . . .

11.3b . . . as the cylinder is removed

11.4 Remove the cylinder base gasket

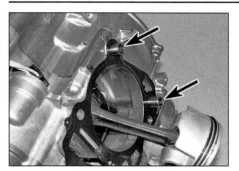

11.5 Remove the dowels (arrowed) if they are loose

11.17 Fit the piston into the cylinder . . .

11.18a . . . until the piston is in the bore completely

5 If they are loose, remove the two dowels from the left-hand edge of the crankcase for safekeeping **(see illustration)**. If either appears to be missing it is probably stuck in the underside of the cylinder.

6 If required, undo the bolts securing the air filter housing support bracket to the rear of the cylinder and remove the bracket.

7 Undo the bolts securing the coolant union to the left-hand side of the cylinder and lift it off. Discard the O-ring seal as a new one must be fitted.

8 Clean any traces of old gasket material from the cylinder and crankcase mating surfaces. If a scraper is used, take care not to scratch or gouge the soft aluminium. Be careful not to let any debris fall into the crankcase.

Inspection

9 Refer to the procedure in Chapter 2A, Section 11, noting the following:
- *When inspecting the cylinder for wear, refer to the Specifications at the beginning of this Chapter.*

Installation

10 If removed, fit a new O-ring into the groove around the coolant union. Lubricate the O-ring with engine coolant, then install the union and tighten the mounting bolts to the torque setting specified at the beginning of this Chapter.

11 If removed, install the air filter housing support bracket and tighten the bolts securely.

12 Remove any rag from around the connecting rod.

11.18b Press the cylinder down onto the crankcase

13 If removed, install the two dowels in the crankcase **(see illustration 11.5)**.

14 Fit a new cylinder base gasket **(see illustration 11.4)**.

15 Ensure that the piston ring end gaps are correctly staggered (see Section 13) then lubricate the piston, rings and cylinder bore with clean engine oil.

16 Release the cam chain so that the cylinder can be lowered down over the chain.

17 Support the piston and fit the top edge into the bottom of the cylinder bore **(see illustration)**. Carefully compress and feed it into the bore as the cylinder is pressed down – use your finger-tips and a small screwdriver to do this. Don't press the cylinder down too hard as this will only cause the rings to snag and take care not to score the surface of the piston skirt with the screwdriver.

18 Gradually slide the cylinder over the piston until all the rings are inside **(see illustration)**. Pull the cam chain up through the tunnel, then align the base of the cylinder with the dowels and press it firmly down onto the crankcase **(see illustration)**.

19 Secure the cam chain.

20 Note that the cylinder is not held securely against the crankcase until the cylinder head has been installed. If, for any reason, the crankshaft has to be turned, hold the cylinder in place while doing so.

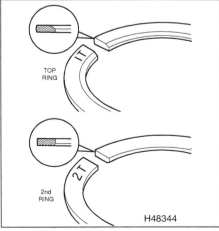

13.1a Piston ring cross-sections

12 Piston

Note: *This procedure can be carried out with the engine in the frame. If the engine has been removed, ignore the steps which do not apply.*
1 Refer to the procedure in Chapter 2A, Section 12, noting the following:
- *When inspecting the piston for wear, refer to the Specifications at the beginning of this Chapter.*

13 Piston rings

1 Refer to the procedure in Chapter 2A, Section 13, noting the following:
- *The upper surface of the top two piston rings should have a manufacturer's mark at one end – the marks on each ring are different, so note which mark is for the top ring and which is for the second. The top ring is marked '1T' and the second ring is marked '2T'. Also note that the rings can be identified by their different cross-sections (see illustration).*
- *When inspecting the piston rings for wear, refer to the Specifications at the beginning of this Chapter.*
- *Once the rings are correctly installed, stagger their end gaps as shown (see illustration).*

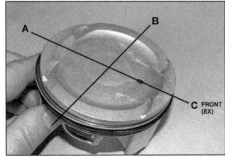

13.1b Position of piston ring end gaps – top ring and upper side rail (A), expander (B), second ring and lower side rail (C)

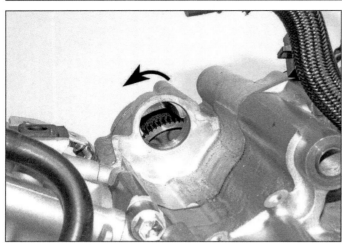

14.1 Gear should rotate freely anti-clockwise

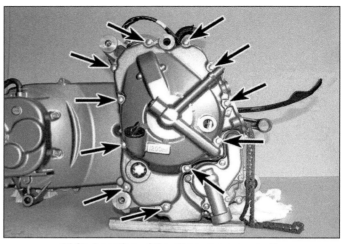

14.6a Location of the alternator cover bolts

14 Starter clutch and gears

Note: *This procedure can be carried out with the engine in the frame. If the engine has been removed, ignore the steps which do not apply.*

Check

1 The operation of the starter clutch can be checked while it is in situ. First remove the starter motor (see Chapter 9). Check that the reduction gear, located inside the starter motor aperture, rotates freely anti-clockwise

(as you look at it from the left-hand side), but locks when rotated clockwise **(see illustration)**. If not, the starter clutch or one of the intermediate gears is faulty and should be removed for inspection.

Removal

2 Remove the right side belly panel and the seat cowling for access (see Chapter 8).
3 Remove the exhaust silencer (see Chapter 4B).
4 Drain the engine oil (see Chapter 1). Position a suitable tray underneath the alternator cover to catch any residual oil when the cover is removed.

5 Trace the wiring from the top of the alternator cover and disconnect the alternator and CKP sensor wiring connectors. Release the wiring from any ties and feed it back to the cover.
6 Undo the alternator cover bolts, noting their locations, and draw off the cover **(see illustration)**. Remove the cover gasket and discard it; note the position of the cover dowels and remove them for safe-keeping if they are loose **(see illustrations)**.
7 Remove the spacer from the reduction gear shaft **(see illustration)**.
8 Note how the smaller pinion on the reduction gear engages with the driven gear on the starter clutch **(see illustration)**. Check the operation of the starter clutch – the driven gear should rotate freely anti-clockwise as you look at it, but should lock when rotated clockwise. If not the starter clutch is faulty and should be removed for inspection.
9 Remove the alternator rotor – the starter clutch is mounted on the back of it (see Chapter 9). **Note:** *Before removing the alternator rotor, slacken the six starter clutch bolts while holding the rotor centre bolt.*
10 Note the location of the key in the slot on the crankshaft, then carefully tap it out using a small chisel **(see illustration)**.

14.6b Remove the cover gasket

14.6c Location of cover dowels (arrowed)

14.7 Remove the spacer

14.8 Smaller pinion engages with starter clutch driven gear

14.10 Remove the key from the crankshaft

14.11 Remove the starter driven gear

14.12a Remove the reduction gear . . .

14.12b . . . and the gear shaft

11 Draw the starter driven gear off the crankshaft, noting how it fits **(see illustration)**.

12 If not already done, remove the reduction gear and its shaft, noting how the larger pinion engages with the starter motor pinion **(see illustrations)**.

Inspection

13 Refer to the procedure in Chapter 2A, Section 14.

Installation

14 Prior to installation, lay the rotor face down and lubricate the clutch assembly with clean engine oil, then fit the driven gear, rotating it clockwise to spread the sprags and allow the gear hub to enter. Ensure that the driven gear rotates freely in a clockwise direction and locks against the rotor in an anti-clockwise direction. Withdraw the driven gear – if it appears stuck, rotate it clockwise to free it from the clutch sprags.

15 Lubricate the reduction gear shaft with clean engine oil, then install the shaft and gear **(see illustrations 14.12b and a)**.

16 Slide the driven gear onto the cranlshaft, then install the key, ensuring it is squarely located in its slot **(see illustrations)**.

17 Clean the tapered section of the crankshaft and inside of the alternator rotor with suitable solvent, then install the rotor (see Chapter 9).

18 Fit the spacer onto the reduction gear shaft **(see illustrations 14.7)**.

19 Clean all old gasket and sealant from the alternator cover and crankcase. If removed, install the cover dowels, then fit the new cover gasket, making sure it locates correctly onto the dowels **(see illustrations 14.6c and b)**. Apply a smear of suitable sealant across the wiring grommet in the alternator cover.

20 Install the cover and cover bolts as noted on removal. Tighten the bolts evenly in a criss-cross pattern to the specified torque setting.

21 Install the remaining components in the reverse order of removal – don't forget to refill the engine oil (see Chapter 1).

14.16a Press the key into its slot firmly . . .

14.16b . . . ensuring it is correctly located

15 Cam chain, chain guide and tensioner blade

Note: *This procedure can be carried out with the engine in the frame. If the engine has been removed, ignore the steps which do not apply.*
1 Except in cases of oil starvation, the cam chain wears very little. If the chain has stretched excessively and can no longer be correctly tensioned by the cam chain tensioner, it is likely that the chain guide and tensioner blades will be worn and in need of renewal as well. Also check the condition of the camshaft sprockets and upper cam chain guide (see Section 8), and crankshaft sprocket (see Step 9). **Note:** *Check the operation of the cam chain tensioner if the chain is slack*

but appears to be in good condition (see Section 7).

Removal

2 To remove the cam chain guide blade, follow the procedure in Section 9 and remove the cylinder head, then lift out the guide blade **(see illustration 9.10)**.

3 To remove the cam chain tensioner blade, first remove the cylinder head (see Section 9), then remove the alternator rotor and starter driven gear (see Section 14).

4 Undo the bolt securing the cam chain tensioner blade and and lift out the blade **(see illustrations)**.

5 To remove the cam chain, first follow Steps 3 and 4. Mark the chain so that it can be fitted the same way around, then feed it

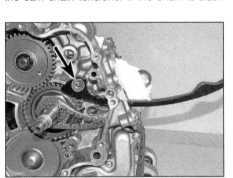

15.4a Undo the bolt (arrowed) . . .

15.4b . . . and remove the cam chain tensioner blade

15.5 Remove the cam chain through the crankcase

15.6 Location of the cam chain guide blade bolt

down into the crankcase and remove it (see illustration).

6 Note the location of the cam chain guide blade bolt and ensure it is tight (see illustration).

Inspection

7 Examine the sliding surface of the guide and tensioner blades for signs of wear or damage. Check them carefully for cracks in the surface and along the edges. Install new components if necessary.

8 Lay the chain on the work surface and pull it taut. Check all round the chain – if there is any discernible slack between the links, or if there is any doubt about its condition, fit a new chain.

9 Inspect the teeth of the crankshaft sprocket. If there are any signs of wear or damage, a new crankshaft will have to be fitted.

10 Inspect the teeth on the camshaft sprockets and renew the camshafts if necessary (see Section 8).

Installation

11 Fit the cam chain onto the crankshaft sprocket, then feed the chain up through the aperture in the crankcase and secure it (see illustration 15.5).

12 Clean the threads of the tensioner blade bolt and apply a suitable non-permanent thread-locking compound. Position the blade, ensuring it is the correct way round, and tighten the bolt to the torque setting specified at the beginning of this Chapter.

13 If required, unscrew the guide blade bolt and clean the threads. Apply a suitable non-permanent thread-locking compound and tighten the bolt to the torque setting specified at the beginning of this Chapter.

14 Install the guide blade once the cylinder has been fitted (see illustration 9.17).

15 Install the remaining components in the reverse order of removal.

16 Balancer shaft and oil pump driven gears

Note: *This procedure can be carried out with the engine in the frame. If the engine has been removed, ignore the steps which do not apply.*

1 Remove the alternator rotor and starter driven gear (see Section 14).

2 The balancer shaft and the oil pump are located inside the crankcases (see Section 17). However, before the crankcase halves can be separated, the balancer shaft and oil pump driven gears must be removed.

Balancer shaft driven gear

Removal

3 To prevent the crankshaft from turning while the driven gear nut is loosened, position the crankshaft so that a suitable 12 mm bolt or steel bar can be inserted through the right-hand crankcase half and the crankshaft webs into the recess in the left-hand crankcase half (see illustrations).

4 Undo the driven gear nut and remove the washer (see illustration).

5 The gear is a two-piece, spring loaded assembly designed to eliminate backlash between the crankshaft and the balancer shaft. Insert a suitable bolt into the hole in the two halves of the driven gear to hold them in alignment, then pull the gear off the balancer shaft (see illustration).

6 Note the location of the key in the slot on the shaft, then carefully tap it out using a small chisel (see illustration).

Inspection

7 Refer to the procedure in Chapter 2A, Section 17.

Installation

8 Fit the rear gear onto the front gear, ensuring it is the correct way round, and align the holes in the two gears. Fit the springs into the rear gear and press them into the recesses in the front gear.

16.3a Insert the bar through the right-hand side . . .

16.3b . . . into the recess (arrowed) on the left-hand side

16.4 Remove the nut and washer

16.5 Align the gears and pull the assembly off

16.6 Remove the key from the balancer shaft

16.10a Press the key into its slot firmly . . .

16.10b . . . ensuring it is correctly located

16.12 Register marks (arrowed) must align exactly

16.16a Undo the screws (arrowed) . . .

16.16b . . . and remove the cover plate

16.17 Undo the nut . . .

9 Install the plain washer and secure the assembly with a new circlip.

10 Install the key, ensuring it is squarely located in its slot in the balancer shaft (see illustrations).

11 Align the teeth on the two halves of the driven gear and insert a suitable bolt into the hole to hold them in position.

12 Align the keyway in the centre of the driven gear with the key in the balancer shaft, then align the register mark on the driven gear with the mark on the crankshaft gear and press the driven gear firmly onto its shaft (see illustration). Remove the bolt. Ensure the balancer shaft driven gear and the crankshaft gear are aligned exactly.

13 Install the washer and driven gear nut finger-tight (see illustration 16.4).

14 Lock the crankshaft to prevent it turning (see Step 3) and tighten the driven gear nut to

the torque setting specified at the beginning of this Chapter. Remove the locking piece.

15 Install the remaining components in the reverse order of removal.

Oil pump driven gear

Removal

16 Undo the screws securing the gear cover plate and remove the plate (see illustrations).

17 If not already done, follow the procedure in Step 3 to lock the crankshaft, then undo the driven gear nut (see illustration).

18 Remove the gear, withdraw the drive pin from the pump shaft and remove the spacer (see illustrations).

Installation

19 Installation is the reverse of removal, noting the following:

• With the crankshaft locked, tighten the driven gear nut to the torque setting specified at the beginning of this Chapter.

17 Crankcase separation and reassembly

Note: To separate the crankcase halves, the engine must be removed from the frame.

Special tools: A 46 mm deep socket will be required to undo the nut securing the crankshaft gear (see Step 6). Pullers may be required to separate the crankcase halves (see Step 10), press the crankshaft out of the crankcase (see Step 16) and draw the crankshaft into the crankcase on reassembly (see Step 21).

16.18a . . . remove the oil pump driven gear . . .

16.18b . . . the drive pin . . .

16.18c . . . and the spacer

17.6a Undo the crankshaft gear nut . . .

17.6b . . . using a 46 mm deep socket

17.7a Remove the washer . . .

Separation

1 To gain access to the connecting rod, crankshaft and bearings, balancer shaft and oil pump, the crankcase must be split into two parts.
2 Remove the engine from the frame (see Section 4).
3 Before the crankcases can be separated the following components must be removed:
• Oil filter (Chapter 1)
• Cylinder head (Section 9)
• Cylinder (Section 11)
• Piston (Section 12)

17.7b . . . and the gear . . .

• Water pump (Chapter 3)
• Alternator rotor and starter motor (Chapter 9)
• Balancer shaft and oil pump driven gears (Section 16)
• Variator and drive belt (Chapter 2C)

4 Lock the crankshaft to prevent it turning using a 12 mm bolt as described in Section 16.
5 A 46 mm deep socket is required to undo the nut securing the crankshaft gear. Suzuki produces a service tool (Part No. 09922-21410) to do this. Alternatively a suitable tool can be made from a socket and a length of tube (see Chapter 2A, Section 18).

17.7c . . . and pull out the pin

6 Slide the socket over the end of the crankshaft and undo the nut (see illustrations).
7 Lift off the washer and the gear, noting how the gear locates over the pin in the crankshaft, then remove the pin (see illustrations).
8 Support the crankcases on the work surface with the left-hand side uppermost. Undo the 6 mm crankcase bolts, then undo the 8 mm bolts (see illustration). **Note:** *As each bolt is removed, store it in its relative position in a cardboard template of the crankcases. This will ensure all bolts are installed in the correct location on reassembly.*
9 Turn the engine over so that the right-hand side is uppermost. Undo the 8 mm bolts evenly in a criss-cross pattern (see illustration).
10 Carefully lift the right-hand crankcase half off the left-hand half (see illustration). If it is stuck, tap around the joint with a soft-faced mallet to dislodge it. If the halves do not separate easily, first make sure all fasteners have been removed. Do not try and separate the halves by levering between the sealing surfaces as they are easily damaged and will leak on reassembly. If required, Suzuki produces a service tool to help with crankcase separation (Part No. 09920-13120). Alternatively, a suitable puller can be made from a piece of steel bar and two lengths of threaded rod (see Chapter 2A, Section 18).

17.8 Left-hand side crankcase bolts – 8 mm bolts (A)

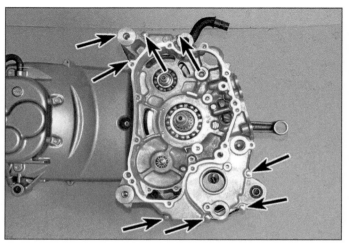

17.9 Right-hand side crankcase bolts

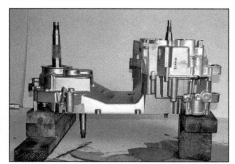

17.10 Lift off the right-hand crankcase half

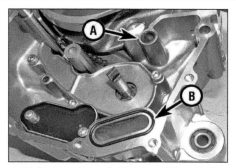

17.11 Location of oil gallery (A) and oil cooler (B) O-rings

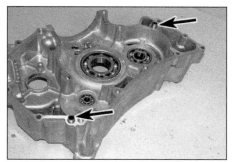

17.12 Location of crankcase dowels

17.13a Remove the balancer shaft . . .

17.13b . . . and inspect the journals and key slot

17.14a Undo the screws . . .

11 The right-hand crankcase half will come away leaving the crankshaft, balancer shaft and oil pump in the left-hand crankcase. Note the location of the oil gallery and oil cooler O-rings and discard them as new ones must be fitted **(see illustration)**.

12 Note the location of the crankcase dowels in the right-hand crankcase half and remove them for safekeeping if they are loose **(see illustration)**.

13 Lift out the balancer shaft **(see illustration)**. Inspect the shaft journals for wear and pitting, especially if the shaft bearings in the crankcase are worn or damaged (see Chapter 2A, Section 20). Ensure that the key slot in the shaft is not damaged **(see illustration)**.

14 Undo the screws securing the oil sump filter cover and remove the cover **(see illustrations)**. Draw out the filter element, noting how it fits **(see illustration)**. Wash

17.14b . . . and remove the sump filter cover

17.14c Note how the filter element fits

the element with a suitable solvent and dry it with compressed air, if available. Ensure any particles of dirt or metal swarf are removed completely. If the element is damaged a new filter must be fitted.

15 Undo the screws securing the oil pump chain cover and remove the cover **(see illustrations)**. Undo the bolts securing the oil pump, then lift the pump out, disengaging the chain from the pump sprocket **(see**

17.15a Undo the screws . . .

17.15b . . . and remove the oil pump chain cover

17.15c Undo the bolts . . .

17.15d . . . and lift out the pump

17.15e Lift out the drive shaft and chain

17.17 Remove the breather gauze filter

illustrations). Lift out the oil pump drive shaft and chain **(see illustration)**. Refer to Section 20 for details on the oil pump.

16 The crankshaft should be a tight fit in the left-hand main bearing and a tool, simiilar to the one used to separate the crankcase halves should be used to press it out (see Chapter 2A, Section 18). **Note:** *If either of the main bearings remains on the crankshaft during disassembly an external bearing puller will be required to remove it (see Chapter 2A, Section 19).*

17 Note the location of the crankcase breather gauze and remove it for cleaning **(see illustration)**. Wash the gauze with a suitable solvent and dry it with compressed air, if available.

18 Refer to Section 18 for details on the crankshaft and connecting rod and Section 19 for details on the crankcases and bearings.

19 If required, follow the procedure in Chapter 2C to remove the transmission components.

17.21 Installed position of the crankshaft left-hand side

Reassembly

20 Remove all traces of old sealant from the crankcase mating surfaces with a suitable solvent and clean the threads of all the crankcase bolts.

21 A special tool will be required to draw the crankshaft into the crankcase. Suzuki produces service tools to do this (Part Nos. 09910-32812, 09910-32870 and 09913-70210). A similar tool can be made utilising the deep socket used to undo the crankshaft gear nut combined with a sleeved extension and a fabricated drawbolt (see Chapter 2A, Section 18). It is essential to keep the crankshaft aligned exactly with the crankcase during installation and to ensure the crankshaft passes all the way through the main bearing **(see illustration)**.

22 Install the crankcase breather gauze and the balancer shaft **(see illustrations 17.17 and 13a)**.

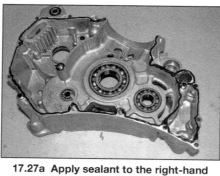

17.27a Apply sealant to the right-hand crankcase half

23 Install the oil pump drive shaft and chain as an assembly, then install the pump and tighten the bolts to the torque setting specified at the beginning of this Chapter **(see illustrations 17.15e, d and c)**. Fit the pump chain cover and tighten the screws securely.

24 Install the oil sump filter element narrow edge first, with the outside lip facing down **(see illustration 17.14c)**. Fit the cover and tighten the screws securely.

25 Fit new oil gallery and oil cooler O-rings in their grooves in the left-hand crankcase half **(see illustration 17.11)**.

26 If removed, install the crankcase dowels **(see illustration 17.12)**.

27 Apply a thin coating of suitable sealant to the mating surface of the right-hand crankcase as shown **(see illustration)**. Also apply sealant around the top edge of the left-hand crankcase half and on the mating surface below the oil cooler aperture **(see illustrations)**.

Caution: Do not apply an excessive amount of sealant as it will ooze out when the case halves are assembled and may obstruct oil passages.

28 Use a hot air gun to heat the right-hand main bearing.

29 Apply a freeze spray to the right-hand crankshaft journal, then immediately install the crankcase half, ensuring the balancer shaft, oil pump drive shaft and the crankcase dowels align correctly **(see illustration)**. Ensure the crankshaft passes all the way through the main bearing and that the crankcase halves are correctly seated. If necessary, tap around

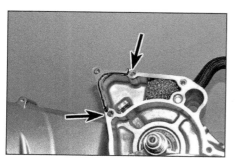

17.27b Apply sealant to the left-hand crankcase half between the arrows at the top . . .

17.27c . . . and below the oil cooler aperture

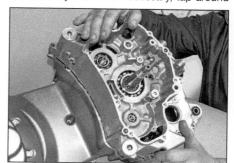

17.29a Ensure the crankcases are correctly aligned

17.29b Tap around the bearing inner race

18.2 Location of the cam chain sprocket

- When inspecting the crankshaft assembly for wear, refer to the Specifications at the beginning of this Chapter.
- The cam chain sprocket is located on the crankshaft **(see illustration)**.
- When inspecting the connecting rod small-end and piston pin for wear, refer to Section 12 and the Specifications in this Chapter.
- When inspecting the cam chain, refer to Section 15 in this Chapter.
- Follow the procedure in Section 17 to install the crankshaft assembly.

the inner race of the main bearing with a flat-nosed punch to ensure the crankcase is seated **(see illustration)**. Note: *The crankcases should fit together without being forced. If the casings are not correctly seated, remove the right-hand half and investigate the problem. Do not attempt to pull the casings together using the crankcase bolts as they will crack and be ruined.*

30 Install the crankcase bolts as noted on removal **(see illustration 17.9)**. Secure all the bolts finger-tight, then tighten the 8 mm bolts evenly in a criss-cross pattern to the torque setting specified at the beginning of this Chapter.

31 Turn the engine over so that the left-hand side is uppermost. Install the crankcase bolts as noted on removal **(see illustration 17.8)**. Secure all the bolts finger-tight, then tighten the 8 mm bolts evenly in a criss-cross pattern to the torque setting specified. Now tighten the 6 mm bolts to the torque setting specified.

32 Support the engine the right way up. Lubricate the main bearings and connecting rod big-end bearing with clean engine oil. Hold the connecting rod to prevent it hitting the crankcase and check that the crankshaft rotates smoothly and easily. If there are any signs of undue stiffness, tight or rough spots, or of any other problem, the fault must be rectified before proceeding further.

33 Fit the crankshaft gear pin **(see illustration 17.7c)**. Install the gear and the washer – the outer rim of the washer should be placed

against the gear **(see illustration 17.7b and a)**. Fit the gear nut finger-tight.

34 Lock the crankshaft to prevent it turning using a 12 mm bolt as on disassembly, then tighten the nut to the specified torque setting **(see illustrations 17.6a and b)**.

35 Install the remaining components in the reverse order of removal.

18 Crankshaft and connecting rod

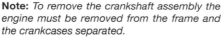

Note: *To remove the crankshaft assembly the engine must be removed from the frame and the crankcases separated.*
Special tool: *If necessary, an external bearing puller will be required to remove the main bearings from the crankshaft.*

1 The crankshaft assembly is a pressed-together unit for which a new connecting rod, crankpin and big-end bearing are available if required. However, because of the complex nature of the job and the special tools and equipment involved, rebuilding the crankshaft should only be undertaken by a dealer service department or engine specialist. Nevertheless, once the crankshaft has been removed (see Section 17) it can be checked for wear and the need for repair assessed.

Inspection and installation

2 Refer to the procedure in Chapter 2A, Section 19, noting the following:

19 Crankcases and bearings

Special tool: *A slide-hammer and knife-edged bearing puller attachment will be required to remove some bearings and seals .*

1 After the crankcase halves have been separated (see Section 17), remove all traces of old gasket from the sealing surfaces, taking care not to nick or gouge the soft aluminium if a scraper is used. Wash the components in a suitable solvent and dry them with compressed air, paying particular attention to the housing for the oil sump filter housing and the cavity for the crankcase breather gauze **(see illustrations 17.14c and 17.17)**.

2 If not already done, release the clip securing the crankcase breather hose and disconnect the hose **(see illustration)**. If the hose is cracked or perished a new one must be fitted.

Inspection

3 Refer to the procedure in Chapter 2A, Section 20, noting the following:
- If the engine mounting bushes need renewing, make a note of any offset before removing the old bushes **(see illustration)**.
- Check the condition of the oil pump drive shaft bearings. Note that the bearing in the left-hand casing is fitted in a blind hole **(see illustration)** and will require a slide-hammer and knife-edged bearing puller to remove it (see Tools and Workshop Tips in the Reference section).

19.2 Check the crankcase breather hose

19.3a Note installed position of mounting bushes

19.3b Location of the left-hand oil pump drive shaft bearing

20 Oil pump

Note: *To remove the oil pump the engine must be removed from the frame and the crankcases separated.*

Removal

1 The oil pump is located inside the crankcase halves. Follow the procedure in Section 17 to remove the pump, drive shaft and chain.

Inspection

2 Lay the chain on the work surface and pull it taut. Check all round the chain – if there is any discernible slack between the links, or if there is any doubt about its condition, fit a new chain.

3 Inspect the teeth of the pump and driveshaft sprockets. If there are any signs of wear or damage, fit a new driveshaft and pump sprocket.

4 If required, remove the circlip securing the pump sprocket and lift off the sprocket **(see illustration)**. Remove the drive pin and washer.

5 Clean the pump in a suitable solvent and dry it with compressed air, if available. Lubricate the pump rotors with clean engine oil and check that the shaft rotates freely, without any side-to-side play, excessive endfloat or binding **(see illustration)**.

6 If any wear or damage is evident, a new pump will have to be fitted – individual components are not available. **Note:** *If required, follow the procedure in Chapter 2A, Section 15, to disassemble the pump.*

Installation

7 Install the washer, drive pin and sprocket in the reverse order of removal and secure the sprocket with a new circlip. Ensure the circlip is correctly located in its groove.

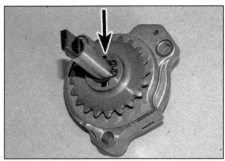

20.4 Circlip (arrowed) secures oil pump sprocket

8 Follow the procedure in Section 17 to install the pump, drive shaft and chain.

21 Start-up and running-in procedure

Initial start-up

1 Make sure the engine oil level and coolant level are correct (see *Pre-ride checks*). Make sure there is fuel in the tank.

2 Pull the cap off the spark plug, then turn the ignition switch ON and crank the engine over with the starter for a few seconds to prime the lubrication system. Turn the ignition OFF and reconnect the plug cap.

3 Start the engine and let it run at idle until it reaches normal operating temperature. Check carefully that there are no oil or coolant leaks. Do not be alarmed if there is a little smoke from the exhaust – this will be due to the oil used to lubricate the piston and bore during assembly and should subside after a while.

4 If the engine proves reluctant to start, remove the spark plug and check that it has not become wet and oily. If it has, clean it and try again. If the engine refuses to start, go

20.5 Inspect the pump for wear and stiffness

through the fault finding charts at the end of this manual to identify the problem.

5 Make sure the transmission and controls, especially the throttle and brakes, function properly before road testing the machine.

Recommended running-in procedure

6 Treat the machine gently for the first few miles to make sure that the oil is circulating and any new parts have started to seat.

7 Even greater care is necessary if a major engine overhaul has been undertaken. In the case of a new crankshaft or piston and cylinder, the bike will have to be run in as when new. This means a restraining hand on the throttle until at least 500 miles (800 km) have been covered.

8 There's no point in keeping to any set speed limit – the main idea is to keep from labouring the engine and to gradually increase performance up to the 1000 mile (1600 km) mark. Make sure that the throttle position is varied to vary engine speed, and use full throttle only for short bursts to start with. Experience is the best guide, since it's easy to tell when an engine is running freely.

9 Pay particular attention to the *Pre-ride checks* at the beginning of this manual. Check the tightness of all relevant nuts and bolts.

Chapter 2C
Transmission

Contents

Degrees of difficulty

Easy, suitable for novice with little experience 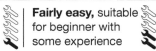	Fairly easy, suitable for beginner with some experience	Fairly difficult, suitable for competent DIY mechanic	Difficult, suitable for experienced DIY mechanic	Very difficult, suitable for expert DIY or professional

Specifications

Variator
Roller diameter
  AN250 models . . . . 23.72 to 23.88 mm
  AN400X to K2 models . . . . not available
  AN400K3 model onward . . . . 26.00 to 26.16 mm
Drive face warpage (service limit). . . . . 0.4 mm

Clutch and driven pulley
Clutch drum inside diameter (service limit)
  AN250 models . . . . 135.5 mm
  AN400X to K2 models . . . . 150.5 mm
  AN400K3 to K6 models . . . . 135.5 mm
  AN400K7 model onward . . . . 160.5 mm
Drive face warpage (service limit)
  AN400 models . . . . 0.4 mm
Spring free length (service limit)
  AN250W to Y models . . . . 99.9 mm
  AN250K1 and K2 models . . . . 104.5 mm
  AN400X to K2 models . . . . 129.4 mm
  AN400K3 to K6 models . . . . 118.7 mm
  AN400K7 to K8 models . . . . 142.5 mm
  AN400K9 model onward . . . . 137.8 mm
Clutch shoe lining thickness (service limit). . . . . 2.0 mm

Drive belt width
All models. . . . . see Chapter 1

Torque settings
Drive pulley nut
  AN250 models . . . . 95 Nm
  AN400 models . . . . 105 Nm
Clutch drum nut
  AN250 models . . . . 75 Nm
  AN400 models . . . . 85 Nm
Clutch assembly nut
  AN250 models . . . . 78 Nm
  AN400 models . . . . 105 Nm
Drive belt inner and outer cover bolts . . . . 11 Nm
Gearbox cover bolts. . . . . 22 Nm

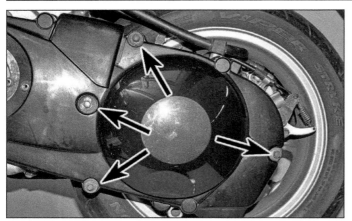

2.2a Undo the screws . . .

2.2b . . . noting the washers . . .

1 General information

The transmission on all models covered by this manual is fully automatic in operation. Power is transmitted from the engine to the rear wheel by belt, via a variable size drive pulley (the variator), an automatic clutch on the driven pulley, and a reduction gearbox. Both the variator and the automatic clutch work on the principal of centrifugal force.

Note: *On some models the internal components of the gearbox may differ slightly to those components described or shown. When dismantling always note the fitted position, order and way round of each component as it is removed.*

2 Drive belt covers

Removal

1 Remove the left-hand belly panel for access

2.2c . . . and lift off the outer cover

2.3 Note location of the cover seal

(see Chapter 8). Remove the drive belt cooling fan filter (see Chapter 1).

AN250 models and AN400X to K6 models

2 Undo the screws securing the outer drive belt cover, noting the location of the washers, and remove the cover **(see illustrations).**

3 Note the location of the cover seal – the seal does not extend around the lower rear edge of the cover **(see illustration)**. Note the location of the sound deadening material inside the

cover but do not try to remove it unless it is torn or damaged.

4 Note the location of the seal for the cooling fan filter but do not try to remove it unless it is torn or damaged. Undo the screws securing the inner drive belt cover and lift it off **(see illustration)**. If it will not lift away easily, the cover dowels may have corroded in the rear half of the cover – use penetrating fluid around the dowels and tap the edge of the cover gently with a soft-faced hammer. Note the location of the cover dowels and remove them for safekeeping if they are loose **(see illustration)**.

2.4a Undo the inner cover screws

2.4b Note location of the cover dowels

2.5a Undo the screws . . .

2.5b . . . and lift off the outer cover

2.7a Undo the inner cover screws

2.7b Draw the inner cover off

AN400K7 model onward

5 Undo the screws securing the outer drive belt cover and remove the cover **(see illustrations)**.

6 Note the location of the sound deadening material inside the cover but do not try to remove it unless it is torn or damaged. Note the location of the speed sensor wiring on the inner cover – either unclip the wiring from the cover or disconnect it at both ends and remove it with the cover.

7 Undo the screws securing the inner drive

2.11 Location of the gearbox input shaft bearing

belt cover **(see illustration)**. To help draw the cover off, thread two screws into the holes in the clutch dome **(see illustration)**. If the inner cover will not lift away easily, the cover dowels may have corroded in the rear half of the cover – use penetrating fluid around the dowels and tap the edge of the cover gently with a soft-faced hammer.

8 Note the location of the cover gasket and discard it as a new one must be fitted. Note the location of the cover dowels and remove them for safekeeping if they are loose **(see illustration 2.4b)**.

Inspection

9 Clean any dust or dirt from the inside of the covers with a stiff brush. Any evidence of oil inside the casing suggests a worn seal either on the crankshaft or the gearbox input shaft which must be rectified. Evidence of grease inside the casing suggests worn seals in the clutch centre which should also be rectified.

10 Examine the drive belt for wear (see Chapter 1).

11 On AN400 engines, an extra bearing for the gearbox input shaft is located in the inner cover **(see illustration)**. Check the condition of the bearing – it should spin freely and

smoothly without any rough spots (see *Tools and Workshop Tips* in the *Reference* section). Renew the bearing if there is any doubt about its condition.

12 Note which way round the bearing is fitted, then undo the screws and remove the bearing retainers.

13 Lay the cover inside face down, heat the bearing housing with a hot air gun then strike the bearing housing sharply with a piece of wood to dislodge the bearing. Alternatively, use a slide-hammer and knife-edged bearing puller to remove the bearing from the inside of the cover (see *Tools and Workshop Tips* in the *Reference* section).

 Warning: Be careful when handling the cover and wear protective gloves – when heated, the cover could cause severe burns.

14 Prior to installing the new bearing, check that the housing is clean and free from surface damage. If the bearing was loose in its housing, use a suitable bearing lock compound to secure it.

15 Lay the cover inside face up and support it securely, then heat the housing. Drive the new bearing in squarely until it

3.2 Holding the drive pulley with a strap wrench

3.3 Note which way round the washer is fitted

seats – ensure pressure is only applied to the bearing's outer race. Install the bearing retainers and tighten the screws securely.

Installation

16 If removed, lubricate the dowels with a smear of grease and fit them into the rear half of the inner cover.
17 Clean the threads of the cover screws and lubricate them with a smear of grease.
18 On AN400K7 models onward, fit a new inner cover gasket over the dowels **(see illustration 2.4b)**.
19 Install the inner cover and tighten the screws securely **(see illustration 2.4a or 7a as applicable)**.
20 On AN400K7 models onward, install the speed sensor wiring as noted on removal (see

Step 6), then install the outer drive belt cover and tighten the screws securely.
21 On AN250 and AN400X to K6 models, press the outer cover seal firmly into the groove around the edge of the cover **(see illustration 2.3)**. Install the cover and secure it with the washers and screws **(see illustrations 2.2b and a)**.
22 Install the remaining components in the reverse order of removal.

3 Drive pulley and variator

Special tools: *To avoid removing the alternator cover, a strap wrench will be required to hold the drive pulley (see Step 2).*

Removal

Note: *It is not necessary to remove the drive belt from the machine during this procedure. If the belt is removed, note any directional arrows or mark the belt so that it can be installed the same way round.*
1 Remove the drive belt covers (see Section 2).
2 To remove the drive pulley nut, the crankshaft must be held to prevent it turning. If available, fit a strap wrench around the outside of the pulley to do this, taking great care not to damage the fins **(see illustration)**. Alternatively, remove the alternator cover (see Chapter 2A or 2B as applicable) and counter-hold the alternator rotor nut.
3 Unscrew the drive pulley nut. Note which way round the spring washer is fitted and mark it with a dab of paint to aid reassembly **(see illustration)**.
4 Hold the inner half of the pulley to prevent the variator rollers from being displaced and lift off the outer half **(see illustration)**.
5 Move the drive belt aside (see **Note** above).
6 Grip the variator assembly so that the ramp plate at the back is held into the housing, then draw the assembly, including the centre sleeve, off the crankshaft **(see illustrations)**.

Inspection

7 Inspect the faces of the pulley for signs of wear, scoring or overheating **(see illustration)**. Check the condition of the splines in the centre

3.4 Lift off the outer half of the pulley

3.6a Grip the variator assembly from the back . . .

3.6b . . . then draw the assembly off . . .

3.6c . . . and slide out the centre sleeve

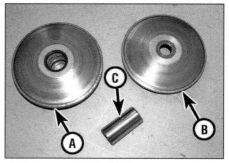

3.7 Inner pulley half (A), outer puller half (B) and centre sleeve (C)

3.8a Undo the screws . . .

3.8b . . . and lift off the variator cover

3.9 Lift out the ramp plate

3.10a Check the splines for wear

3.10b Note location of the ramp guides

3.11 Note location of the rollers

of the outer half of the pulley and examine
the centre sleeve for wear. Renew the pulley
assembly if it is damaged. **Note:** *The centre of
the pulley inner half is lubricated with grease.
If there is evidence of grease leaking onto the
pulley or drive belt the seals must be renewed
(see Step 16).*
8 To disassemble the variator, first undo
the screws and lift off the cover **(see
illustrations)**.
9 Lift out the ramp plate, noting how it fits
(see illustration).
10 Check the condition of the splines in the
centre of the ramp plate and renew it if they
are worn **(see illustration)**. Remove the ramp
guides if they are loose **(see illustration)**.
11 Lift out the rollers, noting how they fit **(see
illustration)**. There are six rollers in the AN250
variator and eight in the AN400 variator.
12 Clean all the components using a suitable
solvent.
13 Inspect the surface of each roller for wear
and flat spots **(see illustration)**. Measure the
diameter of the rollers and compare the result
to the specifications at the beginning of this
Chapter **(see illustration)**. Renew the rollers
as a set if any are damaged or worn below the
minimum diameter. **Note:** *No specification is
available for the rollers fitted to AN400X to K2
models.*
14 Inspect the surface of the ramps in the
variator body and the ramp plate for wear or
damage.
15 Check the slots in the ramp guides
where they fit in the variator body and

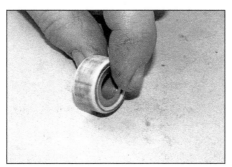
3.13a Inspect the rollers . . .

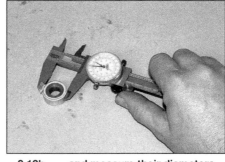
3.13b . . . and measure their diameters

renew the guides as a set if necessary **(see
illustration)**.
16 If required, lever out the seals fitted to both

sides of the inner pulley **(see illustration)**.
Locate the new seals squarely in the housing
and press them in firmly with a suitably-sized

3.15 Check the slots in the ramp guides

3.16a Lever out the old seals

3.16b Locate the new seals squarely . . .

3.16c . . . and press them in with a suitably-sized socket

3.17 Examine the crankshaft splines for wear

socket **(see illustrations)**. Lubricate the centre of the pulley with a small amount of high melting point grease.

17 Examine the splines on the crankshaft for wear **(see illustration)**. If the splines in the outer half of the pulley or in the ramp plate are damaged it is likely the splines on the crankshaft are worn.

Installation

18 Ensure the inner surfaces of both pulley halves and the centre sleeve are clean and grease-free.

19 Fit the rollers into the housing **(see illustration 3.11)**. Check that the ramp guides are correctly fitted on the ramp plate, then install the plate **(see illustration 3.10b and 3.15)**.

20 Install the cover and secure it with the screws **(see illustrations 3.8b and a)**.

21 Grip the variator so that the ramp plate is held into the housing, slide in the centre sleeve, then slide the assembly all the way onto the crankshaft **(see illustrations 3.6c, b and a)**. Ensure the splines in the centre of the ramp plate are aligned with the splines on the crankshaft. **Note:** *If the ramp plate moves and the rollers are dislodged, disassemble the variator and reposition the rollers correctly.*

22 Position the drive belt around the crankshaft **(see illustration)**. Ensure there is sufficient slack in the belt to avoid it being trapped when the outer half of the pulley is installed – if necessary, press the drive belt into the clutch pulley to facilitate fitting it over the variator pulley.

23 Install the outer half of the drive pulley **(see illustration)**. Fit the spring washer with the marked side outermost and tighten the drive pulley nut finger-tight.

24 Make sure the outer pulley half butts against the centre sleeve and is not skewed by the drive belt **(see illustration)**.

25 Use the method employed on removal to prevent the crankshaft turning and tighten the drive pulley nut to the torque setting specified at the beginning of this Chapter **(see illustration)**.

26 Ease the drive belt out of the clutch pulley to reduce the slack in the belt **(see illustration)**.

27 Install the drive belt covers (see Section 2).

3.22 Position the drive belt around the crankshaft . . .

3.23 . . . and install the outer half of the pulley

3.24 Ensure the belt does not restrict fitment of the pulley

3.25 Tighten the drive pulley nut to the specified torque setting

3.26 Installed position of the drive belt

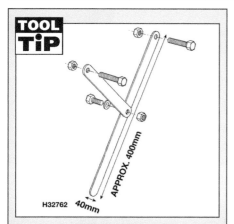

TOOL TiP

H32762

Bolt two strips of steel together so that the shorter one can pivot, making the tool adjustable. Attach bolts through the ends of the strips and lock them in position with two nuts each – the bolts locate in the slots or holes of the component to be held.

4 Clutch and driven pulley

Special tools: *A holding tool will be required to prevent the clutch drum turning during disassembly (see Step 3). A 55 mm socket will be required to undo the clutch assembly nut (see Step 8).*

Removal

1 Remove the drive belt covers (see Section 2).
2 Follow the procedure in Section 3 and remove the outer half of the drive pulley **(see illustration 3.4)**.
3 To remove the clutch drum nut it is necessary to hold the clutch and stop it from turning. Suzuki produces a service tool (Part No. 09930-40113) to do this. Alternatively, use a proprietary holding tool which engages the holes in the clutch drum, or a home-made equivalent (see **Tool Tip**).

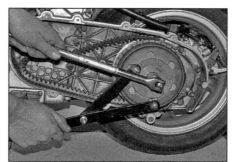
4.4a Hold the clutch securely . . .

4.5 Remove the clutch drum

4 With the drum held securely, unscrew the nut and remove the washer, noting which way round it fits **(see illustrations)**. Mark the washer with a dab of paint to aid reassembly.
5 Remove the clutch drum **(see illustration)**.
6 The clutch drum and clutch shoes can be inspected at this stage (see Steps 17 to 19). If disassembly of the clutch and driven pulley assembly is required, loosen the assembly nut before removing the assembly from the gearbox input shaft (see Step 8).

 Warning: The clutch assembly is under pressure from the centre spring – do not attempt to unscrew the nut completely without first clamping the assembly together.

7 To remove the drive belt, slide the clutch

4.4b . . . unscrew the nut and remove the washer

4.7 Slide out the clutch and driven pulley assembly and lift off the belt

and driven pulley assembly out from the casing and lift off the belt **(see illustration)**. **Note:** *When the belt is removed from the machine, note any directional arrows or mark the belt so that it can be installed the same way round.*
8 To disassemble the clutch and driven pulley assembly, locate the holding tool (see Step 3) in two holes in the clutch backplate and loosen the assembly nut **(see illustration)**.
9 Draw the assembly off the gearbox input shaft **(see illustration)**. If not already done, disengage the drive belt from the pulley.
10 To separate the backplate from the driven pulley, it is necessary to compress the clutch spring while the assembly nut is undone. Suzuki produces a service tool (Part

4.8 Locate the holding tool in the clutch backplate

4.9 Draw the assembly off the gearbox input shaft

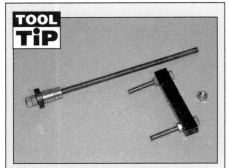

Drill three holes through the tube with centres 55 mm apart. Cut two 90 mm lengths of 10 mm threaded rod and secure them in the holes in either end of the tube with nuts and washers to make a bridge-piece. Cut a 110 mm length of threaded rod and lock two nuts together at one end. Slide on a thick washer to act as a stop and a length of tube or small socket to act as a sleeve inside the driven pulley needle bearing.

No. 09922-31420) to do this. Alternatively, a suitable tool can be made from a piece of square section tube and three lengths of threaded rod (see **Tool Tip**).

11 Secure the long rod upright in a vice. Lower the clutch and driven pulley assembly down the rod so that it sits against the stop with the tube or small socket inside the bearing **(see illustration)**. Take great care not to damage the bearing seal **(see illustration 4.20b)**. Install the bridge-piece and thread a nut down

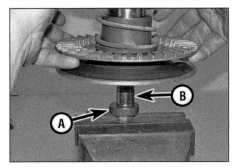

4.11a Lower the assembly over the sleeve (B) and onto the stop (A)

4.11c Unscrew the assembly nut . . .

the long rod **(see illustration)**. Tighten the nut onto the bridge-piece to compress the clutch spring and take the pressure off the assembly nut, then unscrew the assembly nut by hand **(see illustrations)**.

12 Unscrew the nut above the bridge-piece to release the tension in the clutch spring and remove the bridge-piece **(see illustration)**.

4.11b Install the bridge-piece and tighten the nut (arrowed)

4.11d . . . and free it from the threads

Lift the clutch and driven pulley assembly off the long rod.

13. Remove the clutch backplate and the spring **(see illustrations)**.

14 Lift off the centre sleeve then pull out the guide pins **(see illustrations)**. Note the location of the O-rings and discard them as new ones must be fitted

4.12 Release the clutch spring tension

4.13a Remove the clutch backplate . . .

4.13b . . . and lift off the spring

4.14a Lift off the centre sleeve

4.14b Pull out the guide pins . . .

4.14c . . . and remove the O-rings

4.15a Lift off the outer pulley half

4.15b Note location of seals . . .

4.15c . . . and lever them out

15 Separate the pulley halves **(see illustration)**. Note the location of the seals at both ends of the outer pulley shaft **(see illustrations)**. Lever out the seals as new ones should be fitted on reassembly.
16 Clean all the components with a suitable solvent.

Inspection

17 Check the inner surface of the clutch drum for damage and scoring **(see illustration)**. Measure the internal diameter of the drum at several points to determine if it is worn or out-of-round **(see illustration)**. If the drum is out-of-round, or if the results are outside the specification listed at the beginning of this Chapter, renew it.
18 Inspect the splines in the centre of the clutch drum – it should be a firm fit on the gearbox input shaft, with no backlash between the drum and the shaft.
19 Measure the amount of friction material remaining on the clutch shoes and compare the result with the specifications **(see illustration)**. Inspect the shoe springs for wear and stretching. Ensure that the shoes are not seized on their pivot pins and that the retaining circlips are secure on the ends of the pins **(see illustration)**. Clutch components are not available as individual items; if any parts are worn or damaged, fit a new clutch backplate assembly.
20 Inspect the inner faces of the clutch pulley for signs of overheating or blueing, caused by the pulley running out of alignment **(see illustration)**. If the pulley has run out of

4.17a Check the inner surface for damage

4.17b Measuring the internal diameter of the clutch drum

4.19a Measure the thickness of the friction material

4.19b Ensure circlips are secure

alignment, check the condition of the bearings in the hub of the pulley inner half. A needle roller bearing and a sealed ball bearing are fitted in the hub **(see illustrations)**. Inspect the bearing rollers for flat spots and pitting and

check that the ball bearing turns smoothly. If either bearing is worn or damaged new ones must be fitted.
21 Support the pulley inner half on blocks of wood with the hub uppermost and drive out

4.20a Inspect the faces of both pulley halves

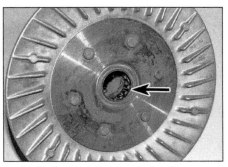

4.20b Inspect the needle bearing . . .

4.20c . . . and the sealed ball bearing

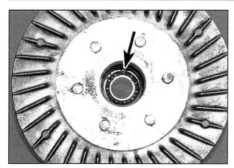

4.21a Remove the circlip . . .

4.21b . . . and drive out the bearing

4.22 Sealed lip of needle bearing should be uppermost

the roller bearing using a rod or long punch through the centre. Turn the hub over and remove the circlip securing the ball bearing **(see illustration)**. Drive out the ball bearing using a suitably-sized socket, noting which way round it is fitted **(see illustration)**.

22 Install the new ball bearing with the sealed side facing out **(see illustration 4.20c)** and secure it with a new circlip. Install the new roller bearing with the sealed lip facing out – ensure pressure is only applied to the bearing's outer race **(see illustration)**.

23 Inspect the guide pins and rollers and their slots in the pulley outer shaft and renew any components that are worn **(see illustrations)**.

24 Check the condition of the spring. Measure its free length and compare the result with the figure in the Specifications **(see illustration)**. Renew the spring if it is bent or has sagged to less than the service limit.

Installation

25 Lubricate the new seals for the outer pulley shaft with a smear of grease and press them into place **(see illustrations 4.15b and c)**.

26 Slide the outer pulley onto the inner pulley hub **(see illustration 4.15a)**. Lubricate the new O-rings with a smear of grease and install them in their groove in the outer pulley shaft **(see illustration 4.14c)**. Align the holes for the guide pins in the hub with slots in the shaft **(see illustration 4.23b)** then lubricate the guide pins and rollers with high melting point grease and install them in their slots **(see illustration 4.14b)**. Install the centre sleeve **(see illustration 4.14a)**.

27 Lubricate the centre of the inner pulley hub

4.23a Inspect the guide pins and rollers . . .

between the bearings with a small amount of high melting point grease.

28 Install the spring and position the clutch backplate over the spring **(see illustrations 4.13b and a)**.

29 Use the method employed on removal to compress the clutch spring – if using the home-made tool, don't forget to fit the clutch assembly nut on the long rod before installing the bridge-piece **(see illustration 4.12)**. Ensure the flats on the backplate are aligned with the flats on the end of the inner pulley hub. Install the assembly nut finger-tight **(see illustration 4.11d and c)**.

30 Temporarily slide the assembly onto the gearbox input shaft **(see illustration 4.9)**. Locate the holding tool (see Step 3) in two holes in the clutch backplate and tighten the assembly nut to the torque setting specified at the beginning of this Chapter **(see illustration)**.

4.23b . . . and the slots (arrowed) in the pulley outer shaft

31 Ensure the inner surfaces of both pulley halves and the inside surface of the clutch drum are clean and grease-free. Draw the clutch and driven pulley assembly part way off the gearbox shaft and install the drive belt, ensuring it is fitted the correct way round. Press the assembly fully onto the shaft and install the clutch drum **(see illustration 4.5)**. Install the washer, ensuring it fitted the correct way round, and tighten the nut finger-tight **(see illustration 4.4b)**.

32 Use the method employed on removal to prevent the clutch turning and tighten the clutch drum nut to the specified torque setting **(see illustration)**.

33 Fit the drive belt over the drive pulley – ensure the variator ramp plate and rollers are still in position and install the outer half of the pulley (see Section 3).

34 Install the drive belt covers (see Section 2).

4.24 Measure the clutch spring free length

4.30 Tighten the clutch assembly nut to the specified torque

4.32 Tighten the clutch drum nut to the specified torque

5.3 Removing the drive belt – AN400K7-on models

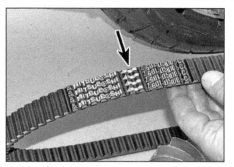

5.6 Note directional arrows on the belt

driven pulley, then install the clutch and driven pulley assembly **(see illustration 4.7)**. Position the belt around the crankshaft and install the outer half of the drive pulley (see Section 3).

9 Ensure the belt is positioned evenly between the two pulleys and not trapped by the pulley outer halves **(see illustration 3.26)**.

10 Install the drive belt covers (see Section 2).

6 Gearbox

Removal

1 Remove the rear wheel and brake disc (see Chapter 7). On AN400X to K6 models, remove the rear hub.

2 Remove the clutch and driven pulley assembly (see Section 4)

3 Drain the gearbox oil (see Chapter 1). Position a suitable tray underneath the gearbox to catch any residual oil when the cover is removed.

4 Undo the bolts securing the gearbox cover and remove the cover – the input shaft will come away with it **(see illustrations)**. Note the location of the cover seal and discard it as a new one must be fitted; note the location of the cover dowels and remove them for safekeeping if they are loose **(see illustrations)**.

5 On AN250 and AN400X to K6 models, remove the thrust washer from the inner end of the input shaft **(see illustration)**.

6 Pull the input shaft out from its bearing in the cover **(see illustration)**.

5 Drive belt

Inspection

1 The drive belt should be inspected according the service schedule (see Chapter 1). A new belt should be fitted if the existing one is worn down to the service limit or damaged. On AN400K3 models onward, the drive belt must be renewed at the specified service interval, irrespective of its apparent condition.

Renewal

2 Follow the procedure in Section 3 to remove the outer half of the drive pulley, then displace the belt from around the crankshaft **(see illustration 3.4)**.

3 On AN400K7 models onward there is

sufficient clearance to lift the belt off the clutch driven pulley **(see illustration)**.

4 On all other models, follow the procedure in Section 4 to remove the clutch drum, then slide the clutch and driven pulley assembly out from the casing and lift off the belt.

5 Clean any dust from inside the casing and ensure the inner surfaces of the drive and driven pulley halves are clean and grease-free.

6 Fit the new belt, making sure any directional arrows point in the direction of normal rotation **(see illustration)**.

7 On AN400K7 models onward, fit the belt onto the clutch driven pulley, pressing it into the pulley as far as possible, then position it around the crankshaft **(see illustration 3.22)**. Follow the procedure in Section 3 to install the outer half of the drive pulley.

8 On all other models, follow the procedure in Section 4 to fit the belt around the clutch

6.4a Undo the gearbox cover bolts . . .

6.4b . . . and remove the cover and gearbox input shaft

6.4c Cover seal fits in groove

6.4d Location of cover dowels

6.5 Remove the thrust washer – AN250 and AN400X to K6 models

6.6 Pull out the input shaft

6.7 Gearbox reduction gear (A) and output shaft (B)

6.9 Remove the output shaft

6.10 Note shim on inner end of reduction gear

6.11a Undo the screw . . .

6.11b . . . and ensure the magnet is clean

7 Remove the shim from the outer end of the reduction gear (see illustration).
8 On AN250 and AN400X to K6 models, remove the thrust washer from the outer end of the output shaft (see illustration 6.7).
9 Lift out the output shaft (see illustration).
10 Lift out the reduction gear and remove the shim from the inner end of the shaft (see illustration).

Inspection

11 Clean all the components with solvent and dry them thoroughly. Don't forget to undo the screw securing the magnet in the bottom of the cover and clean off any metal swarf resulting from wear inside the gearbox (see illustrations). Tighten the screw securely on installation.

12 Lay the shafts, shims and washers in order on a clean surface so that related components can be checked together (see illustration).
13 Check the gear pinion teeth for cracking, chipping, pitting and other obvious wear or damage (see illustration). Where pinions mesh together, check for wear on both shafts (see illustration 6.12).
14 On AN250 models and AN400X and Y

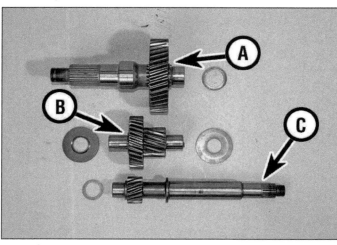

6.12 Gearbox components – output shaft (A), reduction gear (B) and input shaft (C)

6.13 Inspect the gear pinions for wear and damage

6.14 Circlip retains pinion on shaft

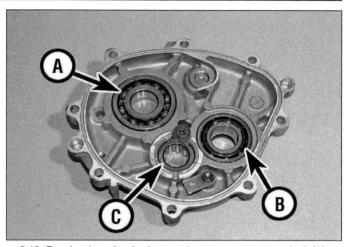

6.18 Bearing location in the gearbox cover – output shaft (A), input shaft (B) and reduction gear (C)

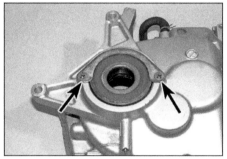

6.20a Undo the screws . . .

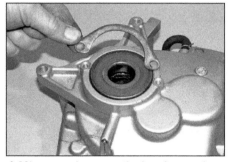

6.20b . . . and remove the bearing retainer

6.20c Remove the bearing with a knife-edged puller

models the pinions on the reduction gear and output shafts are listed as separate items. To renew a damaged or worn pinion, remove the retaining circlip, then slide the pinion off the shaft, noting how it fits **(see illustration)**. On the output shaft, note the location of the shims behind the pinion and ensure they are in position when the new pinion is fitted. Secure the pinion with a new circlip.

15 On all other models the shafts and pinions are listed as assemblies – if a pinion is damaged the shaft must be renewed.

16 Check the surface of the shafts and the splines for wear and damage. Check for signs

of scoring or bluing on the pinions and shafts. This could be caused by overheating due to inadequate lubrication.

17 If there is evidence of oil leaking along the input shaft into the drive belt casing, lever out the input shaft seal carefully, noting which way round it fits.

18 Check the condition of the input shaft bearing **(see illustration)** – it should spin freely and smoothly without any rough spots (see *Tools and Workshop Tips* in the *Reference* section). To renew the bearing, heat the bearing housing with a hot air gun, then drive the bearing out from the outside

using a suitably-sized socket. Note which way round the bearing is fitted. Install the new bearing from the inside with its marked side uppermost. Drive it in squarely until it seats – ensure pressure is only applied to the bearing's outer race.

19 Lubricate the new input shaft seal with a smear of oil and press it into its housing with a suitably-sized socket or driver.

20 If there is evidence of oil leaking from the gearbox along the output shaft, renew the output shaft bearing and seal as follows. Undo the screws securing the bearing retainer and remove the retainer, noting how it fits **(see illustrations)**. Heat the bearing housing with a hot air gun, then use a slide-hammer and knife-edged bearing puller to draw the bearing out **(see illustration)** (see *Tools and Workshop Tips* in the *Reference* section).

21 Note which way round the seal is fitted, then drive it out from inside the casing **(see illustration)**.

22 Check that the housing is clean and free from corrosion. Lubricate the new seal with a smear of oil and press it into its housing from the outside with a suitably-sized socket **(see illustration)**.

23 Heat the bearing housing and install the new bearing with its sealed side facing out. Drive it in squarely until it seats – ensure

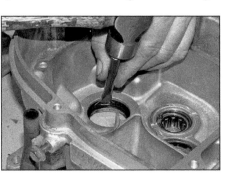

6.21 Removing the old shaft seal

6.22 Install the new seal from the outside

6.23 Drive in the new bearing with a suitably-sized socket

pressure is only applied to the bearing's outer race **(see illustration)**.

24 Inspect the remaining transmission bearings and renew them if there is any doubt about their condition. **Note:** *All the transmission bearings should be a tight fit in their housings. If a bearing is loose, and the housing is not damaged, use a suitable bearing locking compound to hold it in place.*

25 The bearings are fitted in blind holes and will require a slide-hammer and knife-edged bearing puller to remove them (see *Tools and Workshop Tips* in the *Reference* section). Heat the housings to assist removal and installation.

26 Before removing the reduction gear bearing in the cover, undo the screw and remove the retainer **(see illustration)**.

27 Before removing the reduction gear bearing in the casing, remove the retaining circlip **(see illustration)**. Secure the new bearing with a new circlip.

Installation

28 Fit the shim onto the inner end of the reduction gear and install the gear **(see illustration 6.10)**.

29 Install output shaft taking care not to damage the shaft seal **(see illustration 6.9)**. Ensure the output shaft and reduction gear pinions are correctly engaged.

30 Fit the shim onto the outer end of the reduction gear shaft **(see illustration 6.7)**.

31 On AN250 and AN400X to K6 models, fit the thrust washer onto the outer end of the output shaft **(see illustration 6.7)**.

32 Fit the input shaft into its bearing in the cover **(see illustration 6.6)**.

33 On AN250 and AN400X to K6 models, fit the thrust washer onto the inner end of the input shaft **(see illustration 6.5)**.

34 If removed, fit the cover dowels **(see illustration 6.4d)**.

35 Press a new cover seal into the groove around the edge of the cover **(see illustration 6.4c)**.

36 Install the cover, ensuring the shafts are aligned with their bearings – rotate the input shaft to engage its pinion with the reduction gear **(see illustration 6.4b)**.

37 Install the cover bolts, then tighten them evenly and in a criss-cross pattern to the torque setting specified at the beginning of this Chapter. Ensure the input and output shafts turn freely.

38 Fill the gearbox with the specified amount and type of oil (see Chapter 1).

39 Install the clutch and driven pulley (see Section 4).

40 Install the remaining components in the reverse order of removal.

6.26 Reduction gear bearing retainer (arrowed)

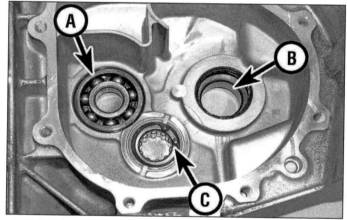

6.27 Bearing location in gearbox casing – input shaft (A), output shaft (B) and reduction gear (C)

Chapter 3
Cooling system

Contents

Degrees of difficulty

Easy, suitable for novice with little experience 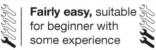	**Fairly easy,** suitable for beginner with some experience	**Fairly difficult,** suitable for competent DIY mechanic	**Difficult,** suitable for experienced DIY mechanic	**Very difficult,** suitable for expert DIY or professional

Specifications

Coolant temperature gauge resistance

AN250W to K2 models and AN400X to K2 models
  Needle position 1* . . . . 152 ohms approx
  Needle position 2* . . . . 39 ohms approx
  Needle position 3* . . . . 18 ohms approx
AN250RK2 models and AN400RK2 models
  Gauge reading HOT . . . . 180 ohms
  Gauge reading COLD . . . . 18 ohms
AN400K3 to K6 models
  Needle position 1* . . . . 770 ohms approx
  Needle position 2* . . . . 155 ohms approx
  Needle position 3* . . . . 75 ohms approx
*see text

Coolant temperature (ECT) sensor

Resistance
  AN250 models and AN400X to K2 models
    At 50°C (122°F). . . . . 140 to 310 ohms
    At 115°C (239°F). . . . . 24.1 to 28.2 ohms
  AN400K3 to K6 models
    At 20°C (68°F). . . . . 2.58 K-ohms (approx)
    At 40°C (104°F). . . . . 1.14 K-ohms (approx)
    At 80°C (176°F). . . . . 0.28 K-ohm (approx)
    At 100°C (212°F). . . . . 0.16 K-ohm (approx)
  AN400K7 model onward
    At 20°C (68°F). . . . . 2.58 K-ohms (approx)
    At 50°C (104°F). . . . . 0.77 K-ohm (approx)
    At 80°C (176°F). . . . . 0.28 K-ohm (approx)
    At 110°C (212°F). . . . . 0.12 K-ohm (approx)

Cooling fan switch operating temperatures

AN250W to K2 models
OFF-ON . . . . 100 to 110°C
ON-OFF . . . . 95 to 105°C
AN250RK2 and AN400RK2 models
OFF-ON . . . . 98°C
ON-OFF . . . . 92°C
AN400X to K6 models
OFF-ON . . . . 93 to 103°C
ON-OFF . . . . 87 to 97°C
AN400K7 model onward
OFF-ON . . . . 98°C approx
ON-OFF . . . . 92°C approx

Thermostat

Opening temperature
AN250W to K2 models. . . . . 70 to 80°C
AN400X to K2 models . . . . 72 to 78°C
AN250RK2 and AN400RK2 models . . . . 82°C
AN400K3 model onward . . . . 82°C
Valve lift
AN250 models and AN400X to K2 models . . . . 3.0 mm at 90°C
AN400K3 model onward . . . . 3.0 mm at 95°C

Torque settings

Cooling fan switch . . . . 18 Nm
Cooling fan mounting bolts . . . . 10 Nm
Engine coolant temperature sensor
AN250 models and AN400X to K2 models . . . . 8 Nm
AN400K3 model onward . . . . 12 Nm
Radiator mounting bolts. . . . . 10 Nm
Thermostat housing bolts. . . . . 10 Nm
Water pump mounting bolts. . . . . 10 Nm
Water pump impeller bolt. . . . . 10 Nm

1 General information

The cooling system uses a water/anti-freeze coolant to carry away excess heat from the engine and maintain as constant a temperature as possible. The cylinder and cylinder head are surrounded by a water jacket through which the coolant is circulated by thermo-syphonic action in conjunction with a water pump. The pump is driven off the oil pump shaft.

The heated coolant passes upwards to the thermostat in the cylinder head and through to the radiator. The coolant then flows across the radiator core, where it is cooled by the passing air, then down to the water pump where the cycle is repeated.

The thermostat is fitted in the system to prevent the coolant flowing through the radiator when the engine is cold, therefore accelerating the speed at which the engine reaches normal operating temperature. On carburettor models, a coolant temperature sensor, mounted in the cylinder head, transmits information to the temperature gauge on the instrument panel. On fuel-injected models, the temperature sensor is part of the engine

management system and for this reason is covered in Chapter 4B.

A fan fitted to the back of the radiator aids cooling in extreme conditions by drawing extra air through the radiator core. The fan motor is activated by a thermo-switch mounted in the lower right-hand side of the radiator.

⚠️ **Warning: Do not remove the reservoir cap when the engine is hot. Scalding hot coolant and steam may be blown out under pressure, which could cause serious injury.**

⚠️ **Warning: Do not allow antifreeze to come in contact with your skin or painted or plastic surfaces of the scooter. Rinse off any spills immediately with plenty of water. Antifreeze is highly toxic if ingested. Never leave antifreeze lying around in an open container or in puddles on the floor; children and pets are attracted by its sweet smell and may drink it. Check with the local authorities about disposing of used antifreeze. Many communities will have collection centres which will see that antifreeze is disposed of safely.**
Caution: At all times use the specified type of antifreeze, and always mix it with distilled water in the correct proportion.

The antifreeze contains corrosion inhibitors which are essential to avoid damage to the cooling system. A lack of these inhibitors could lead to a build-up of corrosion which would block the coolant passages, resulting in overheating and severe engine damage. Distilled water must be used as opposed to tap water to avoid a build-up of scale which would also block the passages.

2 Cooling fan and fan switch

1 If the engine is overheating and the cooling fan isn't coming on, first check the ignition fuse (see Chapter 9). If the fuse has blown, check the fan circuit for a short to earth (see the *Wiring Diagrams* at the end of Chapter 9). If the fuse is good, check the fan motor, then check the switch as follows.

Cooling fan motor

Check

2 To test the fan motor, first remove the kick panel (see Chapter 8).
3 Locate the fan wiring on the lower

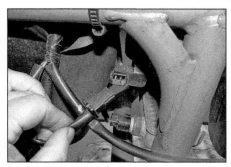

2.3 Disconnect the fan wiring connector

2.5 Radiator fan switch

2.6a Fan assembly mounting bolts

right-hand side of the radiator and disconnect the fan wiring connector **(see illustration)**.
4 Using jumper wires and a fully-charged 12 volt battery, connect the blue wire terminal on the fan side of the connector to the battery positive (+) terminal and the black wire terminal to the battery negative (-) terminal. The fan should turn – if not, the motor is faulty and a new one must be fitted.

Renewal

5 Remove the radiator (see Section 6). If not already done, disconnect the fan switch wiring connector **(see illustration)**.
6 Undo the bolts securing the fan assembly to the radiator – if fitted, note the location of the wiring clip secured by the left-hand bolt **(see illustrations)**.
7 Installation is the reverse of removal. Tighten the fan mounting bolts to the torque setting specified at the beginning of this Chapter
8 Install the radiator (see Section 6).

Fan switch

Check

9 As the coolant temperature rises the switch completes the fan motor circuit to earth (ground) and the fan comes on (see the *Wiring Diagrams* at the end of Chapter 9). If the switch is thought to be faulty, remove it (see Steps 14 and 15) and test it as follows.
10 Fill a small heatproof container with oil and place it on a stove. Using some wire or other support, suspend the switch in the oil so that just the sensing portion and the threads are submerged **(see illustration)**. Also place a

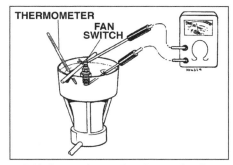

2.6b Note the wiring clip

thermometer capable of reading temperatures up to 120°C in the oil so that its bulb is close to the switch. **Note:** *None of the components should be allowed to touch the container directly.*
11 Using a multimeter, check for continuity between the switch terminals – there should be no continuity (infinite resistance).
12 Heat the oil slowly, stirring it gently, and note the temperature at which the switch closes (zero resistance – cooling fan ON). Turn the heat off and note the temperature at which the switch opens (infinite resistance – cooling fan OFF).
13 Compare the results with the specifications at the beginning of this Chapter. If the switch opens and closes at different temperatures it is faulty and must be renewed. If it operates as specified, refer to *Wiring Diagrams* at the end of Chapter 9 and check the switch and fan motor wiring for continuity.

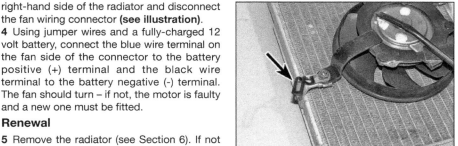

2.10 Set-up for testing the cooling fan switch

Renewal

14 Drain the cooling system (see Chapter 1).
15 Disconnect the wiring connector from the switch **(see illustration 2.5)**. Unscrew the switch and discard the O-ring as a new one must be fitted.
16 Installation is the reverse of removal. Fit a new O-ring onto the switch and tighten it to the torque setting specified at the beginning of this Chapter. Ensure the wiring connector is secure.
17 Follow the procedure in Chapter 1 to refill the system and check the switch for leaks.

3 Temperature gauge and sensor

1 The circuit consists of the engine coolant temperature sensor mounted on the thermostat housing on AN250 models and AN400X to K2 models, and on the cylinder on AN400K3 models onward, and the gauge located in the instrument cluster. If the system malfunctions check first that the battery is fully charged and that the fuses are all good.

Temperature gauge

AN250 models and AN400X to K6 models

2 Remove the left-hand side cover (see Chapter 8).
3 Disconnect the engine coolant temperature (ECT) sensor wiring connector **(see illustrations)**.

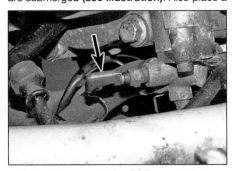

3.3a Disconnect the ECT connector – AN250 and AN400X to K2 models

3.3b Disconnect the ECT connector – AN400K3 to K6 models

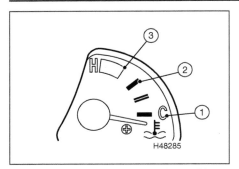

3.5a Temperature gauge needle positions – AN250W to K2 and AN400X to K2 models

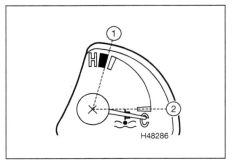

3.5b Temperature gauge needle positions – AN250RK2 and AN400RK2 models

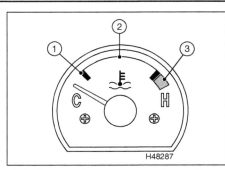

3.5c Temperature gauge needle positions – AN400K3 to K6 models

4 On AN250 and AN400X to K2 models, connect a variable resistance tester between the black/green wire terminal on the loom side of the connector and earth (ground). On AN400K3 to K6 models, connect the tester between the green and black/brown wire terminals on the loom side of the connector.

5 Refer to the appropriate gauge resistance range in the *Specifications* at the beginning of this Chapter and set the tester to the highest ohms setting. Turn the ignition ON and note the reading on the temperature gauge. Carry out the test for the other ohms setting(s). Compare the results with the appropriate gauge needle positions for your machine **(see illustrations)**.

6 If the gauge readings vary greatly from the specifications a new gauge will have to be fitted. Individual components for the instrument cluster are available for AN250 models and AN400X to K2 models, but on AN400K3 to K6 models a new instrument panel will have to be fitted. Refer to Chapter 9 for details.

AN400K7 model onward

7 No individual test procedure is available for the temperature gauge. When the ignition is first switched ON the needle should swing around the scale and then return to zero as part of the instrument's self-checking procedure. If the needle does not move, but the fuel gauge, speedometer and tachometer function as described, have the instrument cluster checked by a Suzuki dealer.

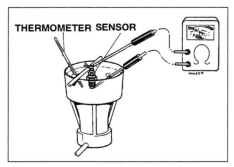

3.14 Set-up for testing the ECT sensor

Temperature sensor

8 The resistance of the engine coolant temperature (ECT) sensor should change with engine temperature. If the sensor is thought to be faulty it can be tested as follows. Note that on fuel-injected models (AN400K3 onward) a fault with the ECT sensor should be indicated by the FI warning light (see Chapter 4B).

 Warning: Allow the engine to cool completely before performing this procedure.

9 On AN250 models and AN400X to K6 models, remove the left-hand side cover (see Chapter 8) to access the sensor **(see illustrations 3.3a or b)**. On AN400K7 onward, remove the air filter housing (see Chapter 4B).

10 Drain the cooling system (see Chapter 1).

11 Disconnect the sensor wiring connector, then unscrew the sensor. On AN400K3 to models onward, note the location of the O-ring and discard it as a new one must be fitted.

12 Fill a small heatproof container with oil and place it on a stove. Set a multimeter to the appropriate ohms range (see *Specifications* at the beginning of this Chapter).

13 If the sensor has a single wire terminal, connect the positive (+) meter probe to the terminal and the negative (-) meter probe to the sensor body. If the sensor has two wire terminals, connect the meter probes between the terminals.

14 Using some wire or other support, suspend the sensor in the oil so that just the sensing portion and the threads are submerged **(see illustration)**. Also place a thermometer capable of reading temperatures up to 120°C in the oil so that its bulb is close to the sensor. **Note:** *None of the components should be allowed to directly touch the container.*

15 Refer to the specifications for the lowest oil temperature for the test and note the resistance reading of the sensor. If required, heat the oil gently to raise the temperature to the minimum specified, then keep the temperature constant for a few minutes before continuing the test.

16 Now increase the heat gradually, stirring the oil gently. As the temperature of the oil

rises, the resistance of the sensor should fall. Check that the correct resistance is obtained at the temperatures specified. If the meter readings obtained are different, or they are obtained at different temperatures, then the sensor is faulty and must be renewed.

 Warning: This must be done very carefully to avoid the risk of personal injury.

17 Prior to installation, on AN250 models and AN400-X to K2 models, ensure the sensor threads are clean and apply a non-permanent thread-locking compound. On AN400K3 models onward, fit a new O-ring. Install the sensor and tighten it to the specified torque setting. Connect the sensor wiring.

18 Refill the cooling system and check the sensor for leaks (see Chapter 1).

19 Install the remaining components in the reverse order of removal.

4 Thermostat

Removal

1 The thermostat is automatic in operation and should give many years service without requiring attention. In the event of a failure, the valve will probably jam open, in which case the engine will take much longer than normal to warm up. Conversely, if the valve jams shut, the coolant will be unable to circulate and the engine will overheat. Neither condition is acceptable, and the fault must be investigated promptly.

2 The thermostat is located on the left-hand side of the cylinder head – remove the left-hand side cover for access (see Chapter 8).

 Warning: Allow the engine to cool completely before performing this procedure.

3 On AN250 models and AN400X to K2 models, disconnect the coolant temperature sensor wiring connector **(see illustration 3.3a)**.

4 Drain the cooling system (see Chapter 1).

4.5 Disconnect the hose from the thermostat cover

4.6 Remove the thermostat cover

4.7 Note location of thermostat

5 If required, disconnect the coolant hose from the thermostat cover **(see illustration)**.
6 Undo the bolts or nuts securing the cover and displace it or lift it off **(see illustration)**. Where fitted, note the location of the guide for the HT lead.
7 Note the location of the thermostat then lift it out from its housing, noting how it fits **(see illustration)**.

Check

8 Inspect the thermostat and its seal for any cracks or splits and renew it if necessary **(see illustration)**. Check the position of the valve before carrying out the test – if it remains in the open position at room temperature, the thermostat should be renewed **(see illustration)**.
9 To test the thermostat, suspend it in a container of cold water. Place a thermometer capable of reading temperatures up to 100°C in the water so that the bulb is close to the thermostat **(see illustration)**. Heat the water, noting the temperature when the thermostat opens. Also check the amount the valve opens after it has been heated at the temperature specified at the beginning of this Chapter for a few minutes. If the results obtained differ greatly from those given in *Specifications*, the thermostat is faulty and must be replaced with a new one.
10 In the event of the thermostat jamming closed, *as an emergency measure only*, it can be removed and the machine used without it. **Note:** *Take care when starting the*

4.8a Inspect the thermostat for damage

engine from cold, as it will take much longer than usual to warm up. Ensure that a new unit is installed as soon as possible.

Installation

11 Clean the thermostat cover and the seat in its housing.
12 Install the thermostat, ensuring the bleed hole is at the top **(see illustration)**.
13 Install the housing and tighten the housing bolts to the specified torque setting. If removed, connect the coolant hose.
14 On AN250 models and AN400X to K2 models, connect the coolant temperature sensor wiring connector **(see illustration 3.3a)**.
15 Refill the cooling system and check the thermostat housing for leaks (see Chapter 1).
16 Install the remaining components in the reverse order of removal.

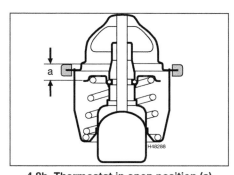

4.8b Thermostat in open position (a)

5 Coolant reservoir

Removal

⚠ *Warning: Allow the engine to cool completely before performing this procedure.*

1 The coolant reservoir on all models is located at the front of the scooter and is housed within the front bodywork panels **(see illustration)**. Remove the headlight panel and cockpit trim panel for access (see Chapter 8).
2 Disconnect the vent hose from the union on the top of the reservoir – secure the hose to prevent it being displaced.
3 Release the clip securing the feed and return

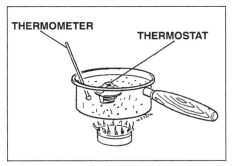

4.9 Set-up for testing the thermostat

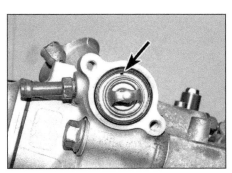

4.12 Location of thermostat bleed hole

5.1 Location of the coolant reservoir – AN400K6 shown

5.3 Disconnect the feed and return hose

hose from its union on the radiator filler neck and disconnect the hose **(see illustration)**. Support the hose upright to prevent leakage of residual coolant.

4 Undo the screws securing the reservoir to its bracket and lift it off. Remove the reservoir cap and drain out the coolant. Note the **Warning** at the beginning of the *Coolant change* sub-section in Chapter 1.

5 Do not dispose of the old coolant by pouring it down the drain. Instead pour it into a heavy plastic container, cap it tightly and take it into an authorised disposal site or service station.

Installation

6 Installation is the reverse of removal. Make sure the hoses are correctly installed and secured. If the clips on the feed and return hose are loose or corroded replace them with new ones.

7 On completion, refill the reservoir as described in Chapter 1.

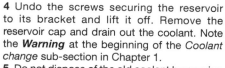

6 Radiator

Removal

⚠️ *Warning: Allow the engine to cool completely before performing this procedure.*

1 The radiator on all models is located at the front of the scooter and is housed within the front bodywork panels. Remove the headlight panel, cockpit trim panel, belly panel and radiator panel for access (see Chapter 8).

2 Drain the cooling system (see Chapter 1).

3 Release the clips securing the coolant hoses and filler neck hose to the unions on the radiator and detach them **(see illustrations)**. If the hoses are being removed from the machine, mark or tag them as a reminder of where they connect.

Caution: The radiator unions are fragile. Do not use excessive force when attempting to remove the hoses.

> **HAYNES HiNT** *If a radiator hose is corroded in place on its union, slit it with a sharp knife and peel it off the union. A new hose will obviously be needed.*

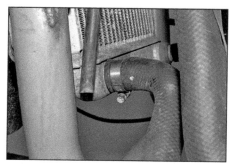

6.3a Radiator bottom hose

6.3b Radiator top hose

4 On AN250 models and AN400X to K2 models, disconnect the cooling fan and fan switch wiring connectors. Undo the four mounting bolts, noting the location of the grommets and spacers in the mounting brackets, and lift the radiator off.

5 On AN400K3 to K6 models, disconnect the combined cooling fan and fan switch wiring connector **(see illustration)**. Undo the top mounting bolt, noting the location of the grommet and spacer in the mounting bracket, and lift the radiator off the lower supports **(see illustrations)**. Note the location of the heat shield strapped to the frame behind the radiator **(see illustrations)**.

6.3c Radiator filler neck hose

6.5a Disconnect the wiring connector(s)

6.5b Undo the mounting bolt . . .

6.5c . . . and lift the radiator off . . .

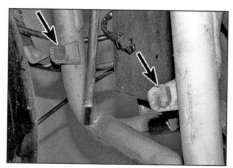

6.5d . . . the lower supports. Note support rubbers

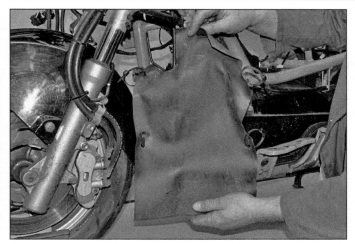

6.5e Heat shield . . .

6.5f . . . is secured by cable-ties

If the shield is damaged replace it with a new one.

6 On AN400K7 models onward, remove the left and right-hand radiator side panels (see Chapter 8). Disconnect the combined cooling fan and fan switch wiring connector. Release the trim clips securing the heat shield to access the top mounting bolt **(see illustrations)**. Undo the top mounting bolt and two lower mounting bolts, noting the location of the grommets and spacers in the mounting brackets, and lift the radiator off **(see illustration)**.

Inspection

7 Check the radiator for signs of damage and clear any dirt or debris that might obstruct air flow and inhibit cooling (see Chapter 1, Section 5). If the radiator fins are badly damaged the radiator must be renewed.

8 Check the condition of the grommets in the mounting brackets and renew them if they are cracked, damaged or distorted **(see illustration)**. On AN400K3 to K6 models, ensure the rubbers in the lower supports are in good condition **(see illustration 6.5d)**.

Installation

9 Installation is the reverse of removal, noting the following:

- *Ensure the coolant hoses are in good condition (see Chapter 1, Section 10). If necessary, follow the procedure in Section 8 of this Chapter to renew the hoses.*
- *Refill the cooling system (see Chapter 1).*

7 Water pump

Check

1 The water pump is located on the lower right-hand side of the engine **(see illustration)**. Remove the belly panel for access (see Chapter 8).

2 Check the area around and below the pump for signs of leakage. If the cover is leaking, check that the bolts are tight. If they are, remove the cover and replace the seal with a new one **(see illustration 7.22)**.

3 To prevent leakage of coolant from the cooling system to the lubrication system and vice versa, two seals are fitted on the pump shaft. If either seal fails, a drain hole in the back of the pump allows the coolant or oil to escape and prevents them mixing.

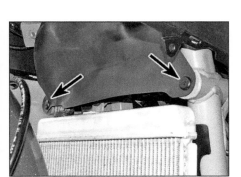

6.6a Release the heat shield trim clips

6.6b Location of top mounting bolt

6.6c Note location of grommets and spacers

6.8 Inspect grommets for wear and damage

7.1 Location of the water pump

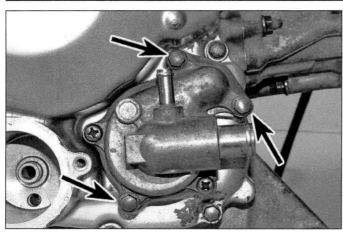

7.7a Undo the mounting bolts . . .

7.7b . . . and pull the pump out

4 The outer seal on the pump shaft is a mechanical-type water seal which bears on the rear face of the impeller. The inner seal, which is mounted behind the water seal, is a conventional feathered-lip oil seal. If on inspection the drain shows signs of leakage, remove the pump and renew the seals.

Removal

5 Drain the coolant (see Chapter 1).

6 Release the spring clip securing the small bore hose to the pump cover and detach the hose **(see illustration 7.1)**.
7 Undo the pump mounting bolts and pull the pump out **(see illustrations)**. Note the location of the pump body O-rings and discard them as new ones must be fitted **(see illustration)**.
8 Undo the cover screws and remove the cover **(see illustrations)**. Discard the cover seal as a new one must be used.

9 Wiggle the pump impeller back-and-forth and up-and-down to check for freeplay in the pump shaft bearing **(see illustration)**. Any freeplay or roughness indicates a worn bearing and will lead to wear in the pump shaft seals. **Note:** *Do not remove the bearing or seals unless they need to be replaced with new ones – once removed they cannot be re-used.*
10 Inspect the impeller for damage. On AN250 models and AN400X to K2 models, if

7.7c Note location of the O-rings

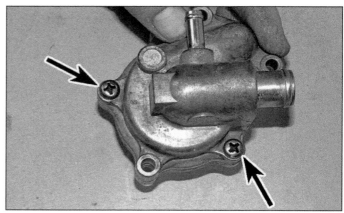

7.8a Undo the cover screws . . .

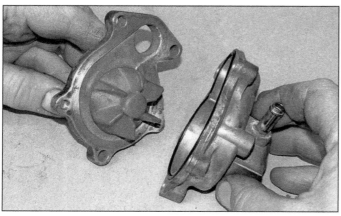

7.8b . . . and remove the cover

7.9 Location of the water pump impeller

7.12a Remove the E-clip . . .

7.12b . . . and draw out the pump shaft

required, a new impeller can be fitted. Undo the impeller bolt and remove the seal and washer, noting which way round the seal is fitted. Pull the impeller off the shaft. On installation, fit a new seal and tighten the impeller bolt to the torque setting specified at the beginning of this Chapter.

11 On AN400K3 to K6 models, if the impeller is damaged, a new impeller and shaft assembly will have to be fitted (see Step 12).

12 Remove the E-clip securing the pump shaft and draw the shaft out **(see illustrations)**.

13 Inspect the contact surface of the water seal on the underside of the pump impeller **(see illustration)**. If it is scratched or pitted, fit a new seal.

Seal and bearing renewal

14 Ease the old ceramic seal off the back of the impeller **(see illustration)**. Lubricate the new seal with coolant and press it into position.

15 Use a knife-edged bearing puller to remove the outer mechanical water seal (see *Tools and Workshop Tips* in the *Reference* section). Install the puller, then slide on a suitably-sized deep socket or length of tube **(see illustrations)**. Install a nut, bolt and large washer as show, thread the bolt into the puller, then tighten the nut down to draw the seal out of the pump **(see illustrations)**.

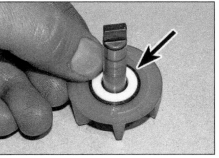
7.13 Inspect water seal contact surface (arrowed)

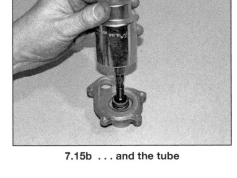
7.14 Ease off the old ceramic seal

7.15a Install the knife-edged puller . . .

7.15b . . . and the tube

7.15c Install the nut, bolt and washer

7.15d Tighten the nut down . . .

7.15e . . . to draw the seal out

7.16 Remove the inner oil seal

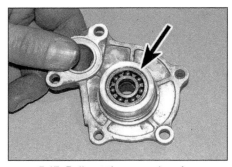

7.17 Pull out the pump bearing

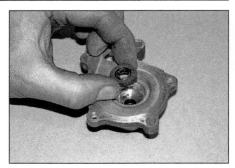

7.19a Press in the new oil seal . . .

7.19b . . . with a suitably-sized socket

7.19c Note drain hole on the inside . . .

7.19d . . . and outside of the pump body

16 Use the same method to remove the inner oil seal **(see illustration)**.

17 Turn the pump body over and pull out the bearing, noting how it fits **(see illustration)**.

18 Install the new bearing, marked side uppermost, ensuring it is pressed all the way into its housing.

19 Lubricate the new oil seal with a smear of multi-purpose grease, then press it into place, closed side uppermost, with a suitably-sized socket **(see illustrations)**. Note the location of the drain hole in the pump body **(see illustrations)**.

20 Install the new mechanical seal carefully to avoid damaging the sealant around its edge **(see illustration)**. Position the seal in the pump body, ensuring it is square with its housing, then fit a socket that bears on the outer lip of the seal only and secure the assembly in a G-clamp or vice **(see illustrations)**. Ease the seal in slowly until the outer lip is seated against the pump body **(see illustration)**.

Installation

21 Install the impeller shaft and secure it with a new E-clip **(see illustrations 7.12b and a)**.

22 Fit a new seal into the groove in the pump cover **(see illustration)**. Lubricate the seal with a smear of grease, install the cover and

7.20a Note sealant around outside edge of new mechanical seal

7.20b Socket must bear on outer lip of seal

7.20c Using a G-clamp to install the seal

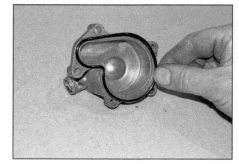

7.20d Installed position of the mechanical seal

7.22 Fit a new pump cover seal

7.24 Note slot (arrowed) in oil pump shaft

secure it with the screws **(see illustrations 7.8b and a)**.

23 Lubricate new pump body O-rings with grease and install them in their grooves **(see illustrations 7.7c)**.

24 Align the end of the water pump shaft with the slot in the end of the oil pump shaft **(see illustration)**. Press the pump into the engine cover and tighten the mounting bolts to the torque setting specified at the beginning of this Chapter **(see illustrations 7.7a)**.

25 Install the coolant hose(s).
26 Refill the cooling system and check for leaks (see Chapter 1).

8 Coolant hoses

1 Before removing a hose, drain the coolant (see Chapter 1).
2 Use a screwdriver or small socket to loosen the large-bore coolant hose clips **(see illustration)**, then slide each clip back along the hose so that it is clear of the union.
3 The small-bore hoses are secured by spring clips – release the clip by squeezing the ears together with pliers, then slide it back along the hose so that it is clear of the union **(see illustration)**.
4 Renew any clips that are sprained or corroded.
5 Take care detaching the hoses from the unions. If a hose appears to be stuck, apply aerosol lubricant, such as WD-40, between the hose and the union, then release the hose

by rotating it on the union before working it off. If all else fails, cut the hose with a sharp knife. Whilst this means fitting a new hose, it is preferable to buying a more expensive item such as a new radiator.
Caution: The radiator unions are fragile. Do not use excessive force when attempting to remove the hoses.
6 On installation, slide the clips onto the hose, then work the hose fully onto its union **(see illustration)**.

> **HAYNES HiNT** *If the hose is difficult to push on its union, soften it by soaking it in very hot water, or alternatively a little soapy water on the union can be used as a lubricant.*

7 Rotate the hose on its unions to settle it in position before sliding the clips into place. On the large-bore hoses, tightening the clips securely.
8 Refill the cooling system and check for leaks (see Chapter 1).

8.2 Large-bore hoses are secured by conventional clips

8.3 Small-bore hoses are secured by spring clips

8.6 Ensure hose is pushed fully onto its union

Notes

Chapter 4A
Fuel system and exhaust – carburettor models

Contents

Degrees of difficulty

Easy, suitable for novice with little experience	Fairly easy, suitable for beginner with some experience	Fairly difficult, suitable for competent DIY mechanic	Difficult, suitable for experienced DIY mechanic	Very difficult, suitable for expert DIY or professional

Specifications

Fuel
Grade . . . . Unleaded. Minimum 91 RON (Research Octane Number)
Fuel tank capacity . . . . 13 litres

Carburettor – AN250
Type . . . . Keihin CVK30
Size (throttle bore) . . . . 30 mm
ID number
  AN250W to Y models
    UK, France and Italy 14F0
    Germany 14F2
    Switzerland 14F3
  AN250RY models
    Italy (with catalytic converter) 14F5
  AN250K1 and K2 models 14F7
Pilot screw setting
  AN250W to Y models . . . . 2 3/4 turns out
  AN250K1 and K2 models . . . . 1 5/8 turns out
Float height
  AN250W and X models . . . . 22 to 24 mm
  AN250Y to K2 models . . . . 17.8 to 19.8 mm
Fuel level . . . . 5.5 to 7.5 below datum line
Idle speed . . . . see Chapter 1
Main jet
  AN250W to Y models
    UK, France and Italy 105
    Germany and Switzerland 108
  AN250K1 and K2 models 108
Needle jet 2.1
Pilot jet
  AN250W to Y models
    UK, France, Italy and Germany 38
    Switzerland 40
  AN250K1 and K2 models 38
Needle
  AN250W to Y models N7AD
  AN250K1 and K2 models N7AE

Carburettor – AN400

Type	Keihin CVK36
Size (throttle bore)	36.5 mm
ID number	
AN400X and Y models	
UK, France and Italy	15F1
Germany	15F2
Switzerland	15F3
AN400RY models	
Italy (with catalytic converter)	15F4
AN400K1 and K2 models	15F7
Pilot screw setting	
AN400X and Y models	1 3/4 turns out
AN400Y models	
Switzerland	2 1/2 turns out
AN400K1 and K2 models	2 1/4 turns out
Float height	16 to 18 mm
Fuel level	0.5 to 2.5 mm above datum line
Idle speed	see Chapter 1
Main jet	108
Needle jet	
AN400X and Y models	3.8
AN400K1 and K2 models	2.6
Pilot jet	38
Needle	N8CA

Carburettor heater

AN250 models	
Resistance	12 to 18 ohms
AN400 models	
Resistance	12 to 16 ohms

Carburettor thermo-switch

No continuity (off)	10 to 16°C and above
Continuity (on)	9 to 3°C and below

Choke resistor

Resistance	7.2 to 8.8 ohms

Fuel level gauge resistance

AN250W to K2 models	
Needle position 1*	103 ohms approx
Needle position 2*	32.5 ohms approx
Needle position 3*	5 ohms approx
AN400X to K2 models	
Needle position 1*	103 ohms approx
Needle position 2*	not available
Needle position 3*	5 ohms approx

see text

Fuel level sensor

Resistance	
Float up (tank full)	1 to 5 ohms
Float down (tank empty)	103 to 117 ohms

Fuel pump

Resistance	1.0 to 2.5 ohms
Delivery rate (minimum)	600 ml per minute

Throttle position sensor

Resistance	
Throttle closed	5 ohms approx
Throttle open	3.09 to 4.63 K-ohms

Torque settings

Fuel cut valve bolts	3.5 Nm
Fuel level sensor bolts	3.5 Nm
Fuel tank mounting bolts	10 Nm
Exhaust system fixings	23 Nm
Exhaust mounting bracket bolts	50 Nm

1 General information and precautions

General information

The fuel system consists of the fuel tank, fuel pump, fuel filter, fuel hose, a constant velocity (CV) carburettor and the throttle cables.

A combination of fuel cut-off valve and pressure control vale on the tank allows air into the tank as the fuel level drops, but prevents petrol fumes escaping into the atmosphere and fuel spillage if the machine falls over. The fuel pump and filter are mounted outside of the tank.

Opening and closing cables from the throttle twistgrip are connected to a pulley on the carburettor which actuates the throttle valve. When the engine is running and the valve is opened, air drawn in by the engine creates a vacuum above the carburettor diaphragm and the diaphragm raises the throttle slide. When the valve is closed the vacuum is reduced and the slide spring lowers the slide.

The carburettor is fitted with an automatic, electronically actuated choke to assist cold starting. Some market models are also fitted with an electronic carburettor heater.

Air is drawn into the carburettor via an air filter which is housed underneath the seat.

The exhaust system is a two-piece design comprising a short header pipe and a silencer. Machines designated AN250R and AN400R have a catalytic converter located inside the silencer. On these scooters a secondary air system introduces filtered air into the exhaust port to improve exhaust gas burning and reduce emissions.

Several of the fuel system service procedures are considered routine maintenance items and for that reason are covered in Chapter 1.

Precautions

 Warning: Petrol (gasoline) is extremely flammable, so take extra precautions when you work on any part of the fuel system. Always remove the battery (see Chapter 9). Don't smoke or allow open flames or bare light bulbs near the work area, and don't work in a garage where a natural gas-type appliance is present. If you spill any fuel on your skin, rinse it off immediately with soap and water. When you perform any kind of work on the fuel system, wear safety glasses and have a fire extinguisher suitable for a class B type fire (flammable liquids) on hand.

Some residual fuel will remain in the fuel hoses and carburettor after the scooter has been used. Before disconnecting any fuel hose, ensure the ignition is switched OFF, and have some absorbent rag handy to catch any fuel. It is vital that no dirt or debris is allowed to enter the fuel tank or the carburettor. Any foreign matter in the fuel system components could result in damage or malfunction.

Always perform service procedures in a well-ventilated area to prevent a build-up of fumes.

Never work in a building containing a gas appliance with a pilot light, or any other form of naked flame. Ensure that there are no naked light bulbs or any sources of flame or sparks nearby.

Do not smoke (or allow anyone else to smoke) while in the vicinity of petrol (gasoline) or of components containing it. Remember the possible presence of vapour from these sources and move well clear before smoking.

Check all electrical equipment belonging to the house, garage or workshop where work is being undertaken (see the *Safety first!* section of this manual). Remember that certain electrical appliances such as drills, cutters etc, create sparks in the normal course of operation and must not be used near petrol (gasoline) or any component containing it. Again, remember the possible presence of fumes before using electrical equipment.

Always mop up any spilt fuel and safely dispose of the rag used.

Any stored fuel that is drained off during servicing work must be kept in sealed containers that are suitable for holding petrol (gasoline), and clearly marked as such; the containers themselves should be kept in a safe place. Note that this last point applies equally to the fuel tank if it is removed from the machine; also remember to keep its filler cap closed at all times.

Read the *Safety first!* section of this manual carefully before starting work.

2 Air filter housing

Removal

1 Remove the seat, storage compartment, underseat panel and right-hand side panel (see Chapter 8).

2 On machines fitted with a secondary air system, undo the 6 mm cylinder head nuts securing the air system valve bracket and displace the bracket, then release the clip and disconnect the flexible hose from the outlet union on the valve **(see illustration)**. Disconnect the vacuum hose.

3 If required, follow the procedure in Chapter 1 to remove the air filter cover and element.

4 Loosen the clip securing the air filter housing outlet tube to the carburettor **(see illustration)**.

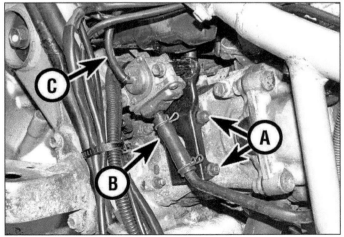

2.2 Undo nuts (A) and disconnect the outlet hose (B) and vacuum hose (C)

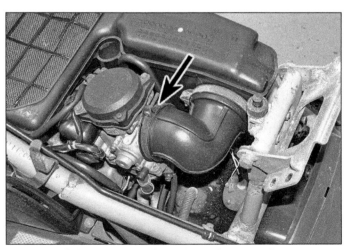

2.4 Loosen the clip on the carburettor tube

2.5a Undo the centre . . .

2.5b . . . and rear mounting bolts

2.6 Disconnect the engine breather hose

2.7 Remove the air filter housing

2.8 Disconnect the secondary air system intake hose

2.9 Housing drain tube (A) and drain plug (B)

5 Undo the central and rear housing mounting bolts (see illustrations).
6 Release the clip and disconnect the engine breather hose from the back of the housing (see illustration).
7 Manoeuvre the housing out (see illustration).
8 Where fitted, release the clip securing the secondary air system valve intake hose and disconnect the hose (see illustration).
9 If required, release the clips securing the drain tube and drain plug(s) (see illustration). Have some rag ready to catch any residual water or oil in the tube and plug(s).

Installation

10 Ensure the inside of the housing is clean and dry. Ensure the drain tube and drain plug(s) are secured with their clips.
11 If applicable, connect the secondary air

system valve to the underside of the housing (see illustration 2.8).
12 Manoeuvre the housing into position and connect the engine breather hose (see illustration 2.6). Ensure the outlet tube is aligned with the carburettor, push it all the way on and tighten the clip securely (see illustration 2.4).
13 If applicable, connect the secondary air system hose to the valve outlet union and reconnect the vacuum hose (see illustration 2.2). Install the valve bracket and tighten the 6 mm cylinder head nuts to the torque setting specified at the beginning of Chapter 2A.
14 Install the central and rear housing mounting bolts and tighten them securely (see illustrations 2.5a and b).
15 Install the remaining components in the reverse order of removal.

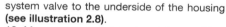

3 Fuel filter

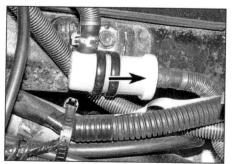

Warning: Refer to the precautions given in Section 1 before starting work.

1 The fuel filter is secured to a bracket on the right-hand side of the fuel tank (see illustration). Remove the centre floor panel and right-hand side belly panel for access (see Chapter 8).
2 Note the arrow on the filter body indicating the direction of fuel flow (see illustration).
3 Release the clips securing the hoses to the intake and outlet unions on the filter and disconnect the hoses (see illustration). If the clips are corroded or sprained new ones must be fitted.

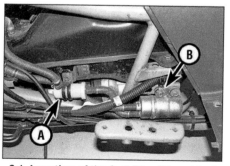

3.1 Location of the fuel filter (A) and fuel pump (B)

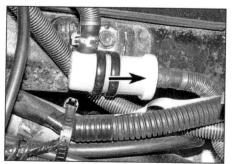

3.2 Arrow indicates direction of fuel flow

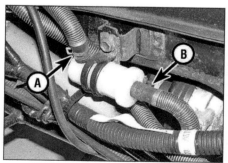

3.3 Fuel filter intake (A) and outlet (B) unions

4 Undo the bolt securing the filter and remove it.

5 Installation is the reverse of removal. Push the hoses all the way onto their unions and secure them with the clips.

4 Fuel pump

4.2 Disconnect the fuel pump wiring connectors

4.5 Disconnect the pump outlet hose

> ⚠ **Warning: Refer to the precautions given in Section 1 before starting work.**

1 The fuel pump is secured to a bracket on the right-hand side of the fuel tank **(see illustration 3.1)**. Remove the centre floor panel and right-hand side belly panel for access (see Chapter 8).

Check

2 Disconnect the wiring connectors from the terminals on the front of the pump, noting how they fit **(see illustration)**.

3 Using a multimeter set the ohms scale, test the resistance between the terminals and compare the result with the specification at the beginning of this Chapter. If the result is outside the specified range the pump is faulty and a new one must be fitted.

4 To check the pump delivery rate, first ensure that the fuel filter is clear (see Section 3).

5 Release the clip and disconnect the outlet fuel hose from the pump **(see illustration)**. Connect a length of fuel hose to the outlet union and place the open end in a calibrated container capable of holding at least 1 litre of fuel.

6 If not already done, disconnect the pump wiring connectors (see Step 2). Using a fully charged 12 volt battery and insulated jumper wires, connect the battery positive (+) terminal to the orange/white wire terminal on the pump and the negative (-) terminal to the black/white wire terminal. The pump should run and discharge at least the specified minimum amount of fuel within 1 minute. If not, the pump is faulty and a new one must be fitted.

7 On completion, reconnect the outlet fuel hose and secure it with the clip. Reconnect the wiring connectors.

Removal and installation

8 Refer to Step 1 to access the pump.

9 Disconnect the pump wiring connectors (see Step 2).

10 Release the clips and disconnect the intake and outlet fuel hoses from the pump **(see illustration 4.5)**. If the clips are corroded or sprained new ones must be fitted.

11 Undo the pump mounting bolts and remove it **(see illustration 4.2)**. Note the location of the grommets and spacers in the mounting bracket – renew the grommets if they are cracked, damaged or distorted.

12 Installation is the reverse of removal. Push the hoses all the way onto their unions and secure them with the clips.

5 Fuel cut-off and pressure control valves

> ⚠ **Warning: Refer to the precautions given in Section 1 before starting work.**

Removal

1 The fuel cut-off and pressure control valves are located on the top of the fuel tank. Remove the centre floor panel for access (see Chapter 8).

2 Temporarily remove the fuel filler cap. Release the spring clip and disconnect the hose from the union on the cut-off valve, then disconnect the drain hose from the spill tray **(see illustrations)**.

3 Unclip the spill tray from the tabs on the frame and lift it off the tank filler neck **(see illustrations)**. The pressure control valve is located on the underside of the spill tray **(see illustration)**.

5.2a Disconnect the hose from the cut-off valve . . .

5.2b . . . and the drain hose from the spill tray

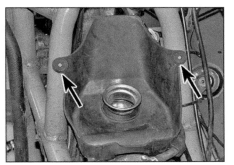

5.3a Unclip the spill tray . . .

5.3b . . . and lift it off

5.3c Location of the pressure control valve

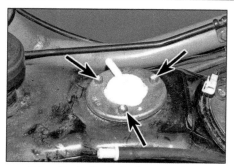

5.4a Undo the bolts (arrowed) . . .

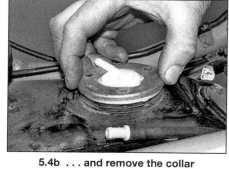

5.4b . . . and remove the collar

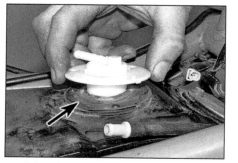

5.4c Lift out the cut-off valve – note fitment of the gasket (arrowed)

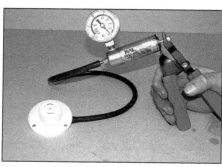

5.5 Checking the cut-off valve with a vacuum pump

4 Undo the bolts securing the cut-off valve and remove the collar, noting how it fits **(see illustrations)**. Lift out the cut-off valve **(see illustration)**. Note the location of the gasket and discard it as a new one must be fitted.

Check

5 To check the operation of the cut-off valve, attach a vacuum pump as shown **(see illustration)**. Hold the valve upside down and apply a vacuum – the gauge needle should be seen to fluctuate.

6 Hold the valve upside down and blow air into the hose union – resistance should be felt.

7 If the results are not as described the cut-off valve is faulty and a new one must be fitted.

8 To check the operation of the pressure control valve, blow air into the outer (orange) end – there should be no resistance. Now blow air through the hose into the inner end – resistance should be felt.

9 If the results are not as described the pressure control valve is faulty and a new one must be fitted.

Installation

10 Fit the gasket for the cut-off valve onto the tank with the flat edge at the front and the notch on the left-hand side **(see illustration 5.4c)**. Install the valve so that the tab on the underside aligns with the notch in the gasket.

11 Fit the collar over the valve, install the bolts and tighten then evenly **(see illustration 5.4b and a)**.

12 Ensure the pressure control valve and hose are correctly located on the underside of the spill tray **(see illustration 5.3c)**. Install the spill tray and secure it to the tabs on the frame **(see illustration 5.3a)**. Connect the drain hose to the spill tray **(see illustration 5.2b)**.

13 Connect the pressure control valve hose to the union on the cut-off valve and secure it with the clip **(see illustration 5.2a)**. Install the fuel filler cap

14 Install the remaining components in the reverse order of removal.

---

6 Throttle cables

Removal

1 Remove the handlebar covers, headlight panel, seat, underseat panel and floor centre panel for access (see Chapter 8).

2 Remove the air filter housing (see Section 2)

3 Loosen the lockrings on the throttle opening and closing cables at the twistgrip end and turn the adjusters all the way in **(see illustration)**.

4 Undo the throttle twistgrip/switch housing screws, noting how they fit, and separate the two halves of the housing **(see illustrations)**. Note the location of the peg in the upper half of the housing with the hole in the handlebar.

5 Note the location of the throttle opening and closing cables on the twistgrip pulley, then detach the inner cable ends from the pulley **(see illustration)**.

6 Undo the screw securing the opening cable elbow in the lower half of the housing, then unscrew the knurled retainer on the closing cable

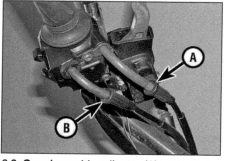

6.3 Opening cable adjuster (A) and closing cable adjuster (B)

6.4a Undo the housing screws . . .

6.4b . . . and separate the two halves of the housing

6.5 Detach the inner cable ends from the pulley

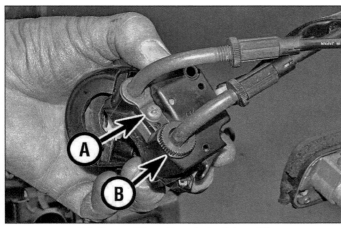

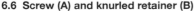

6.6 Screw (A) and knurled retainer (B)

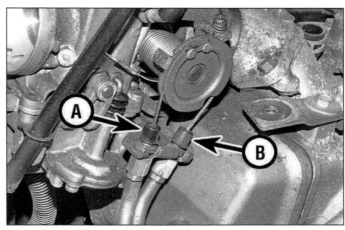

6.7 Closing cable (A), opening cable (B)

(see illustration). Draw both cables out from the housing and feed them through the opening in the lower right-hand handlebar cover.

7 Note the location of the opening and closing cables on the carburettor pulley (see illustration).

8 Working on one cable at a time, displace the boot covering the end of the outer cable, unscrew the locknut and separate the cable from the mounting bracket (see illustration). Detach the inner cable end from the pulley.

9 Note the routing of the cables from the handlebars to the carburettor, especially where they are secured by ties. Withdraw the cables carefully from the scooter, noting the correct routing.

 HAYNES HINT *When fitting a new cable, tape the lower end of the new cable to the upper end of the old cable before removing it from the machine. Slowly pull the lower end of the old cable out, guiding the new cable down into position. Using this method will ensure the cable is routed correctly.*

Installation

10 Fit the lower end of the opening outer cable onto the carburettor bracket, secure it with the locknut and fit the boot. Fit the end of the opening inner cable onto the pulley (see illustration).

11 Follow the same procedure to install the lower end of the closing cable.

12 Ensure the adjusters on the upper ends of the cables are screwed fully in. Pass both cables through the opening in the lower right-hand handlebar cover, then feed the inner cables into the twistgrip/switch housing, ensuring the opening cable is fitted at the front (see illustration). Secure the opening cable elbow with the plate and screw, and the closing cable elbow with the knurled retainer (see illustration 6.6). Fit the Inner cable ends into the throttle pulley (see illustration 6.5).

13 Assemble the housing on the handlebar, making sure the peg in the upper half locates in the hole, then fit the screws with the longest one at the front and tighten them (see illustration 6.4b and a).

14 Adjust the cable freeplay (see Chapter 1).

6.8 Separate the outer cable from the bracket and disconnect the inner cable from the pulley

15 Operate the throttle twistgrip to check that it opens and closes freely.

16 Check the alignment of the closing cable elbow, adjust it if necessary and tighten the knurled retainer.

17 Turn the handlebars from lock-to-lock to make sure the cables don't cause the steering to bind.

18 Lubricate the exposed ends of the inner cables on the carburettor pulley with

6.10 Installed location of the opening cable

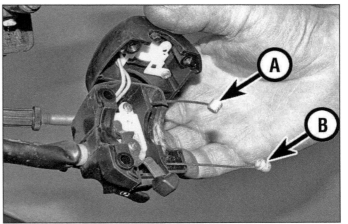

6.12 Fit the opening (A) and closing (B) cables into the twistgrip housing

7.1 Location of the automatic choke unit

7.3 Disconnect the choke unit wiring connector

7.4 Remove the choke unit cover

7.5a Undo the screw . . .

7.5b . . . and ease the choke unit out

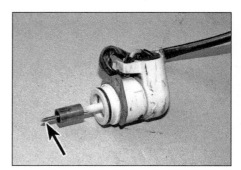

7.8 Check the unit by measuring needle protrusion (arrowed)

multi-purpose grease, then install the air filter housing (see Section 2)

19 Start the engine and check that the idle speed does not increase as the handlebars are turned. If it does, the cables are routed incorrectly. Correct the problem before riding the machine.

20 Install the remaining components in the reverse order of removal.

7 Automatic choke and resistor

1 The automatic choke unit is located on the right-hand side of the carburettor (see illustration). If the unit is thought to be faulty remove it and test as follows. A resistor is fitted in the choke wiring circuit on all machines except AN250X and Y models (see Wiring Diagrams at the end of Chapter 9).

Removal and installation

2 Remove the seat, underseat panel and right-hand side panel for access (see Chapter 8).

3 Trace the wiring from the choke unit and disconnect it at the connector (see illustration). Release the wiring from any ties and feed it back to the carburettor.

4 Ease off the cover, noting how it fits (see illustration).

5 Undo the screw securing the unit and ease it out from the carburettor body (see illustrations). Note the location of the O-ring and fit a new one on reassembly if it is damaged.

6 Installation is the reverse of removal.

Check

7 Inspect the needle for signs of wear or corrosion.

8 No specifications are available for testing the choke unit, however its operation can be

checked as follows. Measure the protrusion of the needle from the body (see illustration). Next, using a fully charged 12 volt battery and insulated jumper wires, connect the battery positive (+) terminal to the yellow/white wire terminal on the unit and the negative (-) terminal to the black/white wire terminal.

9 Measure the protrusion again after 5 minutes. If the measurement has not increased the unit is probably faulty and should be tested by a Suzuki dealer.

Resistor

10 Remove the kick panel for access (see Chapter 8).

11 The resistor is located on the top of the frame behind the steering head.

12 Disconnect the wiring connectors. Using a multimeter set the ohms scale, test the resistance between the terminals and compare the result with the specification at the beginning of this Chapter. If the result is outside the specified range the resistor is faulty and a new one must be fitted.

8 Carburettor heater and thermo-switch

1 The carburettor heater is located on the underside of the carburettor (see illustration). The thermo-switch is located on the right-hand side of the scooter underneath the storage compartment (see illustration). When the air temperature is extremely low,

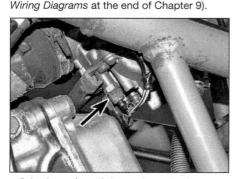

8.1a Location of the carburettor heater

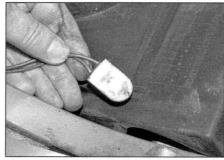

8.1b Location of the thermo-switch

8.7 Disconnect the wiring from the heater terminals

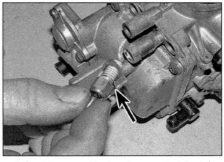

8.8a Unscrew the heater – note black/white wire terminal (arrowed)

...ector

...urettor ...n (see ...pter 9). ...switch ...either ...t them

...el and ...Chapter ...switch,

7 Disconnect the wiring from the heater terminals **(see illustration)**.
8 Unscrew the heater unit from its mounting, noting the location of the black/white wire terminal **(see illustration)**. If required, unscrew the mounting from the carburettor **(see illustration)**.
9 Prior to installation, coat the threads of the heater unit with thermal grease – this greatly increases the conductivity of heat from the heater to the carburettor. Ensure the wiring terminals are clean and free from corrosion.
10 If removed, install the heater mounting and tighten it securely. Install the heater and black/white wire terminal, position the terminal as noted on disassembly and tighten the heater securely **(see illustration)**.
11 Reconnect the wiring to the heater terminals, then install the carburettor (see Section 9).

...pletely

...er unit ...r **(see**

...ery and ...battery ...ite wire ...ctor and ...hite wire ...cold at

...it again ...sed the ...ested by

...n 9).

Thermo-switch

12 Trace the wiring from the thermo-switch and disconnect it at the connector **(see illustration 8.1b)**.
13 To test the thermo-switch, suspend it in a container of iced water. Place a thermometer in the water so that the bulb is close to the switch.
14 Using a multimeter, check for continuity between the switch terminals as the water temperature rises and compare the results with the specifications at the beginning of this Chapter. If the switch remains open or

closed all the time, or closes at a different temperature to that specified, it is faulty and must be renewed.
15 Installation is the reverse of removal.

9 Carburettor removal and installation

⚠ *Warning: Refer to the precautions given in Section 1 before starting work.*

Removal

1 Remove the seat, storage compartment, underseat panel and right-hand side panel (see Chapter 8).
2 Remove the air filter housing (see Section 2)
3 Disconnect the throttle cables from the carburettor pulley (see Section 6).
4 Release the clip securing the fuel supply hose and disconnect the hose **(see illustration)**. Plug the open end of the hose and support it upright to avoid leakage. Place a suitable container below the carburettor drain hose, loosen the drain screw and empty any residual fuel from the float chamber.
5 Trace the wiring from the automatic choke and carburettor heater and disconnect it at the connectors (see Sections 7 and 8).
6 On AN400 models, trace the wiring from the

...nting

8.10 Installed position of the heater and black/white wire terminal

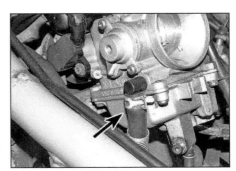

9.4 Disconnect the fuel supply hose

9.6a Trace the wiring from the throttle position sensor . . .

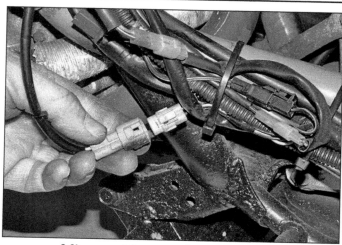

9.6b . . . and disconnect it at the connector

throttle position sensor and disconnect it at the connector (see illustrations).

7 Release the clip securing the secondary air system vacuum hose and disconnect the hose from the carburettor (see illustration).

8 Release the clip securing the drain hose and disconnect the hose from the carburettor (see illustration).

9 Loosen the clamp securing the carburettor to the intake manifold (see illustration). Ensure all the wiring for the carburettor components is free from any clips or ties and feed it back to the carburettor. Ease the carburettor out from the intake manifold, noting how it locates, and lift it off (see illustration).

Caution: Stuff clean rag into the intake manifold after removing the carburettor to prevent anything from falling inside.

Installation

10 Installation is the reverse of removal, noting the following.

- Check for cracks or splits in the intake manifold and replace it with new one if necessary.

- Make sure the intake manifold clamp is positioned correctly (see illustration 9.9a).
- Align the peg on the carburettor with the notch in the manifold, then press the carburettor in firmly to ensure it is fully engaged with the manifold – a squirt of WD-40 or a smear of oil will ease installation.
- Tighten the clamp screw securely.
- Make sure all wiring is correctly routed and secured and not trapped or kinked.
- Push the drain, vacuum and fuel supply hoses fully onto their unions and secure them with the clips – if any of the clips are corroded, replace them with new ones (see illustrations 9.8, 7 and 4).
- Refer to Section 6 for installation of the throttle cables.
- Check the idle speed and adjust as necessary (see Chapter 1).

9.7 Disconnect the secondary air system vacuum hose

9.8 Disconnect the carburettor drain hose

10 Carburettor overhaul

Note: *A Keihin CVK36 carburettor, as fitted to AN400 models, is used to illustrate this procedure. The Keihin CVK30 carburettor, as fitted to AN250 models, is essentially the same although the location of some components may vary.*

1 Poor engine performance, hesitation, hard starting, stalling and flooding are all signs that carburettor overhaul may be required (see *Fault Finding* in the *Reference* section).

2 Before disassembling the carburettor, make sure you have all the necessary O-rings and gaskets, some carburettor cleaner, a supply of clean rags, some means of blowing out the carburettor jets and passages and a clean place to work. Take care when removing components to note their exact locations and any springs or O-rings that may be fitted.

9.9a Loosen the carburettor-to-manifold clamp

9.9b Ease the carburettor off the intake manifold

10.5 Remove the throttle cable bracket

10.6a Undo the screws . . .

10.6b . . . and lift off the cover

Disassembly

3 Remove the carburettor (see Section 9).

4 Remove the automatic choke unit (see Section 7) and the carburettor heater (see Section 8).

5 Undo the screws securing the throttle cable bracket and remove the bracket **(see illustration)**.

6 Undo the screws securing the top cover, noting the location of the cable guide if fitted, and lift the cover off **(see illustrations)**. Remove the slide spring.

7 Carefully peel the diaphragm away from its sealing groove in the carburettor and withdraw the diaphragm/slide assembly **(see illustration)**.

Caution: Do not use a sharp instrument to displace the diaphragm as it is easily damaged.

8 Remove the spring seat, noting how it locates inside the bottom of the slide, and remove the needle **(see illustrations)**.

9 Undo the screws securing the coasting enrichment valve cover and remove the cover and spring **(see illustrations)**. Remove the O-ring from the fuel passage and lift out the diaphragm, noting how it fits **(see illustrations)**.

10 On CVK36 carburettors, if required, undo the tamper-proof screws securing the throttle position sensor. **Note:** *A special screwdriver bit will be required to undo these screws.*

10.7 Withdraw the diaphragm/slide assembly

10.8a Remove the spring seat . . .

10.8b . . . and the needle

10.9a Undo the screws . . .

10.9b . . . and remove the coasting enrichment valve cover and spring

10.9c Remove the O-ring . . .

10.9d . . . and lift out the diaphragm

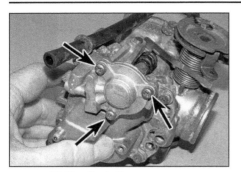

10.11a Undo the screws . . .

10.11b . . . and remove the accelerator pump cover and spring

1

Lift the sensor off, noting how the slot in the sensor fits over the end of the throttle pulley shaft. Note the location of the O-ring.

11 Undo the screws securing the accelerator pump cover and remove the cover and spring (see illustrations). Remove the O-ring from the fuel passage and lift out the diaphragm, noting how it fits (see illustrations).

12 Undo the screws securing the float chamber and remove it (see illustrations). Discard the seal as a new one must be fitted.

13 On CVK30 carburettors, undo the screw securing the float pin, then lift out the float assembly, noting how it fits. Unhook the needle valve from the tab on the float.

14 On CVK36 carburettors, withdraw the float pin and remove the float assembly, noting how it fits (see illustrations). Unhook the needle valve from the tab on the float.

15 Unscrew the pilot jet, the main jet from the top of the jet holder, and then the jet holder (see illustration).

16 The pilot screw can be removed from the carburettor, but note that its setting will be disturbed (see illustration 10.15). To record the pilot screw's current setting, turn the screw in until it seats lightly, counting the exact number of turns. Unscrew and remove the pilot screw along with its spring, washer and O-ring. Discard the O-ring, as a new one must be used. Note: On CVK30 carburettors the pilot screw is located on the right-hand side of the carburettor body.

 Warning: Do not undo the screws securing the butterfly valve to the throttle pulley shaft.

Cleaning

Caution: Use only a dedicated carburettor

cleaner
for carl
manufa
caustic
17 Squi
fuel and
18 Subr
cleaner
any varn
the float
using a
stubbor
compone
19 Use c
and air pa
Caution:
with a p
will be e
metering

10.11d . . . and lift out the diaphragm

10.12a Undo the screws . . .

10.12b

10.14a Withdraw the float pin . . .

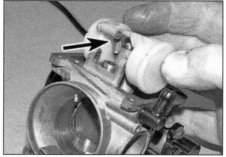

10.14b . . . and remove the float assembly. Note location of needle valve (arrowed)

10.15 P
(B) and p

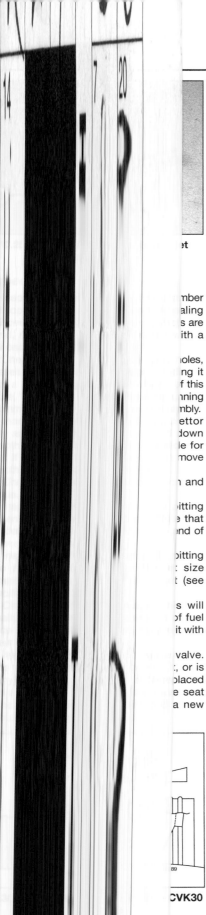

10.29a Coasting enrichment valve diaphragm, spring, cover and O-ring

10.29b Accelerator pump diaphragm, O-ring, spring and cover

28 If removed, check the tapered end of the pilot screw and the spring for wear or damage. Renew the pilot screw and spring if necessary.

29 Check the coasting enrichment valve diaphragm for splits and general deterioration and fit a new one if necessary **(see illustration)**. Similarly, inspect the accelerator pump diaphragm **(see illustration)**.

30 Operate the throttle pulley to make sure it turns smoothly under spring pressure.

31 If required, check the operation of the automatic choke unit (see Section 7) and the carburettor heater (see Section 8).

32 Check the condition of the hoses and hose clips and replace them with new ones if they are damaged, deformed or deteriorated.

Reassembly, float height and fuel level checks

Note: *When reassembling the carburettor, be sure to use the new O-rings, seals and other parts supplied in the rebuild kit. Do not over-tighten the carburettor jets and screws, as they are easily damaged.*

33 If removed, fit the spring, washer and O-ring onto the pilot screw, then thread the screw in until it seats lightly. Now, turn the screw out the number of turns previously recorded, or to the initial setting (see *Specifications*).

34 Install the jet holder, main jet and pilot jet **(see illustrations 10.25 and 10.15)**.

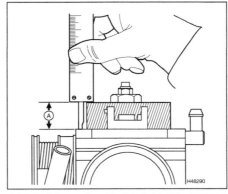

10.36b Measuring float height (A) – CVK36 carburettor

35 Hook the needle valve onto the float, then position the float assembly in the carburettor, making sure the needle valve locates in its seat **(see illustration 10.14b)**. On CVK30 carburettors, install the screw to secure the float pin. On CVK36 carburettors, install the float pin.

36 To check the float height, hold the carburettor upside down. Measure the distance between the top edge of the float and the sealing surface of the float chamber **(see illustrations)**. The height should be as specified at the beginning of this Chapter. If not, bend the needle valve tab on the float to correct it.

37 Fit a new seal onto the float chamber, making sure it is seated properly in its groove **(see illustration)**. Fit the chamber onto the carburettor and tighten the screws securely **(see illustration 10.12a)**.

38 The carburettor fuel level should be checked at this point to ensure that the float and needle valve are working correctly. Support the carburettor upright in a vice and connect a length of hose to the fuel union. Connect a length of clear fuel hose to the drain union on the base of the float chamber. Secure the hose up against the side of the carburettor and mark it level with the fuel level datum line **(see illustrations 10.40 or 10.41 as appropriate)**.

39 Carefully pour a small amount of fuel into the carburettor via the fuel hose union, then undo the drain screw in the bottom of the float chamber enough to allow fuel to flow into the clear hose. Continue pouring fuel into the carburettor until the float needle valve shuts off the supply.

10.37 Install the float chamber seal in its groove

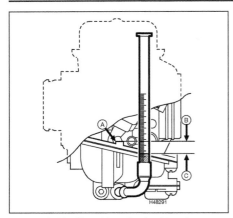

**10.40 Checking the fuel level –
CVK30 carburettor**

A Datum mark on carburettor
B Zero on gauge aligned with datum mark
C Level of fluid

40 On AN250 models **(see illustration)**, the level in the clear hose should be the specified distance below the datum line (see *Specifications* at the beginning of this Chapter). If the fuel level is incorrect, and the float needle valve and the valve seat are good, check the float tab and float pin for wear or damage.

41 On AN400 models **(see illustration)**, the level in the clear hose should be the specified distance above the datum line (see *Specifications* at the beginning of this Chapter). If the fuel level is incorrect, and the float needle valve and the valve seat are good, check the float tab and float pin for wear or damage.

42 Once the fuel level has been confirmed as correct, drain out any residual fuel, then tighten the float chamber drain screw securely.

43 Hold the carburettor upside down and install the accelerator pump diaphragm and a new O-ring **(see illustrations 10.11d and c)**. Install the spring and cover and tighten the cover screws securely.

44 Install the coasting enrichment valve diaphragm and a new O-ring **(see illustrations 10.9d and c)**. Install the spring and cover and tighten the cover screws securely.

45 On CVK36 carburettors, if removed, install the throttle position sensor with a new O-ring. Tighten the screws finger-tight, then check

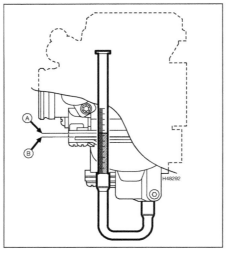

**10.41 Checking the fuel level –
CVK36 carburettor**

A Level of fluid
B Datum mark (level with float chamber mating surface)

the operation of the sensor as follows. Using a multimeter set to the ohms scale, connect the probes between the terminals in the sensor wiring connector as shown **(see illustration)**. Note the meter reading with the throttle valve closed (connection A) and compare it with the specification at the beginning of this Chapter. Now turn the throttle pulley to open the throttle valve fully and note the meter reading between the terminals (connection B). Twist the sensor until the reading is as specified, then tighten the screws securely.

46 Install the needle in the slide and secure it with the spring seat **(see illustrations 10.8b and a)**. Ensure the spring seat is correctly located in the bottom of the slide.

47 Align the slide with the carburettor body and lower it into the carburettor, making sure the needle is aligned with the jet holder **(see illustrations)**. Press the rim of the diaphragm into its groove, making sure it is correctly seated, then install the spring and cover and secure it with the screws **(see illustrations 10.6b and a)**.

48 Check that the piston moves smoothly in the carburettor body by pushing it up with your

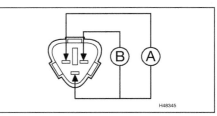

10.45 Check throttle position sensor resistance – throttle closed (A), throttle fully open (B)

finger. Note that the piston should descend slowly and smoothly as the diaphragm draws air into the chamber – it should not drop sharply under spring pressure.

49 Clean the threads of the screws securing the throttle cable bracket and apply a suitable non-permanent thread-locking compound. Install the bracket and tighten the screws securely.

50 Install the carburettor heater (see Section 8) and the automatic choke unit (see Section 7).

51 Install the carburettor (see Section 9).

11 Fuel level gauge and sensor

1 The circuit consists of the fuel level sensor mounted inside the fuel tank and the gauge located in the instrument cluster. If the system malfunctions check first that the battery is fully charged and that the fuses are all good.

Fuel level gauge

2 To check the operation of the gauge, first remove the floor centre panel (see Chapter 8).
3 Trace the wiring from the sensor located in the fuel tank and disconnect it at the connector.
4 Connect a variable resistance tester between the terminals on the gauge side of the connector.
5 Refer to the appropriate gauge resistance range in the *Specifications* at the beginning of this Chapter and set the tester to the highest ohms setting. Turn the ignition ON and note the reading on the fuel gauge. **Note:** *Allow at least 20 seconds for the gauge to register a reading.* Carry out the test at the other ohms setting(s). Compare the results with the appropriate gauge needle positions for your machine **(see illustration)**.

10.47a Lower the slide into the carburettor . . .

10.47b . . . making sure the needle (arrowed) is aligned with the jet holder

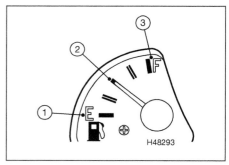

11.5 Fuel level gauge needle positions

the headlight panel, cockpit trim panel, belly panel and radiator panel (see Chapter 8) then remove the radiator (see Chapter 3).

2 Remove the left and right-hand side panels and the front mudguard (see Chapter 8).

3 Disconnect the fuel level sensor wiring connector (see Section 11).

4 Remove the fuel filter (see Section 3). Plug the open end of the intake hose to prevent leakage.

5 Undo the front and rear mounting bolts on the right-hand side and the rear mounting bolt on the left-hand side. Note the location of the grommets and spacers in the tank mounting lugs.

6 Draw the tank forwards and off the machine.

Installation

7 Prior to installation, check the tank mounting grommets and bushes for signs of damage or deterioration and renew them if necessary. Check the condition of the fuel hoses and hose clips.

8 Ease the tank into position and align the mounting lugs with the mounts on the frame. Tighten the mounting bolts to the torque setting specified at the beginning of this Chapter.

9 Install the fuel filter (see Section 3).

10 Connect the fuel level sensor wiring connector (see Section 11).

11 Install the remaining components in reverse order of removal.

Tank repair

12 All repairs to the fuel tank should be carried

out by a professional who has experience in this critical and potentially dangerous work. Even after cleaning and flushing of the fuel system, explosive fumes can remain and ignite during repair of the tank.

13 Exhaust system

 Warning: If the engine has been running the exhaust system will be very hot. Allow the system to cool before carrying out any work.

Removal

1 Undo the nuts securing the silencer front pipe to the header pipe flange **(see illustration)**.

2 Counter-hold the bolts and undo the nuts securing the silencer to its mounting bracket **(see illustration)**. On AN250 models, there are two mounting bolts on the underside of the silencer. On AN400 models, a third mounting bolt is located above the silencer.

3 Pull the front pipe flange off the studs on the header pipe and lift the silencer off **(see illustration)**. Note the location of the sealing washer and discard it as a new one must be fitted **(see illustration)**.

Note 1: *The exhaust sealing washer can become extremely compacted in the pipe flange - ensure all traces of the sealing washer are removed prior to installation.*

Note 2: *On machines fitted with a catalytic*

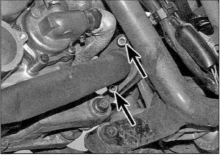
13.1 Undo the exhaust flange nuts

13.2 Location of silencer mounting bolts

13.3a Lift off the silencer

13.3b Note location of sealing washer

13.4a Undo the bolts . . .

13.4b . . . and remove the header pipe

13.5 Location of exhaust mounting bracket bolts

converter take care not to strike or drop the silencer - the catalytic converter is fragile.

4 If required, remove the belly panel (see Chapter 8), then undo the bolts securing the header pipe to the cylinder head and remove the pipe **(see illustrations)**. Note the location of the sealing washer and discard it as a new one must be fitted.

5 If required, undo the bolts securing the exhaust mounting bracket to the engine housing and lift it off **(see illustration)**.

Installation

6 Installation is the reverse of removal, noting the following:

- *If removed, tighten the mounting bracket bolts to the torque setting specified at the beginning of this Chapter.*
- *Apply a dab of grease to the exhaust seals to hold them in place.*
- *Apply a smear of copper or nickel based grease to all nuts and studs to prevent them from seizing.*
- *If removed, install the header pipe and tighten the bolts to the specified torque setting.*
- *Install the silencer and fit the flange nuts and mounting bolts finger-tight.*
- *Ensure the system is correctly aligned, then tighten the flange nuts to the specified torque setting.*
- *Tighten the silencer mounting nuts to the specified torque.*
- *Run the engine and check the system for leaks.*

14 Secondary air system

1 The secondary air system is fitted to reduce the amount of unburned hydrocarbons released in the exhaust gases. A description of the system is given in Chapter 1. The hoses and their unions should be checked at the specified service interval.

2 The control valve is located on the right-hand side of the engine **(see illustration)**. Remove the underseat cover, front frame cover and right-hand side panel for access (see Chapter 8).

3 To remove the valve, first follow the procedure In Section 2 and remove the air filter housing, then separate the valve from the housing **(see illustration)**.

4 To check the operation of the valve, blow air into the inlet hose union and ensure that it flows out through the outlet union. Using a vacuum pump **(see illustration 5.5)**, apply a vacuum of 280 to 450 mmHg via the vacuum hose union and repeat the check – no air should flow through the valve if it is functioning correctly. Replace the valve with a new one if it is faulty.

5 Installation is the reverse of removal.

15 Catalytic converter

Note: *The AN250RK2 and AN400RK2 have a catalytic converter located inside the silencer.*

General information

1 A catalytic converter is incorporated in the exhaust system to minimise the level of exhaust pollutants released into the atmosphere.

2 The catalytic converter consists of a heat tube impregnated with a catalyst material, over which the hot exhaust gases pass. The catalyst speeds up the oxidation of harmful carbon monoxide, unburned hydrocarbons and soot, effectively reducing the quantity of harmful products

released into the atmosphere via the exhaust gases.

3 The catalytic converter is of the open-loop type, providing no feedback to the fuel system.

Precautions

4 The catalytic converter is a reliable device which needs no maintenance in itself, but there are some facts of which an owner should be aware if the converter is to function properly for its full service life.

- *DO NOT use leaded or lead replacement petrol (gasoline) – the additives will coat the precious metals, reducing their converting efficiency and will eventually destroy the catalytic converter.*
- *Always keep the ignition and fuel systems well-maintained in accordance with the manufacturer's schedule – if the fuel/air mixture is suspected of being incorrect have it checked on an exhaust gas analyser.*
- *If the engine develops a misfire, do not ride the scooter (or at least as little as possible) until the fault is cured.*
- *DO NOT use fuel or engine oil additives – these may contain substances harmful to the catalytic converter.*
- *DO NOT continue to use the scooter if the engine burns oil to the extent of leaving a visible trail of blue smoke.*
- *Remember that the catalytic converter Is FRAGILE – handle the silencer with care when it is of the machine.*

14.2 Location of the secondary air system control valve

14.3 Remove control valve with the air filter housing

ement system – fuel injected models

ulty

asy, suitable ner with perience	**Fairly difficult,** suitable for competent DIY mechanic	**Difficult,** suitable for experienced DIY mechanic	**Very difficult,** suitable for expert DIY or professional

. . . .	Unleaded. Minimum 91 RON (Research Octane Number)
. . . .	13 litres
. . . .	95 ohms approx
. . . .	51 ohms approx
. . . .	10 ohms approx
. . . .	130 ohms approx
. . . .	not available
. . . .	10 ohms approx
. . . .	4 to 10 ohms approx
. . . .	40 to 50 ohms approx
. . . .	90 to 100 ohms approx
. . . .	9 to 11 ohms approx
. . . .	129 to 131 ohms approx
. . . .	43 psi (3.0 Bar)
. . . .	35 ml every 10 seconds
. . . .	2 turns out

Engine management system

Crankshaft position (CKP) sensor
    Peak voltage.. 4.5 volts (min)
    Resistance .... 180 to 280 ohms
Engine coolant temperature (ECT) sensor
    Input voltage...................................... 4.5 to 5.5 volts
    Resistance .... 2.58 K-ohms approx at 20°C
Idle air control (IAC) valve
    Resistance
        AN400K3 to K6 models .... 3 to 9 ohms at 20 to 24°C
        AN400K7 model onward........................ 80 ohms (approx) at 20 to 24°C
Ignition coil
    Minimum primary peak voltage .... 150 volts or more
    Primary resistance
        AN400K3 to K6 models .... 3 to 5 ohms
        AN400K7 model onward........................ 1.2 to 3.5 ohms
    Secondary resistance
        AN400K3 to K6 models .... 17 to 30 K-ohms
        AN400K7 model onward........................ 15 to 30 K-ohms
Intake air pressure (IAP) sensor
    Input voltage .... 4.5 to 5.5 volts
    Output voltage
        AN400K3 to K6 models .... 2.6 volts (approx) at idle
        AN400K7 model onward........................ 1.5 to 3.5 volts at idle
Intake air temperature (IAT) sensor
    Input voltage...................................... 4.5 to 5.5 volts
    Resistance
        At 20°C (68°F).............................. 2.58 K-ohms
        At 40°C (104°F)............................. 1.14 K-ohms
        At 80°C (176°F)............................. 0.28 K-ohm
        At 100°C (212°F)............................ 0.155 K-ohm
Oxygen sensor
    Output voltage
        AN400K3 to K6 models
            At idle .... 0.4 volt
            At 3000 rpm .... 0.6 volt
        AN400K7 model onward
            At idle .... 0.3 volt
            At 3000 rpm .... 0.7 volt
    Heater resistance .... 11.5 to 14.5 ohms at 23°C
Secondary throttle position sensor
    Input voltage .... 4.5 to 5.5 volts
    Output voltage
        Valve fully open............................. 3.9 volts (approx)
        Valve fully closed .... 0.5 volt (approx)
Secondary throttle valve actuator
    Resistance .... 6.5 ohms (approx)
Throttle position sensor
    Input voltage .... 4.5 to 5.5 volts
    Output voltage
        Valve fully closed .... 0.6 volt (approx)
        Valve fully open............................. 3.8 volts (approx)
    Resistance
        Valve fully closed .... 0.6 K-ohm (approx)
        Valve fully open............................. 3.8 K-ohms (approx)
Tip over (TO) sensor
    Resistance
        AN400K3 to K6 models .... 19.1 to 19.7 K-ohms
        AN400K7 model onward........................ 16.5 to 22.3 K-ohms
    Output voltage
        AN400K3 to K6 models
            Sensor upright .... 1.3 volts or less
            At 70° .... 3.8 volts or more
        AN400K7 model onward
            Sensor upright .... 0.4 to 1.4 volts
            At 65° .... 3.7 to 4.4 volts
Fuel injector
    Resistance
        AN400K3 to K6 models .... 10.0 to 18.0 ohms at 20°C
        AN400K7 model onward........................ 10.3 ohms at 20°C
Secondary air system control valve
    Resistance .... 20 to 24 ohms at 20°C

. . . .	5 Nm
. . . .	12 Nm
. . . .	3.5 Nm
. . . .	4.5 Nm
. . . .	10 Nm
. . . .	48 Nm
. . . .	23 Nm
. . . .	30 Nm
. . . .	23 Nm
. . . .	23 Nm

into the exhaust port to improve exhaust gas burning and reduce emissions.

Several of the fuel system service procedures are considered routine maintenance items and for that reason are covered in Chapter 1.

Ignition system

The ignition circuit consists of the crankshaft position (CKP) sensor, ignition coil and spark plug.

The triggers on the alternator rotor, which is fitted to the right-hand end of the crankshaft, activate signals in the CKP sensor as the crankshaft rotates. The sensor sends those signals to the ECM which, in conjunction with information received from the throttle position and engine coolant temperature sensor, calculates the ignition timing and supplies the ignition coil with the power necessary to produce a spark at the plug. There is no provision for checking or adjusting the ignition timing.

Note: *Individual engine management system components can be checked but not repaired. If system troubles occur, and the faulty component can be isolated, the only cure for the problem in most cases is to replace the part with a new one. Keep in mind that most electronic parts, once purchased, cannot be returned. To avoid unnecessary expense, make very sure the faulty component has been positively identified before buying a new part.*

Precautions

Warning: Petrol (gasoline) is extremely flammable, so take extra precautions when you work on any part of the fuel system. Always remove the battery (see Chapter 9). Don't smoke or allow open flames or bare light bulbs near the work area, and don't work in a garage where a natural gas-type appliance is present. If you spill any fuel on your skin, rinse it off immediately with soap and water. When you perform any kind of work on the fuel system, wear safety glasses and have a fire extinguisher suitable for a class B type fire (flammable liquids) on hand.

Ensure the ignition is switched OFF before disconnecting or reconnecting any fuel injection system wiring connector. If a connector is disconnected or reconnected with the ignition switched ON, the ECM may be damaged.

Always perform service procedures in a well-ventilated area to prevent a build-up of fumes.

Never work in a building containing a gas appliance with a pilot light, or any other form of naked flame. Ensure that there are no naked light bulbs or any sources of flame or sparks nearby.

Do not smoke (or allow anyone else to smoke) while in the vicinity of petrol (gasoline) or of components containing it. Remember the possible presence of vapour from these sources and move well clear before smoking.

Check all electrical equipment belonging to the house, garage or workshop where work is being undertaken (see the *Safety first!* section of this manual). Remember that certain electrical appliances such as drills, cutters etc, create sparks in the normal course of operation and must not be used near petrol (gasoline) or any component containing it. Again, remember the possible presence of fumes before using electrical equipment.

Always mop up any spilt fuel and safely dispose of the rag used.

Any stored fuel that is drained off during servicing work must be kept in sealed containers that are suitable for holding petrol (gasoline), and clearly marked as such; the containers themselves should be kept in a safe place. Note that this last point applies equally to the fuel tank if it is removed from the machine; also remember to keep its filler cap closed at all times.

Read the *Safety first!* section of this manual carefully before starting work.

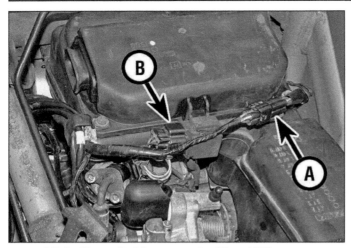

2.3 Ignition coil wiring connector (A) and IAP sensor connector (B)

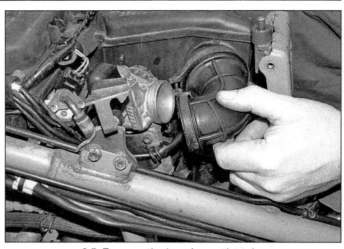

2.5 Remove the housing outlet tube

2 Air filter housing

Removal

1 Remove the seat, storage compartment, underseat panel and right-hand side panel (see Chapter 8).
2 Follow the procedure in Chapter 1 to remove the air filter cover and element.

AN400K3 to K6

3 Disconnect the ignition coil wiring connector (see illustration).
4 Disconnect the intake air pressure (IAP) sensor wiring connector and unclip the sensor from the air filter housing (see illustration 2.3).
5 Loosen the clips securing the air filter housing outlet tube to the housing and the throttle body and remove the tube (see illustration).
6 Disconnect the intake air temperature (IAT) sensor wiring connector (see illustration).
7 Release the clip and disconnect the engine breather hose from the back of the housing (see illustration).
8 Release the clip securing the secondary air system valve intake hose to the underside of the housing and disconnect the hose (see illustration).
9 Undo the central and rear housing mounting bolts and manoeuvre the housing out (see illustrations). Note how the housing locates on its support bracket (see illustration).

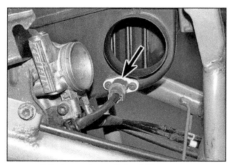

2.6 Location of the IAT sensor

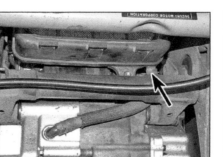

2.7 Disconnect the engine breather hose (arrowed)

2.8 Disconnect the valve hose (arrowed)

2.9a Undo the centre and rear mounting bolts . . .

2.9b . . . and lift the air filter housing out

2.9c Location of the housing support bracket

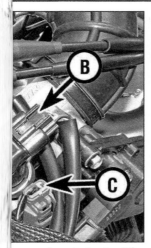

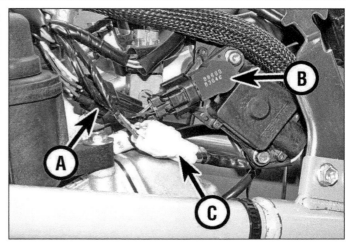

2. ...e speed control valve (B)
...ensor (C)

2.11 Combined wiring connector (A), STP sensor (B) and STVA (C)

AN...

10 ... the
inta... ...alve
and... ...on).
On... the
inta... ...ring
con...

11 ...ing
con... ...ture
(EC... IAT)
sen... ...tors
for... ...TP)

sensor and secondary throttle valve actuator **(see illustration)**.

12 On AN400L0/ZAL0 models onward, undo the screw securing the wiring guide and disconnect the intake air temperature (IAT) sensor wiring connector from the sensor **(see illustration)**.

13 Disconnect the fuel injector wiring connector **(see illustration)**.

14 Release the clip and disconnect the engine breather hose from the back of the housing **(see illustration)**.

15 On AN400L0/ZAL0 models onward, undo

the bolt securing the outlet tube support bracket **(see illustration)**. Loosen the clip securing the air filter housing outlet tube to the throttle body and disconnect the tube **(see illustration)**.

16 On AN400K7 to K9 models, loosen the clips securing the air filter housing outlet tube to the housing and the throttle body and remove the tube **(see illustration 2.5)**.

17 Undo the bolts securing the housing support bracket **(see illustration)**.

18 Undo the right-hand housing mounting bolt and manoeuvre the housing out **(see**

2.13 Fuel injector wiring connector

2.14 Disconnect the engine breather hose

2.15b Loosen the clip (arrowed)

2.17 Bolts secure housing support bracket

2.18a Undo the mounting bolt (arrowed) . . .

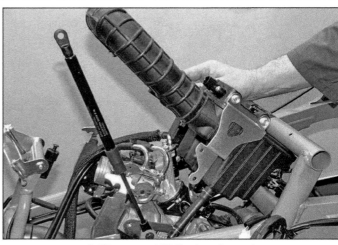
2.18b . . . and lift the housing out

2.18c Location of the housing support bracket

2.19 Ensure the housing drains are clear

illustrations). Note how the housing locates on its support bracket **(see illustration)**.

Installation

19 Prior to installation, ensure the inside of the housing is clean and dry. If required, release the clips securing the drain tube and drain plug(s) **(see illustration)**. Have some rag ready to catch any residual water or oil in the tube and plug(s).

20 Installation is the reverse of removal, noting the following:
• Ensure the drain tube and drain plug(s) are secured with their clips.

• On AN400K3 to K6 models, connect the secondary air system valve to the underside of the housing.
• Ensure the wiring connectors are secure.
• Don't forget to reconnect the engine breather hose.

3 Fuel cut-off and pressure control valves

⚠ *Warning: Refer to the precautions given in Section 1 before starting work.*

1 The fuel cut-off and pressure control valves are located on the top of the fuel tank. Remove the underseat panel and kickpanel for access (see Chapter 8).
2 Follow the procedures in Chapter 4A, Section 5, to remove, check and install the valves.

4 Fuel pressure and delivery check

⚠ *Warning: Refer to the precautions given in Section 1 before starting work.*
Special Tools: *A fuel pressure gauge, hose and adapter are required for the pressure check (see Step 2). A suitable calibrated container is required for the fuel delivery check (see Step 9).*

1 The fuel pump is located inside the fuel tank. When the ignition is switched ON, it should be possible to hear the pump run for a few seconds until the system is up to pressure. If you can't hear anything, check the pump wiring and wiring connectors (see Section 5). Check the pump relay – a fault with the fuel pump relay should be indicated by the FI warning light (see Section 8).

Fuel pressure check

2 To check the fuel pressure, a suitable gauge, gauge adapter, hoses and hose union are needed. Suzuki produces service tools (Part Nos. 09915-77331, 09940-40211, 09915-74521 and 09940-40230) for this purpose.
3 Remove the underseat panel and kickpanel for access (see Chapter 8).
4 Undo the bolts securing the fuel hose union to the fuel pump backplate and disconnect the hose **(see illustration)**. Note the location of the O-ring and discard it as a new one must be fitted **(see illustration)**.
5 Follow the manufacturer's instructions to connect the gauge and hoses.

4.4a Disconnect the fuel hose . . .

4.4b . . . note location of O-ring

4.9a Fuel hose union – AN400K3 to K6 models

4.9b Fuel hose union – AN400K7-on models

4.10a Fuel pump wiring connector – AN400K3 to K6 models

4.10b Fuel pump wiring connector – AN400K7–on models

pump tested by a Suzuki dealer. If all the components are good it is likely the ECM is faulty – have it checked by a Suzuki dealer.

Removal – all models

3 Remove the underseat panel and kickpanel for access (see Chapter 8).
4 Trace the wiring from the terminal on the fuel pump backplate and disconnect it at the connector **(see illustration 4.10a or b)**.
5 Undo the bolts securing the fuel hose union to the fuel pump backplate and disconnect the hose **(see illustration 4.4a)**. Note the location of the O-ring and discard it as a new one must be fitted **(see illustration 4.4b)**.

⚠️ **Warning: Check the fuel level in the tank before removing the pump. Due to the location of the pump, fuel spillage may occur if the tank is more than half full when the pump is removed.**

6 Note which way round the pump backplate is fitted, then undo the mounting bolts evenly and lift the pump assembly out, taking care not to damage the level sensor float arm **(see illustrations)**. Note the location of the seal and discard it as a new one must be fitted **(see illustration)**.

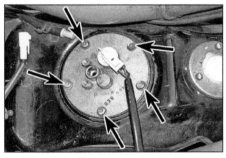

5.6a Undo the pump mounting bolts

5.6c Removing the pump – AN400K7-on models

5.6d Note location of fuel pump seal

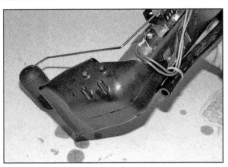

5.7a Location of the fuel pump cover

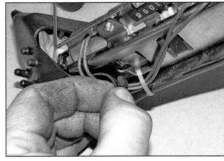

5.7b Unclip the cover . . .

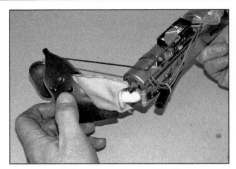

5.7c . . . and ease it off

Overhaul – AN400K3 to K6 models

Disassembly

7 Note the location of the cover on the lower end of the assembly, then unclip it and ease it off the strainer (see illustrations). Release the clip securing the fuel return hose to the pressure regulator and disconnect the hose (see illustration).

8 Note the location of the pump assembly components (see illustration).

9 Undo the screw securing the pump retaining clip and wiring and unhook the clip (see illustrations).

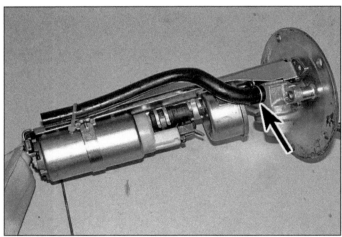

5.7d Disconnect the fuel return hose

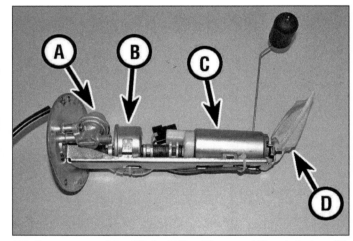

5.8 Pressure regulator (A), fuel filter (B), pump (C) and strainer (D)

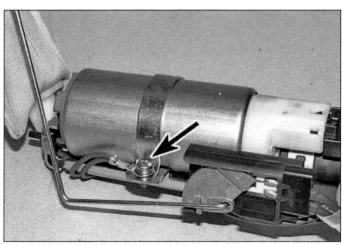

5.9a Undo the screw . . .

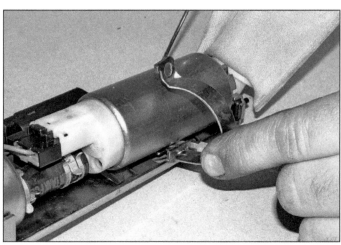

5.9b . . . and unhook the clip

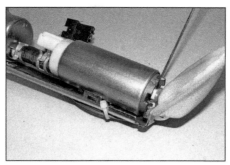

5.11a Note location of pump

5.11b Release the hose clip . . .

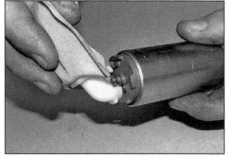

5.12 Twist the strainer anti-clockwise to remove

5.13a Release the clip . . .

10 . . . . . . (see illu . . .

11 . . . loc . . . the . . . ren

12 . . . rele . . . illu . . .

13 . . . be . . . an . . . illu

. . . see

. . . ump . . . ease . . . and

. . . to . . . (see

. . . ose . . . ator . . . (see

14 Undo the screw securing the pressure regulator and draw the regulator off its union on the backplate **(see illustration)**. Note the location of the O-ring and discard it as a new one must be fitted.

Check

15 Allow the strainer to dry, then clean any sediment off the gauze with a soft brush or low pressure compressed air. If the gauze is damaged, or if there is sediment inside the strainer, a new one must be fitted. Also, if there is sediment inside the strainer, it is likely

the filter will contain sediment and a new one should be fitted.

16 Inspect the hoses and renew them if they are cracked or split.

17 Refer to Section 6 to check the operation of the fuel level sensor.

Reassembly

18 Install the pump assembly components in the reverse order of removal, noting the following:

- *Fit a new O-ring onto the pressure regulator union.*
- *Ensure the filter is installed with the side*

. . . e the filter

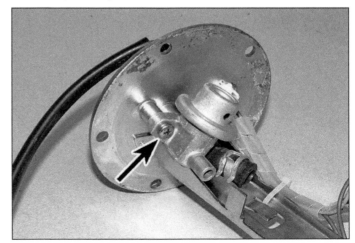

5.14 Screw (arrowed) secures pressure regulator

5.18 OUT marking faces pressure regulator

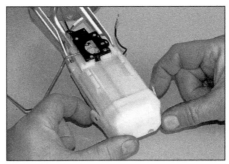

5.19a Unclip the cover . . .

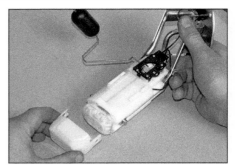

5.19b . . . to access the strainer

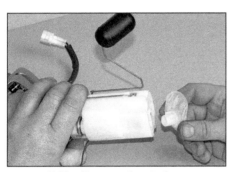

5.19c Remove the strainer

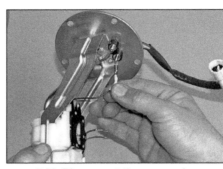

5.20 Disconnect the pump wire

marked *OUT facing the pressure regulator* **(see illustration)**.
- *Fit the strainer onto the pump before installing the pump.*
- *Secure the hoses with the clips.*
- *Don't forget to secure the wiring with the pump retaining clip screw.*

Overhaul – AN400K7 model onward

Disassembly

19 Note the location of the cover on the lower end of the assembly, then unclip it and ease it off the strainer **(see illustrations)**. Ease the strainer off the pump **(see illustration)**.

20 Undo the screw securing the earth wire (black) terminal. Disconnect the pump wire (blue) from the terminal on the backplate **(see illustration)**.

21 Undo the screws securing the pump cover and remove the spacers **(see illustrations)**. Draw off the cover **(see illustration)**.

22 Ease the pump off the union on the pressure regulator **(see illustration)**. Note the location of the O-ring and discard it as a new one must be fitted.

23 Disconnect the fuel level sensor wire (red) from the terminal on the backplate and separate the regulator/sensor assembly from the backplate **(see illustration)**. Note the location of the O-ring on the fuel pipe union and discard it as a new one must be fitted. The pressure regulator and level sensor are not available as separate components.

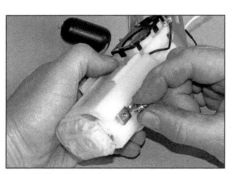

5.21a Undo the cover screws . . .

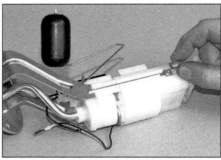

5.21b . . . and remove the spacers . . .

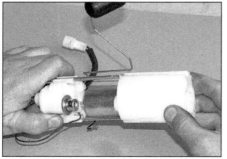

5.21c . . . then draw the cover off

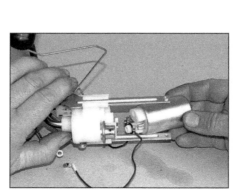

5.22 Ease the fuel pump off

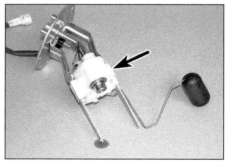

5.23 Separate the regulator/sensor assembly (arrowed) from the backplate

Chec

24 F
and ir
fuel fil
25 R
of the

Reas

26 Ir
in the
follow
• Fit
  fu
• Fit
  ins
• Do
  se
• En
  co

Inst

27 E
are c
with
tank
28 Ir
way
29 T
then
sequ
30 Ir
recor

6

1 Th
mou
locat
malfu
charg

Fue

2 To

first remove the floor centre panel and the kickpanel (see Chapter 8).

3 Trace the wiring from the terminal on the fuel pump backplate and disconnect it at the connector – the sensor is part of the fuel pump assembly (see illustration 4.10a or b). Refer to *Wiring Diagrams* at the end of Chapter 9 and identify the sensor wire terminals in the connector.

4 Connect a variable resistance tester between the terminals on the gauge (loom) side of the connector.

5 Refer to the appropriate gauge resistance range in the *Specifications* at the beginning of this Chapter and set the tester to the highest ohms setting. Turn the ignition ON and note the reading on the fuel gauge. **Note:** *Allow at least 20 seconds for the gauge to register a reading.* Carry out the test at the other ohms setting(s). Compare the results with the appropriate gauge needle positions for your machine (see illustration).

6 If the gauge readings vary greatly from the specifications a new instrument panel will have to be fitted. Individual components for the instrument cluster are not available – refer to Chapter 9 for details.

Fuel level sensor

7 The sensor resistance should change as the fuel level in the tank rises and falls. If the sensor is thought to be faulty, remove the fuel pump assembly (see Section 5) and test the sensor as follows.

> ⚠ **Warning: Refer to the precautions given in Section 1 before starting work.**

8 Inspect the sensor for signs of damage and check that the float arm moves freely up and down.

9 To check the operation of the sensor, refer to *Wiring Diagrams* at the end of Chapter 9 and identify the sensor wire terminals in the connector. Connect the probes of an ohmmeter to the terminals and measure the resistance of the sensor with the float in the

raised (tank full), midway (if appropriate) and lowered (tank empty) positions (see illustration).

10 Compare the readings to the specifications at the beginning of this Chapter. If the tests show the sensor is faulty, replace it with a new one.

11 On AN400K3 to K6 models, the sensor is integral with the fuel pump backplate – follow the procedure in Section 5 to remove the pump components and fit a new backplate.

12 On AN400K7 models onward, the sensor is integral with the fuel pressure regulator – follow the procedure in Section 5 to remove the pump components and fit a new regulator/ sensor assembly.

13 Follow the procedure in Section 5 to install the fuel pump assembly.

7 Engine management system operation

1 The engine management system consists of the fuel system and the ignition circuit, controlled and co-ordinated by the engine control module (ECM). An overview of the engine management system can be found in Section 1.

2 To ensure optimum engine efficiency, the ECM monitors signals from the following components:

• *Crankshaft position (CKP) sensor*
• *Intake air pressure (IAP) sensor*
• *Throttle position (TP) sensor*
• *Engine coolant temperature (ECT) sensor*
• *Intake air temperature (IAT) sensor*
• *Tip-over (TO) sensor*
• *Ignition coil*
• *Fuel injector*
• *Idle air control (IAC) valve*
• *Fuel pump relay*
• *Ignition switch*
• *Oxygen sensor*

3 The FI warning light in the instrument cluster

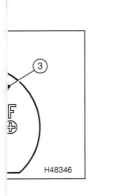

H48346

le positions

values

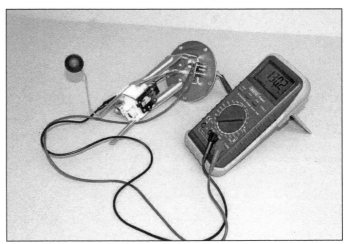

6.9 Checking the operation of the fuel level sensor

8.2a Identify the mode select switch connector . . .

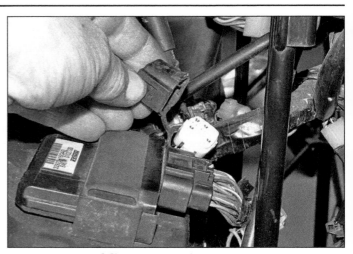

8.2b . . . remove the cover . . .

8.2c . . . and attach the mode select switch

should come on briefly when the ignition is switched ON, then go out – this serves as a check that the engine management system circuit is working correctly. If the warning light does not come on, inspect the instrument cluster wiring and wiring connector (see Chapter 9).

4 In the event of a failure in any of the components or sensor signals, the FI warning light comes on and the letters 'FI' are displayed either on the odometer (AN400K3 to K6 models) or on the multi-function display between the speedometer and tachometer (AN400K7 model onward).

5 The ECM then determines whether the engine can still be run safely. If it can, the warning light will remain ON and the letters 'FI 'will flash. The ECM substitutes the sensor signal with a fixed signal, restricting performance but allowing the scooter to be ridden home or to a dealer. If the fault is serious, the warning light will flash and the letters 'FI 'will be displayed continuously. The ECM shuts down the fuel and ignition systems and the engine will not run.

6 Once a fault has been indicated, the fault code should be accessed from the system and appropriate checks undertaken (see Sections 8 and 9).

7 If the instrument cluster receives no signal

from the ECM when the ignition is switched ON, 'CHEC' is displayed on the odometer. First ensure that the engine stop switch is in the 'RUN' position. If the switch is set correctly, check the ignition fuse (see Chapter 9). If the fuse is good, ensure that the ECM and instrument cluster wiring connectors are secure and that the wiring loom between the two components is not damaged.

8 The system incorporates two safety circuits. The sidestand and brake switch circuits prevent the engine from starting unless the sidestand is up and one of the brake levers is pulled in (see Chapter 9 for component test details). The tip-over sensor circuit, which automatically switches off the fuel pump and cuts power to the ignition and injection circuits if the scooter falls over while the engine is running (see Section 8).

8 Engine management system fault diagnosis

Special tools: *A mode select switch (Suzuki Part No. 09930-82720) is required for this procedure (see Step 2).*

1 To access the fuel injection system fault codes, first remove the headlight panel (see Chapter 8). **Note:** *Do not disconnect the battery leads, the ECM wiring connector or earth (ground) wires, or the main fuse before the fault codes have been read. Disconnecting any of these components will erase the ECM memory.*

2 Refer to *Wiring Diagrams* at the end of Chapter 9 and locate the wiring connector for the fuel injection (FI) mode select switch **(see illustration)**. Remove the connector cover and plug-in the mode select switch **(see illustrations)**. Turn the ignition switch ON and crank the engine for at least 4 seconds, then turn the mode select switch ON.

3 The fault code is displayed on the odometer's LCD display. If there is more than

one fault the codes are displayed in ascending order i.e. C12, C13, C14 etc. Note the fault code(s) then turn the ignition OFF.

4 Compare the codes with the fault code table opposite to identify the faulty components, then refer to Section 8 for checking procedures.

5 To delete a fault code from the system memory once the fault has been corrected, first ensure that the ignition is OFF. Turn the mode select switch ON, then turn the ignition switch ON. If the odometer displays C00 the fault has been cleared.

6 Turn the ignition OFF and disconnect the mode select switch.

9 Engine management system components

Caution: Ensure the ignition is switched OFF before disconnecting/reconnecting any engine management system wiring connectors. If a connector is disconnected/reconnected with the ignition switched ON the engine control module (ECM) could be damaged.

1 If a fault is indicated on any of the system components, first check the wiring and connectors between the appropriate component and the engine control module (ECM) – see *Wiring Diagrams* at the end of Chapter 9. A continuity test (see Chapter 9, Section 2) of all wires will locate a break or short in any circuit. Inspect the terminals inside the wiring connectors and ensure that they are not loose or corroded. Spray the inside of the connectors with a proprietary electrical terminal cleaner before reconnection. Where appropriate, remove the sensor and check the sensor head and clean it if it is dirty – an accumulation of dirt could affect the signal it transmits. Recheck the FI warning light to see if the fault has been cleared before proceeding.

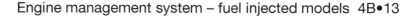

Cod	...onse	Possible causes
C12	...r – engine will not run	Faulty wiring or wiring connector Faulty, damaged or improperly installed sensor Faulty ECM
C13	– engine will run	Faulty vacuum hose or hose connection Faulty wiring or wiring connector Faulty ECM
C14	– engine will run in fail-safe	Faulty wiring or wiring connector Faulty, damaged or improperly installed sensor Faulty ECM
C1	...ECT) sensor – engine hard to ...gnal fixed at 80°C	Faulty wiring or wiring connector Faulty, damaged or improperly installed sensor Faulty ECM
C1		Faulty wiring or wiring connector Faulty, damaged or improperly installed sensor
C2	...) sensor – engine will run, ...C	Faulty wiring or wiring connector Faulty, damaged or improperly installed sensor Faulty ECM
C2	...vill not run	Faulty wiring or wiring connector Faulty, damaged or improperly installed sensor Faulty ECM
C2	...n	Faulty wiring or wiring connector Faulty power supply
C2	...) actuator – engine will run	Faulty wiring or wiring connector Faulty actuator motor
C2	...TP) sensor – engine will run	Faulty wiring or wiring connector Faulty sensor
C3	...un	Faulty wiring or wiring connector Faulty or damaged fuel injector Faulty ECM
C4	...gine will run	Faulty wiring or wiring connector Faulty, damaged or improperly installed valve Blocked air passage Faulty ECM
C4	...ot run	Faulty wiring or wiring connector Faulty, damaged or improperly installed relay Faulty ECM
C4	...t run	Faulty wiring or wiring connector Faulty immobiliser system, if fitted* Faulty ECM
C4	...un	Faulty wiring or wiring connector Faulty or damaged sensor Faulty ECM

* A

4 If the appropriate equipment is not available, the checks should be undertaken by a Suzuki dealer.

5 If, after a thorough check, the source of a fault has not been identified, it is possible that the ECM itself is faulty. No test specifications are available for the ECM. In order to determine conclusively that the unit is defective, take the machine to a Suzuki dealer and have the engine management system checked using the Suzuki Diagnostic System equipment. Note that the ECM must be left in place for the checks to be made. Alternatively, on scooters not fitted with an immobiliser system, the ECM can be substituted for a known good one (see Section 9). If the problem is then rectified, the original unit is faulty.

Fault code C12 – crankshaft position (CKP) sensor
Check
6 The CKP sensor is located on the inside of the alternator cover. Prior to inspecting the sensor, remove the kickpanel (see Chapter 8) and perform the following checks at the sensor wiring connector (see Chapter 9 and trace the wiring to the connector).
7 Disconnect the wiring connector and check the resistance between the terminals on the sensor side of the connector. The result should be within the range specified at the beginning of this Chapter.
8 If the result is good, check for continuity between each terminal and earth (ground). There should be no continuity.

9 If either result is not as specified the CKP sensor is faulty and must be replaced with a new one.

10 To check the sensor peak voltage, connect the peak voltage adapter positive (+) probe to the green wire terminal and the negative (-) probe to the blue wire terminal. Turn the ignition ON, crank the engine for a few seconds and note the peak voltage recorded. Repeat the procedure several times, note the highest voltage recorded and compare this with the specification. Turn the ignition OFF.

11 If the result is below the minimum specified the CKP sensor is faulty and must be replaced with a new one.

12 If the result is good, reconnect the connector, then repeat the check between the green/white (+) and blue (-) wire terminals on the loom side of the ECM connector. If the result is not as specified, check for a fault in the wiring loom.

13 If the peak voltage is as specified it is likely the ECM is faulty – have it checked by a Suzuki dealer.

Removal and installation

14 To remove the CKP sensor, follow the procedure in Chapter 9 to remove the alternator stator. The sensor is integral with the stator assembly and is not available as a separate item.

Fault code C13 – intake air pressure (IAP) sensor

Check

15 On AN400K3 to K6 models, the IAP sensor is located on the front of the air filter housing **(see illustration 2.3)**. Remove the underseat panel for access (see Chapter 8). On AN400K7 models onward, the IAP sensor is located on the throttle body assembly **(see illustration 2.10)**. Remove the underseat cover for access (see Chapter 8).

16 To check the input voltage, disconnect the sensor wiring connector. First connect the meter positive (+) probe to the red wire terminal on the loom side of the connector and the negative (-) probe to earth (ground). Turn the ignition ON and note the voltage. Now connect the negative (-) probe to the black/brown wire terminal and note the voltage. Turn the ignition OFF. Both results should be as specified at the beginning of this Chapter. If either result is outside the specification, refer to *Wiring Diagrams* at the end of Chapter 9 and check both wires for damage.

17 Check the IAP sensor output voltage with the connector connected. Back-probe the green/black wire at the connector with the meter positive (+) probe and the black/brown wire with the meter negative (-) probe. Start the engine and measure the voltage at idle speed. Turn the ignition OFF.

18 On AN400K3 to K6 models, if the result is outside the specification, first examine the vacuum hose for cracks or damage and renew the hose if necessary.

19 On all models, if the result is outside the

specification, check the green/black wire for damage. If the wire is good, the IAP sensor is faulty and must be replaced with a new one.

20 If the output voltage is good have the sensor checked by a Suzuki dealer.

Removal and installation

21 On AN400K3 to K6 models, pull the sensor off its mounting lug, disconnect the vacuum hose and disconnect the wiring connector.

22 On AN400K7 models onward, disconnect the wiring connector, then undo the screw securing the sensor bracket and lift off the sensor. Discard the O-ring as a new one must be fitted.

23 Installation is the reverse of removal.

Fault code C14 – throttle position (TP) sensor

Check

24 The TP sensor is located on the right-hand side of the throttle body assembly (see Section 12). On AN400K3 to K6 models, remove the underseat panel and the right-hand side panel to access the wiring connector (see Chapter 8). On AN400K7 models onward, remove the underseat cover for access (see Chapter 8).

25 To check the input voltage, disconnect the sensor wiring connector **(see illustration 12.6c or 2.10)**. First connect the meter positive (+) probe to the red wire terminal on the loom side of the connector and the negative (-) probe to earth (ground). Turn the ignition ON and note the voltage. Now connect the negative (-) probe to the black/brown wire terminal and note the voltage. Turn the ignition OFF. Both results should be as specified at the beginning of this Chapter. If either result is outside the specification, refer to *Wiring Diagrams* at the end of Chapter 9 and check both wires for damage.

26 On AN400K3 to K6 models, if the result is good, check for continuity between the yellow wire terminal on the sensor side of the connector and earth (ground). There should be no continuity. Next, measure the resistance between the yellow and black/brown wire terminals on the sensor side of the connector with the throttle fully closed and then with it fully open. If either result is outside the specification, follow the procedure in Section 12 and reset the position of the TP sensor. If

the correct result cannot be obtained the TP sensor is faulty and must be replaced with a new one.

27 On all models, check the output voltage with the connector connected. Back-probe the yellow wire at the connector with the meter positive (+) probe and the black/brown wire with the meter negative (-) probe. Turn the ignition ON and note the voltage with the throttle fully closed and then with it fully open. Turn the ignition OFF. If either result is outside the specification, the TP sensor is faulty and must be replaced with a new one.

28 If the output voltage is good, refer to *Wiring Diagrams* at the end of Chapter 9 and check the wiring between the TP sensor and the ECM for damage. Ensure the ECM wiring connector is secure.

Removal and installation

29 To remove the TP sensor, first remove the throttle body assembly (see Section 12).

30 Follow the procedure in Section 12 to remove and install the TP sensor.

Fault code C15 – engine coolant temperature (ECT) sensor

Check

31 On AN400K3 to K6 models, the ECT sensor is located on the left-hand side of the cylinder **(see illustration)**. Remove the left-hand side panel for access (see Chapter 8). On AN400K7 models onward, the ECT sensor is located on the rear of the cylinder **(see illustration)**. Remove the air filter housing for access (see Section 2).

32 To check the input voltage, disconnect the sensor wiring connector. First connect the meter positive (+) probe to the dark green wire terminal on the loom side of the connector and the negative (-) probe to earth (ground). Turn the ignition ON and note the voltage. Now connect the negative (-) probe to the black/brown wire terminal and note the voltage. Turn the ignition OFF. Both results should be as specified at the beginning of this Chapter. If either result is outside the specification, refer to *Wiring Diagrams* at the end of Chapter 9 and check both wires for damage. Ensure the ECM wiring connector is secure.

33 If the input voltage is within the specified range, check the resistance between the

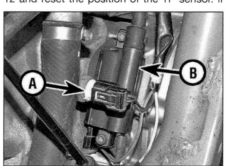

9.31a Location of the ECT sensor (A) and ignition coil (B) – AN400K3 to K6 models

9.31b Location of the ECT sensor – AN400K7-on models

termin
(at a
20°C)
specif
remov
descr

Rem

34 F

Fau

Che

35
of t
moc
the
the
acce
36
on
pos
tem
igni
Turr
37
Wiri
che
rem
dan
38
rem
Bac
sen
pro
the
vol
scr
to
vol
mo
39
de:
wit
the

Re

40
the
the
dra
41

r

d
y
e
r,
s

ear
K7
ove
und
for

nal
ter
vire
the
ge.

r to
and
ise,
for

sor,
ctor.
the
(+)
with
t to
s a
lose
tput
er is

as
ced
sure

cess
ctor,
and

Fault code C21 – intake air temperature (IAT) sensor

Check

42 On AN400K3 to K9 models, the IAT sensor is located on the underside of the air filter housing **(see illustration 2.6)**. Remove the underseat panel for access (see Chapter 8). If required, remove the air filter housing outlet tube (see Section 2).

43 On AN400-L0/ZAL0 models onward, the IAT sensor is located on the top left-hand side of the air filter housing **(see illustration 2.12)**.

43 To check the input voltage, disconnect the sensor wiring connector. First connect the meter positive (+) probe to the black/blue wire terminal on the loom side of the connector and the negative (-) probe to earth (ground). Turn the ignition ON and note the voltage. Now connect the negative (-) probe to the black/brown wire terminal and note the voltage. Turn the ignition OFF. Both results should be as specified at the beginning of this Chapter. If either result is outside the specification, refer to *Wiring Diagrams* at the end of Chapter 9 and check both wires for damage. Ensure the ECM wiring connector is secure.

44 If the input voltage is within the specified range, check the resistance between the terminals on the sensor with the engine cold (at ambient temperature, approximately 20°C). If the result varies greatly from the specification at the beginning of this Chapter, the sensor should be removed and its operation checked using the same set-up as for the ECT sensor (see Chapter 3) referring to the specifications for the IAT sensor.

Removal and installation

45 To remove the IAT sensor, follow the procedure In Section 2 to access the sensor.

46 Undo the screws securing the sensor and withdraw it from the air filter housing. Discard the O-ring as a new one must be fitted.

47 Installation is the reverse of removal.

Fault code C23 – tip-over (TO) sensor

Check

48 The TO sensor is located on the headlight panel bracket **(see illustration)**. Remove the fairing for access (see Chapter 8).

49 Disconnect the sensor wiring connector and check the resistance between the red and black/brown wire terminals on the sensor. If the result is outside the specification given at the beginning of this Chapter the sensor is faulty.

50 If the result is good, reconnect the wiring connector, then back-probe the brown/white wire terminal on the connector with the meter positive (+) probe and the black/brown wire terminal with the meter negative (-) probe. Turn the ignition ON and check the output voltage with the sensor upright. Turn the ignition OFF.

51 Next, remove the sensor from its bracket. With the meter probes connected as before, turn the ignition ON and tilt the sensor both to the left and the right at the specified angle, noting the output voltage.

52 If the results are not as specified, first check the sensor wiring and the ECM connector. If they are good, the sensor is faulty and must be replaced with a new one.

53 If the results are as specified, check the sensor wiring and the ECM connector. If they are good it is likely the ECM is faulty – have it checked by a Suzuki dealer.

Removal and installation

54 To remove the TO sensor, first remove the fairing (see Chapter 8).

55 Remove the sensor from its bracket and disconnect the wiring connector **(see illustration 9.48)**.

56 Installation is the reverse of removal.

Fault code C24 – ignition coil

Check

57 The ignition coil is located on the left-hand side of the engine unit **(see illustration)**. Remove the side panel for access (see Chapter 8).

58 To check the coil peak voltage, first disconnect the cap from the spark plug (see Chapter 1). Fit a new plug into the cap and earth the plug securely against the engine. Connect the peak voltage adapter positive (+) probe to the white wire terminal on the coil and the negative (-) probe to earth (ground). Turn the ignition ON, crank the engine for a few seconds and note the peak voltage recorded. Repeat the procedure several times, note the highest voltage recorded and compare this with the specification. Turn the ignition OFF.

9.48 Location of the TO sensor

9.57 Location of the ignition coil – AN400K7-on models

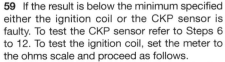

9.69 Location of the secondary throttle valve

9.82a Fuel injector wiring connector – AN400K3 to K6 models

9.82b Fuel injector wiring connector – AN400K7-on models

59 If the result is below the minimum specified either the ignition coil or the CKP sensor is faulty. To test the CKP sensor refer to Steps 6 to 12. To test the ignition coil, set the meter to the ohms scale and proceed as follows.

60 Disconnect the cap from the spark plug and disconnect the white and orange/white wiring connectors from the coil, noting how they fit.

61 To test the coil primary resistance, connect the multimeter positive (+) probe to the white wire terminal on the coil and the negative (-) probe to the orange/white wire terminal and note the result. To test the coil secondary resistance, connect the negative (-) probe to the terminal inside the spark plug cap and note the result.

62 Both results should be as specified at the beginning of this Chapter. If either result is outside the specification, it is likely the ignition coil is faulty – have it checked by a Suzuki dealer.

Removal and installation

63 To remove the ignition coil, first remove the left-hand side panel (see Chapter 8).

64 Disconnect the cap from the spark plug and disconnect the white and orange/white wiring connectors from the coil, noting how they fit (see illustration 9.31a or 57).

65 Undo the bolts securing the coil and lift it off, noting how it fits.

66 Installation is the reverse of removal.

Fault code C28 – secondary throttle valve actuator (STVA)

Check

67 The STV actuator is located on the right-hand side of the throttle body assembly on AN400K7 models onward (see illustration 2.11). Remove the underseat cover and front underseat panel for access (see Chapter 8).

68 To check the operation of the secondary throttle valve in start-up mode, first remove the air filter housing outlet tube (see Section 2).

69 Note the position of the secondary throttle valve (see illustration).

70 Turn the ignition ON – from fully open the valve should move to the 95% open position. Turn the ignition OFF.

71 If the valve does not move as described, check the terminals in the actuator wiring connector and check the wiring between the connector and the ECM.

72 If the wiring is good, disconnect the actuator wiring connector and check for continuity between the terminals on the loom side of the connector and earth (ground). There should be no continuity.

73 To test the actuator resistance, connect the meter positive (+) probe to the black wire terminal on the actuator side of the connector and connect the negative (-) probe to the green wire terminal and note the result. Now connect the meter positive (+) probe to the pink wire terminal on the actuator side of the connector and connect the negative (-) probe to the white/black wire terminal and note the result. If either result is outside the specification, it is likely the STV actuator is faulty – have it checked by a Suzuki dealer. If the results are good it is likely the ECM is faulty.

Removal and installation

74 The STV actuator is an integral part of the throttle body assembly and is not available as a separate item (see Section 12).

Fault code C29 – secondary throttle position (STP) sensor

Check

75 The STP sensor is located on the right-hand side of the throttle body assembly (see illustration 2.11). Remove the underseat cover and front underseat panel for access (see Chapter 8).

76 To check the input voltage, disconnect the sensor wiring connector. First connect the meter positive (+) probe to the red wire terminal on the loom side of the connector and the negative (-) probe to earth (ground). Turn the ignition ON and note the voltage. Now connect the negative (-) probe to the black/brown wire terminal and note the voltage. Turn the ignition OFF. Both results should be as specified at the beginning of this Chapter. If either result is outside the specification, refer to *Wiring Diagrams* at the end of Chapter 9 and check both wires for damage. Ensure the ECM wiring connector is secure.

77 Check the output voltage with the connector connected. Back-probe the yellow/green wire at the connector with the meter positive (+) probe and the black/brown wire with the meter negative (-) probe. Turn the ignition ON and note the voltage with the throttle valve fully closed and then with it fully open. Turn the ignition OFF. If either result is outside the specification, the STP sensor is faulty and must be replaced with a new one.

78 If the results are good, check the terminals in the sensor wiring connector and check the wiring between the connector and the ECM. If the connectors and wiring are good it is likely the ECM is faulty.

Removal and installation

79 To remove the STP sensor, first remove the throttle body (see Section 12)

80 Follow the procedure in Section 12 to remove and install the STP sensor.

Fault code C32 – fuel injector

Check

81 The fuel injector is located on the rear of the throttle body assembly. Remove the underseat panel for access (see Chapter 8).

82 Disconnect the wiring connector (see illustrations). Test the resistance between the terminals on the injector and compare the result with the specification at the beginning of this Chapter. If the result varies greatly from the specification at the beginning of this Chapter it is likely the injector is faulty.

83 Check for continuity between the injector terminals and earth (ground). There should be no continuity.

84 If the injector fails either of these tests it is faulty and must be replaced with a new one.

85 To check the injector voltage, connect the meter (+) probe to the yellow/red wire terminal on the loom side of the connector and the negative (-) probe to earth (ground). Turn the ignition ON and check for battery voltage – voltage will be present for approximately 3 seconds. Turn the ignition OFF. No voltage indicates a fault in the yellow/red wire.

86 If the voltage is good, check the grey/white between the connector and the ECM for damage. If the wiring and connectors are good it is likely the ECM is faulty – have it checked by a Suzuki dealer.

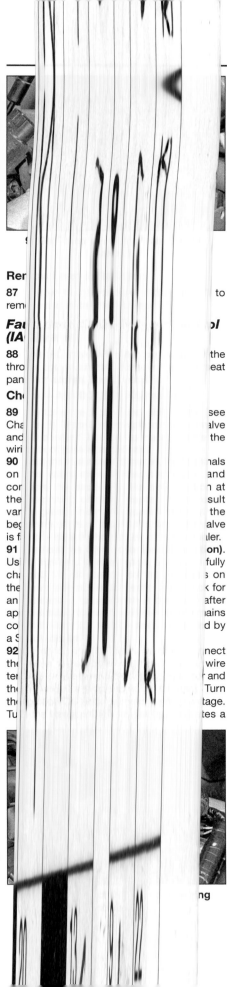

9.89b ... and disconnect it at the connector

9.91 Remove the IAC valve cover

Rer
87
rem

*Fau
(IA*

88
thro
pan

Ch

89
Cha
and
wiri
90
on
cor
the
var
beg
is f
91
Us
cha
the
an
ap
co
a S
92
the
ter
the
Tu

to

the
eat

see
alve
the

nals
and
at
sult
the
alve
ler.
on).
fully
on
for
after
ains
d by

nect
wire
and
Turn
tage.
tes a

ng

fault in the wiring between the connector and the ECM.

Note: *If no faults can be found with the IAC valve and wiring, an air passage in the throttle body may be blocked – refer to Section 12 to examine the throttle body.*

Check – AN400K7 model onward

93 Disconnect the IAC valve wiring connector and examine the terminals for damage and corrosion **(see illustration)**.

94 Disconnect the ECM wiring connector. Refer to *Wiring Diagrams* at the end of Chapter 9 and check the wiring between the IAC valve and ECM connectors for continuity.

95 If the connectors and wiring are good, test the IAC valve resistance. Connect the meter positive (+) probe to the black/light green wire terminal on the valve connector and connect the negative (-) probe to the green wire terminal and note the result. Now connect the meter positive (+) probe to the pink/white wire terminal and connect the negative (-) probe to the white/black wire terminal and note the result. If either result is outside the specification, the IAC valve is faulty and must be replaced with a new one. If the results are good it is likely the ECM is faulty.

Note: *On AN400K7 models onward, further checks on the IAC valve can be undertaken by a Suzuki dealer using the Suzuki Diagnostic System equipment.*

Note: *If no faults can be found with the IAC valve and wiring, an air passage in the throttle body may be blocked – refer to Section 12 to examine the throttle body.*

Removal and installation – all models

96 Follow the procedure in Section 12 to remove and install the IAC valve.

Fault code C41 – fuel pump relay

Check

97 The fuel pump relay is located on the fairing bracket **(see illustration)**. Remove the fairing for access (see Chapter 8).

98 Disconnect the relay wiring connector and examine the terminals for damage and corrosion. **Note:** *The fuel pump and safety relays are mounted side-by-side and are easily transposed. Check the colour-coding of the wiring with the wiring diagrams at the end of Chapter 9 to confirm the identity of the relays.*

99 Disconnect the ECM wiring connector **(see illustration 10.2)**. Refer to *Wiring Diagrams* at the end of Chapter 9 and check the wiring between the relay and ECM connectors for continuity.

100 If the connectors and wiring are good, test the relay operation as follows. Disconnect the relay wiring connector and release the relay from its bracket. Using a multimeter, check for continuity between terminals 1 and 2 on the relay **(see illustration)**. There should be no continuity. Now use jumper wires to connect the positive (+) terminal of a fully charged 12 volt battery to terminal 3 on the relay and the negative (-) battery terminal to relay terminal 4. There should now be continuity between terminals 1 and 2. If the relay fails either of the checks it must be replaced with a new one.

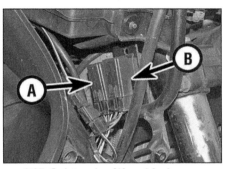

9.97 Safety relay (A) and fuel pump relay (B)

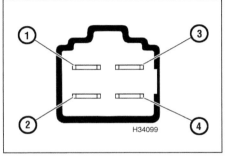

9.100 Fuel pump relay terminal identification

9.108 Location of the oxygen sensor – AN400K3 to K6 models

9.109 Oxygen sensor wiring connector

Removal and installation

101 Follow the procedure in Chapter 8 to remove the fairing.
102 Disconnect the relay wiring connector and release the relay from its bracket.
103 Installation is the reverse of removal.

Fault code C42 – ignition switch

104 Refer to Chapter 9 to check the operation of the ignition switch.
105 On AN400K5 models onward, the fault code could be the result of a fault with the immobiliser system. When the ignition is turned ON, signals between the transponder in the ignition key and the ECM confirm that the identities of the two components are correct. The immobiliser indicator in the instrument cluster flashes to indicate the number of keys registered in the ECM and then remains illuminated for 2 seconds to confirm that the engine is ready to start. If a fault occurs, possibly due to radio interference or low battery power in cold weather, the indicator flashes rapidly. Turn the ignition OFF, then repeat the starting procedure.
106 If the problem persists this may be due to a system failure in the key transponder, immobiliser antenna, wiring loom or ECM. Ensure that the components in the ignition circuit are working correctly – refer to Chapter 9 for details of fuse and switch checks.
107 If the fault cannot be identified, have the system checked by a Suzuki dealer.

Fault code C44 – oxygen sensor

Check

108 On AN400K3 to K6 models, the oxygen sensor is located in the exhaust header pipe **(see illustration)**. On AN400K7 models onward, the oxygen sensor is located in the silencer front pipe (see Section 14). Remove the underseat panel and belly panel for access (see Chapter 8).

109 Run the engine until it reaches normal operating temperature then turn the ignition OFF. Trace the oxygen sensor wiring to the connector **(see illustration)**.
110 On AN400K3 to K6 models, back-probe the black/green wire terminal on the loom side of the connector with the meter positive (+) probe and the yellow/white wire terminal with the meter negative (-) probe. Start the engine and check the output voltage first with the engine idling and then at 3000 rpm. Turn the engine OFF.
111 On AN400K7 models onward, back-probe the black/yellow wire terminal on the loom side of the connector with the meter positive (+) probe and the black/brown wire terminal with the meter negative (-) probe. Start the engine and check the output voltage first with the engine idling and then at 3000 rpm. Turn the engine OFF.
112 Compare the results with the specifications at the beginning of this Chapter. If the results are outside the ranges specified the oxygen sensor is faulty and must be renewed.
113 To check the sensor heater voltage, back-probe the orange/white wire terminal on the loom side of the connector with the meter positive (+) probe and connect the meter negative (-) probe to earth (ground). Turn the ignition ON – there should be battery voltage for a few seconds. If no voltage is indicated the sensor is faulty and must be renewed.
114 If the output and heater voltages are good, allow the sensor to cool to ambient temperature, then disconnect the wiring connector and test the resistance between the white wire terminals on the sensor side of the connector.
115 Compare the result with the specification at the beginning of this Chapter. If the result is outside the range specified the oxygen sensor is faulty and must be renewed.
116 If the result is good, inspect the wiring between the connector and the oxygen

sensor, and between the connector and the ECM for damage.

Removal and installation

117 Follow the procedure in Section 14.

10 Engine control module (ECM)

1 No test details are available for the ECM. If the unit is thought to be faulty, have it checked by a Suzuki dealer.
2 The ECM is located above the battery housing in the kickpanel **(see illustration)**. Remove the headlight panel for access (see Chapter 8).
3 For the purpose of testing the continuity of the ECM wiring, ensure the ignition is OFF, then disconnect the ECM multi-pin connector.
4 Inspect the terminals on the ECM and inside the wiring connector for damage and corrosion.
5 When testing with a multimeter, use needle probes to contact the connector terminals. Take great care not to damage the terminals.
6 On installation, align the connector terminals carefully, then press the connector into place, ensuring it is secure.

10.2 Location of the engine control module (ECM)

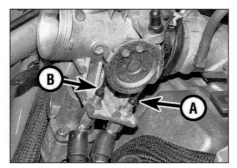

11.4a Throttle opening (A) and closing cable (B)

11.4b Free each cable from the bracket and then the pulley

11.5a Undo the screw (arrowed)

11 Throttle cables

Removal

1 Remove the handlebar covers, headlight panel, seat, underseat panel and floor centre panel for access (see Chapter 8).
2 Remove the air filter housing (see Section 2)
3 Follow the procedure in Chapter 4A, Section 6, to disconnect the cables from the twistgrip pulley and separate the cable elbows from the lower half of the throttle twistgrip/switch housing. Note that on AN400K7 models onward, there is no adjuster on the closing cable.
4 On AN400K3 to K6 models, note the location of the opening and closing cables on the throttle body pulley (see illustration). Working on one cable at a time, unscrew the locknut and separate the cable from the mounting bracket, then detach the inner cable end from the pulley (see illustration).
5 On AN400K7 models onward, undo the screw securing the cable retaining plate and separate the cables from the mounting bracket (see illustrations). Detach the inner cable ends from the pulley (see illustration). **Note:** The retaining plate is attached to the rear opening cable.
6 Note the routing of the cables from the handlebars to the throttle body, especially where they are secured by ties. Withdraw the

cables carefully from the scooter, noting the correct routing.

> **HAYNES HiNT** When fitting a new cable, tape the lower end of the new cable to the upper end of the old cable before removing it from the machine. Slowly pull the lower end of the old cable out, guiding the new cable down into position. Using this method will ensure the cable is routed correctly.

Installation

7 On AN400K3 to K6 models, working on one cable at a time, fit the lower end of the inner cable onto the pulley, then fit the end of the outer cable onto the bracket and secure it with the locknut (see illustration 11.4b).
8 On AN400K7 models onward, fit the lower ends of the inner cables onto the pulley, ensuring they are the correct way round (see illustration 11.5c). Fit the ends of the outer cables onto the bracket and secure the retaining plate with the screw (see illustration 11.5b and a).
9 Follow the procedure in Chapter 4A, Section 6, to connect the cables to the twistgrip pulley
10 Adjust the cable freeplay (see Chapter 1).
11 Operate the throttle twistgrip to check that it opens and closes freely.
12 Check the alignment of the closing cable elbow, adjust it if necessary and tighten the knurled retainer.
13 Turn the handlebars from lock-to-lock to

make sure the cables don't cause the steering to bind.
14 Lubricate the exposed ends of the inner cables on the throttle body pulley with multi-purpose grease, then install the air filter housing (see Section 2).
15 Start the engine and check that the idle speed does not increase as the handlebars are turned. If it does, the cables are routed incorrectly. Correct the problem before riding the machine.
16 Install the remaining components in the reverse order of removal.

12 Throttle body

> ⚠ **Warning: Refer to the precautions given in Section 1 before starting work.**

Removal

1 Remove the seat, storage compartment, underseat panel and right-hand side panel (see Chapter 8).
2 Remove the air filter housing (see Section 2).
3 Disconnect the throttle cables from the throttle pulley (see Section 11).

AN400K3 to K6 models

4 Disconnect the fuel injector wiring connector (see illustration 9.82a).
5 Undo the bolts securing the fuel hose union to the fuel injector and disconnect the hose (see illustration 4.9a). Note the location of

11.5b Free the cables from the bracket

11.5c Detach the cables from the pulley

12.5 Location of the fuel hose O-ring

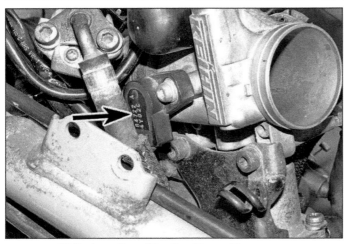

12.6a Location of the throttle position sensor

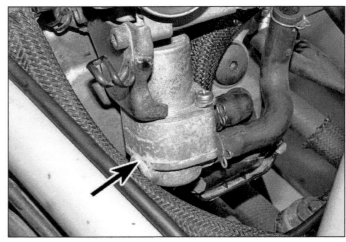

12.6b Location of the secondary air system control valve

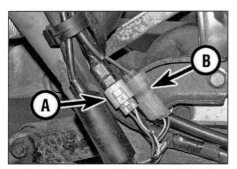

12.6c Throttle position sensor (A) and secondary air system valve (B) connectors

12.7a Intake manifold bolts

12.7b Note the O-ring in intake manifold . . .

the O-ring and discard it as a new one must be fitted **(see illustration)**.

6 Trace the wiring from the throttle position sensor and secondary air system control valve to the wiring connectors and disconnect them **(see illustrations)**. Disconnect the idle air control valve wiring connector **(see illustrations 9.89a and b)**. Free the wiring from any clips or ties and feed it back to the throttle body. Release the clip securing the outlet hose to the secondary air system control valve and disconnect the hose.

7 Undo the bolts securing the intake manifold to the cylinder head and lift the throttle body

assembly off **(see illustration)**. Note the location of the O-rings in the intake manifold and insulator and discard them as new ones must be fitted **(see illustrations)**.

AN400K7 model onward

8 Ensure that all the wiring connectors on the throttle body sub-loom have been disconnected (see Section 2).

9 Undo the bolts securing the fuel hose union to the fuel injector and disconnect the hose **(see illustration 4.9b)**. Note the location of the O-ring and discard it as a new one must be fitted **(see illustration 12.5)**.

10 Loosen the clamp securing the throttle body assembly to the intake manifold and ease the assembly off, noting how it fits **(see illustrations)**.

Caution: Stuff clean rag into the cylinder head intake manifold after removing the throttle body assembly to prevent anything from falling inside.

Disassembly and inspection

AN400K3 to K6 models

11 Pull the cover off the idle air control (IAC) valve, then undo the screw securing the valve

12.7c . . . and the insulator

12.10a Loosen the clamp . . .

12.10b . . . and ease the throttle body off

12.11a Undo the screw . . .

12.11b . . . and ease the IAC valve out

and ease it out **(see illustrations)**. Note the location of the O-ring and discard it as a new one must be fitted. Check that the valve passage in the throttle body is clear.

12 Before removing the throttle position (TP) sensor, mark its position against the throttle body **(see illustration)**. Undo the screw securing the sensor and remove it **(see illustration)**.

13 Inspect the intake air pressure (IAP) sensor vacuum hose for cracks or damage and renew the hose if necessary **(see illustration)**.

14 Note the location of the secondary air system control valve, then undo the valve bracket bolts and remove the assembly **(see illustration)**. Refer to Section 16 to check the operation of the valve.

15 Undo the screw securing the fuel injector and remove the insulator **(see illustrations)**. Ease the injector out **(see illustration)**. Refer to Section 13 to check the injector.

16 If required, loosen the clamp securing the throttle body to the intake manifold and ease

12.12a Mark the position of the TP sensor

12.12b Remove the TP sensor, noting how it fits

12.13 Inspect the IAP sensor hose

12.14 Location of the secondary air system control valve

12.15a Undo the screw . . .

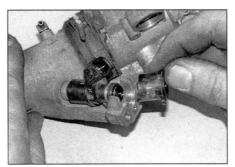

12.15b . . . remove the insulator . . .

12.15c . . . and ease out the injector

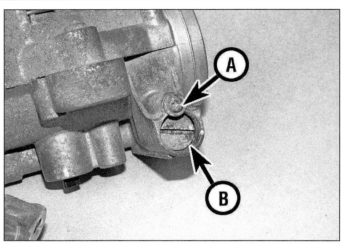

12.16 Clamp (A) secures throttle body (B) to intake manifold (C)

12.17a Screw (A) secures idle speed adjuster (B)

it off, noting how it fits (see illustration). Note the location of the O-ring and discard it as a new one must be fitted.

17 Undo the screw securing the idle speed adjuster (see illustration). Before removing the adjuster, turn it clockwise until it seats, counting the number of turns, then unscrew it

all the way (see illustration). Note the location of the O-ring and spring – discard the O-ring as a new one must be fitted.

18 Do not disturb the setting of the throttle pulley stop screw (see illustration). Do not remove the throttle valve.

19 Clean the assembly with suitable solvent

using a nylon-bristled brush to remove stubborn deposits.

Caution: Use only a dedicated fuel system cleaner or petroleum-based solvent for cleaning, following the manufacturer's instructions. DO NOT use caustic cleaners.

20 Inspect the throttle body for cracks or any other damage which may result in air leaks.

21 Check that the throttle pulley moves smoothly and freely in the body (see illustration). Inspect the valve shaft and throttle body for wear. Check the condition of the valve shaft spring.

22 Inspect the clip on the intake manifold – if it is corroded or damaged it must be renewed. If the manifold union is hardened or split a new manifold should be fitted.

AN400K7 model onward

23 Undo the screw securing the fuel injector and remove the insulator (see illustration). Ease the injector out. Refer to Section 13 to check the injector.

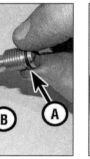

12.17b Location of O-ring (A) and spring (B)

12.18 Throttle pulley stop screw is pre-set – do not disturb

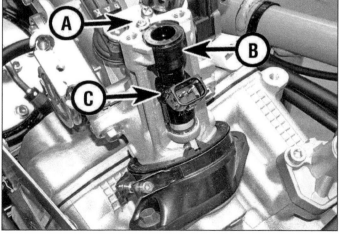

12.21 Check the operation of the throttle pulley

12.23 Undo the screw (A) and remove the insulator (B) and injector (C)

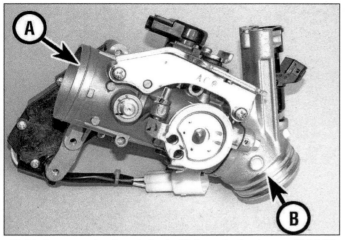

12.24 Separate the throttle body (A) from the intake manifold (B)

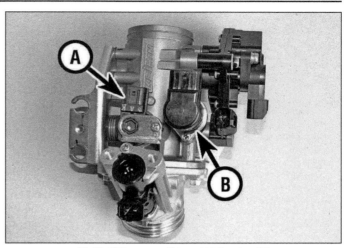

12.25 IAP sensor (A) and IAC valve (B)

24 Undo the bolts securing the throttle body to the intake manifold **(see illustration)**. Note the location of the throttle body seal and discard it as a new one must be fitted.

25 Undo the screw securing the intake air pressure (IAP) sensor bracket and lift off the sensor **(see illustration)**. Discard the O-ring as a new one must be fitted.

26 Undo the screw securing the idle air control (IAC) valve and remove the valve **(see illustration 12.25)**. Discard the O-ring as a new one must be fitted. Inspect the tip of the valve for carbon deposits and clean it if necessary.

27 Before removing the throttle position (TP) and secondary throttle position (STP) sensors, mark their positions against the throttle body **(see illustration)**. Undo the screws securing the sensors and remove them. Discard the O-rings as new ones must be fitted.

28 Do not remove the secondary throttle valve actuator (STV) actuator **(see illustration 12.27)**. Do not remove the throttle valve or the secondary throttle valve.

29 Clean the assembly with suitable solvent using a nylon-bristled brush to remove stubborn deposits.
Caution: Use only a dedicated fuel system cleaner or petroleum-based solvent for

cleaning, following the manufacturer's instructions. DO NOT use caustic cleaners.

30 Inspect the throttle body for wear and damage and check the operation of the throttle pulley **(see illustration)**. Do not disturb the secondary throttle valve, its action is controlled by the STV actuator. If required, check the operation of the STV actuator as described in Section 9.

31 Inspect the clamp on the intake manifold – if it is corroded or damaged it must be renewed. If the manifold is hardened or split a new manifold should be fitted.

Installation

AN400K3 to K6 models

32 Installation is the reverse of removal, noting the following:
- *Fit new O-rings as noted on removal. Lubricate the O-rings with a smear of engine oil.*
- *Follow the procedure in Section 13 to install the fuel injector.*
- *Ensure the throttle valve is fully closed, then align the TP sensor with the throttle body as noted on removal (see Step 12) and tighten the screw. Check the position of the TP sensor as described below.*

- *If the throttle body and intake manifold have been separated, make sure the manifold clip is positioned correctly. Align the throttle body correctly and press it in firmly to ensure it is fully engaged with the manifold – a squirt of WD-40 or a smear of oil will ease entry.*
- *Tighten the clamp securely.*
- *Route the wiring as noted on removal and ensure the connectors are secure.*

33 Install the throttle cables (see Section 11). Check the operation of the cables and adjust them as necessary (see Chapter 1).

34 Install the air filter housing (see Section 2).

35 Check and adjust the idle speed (see Chapter 1).

36 With the engine at normal operating temperature, turn the ignition OFF, then follow the procedure in Section 8 and connect the fuel injection mode select switch.

37 Turn the mode select switch ON, note the code displayed on the odometer and compare it with the diagram **(see illustration)**.

38 To adjust the position of the TP sensor, loosen the mounting screw and twist the sensor clockwise or anti-clockwise until the correct position code is displayed. Tighten the mounting screw. Turn the mode select switch OFF.

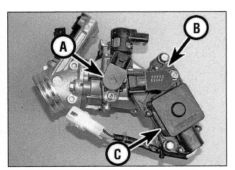

12.27 TP sensor (A), STP sensor (B) and STV actuator (C)

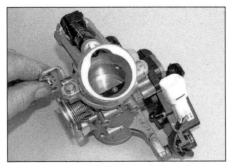

12.30 Check the operation of the throttle pulley

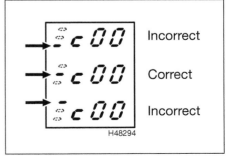

12.37 Throttle position sensor adjustment codes

39 Install the remaining components in the reverse order of removal.

AN400K7 model onward

40 Installation is the reverse of removal, noting the following:

• *Fit new O-rings as noted on removal. Lubricate the O-rings with a smear of engine oil.*

• *Ensure the secondary throttle valve is fully open, then align the STP sensor with the throttle body as noted on removal (see Step 27) and tighten the screw. Check the position of the STP sensor as described in Steps 42 to 44.*

• *Ensure the throttle valve is fully closed, then align the TP sensor with the throttle body as noted on removal (see Step 27) and tighten the screw. Check the position of the TP sensor as described in Steps 45 to 47.*

• *Install the IAC valve. Check the valve setting as described in Steps 48 and 49.*

• *Follow the procedure in Section 13 to install the fuel injector.*

• *Ensure the manifold clamp is positioned correctly. Align the throttle body assembly correctly and press it in firmly to ensure it is fully engaged with the manifold – a squirt of WD-40 or a smear of oil will ease entry.*

• *Tighten the clamp securely.*

• *Install the air filter housing (see Section 2).*

• *Route the wiring as noted on removal and ensure the connectors are secure.*

41 Install the throttle cables (see Section 11). Check the operation of the cables and adjust them as necessary (see Chapter 1).

42 To check the position of the STP sensor,

first remove the air filter housing outlet tube (see Section 2). Disconnect the STV actuator wiring connector.

43 Using a multimeter set to the volts scale, back-probe the wires in the STP sensor connector – connect the positive (+) probe to the yellow/green wire and the negative (-) probe to the black/brown wire. Turn the ignition ON. Note the output voltage with the valve open, then close the valve by hand and note the output voltage. Compare the results with the specifications at the beginning of this Chapter.

44 If the result (valve fully closed) is outside the specification, loosen the mounting screw and twist the sensor clockwise or anti-clockwise until the correct voltage is displayed. Tighten the mounting screw.

45 To check the position of the TP sensor, first warm the engine to normal operating temperature, then follow the procedure in Section 8 and connect the fuel injection mode select switch.

46 Turn the mode select switch ON, note the code displayed on the odometer and compare it with the diagram **(see illustration 12.37)**.

47 To adjust the position of the TP sensor, loosen the mounting screw and twist the sensor clockwise or anti-clockwise until the correct position code is displayed. Tighten the mounting screw. Turn the mode select switch OFF.

48 To check the IAC valve setting, follow the procedure in Section 8 and connect the fuel injection mode select switch.

49 Turn the mode select switch ON. Open the throttle fully and turn the ignition switch ON. Hold the throttle open for at least 10 seconds,

then close the throttle and turn the ignition OFF. The IAC valve is now in its pre-set position. Turn the mode select switch OFF.

50 Install the remaining components in the reverse order of removal.

13 Fuel injector

 Warning: Refer to the precautions given in Section 1 before starting work.

1 The fuel injector is located in the intake manifold which is part of the throttle body assembly (see Section 12). A fault with the injector should be indicated by the FI warning light (see Section 8). Follow the procedure in Section 9 to test the injector.

Removal

2 Remove the throttle body assembly and follow the procedure in Section 12 to remove the injector.

3 Note the location of the upper O-ring and lower seal on the injector and discard them as new ones must be fitted **(see illustration)**.

4 Inspect the end of the fuel injector for accumulations of carbon. Check that the terminals in the wiring connector are clean.

5 Modern fuels contain detergents which should keep the injector clean and free of gum or varnish from fuel residue. If an injector is suspected of being blocked, clean it through with injector cleaner. If the injector is clean but its performance is suspect, take it to a Suzuki dealer for assessment.

Installation

Note: *Apply a smear of engine oil to the new seal and O-ring before reassembly.*

6 Installation is the reverse of removal, noting the following:

• *Install the new seal and O-ring onto the injector carefully.*

• *Align the insulator with the injector and press the insulator on firmly* **(see illustrations)**.

• *Align the injector with the intake manifold and press it on firmly* **(see illustration)**. *Do not twist the injector during installation.*

• *Secure the injector with the screw* **(see illustration)**.

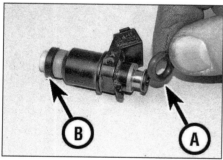

13.3 Injector upper O-ring (A) and lower seal (B)

13.6a Press the insulator over the O-ring

13.6b Installed location of the injector insulator

13.6c Press the injector into the manifold firmly

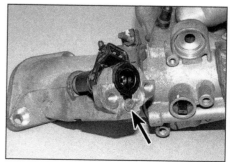

13.6d Installed position of the injector – note the fixing screw (arrowed)

14.4a Oxygen sensor wiring connector – AN400K7-on models

14.4b Feed the wiring back to the sensor (arrowed)

14.5a Loosen the clamp (arrowed) . . .

14.5b Remove the lower . . .

14.5c . . . and upper mounting bolts

14.5d Location of exhaust seal on header pipe

14 Exhaust system

⚠️ *Warning: If the engine has been running the exhaust system will be very hot. Allow the system to cool before carrying out any work.*

1 The procedure for removal and installation of the exhaust system is the same as described in Chapter 4A, Section 13, noting the following.

2 Remove the right side belly panel and the seat cowling for access (see Chapter 8).

3 Fuel injected models are fitted with oxygen sensors **(see illustration 9.108)**.

4 Before removing the silencer on AN400K7 models onward, trace the wiring from the sensor and disconnect it at the connector **(see illustration)**. Release the wiring from any clips or ties and feed it back to the sensor **(see illustration)**.

5 On AN400K7 models onward, loosen the clamp securing the silencer front pipe to the header pipe, undo the bolts securing the silencer to the rear sub-frame, then draw the silencer off **(see illustrations)**. Note the location of the exhaust seal and discard it as a new one must be fitted **(see illustration)**.

6 A catalytic converter is incorporated in the silencer. The catalytic converter is FRAGILE – do not strike or drop the silencer.

7 On AN400K3 to K6 models, note the location of the spacers and grommets in the mounting bracket **(see illustration)**.

Renew the grommets if they are damaged or deteriorated.

8 On AN400K7 models onward, note the location of the spacers and grommets in the silencer mountings **(see illustration)**. Renew the grommets if they are damaged or deteriorated.

9 Before removing the header pipe on AN400K3 to K6 models, trace the wiring from the oxygen sensor and disconnect it at the connector **(see illustration 9.109)**. Release the wiring from any clips or ties and feed it back to the sensor.

10 If required, unscrew the oxygen sensor using one of the commercially available ring spanners or deep sockets **(see illustration)**. Take care not to damage the exhaust pipe. DO NOT apply oil or grease to the sensor threads

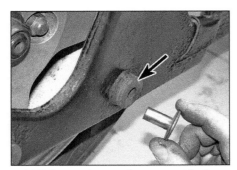

14.7 Spacer locates in grommet in the mounting bracket – AN400K3 to K6 models

14.8 Spacer locates in grommet in the silencer mounting – AN400K7-on models

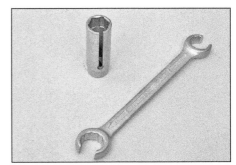

14.10a Oxygen sensor spanner and deep socket

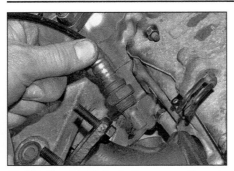

14.10b Do not lubricate the sensor threads

on installation **(see illustration)**. If available, use the deep socket and tighten the sensor to the torque setting specified at the beginning of this Chapter.
11 Tighten the header pipe flange bolts, the silencer mounting nuts and the clamp bolt to the torque settings specified at the beginning of this Chapter.
12 Once the exhaust system has been installed, secure the sensor wiring as noted on removal.
13 Run the engine and check the system for leaks.

15 Catalytic converter

General information

1 A catalytic converter is incorporated in the exhaust system to minimise the level of exhaust pollutants released into the atmosphere.
2 All fuel injected machines have a three-way catalytic converter located in the silencer. Hot exhaust gasses pass through the flow channels in the converter which are coated with a precious metal catalyst. The catalyst reduces nitrous oxides into nitrogen and oxygen, and oxidises unburned harmful hydrocarbons and carbon monoxide into water and carbon dioxide. The efficiency of the catalyst is reduced if the flow channels become clogged or if the precious metal coating becomes covered with carbon, lead or oil.

Precautions

3 The catalytic converter is a reliable device which needs no maintenance in itself, but there are some facts of which an owner should be aware if the converter is to function properly for its full service life.
• *DO NOT use leaded or lead replacement petrol (gasoline) – the additives will coat the precious metals, reducing their converting efficiency and will eventually destroy the catalytic converter.*
• *Always keep the ignition and fuel systems well-maintained in accordance with the manufacturer's schedule – if the fuel/air mixture is suspected of being incorrect*

have it checked on an exhaust gas analyser.
• *If the engine develops a misfire, do not ride the scooter (or at least as little as possible) until the fault is cured.*
• *DO NOT use fuel or engine oil additives – these may contain substances harmful to the catalytic converter.*
• *DO NOT continue to use the scooter if the engine burns oil to the extent of leaving a visible trail of blue smoke.*
• *Remember that the catalytic converter is FRAGILE – handle the silencer with care when it is off the machine.*

16 Secondary air system

1 The secondary air system is fitted to AN400K3 to K6 models reduce the amount of unburned hydrocarbons released in the exhaust gases. A description of the system is given in Chapter 1. The hoses and their unions should be checked at the specified service interval.

Removal

2 The control valve is located on the underside of the throttle body assembly **(see illustration 12.6b)**. Remove the seat, storage compartment, underseat panel and right-hand side panel for access (see Chapter 8).
3 Remove the air filter housing (see Section 2).
4 To remove the control valve, first trace the wiring to the connector and disconnect it **(see illustration 12.6c)**. Free the wiring from any clips or ties and feed it back to the valve.
5 Release the clip securing the outlet hose and disconnect the hose from the union on the valve.
6 Undo the bolts securing the valve bracket to the throttle body and remove the assembly **(see illustration 12.14)**.

Check

7 Using a multimeter set to the ohms scale, measure the resistance between the control valve terminals and compare the result with the specification at the beginning of this Chapter. If the result is not within the specified range the control valve is faulty.
8 To check the operation of the valve, blow into the (lower) inlet union and ensure air flows out of the (upper) outlet union. Now use insulated jumper wires to connect a fully charged 12 volt battery to the terminals in the valve wiring connector. Blow into the inlet union again – air should not flow out the outlet union.
9 If the control valve does not perform as described it should be renewed.

Installation

10 Installation is the reverse of removal.

Reed valve

11 The secondary air system reed valve is located in the valve cover on top of the cylinder head. To inspect the reed valve, refer to Chapter 2A, Section 6.

17 Fuel tank

⚠️ *Warning: Refer to the precautions given in Section 1 before starting work.*
Note: *If the fuel tank is removed from the bike, it should not be placed in an area where sparks or open flames could ignite the fumes coming out of the tank. Be especially careful inside garages where a natural gas-type appliance is located, because the pilot light could cause an explosion.*

Removal

AN400K3 to K6

1 The fuel tank is located at the front of the scooter behind the radiator. First remove the headlight panel, cockpit trim panel, belly panel and radiator panel (see Chapter 8) then remove the radiator (see Chapter 3).
2 Remove the left and right-hand side panels, kick panel and the front mudguard (see Chapter 8).
3 Undo the bolts securing the fuel hose union to the fuel pump backplate and disconnect the hose **(see illustration 4.4a)**. Note the location of the O-ring and discard it as a new one must be fitted **(see illustration 4.4b)**. Plug the open end of the hose to prevent leakage.
4 Trace the wiring from the terminal on the fuel pump backplate and disconnect it at the connector **(see illustration 4.10a)**. Free the wiring from any clips or ties and feed it back to the fuel pump.
5 Temporarily remove the fuel filler cap. Release the clip and disconnect the hose from the union on the cut-off valve, then disconnect the drain hose from the spill tray.
6 Release the trim clips securing the spill tray to the frame and lift it off the tank filler neck. Note the location of the pressure control valve on the underside of the spill tray. Install the fuel filler cap.
7 Undo the bolt securing the front left-hand mounting bracket and lift it off **(see illustration)**.
8 Undo the rear mounting bolts and the front mounting bolt on the right-hand side

17.7 Fuel tank bracket, front left-hand side

17.8a Fuel tank rear mounting bolts

17.8b Fuel tank front right-hand mounting bolt

17.14 Location of front left-hand side mounting bracket

(see illustrations). Note the location of the grommets and spacers in the tank mounting lugs.

9 Draw the tank forwards and off the machine.

AN400K7 model onward

10 The fuel tank is located at the front of the scooter underneath the floor panels. First remove the underseat panel, side panels, belly panel, floor panels and kick panel (see Chapter 8).

11 Follow the procedure in Chapter 2B and remove the engine.

12 Remove the rear suspension rising rate linkage assembly (see Chapter 6).

13 Follow the procedure in Steps 3 to 6 to disconnect the fuel hose and pump wiring connector and remove the spill tray and pressure control valve.

14 Undo the front mounting bolts and remove the bracket on the left-hand side **(see illustration)**.

15 Undo the rear mounting bolts and remove the rear bracket and the support bracket on the left-hand side **(see illustrations)**. Note the location of the grommets and spacers in the tank mounting lugs.

16 Draw the tank rearwards and lift it out.

Installation

17 Prior to installation, check the tank mounting grommets and bushes for signs of damage or deterioration and renew them if necessary. Check the condition of the fuel hoses and hose clips.

18 Ease the tank into position and align the mounting lugs with the mounts on the frame and the mounting bracket(s). Tighten the mounting bolts to the torque setting specified at the beginning of this Chapter.

19 Fit a new O-ring onto the fuel hose union.

20 Secure the fuel pump wiring as noted on removal.

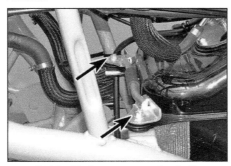

17.15a Undo rear mounting bolts

21 Ensure the spill tray is correctly installed and secured. Connect the pressure control valve hose to the union on the cut-off valve.

22 Install the remaining components in the reverse order of removal.

Tank repair

23 All repairs to the fuel tank should be carried out by a professional who has experience in this critical and potentially dangerous work. Even after cleaning and flushing of the fuel system, explosive fumes can remain and ignite during repair of the tank.

17.15b Location of rear left-hand side support bracket

Notes

Chapter 5
Ignition system –
AN250W to K2 and AN400X to K2 models

Ignition related components fitted to AN400K3-on models are covered in Chapter 4B Engine Management

Contents

Degrees of difficulty

| **Easy,** suitable for novice with little experience | | **Fairly easy,** suitable for beginner with some experience | | **Fairly difficult,** suitable for competent DIY mechanic | | **Difficult,** suitable for experienced DIY mechanic | | **Very difficult,** suitable for expert DIY or professional | |

Specifications

General information
Spark plug . . . .   see Chapter 1

Ignition pulse generator
Peak voltage . . . .   2.4 volts (min)
Resistance . . . .   184 to 276 ohms

Ignition coil
Minimum primary peak voltage . . . .   200 volts
Primary resistance . . . .   3 to 5 ohms
Secondary resistance . . . .   17 to 30 K-ohms

Torque wrench setting
Ignition pulse generator bolts . . . .   5 Nm

1 General information

All models are fitted with a fully transistorised electronic ignition system. The system consists of the pulse generator, ignition control unit (ICU), ignition coil and spark plug.

The triggers on the alternator rotor, which is fitted to the right-hand end of the crankshaft, activate signals in the pulse generator as the crankshaft rotates. The pulse generator sends those signals to the ICU which calculates the ignition timing and supplies the ignition coil with the power necessary to produce a spark at the plug. The ICU incorporates an electronic advance system. There is no provision for checking or adjusting the ignition timing.

The system incorporates a safety interlock circuit which will cut the ignition if the sidestand is extended whilst the engine is running. It also prevents the engine from being started unless the sidestand is up and one of the brake levers is pulled in (see Chapter 9 for component test details).

Because of their nature, the individual ignition system components can be checked but not repaired. If ignition system troubles occur, and the faulty component can be isolated, the only cure for the problem is to replace the part with a new one. Keep in mind that most electrical parts, once purchased, cannot be returned. To avoid unnecessary expense, make very sure the faulty component has been positively identified before buying a replacement part.

2 Ignition system check

⚠️ *Warning: The energy levels in electronic systems can be very high. On no account should the ignition be switched on whilst a plug or plug cap is being held. Shocks from the HT circuit can be most unpleasant. Secondly, it is vital that the engine is not turned over with the plug cap removed, and that the plug is soundly earthed (grounded) when the system is checked for sparking. The ignition system components can be seriously damaged if the HT circuit becomes isolated.*

1 As no means of adjustment is available, any failure of the system can be traced to failure of a system component or a simple wiring fault. Of the two possibilities, the latter is by far the most likely. In the event of failure, check the system in a logical fashion, as described below.
2 Pull the cap off the spark plug (see Chapter 1). Fit a spare spark plug into the cap and lay the plug against the cylinder head with the threads contacting it. If necessary, hold the spark plug with an insulated tool.

⚠️ *Warning: Do not remove the spark plug from the engine to perform this check – atomised fuel being pumped out of the open spark plug hole could ignite, causing severe injury! Make sure the spare plug is securely held against the engine – if it is not earthed when the engine is turned over, the ignition control unit could be damaged.*

3 Support the scooter on its centrestand with the rear wheel off the ground. Turn the ignition switch ON, and turn the engine over on the starter motor. If the system is in good condition a regular, fat blue spark should be evident at the plug electrodes. If the spark appears thin or yellowish, or is non-existent, further investigation will be necessary.
4 The ignition system must be able to produce a spark which is capable of jumping a particular size gap – Suzuki do not give a specification, but a healthy system should produce a spark capable of jumping at least 6 mm. Simple ignition spark gap testing tools are commercially available – follow the manufacturer's instructions and check the strength of the spark (see illustration).
5 If the test results are good the entire ignition system can be considered good. If the spark appears thin or yellowish, or is non-existent, further investigation is necessary.
6 Ignition faults can be divided into two categories, namely those where the ignition system has failed completely, and those which are due to a partial failure. The likely faults are listed below, starting with the most probable source of failure. Work through the list systematically, referring to the subsequent sections for full details of the necessary checks and tests, and to the *Wiring Diagrams* at the end of Chapter 9. Before checking the following items ensure that the battery is fully charged and that all fuses are in good condition.
- Loose, corroded or damaged wiring connections, broken or shorted wiring between any of the component parts of the ignition system (see Chapter 9).
- Faulty HT lead or spark plug cap, faulty spark plug, dirty, worn or corroded plug electrodes, or incorrect gap between electrodes.
- Faulty ignition switch (see Chapter 9).
- Faulty sidestand switch or brake switch (see Chapter 9).
- Faulty ignition coil.
- Faulty ignition pulse generator.
- Faulty ICU.

7 If the above checks don't reveal the cause of the problem, have the ignition system tested by a Suzuki dealer.

3 Ignition coil

Caution: Ensure the ignition is switched OFF before disconnecting/reconnecting any ignition system wiring connectors. If a connector is disconnected/reconnected with the ignition switched ON the ignition control unit (ICU) could be damaged.
Special tools: *A multimeter and peak voltage adapter are required for this procedure (see Step 3).*
1 The ignition coil is located behind the left-hand side panel (see illustration) – remove the side panel for access (see Chapter 8).
2 Ensure that the spark plug and spark plug cap are in good condition (see Chapter 1).

Check

3 Suzuki produces a circuit testing set (Part No. 09900-25008) that includes the facility for recording peak voltages. If this is not available, you will need a peak voltage adapter for your multimeter to carry-out the following check. If the appropriate equipment is not available, have the coil tested by a Suzuki dealer.
4 Disconnect the cap from the spark plug (see Chapter 1). Fit a new plug into the cap and earth the plug securely against the engine. Connect the peak voltage adapter positive (+) probe to the white wire terminal on the coil and the negative (-) probe to earth (ground). Turn the ignition ON, crank the engine for a few seconds and note the peak voltage recorded. Repeat the procedure several times, note the highest voltage recorded and compare this with the specification. Turn the ignition OFF.
5 If the result is below the minimum specified either the ignition coil, the ignition pulse generator (see Section 4) or the ignition control unit (see Section 5) is faulty.

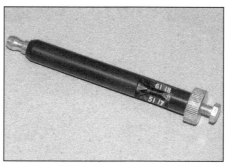

2.4 Spark gap testing tool

3.1 Location of the ignition coil

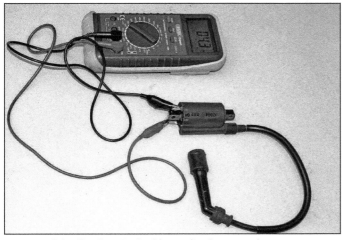

3.8a Testing the ignition coil primary resistance

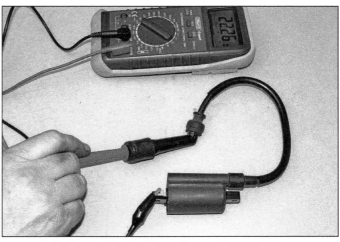

3.8b Testing the ignition coil secondary resistance

6 To test the ignition coil, set the multimeter to the ohms scale and proceed as follows.

7 Disconnect the cap from the spark plug and disconnect the white and orange/white wiring connectors from the coil, noting how they fit.

8 To test the coil primary resistance, connect the meter positive (+) probe to the white wire terminal on the coil and the negative (-) probe to the orange/white wire terminal and note the result **(see illustration)**. To test the coil secondary resistance, connect the negative (-) probe to the terminal inside the spark plug cap and note the result **(see illustration)**.

9 Both results should be as specified at the beginning of this Chapter. If either result is outside the specification, it is likely the ignition coil is faulty – have it checked by a Suzuki dealer.

Removal and installation

10 To remove the ignition coil, first remove the left-hand side panel (see Chapter 8).

11 Disconnect the cap from the spark plug and disconnect the white and orange/white wiring connectors from the coil, noting how they fit **(see illustration 3.1)**.

12 Undo the bolts securing the coil mounting bracket and lift the coil off, noting how it fits.

13 Installation is the reverse of removal.

4   Ignition pulse generator

Caution: Ensure the ignition is switched OFF before disconnecting/reconnecting any engine management system wiring connectors. If a connector is disconnected/ reconnected with the ignition switched ON the ignition control unit (ICU) could be damaged.

Special tools: *A multimeter and peak voltage adapter are required for this procedure (see Step 1).*

Check

1 Suzuki produces a circuit testing set (Part No. 09900-25008) that includes the facility for recording peak voltages. If this is not available, you will need a peak voltage adapter for your multimeter to carry-out the following check. If the appropriate equipment is not available, have the ignition pulse generator tested by a Suzuki dealer.

2 Follow the procedure in Section 5 to access the ICU and disconnect the multi-pin wiring connector **(see illustration 5.3)**. Connect the peak voltage adapter positive (+) probe to the black/white wire terminal in the loom side of the ICU connector and the negative (-) probe to the blue wire terminal.

3 Remove the spark plug (see Chapter 1).

4 Turn the ignition ON, crank the engine for a few seconds and note the peak voltage recorded. Turn the ignition OFF.

5 Compare the result with the specification at the beginning of this Chapter. If the result is below the specified minimum, repeat the test at the pulse generator wiring connector as follows.

6 The ignition pulse generator is located inside the alternator cover on the right-hand side of the engine unit. Remove the storage compartment and the right-hand side panel for access (see Chapter 8).

7 Trace the pulse generator wiring from the alternator cover and disconnect it at the connector.

8 Connect the peak voltage adapter positive (+) probe to the green wire terminal in the pulse generator side of the connector and the negative (-) probe to the blue wire terminal. Repeat the test.

9 If the result in the second test is as specified, inspect the wiring and connections between the wiring connector and the ICU for damage. If the result is again below the specified minimum, it is likely the ignition pulse generator is faulty.

10 Set the multimeter to the ohms scale and check the resistance between the terminals in the pulse generator connector – the result should be within the range specified at the beginning of this Chapter.

11 If the result is good, check for continuity between each terminal and earth (ground). There should be no continuity.

12 If any test results are outside the specifications, it is likely the ignition pulse generator is faulty – have it checked by a Suzuki dealer.

Removal and installation

13 To remove the ignition pulse generator, follow the procedure in Chapter 9 to remove the alternator stator. The pulse generator is integral with the stator assembly and is not available as a separate item.

5   Ignition control unit (ICU)

1 If the tests shown in the preceding Sections have failed to isolate the cause of an ignition fault, it is likely that the ignition control unit (ICU) itself is faulty. The ICU can be checked using the test values shown in this Section, however it must be stressed that satisfactory results can only be guaranteed when using the Suzuki circuit testing set (Part No. 09900-25008). If alternative equipment is used and the results are not as specified, it may be that the test equipment is not suitable for the task. Before condemning the ICU have it checked by a Suzuki dealer.

Check

2 The ICU is located on the right-hand side of the scooter below the storage compartment – remove the storage compartment for access (see Chapter 8).

3 Disconnect the ICU wiring connector and release the ICU from its holder **(see illustration)**.
4 On AN250W to K2 models, the terminals on the ICU are numbered 1 to 8. On AN400X to K2 models, the terminals on the ICU are numbered 1 to 12 **(see illustrations)**.
5 Set the multimeter to the diode test option and check the voltage between pairs of terminals as shown. The correct result for each test can be found where the values for the terminals intersect **(see tables)**.
6 If the ICU is good, make sure the wiring connector terminals are clean and check the wiring between the ICU and the system components for continuity (see *Wiring Diagrams* at the end of Chapter 9).

Removal and installation

7 Make sure the ignition is OFF.
8 Remove the storage compartment for access (see Chapter 8).
9 Disconnect the ICU wiring connector and release the ICU from its holder **(see illustration 5.3)**.
10 Installation is the reverse of removal. Ensure the wiring connector is secure.

5.3 Disconnect the ICU wiring connector

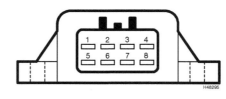

Unit: V (volts)

Tester negative probe	Tester positive probe							
		1	2	3	4	5	6	7	8
1			1.0 to 1.5	1.0 to 1.5	Approx 1.5	Approx 1.5	1.0 to 1.5	1.0 to 1.5	1.0 to 1.5
2		1.0 to 1.5		0.6 to 1.0	Approx 1.5	Approx 1.5	0.7 to 1.3	0.3 to 0.8	0.6 to 1.1
3		1.0 to 1.5	0.7 to 1.0		Approx 1.5	Approx 1.5	0.6 to 1.1	0.4 to 0.9	0 to 0.5
4		1.0 to 1.5	0.9 to 1.3	0.5 to 1.0		Approx 1.5	0.7 to 1.2	0.2 to 0.7	0.4 to 0.9
5		1.0 to 1.5	1.0 to 1.5	0.8 to 1.2	Approx 1.5		0.7 to 1.3	0.4 to 0.9	0.7 to 1.2
6		1.0 to 1.5	0.9 to 1.3	0.6 to 1.0	Approx 1.5	Approx 1.5		0.4 to 0.9	0.6 to 1.1
7		1.0 to 1.5	0.7 to 1.3	0.4 to 0.9	Approx 1.5	Approx 1.5	0.4 to 0.9		0.3 to 0.8
8		1.0 to 1.5	0.5 to 1.0	0 to 0.5	Approx 1.5	Approx 1.5	0.6 to 1.1	0.3 to 0.8	

5.4a ICU diode test terminal identification – AN250 models

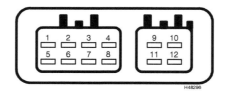

Unit: V (volts)

Tester negative probe	Tester positive probe											
		1	2	3	4	5	6	7	8	9	10	11	12
1			1.5	1.5	0.7 – 1.1	0.9 – 1.5	1.5	1.5	1.5	1.1 – 1.5	0.8 – 1.2	0.7 – 1.1	1.5
2		1.5		1.5	0.8 – 1.2	1.0 – 1.4	1.5	1.5	1.5	1.2 – 1.5	1.1 – 1.5	0.8 – 1.2	1.5
3		1.5	1.5		1.2 – 1.5	1.5	1.5	1.5	1.5	1.5	1.5	1.2 – 1.5	1.5
4		1.0 – 1.4	1.5	1.2 – 1.5		0.5 – 0.9	1.2 – 1.5	1.0 – 1.4	1.5	0.7 – 1.1	0.4 – 0.8	0	1.5
5		1.1 – 1.5	1.5	1.5	0.5 – 0.9		1.5	0.9 – 1.3	1.5	0.5 – 0.9	0.8 – 1.2	0.5 – 0.9	1.5
6		1.5	1.5	1.5	1.1 – 1.5	1.2 – 1.5		1.5	1.5	1.5	1.5	1.1 – 1.5	1.5
7		1.2 – 1.5	1.5	1.5	0.3 – 0.7	0.8 – 1.2	1.5		1.5	1.0 – 1.4	0.8 – 1.2	0.3 – 0.7	1.5
8		1.5	1.5	1.5	0.6 – 1.0	0.8 – 1.2	1.5	1.5		1.1 – 1.5	1.0 – 1.4	0.7 – 1.0	1.5
9		1.5	1.5	1.5	1.5	1.5	1.5	0.5 – 0.9	1.5		1.5	1.5	1.5
10		0.7 – 1.1	1.5	1.5	0.2 – 0.6	0.7 – 1.1	1.2 – 1.5	1.2 – 1.5	1.5	0.9 – 1.3		0.2 – 0.6	1.5
11		1.0 – 1.4	1.5	1.5	0	0.5 – 0.9	1.2 – 1.5	1.0 – 1.4	1.5	0.7 – 1.1	0.4 – 0.8		1.5
12		1.2 – 1.5	1.5	1.5	0.3 – 0.7	0.6 – 1.0	1.5	1.2 – 1.5	1.5	0.8 – 1.2	0.8 – 1.2	0.3 – 0.7	

5.4b ICU diode test terminal identification – AN400X to K2 models

Chapter 6
Frame and suspension

Contents

Degrees of difficulty

Easy, suitable for novice with little experience 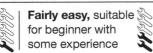	**Fairly easy,** suitable for beginner with some experience	**Fairly difficult,** suitable for competent DIY mechanic	**Difficult,** suitable for experienced DIY mechanic	**Very difficult,** suitable for expert DIY or professional

Specifications

Front forks

Fork oil type	Fork oil SAE10 (G10)
Fork oil capacity	
AN250W and X models	292 cc
AN250Y to K2 models	281 cc
AN400X model	275 cc
AN400Y to K6 models	284 cc
AN400K7 model onward	301 cc
Fork oil level*	
AN250W and X models	98 mm
AN250Y to K2 models	96 mm
AN400X model	102 mm
AN400Y to K6 models	96 mm
AN400K7 model onward	87 mm
Fork spring free length (service limit)	
AN250W and X models	251 mm
AN250Y to K2 models	323 mm
AN400X model	251 mm
AN400Y to K6 models	324 mm
AN400K7 model onward	347.6 mm

*Oil level is measured from the top of the tube with the fork spring removed and the leg fully compressed.

Torque settings

Brake master cylinder clamp bolts.	10 Nm
Engine mounting bolt	
AN250W to Y models.	93 Nm
AN250K1 and K2 models.	75 Nm
AN400 models	93 Nm
Engine mounting bracket bolts	85 Nm
Engine mounting bracket nuts	85 Nm
Fork damper bolt	30 Nm
Fork top bolt.	45 Nm
Fork yoke clamp bolts	23 Nm
Handlebar clamp bolts.	23 Nm
Handlebar bracket cable guide bolts	10 Nm
Handlebar bracket set bolt	
AN250 models	10 Nm
AN400 models	23 Nm
Handlebar bracket clamp bolts	
AN250 models	23 Nm
AN400 models	55 Nm
Rear axle nut	120 Nm
Rear shock adjuster mounting bolts	10 Nm
Rear sub-frame mounting bolts	50 Nm
Rear suspension arm pivot bolt	78 Nm
Rear suspension linkage rod pivot bolts	50 Nm
Shock absorber bolts.	50 Nm
Steering head bearing adjuster (initial setting)	
AN250 models	45 Nm
AN400X to K2 models	45 Nm
AN400K3 model onward	30 Nm
Steering head bearing adjuster locknut	30 Nm

1 General information

All scooters covered by this manual are fitted with a tubular and pressed steel one-piece frame.

Front suspension is by conventional, non-adjustable, oil-damped telescopic forks.

At the rear, the upper end of the crankcase pivots on a bracket fixed to the frame. Suspension movement is controlled by a single oil damped shock absorber located between the engine/transmission unit and the frame via a rising rate linkage and engine pivot mounting. The shock is adjustable for spring preload. On AN400K7 models onward, a sub-frame is mounted on the right-hand side of the engine/transmission unit, supporting the gearbox output shaft/rear wheel axle.

Ancillary items such as stands and handlebars are covered in this Chapter.

2 Frame inspection and repair

1 The frame should not require attention unless accident damage has occurred. In most cases, fitting a new frame is the only satisfactory remedy for such damage. Frame specialists have the jigs and other equipment necessary for straightening a frame to the required standard of accuracy, but even then there is no simple way of assessing to what extent it may have been over-stressed.

2 After a high mileage, the frame should be examined closely for signs of cracking or splitting at the welded joints. Loose engine mounting and suspension bolts can cause ovaling or fracturing of the mounting points. Minor damage can often be repaired by specialised welding, depending on the extent and nature of the damage.

3 Remember that a frame that is out of alignment will cause handling problems. If, as the result of an accident, misalignment is suspected, it will be necessary to strip the machine completely so the frame can be thoroughly checked (see Chapter 7 for wheel alignment checks).

3.1a Location of the centrestand

3 Stands

Centrestand

1 The centrestand pivots on brackets on the underside of the frame (see illustration). Springs between the frame and the stand ensure that it is held in the retracted or extended position. When the stand is retracted the springs should hold a rubber cushion on the stand firmly against the underside of the frame (see illustration).

2 To remove the centrestand, support the scooter securely in an upright position using an auxiliary stand. **Note:** *Do not rest the weight of the machine on the bodywork – if*

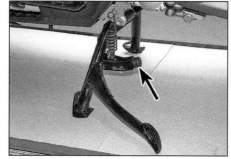

3.1b Note the rubber cushion (arrowed)

necessary, remove the belly panel to expose the frame (see Chapter 8).

3 On all models, the stand is held in position by two springs – take great care when removing the springs as they are under considerable tension **(see illustration)**. With the stand retracted (UP position) lever one end of the spring off using a large screwdriver or steel rod.

AN250 models

4 Remove the split pin and washer securing the pivot pin on the right-hand side, then withdraw the pivot pin and ease the stand off. Clean off all old grease and corrosion, then examine the pivot pin for wear and renew it if it is damaged. Prior to installation, lubricate the pivot pin with multi-purpose grease. Secure the pivot pin with a new circlip.

5 Install the springs. It is essential that the springs are in good condition and are capable of holding the stand up when not in use. A broken or weak spring is an obvious safety hazard.

AN400X to K2 models

6 Counter-hold the pivot bolt and undo the nut on the right-hand side, then withdraw the bolt and ease the stand off. Clean off all old grease and corrosion. Examine the pivot pin and the pivot bushes in the stand lugs for wear and renew them if necessary. Prior to installation, lubricate the pivot bolt and bushes with multi-purpose grease. Tighten the pivot bolt nut securely. Check that the stand pivots freely around the bolt.

7 Install the springs (see Step 5).

AN400K3 to K6 models

8 The stand pivots on two separate bolts – counter-hold the bolts and undo the nuts, then withdraw the bolts and ease the stand off. Clean off all old grease and corrosion. Examine the pivot bolts and the pivot bushes in the stand lugs for wear and renew them if necessary. Prior to installation, lubricate the pivot bolts and bushes with multi-purpose grease. Tighten the pivot bolt nuts securely. Check that the stand pivots freely around the bolts.

9 Install the springs (see Step 5).

3.3 Stand is held in position by two springs

AN400K7 model onward

10 The stand pivots on two separate bolts – undo the bolts and ease the stand off. Clean off all old grease and corrosion. Examine the pivot bolts and the pivot bushes in the stand lugs for wear and renew them if necessary. Prior to installation, lubricate the pivot bolts and bushes with multi-purpose grease. Tighten the pivot bolts securely. Check that the stand pivots freely around the bolts.

11 Install the springs (see Step 5).

Sidestand

12 The sidestand pivots on a bracket on the left-hand side of the frame. Springs between the bracket and the stand ensure that it is held in the retracted or extended position.

13 To remove the sidestand, support the scooter on its centrestand. Ease the lower ends of the springs off the lug on the stand, then remove the springs, noting how they fit **(see illustration)**.

14 Unscrew the pivot bolt locknut, then unscrew the pivot bolt and remove the stand.

15 Inspect the stand carefully for wear and damage. Clean the stand bracket and pivot bolt and inspect them for wear – fit a new bolt if necessary.

16 Prior to installation, lubricate the pivot bolt and bracket with multi-purpose grease. Tighten the pivot bolt, then tighten the locknut. Check that the stand pivots freely around the bolt.

17 Hook the upper ends of the springs over the lug on the stand bracket, then pull the springs down carefully and hook them over

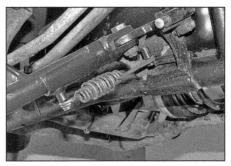

3.13 Sidestand springs are secured between two lugs

the lug on the stand. It is essential that the springs are in good condition and are capable of holding the stand up when not in use – an accident is almost certain to occur if the stand extends while the machine is in motion.

18 Check the operation of the sidestand switch (see Chapter 9).

4 Handlebars

Note 1: *If required, the handlebars can be displaced without having to detach any cables or remove the front and rear brake master cylinders. If this is the case, ignore the Steps which do not apply. Cover the cockpit trim panel and surrounding bodywork to avoid accidental damage. Take great care to avoid spilling brake fluid on the bodywork.*
Note 2: *If you are removing the handlebars completely, note how the wiring is secured before freeing it.*

Removal

1 Remove the handlebar covers and the mirrors (see Chapter 8).

2 Undo the bolts securing the bar-ends and remove them. Where fitted, remove the hand covers (see Chapter 8).

3 Displace the brake lever covers and disconnect the wiring from the front and rear brake light switches **(see illustrations)**.

4 Note the routing of the throttle cables, brake hoses and wiring around the steering stem **(see illustration)**. Release the tie

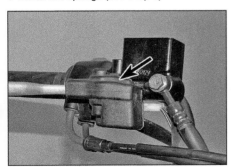

4.3a Displace the brake lever covers . . .

4.3b . . . and disconnect the brake light switch wiring connectors

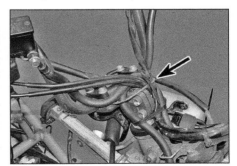

4.4a Note the routing of all cables, hoses and wiring

4.4b Release the cable-tie

4.4c Bolts (arrowed) secure cable guide

4.5 Undo the master cylinder clamp bolts

securing the brake hoses to the steering stem **(see illustration)**. Undo the bolts securing the cable guide and remove it **(see illustration)**.

5 Working on one brake at a time, undo the master cylinder clamp bolts and remove the back of the clamp **(see illustration)**. Secure the master cylinder assembly clear of the handlebar and ensure no strain is placed on the brake hose. Keep the fluid reservoir upright to prevent air entering the system.

6 Follow the procedure in Chapter 4A to detach the throttle cables from the twistgrip pulley. **Note:** *It is not necessary to remove the headlight panel and associated bodywork when removing the handlebars. Slide the twistgrip off the handlebar. Position the twistgrip/switch housing away from the handlebar.*

7 Follow the procedure in Chapter 9 to separate the two halves of the left-hand switch housing and position them away from the handlebar.

8 Pull the left-hand grip off the handlebar. **Note:** *The grip will probably be stuck in place – it may be necessary to slit the grip with a sharp knife in order to remove it.*

9 Support the handlebars, undo the bolts securing the handlebar clamps and remove them **(see illustrations)**.

10 Lift the handlebars off.

Installation

11 Installation is the reverse of removal, noting the following:

* Clean the threads of the handlebar clamp bolts and apply a suitable non-permanent thread-locking compound.
* Align the punch mark on the handlebars with the mating surfaces of the clamp **(see illustration)**.
* Tighten the front handlebar clamp bolts first – tighten the bolts to the torque setting specified at the beginning of this Chapter.

* If a new left-hand grip is being fitted, secure it with a suitable adhesive.
* Follow the procedure in Chapter 9 to install the left-hand switch housing.
* Follow the procedure in Chapter 4A to install the right-hand twistgrip/switch housing.
* Ensure the backs of the brake master cylinder clamps are installed with the UP mark facing up **(see illustrations 4.5)**. Align the clamp joint with the punch mark on the underside of the handlebar **(see illustration)**. Tighten the top clamp bolt first – tighten the bolts to the specified torque setting.
* Check the operation of the brake light switches before riding the scooter.

5 Fork removal and installation

Removal

1 Remove the headlight panel (see Chapter 8).

2 Remove the front wheel and secure the brake caliper to the machine so that it is clear of the front forks (see Chapter 7).

3 On all AN250 models and AN400X to K6 models, note how the speedometer drive housing locates against the right-hand fork outer tube **(see illustration)**. Release the speedometer wire from the guides on the right

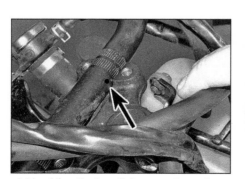

4.9a Undo the bolts . . .

4.9b . . . and remove the handlebar clamps

4.11b Align master cylinder clamp joint with punch mark

5.3 Note how the speedometer drive housing locates against fork tube

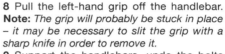

4.11a Align the handlebar punch mark as described

5.5 Fork top bolt (A), fork clamp bolts (B)

5.6 Spring seat (arrowed)

5.7 Pull the fork down out of the yoke

and left-hand outer tube and front mudguard and secure the drive housing clear of the front forks.

4 Remove the front mudguard (see Chapter 8).

5 Working on one fork leg at a time, unscrew the fork top bolt **(see illustration)**. Note the location of the O-ring.

6 On AN250Y to K2 models and AN400K1 models onward, remove the spring seat **(see illustration)**.

7 Loosen the clamp bolts in the fork yoke, then remove the fork leg by twisting it and pulling it down **(see illustration)**. On AN400K7 models onward, note which way round the fork legs are fitted and mark them to aid installation if necessary. On all other models the right-hand fork outer tube has the lugs to secure the brake caliper.

 HAYNES HiNT *If the fork legs are seized in the yoke, spray the area with penetrating oil and allow time for it to soak in before trying again.*

8 Temporarily install the spring seat (if removed) and top bolt to avoid oil spillage.

Installation

9 Prior to installation, remove all traces of corrosion from the fork inner tube and the yoke. Examine the O-ring on the top bolt and

5.9 Note location of O-ring on top bolt

fit a new one if it is damaged or distorted **(see illustration)**.

10 Make sure you install the fork legs the correct way round – see Step 7.

11 Slide the fork leg up into the yoke as far as it will go and tighten the clamp bolts temporarily to secure it **(see illustration)**.

12 Install the spring seat and tighten the top bolt temporarily **(see illustration 5.6)**.

13 Tighten the clamp bolts to the torque setting specified at the beginning of this Chapter.

14 Tighten the top bolt to the specified torque setting.

15 Install the remaining components in the reverse order of removal.

16 Check the operation of the front forks and brake before riding the scooter.

5.11 Slide the fork leg up as far as it will go

6 Fork overhaul

Disassembly

1 Follow the procedure in Section 5 to remove the fork legs.

2 Always dismantle the fork legs separately to avoid interchanging parts. Store all components in separate, clearly marked containers.

3 Start by loosening the damper bolt in the underside of the outer tube **(see illustration)**. To prevent the damper from turning inside the leg, hold the fork leg upside-down and compress it so that the spring exerts maximum pressure on the damper. If the bolt will not loosen, or the damper turns inside the leg, try again once the spring has been removed (see Step 9). Alternatively, use an air-wrench if available.

4 Support the leg upright and unscrew the top bolt.

5 On AN250Y to K2 models and AN400K1 models onward, remove the spring seat.

6 On AN250W and X models and AN400X and Y models, remove the spacer, then compress the fork inner tube down into the outer tube and remove the spring seat.

7 Remove the spring **(see illustration)**.

8 Invert the fork leg over a suitable container and pump the fork to expel as much oil as possible. Support the fork upside down in the container and allow it to drain for a few

6.3 Loosen the damper bolt

6.7 Draw out the spring

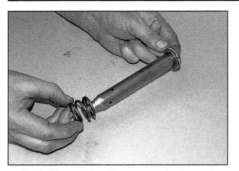

6.10 Tip out the damper and rebound spring

6.11 Prise off the dust seal

6.12 Remove the oil seal retaining clip

minutes. If the oil contains metal particles inspect the internal components for wear (see Steps 16 to 21).

9 Remove the previously loosed damper bolt and its sealing washer (see Step 3). Discard the sealing washer as a new one must be used. If the damper bolt was not loosened earlier, insert a length of wood doweling, tapered on the end to engage the head of the damper, into the fork leg. Press the leg down onto the doweling and undo the bolt.

10 Tip the damper and rebound spring out of the fork leg (see illustration).

11 Carefully prise off the dust seal from the top of the outer tube (see illustration). Discard the seal as a new one must be used.

12 Remove the oil seal retaining clip, taking care not to scratch the surface of the inner tube (see illustration).

13 To separate the inner tube from the outer tube it is necessary to displace the oil seal and top bush. The bottom bush will not pass

through the top bush, and this can be used to good effect. Compress the fork leg fully, then pull the tubes sharply apart so that the bottom bush strikes the top bush. Repeat this operation until the seal and top bush are tapped out of the outer tube and the two tubes can be separated (see illustration).

14 Slide the oil seal, washer and top bush off the inner tube, noting which way up the seal is fitted. Discard the seal as a new one must be used.

Caution: Do not remove the bottom bush from the tube unless it is to be renewed.

15 Tip the damper seat out of the outer tube, noting which way up it fits (see illustration 6.20).

Inspection

16 Clean all parts in solvent and blow them dry with compressed air, if available.

17 Check the fork inner tube for score marks, scratches, flaking of the chrome finish and

excessive or abnormal wear. Look for dents in the tube and renew both fork tubes if any are found.

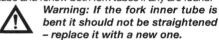 **Warning: If the fork inner tube is bent it should not be straightened – replace it with a new one.**

18 Examine the working surfaces of the two bushes – if worn or scuffed they must be renewed (see illustration). To remove the bottom bush from the fork inner tube, prise it apart at the slit using a flat-bladed screwdriver and slide it off. Make sure the new bush seats properly.

19 Examine the fork seal seat in the outer tube for nicks, gouges and scratches. If damage is evident, leaks will occur. Also check the oil seal washer for damage and renew it if necessary.

20 Check the damper and its piston ring for wear and score marks and renew it if necessary (see illustration). Do not remove the piston ring unless it requires renewal.

21 Check the spring for cracks and other damage. Measure the spring free length and compare the result to the specification at the beginning of this Chapter (see illustration). If either main spring is defective or has sagged below the service limit, replace both springs with new ones. Never renew only one spring. Also check the rebound spring (see illustration 6.20).

Reassembly

22 Slide the rebound spring onto the damper (see illustration 6.10). Insert the damper into the top of the inner tube, slide it down so that it projects from the bottom of the tube, then install the damper seat (see illustration).

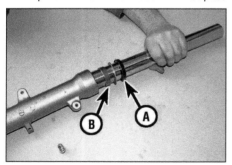

6.13 Separate the fork tubes – note the seal (A) and top bush (B)

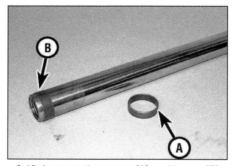

6.18 Inspect the upper (A) and lower (B) fork bushes

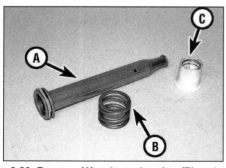

6.20 Damper (A), rebound spring (B) and damper seat (C)

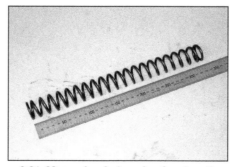

6.21 Measuring fork spring free length

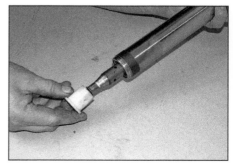

6.22 Install the damper seat on the projecting damper

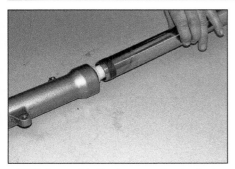

6.23 Assemble the inner and outer fork tubes

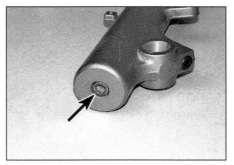

6.24 Install the damper bolt (arrowed) with thread-lock and a new sealing washer

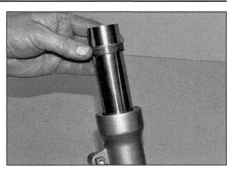

6.25a Install the top bush . . .

6.25b . . . and washer

6.25c Tap the bush into place with a pin punch

23 Lubricate the inner tube and bottom bush with fork oil, then insert the assembly into the outer tube **(see illustration)**.

24 Clean the threads of the damper bolt and apply a suitable non-permanent thread-locking compound. Fit a new sealing washer onto the bolt, then install the bolt into the bottom of the outer tube and thread it into the damper **(see illustration)**. Tighten the damper bolt to the torque setting specified at the beginning of this Chapter. If the damper rotates inside the tube, hold it with spring pressure or a wooden dowel as on disassembly (see Steps 3 and 9).

25 Compress the fork leg fully, then oil the top bush and slide it down the inner tube **(see illustration)**. Press the bush squarely into its seat in the outer tube, then install the washer **(see illustration)**. If necessary, use a pin punch to tap the washer and bush down until the bush is seated **(see illustration)**.

26 Lubricate the inside of the new oil seal with general purpose grease and slide it down the inner tube with its markings facing upwards **(see illustration)**. Press the seal into the outer tube until the retaining clip groove is visible above the seal. Suzuki produces a service tool (Part No. 09940-52861) to do this. Alternatively, use a piece of tubing slightly larger in diameter than the inner tube and slightly smaller in diameter than the seal recess in the outer tube. **Note:** *Take care not to scratch the inner tube during this operation – if the inner tube is pushed fully into the outer tube any accidental scratching is confined to the area above the oil seal.*

27 Fit the retaining clip **(see illustration 6.12)**.

28 Lubricate the inside of the new dust seal with a smear of grease, then slide it down the inner tube and press it into position **(see illustration 6.11)**.

29 Hold the fork leg upright and slowly pour in the specified quantity of the correct grade of fork oil (see Specifications at the beginning of this Chapter) **(see illustration)**. Pump the fork up-and-down several times to expel any trapped air, then compress the inner tube fully and measure the oil level to the top of the tube **(see illustration)**. Add or subtract oil until it is at the level specified at the beginning of this Chapter.

30 Pull the inner tube up and install the spring.

31 On AN250W and X models and AN400X and Y models, install the spring seat and spacer. On AN250Y to K2 models and

AN400K1 models onward, install the spring seat.

32 Fit a new O-ring into the groove in the top bolt and lubricate it with a smear of fork oil.

33 Install the fork legs (see Section 5).

7 Steering stem

Removal

Special tool: *A peg spanner will be required to tighten the bearing adjuster nut to the specified torque setting (see Steps 16 and 17).*

1 Remove or displace the handlebars (see Section 4).

2 Remove the headlight panel and the cockpit trim panel (see Chapter 8).

3 Remove the front fork legs (see Section 5).

6.26 Install the new oil seal

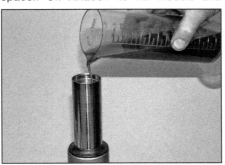

6.29a Pour in a measured amount of oil

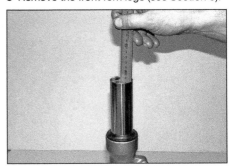

6.29b Measure the fork oil level

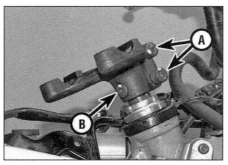

7.4 Detach the brake hose guide from the fork yoke

7.5a Loosen the clamp bolts (A), remove the set bolt (B)

7.5b Lift the handlebar bracket off

4 Undo the bolts securing the front brake hose guide to the fork yoke **(see illustration)**.
5 Loosen the handlebar bracket clamp bolts,

undo the set bolt and lift the bracket off **(see illustrations)**.
6 Using a C-spanner or peg spanner, undo

the bearing adjuster locknut and remove the tab washer **(see illustrations)**. Discard the tab washer as a new one must be fitted.
7 Support the fork yoke and unscrew the bearing adjuster **(see illustration)**.
8 Lift off the dust cover and the upper bearing inner race, then lower the steering stem out of the steering head **(see illustrations)**.
9 On all AN250 models and AN400X to K6 models, the steering head bearings are caged ball bearings. The upper bearing will remain in the outer race on the steering head and the lower bearing will remain on the inner race on the steering stem.
10 AN400K7 models onward are fitted with tapered roller bearings. The upper bearing outer race will remain in the steering head and the lower bearing will remain on the steering stem.
11 Remove all traces of old grease from the bearings and races using a suitable solvent, then check them for wear or damage as described in Section 8.

7.6a Undo the adjuster locknut . . .

7.6b . . . and remove the tab washer

Installation

12 Apply a liberal quantity of multi-purpose grease to the bearing races in the frame and work grease into the upper and lower bearing cages.
13 Lift the steering stem up through the steering head and install the upper bearing **(see illustration)**.
14 On all AN250 models and AN400X to K6

7.7 Unscrew the bearing adjuster

7.8a Lift off the dust cover . . .

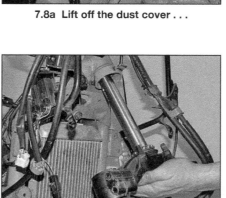

7.8b . . . and the upper bearing inner race

7.8c Lower the steering stem out of the steering head

7.13 Slide the upper bearing down the steering stem

7.15 Tighten the bearing adjuster nut finger-tight

7.16 Use a peg spanner to tighten the adjuster nut

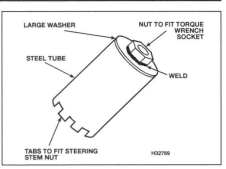

7.17 Details of a home-made peg spanner

models, install the upper bearing inner race **(see illustration 7.8b)**.

15 Fit the dust cover **(see illustration 7.8a)** and tighten the bearing adjuster finger-tight **(see illustration)**.

16 If the Suzuki service tools (Part Nos. 09940-14911 and 09940-11420) or a suitable peg spanner and a torque wrench are available, tighten the adjuster to the initial torque setting specified at the beginning of this Chapter **(see illustration)**. Turn the steering stem through its full lock at least five times to settle the bearings, then slacken the adjuster by 1/4 to 1/2 of a turn. Check that the steering stem moves smoothly from lock-to-lock without any freeplay or binding and adjust the adjuster nut if necessary.

17 If special tools are not available, a peg spanner can be made by cutting castellations into an old socket **(see illustration)**.

18 Alternatively, tighten the adjuster using a C-spanner so that bearing play is eliminated but the steering is able to move freely from lock-to-lock, then slacken the nut so that it is loose. Now tighten it lightly – the nut must be literally on the point of being loose. *Caution: Take great care not to apply excessive pressure because this will cause premature failure of the bearings.*

19 Fit a new tab washer, aligning the tab with the slot in the steering stem, then fit the bearing adjuster locknut. Tighten the locknut to the specified torque setting, then check the bearing adjustment to ensure it is still correct.

20 Install the handlebar bracket and tighten the set bolt to the specified torque setting. Tighten the clamp bolts to the specified torque setting.

21 Secure the front brake hose guide to the fork yoke.

22 Install the remaining components in the reverse of the removal.

23 Recheck the steering head bearing adjustment as described in Chapter 1.

8 Steering head bearings

Note: *Do not attempt to remove the outer races from the steering head or the lower inner*

race from the steering stem unless they are to be renewed.

Inspection

1 Remove the steering stem (see Section 7).

2 On AN250 and AN400X to K6 models, remove the upper bearing from the outer race in the steering head and lift the lower bearing off the steering stem, noting how they fit.

3 On AN400K7 models onward, the upper bearing will have been removed prior to removing the steering stem. The lower bearing is a firm fit on the lower end of the steering stem.

4 Remove all traces of old grease from the bearings and races using a suitable solvent, then inspect them for wear or damage.

8.5a Inspect the outer races in the top . . .

8.6a Examine the upper inner race . . .

5 The outer races in the steering head should be polished and free from indentations **(see illustrations)**.

6 On AN250 and AN400X to K6 models, the inner races should be polished and free from indentations **(see illustrations)**. The ball bearings should be free from signs of wear, pitting or discoloration

7 On AN400K7 models onward, inspect the bearing rollers for wear, discoloration and pitting.

8 For further details refer to *Bearing fault finding* in the *Reference* section.

Renewal

9 The outer races are an interference fit in the steering head – tap them from position using a suitable drift located on the exposed inner lip

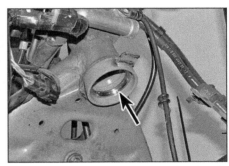

8.5b . . . and bottom of the steering head

8.6b . . . and lower inner race – AN250 and AN400X to K6 models

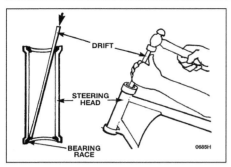

8.9 Using a drift to remove the outer races

of the race **(see illustration)**. Tap firmly and evenly around each race to ensure that it is driven out squarely. Curve the end of the drift slightly to improve access if necessary.

10 Alternatively, remove the outer races using a bearing puller with slide-hammer attachment (see *Tools and Workshop Tips* in the *Reference* section).

11 Install the new outer races using a drawbolt arrangement **(see illustration)**. Ensure the drawbolt washer rests only on the outer edge of the race and does not contact

 HAYNES HiNT *Installation of new bearing outer races is made much easier if the races are left overnight in the freezer. This causes them to contract slightly making them a looser fit. Alternatively, use a freeze spray.*

8.12a Lever the lower race off the steering stem . . .

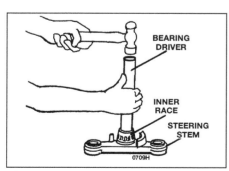

8.14 Installing the new inner race on the steering stem

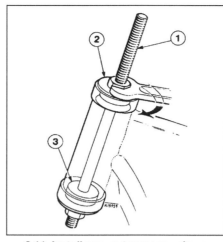

8.11 Install new outer races using a drawbolt

1 Long bolt or threaded bar
2 Thick washer
3 Guide for lower outer race

the bearing surface. Ensure both races are drawn all the way into their seats.

12 To remove the lower inner race from the steering stem, use two screwdrivers placed on opposite sides to work it free, using blocks of wood to improve leverage and protect the yoke, or tap under it using a cold chisel **(see illustrations)**. If the race is firmly in place it will be necessary to use a puller or split the race using an angle grinder – be very careful not to gouge the steering stem

8.12b . . . or dislodge it with a chisel

9.3 Using the C-spanner to adjust shock pre-load

13 Remove the dust seal from the bottom of the stem and replace it with a new one.
14 Fit the new lower inner race onto the steering stem. Tap the new race into position using a length of tubing with an internal diameter slightly larger than the steering stem **(see illustration)**. Ensure that the tube rests only on the inner edge of the race and does not contact the bearing surface.
15 Install the steering stem (see Section 7).

9 Rear shock absorber

⚠ *Warning: Do not attempt to disassemble the shock absorber – no individual components are available. Improper disassembly could result in serious injury.*

1 The rear shock absorber is located underneath the machine, forward of the engine unit.

AN250
Adjustment

2 Support the scooter on its centrestand. Release the trim clip securing the shock absorber access panel in the front of the belly panel and remove the panel.
3 To adjust the spring preload, turn the adjuster cam using the C-spanner supplied in the scooter's toolkit **(see illustration)**. There are seven pre-load settings. Position 1 is the softest and position 7 is the hardest. Standard setting is position 3.

Removal

4 Support the scooter on its centrestand. Position a support under the rear wheel so that the engine unit does not drop when the shock absorber is removed, but also making sure that the weight of the machine is off the rear suspension so that the shock is not compressed.
5 Remove the belly panel, the radiator panel and the floor centre panel (see Chapter 8)
6 Undo the bolts securing the fuel pump and displace the pump (see Chapter 4A).
7 Undo the shock absorber front mounting bolt **(see illustration)**.
8 Unscrew the nuts on the suspension arm pivot bolt and the bolt securing the suspension rods to the crankcase **(see illustrations 9.39a and b)**.

9.7 Undo the shock absorber front mounting bolt

**9.17 Location of the rear shock adjuster –
AN400X to K6 models**

**9.22a Undo the bolts securing the pre-load
adjuster**

**9.22b Unclip the adjuster hose from the
frame**

9 Support the shock, withdraw the bolts and lower the shock off the machine.
10 Unscrew the nut and bolt securing the shock to the suspension arm.

Inspection

11 Inspect the shock absorber for obvious physical damage and oil leakage. Check the spring for looseness, cracks or signs of fatigue, and inspect the damper rod for signs of wear, corrosion or pitting **(see illustration 9.28)**.
12 Ensure that the spring pre-load adjuster is clean and free from corrosion. Using the C-spanner from the scooter's toolkit, check that the adjuster moves freely.
13 Inspect the bush in the shock absorber front mount for wear or damage. Check for elongation of the bolt holes in the rear mount.
14 If any defects are found a new shock must be fitted – individual components are not available.

Installation

15 Prior to installation, check the bearings in the suspension arm (see Section 10).
16 Installation is the reverse of removal, noting the following:
• *Install the suspension arm pivot bolt last.*
• *Tighten the mounting bolts to the torque settings specified at the beginning of this Chapter.*
• *Follow the procedure in Step 3 to adjust the spring pre-load.*

AN400X to K6 models

Adjustment

17 Support the scooter on its centrestand. The adjuster is located on the left-hand side below the side panel **(see illustration)**.
18 Turn the adjuster clockwise to stiffen the pre-load and anti-clockwise to make it softer.
19 To reset the pre-load, turn the adjuster

fully anti-clockwise to the softest position, then turn it clockwise the desired amount. There is a click position for every 1/2 turn of the adjuster. Standard setting is 9 clicks clockwise from the softest position.

Removal

20 Support the scooter on its centrestand as described in Step 4.
21 Remove the belly panel, the radiator panel, the floor centre panel, the side panels and the storage compartment (see Chapter 8).
22 Undo the bolts securing the preload adjuster, unclip the adjuster hose from the frame, noting its routing, and position it at the front of the machine alongside the shock **(see illustrations)**.
23 On AN400X to K2 models, undo the bolts securing the fuel pump and displace the pump (see Chapter 4A).
24 Undo the shock absorber front mounting bolt **(see illustration)**.
25 Unscrew the nuts on the suspension arm pivot bolt and the bolt securing the suspension rods to the crankcase **(see illustrations)**.
26 Support the shock, withdraw the bolts and lower the shock off the machine **(see illustration)**.
27 Unscrew the nut and bolt securing the shock to the suspension arm.

Inspection

28 Inspect the shock absorber for obvious physical damage and oil leakage. Check the spring for looseness, cracks or signs of fatigue, and inspect the damper rod for signs of wear, corrosion or pitting **(see illustration)**.
29 Check the operation of the spring pre-load

**9.24 Undo the shock absorber front
mounting bolt**

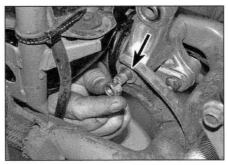

**9.25a Unscrew the nut on the suspension
arm pivot bolt . . .**

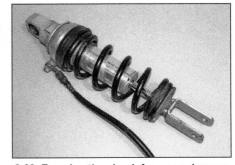

**9.28 Examine the shock for wear, damage
and oil leakage**

**9.25b . . . and the bolt securing the
suspension rods to the crankcase**

9.26 Lower the shock off

9.38 Undo the shock absorber front mounting bolt

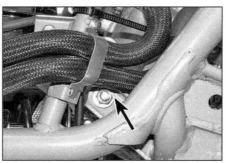

9.39a Unscrew the nut on the suspension arm pivot bolt . . .

9.39b . . . and the bolt securing the suspension rods to the crankcase

9.40 Lower the shock off

adjuster. Do not disconnect the hose from the adjuster unit or the shock. If the hose is damaged a new shock absorber will have to be fitted.

30 Inspect the bush in the shock absorber front mount for wear or damage. Check for elongation of the bolt holes in the rear mount.

31 If any defects are found a new shock must be fitted – individual components are not available.

Installation

32 Prior to installation, check the bearings in the suspension arm (see Section 10).

33 Installation is the reverse of removal, noting the following:
• *Ensure the pre-load adjuster cable is correctly routed.*

• *On AN400X to K2 models, install the suspension arm pivot bolt first.*
• *On AN400K3 to K6 models, install the suspension arm pivot bolt last.*
• *Tighten the mounting bolts to the torque settings specified at the beginning of this Chapter.*
• *Follow the procedure in Steps 18 and 19 to adjust the spring pre-load.*

AN400K7 model onward

Adjustment

34 Support the scooter on its centrestand. Release the catch securing the shock absorber access panel in the front of the belly panel.

35 To adjust the spring pre-load, turn the adjuster cam using the C-spanner supplied in the scooter's toolkit as described in Step 3.

Removal

36 Support the scooter on its centrestand as described in Step 4.

37 Remove the belly panel, the radiator panel and the floor centre panel (see Chapter 8).

38 Undo the shock absorber front mounting bolt **(see illustration)**.

39 Unscrew the nuts on the suspension arm pivot bolt and the bolt securing the suspension rods to the crankcase **(see illustrations)**.

40 Support the shock, withdraw the bolts and lower the shock off the machine **(see illustration)**.

41 Unscrew the nut and bolt securing the shock to the suspension arm **(see illustration)**.

Inspection

42 Follow the procedure in Steps 11 to 14.

Installation

43 Prior to installation, check the bearings in the suspension arm (see Section 10).

44 Installation is the reverse of removal, noting the following:
• *Install the suspension arm pivot bolt last.*
• *Tighten the mounting bolts to the torque settings specified at the beginning of this Chapter.*
• *Follow the procedure in Step 3 to adjust the spring pre-load.*

10 Rear suspension

Suspension arm and rods

1 Remove the rear shock absorber (see Section 9).

2 Undo the nut and bolt securing the linkage rods to the suspension arm.

3 Clean the components thoroughly, removing all traces of dirt, corrosion and grease **(see illustration)**.

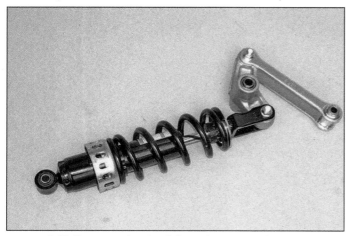

9.41 Separate the shock from the suspension arm

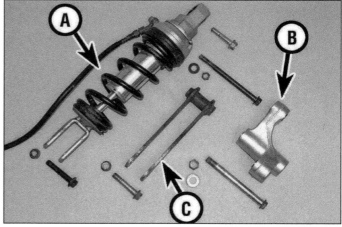

10.3 Rear shock (A), suspension arm (B), linkage rods (C) and mounting hardware

10.6 Remove the bearing sleeves from the suspension arm

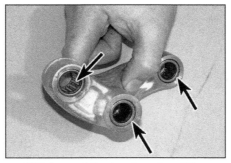

10.7 Inspect the bearings for pitting

4 Inspect the mounting bolts and renew any that are worn or corroded.

5 Inspect the bush in the rear end of the linkage rod – if it is worn or distorted fit a new linkage rod. Check for elongation of the bolt holes in the front of the rods.

6 Withdraw the sleeves from the needle bearings in the suspension arm, noting how they fit **(see illustration)**. Clean the sleeves and bearings with a suitable solvent to remove all traces of dirt and grease. Remove any corrosion from the sleeves with steel wool and dry the needle roller bearings with compressed air, if available.

7 Inspect the bearing needles for pitting **(see illustration)**.

8 Apply clean oil to the sleeves, then slip each one back into its bearing(s) in the suspension arm and check that there is not an excessive amount of freeplay between the two. Ensure the sleeves turn smoothly in the bearings without binding or grating. Replace any components as required with new ones.

9 Only remove the needle bearings if new ones are going to be fitted. Note the position of the bearings before commencing work. The single bearings can be pressed out of the suspension arm, but the two bearings that support the suspension arm should be extracted using a knife-edged puller and slide-hammer – refer to *Tools and Workshop Tips* in the Reference section. Suzuki produces service tools (Part Nos. 09923-73210 and 09930-30104) to do this. Alternatively, insert a drift through the suspension arm and drive each bearing out from the opposite side. The new bearings should be pressed or drawn into place and must not be driven into position.

10 Prior to installation, lubricate the bearings and sleeves with multi-purpose grease. Assemble the linkage rods, suspension arm and rear shock and tighten the pivot bolts to the torque settings specified at the beginning of this Chapter.

Engine pivot mounting

11 The engine pivot mounting is located above the engine unit. Remove the side panels and storage compartment for access.

12 Support the scooter on its centrestand. Position a support under the rear wheel so that the engine unit does not drop when the

pivot mounting is removed, but also making sure that the weight of the machine is off the rear suspension.

AN250

13 On AN250-W to Y models, the pivot mounting is a two-piece assembly located either side of the upper crankcase mounting lug. If applicable, disconnect the parking brake cable from the rear brake caliper (see Chapter 7) and pass it through the guide on the left-hand mounting. On AN250K1 and K2 models, the pivot mounting is a one-piece assembly as fitted to AN400X to K6 models (see Step 35 onwards).

14 Undo the nut on the upper engine mounting bolt and remove the washer (see Chapter 2A). Undo the nuts on the left and right-hand pivot mounting bolts. Loosen the left and right-hand rubber damper bolts **(see illustration 10.36)**.

15 Make sure the rear wheel is properly supported, then withdraw the upper engine mounting bolt.

16 Remove the rubber damper bolts and washers, and the rubber dampers.

17 Remove the pivot mounting bolts and pivot mountings, noting how they are fitted – the knurled end of the centre sleeve should fit against the frame.

18 Clean the components thoroughly, removing all traces of dirt, corrosion and grease.

19 Inspect the mounting bolts and renew any that are worn or corroded.

20 Inspect the rubber dampers – if they

10.28 Install the left-hand pivot mounting bolt

are cracked or distorted, new ones must be fitted.

21 Withdraw the sleeves from the needle bearings in the upper engine mountings, noting how they fit. Clean the sleeves and bearings with a suitable solvent to remove all traces of dirt and grease. Remove any corrosion from the sleeves with steel wool and dry the needle roller bearings with compressed air, if available.

22 Inspect the bearing needles for pitting **(see illustration 10.7)**.

23 Apply clean oil to the sleeves, then slip them back into their bearings and check that there is not an excessive amount of freeplay between the two. Ensure the sleeves turn smoothly in the bearings without binding or grating. Replace any components as required with new ones.

24 Only remove the needle bearings if new ones are going to be fitted. Note the position of the bearings before commencing work. The bearings should be pressed out of the pivot mountings – refer to *Tools and Workshop Tips* in the Reference section. The new bearings should be pressed or drawn into place and must not be driven into position.

25 Prior to installation, lubricate the bearings and sleeves with multi-purpose grease and install the sleeves.

26 Inspect the bushes and bearings in the pivot mountings. If the bushes are cracked or distorted it is likely the bearings are worn also – follow the procedure in Steps 21 to 24 to check the bearings.

27 Refer to *Tools and Workshop Tips* in the Reference section and use a bearing puller with slide-hammer attachment to remove the old bushes and bearings. Use a drawbolt to install the new components. Renew the bushes and bearings in pairs. When installing the bushes, align the edge of the outer sleeve with the edge of the mounting. Ensure the knurled ends of the bush centre sleeves fit against the frame on assembly.

28 Install the left-hand pivot mounting first. Hold the mounting in position, install the bolt and tighten it finger-tight **(see illustration)**.

29 Temporarily install the left-hand rubber damper bolt and washer without the rubber damper **(see illustration)**.

30 Pivot the mounting around anti-clockwise

10.29 Install the left-hand damper bolt and washer without the damper

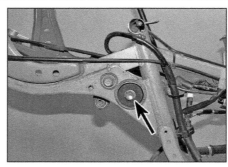

10.30 Pivot the mounting anti-clockwise to set the clearance

10.36 Loosen the rubber damper bolts

10.38a Remove the damper bolts . . .

until a clearance of 2 mm exists between the edge of the damper housing and the washer on the bolt, then tighten the pivot mounting bolt to the torque setting specified at the beginning of this Chapter **(see illustration)**. Remove the rubber damper bolt.

31 Using a length of steel rod or large screwdriver inserted in the hole provided, lever the pivot mounting around clockwise until the thread for the rubber damper bolt is centralised with the damper housing, then install the rubber damper and tighten the bolt to the specified torque setting.

32 Follow the same procedure to install the right-hand pivot mounting, ensuring the two mountings align.

33 Install the upper engine mounting bolt from the left-hand side, install the washer and tighten the nut to the specified torque setting.

34 If applicable, install the parking brake cable (see Chapter 7).

AN400

35 On these machines the pivot mounting is a one-piece assembly located above the upper crankcase mounting lug. If applicable, disconnect the parking brake cable from the rear brake caliper (see Chapter 7) and pass it through the guide on the mounting.

36 Undo the nut on the upper engine mounting bolt and remove the washer (see Chapter 2A). Undo the nut on the pivot mounting bolt. Loosen the left and right-hand rubber damper bolts **(see illustration)**.

37 Make sure the rear wheel is properly

supported, then withdraw the upper engine mounting bolt.

38 Remove the rubber damper bolts and washers, and the rubber dampers **(see illustrations)**.

39 Remove the pivot mounting bolt and manoeuvre out the pivot mounting.

40 Clean the components thoroughly, removing all traces of dirt, corrosion and grease.

41 Inspect the mounting bolts and renew any that are worn or corroded.

42 Inspect the rubber dampers – if they are cracked or distorted, new ones must be fitted.

43 Withdraw the sleeves from the needle bearings in the upper engine mountings, noting how they fit **(see illustration)**. Follow the procedure in Steps 21 to 24 to clean and inspect the bearings. Install new bearings if necessary.

44 Prior to installation, lubricate the bearings and sleeves with multi-purpose grease, then install the sleeves from the inside of the pivot mounting.

45 The pivot mounting bolt is supported by an outer bush and an inner bearing on both ends of the pivot mounting **(see illustration)**. If the bushes are cracked or distorted it is likely the bearings are worn also. Apply clean oil to the pivot mounting bolt, then install it in the mounting and check for freeplay in the bearings.

46 Renew the bushes and bearings as a set. Refer to *Tools and Workshop Tips* in the

Reference section and use a bearing puller with slide-hammer attachment to remove the old bushes and bearings. Note the location of the central bearing spacer.

47 Use a drawbolt to install the new components. Pull the bearings all the way into the mounting against the internal shoulder – don't forget to install the bearing spacer before fitting the second bearing. When installing the bushes, align the edge of the outer sleeve with the edge of the mounting. Ensure the knurled ends of the bush centre sleeves fit against the frame on assembly **(see illustration 10.45)**.

48 Position the pivot mounting in the frame and tighten the pivot mounting bolt finger-tight **(see illustration 10.28)**.

49 Temporarily install the rubber damper bolts and washers without the rubber dampers **(see illustration 10.29)**.

50 On AN400X to K6 models, pivot the mounting backwards until a clearance of 2 mm exists between the edge of the damper housings and the washers on the bolts **(see illustration 10.30)**, then tighten the pivot mounting bolt to the torque setting specified at the beginning of this Chapter. Remove the rubber damper bolts.

51 On AN400K7 models onward, pivot the mounting backwards until a clearance of 14 mm exists between the edge of the damper housings and the washers on the bolts **(see illustration 10.30)**, then tighten the pivot mounting bolt to the torque setting specified at the beginning of this Chapter Remove the rubber damper bolts.

10.38b . . . and the rubber dampers

10.43 Note how the sleeves fit in the bearings

10.45 Pivot mounting bolt outer bush – note knurled centre sleeve

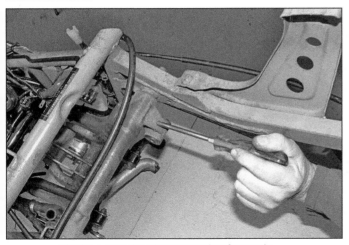

10.52a Lever the pivot mounting forwards . . .

10.52b . . . to centralise the threads for the damper bolts

52 Using a length of steel rod or large screwdriver inserted in the holes provided, lever the pivot mounting forwards until the threads for the rubber damper bolts are centralised with the damper housings **(see illustrations)**, then install the rubber dampers and tighten the bolts to the specified torque setting **(see illustrations 10.38b and a)**.
53 Install the upper engine mounting bolt, install the washer and tighten the nut to the specified torque setting.
54 If applicable, install the parking brake cable (see Chapter 7).

Rear sub-frame

55 On AN400K7 models onward, the right-hand end of the rear wheel axle is supported by a sub-frame. An axle bearing is located inside the sub-frame.
56 Remove the right side belly panel and the seat cowling for access (see Chapter 8).
57 Remove the exhaust system (see Chapter 4B).
58 Apply the rear brake to prevent the rear wheel turning, then undo the rear axle nut **(see illustration)**. **Note:** *The rear axle nut is a self-locking nut – it should be renewed when*

the self-locking section no longer grips the axle.
59 Undo the bolts securing the rear brake hose and parking brake cable clips **(see illustration)**.
60 Displace the rear brake caliper (see Chapter 7).
61 Undo the bolts securing the sub-frame to the crankcase **(see illustration)**.
62 Remove the outer axle spacer and lift the sub-frame off **(see illustrations)**.
63 Remove the inner axle spacer **(see illustration)**.

10.58 Undo the rear axle nut

10.59 Release the rear brake hose and parking brake cable

10.61 Bolts secure the sub-frame to the crankcase

10.62a Remove the outer axle spacer . . .

10.62b . . . and lift the sub-frame off

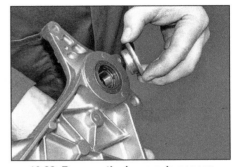

10.63 Remove the inner axle spacer

10.65 Lever out the bearing seals

10.68 Installed location of the smaller axle spacer

64 Clean all old grease off the spacers and bearing seals. Inspect the bearing – check that the inner race turns smoothly, quietly and freely and that the outer race is a tight fit in the sub-frame (see *Tools and Workshop Tips* in the *Reference* section).

65 If the bearing is worn, first lever out the seals on both sides with a flat-bladed screwdriver and discard them as new ones must be fitted **(see illustration)**. Drive or press the bearing out from the inside of the sub-frame with a suitably-sized socket.

66 Drive or press the new bearing in from the outside of the sub-frame with the marked side uppermost. Lubricate the bearing with multi-purpose grease

67 Press in the new seals using a suitable-sized socket. Lubricate the inside edge of the seals with a smear of grease.

68 Prior to installation, press the inner (smaller) axle spacer into the seal **(see illustration)**.

69 Installation is the reverse of removal, noting the following:
• *Install the outer (larger) axle spacer and tighten the axle nut finger-tight.*
• *If necessary, fit a new rear axle nut.*
• *Tighten the sub-frame mounting bolts to the torque setting specified at the beginning of this Chapter.*
• *Install the rear brake caliper, then tighten the axle nut to the specified torque setting.*

Chapter 7
Brakes, wheels and tyres

Degrees of difficulty

Easy, suitable for novice with little experience 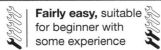	**Fairly easy,** suitable for beginner with some experience 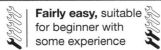	**Fairly difficult,** suitable for competent DIY mechanic 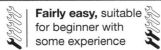	**Difficult,** suitable for experienced DIY mechanic 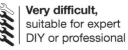	**Very difficult,** suitable for expert DIY or professional

Specifications

Brake system

ABS wheel speed sensor air gap	
Front	0.36 to 1.62 mm
Rear	0.16 to 1.62 mm
Disc thickness (service limit)	
Front.	4.0 mm
Rear	4.5 mm
Disc runout (service limit)	0.3 mm
Fluid type	DOT 4
Pad minimum thickness	1.5 mm

Caliper and master cylinder

AN250 models and AN400X to K6 models

Caliper bore ID	
Front	
Upper	33.960 to 34.010 mm
Lower	22.650 to 22.700 mm
Rear	25.400 to 25.450 mm
Caliper piston OD	
Front	
Upper	33.878 to 33.928 mm
Lower	22.568 to 22.618 mm
Rear	
AN250 models and AN400X to K2 models.	25.335 to 25.368 mm
AN400K3 to K6 models	25.318 to 25.368 mm
Master cylinder bore ID	
Front	11.000 to 11.043 mm
Rear	14.000 to 14.043 mm
Master cylinder piston OD	
Front	10.975 to 10.984 mm
Rear	13.957 to 13.984 mm

Caliper and master cylinder (continued)

AN400K7 model onward

Caliper bore ID
    Front .... 25.400 to 25.450 mm
    Rear .... 27.0 to 27.05 mm
Caliper piston OD
    Front .... 25.318 to 25.368 mm
    Rear .... 26.918 to 26.968 mm
Master cylinder bore ID
    Front
        Non-ABS models .... 12.700 to 12.743 mm
        ABS models .... 14.000 to 14.043 mm
    Rear – all models .... 12.700 to 12.743 mm
Master cylinder piston OD
    Front
        Non-ABS models .... 12.657 to 12.684 mm
        ABS models .... 13.957 to 13.984 mm
    Rear – all models .... 12.657 to 12.684 mm

Wheels

Maximum wheel runout (front and rear)
    Axial (side-to-side) .... 2.0 mm
    Radial (out-of-round) .... 2.0 mm
Maximum front axle runout .... 0.25 mm

Tyres

Tyre pressures and sizes .... see *Pre-ride checks*

Torque settings

Brake caliper bleed valve .... 12 Nm
Brake caliper mounting bolts
    AN250 models and AN400X to K2 models .... 25 Nm
    AN400K3 to K6 models
        Front .... 25 Nm
        Rear .... 28 Nm
    AN400K7 model onward
        Front .... 35 Nm
        Rear .... 23 Nm
Brake master cylinder clamp bolts .... 10 Nm
Brake pad pins .... 18 Nm
Brake delay valve mounting bolts .... 10 Nm
Front brake caliper joining bolts .... 23 Nm
Brake disc mounting bolts .... 23 Nm
Brake hose banjo bolts
    AN250 models and AN400X to K2 models .... 23 Nm
    AN400K3 to K6 models
        Front brake .... 23 nm
        Rear brake .... 28 Nm
    AN400K7 model onward .... 23 nm
Brake pipe gland nut .... 16 Nm
Front axle .... 65 Nm
Front axle pinch bolt .... 23 Nm
Parking brake bracket bolts .... 22 Nm
Rear axle nut
    AN250 models .... 100 Nm
    AN400 models .... 120 Nm
Rear brake lock housing bolts .... 23 Nm
Rear wheel nuts .... 50 Nm

2.1a Unscrew the lower pad pin . . .

2.1b . . . lift out the pad spring . . .

2.1c . . . and draw out the outer . . .

2.1d . . . and inner lower brake pads

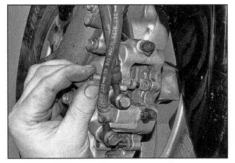

2.2a Unscrew the upper pad pin . . .

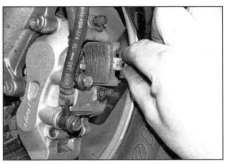

2.2b . . . and remove the two upper pads

1 General information

The front brake on all AN250 models and AN400X to K6 models is a single, hydraulically operated disc brake with an opposed-piston caliper. AN400K7 models onward are fitted with twin front disc brakes with two-piston sliding calipers. The rear brake on all models is a single disc brake with a two-piston sliding caliper.

All AN250 and AN400X to K6 models have a combined braking system whereby the front brake is actuated by the right-hand handlebar lever and both front and rear brakes are actuated by the left-hand lever.

All machines covered in this manual are equipped with a cable-operated parking brake.

From 2009, ABS was available as an optional extra. Scooters with ABS are designated AN400A, e.g. AN400A-K9.

All models covered in this manual are fitted with cast alloy wheels designed for tubeless tyres only.

Caution: Disc brake components rarely require disassembly. Do not disassemble components unless absolutely necessary. If an hydraulic brake hose is loosened, the entire system must be disassembled, drained, cleaned and then properly filled and bled upon reassembly. Do not use solvents on internal brake components.

Solvents will cause the seals to swell and distort. Use only clean brake fluid or denatured alcohol for cleaning. Use care when working with brake fluid as it can injure your eyes and it will damage painted surfaces and plastic parts.

2 Front brake pads

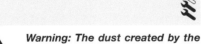

⚠ **Warning: The dust created by the brake may contain asbestos which is harmful to your health. Never blow it out with compressed air and don't inhale any of it. An approved filtering mask should be worn when working on the brakes.**

Removal

Note: *Do not operate the brake levers while the pads are out of the caliper.*

AN250 and AN400X to K6 models

1 Unscrew the lower pan pin, lift out the pad spring and draw out the two lower brake pads, noting how they fit **(see illustrations)**. **Note:** *The lower pads are part of the combined braking system.*

2 Unscrew the upper pad pin and follow the same procedure to remove the two upper pads **(see illustrations)**.

AN400K7 model onward

3 Loosen the brake pad pins, then undo the caliper mounting bolts and slide the caliper off the disc **(see illustrations)**.

4 Unscrew the pad pins and lift out the inner

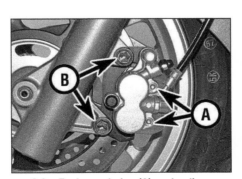

2.3a Brake pad pins (A) and caliper mounting bolts (B)

2.3b Slide the caliper off the disc

2.4a Unscrew the pad pins . . .

2.4b . . . and lift out the inner . . .

2.4c . . . and outer brake pads

2.4d Note location of the pad spring

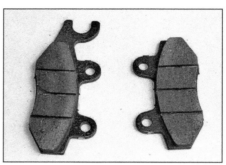

2.5a Check the pads for contamination

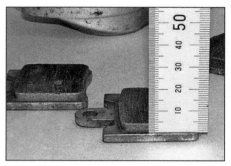

2.5b Measure the thickness of the friction material

and outer brake pads, noting how they fit **(see illustrations)**. Note the location of the pad spring **(see illustration)**. Note the location of the shims clipped to the backs of the brake pads.

Inspection

5 Inspect the surface of each pad for contamination and check that the friction material has not worn to or below the specified minimum thickness **(see illustration)**. The friction material on the original Suzuki pads has wear indicators on the edge next to the backing plate. Some aftermarket pads may not have wear indicators – measure the thickness of the friction material and compare the result with the specification at the beginning of this Chapter **(see illustration)**.

6 If any pad is worn down to, or beyond, the service limit, fouled with oil or grease, or heavily scored or damaged, it must be replaced with a new one. Always renew the pads in pairs.

Note: *It is not possible to degrease the friction material – if the pads are contaminated in any way they must be renewed.*

7 If the pads are in good condition, clean them carefully using a fine wire brush which is completely free of oil and grease to remove all traces of road dirt and corrosion. Any areas of glazing may be removed using emery cloth, bearing in mind the **Warning** above.

8 Check the condition of the brake disc (see Section 4).

9 Remove all traces of corrosion from the pad pins and pad spring. Inspect the pins and spring for signs of wear and renew them if necessary.

Installation

10 If new pads are being fitted, push the pistons as far back into the caliper as possible using hand pressure or a piece of wood for leverage. Due to the increased friction material

thickness of new pads, it may be necessary to remove the master cylinder reservoir cover (see *Pre-ride checks*) and siphon out some brake fluid.

Caution: Never lever the piston against the brake disc to push it back into the caliper as damage to the disc will result.

11 On pads with no backing shims, smear the backs of the pads with copper-based grease, making sure that none gets on the front or sides of the pads. Lubricate the shanks of the pad pins with a smear of copper-based grease.

12 Insert the pads into the caliper so that the friction material faces the disc.

13 On AN250 and AN400X to K6 models, install the pads one pair at a time. Secure the outer pad with the pad pin, then install the pad spring **(see illustration 2.1b)**. Support the inner pad from the back of the caliper and push the pad pin all the way in **(see illustration 2.1a)**. With the pads correctly secured, tighten the pad pins to the torque setting specified at the beginning of this Chapter.

14 On AN400K7 models onward, press the outer pad firmly into place in the caliper bracket **(see illustration)**. Install the inner pad, hooking the upper end over the peg on the caliper bracket **(see illustration 2.4b)**. Tighten the pad pins finger-tight. Ensure there is sufficient space between the pads for the brake disc **(see illustration)**. Install the caliper and tighten the caliper mounting bolts to the torque setting specified at the beginning of this Chapter **(see illustration 2.3a)**. Tighten the pad pins to the specified torque setting.

2.14a Press the outer pad firmly into place

2.14b Leave space between the pads for fitting onto the disc

3.1 Bolt (arrowed) secures the brake hose guide

3.2a Remove the caliper mounting bolts (arrowed) . . .

3.2b . . . and slide the caliper off the disc

15 Operate the brake lever several times to bring the pads into contact with the disc. Check the operation of the brake before riding the scooter.

16 Check the fluid level in the master cylinder reservoir and top-up if necessary (see *Pre-ride checks*).

3 Front brake caliper

⚠ *Warning: If a caliper is in need of an overhaul all old brake fluid should be flushed from the system. Also, the dust created by the brake system may contain asbestos, which is harmful to your health. Never blow it out with compressed air and do not inhale any of it. An approved filtering mask should be worn when working on the brakes. Overhaul of the brake caliper must be done in a spotlessly clean work area to avoid contamination and possible failure of the brake hydraulic system components. Do not, under any circumstances, use petroleum-based solvents to clean brake parts. Use clean DOT 4 brake fluid, dedicated brake cleaner or denatured alcohol only. To prevent damage from spilled brake fluid, always cover paintwork when working on the braking system.*

Special tool: *A source of compressed air is required to ease the pistons out from the brake caliper (see Step 9).*

Note: *If the caliper is being overhauled (usually due to sticking pistons or fluid leaks) read through the entire procedure first and make sure that you have obtained all the new parts required, including some new DOT 4 brake fluid.*

AN250 and AN400X to K6 models

Removal

1 Undo the bolt securing the brake hose guide to the left-hand fork **(see illustration)**.

2 If the caliper assembly is just being displaced from the front forks, unscrew the

mounting bolts and slide it off the disc **(see illustrations)**. Secure the caliper to the scooter with a cable-tie to avoid straining the brake hose. **Note:** *Do not operate the brake levers while the caliper is off the disc.*

3 If the caliper is being overhauled, first remove the brake pads (see Section 2), then, working from the right-hand side of the machine, loosen and lightly retighten the bolts which join the caliper halves **(see illustration 3.7a)**.

4 Unscrew the brake hose banjo bolts and detach the banjo unions, noting their alignment with the caliper **(see illustration)**. Wrap a small plastic bag around each banjo union and secure the hoses in an upright position to minimise fluid loss. Discard the sealing washers as new ones must be fitted on

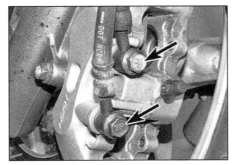

3.4 Unscrew the brake hose banjo bolts

3.7b . . . and separate the caliper halves

reassembly. **Note:** *Do not operate the brake levers while the hoses are disconnected.*

5 Undo the caliper mounting bolts and slide the caliper off the disc **(see illustrations 3.2a and b)**.

Overhaul

6 Clean the exterior of the caliper with denatured alcohol or brake system cleaner.

7 Unscrew the joining bolts and separate the caliper halves **(see illustrations)**.

8 Note the location of the O-rings and discard them as new ones must be fitted **(see illustration)**.

9 Displace the pistons from the caliper body one at a time by directing compressed air into the internal brake fluid galleries. When working on the left-hand caliper half, temporarily install the banjo bolts to prevent the air escaping

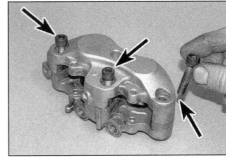

3.7a Unscrew the caliper joining bolts . . .

3.8 Location of caliper O-rings

3.9a Install banjo bolts to prevent air escaping

3.9b Displacing the pistons with compressed air

3.11 Remove the seals carefully to avoid damage

(see illustration). Use only low pressure to ease the pistons out – if the air pressure is too high and the pistons are forced out, the caliper and/or pistons may be damaged. Always place a wad of rag over the piston to act as a cushion **(see illustration)**. Mark each piston head and caliper bore with a felt marker to ensure that the pistons can be matched to their original bores on reassembly. **Note:** *The lower (smaller diameter) pistons are part of the combined braking system.*

10 Do not try to remove a piston by levering it out or by using pliers or other grips. If the piston has completely seized you will have to replace the caliper with a new one.

11 Remove the (outer) dust seal and the (inner) piston seal from each piston bore using a soft wooden or plastic tool to avoid scratching the bore **(see illustration)**. Discard the seals as new ones must be fitted.

12 Clean the pistons and bores with fresh brake fluid and blow compressed air through the fluid galleries in the caliper to ensure they are clear (make sure the air is filtered and unlubricated).

Caution: Do not, under any circumstances, use a petroleum-based solvent to clean brake parts.

13 Inspect each caliper bore and piston for signs of corrosion, nicks and burrs and loss of plating. If surface defects are present, the pistons and/or the caliper assembly must be renewed.

14 If the necessary measuring equipment is available, compare the dimensions of the caliper bores and pistons to those specified at the beginning of this Chapter, and obtain new pistons or a new caliper as necessary.

15 If the caliper is in poor condition the master cylinder should be checked (see Section 5).

16 Prior to installing the pistons and seals, lay the components out to ensure they are fitted correctly – the upper pistons are a larger diameter than the lower pistons **(see illustration)**.

17 Lubricate the new piston seals with fresh brake fluid and install them in their grooves in the caliper bores **(see illustration)**.

18 Follow the same procedure to install the new dust seals **(see illustration)**.

19 Lubricate the pistons with clean brake fluid and install them closed-end first into the caliper bores. Using your thumbs, push the pistons all the way in, making sure they enter the bores squarely and taking care not to displace the seals **(see illustration)**.

20 Fit new O-rings into one half of the caliper body, then join the halves together **(see illustrations 3.8 and 3.7b)**.

21 Clean the threads of the joining bolts and apply a suitable non-permanent thread-locking compound. Tighten the bolts to the torque setting specified at the beginning of this Chapter.

Installation

22 If the caliper has not been overhauled, ease the brake pads apart so that they will fit either side of the disc, then install the caliper assembly **(see illustrations 3.2b and a)**. Tighten the caliper mounting bolts to the torque setting specified at the beginning of this Chapter. Operate the brake lever several times to bring the pads into contact with the disc.

23 If the caliper has been overhauled, install the caliper and tighten the mounting bolts to the specified torque setting. Connect the brake hoses to the caliper using new sealing washers on both sides of the unions **(see illustrations 3.4)**. Tighten the banjo bolts to the specified torque setting. Install the brake pads (see Section 2).

24 Top up the master cylinder reservoir with DOT 4 brake fluid and bleed the system as described in Section 11. Check that there are no fluid leaks.

25 Secure the brake hose guide to the left-hand fork and tighten the bolt securely **(see illustration 3.1)**.

26 Check the operation of the brake before riding the scooter.

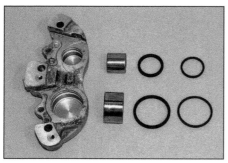

3.16 Lay out the caliper components, noting their sizes

3.17 Install the piston seals in the inner grooves

3.18 Install the dust seals in the outer grooves

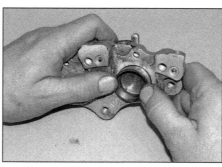

3.19 Install the pistons closed end first

AN400K7 model onward

Removal

27 If the caliper assembly is just being displaced from the front forks, unscrew the mounting bolts and slide it off the disc **(see illustrations 2.3a and b)**. Secure the caliper to the scooter with a cable-tie to avoid straining the brake hose. **Note:** *Do not operate the front brake lever while the caliper is off the disc.*

28 If the caliper is being overhauled, first unscrew the brake hose banjo bolt and detach the banjo union, noting its alignment with the caliper **(see illustration)**. Wrap a small plastic bag around the banjo union and secure the hose in an upright position to minimise fluid loss. Discard the sealing washers as new ones must be fitted on reassembly. **Note:** *Do not operate the front brake lever while the hose is disconnected.*

29 Following the procedure in Section 2, remove the caliper, then remove the brake pads.

Overhaul

30 Follow the procedure in Section 7 to overhaul the caliper.

Installation

31 Installation is the reverse of removal, noting the following:
* *Tighten the caliper mounting bolts and the pad pins to the torque settings specified at the beginning of this Chapter.*

4 Front brake disc

Inspection

1 Inspect the surface of the disc for score marks and other damage **(see illustration)**. Light scratches are normal after use and won't affect brake operation, but deep grooves and heavy score marks will reduce braking efficiency and accelerate pad wear. If a disc is badly grooved it must be machined or renewed.

2 The disc must not be allowed to wear or be machined too thin – a minimum thickness specification is stamped into the surface of the disc **(see illustration)**. Measure the thickness

3.28 Unscrew the brake hose banjo bolt

of the disc in the brake pad contact area with a micrometer and compare the result with the specification at the beginning of this Chapter **(see illustration)**. Fit a new disc if necessary. If no measuring equipment is available, check for a ridge between the rim of the disc and the pad contact area and renew the disc as necessary.

3 If the disc is running out-of-true, the lever will pulse when the brake is applied. To check disc runout, support the scooter on its centrestand with the front wheel raised off the ground. Attach a dial gauge to the front suspension with the gauge pointer touching the surface of the disc close to the outer edge (but clear of any drilled holes). Rotate the wheel slowly and watch the gauge needle, comparing the reading with the limit listed in the Specifications at the beginning of this Chapter. If the runout is greater than the service limit, check the wheel bearings for play (see Section 20). If the bearings are worn, renew them, then repeat this check. If the disc runout is still excessive, the disc will have to be renewed.

Removal

4 Remove the front wheel (see Section 18).
Caution: Do not lay the wheel down and allow it to rest on the disc – the disc could become warped.
5 Mark the relationship of the disc to the wheel, so it can be installed in the same position if required. On AN400K7 models onward, mark the left and right-hand discs accordingly.

4.1 Examine the surface of the disc for damage

6 Unscrew the disc retaining bolts, loosening them evenly, a little at a time to avoid distorting the disc, then remove the disc **(see illustration)**.

Installation

Note: *Fit new brake pads if fitting a new disc.*
7 Ensure the mating surface of the wheel is clean, then install the disc – if applicable, align the previously made reference marks.
8 Clean the threads of the retaining bolts and apply a suitable non-permanent thread-locking compound, then install the bolts and tighten them evenly and progressively to the torque setting specified at the beginning of this Chapter.
9 Clean the disc using acetone or brake system cleaner. If a new disc has been installed, remove any protective coating from its working surfaces.
10 Install the wheel (see Section 18).
11 Operate the front brake lever several times to bring the brake pads into contact with the disc. Check the operation of the brake before riding the scooter.

5 Front and rear brake master cylinders

⚠️ *Warning: If the brake master cylinder is in need of an overhaul all old brake fluid should be flushed from the system. Overhaul must be done in a spotlessly clean work area to avoid contamination and possible failure of*

4.2a Minimum thickness markings

4.2b Measuring thickness of the brake disc

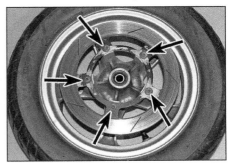

4.6 Loosen the disc retaining bolts evenly

5.4a Remove the lever cover . . .

5.4b . . . and disconnect the brake light switch wiring

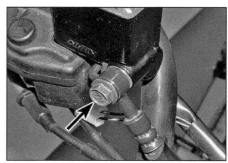

5.6a Unscrew the brake hose banjo bolt . . .

5.6b . . . and detach the banjo union

5.7 Unscrew the master cylinder clamp bolts

5.9a Undo the locknut . . .

the brake hydraulic system components. Do not, under any circumstances, use petroleum-based solvents to clean brake parts; use clean DOT 4 brake fluid, dedicated brake cleaner or denatured alcohol only. To prevent damage from spilled brake fluid, always cover paintwork when working on the braking system.

Removal

Note 1: If the master cylinder is being overhauled (usually due to sticking or poor action, or fluid leaks) read through the entire procedure first and make sure that you have obtained all the new parts required, including some new DOT 4 brake fluid.

Note 2: The procedure for removal, overhaul and installation of the front (right-hand) and rear (left-hand) master cylinders is the same. The left-hand master cylinder part of the combined braking system on AN250 and AN400X to K6 models.

1 If the master cylinder is just being displaced from the handlebars, follow the procedure in Chapter 6, Section 4. Note that it is not necessary to remove the bar-ends if only the master cylinder is being removed.

2 If the master cylinder is being completely removed or overhauled, first remove the handlebar covers (see Chapter 8).

3 Remove the mirror (see Chapter 8).

4 Remove the brake lever cover and disconnect the wiring from the brake light switch **(see illustrations)**.

5 Remove the master cylinder cover, diaphragm plate and diaphragm (see *Pre-ride checks*). Siphon out the brake fluid, then temporarily install the cover.

6 Unscrew the brake hose banjo bolt and detach the banjo union, noting its alignment

with the master cylinder **(see illustrations)**. Wrap a small plastic bag around the banjo union and secure the hose in an upright position to minimise fluid loss. Discard the sealing washers as new ones must be fitted on reassembly.

7 Undo the master cylinder clamp bolts and remove the back of the clamp **(see illustration)**. Lift the master cylinder off the handlebar.

8 Remove the reservoir cover, diaphragm plate and diaphragm and wipe any remaining brake fluid out of the reservoir with a clean rag.

9 Undo the brake lever pivot bolt locknut, then unscrew the pivot bolt and remove the lever **(see illustrations)**.

10 If required, undo the screw securing the brake light switch to the bottom of the master cylinder and remove the switch **(see illustration)**.

5.9b . . . unscrew the pivot bolt . . .

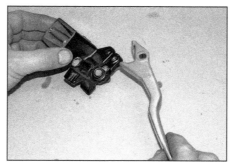

5.9c . . . and remove the lever

5.10 Location of the brake light switch

5.11a Note location of the boot . . .

5.11b . . . then pull it off

5.12a Note location of the circlip

5.12b Remove the circlip . . .

5.12c . . . and the plain washer

5.13 Draw out the piston assembly and spring

Overhaul

11 Note how the rubber boot locates on the master cylinder piston, then remove the boot **(see illustrations)**.

12 Note the location of the circlip securing the master cylinder piston **(see illustration)**. Depress the piston and use circlip pliers to remove the circlip, then remove the plain washer **(see illustrations)**.

13 Draw out the piston assembly and the spring, noting how they fit **(see illustration)**. If the piston is difficult to remove, apply low pressure compressed air to the brake fluid outlet. Lay the parts out in the

proper order to avoid confusion during reassembly.

14 Clean the inside of the master cylinder and reservoir with fresh brake fluid. If compressed air is available, blow it through the fluid galleries to ensure they are clear (make sure the air is filtered and unlubricated).

Caution: Do not, under any circumstances, use a petroleum-based solvent to clean brake parts.

15 Check the master cylinder bore for corrosion, scratches, nicks and score marks. If the necessary measuring equipment is available, compare the dimensions of the piston and bore to

those specified at the beginning of this Chapter. If damage or wear is evident, the master cylinder must be replaced with a new one. If the master cylinder is in poor condition the caliper should be checked (see Sections 3 and 7).

16 The spring, piston and its seals, dust boot, circlip, and washer are all included in the master cylinder rebuild kit **(see illustration)**. Use all of the new parts, regardless of the apparent condition of the old ones.

17 Lubricate the master cylinder bore and the piston assembly with brake fluid, then fit the narrow end of the spring onto the piston **(see illustration)**.

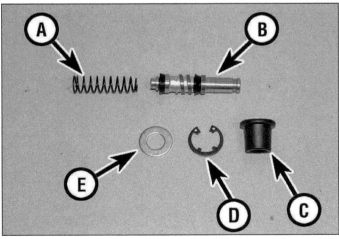

5.16 Master cylinder rebuild kit – spring (A), piston and seals (B), dust boot (C), circlip (D) and washer (E)

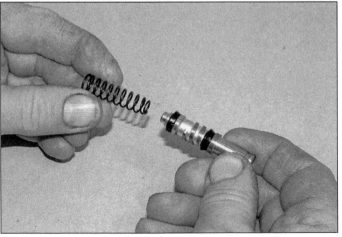

5.17 Fit the narrow end of the spring onto the piston

18 Carefully slide the assembly into the master cylinder **(see illustration 5.13)**.

19 Push the piston all the way in, compressing the spring, then fit the washer and secure It with the new circlip, making sure it locates properly in its groove **(see illustrations 5.12c, b and a)**.

20 Smear the inside of the rubber boot with silicone grease, fit it over the end of the piston and press the wide rim into the master cylinder against the circlip using a suitably-sized socket. The outer rim of the boot should locate in the groove in the outer end of the piston **(see illustration 5.11a)**.

21 Inspect the fluid reservoir diaphragm and fit a new one if it is damaged or deteriorated.

Installation

22 If the master cylinder has just been displaced from the handlebars, follow the procedure in Steps 25 and 27.

23 If the master cylinder has been completely removed or overhauled, fit the brake light switch onto the bottom of the master cylinder and tighten the screw securely **(see illustration 5.10)**.

24 Install the brake lever and secure it with the pivot bolt, then tighten the pivot bolt locknut securely **(see illustrations 5.9c, b and a)**.

25 Align the master cylinder clamp joint with the punch mark on the underside of the handlebar, then fit the back of the clamp with its UP mark facing up **(see illustration 5.7)**. Tighten the upper clamp bolt to the torque setting specified at the beginning of this Chapter, followed by the lower bolt so that any gap is at the bottom of the clamp joint.

26 Connect the brake hose to the master cylinder, using new sealing washers on both sides of the banjo union **(see illustration 5.6b and a)**. Align the hose as noted on removal, then tighten the banjo bolt to the specified torque setting.

27 Connect the brake light switch wiring connectors **(see illustration 5.4b)**.

28 Fill the fluid reservoir with new DOT 4 brake fluid (see *Pre-ride checks*) and bleed the system as described in Section 11. Check that there are no fluid leaks.

29 Install the brake lever cover.

30 Install the mirror and the handlebar covers (see Chapter 8).

31 Check the operation of the brake before riding the scooter.

6 Rear brake pads

⚠️ *Warning: The dust created by the brake system is harmful to your health. Never blow it out with compressed air and don't inhale any of it. An approved filtering mask should be worn when working on the brakes.*
Note: *Do not operate the rear brake lever while the pads are out of the caliper.*

Removal

AN250 and AN400X to K6 models

1 To access the rear brake caliper, first remove the exhaust system (see Chapter 4A or 4B as applicable), then remove the rear wheel (see Section 19).

2 Loosen the brake pad pins, then undo the caliper mounting bolts and slide the caliper off the disc **(see illustrations)**.

3 Unscrew the pad pins and lift out the inner and outer brake pads, noting how they fit **(see illustrations)**. Note the location of the pad spring **(see illustration)**.

AN400K7 model onwards

4 To access the rear brake caliper, first remove the exhaust system (see Chapter 4B).

5 Loosen the brake pad pins, then undo the

6.2a Loosen the brake pad pins . . .

6.2b . . . then undo the caliper mounting bolts . . .

6.2c . . . and slide the caliper off the disc

6.3a Unscrew the pad pins . . .

6.3b . . . and lift out the inner . . .

6.3c . . . and outer brake pads

6.3d Note location of the pad spring

6.5a Loosen the brake pad pins . . .

6.5b . . . then undo the caliper mounting bolts . . .

6.5c . . . and slide the caliper off the disc

caliper mounting bolts and slide the caliper off the disc **(see illustrations)**.

6 Unscrew the pad pins and lift out the inner and outer brake pads, noting how they fit **(see illustrations)**. Note the location of the pad spring **(see illustration)**. Note the location of the shims clipped to the backs of the brake pads **(see illustration)**.

Inspection

7 Follow the procedure in Chapter 2 to examine the pads, brake disc, pad pins and spring.

8 On AN400K7 models onward, note the location of the shims and packing pieces clipped to the backs of the brake pads **(see illustration 6.6d)**.

Installation

9 If new pads are being fitted, retract the

pistons as far back into the caliper as possible. The front piston can be pushed back using hand pressure or a piece of wood for leverage. The rear piston is linked to the parking brake mechanism – using a large, flat-bladed screwdriver, turn it clockwise to wind it into the caliper while holding the front piston in place with a block of wood **(see illustration)**. Due to the increased friction material thickness of new pads, it may be necessary to remove the master cylinder reservoir cover (see *Pre-ride checks*) and siphon out some fluid.

Caution: Never lever the piston against the brake disc to push it back into the caliper as damage to the disc will result.

10 On pads with no backing shims, smear the backs of the pads with copper-based grease, making sure that none gets on the front or sides of the pads. Lubricate the shanks of

the pad pins with a smear of copper-based grease.

11 Insert the pads into the caliper so that the friction material faces the disc – align the peg on the back of the outer pad with the recess in the rear piston **(see illustration)**.

12 Press the outer pad firmly into place in the caliper bracket **(see illustration 6.3c)**. Install the inner pad, press it down onto the pad spring and secure both pads with the pad pins **(see illustrations 6.3b and a)**.

13 Ensure there is sufficient space between the pads for the brake disc, install the caliper and tighten the caliper mounting bolts to the torque setting specified at the beginning of this Chapter. Tighten the pad pins to the specified torque setting.

14 Install the remaining components in the reverse order of removal.

6.6a Unscrew the pad pins . . .

6.6b . . . and lift out the brake pads

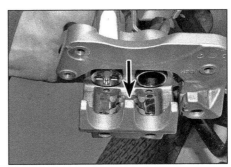

6.6c Note location of the pad spring

6.6d Location of shim on back of brake pad

6.9 Turn rear piston (arrowed) with a large screwdriver

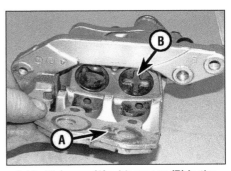

6.11 Align peg (A) with recess (B) in the rear piston

7.3 Unscrew the brake hose banjo bolt

7.5a Unhook the return spring

7.5b Disconnect the cable from the cable stop . . .

7 Rear brake caliper

Warning: If a caliper is in need of an overhaul all old brake fluid should be flushed from the system. Also, the dust created by the brake system may contain asbestos, which is harmful to your health. Never blow it out with compressed air and do not inhale any of it. An approved filtering mask should be worn when working on the brakes. Overhaul of the brake caliper must be done in a spotlessly clean work area to avoid contamination and possible failure of the brake hydraulic system components. Do not, under any circumstances, use petroleum-based solvents to clean brake parts. Use clean DOT 4 brake fluid, dedicated brake cleaner or denatured alcohol only. To prevent damage from spilled brake fluid, always cover paintwork when working on the braking system.

Special tool: *A source of compressed air is required to ease the pistons out from the brake caliper (see Step 17).*

Note: *If the caliper is being overhauled (usually due to sticking pistons or fluid leaks) read through the entire procedure first and make sure that you have obtained all the new parts required, including some new DOT 4 brake fluid.*

Removal

AN250 and AN400X to K6 models

1 First remove the exhaust system (see Chapter 4A or 4B as applicable), then remove the rear wheel (see Section 19).

2 If the caliper assembly is just being displaced, undo the bolt securing the brake hose clip to the top of the drive belt casing, then undo the caliper mounting bolts and slide the caliper off the disc **(see illustrations 6.2b and c)**. Secure the caliper to the scooter with a cable-tie to avoid straining the brake hose. **Note:** *Do not operate the rear brake lever while the caliper is off the disc.*

3 If the caliper is being completely removed or overhauled, unscrew the brake hose banjo bolt and detach the banjo union, noting its alignment with the caliper **(see illustration)**. Wrap a small plastic bag around the banjo union and secure the hose in an upright position to minimise fluid loss. Discard the sealing washers, as new ones must be fitted on reassembly. **Note:** *Do not operate the rear brake lever while the hose is disconnected.*

4 Loosen the brake pad pins, then undo the caliper mounting bolts and slide the caliper off the disc **(see illustrations 6.2a, b and c)**.

5 Unhook the parking brake cable return spring and disconnect the cable from the cable stop and brake arm **(see illustrations)**.

6 Remove the brake pads (see Section 6).

AN400K7 model onward

7 To access to the rear brake caliper, first remove the exhaust system (see Chapter 4B).

8 If the caliper assembly is just being displaced, undo the bolts securing the rear brake hose and parking brake cable clips to the rear sub-frame, then undo the caliper mounting bolts and slide the caliper off the disc **(see illustrations 6.5b and c)**. Secure the caliper to the scooter with a cable-tie to avoid straining the brake hose. **Note:** *Do not operate the rear brake lever while the caliper is off the disc.*

9 If the caliper is being completely removed or overhauled, unscrew the brake hose banjo bolt and detach the banjo union, noting its alignment with the caliper **(see illustration)**. Wrap a small plastic bag around the banjo union and secure the hose in an upright position to minimise fluid loss. Discard the sealing washers, as new ones must be fitted on reassembly. **Note:** *Do not operate the rear brake lever while the hose is disconnected.*

10 Unhook the parking brake cable return spring and disconnect the cable from the cable stop and brake arm **(see illustration)**.

11 Loosen the brake pad pins, then undo the caliper mounting bolts and slide the caliper off the disc **(see illustrations 6.5a, b and c)**.

12 Remove the brake pads (see Section 6).

7.5c . . . and from the brake arm

7.9 Unscrew the brake hose banjo bolt

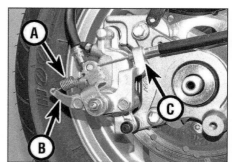

7.10 Parking brake return spring (A), brake arm (B) and cable stop (C)

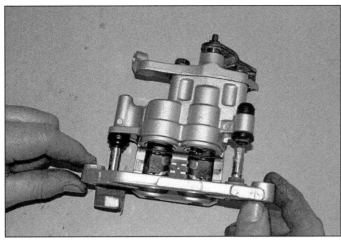

7.13 Separate the caliper and caliper bracket

7.14 Remove the pad spring

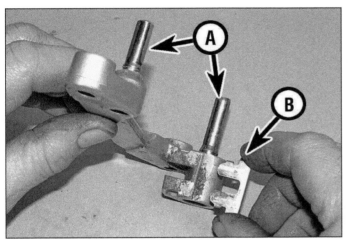

7.15 Slider pins (A) and location of the pad plate (B)

7.16 Check the caliper boots

Overhaul

13 Slide the caliper off the bracket **(see illustration)**.

14 Remove the pad spring, noting how it fits **(see illustration)**. Clean the exterior of the caliper and bracket with denatured alcohol or brake system cleaner. Have some clean rag ready to catch any spilled brake fluid.

15 Clean off all traces of corrosion and hardened grease from the slider pins and make sure they are a tight fit on the bracket **(see illustration)**. Note the location of the pad plate on the caliper bracket.

16 Examine the boots in the caliper and renew them if they are damaged, deformed or deteriorated **(see illustration)**.

17 Place a wad of rag over the front piston to act as a cushion and displace the piston from the caliper body by directing compressed air into the fluid inlet **(see illustration)**. Use only low pressure to ease the piston out – if the air pressure is too high and the piston is

forced out, the caliper and/or piston may be damaged. Do not try to remove the piston by levering it out or by using pliers or other grips. If the piston has completely seized you will have to replace the caliper with a new one.

18 The rear piston is linked to the parking

brake mechanism – using a large, flat-bladed screwdriver, turn it anti-clockwise to wind it out from the caliper **(see illustration)**.

19 Remove the (outer) dust seal and the (inner) piston seal from each piston bore using a soft wooden or plastic tool to avoid

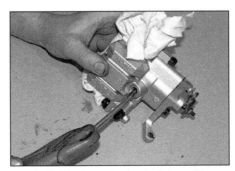

7.17 Displace the front piston with compressed air

7.18 Turn the rear piston anti-clockwise to remove it

7.19 Remove the seals carefully to avoid damage

7.20a Remove the parking brake bracket

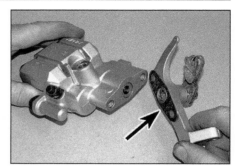

7.20b Note the location of the gasket

scratching the bore (see illustration). Discard the seals as new ones must be fitted.

20 Undo the bolts securing the parking brake bracket assembly and remove the bracket (see illustration). Note the location of the gasket and discard it as a new one must be fitted (see illustration).

21 Unscrew the brake arm from the bracket and discard the O-ring as a new one must be fitted (see illustrations). If required, the brake arm and shaft can be separated after undoing the retaining nut – note the register marks on the arm and shaft and ensure they are correctly aligned on installation.

22 Clean the pistons and bores with fresh brake fluid and blow compressed air through the fluid galleries in the caliper to ensure they are clear (make sure the air is filtered and unlubricated).

Caution: Do not, under any circumstances,

use a petroleum-based solvent to clean brake parts.

23 Inspect each caliper bore and piston for signs of corrosion, nicks and burrs and loss of plating. If surface defects are present, the pistons and/or the caliper assembly must be renewed.

24 If the necessary measuring equipment is available, compare the dimensions of the caliper bores and pistons to those specified at the beginning of this Chapter, and obtain new pistons or a new caliper as necessary.

25 If the caliper is in poor condition the master cylinder should be checked (see Section 5).

26 Fit a new O-ring into the parking brake bracket (see illustration 7.21b) and lubricate the shaft and thread of the brake arm with silicone grease. To install the brake arm, align the register mark on the arm between the two lines on the bracket, then screw the shaft in

(see illustration). On all AN250 models and AN400X to K6 models, screw the shaft in anti-clockwise. On AN400K7 models onward, screw the shaft in clockwise.

27 Fit a new gasket onto the bracket. Clean the threads of the mounting bolts and apply a suitable non-permanent thread-locking compound, then fit the bracket onto the caliper and tighten the mounting bolts to the torque setting specified at the beginning of this Chapter (see illustrations 7.20b and a).

28 Lubricate the new piston seals with fresh brake fluid and install them in their grooves in the caliper bores (see illustration).

29 Follow the same procedure to install the new dust seals.

30 Lubricate the pistons with clean brake fluid. Install the rear piston by screwing it into the caliper (see illustration 7.18). Using your thumbs, push the front piston all the way in, closed-end first (see illustration). Take care not to displace the seals.

31 Install the pad spring, then apply a smear of silicone-based grease to the slider pins and slide the caliper onto the bracket (see illustrations 7.14 and 7.13).

Installation

32 If the caliper has not been overhauled, ease the brake pads apart so that they will fit either side of the disc, then install the caliper assembly (see illustration 6.2c). Tighten the caliper mounting bolts to the torque setting specified at the beginning of this Chapter. Operate the rear brake lever several times to bring the pads into contact with the disc.

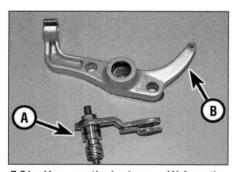

7.21a Unscrew the brake arm (A) from the bracket (B)

7.21b Note location of the O-ring

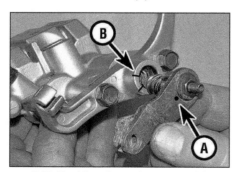

7.26 Position the register mark (A) between the two lines (B)

7.28 Install the piston seals in the lower grooves

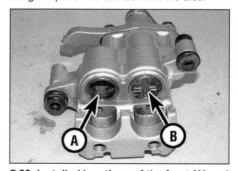

7.30 Installed locations of the front (A) and rear (B) caliper pistons

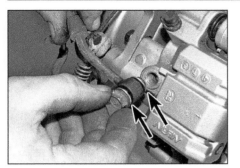

7.35 Fit new sealing washers on both sides of the banjo union

8.2a Examine the surface of the disc for damage

8.2b Minimum thickness markings

33 If the caliper has been overhauled, install the brake pads (see Section 6) then install the caliper and tighten the mounting bolts to the specified torque setting. Tighten the pad pins to the specified torque setting.

34 Install the parking brake cable and the return spring **(see illustration 7.10)**.

35 Connect the brake hose to the caliper using a new sealing washer on both sides of the union **(see illustration)**. Tighten the banjo bolt to the specified torque setting.

36 On AN250 and AN400X to K6 models, secure the brake hose with its clip to the top of the drive belt casing.

37 On AN400K7 models onward, secure the rear brake hose and parking brake cable to the rear sub-frame with the clips.

38 Top up the master cylinder reservoir with DOT 4 brake fluid and bleed the system as described in Section 11. Check that there are no fluid leaks.

39 Check the operation of the parking brake and adjust if necessary (see Chapter 1, Section 11).

40 Install the remaining components in the reverse order of removal.

41 Check the operation of the brake before riding the scooter.

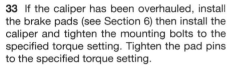

8 Rear brake disc

Inspection

1 To assess the condition of the rear brake

disc it is first necessary to remove the exhaust system (see Chapter 4A or 4B), then remove the rear wheel (see Section 19).

2 Refer to Section 4 of this Chapter to check the disc **(see illustrations)**. To check disc runout on AN250 and AN400X to K6 models, attach the dial gauge to the transmission casing. In AN400K7 models onward, attach the dial gauge to the rear sub-frame.

Removal

AN250 and AN400X to K2 models

3 First remove the exhaust system (see Chapter 4A), then remove the rear wheel (see Section 19).

4 Draw off the disc assembly. If required, undo the bolts securing the disc to the carrier – if you are not replacing the disc with a new one, mark the relationship of the disc to the carrier so it can be installed in the same position. Loosen the bolts evenly and a little at a time in a criss-cross pattern to avoid distorting the disc, then remove the disc. Note which way round it is fitted.

5 Inspect the splines in the centre of the carrier and the splines on the rear axle and renew any components that are worn. The carrier should be a firm sliding fit on the shaft with no freeplay.

6 Prior to installation, clean the threads of the disc mounting bolts and apply a non-permanent thread-locking compound. Tighten the bolts to the torque setting specified at the beginning of this Chapter.

AN400K3 to K6 models

7 First remove the exhaust system (see Chapter 4B), then remove the rear wheel (see Section 19).

8 Apply the rear brake and loosen the rear axle nut, then displace the rear brake caliper assembly (see Section 7).

9 Remove the axle nut and washer **(see illustration)**.

10 Draw off the disc assembly **(see illustration)**. The disc and carrier are a one-piece assembly. If required, draw off the hub **(see illustration)**.

11 Inspect the splines in the centre of the hub and the splines on the axle and renew any components that are worn **(see illustration 8.10b)**. The hub should be a firm sliding fit on the axle with no freeplay.

AN400K7 models onward

12 First remove the exhaust system (see Chapter 4B), then remove the rear wheel (see Section 19).

Caution: Don't lay the wheel down and allow it to rest on the disc – it could become warped. Set the wheel on wood blocks so the wheel rim supports the weight of the wheel.

13 If you are not replacing the disc with a new one, mark the relationship of the disc to the wheel so it can be installed in the same position. Unscrew the disc retaining bolts, loosening them evenly and a little at a time in a criss-cross pattern to avoid

8.9 Remove the axle nut and washer

8.10a Draw off the disc and disc carrier

8.10b Note location of the rear wheel hub

8.13 Loosen the disc retaining bolts evenly

distorting the disc, then remove the disc **(see illustration)**.

14 Before installing the disc, make sure there is no dirt or corrosion where it seats on the wheel. If the disc does not sit flat when it is bolted down, it will appear to be warped when checked or when the rear brake is used.

15 Install the disc on the wheel with its marked side facing out, aligning the previously applied matchmarks (if you're reinstalling the original disc).

16 Clean the threads of the disc mounting bolts, then apply a suitable non-permanent thread-locking compound. Install the bolts and tighten them evenly and a little at a time in a criss-cross pattern to the torque setting specified at the beginning of this Chapter.

Installation

17 Installation is the reverse of removal, noting the following:

• *Clean the disc using acetone or brake system cleaner.*
• *If a new disc has been installed, remove any protective coating from its working surfaces.*
• *Always fit new brake pads with a new disc.*
• *Tighten the axle nut to the specified torque setting.*

9 Combined braking system delay valve

General description

1 All AN250 models and AN400X to K6 models have a combined braking system whereby the lower pair of brake pads in the front brake caliper and the pads in the rear brake caliper are actuated by the left-hand handlebar lever via a delay valve.

2 The purpose of the delay valve is to distribute hydraulic pressure between the front and rear brake calipers according to the amount of force applied to the brake lever.

3 During light braking the delay valve remains static; hydraulic pressure is uninterrupted and both brakes are applied equally.

4 As more force is applied to the lever, the delay valve descends, closing the feed to the front caliper and directing all hydraulic pressure to the rear caliper.

5 With full force applied to the lever, the delay valve descends further, opening the feed to the front caliper and directing hydraulic pressure to both brakes in such a way that balanced front/rear braking is achieved.

6 If braking performance is not as described, first examine the front (lower) and rear brake pads for uneven wear (see Sections 2 and 6). Next, ensure the brake pistons are not sticking in the caliper bores and that the left-hand brake master cylinder is working correctly (see Sections 3, 7 and 5).

7 If all the components are in good working condition it is likely the delay valve is faulty – have the brake system tested by a Suzuki dealer.

Removal and installation

8 The delay valve is located on the steering head at the front of the frame **(see illustration)**. Remove the headlight panel for access (see Chapter 8). If required, cover or remove the front mudguard to avoid damage from spilled brake fluid.

9 Release the speedometer wiring from the clip secured by the delay valve mounting bolt.

10 Unscrew the brake hose banjo bolts and detach the banjo unions, noting their alignment with the valve body **(see illustration)**. Wrap a small plastic bag around each banjo union and secure the hoses in an upright position to minimise fluid loss. Discard the sealing washers as new ones must be fitted on reassembly. **Note:** *Do not operate the rear brake lever while the hose is disconnected.*

11 Unscrew the brake pipe gland nut and disconnect the pipe from the valve body **(see illustration 9.10)**. Cover the open end of the pipe to minimise fluid loss.

12 Undo the delay valve mounting bolts and remove the valve.

13 Installation is the reverse of removal, noting the following:

• *Tighten the mounting bolts to the torque setting specified at the beginning of this Chapter.*
• *Fit new sealing washers to both sides of the hose unions.*
• *Tighten the banjo bolts to the specified torque setting.*
• *Tighten the gland nut to the specified torque setting.*

10 Brake hoses, pipes and unions

Inspection

1 Brake hose and pipe condition should be checked regularly and the hoses renewed at the specified interval (see Chapter 1). Remove any body panels as necessary to inspect the full length of the brake hoses.

2 Inspect the hoses carefully in the area of the steering head – if a hose is not correctly routed or secured it can become trapped and

9.8 Location of the braking system delay valve

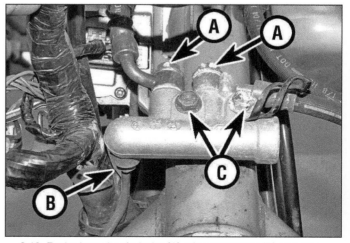

9.10 Brake hose banjo bolts (A), pipe gland nut (B) and valve mounting bolts (C)

will wear between the frame and an adjacent body panel.

3 Twist and flex the hose while looking for cracks, bulges and seeping fluid. Check extra carefully around the areas where the hose connects with the master cylinder and caliper banjo unions, as these are common areas for hose failure (see Sections 5, 3 and 7).

4 Inspect the unions connected to the brake hose. If the unions are rusted, scratched or cracked, renew the hoses.

Renewal

5 Cover the surrounding area with plenty of rags, then unscrew the banjo bolt at each end of the hose, noting the alignment of the banjo union. Discard the sealing washers as new ones must be used. Free the hose from any clips or guides and remove it.

6 Position the new hose, making sure it isn't twisted or otherwise strained. Align the banjo unions as noted on removal, then install the banjo bolts using new sealing washers on both sides of the unions. Tighten the banjo bolts to the torque setting specified at the beginning of this Chapter.

7 Make sure the hose is correctly aligned and routed clear of all moving components. Secure the hose with any clips or guides.

8 Top-up the appropriate fluid reservoir (see *Pre-ride checks*) and bleed the brake system (see Section 11). Check for leaks and test the operation of the brake before riding the scooter.

---

11 Brake system bleeding and fluid change

Caution: Support the scooter in an upright position and ensure that the fluid reservoir is level while carrying-out these procedures.

Brake bleeding

Note: *If bleeding the brake system the conventional way does not work sufficiently well, it is advisable to obtain a commercially available vacuum-type bleeding tool and repeat the procedure. Follow the manufacturer's instructions for using the tool.*

1 Bleeding the brakes is simply the process of removing all the air bubbles from the fluid reservoir, master cylinder, the hose and the brake caliper. Bleeding is necessary whenever a brake system connection is loosened, when a component or hose is renewed, or when the master cylinder or caliper is overhauled. Leaks in the system may also allow air to enter, but leaking brake fluid will reveal their presence and warn you of the need for repair.

2 To bleed the brakes, you will need some new DOT 4 brake fluid, a length of clear flexible hose, a small container partially filled with clean brake fluid, some rags, a spanner to fit the brake caliper bleed valve, and help from an assistant **(see illustration)**. Alternatively, bleeding kits that include the hose, a one-way

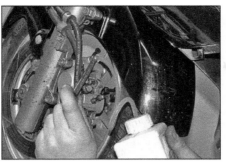

11.2 Set-up for bleeding the brakes – front brake shown

valve and a container are available and greatly simplify the task.

3 Cover or remove the handlebar covers to avoid damage from spilled brake fluid (see Chapter 8).

AN250 and AN400X to K6 models – front brake

4 Remove the right-hand reservoir cover, diaphragm plate and diaphragm (see *Pre-ride checks*). Slowly pump the brake lever a few times, until no air bubbles can be seen floating up from the holes in the bottom of the reservoir **(see illustration)**. Doing this bleeds any air from the master cylinder end of the system. Temporarily refit the reservoir cover.

5 Pull the dust cap off the upper caliper bleed valve **(see illustration)**. Attach one end of the clear vinyl or plastic tubing to the bleed valve and submerge the other end in the brake fluid in the container. **Note:** *To avoid damaging the bleed valve during the procedure, loosen it and then tighten it temporarily with a ring spanner before attaching the hose. With the hose attached, the valve can then be opened and closed with an open-ended spanner.*

6 Check the fluid level in the reservoir. Do not allow the fluid level to drop below the lower mark during the procedure.

7 Pump the brake lever three or four times in rapid succession, then hold it in while opening the caliper bleed valve. When the valve is opened, brake fluid will flow out of the caliper into the clear tubing and the lever will move toward the handlebar. If there is air in the system there will be air bubbles in the brake fluid coming out of the caliper.

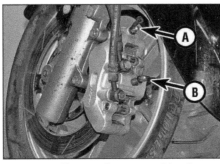

11.5 Front caliper upper bleed valve (A) and lower bleed valve (B)

11.4 Check for air bubbles in the bottom of the reservoir

8 Tighten the bleed valve, then release the brake lever gradually.

9 Repeat the process, topping-up the reservoir when necessary, until no air bubbles are visible in the brake fluid leaving the caliper and the lever is firm when applied. On completion, disconnect the hose, ensure the bleed valve is tightened securely and fit the dust cap.

10 Top-up the reservoir, install the diaphragm, diaphragm plate and cover, then wipe up any spilled brake fluid. Check for leaks and check the operation of the brake before riding the scooter.

> **HAYNES HINT** *If it's not possible to produce a firm feel to the lever the fluid may be aerated. Let the brake fluid in the system stabilise for a few hours and then repeat the procedure when the tiny bubbles in the system have settled out. To speed this process up, tie the front brake lever to the handlebar so that the system is pressurised.*

AN250 and AN400X to K6 models – combined braking system

11 Remove the left-hand reservoir cover, diaphragm plate and diaphragm (see *Pre-ride checks*), then follow the procedure in Step 4 to bleed any air from the master cylinder end of the system. Temporarily refit the reservoir cover.

12 Where fitted, remove the rear brake caliper cover, then pull the dust cap off the caliper bleed valve **(see illustration)**. Follow

11.12 Rear caliper bleed valve

**11.16 Front caliper bleed valve –
right-hand side**

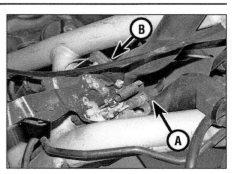

**12.6 Outer parking brake cable locknuts
(A), light switch connectors (B)**

11.19 Rear caliper bleed valve

the procedure in Steps 5 to 9 to bleed any air from the rear brake system.

13 Pull the dust cap off the lower front caliper bleed valve **(see illustration 11.5)**, then follow the procedure in Steps 5 to 9 to bleed any air from the front section of the combined braking system.

14 Top-up the reservoir, install the diaphragm, diaphragm plate and cover, then wipe up any spilled brake fluid. Check for leaks and check the operation of the brakes before riding the scooter.

AN400K7 model onward – front brakes

15 Remove the right-hand reservoir cover, diaphragm plate and diaphragm (see *Pre-ride checks*), then follow the procedure in Step 4 to bleed any air from the master cylinder end of the system. Temporarily refit the reservoir cover.

16 Working on one caliper at a time, pull the dust cap off the bleed valve **(see illustration)**. Follow the procedure in Steps 5 to 9 to bleed any air from the system, then repeat the procedure on the other front brake caliper.

17 Top-up the reservoir, install the diaphragm, diaphragm plate and cover, then wipe up any spilled brake fluid. Check for leaks and check the operation of the front brake before riding the scooter.

AN400K7 model onward – rear brake

18 Remove the left-hand reservoir cover, diaphragm plate and diaphragm (see *Pre-ride checks*), then follow the procedure in Step 4 to bleed any air from the master cylinder end of the system. Temporarily refit the reservoir cover.

19 Pull the dust cap off the caliper bleed valve **(see illustration)**. Follow the procedure in Steps 5 to 9 to bleed any air from the rear brake system.

20 Top-up the reservoir, install the diaphragm, diaphragm plate and cover, then wipe up any spilled brake fluid. Check for leaks and check the operation of the rear brake before riding the scooter.

Fluid change

21 Changing the brake fluid is a similar process to bleeding the brakes and requires the same materials (see Step 2) plus a suitable

syringe for siphoning the fluid out of the master cylinder reservoirs. Also ensure that the container is large enough to take all the old fluid when it is flushed out of the system.

22 Cover or remove the handlebar covers to avoid damage from spilled brake fluid (see Chapter 8).

23 Working on one brake at a time, remove the reservoir cover, diaphragm plate and diaphragm and siphon the old fluid out of the reservoir. Wipe the reservoir clean and fill it with new brake fluid.

24 Connect the tubing and container to the appropriate bleed valve, then open the valve and pump the brake lever to expel the old fluid from the system. Keep the reservoir topped-up with new fluid to above the LOWER level at all times or air may enter the system and greatly increase the length of the task. Repeat the process until new fluid can be seen emerging from the caliper bleed valve.

25 Tighten the bleed valve securely, disconnect the hose and install the dust cap.

26 On AN250 and AN400X to K6 models, when changing the fluid in the combined braking system, change the fluid in the front section first (see Step 13), then change the fluid in the rear brake system (see Step 12).

> **HAYNES HiNT** *Old brake fluid is invariably much darker in colour than new fluid, making it easy to see when all old fluid has been expelled from the system.*

27 On completion, ensure the master cylinder reservoirs are topped-up. Wipe up any spilled brake fluid. Check for leaks and check the operation of the brakes before riding the scooter.

12 Parking brake

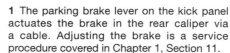

1 The parking brake lever on the kick panel actuates the brake in the rear caliper via a cable. Adjusting the brake is a service procedure covered in Chapter 1, Section 11.

2 To examine the brake mechanism in the rear caliper refer to Section 7.

Brake cable

3 To check and remove the brake cable, first remove the storage compartment, seat cowling, floor panels and kick panel (see Chapter 8).

4 Note the routing of the cable, especially where it passes through a guide on the engine pivot mounting (see Chapter 6, Section 10).

5 To remove the cable, first unhook the return spring from the brake arm on the rear caliper, then disconnect the lower end of the outer cable from the cable stop and the inner cable from the brake arm (see Section 7).

6 Note how the upper end of the cable is secured in the lever bracket, then loosen the locknuts and disconnect the outer cable from the bracket **(see illustration)**.

7 Disconnect the end of the inner cable from the lever mechanism.

8 Release the cable from any clips or ties and draw it off, noting the routing.

9 Installation is the reverse of removal, noting the following:

- *Apply some multi-purpose grease to the upper and lower ends of the inner cable.*
- *Ensure the upper end of the outer cable is held securely in the lever bracket.*
- *Press the lower end of the outer cable fully into the cable stop.*
- *Check that the cable is correctly routed and secured.*
- *Don't forget to install the return spring on the brake arm.*

10 Follow the procedure in Chapter 1 to adjust the brake mechanism.

11 Check the operation of the brake before riding the scooter.

> **HAYNES HiNT** *When fitting a new cable, tape the lower end of the new cable to the upper end of the old cable before removing it from the machine. Slowly pull the lower end of the old cable out, guiding the new cable down into position. Using this method will ensure the cable is routed correctly.*

Lever ratchet

11 The ratchet mechanism should hold the brake ON until the lever is pulled to release it.

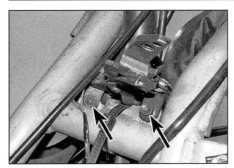

12.15 Bolts (arrowed) secure parking brake mechanism

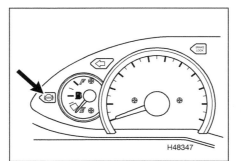

13.2 Location of the ABS indicator light

13.6 Connect the mode select switch to the ABS service check connector

If the ratchet is faulty, follow the procedure in Chapter 8 to remove the kick panel.

12 Follow the procedure in Steps 5 to 7 to disconnect both ends of the cable.

13 Inspect the ratchet mechanism and return spring. Clean off any corrosion and lubricate the mechanism with light oil. If the mechanism is damaged or worn it must be renewed.

14 Disconnect the brake warning light switch wiring connectors **(see illustration 12.6)**.

15 Undo the bolts securing the ratchet mechanism and remove it **(see illustration)**.

16 Prior to installation lubricate the mechanism with multi-purpose grease.

17 Installation is the reverse of removal.

13 ABS fault finding

1 The ABS prevents the wheels from locking up under hard braking or on uneven road surfaces. A sensor on each wheel transmits information about the speed of rotation to the ABS control unit; if the unit senses that a wheel is about to lock, it releases brake pressure to that wheel momentarily, preventing a skid.

2 The ABS is self-checking and is activated when the ignition switch is turned on – the ABS indicator light in the instrument cluster will come on and will remain on until road speed increases above 6 mph (10 kph) at which point, if the ABS is normal, the light will go off **(see illustration)**. **Note:** *If the ABS indicator light does not come on initially there is a fault in the system - see Section 14.*

3 If the indicator light remains on, or starts flashing while the machine is being ridden, there is a fault in the system and the ABS function will be switched off – the brakes will still operate but take extra care when using them.

4 If a fault is indicated, details will be stored in the control unit memory. To access the fault codes, a Suzuki mode select switch (Part No. 09930-82710) is required. The mode select switch is inexpensive and will be required for a number of test procedures.

5 Ensure the ignition switch is OFF. Remove the cockpit trim panel and instrument panel (see Chapter 8).

6 Trace the orange and black/white wires to the ABS service check connector and pull the connector out of its holder. Ensure the mode select switch is OFF, then connect it to the service check connector **(see illustration)**. Reconnect the instrument cluster wiring connector

7 Turn the mode select switch ON, then turn the ignition switch ON. The fault code will be represented as a series of flashes of the ABS indicator light.

8 All fault codes are represented by two-digit numbers (see Section 14). When the ignition is switched ON the ABS indicator light will come on initially for 2 seconds, then go off for approximately 3.6 seconds. It will then display the fault code in a series of 0.4 second flashes with a delay of 1.6 seconds between the 'tens' and the 'ones'. For example, fault code 13 will appear as one 0.4 second flash followed by a 1.6 second delay followed by three 0.4 second flashes. The fault code will be repeated after a further 3.6 second delay.

9 If there is more than one fault, the flashes will appear in groups in ascending order, with a 3.6 second delay between each group.

10 Record the code(s) and identify the fault(s) from the table in Section 14.

11 Turn the ignition switch OFF. **Note:** *Don't disconnect the battery or the ABS control unit connector until the fault code has been confirmed – disconnection will erase the control unit memory.*

12 Once the faults have been corrected, delete the fault codes from the control unit memory as follows. Follow the procedure in Step 7 to display the fault codes, and, while they are being displayed, turn the mode select switch OFF. Now turn the switch ON and OFF three times at 1 second intervals to start the deletion process. When the fault codes have been deleted the ABS indicator light should flash to confirm this.

13 To confirm that the control unit memory has been cleared, follow the procedure in Step 7 – the ABS indicator light should come on but not flash.

14 Once the reset procedure has been confirmed, turn the ignition switch OFF, disconnect the mode select switch and install the service check connector in its holder. Install the cockpit panel and instrument panel (see Chapter 8).

15 Check that the ABS is operating normally (see Step 2).

14 ABS system checks

1 Refer to Chapter 9, Section 2, for general fault finding procedures and equipment.

2 If a fault is indicated in the ABS (see Section 13), first check that the battery is fully charged.

3 Ensure the ignition switch is OFF. Remove the cockpit trim panel and instrument panel (see Chapter 8).

4 Disconnect the battery negative (-) lead (see Chapter 9). Lift the catch on the ABS control unit wiring connector and disconnect the connector. Check for continuity between terminals 24 and 25 on the loom side of the connector **(see illustration)** and the terminal on the battery negative lead. There should be continuity. If there is no continuity, inspect the black/white wires for damage (see *Wiring Diagrams* at the end of Chapter 9).

5 Having obtained the fault code following the procedure in Section 13, refer to the table below and the relevant Steps to identify and correct the faulty component. Unless specified otherwise, carry-out all checks with the ignition switch OFF.

6 If, after a thorough check, the source of a fault has not been identified, have the ABS control unit tested by a Suzuki dealer.

Note: *The ABS control unit may diagnose a fault if tyre sizes other than those specified by Suzuki are fitted, if the tyre pressures are incorrect or if the machine has been run continuously over bumpy roads. A fault may also be diagnosed if the rear wheel turns while the engine is running with the machine on its centrestand.*

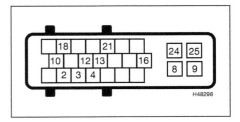

14.4 ABS control unit wiring connector – loom side

Fault code/ flashes	Faulty component - symptoms	Possible causes
Light does not come on	No voltage at instrument cluster No voltage at control unit	Damaged fuse Faulty wiring or wiring connector Damaged earth (ground) wire
Light stays on continuously	Service check connector No voltage at control unit ABS control unit	Faulty wiring or wiring connector Damaged earth (ground) wire Internal fault
13	Tyre size Front wheel speed sensor	Incorrect tyre size/tyre pressure Faulty wiring or wiring connector Dirty or damaged sensor Damaged rotor
14	Tyre size Rear wheel speed sensor	Incorrect tyre size/tyre pressure Faulty wiring or wiring connector Dirty or damaged sensor Damaged rotor
22	Front brake binding/locking ABS wiring circuit	Faulty brake disc or caliper Faulty speed sensor wiring or wiring connector Faulty control unit
23	Rear brake binding/locking ABS wiring circuit	Faulty brake disc or caliper Faulty speed sensor wiring or wiring connector Faulty control unit
25	Tyre size Speed sensors	Incorrect tyre size/tyre pressure Dirty or damaged sensor Damaged rotor Faulty control unit
35	ABS motor fuse No voltage at control unit ABS control unit	Damaged fuse Faulty wiring or wiring connector Internal fault
41	Front wheel speed sensor	Dirty or damaged sensor Damaged rotor
42	Front wheel speed sensor circuit	Faulty wiring or wiring connector
43	Front wheel speed sensor circuit	Faulty wiring or wiring connector Faulty sensor Faulty control unit
44	Rear wheel speed sensor	Dirty or damaged sensor Damaged rotor
45	Rear wheel speed sensor circuit	Dirty or damaged sensor Faulty wiring or wiring connector
46	Rear wheel speed sensor circuit	Faulty wiring or wiring connector Faulty sensor Faulty control unit
47, 48	Supply voltage	Faulty battery Faulty alternator Faulty wiring Faulty control unit
55	ABS control unit	Internal fault
61	ABS solenoid valve fuse ABS solenoid	Damaged ABS fuse Faulty wiring or wiring connector

ABS indicator light does not come on

7 First check the 15A signal fuse (No. 5) in the main fusebox (see Chapter 9).

8 If the fuse is good, remove the cockpit trim panel and instrument panel (see Chapter 8). Lift the catch on the ABS control unit wiring connector and disconnect the connector.

9 Using a multimeter set to the volts scale, connect the positive (+) probe to terminal 16 (orange/yellow wire) on the loom side of the connector and the negative probe to terminal 24 (black/white wire) **(see illustration 14.4)**. Turn the ignition ON and check for battery voltage. Turn the ignition OFF. If there is no voltage, inspect the wiring for damage.

10 If there is voltage, reconnect the instrument cluster wiring connector. Connect the positive (+) meter probe to terminal 21 (brown wire) on the loom side of the ABS control unit connector and the negative (-) probe to terminal 24 (black/white wire). Turn the ignition ON and note the voltage. Turn the ignition OFF. The meter should register 8 volts or more. If not, inspect the brown wire between the connector and the instrument cluster, and the terminals of the instrument cluster connector, for damage. If the wiring and terminals are good it is likely the indicator LED has failed and a new instrument panel will have to be fitted (see Chapter 9).

11 If the voltage is as specified, test for continuity between terminals 24 and 25 on the loom side of the connector and earth (ground). If there is no continuity, check for a fault in the wires. If there is continuity it is likely the ABS control unit is faulty – have it tested by a Suzuki dealer.

ABS indicator light stays on continuously

12 First check the 15A signal fuse (No. 5) in the main fusebox (see Chapter 9).

13 If the fuse is good, follow the procedure in Step 8 and disconnect the ABS control unit wiring connector.

14 Using a multimeter set to the volts scale, connect the positive (+) probe to terminal 16 (orange/yellow wire) on the loom side of the connector and the negative (-) probe to terminal 24 (black/white wire) **(see illustration 14.4)**. Turn the ignition ON and check for battery voltage. Turn the ignition OFF. If there is no voltage, inspect the wiring for damage.

15 If there is voltage, reconnect the instrument cluster wiring connector. Connect the positive (+) meter probe to terminal 21 (brown wire) on the loom side of the ABS control unit connector and the negative (-) probe to terminal 24 (black/white wire). Turn the ignition ON and note the voltage. Turn the ignition OFF. The meter should register 8 volts or more. If not, inspect the brown wire between the connector and the instrument cluster, and the terminals of the instrument cluster connector, for damage.

16 If the voltage is as specified, follow the procedure in Section 13 and connect the mode select switch to the service check connector. Turn the switch ON. Check for continuity between the orange (No. 13) and black/white (No. 24) wire terminals in the ABS control unit connector. If there is no continuity, check for a fault in the wiring. If there is continuity it is likely the ABS control unit is faulty – have it tested by a Suzuki dealer.

Fault code 13 – front wheel speed sensor and rotor

Note: *First ensure that the tyre size and pressure are correct (see Scooter spec and Pre-ride checks (Tyres) at the beginning of this manual). Next, follow the procedure in Section 13 to reset the control unit memory, then activate the self-checking procedure. If the fault code is the result of incorrect tyre fitment or unusual riding conditions and the ABS is normal, the indicator light will go off. Otherwise perform the following checks.*

Check

17 Measure the air gap between the speed sensor on the left-hand side of the front fork and the rotor on the wheel hub with a feeler gauge, then compare the result with the specification at the beginning of this Chapter. Rotate the wheel to a new position and measure the air gap again to ensure the rotor is not out-of-true.

18 The gap is not adjustable – if it is outside the specification, check that the speed sensor and rotor fixings are tight, that the components are not damaged and that there is no dirt on the sensor tip or between the slots in the rotor.

19 If the checks fail to identify the fault, have the ABS system checked by a Suzuki dealer.

Removal and installation

20 To remove the front wheel speed sensor, first remove the headlight panel (see Chapter 8).

21 Trace the wiring from the sensor and disconnect it at the connector. Release the wiring from any clips or ties, noting its routing.

22 Undo the bolts securing the speed sensor to its mounting bracket and withdraw the sensor.

23 Install the new speed sensor and tighten the mounting bolts securely. Feed the wiring up the front fork and secure it as noted on removal. Connect the wiring at the connector.

24 Check the air gap (see Step 17). Install the headlight panel (see Chapter 8)

25 To remove the speed sensor rotor, first remove the front wheel (see Section 18).

26 Undo the screws securing the rotor and lift it off, noting which way round it fits.

27 Ensure there is no dirt or corrosion where the rotor seats on the hub – if the rotor does not sit flat when it is installed the sensor air gap will be incorrect. Ensure the marking 50T on the rotor faces out. Tighten the screws securely.

28 Install the front wheel (see Section 18). Check the speed sensor air gap (see Step 17).

Fault code 14 – rear wheel speed sensor and rotor

Note: *First ensure that the tyre size and pressure are correct (see Scooter spec and Pre-ride checks (Tyres) at the beginning of this manual). Next, follow the procedure in Section 13 to reset the control unit memory, then activate the self-checking procedure. If the fault code is the result of incorrect tyre fitment or unusual riding conditions and the ABS is normal, the indicator light will go off. Otherwise perform the following checks.*

Check

29 Measure the air gap between the speed sensor on the top of the transmission casing and the rotor on the left-hand side of the wheel hub with a feeler gauge, then compare the result with the specification at the beginning of this Chapter. Rotate the wheel to a new position and measure the air gap again to ensure the rotor is not out-of-true.

30 The gap is not adjustable – if it is outside the specification, check that the speed sensor

and rotor fixings are tight, that the components are not damaged and that there is no dirt on the sensor tip or between the slots in the rotor.

31 If the checks fail to identify the fault, have the ABS system checked by a Suzuki dealer.

Removal and installation

32 To remove the rear wheel speed sensor, first remove the seat cowling (see Chapter 8).

33 Trace the wiring from the sensor and disconnect it at the connector. Release the wiring from any clips or ties, noting its routing.

34 Undo the bolt securing the sensor bracket and lift the assembly off. Undo the bolts securing the sensor to the bracket and withdraw the sensor, noting how the wiring clip locates.

35 Install the new speed sensor on its bracket, ensuring the wiring clip is correctly located, and tighten the mounting bolt securely. Install the assembly on the machine and tighten the mounting bolts securely. Feed the wiring up the connector and secure it as noted on removal.

36 Check the air gap (see Step 29). Install the seat cowling (see Chapter 8).

37 To remove the speed sensor rotor, first remove the rear wheel (see Section 19).

38 Undo the screws securing the rotor and lift it off, noting which way round it fits.

39 Ensure there is no dirt or corrosion where the rotor seats on the hub – if the rotor does not sit flat when it is installed the sensor air gap will be incorrect. Ensure the marking 72T on the rotor faces out. Tighten the screws securely.

40 Install the rear wheel (see Section 19). Check the speed sensor air gap (see Step 29).

Fault code 22 – front brake binding/ABS circuit malfunction

41 Remove the belly panel (see Chapter 8). Place the scooter on its centrestand, then position a support under the front of the frame to raise the front wheel off the ground.

42 Turn the wheel in the normal direction of rotation and ensure that it spins freely. If not, remove the brake pads and clean the inside of the calipers (see Section 2). If the pads are wearing unevenly, or there are signs that a piston is sticking in its bore, overhaul the calipers (see Section 3). Follow the procedure in Section 4 and check the runout of the front brake discs.

43 Follow the procedure in Steps 17 and 18 and check the speed sensor and rotor.

44 Follow the procedure in Steps 20 and 21 and check the sensor wiring and wiring connector.

45 If the checks fail to identify the fault, have the ABS control unit checked by a Suzuki dealer.

Fault code 23 – rear brake binding/ABS circuit malfunction

46 Support the scooter on its centrestand with the rear wheel off the ground.

47 Turn the wheel in the normal direction of rotation and ensure that it rotates freely – note that transmission drag will slow the rotation of the wheel. If the wheel does not rotate freely, remove the brake pads and clean the inside of the caliper (see Section 6). If the pads are wearing unevenly, or there are signs that a piston is sticking in its bore, overhaul the caliper (see Section 7). Follow the procedure in Section 8 and check the runout of the rear brake disc.

48 Follow the procedure in Steps 29 and 30 and check the speed sensor and rotor.

49 Follow the procedure in Steps 32 and 33 and check the sensor wiring and wiring connector.

50 If the checks fail to identify the fault, have the ABS control unit checked by a Suzuki dealer.

Fault code 25 – speed sensor malfunction

51 Ensure that the front and rear tyre sizes and pressures are correct (see *Scooter spec* and *Pre-ride checks (Tyres)* at the beginning of this manual).

52 Follow the procedure in Steps 17 and 18 and check the front wheel speed sensor and rotor.

53 Follow the procedure in Steps 29 and 30 and check the rear wheel speed sensor and rotor.

54 If the checks fail to identify the fault, have the ABS control unit checked by a Suzuki dealer.

Fault code 35 – ABS motor

55 The ABS pump motor is integral with the ABS control unit which is located on the steering head at the front of the frame. Remove the headlight panel for access (see Chapter 8). Turn the ignition ON and listen for any turning noise from the motor. If there is any noise with the machine at a standstill, have the control unit checked by a Suzuki dealer.

56 If no noise is heard from the pump motor, if not already done, remove the cockpit trim panel (see Chapter 8) to access the ABS fusebox. Check the 20A motor fuse (No.7) in the fusebox (see Chapter 9).

57 If the fuse is good, follow the procedure in Step 8 to access the ABS control unit wiring connector. Ensure that the connector is secure, then disconnect it and check that the contacts are clean and undamaged.

58 Using a multimeter set to the volts scale, connect the positive (+) probe to terminal 9 (red/black wire) on the loom side of the connector and the negative probe to terminal 25 (black/white wire) **(see illustration 14.4)**. Turn the ignition ON and check for battery voltage. Turn the ignition OFF. If there is no voltage, inspect the wiring for damage.

59 If there is voltage, it is likely the ABS control unit is faulty – have it tested by a Suzuki dealer.

Fault code 41 – front wheel speed sensor signal malfunction

60 Follow the procedure in Steps 17 and 18 and check the front wheel speed sensor and rotor.

61 Follow the procedure in Steps 20 and 21 and check the sensor wiring and wiring connector.

62 If no fault can be found, inspect the speed sensor circuit (see Fault code 42).

Fault code 42 – front wheel speed sensor broken circuit

63 Follow the procedure in Steps 20 and 21 and inspect the sensor wiring and wiring connector.

64 Follow the procedure in Step 8 to access the ABS control unit wiring connector. Ensure that the connector is secure, then disconnect it and check that the contacts are clean and undamaged.

65 Test for continuity between terminal 12 (black/red wire) on the loom side of the connector and earth (ground) **(see illustration 14.4)**. There should be no continuity (infinite resistance).

66 If there is continuity, disconnect the speed sensor connector. Test for continuity between the white wire terminal in the sensor side of the connector and earth (ground). If there is continuity, the front wheel speed sensor is faulty and must be renewed. If there is no continuity, inspect the black/red wire between the loom side of the sensor connector and the ABS control unit connector for damage.

67 If no continuity is found in the test in Step 65, test for continuity between terminal 3 (white/red wire) on the loom side of the ABS control unit wiring connector and earth (ground). There should be no continuity (infinite resistance).

68 If there is continuity, test for continuity between the blue wire terminal on the sensor side of the speed sensor connector and earth (ground). If there is continuity, the front wheel speed sensor is faulty and must be renewed. If there is no continuity, inspect the white/red wire between the loom side of the sensor connector and the ABS control unit connector for damage.

69 If no continuity is found in the test in Step 67, inspect the black/red wire between the loom side of the sensor connector and the ABS control unit connector for damage. If the black/red wire is good, inspect the white/red wire between the loom side of the sensor connector and the ABS control unit connector for damage.

70 If no fault can be traced in the speed sensor circuit it is likely the ABS control unit is faulty – have it checked by a Suzuki dealer.

Fault code 43 – front wheel speed sensor short circuit

71 Follow the procedure in Step 8 to access the ABS control unit wiring connector. Ensure that the connector is secure, then disconnect it and check that the contacts are clean and undamaged.

72 Test for continuity between terminals 3 (white/red wire) and 12 (black/red wire) on the loom side of the connector **(see illustration 14.4)**. If there is continuity, inspect the wiring to the front wheel sensor for damage (see Fault code 42). If the wiring is good, it is likely the speed sensor is faulty.

73 If there is no continuity, test for continuity between terminals 2 (black/yellow wire) and 3 (white/red wire). If there is continuity, inspect the wiring loom for damage. If the wiring is good, it is likely the speed sensor is faulty

74 If no fault can be found, set a multimeter to the volts scale, then connect the positive (+) probe to terminal 3 (white/red wire) on the loom side of the connector and the negative probe to terminal 24 (black/white wire) **(see illustration 14.4)**. Turn the ignition ON and check for voltage. Turn the ignition OFF. There should be no voltage. If voltage is indicated, inspect the sensor circuit and power supply wiring for damage. If no voltage is indicated, it is likely the ABS control unit is faulty – have it checked by a Suzuki dealer.

Fault code 44 – rear wheel speed sensor signal malfunction

75 Follow the procedure in Steps 29 and 30 and check the rear wheel speed sensor and rotor. If no fault can be found, inspect the speed sensor circuit (see Fault code 45).

Fault code 45 – rear wheel speed sensor broken circuit

76 Follow the procedure in Steps 32 and 33 to inspect the sensor wiring and wiring connector.

77 Follow the procedure in Step 8 to access the ABS control unit wiring connector. Ensure that the connector is secure, then disconnect it and check that the contacts are clean and undamaged.

78 Test for continuity between terminal 2 (black/yellow wire) on the loom side of connector and earth (ground) **(see illustration 14.4)**. There should be no continuity (infinite resistance).

79 If there is continuity, disconnect the speed sensor connector. Test for continuity between the white wire terminal in the sensor side of the connector and earth (ground). If there is continuity, the rear wheel speed sensor is faulty and must be renewed. If there is no continuity, inspect the black/yellow wire between the loom side of the sensor connector and the ABS control unit connector for damage.

80 If no continuity is found in the test in Step 78, test for continuity between terminal 18 (white/yellow wire) on the loom side of the ABS control unit wiring connector and earth (ground). There should be no continuity (infinite resistance).

81 If there is continuity, test for continuity between the blue wire terminal in the sensor side of the connector and earth (ground). If there is continuity, the rear wheel speed sensor is faulty and must be renewed. If there is no continuity, inspect the white/yellow wire between the loom side of the sensor connector and the ABS control unit connector for damage.

82 If no continuity is found in the test in Step 80, inspect the black/yellow wire between the loom side of the sensor connector and the ABS control unit connector for damage. If the black/yellow wire is good, inspect the white/yellow wire between the loom side of the sensor connector and the ABS control unit connector for damage.

83 If no fault can be traced in the speed sensor circuit it is likely the ABS control unit is faulty – have it checked by a Suzuki dealer.

Fault code 46 – rear wheel speed sensor short circuit

84 Follow the procedure in Step 8 to access the ABS control unit wiring connector. Ensure that the connector is secure, then disconnect it and check that the contacts are clean and undamaged.

85 Test for continuity between terminals 2 (black/yellow wire) and 18 (white/yellow wire) on the loom side of the connector **(see illustration 14.4)**. If there is continuity, inspect the wiring to the rear wheel sensor for damage (see Fault code 45). If the wiring is good, it is likely the speed sensor is faulty.

86 If there is no continuity, test for continuity between terminals 12 (black/red wire) and 18 (white/yellow wire). If there is continuity, inspect the wiring loom for damage. If the wiring is good, it is likely the speed sensor is faulty

87 If no fault can be found, set a multimeter to the volts scale, then connect the positive (+) probe to terminal 2 (black/yellow wire) on the loom side of the connector and the negative probe to terminal 24 (black/white wire) **(see illustration 14.4)**. Turn the ignition ON and check for voltage. Turn the ignition OFF. There should be no voltage. If voltage is indicated, inspect the sensor circuit and power supply wiring for damage. If no voltage is indicated, it is likely the ABS control unit is faulty – have it checked by a Suzuki dealer.

Fault codes 47 and 48 – supply voltage

88 Check the battery voltage (see Chapter 9, Section 3). If the voltage is good, check the regulated voltage of the charging system (see Chapter 9, Section 28).

89 If the charging system is good, follow the procedure in Step 8 to access the ABS control unit wiring connector. Ensure that the connector is secure, then disconnect it and check that the contacts are clean and undamaged.

90 Reconnect the instrument cluster wiring connector, but leave the ABS control unit wiring connector disconnected. Start the engine and warm it up to normal operating temperature. Switch the headlight main (HI) beam ON and increase the engine speed to 5000 rpm.

Warning: Ensure the scooter is positioned on its centrestand and with the rear wheel/tyre clear of the ground when performing this test.

91 Using a multimeter set to the volts scale, connect the positive (+) probe to terminal 16 (orange/yellow wire) on the loom side of the ABS control unit connector and the negative probe to terminal 24 (black/white wire) **(see illustration 14.4)**. The regulated charging system voltage should be shown on the meter (see Chapter 9 Specifications).

92 If the voltage is outside the specifications, inspect the ABS wiring loom for damage. If the voltage is good it is likely the ABS control unit is faulty – have it checked by a Suzuki dealer.

Fault code 55 – control unit malfunction

93 Follow the procedures in Steps 17, 18, 29 and 30 to ensure that the front and rear speed sensor air gaps are correct, that the components are not damaged and that the speed sensor and rotor fixings are tight.

94 If the checks fail to identify the fault, follow the procedure in Section 13 to reset the control unit memory, then turn the ignition switch ON to activate the self-checking procedure. If the fault code remains it is likely the ABS control unit is faulty – have it checked by a Suzuki dealer.

Fault code 61 – ABS solenoid malfunction

95 Remove the cockpit trim panel (see Chapter 8) to access the ABS fusebox. Check the 15A valve fuse (No. 8) in the fusebox (see Chapter 9).

96 If the fuse is good, follow the procedure in Step 8 to access the ABS control unit wiring connector. Ensure that the connector is secure, then disconnect it and check that the contacts are clean and undamaged.

97 Using a multimeter set to the volts scale, connect the positive (+) probe to terminal 8 (red/blue wire) on the loom side of the connector and the negative (-) probe to terminal 24 (black/white wire) **(see illustration 14.4)**. The meter should register battery voltage.

98 If there is voltage, it is likely the ABS control unit is faulty – have it tested by a Suzuki dealer.

15 ABS control unit

Note: *Before the control unit can be removed from the bike, the brake fluid must be drained from the hydraulic system. When refilling and bleeding the ABS-equipped brake system it may be helpful to use a vacuum-type brake bleeder kit. Alternatively, removal and installation of the control unit should be entrusted to a Suzuki dealer.*

1 The ABS control unit is located on the

steering head at the front of the frame. Remove the cockpit trim panel, instrument panel and headlight panel for access (see Chapter 8). If required, cover or remove the front mudguard to avoid damage from spilled brake fluid.

2 Lift the catch on the ABS control unit wiring connector and disconnect the connector.

3 Refer to the procedure in Section 11 for changing the brake fluid – siphon the fluid out of the front and rear reservoirs and pump any residual fluid out through the brake calipers, but do not refill the system at this stage.

4 Undo the bolts securing the brake hose-to-brake pipe unions.

5 Unscrew the four brake pipe gland nuts and disconnect the pipes from the control unit. Have some rag ready to catch any residual brake fluid. Plug the openings in the control unit to prevent dirt entering.

6 Undo the four bolts securing the control unit carrier and lift the assembly off. Undo the bolts securing the control unit in the carrier.

7 Installation is the reverse of removal, noting the following:

• *Check the condition of the mounting grommets and fit new ones if they are damaged or deteriorated.*

• *Tighten the brake pipe gland nuts to the torque setting specified at the beginning of this Chapter.*

• *Ensure the control unit wiring connector is secure.*

• *Follow the procedure in Section 11 to refill and bleed the brake system using a vacuum-type brake bleeder kit.*

16 Wheel inspection

Note: *If, when checked in place on the scooter, wheel runout is excessive, check the wheel bearings for wear before renewing the wheel (see Section 20).*

1 In order to carry out a proper inspection of the wheels, support the scooter upright with the wheel being checked raised off the ground. Clean the wheels thoroughly to remove mud and dirt that may interfere with the inspection procedure or mask defects. Make a general check of the wheels and tyres (see Chapter 1).

2 To check front wheel runout, attach a dial gauge to the front fork, with the gauge pointer touching the side of the rim. When checking rear wheel runout, attach the gauge to the transmission casing (AN250 and AN400X to K6 models) or rear sub-frame (AN400K7 models onward). Rotate the wheel slowly and check the axial (side-to-side) runout of the rim **(see illustration)**. In order to accurately check radial (out of round) runout with the dial gauge, the wheel should be removed from the machine, and the tyre from the wheel. With a suitable axle clamped in a vice or jig and the dial gauge positioned on the top of the rim, the wheel can be rotated to check the runout.

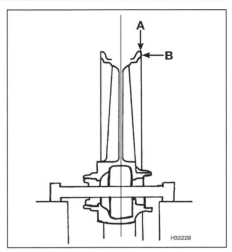

16.2 Check the wheel for radial (out-of-round) runout (A) and axial (side-to-side) runout (B)

3 An easier, though slightly less accurate, method is to use a stiff wire pointer in place of the dial gauge. Attach the pointer as required and position the end of the pointer a fraction of an inch from the wheel rim where the wheel and tyre join. If the wheel is true, the distance from the pointer to the rim will be constant as the wheel is rotated.

4 Inspect the wheels for cracks, flat spots on the rim and other damage. Look very closely for dents in the area where the tyre bead contacts the rim. Dents in this area may prevent complete sealing of the tyre against the rim, which leads to deflation of the tyre over a period of time. If damage is evident, or if runout in either direction is excessive, the wheel will have to be replaced with a new one. Never attempt to repair a damaged cast alloy wheel.

17 Wheel alignment check

1 Misalignment of the wheels can cause strange and potentially dangerous handling problems and will most likely be due to bent frame or suspension components as the result of an accident. If the frame or suspension is at fault, repair by a frame specialist or replacement with new parts are the only options.

2 To check wheel alignment you will need an assistant, a length of string or a perfectly straight piece of wood or metal bar, and a ruler. A plumb bob or spirit level for checking that the wheels are vertical will also be required. Support the scooter in an upright position on its centrestand.

3 If a string is used, have your assistant hold one end of it about halfway between the floor and the centre of the rear wheel, with the string touching the back edge of the rear tyre sidewall.

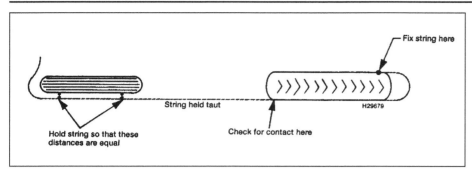

Fix string here

String held taut

Hold string so that these distances are equal

Check for contact here

H29679

17.4 Wheel alignment check using the string method

4 Run the other end of the string forward and pull it tight so that it is roughly parallel to the floor. Slowly bring the string into contact with the front sidewall of the rear tyre, then turn the front wheel until it is parallel with the string. Measure the distance (offset) from the front tyre sidewall to the string **(see illustration)**. **Note:** *Where the same size tyre is fitted front and rear, there should be no offset.*

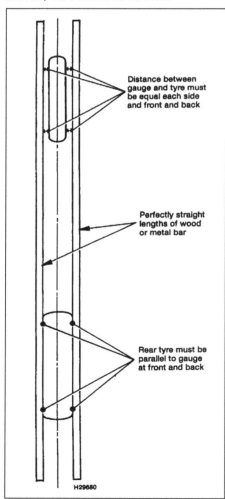

Distance between gauge and tyre must be equal each side and front and back

Perfectly straight lengths of wood or metal bar

Rear tyre must be parallel to gauge at front and back

H29680

17.6 Wheel alignment check using a straight-edge

5 Repeat the procedure on the other side of the machine. The distance from the front tyre sidewall to the string should be equal on both sides.
6 As mentioned, a perfectly straight length of wood or metal bar may be substituted for the string **(see illustration)**.
7 If the distance between the string and tyre is greater on one side, or if the rear wheel appears to be out of alignment, have your machine checked by a Suzuki dealer.
8 If the front-to-back alignment is correct, the wheels still may be out of alignment vertically.
9 Using a plumb bob or spirit level, check the rear wheel to make sure it is vertical. To do this, hold the string of the plumb bob against the tyre upper sidewall and allow the weight to settle just off the floor. If the string touches both the upper and lower tyre sidewalls and is perfectly straight, the wheel is vertical. If it is not, adjust the centrestand until it is.

18.3 Loosen the axle pinch bolt

18.5 Remove the spacer from the left-hand side

10 Once the rear wheel is vertical, check the front wheel in the same manner. If both wheels are not perfectly vertical, the frame and/or major suspension components are bent.

18 Front wheel

Removal

1 Remove the belly panel (see Chapter 8). Place the scooter on its centrestand, then position a support under the front of the frame to raise the front wheel off the ground.
2 Displace the front brake caliper(s) (see Section 3). **Note:** *Do not operate the front brake lever while the caliper is off the disc.*
3 Loosen the axle pinch bolt **(see illustration)**.
4 Working on the right-hand side, loosen the axle, then support the wheel and draw the axle out **(see illustration)**.
5 Lower the wheel and remove the spacer from the seal in the left-hand side of the hub **(see illustration)**.
6 Where fitted, lift the speedometer drive housing off the right-hand side of the hub, noting how it fits **(see illustration)**. **Note:** *Do not try to disconnect the speedometer wire from the drive housing. Secure the speedometer drive housing to the scooter to avoid straining the wire.*
Caution: Don't lay the wheel down and allow it to rest on the disc – the disc could become warped. Set the wheel on wood

18.4 Loosen the axle then pull it out

18.6 Note the location of the speedometer drive housing

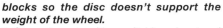

18.13 Installed location of the speedometer drive housing

19.5 Undo the wheel nuts

19.6 Lift the wheel off the hub

blocks so the disc doesn't support the weight of the wheel.

7 Clean the axle with a suitable solvent and remove any corrosion using steel wool. Check the axle for straightness by rolling it on a flat surface such as a piece of plate glass. If available, check the axle for runout using V-blocks and a dial gauge. If the axle is bent or the runout is excessive, renew it.

8 Check the condition of the wheel bearings (see Section 20).

9 Prior to installation, clean any old grease out of the speedometer drive housing and lubricate it with a smear of multi-purpose grease.

Installation

10 Apply a thin coat of multi-purpose grease to the axle.

11 Manoeuvre the wheel between the fork legs. Install the spacer in the seal on the left-hand side of the hub **(see illustration 18.5)**.

12 Where fitted, install the speedometer drive housing onto the hub, making sure the drive tabs locate correctly **(see illustration 18.6)**.

13 Lift the wheel into position, making sure the tabs on the speedometer housing locate correctly against the tabs on the inside of the fork outer tube **(see illustration)**. Install the axle and press it all the way through the hub and spacer, then screw it by hand into the left-hand fork outer tube.

14 Ensure everything is correctly aligned, then tighten the axle to the torque setting specified at the beginning of this Chapter.

15 Tighten the axle pinch bolt to the specified torque setting.

16 Install the brake caliper(s) (see Section 3).

17 Operate the front brake lever several times to bring the pads into contact with the disc(s). Check the operation of the brake before riding the scooter.

19 Rear wheel

Note: *The rear axle nut is a self-locking nut. The nut should be renewed when the self-locking section no longer grips the rear axle.*

Removal

AN250 and AN400X to K2 models

1 First remove the exhaust system and the exhaust mounting bracket (see Chapter 4A).

2 Apply the rear brake and undo the rear axle nut.

3 Draw the wheel off the rear axle.

AN400K3 to K6 models

4 First remove the exhaust system and the exhaust mounting bracket (see Chapter 4B).

5 Apply the rear brake and undo the wheel nuts **(see illustration)**.

6 Lift the wheel off the rear hub **(see illustration)**.

AN400K7 model onward

7 First remove the exhaust system (see Chapter 4B).

8 Remove the rear sub-frame (see Chapter 6, Section 10).

9 Draw the wheel off the rear axle **(see illustration)**.

Caution: Don't lay the wheel down and allow it to rest on the disc – it could become warped. Set the wheel on wood blocks so the wheel rim supports the weight of the wheel.

Inspection

10 Refer to Section 16 and to Chapter 1, Section 12, to check the condition of the wheel.

11 On AN250 models, AN400X to K2 and AN400K7 models onward, inspect the splines on the rear axle and on the inside of the wheel and renew any components that are worn. The wheel should be a firm sliding fit on the shaft

19.9 Draw the wheel off the rear axle

with no freeplay. Prior to installation, clean any old grease or corrosion off the axle and lubricate it with a smear of multi-purpose grease.

12 AN400K7 models onward, note the location of the O-ring inside the right-hand end of the wheel hub and discard it as a new one must be fitted **(see illustration)**. Lubricate the new O-ring with a smear of multi-purpose grease.

Installation

13 Installation is the reverse of removal, noting the following:

- *On AN400X to K2 models, lubricate the threads of the rear axle nut with engine oil.*
- *Tighten all nuts to the torque settings specified at the beginning of this Chapter.*
- *Check the operation of the brake before riding the scooter.*

20 Wheel bearings

Check

1 Wheel bearings will wear over a period of time and cause handling problems.

2 Support the scooter upright on its centrestand. Check for any play in the bearings by pushing and pulling the wheel against the hub.

3 Now rotate the wheel and check that it turns smoothly; note that slight resistance may be due to brake drag or, when checking the rear wheel, transmission drag.

4 The front wheel bearings are housed in the wheel hub. There are no rear wheel bearings as

19.12 Location of the hub O-ring

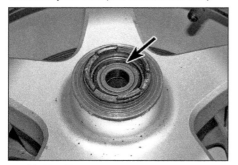

20.8 Lever out the bearing seal

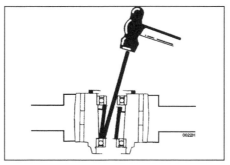

20.9 Locate the drift as shown when driving out the bearings

20.12a Installing the wheel bearing using a suitably-sized socket

such – the wheel is mounted on the rear axle/ gearbox output shaft which turns on bearings located inside the gearbox (see Step 16).

5 If any play or roughness is detected, first check that the axle and wheel mountings are tight, then remove the wheel and check the bearings carefully.

Removal and installation

Front wheel bearings

Note: *Only remove the bearings if they are going to be renewed. Always renew the wheel bearings in pairs – never renew bearings individually. Refer to Tools and Workshop Tips in the Reference section for further information on bearings.*

6 Remove the wheel (see Section 18).

7 Set the wheel on blocks – never allow the weight of the wheel to rest on the brake disc. If not already done, remove the left-hand spacer retained by the seal **(see illustration 18.5)**.

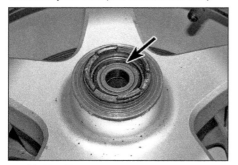

20.12b Ensure the sealed side faces outwards

20.14b . . . and press them in firmly

8 Lever out the left-hand bearing seal, taking care not to damage the hub **(see illustration)**. Note which way round the seal is fitted. On AN400K7 models onward, remove the right-hand seal. Discard the seals as new ones must be fitted.

9 To remove the bearings use either an expanding bearing puller and slide-hammer, or a suitable drift (such as a metal or brass rod or punch) inserted from the opposite side to the bearing being removed **(see illustration)**. Tap evenly around the inner race of the bearing and drive it out of the hub, then remove the central spacer. Turn the wheel over and remove the other bearing.

10 Thoroughly clean the hub area of the wheel.

11 Lubricate the inner (unsealed) side of the new bearings with multi-purpose grease.

12 On AN250 and AN400X to K6 models, install the left-hand bearing first. On AN400K7

20.14a Lubricate the inside of the seals . . .

20.16 Checking for play in the output shaft bearings

models onward, install the right-hand bearing first. Install the bearings using a bearing driver or a socket large enough to contact the outer race of the bearing – ensure the sealed side of the bearing faces outwards **(see illustrations)**. Alternatively, use the drawbolt method (see *Tools and Workshop Tips* in the *Reference* section).

13 Install the first bearing, ensuring it is completely seated. Turn the wheel over and install the central spacer, then install the second bearing.

14 Install the bearing seals, where fitted, making sure the marked or closed side is facing outwards **(see illustrations)**. Lubricate the inside of each seal with a smear of multi-purpose grease.

15 Clean the brake disc with acetone or brake system cleaner, then install the wheel (see Section 18).

Rear wheel bearings

16 Ensure the wheel fixings are tightened securely, then check for any play in the rear axle/gearbox output shaft bearings by pushing and pulling the wheel against the hub **(see illustration)**.

17 If any freeplay is noted, remove the rear wheel (see Section 19). On AN400K3 to K6 models, remove the brake disc assembly (see Section 8).

18 Grasp the axle/output shaft and try to move it up and down – if any freeplay is noted, the shaft bearings are worn **(see illustration)**. Refer to Chapter 2C for renewal of the output shaft bearings.

20.18 Freeplay in the output shaft (arrowed) indicates worn gearbox bearings

MANUFACTURER'S NAME
OR BRAND NAME

PATTERN CODE

LOAD AND PRESSURE
MARKING REQUIREMENT (NOT
APPLICABLE IN U.K.)

COUNTRY OF
MANUFACTURE

TYRE CONSTRUCTION DETAIL
(NOT REQUIRED IN U.K.)

NORTH AMERICAN
TYRE IDENTIFICATION
NUMBER

TYRE SIZE DESIGNATION

NORTH AMERICAN
DEPARTMENT OF
TRANSPORTATION
COMPLIANCE SYMBOL

ARROW DENOTING
THE DIRECTION OF
WHEEL ROTATION

LOAD INDEX/
SPEED SYMBOL

THE WORD TUBELESS
WHERE APPLICABLE

TYRE TYPE

ADVANCED VARIABLE BELT
DENSITY
WHERE APPLICABLE

ECE TYPE APPROVAL MARK
AND NUMBER

21.3 Common tyre sidewall markings

21 Tyres

General information

1 The wheels are designed for tubeless tyres only. Tyre sizes are given in the *Scooter spec* section at the beginning of this manual.
2 Refer to *Pre-ride checks* at the beginning of this manual for tyre maintenance.

Fitting new tyres

3 When selecting new tyres, refer to the tyre information label on the scooter and the tyre options listed in the owners handbook. Ensure that front and rear tyre types are compatible, the correct size and correct speed rating **(see illustration)**; if necessary seek advice from a Suzuki dealer or tyre fitting specialist.
4 It is recommended that tyres are fitted by a motorcycle tyre specialist rather than attempted in the home workshop. This is

particularly relevant in the case of tubeless tyres because the force required to break the seal between the wheel rim and tyre bead is substantial, and is usually beyond the capabilities of an individual working with normal tyre levers. Additionally, the specialist will be able to balance the wheels after tyre fitting.
5 Note that punctured tubeless tyres can in some cases be repaired although such repairs must be carried out by a tyre specialist.

Notes

Chapter 8
Bodywork

Contents

Degrees of difficulty

Easy, suitable for novice with little experience	Fairly easy, suitable for beginner with some experience	Fairly difficult, suitable for competent DIY mechanic	Difficult, suitable for experienced DIY mechanic	Very difficult, suitable for expert DIY or professional

Specifications

Torque settings

Passenger handle bolts . . . . 23 Nm
Passenger backrest bolts. . . . . 23 Nm

---

1 General information

1 Almost all the functional components of the scooters covered by this manual are enclosed by body panels, making removal of relevant panels a necessary part of most servicing and maintenance procedures. Panel removal is straightforward, and as well as facilitating access to mechanical components, it avoids the risk of accidental damage to the panels.
2 Before attempting to remove any body panel, study it closely, noting any fasteners and associated fittings. Most panels are retained by screws and inter-locking tabs, although in some cases trim clips are used

(see overleaf). Once the evident fasteners have been removed, try to withdraw the panel as described but DO NOT FORCE IT – if it will not release, check that all fasteners have been removed and try again. Where a panel engages another by means of tabs, be careful not to break the tab or its mating slot. Remember that a few moments of patience at this stage will save you a lot of money in replacing broken body panels! In some cases the aid of an assistant will be required when removing panels.
3 When installing a body panel, check the fasteners and associated fittings removed with it, to be sure of returning everything to its correct place. Ensure all the fasteners are in good condition, including all trim clips, U-clips, grommets and wellnuts – any of these

should be renewed if faulty before the panel is reassembled. Check also that all mounting brackets are straight and repair or renew them if necessary before attempting to install the panel. Where assistance was required to remove a panel, make sure your assistant is on hand to install it.
4 Tighten the fasteners securely, but be careful not to overtighten any of them or the panel may break (not always immediately) due to the uneven stress.

HAYNES HiNT *Note that a small amount of lubricant (liquid soap or similar) applied to rubber mounting grommets will assist the lugs to engage without the need for undue pressure.*

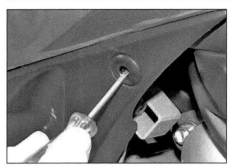

1.5a Push the centre pin in . . .

1.5b . . . to release the clip

1.6 Lift the head to release the clip

1.7 X-head clips – unscrew the centre to release the clip

1.9 Ensure U-clips are a secure fit

the condition of each lug and ensure it is not split or the thread stripped. If necessary, repair a damaged lug with a proprietary repair kit.

9 If the screws engage in U-clips, check that the clips are a firm fit on the mounting lug and that they are not sprained **(see illustration)**. If necessary, fit new U-clips.

Wellnuts

10 Wellnuts have a metal thread retained inside a rubber bush. The bush is a firm press fit in a body panel or windshield **(see illustration)**. Avoid overtightening the screw, otherwise the bush will twist in the panel and damage the locating hole.

Panel repair

11 In the case of damage to the body parts, it is usually necessary to remove the broken component and replace it with a new (or used) one. There are however some shops that specialise in 'plastic welding', so it may be worthwhile seeking the advice of one of these specialists before consigning an expensive component to the bin. Additionally, proprietary repair kits can be obtained for repair of small components **(see illustration)**.

Trim clips

5 Three types of trim clips are used. If the centre pin is level with the head of the trim clip, push the centre into the body, then draw the clip out of the panel **(see illustrations)**. Before installing the trim clip, push the centre back out so that it protrudes from the top of the clip. Fit the clip into its hole, then push the centre in so that it is flush with the top of the clip.

6 If the centre pin has a round, flat head, prise it up, then draw the clip out of the panel **(see illustration)**. On installation, fit the clip into its

hole, then push the head down to secure the clip.

7 If the centre pin has an X-head, unscrew it to release the clip, then draw the clip out of the panel **(see illustration)**. On installation, fit the clip into its hole, then screw the centre pin in to secure the clip.

Self-tapping screws

8 When the panel is removed, note the location of the screws. If they engage in plastic lugs on the back of an adjacent panel, check

1.10 Wellnut threads are retained inside a rubber bush

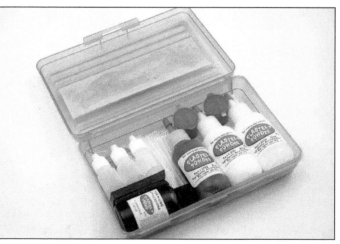

1.11 A typical repair kit for plastic panels

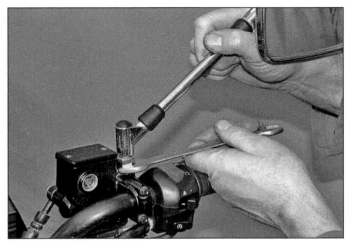

2.1a Loosen the lower end of the mirror stem . . .

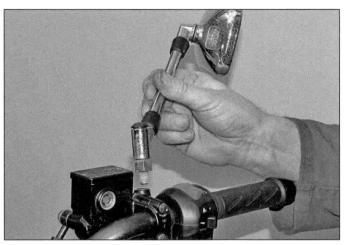

2.1b . . . then unscrew the mirror from its socket

2 Mirrors

1 Loosen the lower end of the mirror stem with an open-ended spanner, then unscrew the mirror from the socket on the brake master cylinder (see illustrations).
2 Installation is the reverse of removal. Screw the mirror stem into the socket in the master cylinder, then tighten the lower end securely. The mirror stem is spring loaded – adjust it to the required position.

3 AN250 and AN400X to K2 body panels

Handlebar covers

1 Follow the procedure in Chapter 4A and disconnect the throttle cables from the twistgrip pulley.
2 Undo the screws securing the left and right-hand lower handlebar covers and remove the covers (see illustration).

3 Undo the screws securing the upper handlebar cover to the handlebars, then unclip the upper handlebar cover, noting how it fits.
4 Installation is the reverse of removal, noting the following:
• Don't forget to pass the throttle cables through the opening in the lower right-hand cover.

Windshield panels

5 Undo the screws at the front and back on both sides of the lower windshield

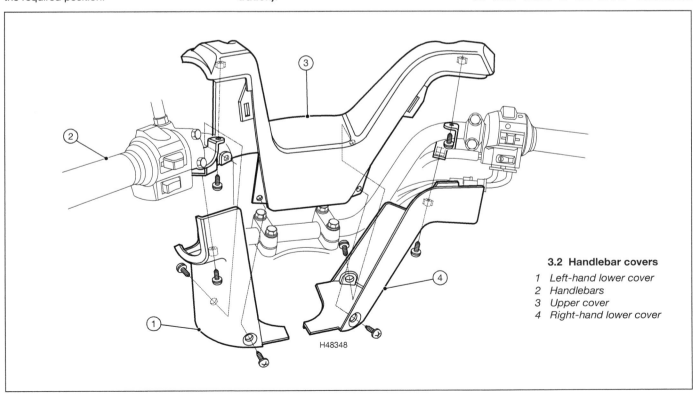

3.2 Handlebar covers

1 Left-hand lower cover
2 Handlebars
3 Upper cover
4 Right-hand lower cover

H48348

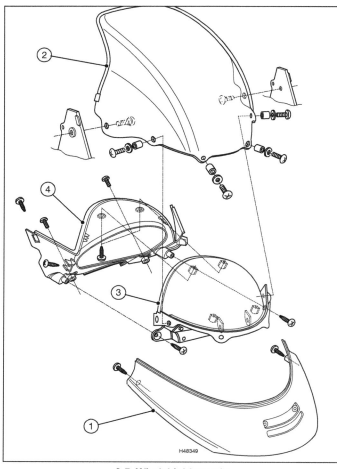

3.5 Windshield panels

1 *Lower windshield panel*   3 *Instrument panel*
2 *Windshield*   4 *Cockpit trim panel*

3.10 Headlight panel

1 *Headlight panel*   3 *Radiator panel*
2 *Kick panel*

panel and lift the panel off **(see illustration)**.

6 Undo the screws securing the windshield, noting the location of the plastic washers. The front four screws are secured by wellnuts (see Section 1). The two rear screws locate in the fairing bracket.

7 If the wellnuts remain in the lower edge of the instrument panel, pull them out prior to installation, noting how they fit.

8 Installation is the reverse of removal, noting the following:

• *Hold the windshield in position and press the wellnuts through the holes in the windshield into the instrument panel.*

• *Take care not to over-tighten the screws in the wellnuts.*

Headlight panel

9 Remove the lower windshield panel (see Step 5).

10 Remove the front floor mats, noting how they fit. Undo the left and right-hand screws securing the lower edge of the headlight panel to the kick panel **(see illustration)**.

11 Release the trim clips securing the inner edge of the headlight panel to the radiator panel.

12 Undo the screws securing the outer edge of the headlight panel to the kick panel.

13 Undo the screws securing the inner and upper edges of the headlight panel to the kick panel.

14 Draw the headlight panel forwards and

disconnect the headlight unit wiring connector **(see illustrations)**.

15 If required, follow the procedure in Chapter 9 to remove the headlight unit.

16 Installation is the reverse of removal, noting the following:

• *Ensure the headlight unit wiring connector is secure.*

• *Check the operation of the lights before riding the scooter.*

3.14a Draw the headlight panel forwards . . .

3.14b . . . and disconnect the headlight unit wiring connector

Instrument panel and cockpit trim panel

17 Remove the windshield panels (see Steps 5 to 7) and the headlight panel (see Steps 10 to 14).
18 Disconnect the instrument cluster wiring connector.
19 Undo the screws securing the instrument cluster to the cockpit trim panel, then lift off the instrument panel assembly **(see illustration 3.5)**.
20 Undo the screws securing the cockpit trim panel and remove the panel.
21 Installation is the reverse of removal, noting the following:
• *Ensure the instrument cluster wiring connector is secure.*

Radiator panel

22 Remove the headlight panel (see Steps 9 to 14).
23 Release the trim clips on the underside of the radiator panel **(see illustration 3.10)**.
24 Undo the left and right-hand screws securing the edge of the radiator panel to the kick panel.
25 Draw the panel forwards to release the tabs on the upper rear edge from the kick panel.
26 Installation is the reverse of removal, noting the following:
• *Ensure the tabs on the upper rear edge are correctly secured before installing the trim clips.*

Belly panels

27 Working on one side at a time, remove the front and rear floor mats, noting how they fit. Undo the screw securing the rear edge of the belly panel to the underside of the floor panel **(see illustration)**.
28 Release the trim clips securing the front underside of the side belly panel to the centre belly panel.
29 Release the trim clips securing the side belly panel through the floor panel.
30 Pull the side belly panel away from the machine to release the tabs along the top edge and lift it off **(see illustration)**.
31 Release the trim clips securing the front edge of the centre belly panel to the frame.
32 Lower the front edge of the centre belly panel, then draw the panel forwards to release the clip on the rear edge from the frame **(see illustration)**.
33 Installation is the reverse of removal.

Underseat panel

34 Raise the seat.
35 Undo the screws securing the rear top edge of the panel to the seat cowling on both sides **(see illustration)**.
36 Where fitted, undo the screw securing the centre of the panel to the centre floor panel.
37 Lower the seat. Push the panel back to

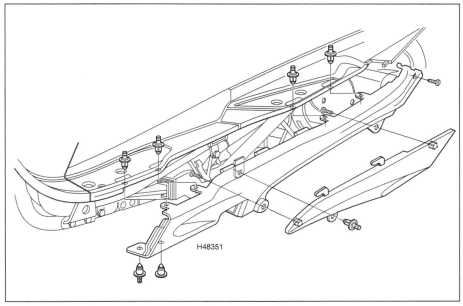

3.27 Belly panel fixings – left-hand side

release the tabs on the front edge from the back edge of the floor centre panel, then manoeuvre the underseat panel off **(see illustration)**.
38 Installation is the reverse of removal.

Seat and underseat cover

39 The underseat cover is secured by trim clips on the left and right-hand sides. Release the trim clips, then draw the cover back to remove it.
40 To remove the seat, first remove the underseat cover (see Step 39) and the underseat panel (see Steps 35 to 37).
41 Raise the seat. Trace the wiring from the underseat light and disconnect it at the

3.30 Release tabs along the top edge of the panel

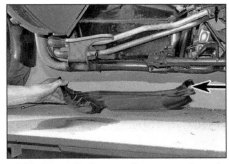

3.32 Note clip (arrowed) on rear edge of centre belly panel

3.35 Undo the screws on both sides

3.37 Lift the underseat panel off

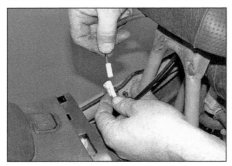

3.41 Disconnect the underseat light wiring connector

3.42 Pull out the R-clip

3.43 Undo the seat hinge nuts

connector **(see illustration)**. Release the wiring from any clips or ties and feed it back to the seat.

42 Pull out the R-clip securing the seat damper rod to the underside of the seat

(see illustration). Remove the washer and disconnect the damper rod from the seat.

43 Fold the seat all the way forwards, then undo the nuts securing the seat to the hinge and lift the seat off **(see illustration)**.

44 Installation is the reverse of removal.

Passenger handles and backrest

45 Raise the seat. The handles and backrest must be removed in the following order.

46 Release the trim clips securing the panel at the rear of the backrest and remove the panel **(see illustration)**.

47 Undo the screw securing the backrest cushion bracket, then pull the cushion forwards to unclip it from the backrest **(see illustrations)**.

48 Undo the screws securing the panel at the front of the backrest and remove the panel **(see illustrations)**.

49 Remove the blanking plug from the front handle mounting **(see illustration)**. Undo the front and rear handle mounting bolts, noting the location of the spacers, and lift the handle off **(see illustrations)**.

3.46 Release the trim clips

3.47a Undo the screw (arrowed) . . .

3.47b . . . then pull the cushion off

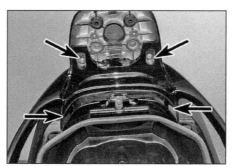

3.48a Undo the screws . . .

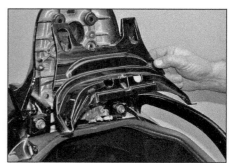

3.48b . . . and remove the panel

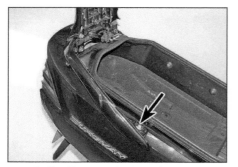

3.49a Remove the blanking plug

3.49b Note location of spacers on rear . . .

3.49c . . . and front handle mounting bolts

3.50 Displace the seat catch

3.51 Undo the backrest mounting bolts

3.54 Undo the screw (arrowed) on both sides

50 To remove the backrest, first undo the screws securing the seat catch and displace the catch **(see illustration)**. Alternatively, disconnect the seat lock cable from the catch, noting how it fits **(see illustrations 4.50a and b)**.
51 Undo the bolts securing the backrest and lift it off **(see illustration)**.
52 Installation is the reverse of removal, noting the following:
- *Clean the threads of the mounting bolts and apply a suitable non-permanent thread-locking compound.*
- *Tighten the mounting bolts to the torque setting specified at the beginning of this Chapter – don't forget to fit the spacers on the passenger handle mounting bolts.*

- *Check the operation of the seat catch before lowering the seat.*

Seat cowling
53 Remove the underseat panel (see Steps 34 to 37) and the passenger handles and backrest (see Steps 45 to 51).
54 Undo the screws securing the left and right-hand sides of the cowling to the rear floor panels **(see illustration)**.
55 Undo the screws on the inside of the storage compartment securing the storage compartment to the cowling side panels **(see illustrations)**. Note the location of the washers. Where fitted, release the trim clips securing the top edge of the cowling side panels to the rim of the storage compartment.
56 Counter-hold the nuts on the inside of

the storage compartment and undo the bolts securing the top rear edges of the storage compartment to the sides of the cowling **(see illustration)**.
57 Undo the screws securing the left and right-hand sides of the cowling to the lower edges of the rear floor panels and release the trim clips securing the lower edges of the cowling side panels to the mudguard **(see illustration)**.
58 Draw the cowling assembly back carefully and release the tabs securing the cowling to the upper rear edges of the floor panels **(see illustration 3.68b)**. Disconnect the tail light unit wiring connector, then remove the cowling assembly **(see illustrations)**.
59 If required, disconnect the release cable from the seat lock, then pull up the spring

3.55a Undo the screws on both sides

3.55b Note location of the washers

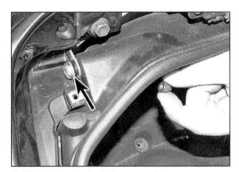

3.56 Undo the bolt (arrowed) – note nut on inside

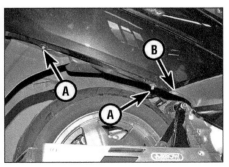

3.57 Trim clips (A), screw (B)

3.58a Disconnect the tail light assembly wiring connector . . .

3.58b . . . and draw the cowling assembly off

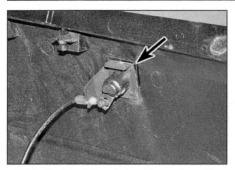

3.59 Seat lock is retained by spring clip (arrowed)

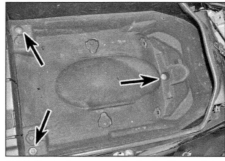

3.63 Undo the screws in the bottom of the storage compartment

3.64a Undo the bolts on both sides

3.64b Manoeuvre the storage compartment out

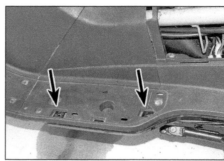

3.67a Undo the bolts securing the front . . . .

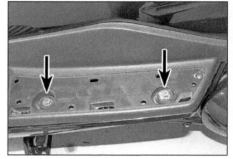

3.67b . . . and rear of the floor panels to the support brackets

clip securing the lock in the left-hand cowling panel **(see illustration)**.

60 If required, follow the procedure in Chapter 9 to remove the tail light unit.

61 Installation is the reverse of removal, noting the following:

• *Ensure the tail light assembly wiring connector is secure.*
• *Check the operation of the seat catch before lowering the seat.*
• *Check the operation of the lights before riding the scooter.*

Storage compartment

62 Remove the underseat panel (see Steps 34 to 37), passenger handles and backrest (see Steps 45 to 51) and the seat cowling (see Steps 54 to 58).

63 Undo the screws securing the bottom of the storage compartment to the frame **(see illustration)**. Note the location of the washers and spacers.

64 Undo the bolts securing the rear mudguard to the frame **(see illustration)**. Tilt the rear of the storage compartment down and manoeuvre it out **(see illustration)**.

65 Installation is the reverse of removal.

Floor panels

Note: *On AN250W to Y models and AN400X and Y models the floor panels are a one-piece unit.*

66 Remove the left and right-hand side belly panels (see Steps 27 to 30) and the underseat panel (see Steps 34 to 37). On AN250W to Y models, and AN400X and Y models, remove the passenger handles and backrest (see Steps 45 to 51) and the seat cowling (see Steps 54 to 58).

67 Undo the bolts securing the floor panels to the front and rear support brackets on both sides **(see illustrations)**. Note the location of the washers and spacers.

68 On AN250K1 and K2 models and AN400K1 and K2 models, working on one side at a time, undo the screws securing the left and right-hand floor panels to the floor centre panel **(see illustration)**. Ease each panel back and unclip it from the floor centre panel and the lower edge of the seat cowling **(see illustration)**.

69 Undo the screws securing the centre

3.68a Undo the screw . . .

3.68b . . . then ease the floor panel off – AN400K1 and K2 models

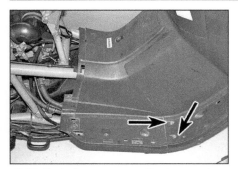

3.69 Undo the screws on the lower edge of the kickpanel

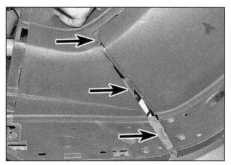

3.71a Ease the floor centre panel back to release the tabs (arrowed) . . .

3.71b . . . then lift the panel off

panel to the lower edge of the kick panel on both sides **(see illustration)**.

70 On AN250W to Y models, and AN400X and Y models, ease the floor panel unit back, noting how the tabs along the front edge locate in the slots in the kick panel. Remove the floor panel unit. Note the location of the cushion block below the lock for the fuel filler flap.

71 On AN250K1 and K2 models and AN400K1 and K2 models, ease the floor centre panel back noting how the tabs along the front edge locate in the slots in the kick panel **(see illustration)**. Remove the floor centre panel unit **(see illustration)**.

72 If required, undo the bolts securing the rear support brackets and remove them **(see illustration)**.

73 Installation is the reverse of removal.

Kick panel

74 Remove all other panels and the seat to gain access to the kick panel.

75 Remove the battery (see Chapter 9). Pass the battery terminal leads through the back of the panel.

76 Insert a T-25 Torx driver into the hole on the right-hand side of the steering stem and undo the screw securing the ignition switch cover. Undo the screw securing the parking brake handle and draw the handle off the lever.

77 Undo the screws securing the left and right-hand sides of the kick panel to the frame **(see illustration)**. Undo the screw in the

3.72 Remove the rear support brackets

centre of the glove compartment securing the kick panel to the frame.

78 Ensure all wiring is clear of the panel assembly, then ease the rear edge of the kick panel up over the seat pivot bracket and lift it off.

79 Installation is the reverse of removal.

Front mudguard

80 Remove the front wheel (see Chapter 7).

81 If applicable, release the speedometer wire from the guides on the right and left-hand fork legs and release the clip from the top of the mudguard. Secure the speedometer drive housing to the scooter to avoid straining the wire.

82 Undo the mounting bolts at the front (outside) and rear (inside) of the mudguard **(see illustration)**.

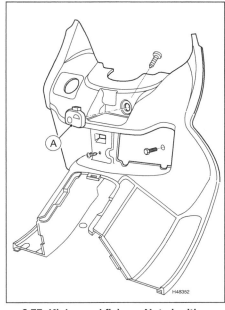

3.77 Kick panel fixings. Note ignition switch cover (A)

83 Draw the mudguard forwards and off **(see illustration)**.

84 Installation is the reverse of removal, noting the following:

• *Ensure the speedometer wire is correctly routed and secured.*

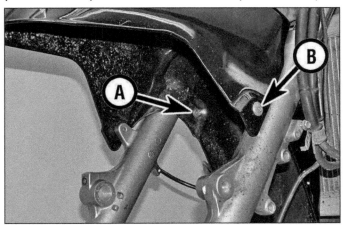

3.82 Mounting bolts inside (A) and outside (B) the mudguard

3.83 Draw the mudguard forwards

4.2a Release the trim clip . . .

4.2b . . . and lift off the centre panel

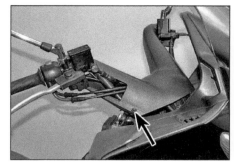

4.3a Release the trim clips on both sides

4 AN400K3 to K6 body panels

Handlebar covers

1 Open the battery storage compartment.
2 Release the trim clip securing the centre cockpit panel, then lift the panel to release the spring clips and lift it off (see illustrations).
3 Release the trim clips on both sides securing the front and rear halves of the handlebar cover and unclip the rear half (see illustrations).
4 Unclip the front half of the cover from the handlebars (see illustration).
5 Installation is the reverse of removal, noting the following:
• *Ensure the covers are correctly aligned before installing the trim clips.*

4.3b Unclip the rear half of the cover . . .

4.3c . . . and lift it off

Windshield panels

6 Undo the screws on the inside of the cockpit securing the lower windshield panel and unclip the panel (see illustrations).

7 Undo the screws securing the windshield, noting how they fit, and lift it off (see illustrations). Note the location of the plastic washers. The screws are secured by wellnuts (see illustration) (see Section 1).

4.4 Unclip the front half

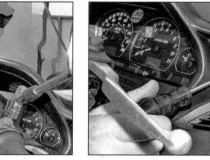

4.6a Undo the screws on both sides

4.6b Pull the panel off

4.7a Undo the windshield screws . . .

4.7b . . . and lift the windshield off

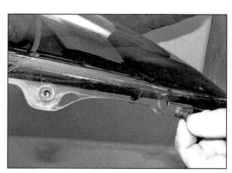

4.7c Note location of the wellnuts

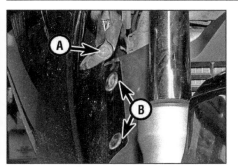

4.11 Remove the screw (A) and trim clips (B)

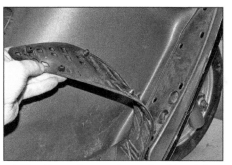

4.12a Note clips on the underside of the floor mats

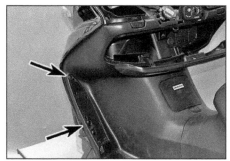

4.12b Undo the screws (arrowed) on both sides

Headlight panel

10 Remove the lower windshield panel (see Step 6).

11 Undo the screws and release the trim clips securing the left and right-hand inner edges of the headlight panel (**see illustration**).

12 Remove the front floor mats, noting how they fit (**see illustration**). Undo the screws securing the outer edges of the headlight panel to the kick panel (**see illustration**).

13 Undo the screws on both sides securing the upper edge of the headlight panel to the fairing bracket (**see illustration**).

14 Open the small box lids and undo the screws securing the back of the headlight panel (**see illustration**).

15 Reach up underneath the headlight panel and disconnect the headlight and parking light wiring connectors (**see illustration**).

16 Draw the headlight panel forwards and disconnect the turn signal wiring connectors (**see illustrations**). If required, follow the procedure in Chapter 9 to remove the headlight unit.

17 Installation is the reverse of removal, noting the following:

- *Ensure the wiring connectors are secure.*
- *Check the operation of the lights before riding the scooter.*

Instrument panel and cockpit trim panel

18 Remove the windshield panels (see Steps 6 to 7) and the headlight panel (see Steps 11 to 16).

19 Disconnect the instrument cluster wiring connector (**see illustration**).

20 Undo the screw on the lower front edge of the instrument panel (**see illustration**).

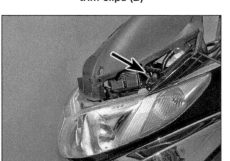

4.13 Screw secures upper edge of panel

4.14 Undo the screws inside the small boxes

8 If the wellnuts remain in the lower edge of the instrument panel, pull them out prior to installation, noting how they fit.

9 Installation is the reverse of removal, noting the following:

- *Hold the windshield in position and press the wellnuts through the holes in the windshield into the instrument panel.*
- *Take care not to over-tighten the screws in the wellnuts.*

4.15 Disconnect the lighting wiring connectors

4.16a Draw the headlight panel forwards . . .

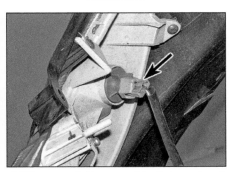

4.16b . . . and disconnect both turn signal wiring connectors

4.19 Instrument cluster wiring connector

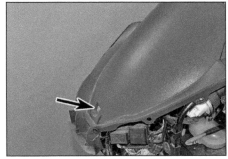

4.20 Undo the screw

4.21a Undo the left . . .

4.21b . . . and right-hand screws

4.21c Lift off the instrument panel assembly

4.22a Undo the screws (arrowed) . . .

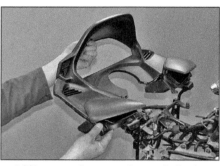
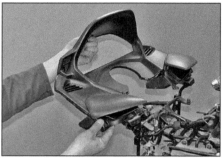
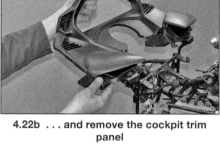

4.22b . . . and remove the cockpit trim panel

21 Undo the screws securing the instrument cluster to the cockpit trim panel, then lift off the instrument panel assembly **(see illustrations)**.

22 Undo the screws securing the cockpit trim panel and remove the panel **(see illustrations)**.

23 Installation is the reverse of removal, noting the following:
* *Ensure the instrument cluster wiring connector is secure.*

Belly panels

24 Working on one side at a time, remove the front and rear floor mats, noting how they fit.

25 Undo the screws and release the trim clips securing the side belly panel through the floor panel **(see illustrations)**.

26 Release the trim clips securing the front underside of the side belly panel to the centre belly panel and radiator panel **(see illustration)**.

27 Release the trim clips on the rear underside of the side belly panel **(see illustrations)**.

28 Pull the side belly panel away from the machine to release the tabs along the top edge and lift it off **(see illustrations)**.

29 Once the left and right-hand side belly panels have been removed, separate the front edge of the centre belly panel from the lower edge of the radiator panel **(see illustration)**.

30 Lower the front edge of the centre belly

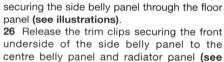

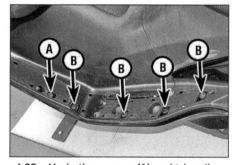

4.25a Undo the screws (A) and trim clips (B) at the front . . .

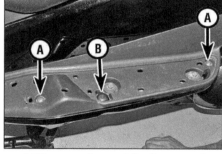

4.25b . . . and rear of the floor panel

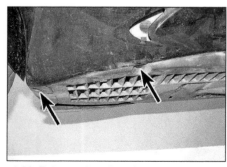

4.26 Release the trim clips on both sides

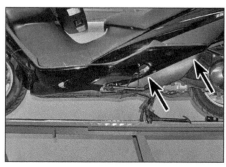

4.27a Trim clips on the rear left . . .

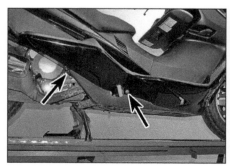

4.27b . . . and right-hand sides

4.28a Release the tabs along the top edge . . .

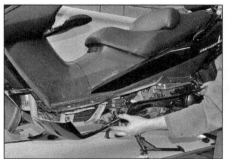

4.28b . . . and ease the belly panel off

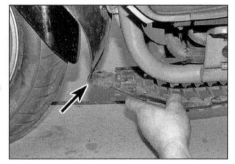

4.29 Separate the centre belly panel from the radiator panel (arrowed)

panel, then draw the panel forwards to release the clip on the rear edge from the frame **(see illustrations)**.

31 Installation is the reverse of removal.

Radiator panel

32 Remove the headlight panel (see Steps 10 to 16).

33 Remove the belly panels (see Steps 24 to 30).

34 Ease the tabs on the side of the radiator panel off the brackets on the frame and lower the panel off **(see illustration)**.

35 Installation is the reverse of removal, noting the following:

• *Ensure the tabs on the upper edge are correctly secured before installing the trim clips and screws.*

Underseat panel

36 Raise the seat.

37 Release the trim clips securing the rear top edge of the panel to the side panels on both sides **(see illustration)**.

38 Lower the seat. Push the panel back to release the tabs on the front edge from the back edge of the kick panel, then manoeuvre the underseat panel off **(see illustration)**.

39 Installation is the reverse of removal.

Seat and underseat cover

40 The underseat cover is secured by trim clips on the left and right-hand sides. Release

the trim clips, then draw the cover back to remove it.

41 To remove the seat, first remove the underseat cover (see Step 40) and the underseat panel (see Steps 37 and 38).

42 Raise the seat. Trace the wiring from the underseat light and disconnect it at the connector **(see illustration 3.41)**. Release the wiring from any clips or ties and feed it back to the seat.

43 Pull out the R-clip securing the seat damper rod to the underside of the seat **(see illustration 3.42)**. Remove the washer and disconnect the damper rod from the seat.

44 Fold the seat all the way forwards, then

undo the nuts securing the seat to the hinge and lift the seat off **(see illustration 3.43)**.

45 Installation is the reverse of removal.

Passenger backrest and handles

46 Raise the seat. The handles and backrest must be removed in the following order.

47 Release the trim clips securing the panel at the rear of the backrest and remove the panel **(see illustration 3.46)**.

48 Undo the screw securing the backrest cushion bracket, then pull the cushion forwards to unclip it from the backrest **(see illustrations 3.47a and b)**.

49 Undo the screws and release the trim clips

4.30a Draw the centre belly panel forwards . . .

4.30b . . . to release the clip on the rear edge from the frame

4.34 Lower the radiator panel off

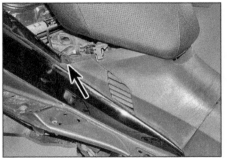

4.37 Release the trim clips on both sides

4.38 Lift the underseat panel off

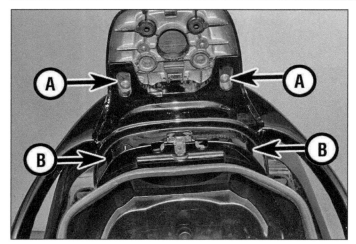

4.49a Undo the screws (A) and trim clips (B) . . .

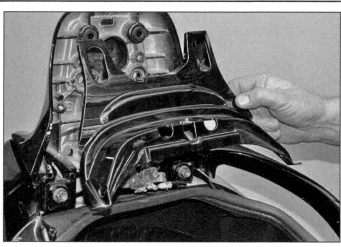

4.49b . . . and remove the panel

4.50a Disconnect the seat lock cable from the catch . . .

4.50b . . . noting how the outer cable end fits in the bracket

securing the panel below the backrest cushion and remove the panel **(see illustrations)**.

50 Disconnect the seat lock cable from the catch, noting how it fits **(see illustrations)**. Alternatively, undo the screws securing the seat catch and displace the catch.

51 Undo the bolts securing the backrest and lift it off **(see illustrations)**.

52 To remove the passenger handles, first remove the blanking plugs from the front handle mountings **(see illustration)**.

53 Undo the front and rear handle mounting bolts, noting the location of the spacers, and lift the handles off **(see illustrations)**.

54 Installation is the reverse of removal, noting the following:

- *Clean the threads of the mounting bolts and apply a suitable non-permanent thread-locking compound.*
- *Tighten the mounting bolts to the torque setting specified at the beginning of this Chapter.*
- *Check the operation of the seat catch before lowering the seat.*

Rear bodywork panels

Note: *The rear bodywork panels interlock and must be removed in the following general order.*

4.51a Undo the backrest mounting bolts . . .

4.51b . . . and lift the backrest off

4.52 Remove the blanking plugs

4.53a Remove bolts, noting location of spacers . . .

4.53b . . . and lift the handles off

4.55a Release the trim clips on both sides

4.55b Pull the panel back – note hooks on upper edge

Rear panel
55 Release the trim clips on both sides, then pull the panel to the rear to release the hooks on the upper edge **(see illustrations)**.

Floor panels
56 Remove the left and right-hand side belly panels (see Steps 24 to 28).
57 Working on one side at a time, release the trim clip at the rear of the panel **(see illustration)**.
58 Undo the screws securing the floor panel to the lower edges of the kick panel, then undo the bolts securing the floor panel to the frame **(see illustrations)**.
59 Ease the floor panel forwards to release the hooks on the rear upper edge from the lower edge of the side panel **(see illustration)**.
60 Now draw the floor panel rearwards to release the hooks on the lower edge from the kick panel **(see illustration)**.
61 If required, undo the bolts securing the rear support brackets and remove them **(see illustration)**.

Side panels
62 Remove the underseat panel (see Steps 36 to 38) and the passenger backrest and handles (see Steps 46 to 53).
63 The left and right-hand side panels and tail light unit are removed as an assembly **(see illustration)**.

4.57 Release the trim clip

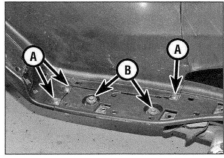

4.58a Undo the screws (A) and bolts (B) at the front . . .

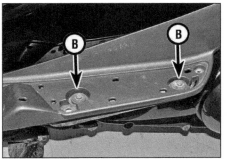

4.58b . . . and rear of the floor panels

4.59 Detach the floor panel from the side panel

4.60 Hooks (arrowed) locate in the kick panel

4.61 Rear support bracket mounting bolts

4.63 Remove the side panels and tail light unit as an assembly

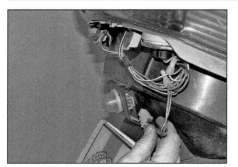

4.64a Licence plate light wiring connector

4.64b Tail light wiring connector

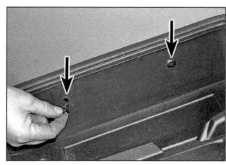

4.65 Release the trim clips on both sides

64 Disconnect the licence plate light and tail light unit wiring connectors **(see illustrations)**.

65 Release the trim clips on the inside of the storage compartment securing the storage compartment to the cowling side panels **(see illustration)**. Note the location of the washers. Where fitted, release the trim clips securing the top edge of the cowling side panels to the rim of the storage compartment.

66 Release the trim clips securing the upper and lower rear edges of the side panels **(see illustrations)**.

67 Draw the assembly back and off the scooter, noting the routing of the seat lock release cable – this must be routed correctly on assembly, otherwise it will become trapped between the left-hand side panel and the frame.

68 If required, follow the procedure in Chapter 9 to remove the tail light unit.

Installation

69 Installation is the reverse of removal, noting the following:
- *Ensure the tail light assembly and licence plate light wiring connectors are secure.*
- *Check the operation of the lights before riding the scooter.*

Storage compartment

70 Remove the underseat panel (see Steps 36 to 38), passenger backrest and handles (see Steps 46 to 53), rear panel (see Step 55), floor panels (see Steps 56 to 60) and side panels (see Steps 63 to 67).

71 Unclip the compartment liner and remove it.

72 Undo the screws securing the bottom of the storage compartment to the frame **(see illustration)**. Note the location of the washers and spacers.

73 Undo the nuts and bolts securing the rear of the storage compartment to the frame **(see illustration)**.

74 Lift the storage compartment out – note that the rear mudguard is an integral part of the storage compartment **(see illustration)**.

75 Installation is the reverse of removal.

Kick panel

76 Remove all other panels and the seat to gain access to the kick panel.

77 Remove the battery (see Chapter 9). Pass the battery terminal leads through the back of the panel **(see illustration)**.

78 Disconnect the ECM multi-pin wiring

4.66a Release the trim clips on the upper . . .

4.66b . . . and lower rear edges of the side panels

4.72 Note location of washers and spacers

4.73 Undo the nuts and bolts on both sides

4.74 Storage compartment and rear mudguard are an integral unit

4.77 Draw the battery leads out through the back of the panel

4.78 Remove the ECM

4.79 Disconnect the accessory socket wiring connector

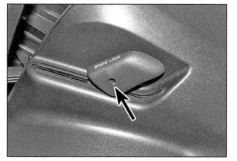

4.80 Undo the screw (arrowed) and remove the lever

connector and release the ECM from its holder **(see illustration)**.
79 Trace the wiring from the accessory socket inside the glove compartment and disconnect it **(see illustration)**.
80 Undo the screw securing the parking brake handle and draw the handle off the lever **(see illustration)**.
81 Undo the bolts inside the glove compartment securing the kick panel to the frame **(see illustration)**.
82 Ease the rear edge of the kick panel up over the seat pivot bracket and lift it off **(see illustration)**.
83 Installation is the reverse of removal.

Front mudguard

84 Follow the procedure in Section 3, Steps 80 to 84, to remove and install the front mudguard.

5   AN400K7 model onward body panels

Handlebar covers

1 Release the trim clips on both sides securing the front and rear halves of the handlebar cover and unclip the rear half **(see illustrations)**.
2 Unclip the front half of the handlebar cover and lift it off **(see illustrations)**.

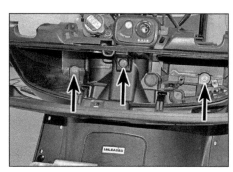

4.81 Undo the bolts inside the glove compartment

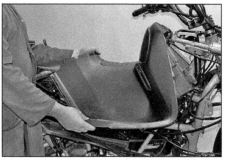

4.82 Lift the rear edge of the kick panel and manoeuvre it off

5.1a Release the trim clips on both sides . . .

5.1b . . . and unclip the rear half of the cover

5.2a Unclip the front half of the cover . . .

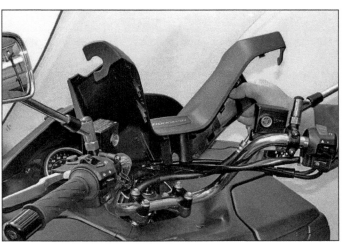

5.2b . . . and lift it off

3 Installation is the reverse of removal, noting the following:
- *Ensure the covers are correctly aligned before installing the trim clips.*

Windshield panels

4 The lower instrument trim panel is secured by four clips – ease the panel back to release the clips and remove the panel **(see illustration)**.

5 Undo the screws securing the lower windshield panel **(see illustration)**. Ease the panel forwards to release the clips and lift it off **(see illustrations)**.

6 Undo the screws securing the windshield, noting how they fit, and lift it off **(see illustrations)**. Note the location of the plastic washers. The screws are secured by wellnuts (see Section 1).

7 If the wellnuts remain in the lower edge of the instrument panel, pull them out prior to installation, noting how they fit **(see illustration)**.

8 Installation is the reverse of removal, noting the following:
- *Hold the windshield in position and press the wellnuts through the holes in the windshield into the instrument panel.*
- *Take care not to over-tighten the screws in the wellnuts.*

Cockpit trim panel and instrument panel

9 Remove the handlebar covers (see Steps 1 and 2).

10 Open the glove compartment and undo the screw securing the trim panel **(see illustration)**.

5.4 Ease the lower instrument trim panel out

5.5a Undo the screws (arrowed)

5.5b Ease the lower windshield panel forwards . . .

5.5c . . . to release the clips

11 Undo the screw securing the parking brake handle and draw the handle off the lever **(see illustration)**.

12 Draw the trim panel backwards to release the tabs on the front edge **(see illustration)**.

13 To remove the instrument panel, first remove the handlebar covers (see Steps 1 and 2), windshield panels (see Steps 4 to 6) and cockpit trim panel.

14 Undo the screws and trim clips securing

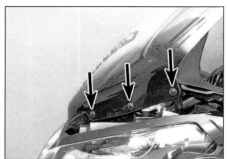

5.6a Undo the screws on both sides . . .

5.6b . . . and lift the windshield off

5.7 Remove the wellnuts from the instrument panel

5.10 Undo the screw securing the trim panel

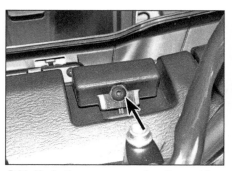

5.11 Undo the screw securing the parking brake handle

5.12 Pull the trim panel off

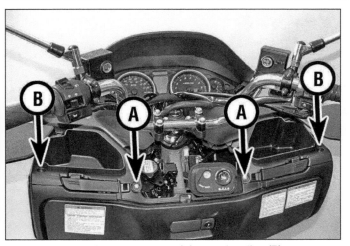

5.14 Undo the screws (A) and trim clips (B)

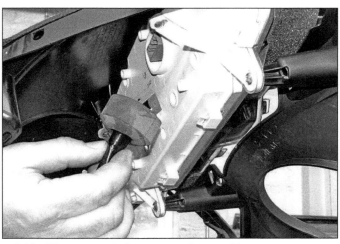

5.15a Disconnect the instrument cluster wiring connector . . .

5.15b . . . and remove the instrument panel

5.18 Remove the front floor mats

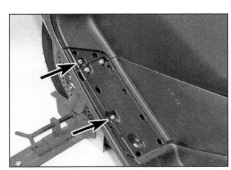

5.19 Undo the screws (arrowed) on both sides

the instrument panel on both sides (see illustration).

15 Ease the panel assembly off, disconnect the instrument cluster wiring connector, and remove the panel (see illustrations).

16 Installation is the reverse of removal, noting the following:

• Ensure the instrument cluster wiring connector is secure.

Headlight panel

17 Remove the handlebar covers (see Steps 1 and 2), windshield panels (see Steps 4 to 6), cockpit trim panel and instrument panel (see Steps 10 to 15).

18 Remove the front floor mats, noting how they fit (see illustration).

19 Undo the left and right-hand screws securing the lower edge of the headlight

panel to the kick panel (see illustration).

20 Undo the screws securing the upper edge of the panel to the fairing bracket (see illustration).

21 Undo the screws and release the trim clips securing the inner edges of the headlight panel to the kick panel and radiator panel (see illustration).

5.20 Undo the screws

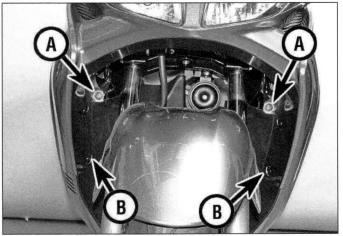

5.21 Undo the screws (A) and trim clips (B)

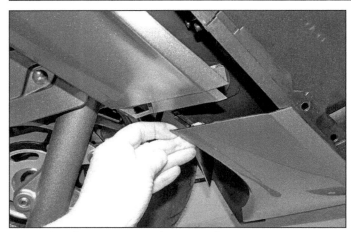

5.22a Detach the headlight panel from the belly panel

5.22b Draw the panel forwards and disconnect the wiring connectors

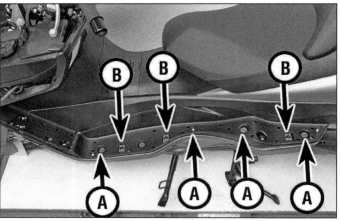

5.26 Screws (A) and trim clips (B) securing the side belly panel

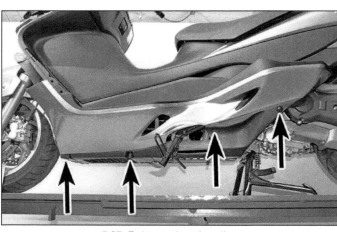

5.27 Release the trim clips

22 Draw the panel upwards to release the tabs on the lower edges (see illustration). Disconnect the wiring connectors for the turn signals, parking lights and headlights, and lift the headlight panel off (see illustration).
23 If required, follow the procedure in Chapter 9 to remove the headlight unit.
24 Installation is the reverse of removal, noting the following:
• Ensure the headlight unit wiring connectors are secure.

• Check the operation of the lights before riding the scooter.

Belly panels

25 Working on one side at a time, remove the front and rear floor mats, noting how they fit (see illustration 5.18).
26 Undo the screws and release the trim clips securing the side belly panel through the floor panel (see illustration).
27 Release the trim clips securing the side

belly panel to the centre belly panel (see illustration).
28 Ease the side belly panel away from the machine to release the tabs along the top and bottom edges and lift it off (see illustration). Note the location of the centre belly panel (see illustration).
29 Once the left and right-hand side belly panels have been removed, separate the front edge of the centre belly panel from the lower edge of the radiator panel (see illustration).

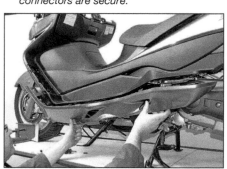

5.28a Remove the side belly panel carefully, noting the tabs

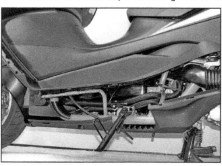

5.28b Note location of centre belly panel

5.29 Separate the centre belly panel from the radiator panel (arrowed)

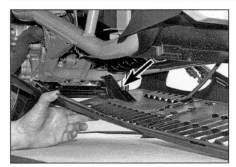

5.30 Draw the centre belly panel forwards to release the clip (arrowed) from the frame

30 Lower the front edge of the centre belly panel, then draw the panel forwards to release the clip on the rear edge from the frame **(see illustration)**.
31 Installation is the reverse of removal.

Radiator panels

32 Remove the handlebar covers (see Steps 1 and 2), windshield panels (see Steps 4 to 6), cockpit trim panel and instrument panel (see Steps 10 to 15), headlight panel (see Steps 18 to 22) and belly panels (see Steps 25 to 30).
33 Ease the pegs on the side of the front radiator panel off the fairing bracket and lower the panel off **(see illustration)**.
34 Note the location of the radiator side panels. To remove the side panels, release the trim clip, then unhook the tabs on the back of the panels from the slots in the radiator fan housing **(see illustrations)**.
35 Installation is the reverse of removal.

Underseat panel

36 Raise the seat.
37 Release the trim clips securing the rear top edge of the panel to the seat cowling on both sides **(see illustration)**.
38 Lower the seat. Push the panel back to release the tabs on the front edge from the back edge of the kick panel, then manoeuvre the underseat panel off **(see illustration)**.
39 Installation is the reverse of removal.

Seat and underseat cover

40 The underseat cover is secured by trim clips on the left and right-hand sides. Release

5.40b ... and lift the cover out

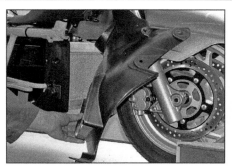

5.33 Lower the radiator panel off

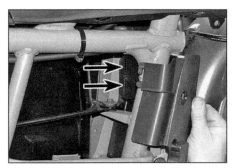

5.34b Unhook the tabs from the slots (arrowed)

the trim clips, then draw the cover back to remove it **(see illustrations)**.
41 To remove the seat, first remove the underseat cover (see Step 40) and the underseat panel (see Steps 37 and 38).
42 Raise the seat. Trace the wiring from the underseat light and disconnect it at the

5.38 Lift the underseat panel off

5.42 Disconnect the underseat light wiring connector

5.34a Release the trim clip

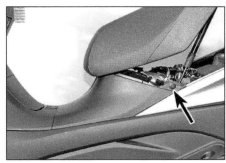

5.37 Release the trim clips on both sides

connector **(see illustration)**. Release the wiring from any clips or ties and feed it back to the seat.
43 Pull out the R-clip securing the seat damper rod to the underside of the seat **(see illustration)**. Remove the washer and disconnect the damper rod from the seat.

5.40a Release the trim clips ...

5.43 Remove the R-clip

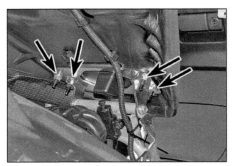

5.44 Undo the nuts securing the seat hinge

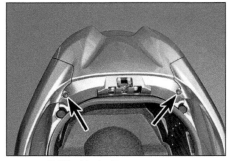

5.47a Undo the screws . . .

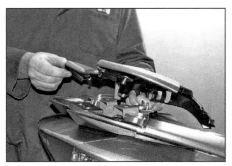

5.47b . . . then lift the panel to release the pegs

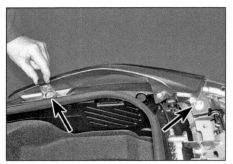

5.48a Remove the plugs and mounting bolts on both sides

5.48b Note the location of the spacers

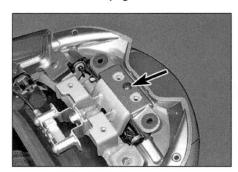

5.49a Undo the screw . . .

44 Fold the seat all the way forward, then undo the nuts securing the seat to the hinge and lift the seat off **(see illustration)**.
45 Installation is the reverse of removal.

Passenger handles
46 Raise the seat.
47 Undo the screws securing the top rear panel, then lift the panel to release

the pegs on the underside from the grommets in the handle assembly **(see illustrations)**.
48 The passenger handles are a single component. Remove the blanking plugs from the front handle mountings, then undo the front and rear handle mounting bolts, noting the location of the spacers **(see illustrations)**.
49 Undo the screw in the centre rear of the handle assembly and lift the handles off **(see illustrations)**.
50 Installation is the reverse of removal, noting the following:
• *Clean the threads of the mounting bolts and apply a suitable non-permanent thread-locking compound.*
• *Tighten the mounting bolts to the torque setting specified at the beginning of this Chapter.*

5.49b . . . and lift the handles off

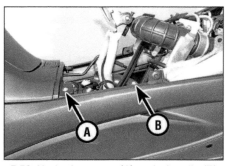

5.52 Undo the screw (A) and trim clip (B)

Seat cowling
51 Remove the underseat panel (see Steps 36 to 38) and the passenger handles (see Steps 46 to 49).
52 Working on one side at a time, undo the screw and release the trim clip securing the lower side panel **(see illustration)**.
53 Ease the lower side panel away from the machine to release the tabs along the top edge and the spring clips **(see illustrations)**.
54 Ease the turn signals access panel away from the tail light assembly to release the

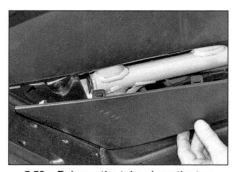

5.53a Release the tabs along the top edge . . .

5.53b . . . and the clips on the back of the panel

5.54a Ease the panel back . . .

5.54b . . . to release the spring clips

5.55 Remove the tail light access panel

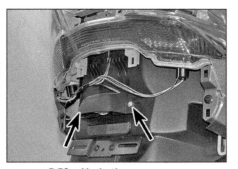

5.56a Undo the screws . . .

5.56b . . . and disconnect the licence plate light connector

5.57 Remove the heat shield

retaining spring clips and remove the panel **(see illustrations)**.

55 Ease the tail light unit access panel away from the tail light unit to release the retaining spring clips and remove the panel **(see illustration)**.

56 Undo the screws securing the licence plate light, lift off the light assembly and disconnect the wiring connector **(see illustrations)**.

57 Release the trim clips securing the heat shield on the right-hand side **(see illustration)**.

58 Release the trim lips on the inside of the storage compartment securing the storage compartment to the upper side panels **(see illustration)**.

59 Release the trim clips securing the inside edges of the upper side panels to the rear of the floor panels **(see illustration)**.

60 Draw the cowling assembly back, disconnect the tail light unit wiring connector, then remove the cowling assembly **(see illustrations)**.

61 If required, follow the procedure in Chapter 9 to remove the tail light unit.

62 Installation is the reverse of removal, noting the following:

• *Ensure the tail light assembly and licence plate light wiring connectors are secure.*

• *Check the operation of the lights before riding the scooter.*

Storage compartment

63 Remove the underseat panel (see Steps 36 to 38), passenger handles (see Steps

46 to 49) and the seat cowling (see Steps 52 to 60).

64 Unclip the compartment liner and remove it.

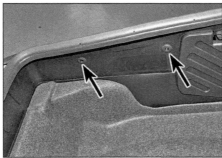

5.58 Release the trim clips on both sides

5.60a Disconnect the tail light wiring connector . . .

65 Undo the screws inside the storage compartment securing the bottom of the compartment to the frame. Note the location of the washers and spacers.

5.59 Trim clip is located on the inside of the panels

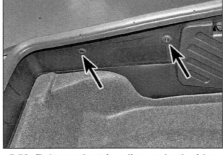

5.60b . . . then lift off the seat cowling assembly

5.66a Bolts (arrowed) secure storage compartment to frame

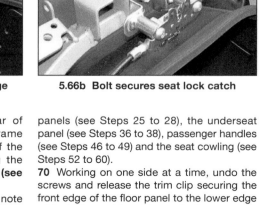

5.66b Bolt secures seat lock catch

5.67 Lift out the storage compartment

66 Undo the bolts securing the rear of the storage compartment to the frame **(see illustration)**. Note the location of the captive nuts. Undo the bolt securing the seat lock catch and displace the catch **(see illustration)**.

67 Lift the storage compartment out – note that the rear mudguard is an integral part of the storage compartment **(see illustration)**.

68 Installation is the reverse of removal.

• *Check the operation of the seat catch before lowering the seat.*

Floor panels

69 Remove the left and right-hand side belly panels (see Steps 25 to 28), the underseat panel (see Steps 36 to 38), passenger handles (see Steps 46 to 49) and the seat cowling (see Steps 52 to 60).

70 Working on one side at a time, undo the screws and release the trim clip securing the front edge of the floor panel to the lower edge of the kick panel **(see illustration)**.

71 Undo the bolts securing the floor panel to the front and rear support brackets and lift the panel off **(see illustrations)**. Note the location of the washers and spacers.

72 If required, undo the bolts securing the rear support brackets and remove them **(see illustration)**.

73 Installation is the reverse of removal.

Kick panel

74 Remove all other panels and the seat to gain access to the kick panel.

75 Remove the battery (see Chapter 9). Pass the battery terminal leads through the back of the panel.

76 Displace the ambient temperature sensor from the front right-hand side of the panel.

77 Displace the ECM from the front left-hand side of the panel **(see illustration)**.

78 Undo the three bolts inside the glove compartment securing the kick panel to the frame.

79 Ensure all wiring is clear of the panel assembly, then ease the rear edge of the kick panel up over the seat pivot bracket and lift it off.

80 Installation is the reverse of removal.

Front mudguard

81 Follow the procedure in Section 3, Steps 80 to 84, to remove and install the front mudguard, noting the following:

• *There is no speedometer drive housing and wire fitted to the front of these models.*

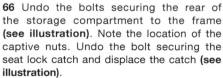

5.70 Undo the screws (A) and trim clip (B)

5.71a Undo the bolts . . .

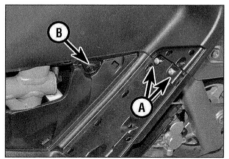

5.71b . . . and lift the floor panel off

5.72 Bolts (arrowed) secure rear support brackets

5.77 Location of the ECM

Chapter 9
Electrical system

Contents

Degrees of difficulty

| Easy, suitable for novice with little experience | 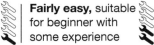 | Fairly easy, suitable for beginner with some experience | | Fairly difficult, suitable for competent DIY mechanic | | Difficult, suitable for experienced DIY mechanic | | Very difficult, suitable for expert DIY or professional | |

Specifications

Battery
Capacity
AN250W and X models	12 V, 6 Ah
AN250Y to K2 models	12 V, 8 Ah
AN400X to K2 models	12 V, 8 Ah
AN400K3 to K6 models	12 V, 10 Ah
AN400K7 model onward	12 V, 9 Ah

Charging rate
AN250 models	0.7 A for 5 to 10 hrs
AN400X to K2 models	0.9 A for 5 to 10 hrs
AN400K3 to K6 models	1.2 A for 5 to 10 hrs
AN400K7 model onward	0.9 A for 5 to 10 hrs
Leakage rate	3 mA

Alternator
AN250 models
Unregulated voltage	56 volts AC @ 5000 rpm
Regulated voltage	13.5 to 15 volts DC @ 5000 rpm

AN400X to K2 models
Unregulated voltage	56 volts AC @ 5000 rpm
Regulated voltage	13.5 to 15 volts DC @ 5000 rpm
Stator coil resistance	0.15 to 0.45 ohms

AN400K3 to K6 models
Unregulated voltage	56 volts AC @ 5000 rpm
Regulated voltage	14.0 to 15.5 volts DC @ 5000 rpm
Stator coil resistance	0.2 to 0.6 ohms

AN400-K7 model onward
Unregulated voltage	55 volts AC @ 5000 rpm
Regulated voltage	14.0 to 15.5 volts DC @ 5000 rpm
Stator coil resistance	0.1 to 1.0 ohms

Starter relay

Resistance
AN250 models .... 2 to 6 ohms
AN400X to K2 models .... 1 to 7 ohms
AN400K3 model onward .... 3 to 6 ohms

Starter motor

Brush length (min) .... 3.5 mm

Fuses

AN250 models
Main .... 30 A
Headlight (No. 1).................................... 15 A
Headlight (No. 2).................................... 15 A
Ignition (No. 3) .... 10 A
Signal (No. 4) .... 15 A
Instruments and tail light (No. 5)..................... 10 A
AN400X to K2 models
Main .... 30 A
Headlight (No. 1).................................... 15 A
Headlight (No. 2).................................... 15 A
Ignition (No. 3) .... 10 A
Signal (No. 4) .... 15 A
Instruments and tail light (No. 5)..................... 10 A
AN400K3 to K6 models
Main .... 30 A
Headlight (No. 1).................................... 10 A
Headlight (No. 2).................................... 10 A
Instruments (No. 3).................................. 10 A
Ignition (No. 4) .... 10 A
Signal (No. 5) .... 15 A
Accessory socket (No. 6) .... 10 A
AN400K7 model onward
Main .... 30 A
Headlight (No. 1).................................... 10 A
Headlight (No. 2).................................... 10 A
Instruments (No. 3).................................. 10 A
Ignition (No. 4) .... 10 A
Signal (No. 5) .... 15 A
Accessory socket (No. 6) .... 10 A
ABS motor (No. 7)................................... 20 A
ABS valve (No. 8) .... 15 A

Bulbs

Headlight
AN250 models and AN400X to K2 models .... 60/55 W H4
AN400K3 to K6 models .... 35/35 W x 2
AN400K7 model onward
High beam .... 60/55 W
Low beam....................................... 55 W
Sidelight .... 5 W
Brake/tail light .... 21/5 W
Turn signals .... 21 W
Licence plate light .... 5 W
Storage compartment
AN250W to Y models .... 2 W
AN250K1 and K2 models.............................. 5 W
AN400X and Y models .... 2 W
AN400K1 model onward .... 5 W
Instrument cluster
AN250 models and AN400X to K6 models
Warning lights.................................... 1.7 W
Cluster illumination .... 1.7 W
AN400K7 model onward
Warning lights.................................... LED
Cluster illumination .... LED
Immobiliser light..................................... LED

Torque wrench settings

Alternator rotor nut	160 Nm
Alternator stator bolts	
AN250 models and AN400X to K6 models	10 Nm
AN400K7 model onward	11 Nm
Alternator wiring sub-loom clamp bolt	10 Nm
CKP sensor bolts	6 Nm
Ignition pulse generator bolts	5 Nm

1 General information

All models covered in this manual have a 12-volt electrical system charged by a three-phase alternator with a separate regulator/rectifier.

The regulator maintains the charging system output within the specified range to prevent overcharging, and the rectifier converts the ac (alternating current) output of the alternator to dc (direct current) to power the lights and other components and to charge the battery. The alternator rotor is mounted on the right-hand end of the crankshaft.

All models are fitted with an electric starter motor. The starting system includes the motor, the battery, the relay and the various wires and switches. Some of the switches are part of an ignition safety interlock circuit which prevents the engine from being started if the sidestand is down or if the front or rear brake is not applied. The system will also cut the engine should the sidestand extend while the scooter is being ridden – see Section 20.

Note: *Keep in mind that electrical parts, once purchased, cannot be returned. To avoid unnecessary expense, make very sure the faulty component has been positively identified before buying a replacement part.*

2 Fault finding

 Warning: To prevent the risk of short circuits, the ignition switch must always be OFF and the battery negative (-ve) terminal should be disconnected before any of the bike's other electrical components are disturbed. Don't forget to reconnect the terminal securely once work is finished or if battery power is needed for circuit testing.

1 A typical electrical circuit consists of an electrical component, the switches, relays, etc, related to that component and the wiring and connectors that link the component to the battery and the frame.

2 Before tackling any troublesome electrical circuit, first study the wiring diagram thoroughly to get a complete picture of what makes up that individual circuit. Trouble spots, for instance, can often be narrowed down by noting if other components related to that circuit are operating properly or not. If several components or circuits fail at one time, chances are the fault lies either in the fuse or in the common earth (ground) connection, as several circuits are often routed through the same fuse and earth (ground) connections.

3 Electrical problems often stem from simple causes, such as loose or corroded connections or a blown fuse. Prior to any electrical fault finding, always visually check the condition of the fuse, wires and connections in the problem circuit. Intermittent failures can be especially frustrating, since you can't always duplicate the failure when it's convenient to test. In such situations, a good practice is to clean all connections in the affected circuit, whether or not they appear to be good. All of the connections and wires should also be wiggled to check for looseness which can cause intermittent failure.

4 A multimeter will enable a full range of electrical tests to be made. If you don't have a multimeter it is highly advisable to obtain one – they are not expensive and will enable a full range of electrical tests to be made. Go for a modern digital one with LCD display as they are easier to use. A continuity tester and/or test light are useful for certain electrical checks as an alternative, though are limited in their usefulness compared to a multimeter **(see illustrations)**.

Continuity checks

5 The term continuity describes the uninterrupted flow of electricity through an electrical circuit. Continuity can be checked with a multimeter set either to its continuity function (a beep is emitted when continuity is found), or to the resistance (ohms / Ω) function, or with a dedicated continuity tester. Both instruments are powered by an internal battery, therefore the checks are made with the ignition OFF. As a safety precaution, always disconnect the battery negative (-) lead before making continuity checks, particularly if ignition system checks are being made.

6 If using a multimeter, select the continuity function if it has one, or the resistance (ohms) function. Touch the meter probes together and check that a beep is emitted or the meter reads zero ohms (no resistance), which indicates continuity. If there is no continuity there will be no beep or the meter will show infinite resistance. After using the meter, always switch it OFF to conserve its battery.

7 A continuity tester can be used in the same way – its light should come on or it should beep to indicate continuity in the switch ON position, but should be off or silent in the OFF position.

8 Note that the polarity of the test probes doesn't matter for continuity checks, although care should be taken to follow specific test procedures if a diode or solid-state component is being checked.

Switch continuity checks

9 If a switch is at fault, trace its wiring to the wiring connectors. Separate the connectors

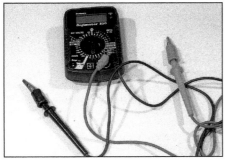

2.4a A digital multimeter can be used for all electrical tests

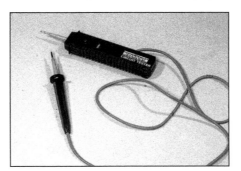

2.4b A battery powered continuity tester

2.4c A simple test light is useful for voltage tests

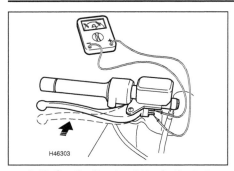

2.10 Continuity should be indicated across switch terminals when the lever is operated

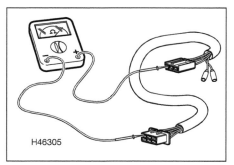

2.12 Wiring continuity check. Connect the meter probes across each end of the same wire

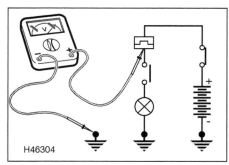

2.15 Voltage check. Connect the meter positive probe to the component and the negative probe to earth

and inspect them for security and condition. A build-up of dirt or corrosion here will most likely be the cause of the problem – clean up and apply a water dispersant such as WD-40, or alternatively use a dedicated contact cleaner and protection spray.

10 If using a multimeter, select the continuity function if it has one, or the resistance (ohms) function, and connect its probes to the terminals in the connector **(see illustration)**. Simple ON/OFF type switches, such as brake light switches, only have two wires whereas combination switches, like the handlebar switches, have many wires. Study the wiring diagram to ensure that you are connecting to the correct pair of wires. Continuity should be indicated with the switch ON and no continuity with it OFF.

Wiring continuity checks

11 Many electrical faults are caused by damaged wiring, often due to incorrect routing or chaffing on frame components. Loose, wet or corroded wire connectors can also be the cause of electrical problems.

12 A continuity check can be made on a single length of wire by disconnecting it at each end and connecting the meter or continuity tester probes to each end of the wire **(see illustration)**. Continuity should be indicated if the wire is good. If no continuity is shown, suspect a broken wire.

13 To check for continuity to earth (ground) in any earth wire, connect one probe of your meter or tester to the earth wire terminal in the connector and the other to the frame, engine, or battery earth (-) terminal. Continuity should be indicated if the wire is good. If no continuity is shown, suspect a broken wire or corroded or loose earth point (see below).

Voltage checks

14 A voltage check can determine whether power is reaching a component. Use a multimeter set to the dc (direct current) voltage scale to check for power from the battery or regulator/rectifier, or set to the ac (alternating current) voltage scale to check for power from the alternator. A test light can be used to check for dc voltage. The test light is the cheaper component, but the meter has

the advantage of being able to give a voltage reading.

15 Connect the meter or test light in parallel, i.e. across the load **(see illustration)**.

16 First identify the relevant wiring circuit by referring to the wiring diagram at the end of this manual. If other electrical components share the same power supply (i.e. are fed from the same fuse), take note whether they are working correctly – this is useful information in deciding where to start checking the circuit.

17 If using a meter, check first that the meter leads are plugged into the correct terminals on the meter – red to positive (+), black to negative (-). Set the meter to the appropriate volts function (dc or ac), where necessary at a range suitable for the battery voltage – 0 to 20 volts dc. Connect the meter red probe (+) to the power supply wire and the black probe to a good metal earth (ground) on the scooter's frame or directly to the battery negative terminal. Battery voltage, or the specified voltage, should be shown on the meter with the ignition switch, and if necessary any other relevant switch, ON.

18 If using a test light **(see illustration 2.4c)**, connect its positive (+) probe to the power supply terminal and its negative (-) probe to a good earth (ground) on the scooter's frame. With the switch, and if necessary any other relevant switch, ON, the test light should illuminate.

19 If no voltage is indicated, work back towards the power source continuing to check for voltage. When you reach a point where

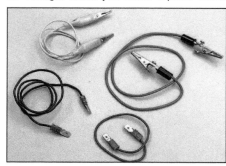

2.23 A selection of insulated jumper wires

there is voltage, you know the problem lies between that point and your last check point.

Earth (ground) checks

20 Earth connections are made either directly to the engine or frame (such as the starter motor which only has a positive feed) or by a separate wire into the earth circuit of the wiring harness. Alternatively a short earth wire is sometimes run from the component directly to the scooter's frame.

21 Corrosion is a common cause of a poor earth connection, as is a loose earth terminal fastener.

22 If total or multiple component failure is experienced, check the security of the main earth lead from the negative (-) terminal of the battery, the earth lead bolted to the engine, and the main earth point(s) on the frame. If corroded, dismantle the connection and clean all surfaces back to bare metal. Remake the connection and prevent further corrosion from forming by smearing battery terminal grease over the connection.

23 To check the earthing of a component, use an insulated jumper wire to temporarily bypass its earth connection **(see illustration)** – connect one end of the jumper wire to the earth terminal or metal body of the component and the other end to the scooter's frame. If the circuit works with the jumper wire installed, the earth circuit is faulty.

24 To check an earth wire first check for corroded or loose connections, then check the wiring for continuity between each connector in the circuit in turn, and then to its earth point, to locate the break (see Steps 12 and 13).

>
> **HAYNES HiNT** *Remember that all electrical circuits are designed to conduct electricity from the battery, through the wires, switches, relays, etc. to the electrical component (light bulb, starter motor, etc). From there it is directed to the frame (earth) where it is passed back to the battery. Electrical problems are basically an interruption in the flow of electricity from the battery or back to it.*

3 Battery

Caution: Be extremely careful when handling or working around the battery. The electrolyte is very caustic and an explosive gas (hydrogen) is given off when the battery is charging. Always disconnect the battery negative (-ve) lead first, and reconnect it last.

Removal and installation

1 Make sure the ignition is switched OFF.
2 On AN250 models and AN400X to K6 models, open the glove compartment, then undo the screw securing the battery cover and remove the cover **(see illustrations)**. Unscrew the negative (-) terminal bolt first and disconnect the lead from the battery, then unscrew the positive (+) terminal bolt and disconnect the lead **(see illustration)**. Lift the battery from its holder **(see illustration)**.
3 On AN400K7 models onward, open the glove compartment, then undo the screw securing the battery cover and remove the cover **(see illustration)**. Unscrew the negative (-) terminal bolt first and disconnect the lead from the battery, then unscrew the positive (+) terminal bolt and disconnect the lead **(see illustration)**. Pull the battery tray out to remove the battery **(see illustration)**.
4 Prior to installation, ensure the battery terminals and lead ends are clean (see Step 7). Fit the battery into its holder and reconnect the leads, connecting the positive (+) terminal first.

 Battery corrosion can be kept to a minimum by applying a layer of battery terminal grease or petroleum jelly (Vaseline) to the terminals after the leads have been connected. DO NOT use a mineral based grease.

Inspection

5 The battery fitted to all models covered in this manual is of the maintenance-free (sealed) type – however, the following checks should still be performed.
6 Check the condition of the battery by measuring the voltage at the terminals. Connect the voltmeter positive (+) probe to the battery positive (+) terminal, and the negative (-) probe to the negative (-) terminal **(see illustration)**. When fully-charged there should be approximately 12.6 volts present. If the voltage falls below 12.3 volts remove the battery and recharge it (see Steps 11 to 13).
7 Check the battery terminals and leads are tight and free of corrosion. If corrosion is evident, remove the battery and clean the terminals and lead ends with a wire brush, penknife or wire wool.

3.2a Undo the screw . . .

3.2b . . . and remove the battery cover

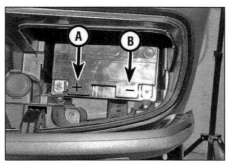
3.2c Battery positive (A) and negative (B) terminals

3.2d Pull the battery out

8 Keep the battery case clean to prevent current leakage, which can discharge the battery over a period of time (especially when it sits unused).
9 Look for cracks in the case and replace the battery with a new one if any are found. If acid has been spilled on the frame or battery holder, neutralise it with a baking soda and water solution, dry it thoroughly, then touch up any damaged paint.

3.3a Remove the battery cover

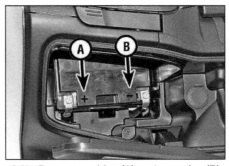
3.3b Battery positive (A) and negative (B) terminals

3.3c Pull the battery out on its tray

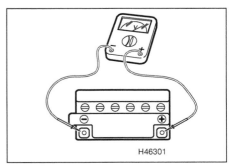
3.6 Checking the battery voltage

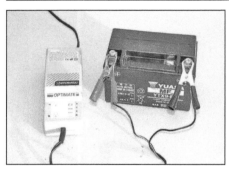

3.12 Battery connected to a charger

4.4 Location of the starter relay – early models

4.6 Location of the starter relay – AN400K7-on models

10 If the scooter sits unused for long periods of time, disconnect the leads from the battery terminals, negative (-) terminal first. Check the battery condition regularly and charge the battery once every month.

Charging

11 Ensure the battery charger is suitable for charging a 12 volt battery.
12 Remove the battery (see Steps 1 to 3). Before switching the charger ON, connect it to the battery, making sure that the positive (+) lead on the charger is connected to the positive (+) terminal on the battery, and the negative (-) lead is connected to the negative (-) terminal **(see illustration)**.
13 The recommended battery charging rate for each model is shown at the beginning of this Chapter. Exceeding this figure can cause the battery to overheat, buckling the plates and rendering it useless. Few owners will have access to an expensive current controlled charger, so if a normal domestic charger is used, check that after a possible initial peak, the charge rate falls to a safe level. **Note:** *In emergencies the battery can be charged at a maximum rate of 3.0 amps for a period of 1 hour. However, this is not recommended and the low amp charge is by far the safer method of charging the battery.*
14 If the battery becomes hot during charging **STOP**. Further charging will cause damage
15 After charging, allow the battery to stand for 30 minutes, then measure its terminal voltage (see Step 6). If the voltage is below 12.3 volts, charge the battery again and repeat

the voltage measuring process. If the voltage is still low, the battery is failing and should be replaced with a new one.
16 Install the battery (see Step 4).
17 If the recharged battery discharges rapidly when left disconnected, it is likely that an internal short caused by physical damage or sulphation has occurred. A new battery will be required.

4 Fuses

1 The electrical circuits are protected by fuses. If a fuse blows, be sure to check the appropriate wiring circuit very carefully for evidence of a short-circuit (see *Wiring Diagrams* at the end of this Chapter). Look for bare wires and chafed, melted or burned insulation, or a damaged switch. If the fuse is renewed before the cause is located, the new fuse will blow immediately.
2 Occasionally a fuse will blow or cause an open-circuit for no obvious reason. Corrosion of the fuse and fusebox terminals may occur and cause poor electrical contact. If this happens, remove the corrosion with a knife or wire wool, then spray the terminals with electrical contact cleaner.

Main fuse

3 The main fuse is integral with the starter relay.

4 On AN250 models and some AN400X to K2 models, the starter relay is located on the right-hand side behind the underseat panel – remove the panel for access (see Chapter 8). Alternatively, the starter relay is located on the right-hand side behind the lower windshield panel **(see illustration)** – remove the panel for access (see Chapter 8).
5 On AN400K3 to K6 models, the starter relay is located on the right-hand side behind the lower windshield panel **(see illustration 4.4)** – remove the panel for access (see Chapter 8).
6 On AN400K7 models onward, the starter relay is located on the right-hand side behind the lower instrument trim panel **(see illustration)** – remove the panel (part of the windshield panel removal procedure) for access (see Chapter 8).
7 To remove the main fuse, first disconnect the battery negative (-) lead (see Section 3). Displace the relay terminal cover, disconnect the relay wiring connector and pull out the fuse **(see illustrations)**. **Note:** *A spare main fuse is located in an adjacent holder on the relay.* To check the fuse, see Step 13.

Circuit fuses

Note: *The fuse numbering in Specifications relates to the fuses as shown in the Wiring Diagrams at the end of this Chapter.*
8 The circuit fuses are housed in the fusebox.
9 On AN250 models and some AN400X to K2 models, the fusebox is located centrally behind the lower windshield panel – remove the panel for access (see Chapter 8). Alternatively, the fusebox is located on the

4.7a Displace the relay terminal cover . . .

4.7b . . . disconnect the relay wiring connector . . .

4.7c . . . and pull out the fuse

left-hand side behind the lower windshield panel **(see illustration)**.

10 On AN400K3 to K6 models, the fusebox is located on the left-hand side behind the lower windshield panel **(see illustration 4.9)** – remove the panel for access (see Chapter 8).

11 On AN400K7 models onward, the fusebox is located on the left-hand side behind the lower instrument trim panel **(see illustration)** – remove the panel (part of the windshield panel removal procedure) for access (see Chapter 8).

12 To remove any of the circuit fuses, unclip the fusebox lid and pull out the fuse – fuse locations are detailed on a label inside the lid **(see illustration)**. **Note:** *Spare fuses are located inside the fusebox.*

Check

13 The fuses should be removed and checked visually. If you can't pull the fuse out with your fingertips, use a pair of long-nose pliers.

14 A blown fuse is easily identified by a break in the element **(see illustration)**. Each fuse is clearly marked with its rating and must only be replaced by a fuse of the correct rating. If a spare fuse is used, always replace it with a new one so that a spare of each rating is carried on the scooter at all times.

 Warning: Never put in a fuse of a higher rating or bridge the terminals with any other substitute, however temporary it may be. Serious damage may be done to the circuit, or a fire may start.

5 Lighting system check

Note: *On AN250 models and AN400X to K2 models, the lighting is switched ON and OFF by a handlebar mounted switch. On all other models covered in this manual the lighting is controlled by the ignition switch - on these machines the headlight will go OFF temporarily when the starter button is pressed.*

1 The battery provides power for operation of the lights. If none of the lights work, always check battery voltage before proceeding. Low battery voltage indicates either a faulty battery or a defective charging system. Refer to Section 3 for battery checks and Section 28 for charging system tests. Also, check the condition of the fuses (see Section 4) – if there is more than one problem at the same time, it is likely to be a fault relating to a multi-function component, such as one of the fuses governing more than one circuit, or the ignition switch.

2 When checking for a blown filament in a bulb, it is advisable to back up a visual check with a continuity test of the filament as it is not always apparent that a bulb has blown. When testing for continuity, remember that on single terminal bulbs it is the metal body of the bulb that is the earth (ground).

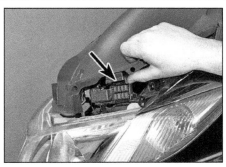
4.9 Location of the fusebox – early models

4.12 Fuse locations are detailed inside the fusebox lid

Headlight

3 AN250 models and AN400X to K2 models have one twin filament bulb. AN400K3 to K6 models have two twin filament bulbs. AN400K7 models onward have one twin filament bulb (right-hand headlight) and one single filament bulb (left-hand headlight).

4 If one headlight beam fails to work, first check the bulb (see Section 6). If both headlight beams fail to work, first check the fuse (see Section 4), and then the bulb(s) (see Section 6). If they are good, the problem lies in the wiring or connectors, or one of the switches in the lighting circuit.

5 On AN250 models and AN400X to K2 models, disconnect the headlight unit wiring connector (see Section 6) and check for battery voltage on the supply (loom) side of the connector. On AN400K3 models onward, disconnect the headlight bulb wiring connector (see Section 6) and check for battery voltage on the supply side of the connector. Using a multimeter set to the volts scale, connect the negative (-) probe to the black/white wire (earth) terminal and the positive (+) probe to the yellow wire terminal for the high beam, or the white wire terminal for the low beam. Don't forget to select either high or low beam as appropriate at the dimmer switch.

6 Turn the ignition and/or lighting ON – if no voltage is indicated, check for continuity between the black/white wire terminal and earth (ground). If there is no continuity, check the earth (ground) circuit for an open or poor connection.

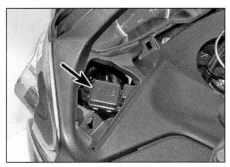
4.11 Location of the fusebox – AN400K7-on models

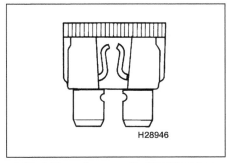
4.14 A blown fuse can be identified by a break in the element

7 If the earth circuit is good, refer to *Wiring Diagrams* at the end of this chapter and check the wiring between the components in the lighting circuit, and check the components themselves.

8 On AN250 models and AN400X to K2 models, if voltage is indicated, check for continuity between the terminals on the headlight side of the wiring connector and the corresponding terminals in the bulb connector – no continuity indicates a break in the circuit.

Sidelight

9 If the sidelight(s) fail(s) to work, first check the bulb(s) (see Section 6) then the signal fuse (see Section 4). If they are good, the problem lies in the wiring or connectors, or one of the switches in the lighting circuit.

10 On AN250 models and AN400X to K2 models, disconnect the headlight unit wiring connector (see Section 6) and check for battery voltage on the supply (loom) side of the connector. On AN400K3 models onward, disconnect the sidelight bulb wiring connector (see Section 6) and check for battery voltage on the supply side of the connector. Using a multimeter set to the volts scale, connect the negative (-) probe to the black/white wire (earth) terminal, and the positive (+) probe to the brown wire terminal.

11 Turn the ignition and/or lighting ON – if no voltage is indicated, check for continuity between the black/white wire terminal and earth (ground). If there is no continuity, check the earth (ground) circuit for an open or poor connection.

12 If the earth circuit is good, refer to *Wiring Diagrams* at the end of this chapter and check the wiring between the components in the lighting circuit, and check the components themselves.

13 On AN250 models and AN400X to K2 models, if voltage is indicated, check for continuity between the terminals on the sidelight side of the wiring connector and the corresponding terminals in the bulbholder – no continuity indicates a break in the circuit.

Tail light

14 If the tail light(s) fail(s) to work, first check the bulb(s) (Section 8), then the signal fuse (Section 4). If they are good, the problem lies in the wiring or connectors, or one of the switches in the lighting circuit.

15 On AN250 models and AN400X to K2 models, remove the seat cowling (see Chapter 8). On AN400K3 to K6 models, follow the procedure in Chapter 8 to remove the rear bodywork panels to access the tail light assembly wiring connector. On AN400K7 models onward, remove the seat cowling (see Chapter 8).

16 Disconnect the tail light wiring connector and check for battery voltage on the supply side of the connector. Using a multimeter set to the volts scale, connect the negative (-) probe to the black/white wire (earth) terminal, and the positive (+) probe to the brown wire terminal.

17 Turn the ignition and/or lighting ON – if no voltage is indicated, check for continuity between the black/white wire terminal and

earth (ground). If there is no continuity, check the earth (ground) circuit for an open or poor connection.

18 If the earth circuit is good, refer to *Wiring Diagrams* at the end of this chapter and check the wiring between the components in the lighting circuit, and check the components themselves.

19 If voltage is indicated, remove the tail light bulb (see Section 8) and check for continuity between the terminals on the tail light side of the wiring connector and the corresponding terminals in the bulbholder – no continuity indicates a break in the circuit.

Brake light

20 If the brake light fails to work, first check the bulb (Section 8), then the signal fuse (Section 4).

21 If they are good, follow the appropriate procedure in Step 15 to access the brake/tail light wiring connector.

22 Disconnect the brake/tail light wiring connector and check for battery voltage on the supply side of the connector. Using a multimeter set to the volts scale, connect the negative (-) probe to the black/white wire (earth) terminal, and the positive (+) probe to the white/black wire terminal.

23 Turn the ignition ON. Check first with the front and then with the rear brake lever pulled in.

24 If no voltage is indicated in either test, check the appropriate brake light switch (see Section 21), then the wiring between the brake light connector and the switches.

25 Check for continuity to earth (ground) in the black/white wire on the loom side of the wiring connector. If there is no continuity, check the earth (ground) circuit for a broken or poor connection.

26 If voltage is indicated, check for continuity between the terminals on the brake/tail light side of the wiring connector and the corresponding terminals in the bulbholder (see Step 21) – no continuity indicates a break in the circuit.

Licence plate light

Note: *On AN250W to Y models and AN400X and Y models, the licence plate is illuminated by the tail light bulbs (see Steps 14 to 19).*

27 If the licence plate light fails to work, first check the bulb (Section 10), then the signal fuse (Section 4).

28 If they are good, follow the appropriate procedure in Step 15 to access the brake/tail light wiring connector.

29 Follow the procedure in Steps 16 to 19 to check the voltage supply and earth circuits. If they are good, disconnect the wiring connector from the licence plate light (see Section 10) and check for continuity in the sub loom between the brake/tail light wiring connector and the licence plate light connector.

Turn signals

30 See Section 11 for the turn signal circuit check.

Instrument and warning lights

31 See Section 14 for instrument and warning light bulb renewal.

6   Headlight and sidelight bulbs

Note 1: *The headlight bulb is of the quartz-halogen type – do not touch the bulb glass as skin acids will shorten the bulb's service life. If the bulb is accidentally touched, it should be wiped carefully when cold with a rag soaked in methylated spirit and dried before fitting. Use a paper towel or dry cloth when handling new bulbs to prevent injury if the bulb should break and to increase bulb life.*

Note 2: *Access to the bulbs located in the headlight unit is extremely restricted and is best undertaken after first removing the headlight panel (see Chapter 8).*

AN250 models and AN400X to K2 models

Headlight

1 Disconnect the bulb wiring connector **(see illustration)**.

2 Note which way round the dust cover is fitted, then remove the cover **(see illustration)**.

3 Release the spring clip, noting how it fits, then lift out the bulb **(see illustrations)**.

6.1 **Disconnect the bulb wiring connector**

6.2 **Remove the dust cover**

6.3a **Release the spring clip . .**

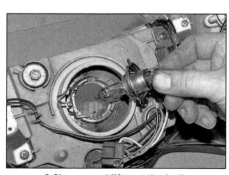

6.3b **. . . and lift out the bulb**

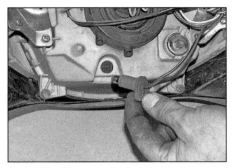

6.5a Remove the bulbholder . . .

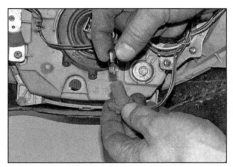

6.5b . . . then pull out the bulb

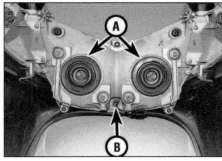

6.8 Location of headlight (A) and sidelight bulbs (B)

4 Installation is the reverse of removal, noting the following:
- *Line up the tabs of the new bulb with the slots in the headlight.*
- *Ensure the bulb is clipped securely in place.*
- *Check that the dust cover is correctly installed.*
- *Check the operation of the headlight before riding the motorcycle.*

Sidelight

5 Pull the bulbholder out of its socket in the headlight unit, then carefully pull the bulb out of the holder **(see illustrations)**.
6 Carefully press the new bulb into the bulbholder, then install the bulbholder by pressing it in.
7 Check the operation of the sidelight.

AN400K3 to K6 models
Headlight

8 The procedure for removing and installing

the left and right-hand bulbs is the same for both **(see illustration)**.
9 Note which way round the dust cover is fitted, then remove the cover **(see illustration)**.
10 Release the spring clip, noting how it fits, then lift out the bulb **(see illustrations)**.
11 Installation is the reverse of removal (see Step 4).

Sidelight

12 Follow the procedure in Steps 5 to 7 to remove and install the sidelight bulb.

AN400K7 model onward
Headlight – left-hand side

13 Note the location of the bulbs in the back of the headlight unit **(see illustration)**.
14 Remove the dust cover, noting how it fits **(see illustration)**.

6.9 Remove the dust cover

15 Release the spring clip, noting how it fits, then lift out the bulbholder **(see illustration)**.
16 Carefully pull the bulb out of the holder, noting how it fits **(see illustration)**.

6.10a Release the spring clip . .

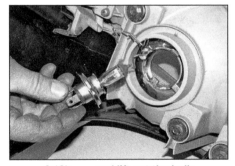

6.10b . . . and lift out the bulb

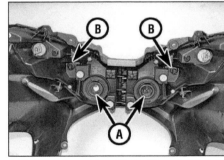

6.13 Location of headlight (A) and sidelight bulbs (B)

6.14 Remove the dust cover

6.15 Release the spring clip and lift out the bulbholder

6.16 Pull the bulb out of the holder

6.17 Ensure the bulb is clipped securely in place

6.19 Lift out the bulb

17 Installation is the reverse of removal, noting the following:
• *Align the new bulb with the bulbholder as noted on removal.*
• *Line up the tab of the new bulb with the slot in the headlight.*
• *Ensure the bulb is clipped securely in place (see illustration).*
• *Check that the dust cover is correctly installed.*

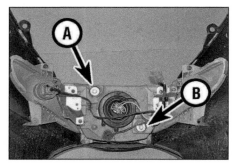

7.4 Vertical (A) and horizontal (B) adjusters – AN250 and AN400X to K2

• *Check the operation of the headlight before riding the motorcycle.*

Headlight – right-hand side

18 Remove the dust cover, noting how it fits **(see illustration 6.14)**, then release the spring clip.
19 Lift out the bulb **(see illustration)**.
20 Installation is the reverse of removal (see Step 4).

Sidelight

21 Follow the procedure in Steps 5 to 7 to remove and install the sidelight bulbs.

7 Headlight

Headlight aim

Note: *An improperly adjusted headlight may cause problems for oncoming traffic or provide poor, unsafe illumination of the road ahead. Before adjusting the headlight aim, be sure to consult with local traffic laws and regulations*

– for UK models refer to MOT Test Checks in the Reference section.

1 Before making any adjustment, check that the tyre pressures are correct and the suspension is adjusted as required. Make any adjustments to the headlight aim with the machine on level ground, with the fuel tank half full and with an assistant sitting on the seat.
2 Adjust the beam vertically first, then horizontally.
3 If an adjuster appears seized, do not force it. Remove the headlight panel (see Chapter 8) and lubricate the adjuster mechanism with WD-40.

AN250 models and AN400X to K2 models

4 The headlight adjusters are located on the back of the headlight unit **(see illustration)**. Remove the lower windshield panel for access (see Chapter 8).
5 Insert a long cross-head screwdriver into the appropriate adjuster via the guide channel and turn the adjuster as required.

AN400K3 to K6 models

6 Adjusters for the left and right-hand headlights are located on the back of the headlight unit **(see illustration)**. Access the adjusters from the underside of the of the headlight panel.
7 Insert a long cross-head screwdriver into the appropriate adjuster via the guide channel and turn the adjuster as required.

AN400K7 model onward

8 Adjusters for the left (LO beam) and right-hand (HI beam) headlights are located on the back of the headlight unit **(see illustration)**. Access the adjusters from the underside of the of the headlight panel.
9 Insert a long cross-head screwdriver into the appropriate adjuster via the guide channel and turn the adjuster as required.

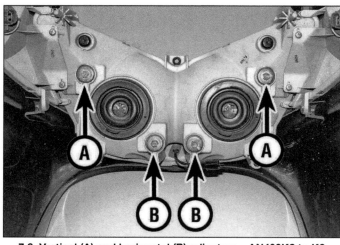

7.6 Vertical (A) and horizontal (B) adjusters – AN400K3 to K6

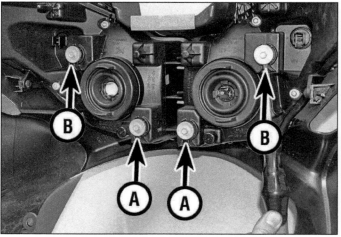

7.8 Vertical (A) and horizontal (B) adjusters – AN400K7-on

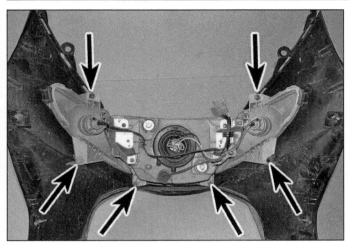

7.11 Location of the headlight unit screws –
AN250 and AN400X to K2

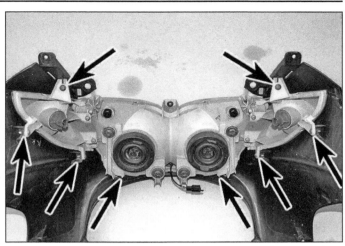

7.13 Location of the headlight unit screws – AN400K3 to K6

Removal

10 Follow the procedure in Chapter 8 to remove the headlight panel.

AN250 models and AN400X to K2 models

11 The headlight unit and front turn signals assembly is secured in the headlight panel by six screws **(see illustration)**. Undo the screws and lift the assembly out.
12 If required, undo the screws securing the joining plates and separate the components.

AN400K3 to K6 models

13 The headlight unit and front turn signals assembly is secured in the headlight panel by eight screws **(see illustration)**. Undo the screws and lift the assembly out.
14 If required, undo the screws securing the

turn signals to the headlight and separate the components.

AN400K7 model onward

15 Left and right-hand headlight units are fitted with integral turn signals. Each unit is secured by five screws **(see illustration)**. Undo the screws and lift the units out individually, noting how they interlock in the centre.

Installation

16 Installation is the reverse of removal. Make sure the headlight unit is correctly aligned with the aperture in the headlight panel before tightening the mounting screws. Take great care not to over-tighten the screws.
17 Check the operation of the lights before riding the scooter.
18 Check the headlight aim (see Steps 1 to 9).

8 Brake/tail light bulbs

Note: *It is a good idea to use a paper towel or dry cloth when handling bulbs to prevent injury if the bulb should break.*
1 On AN250W to Y models and AN400X and Y models, undo the screws securing the tail light lens and lift it off, noting that the left and right-hand turn signal lenses are secured by the tail light lens. Both brake/tail light bulbs have twin filaments. Push the bulb into its holder and twist it anti-clockwise to remove it.
2 On AN250K1 and K2 models and AN400K1 to K6 models, first follow the procedure in Chapter 8 to remove the rear panel **(see illustration)**. Turn the bulbholder anti-

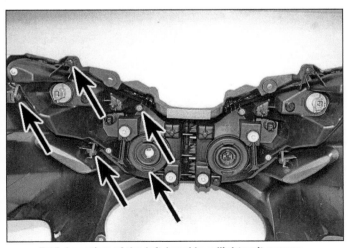

7.15 Location of the left-hand headlight unit screws –
AN400K7-on

8.2a Remove the rear panel

8.2b Turn the bulbholder (arrowed) anti-clockwise

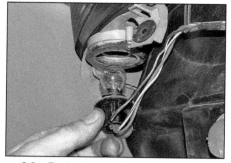

8.2c Push the bulb into its holder . . .

8.2d . . . and twist it anti-clockwise

clockwise to remove it, then push the bulb into its holder and twist it anti-clockwise to remove it **(see illustrations)**.

3 On AN400K7 models onward, first follow the procedure in Chapter 8 to remove the tail light access panel section of the seat cowling. Follow the procedure in Step 2 to remove the bulbholder and bulb.

4 Check the socket terminals for corrosion and clean them if necessary. Line up the pins of the new bulb with the slots in the socket, then push the bulb in and turn it clockwise until it locks into place. **Note:** *The pins on the bulb are offset, the bulb can only be installed one way round.*

5 Install the remaining components in the reverse order or removal. On AN250W to Y models and AN400X and Y models, ensure both turn signal lenses are correctly positioned

before installing the tail light lens. Take great care not to over-tighten the lens screws.

6 Check the operation of the tail light and the brake light.

9 Brake/tail light unit

Note: *When disconnecting any wiring, it is advisable to mark or tag the wires as a reminder of where they connect.*

1 On AN250 models and AN400X to K2 models, first remove the seat cowling (see Chapter 8). Undo the screws securing the cowling side panels to the tail light assembly and separate the components **(see illustration)**.

2 On AN400K3 to K6 models, first remove the rear bodywork panels (see Chapter 8). Undo the screws securing the cowling side panels to the tail light assembly and separate the components **(see illustration)**.

3 On AN400K7 models onward, first remove the seat cowling (see Chapter 8). Undo the screws securing the cowling side panels to the tail light assembly and separate the components.

4 Installation is the reverse of removal. Check the operation of the lights.

10 Licence plate light

Note: *When disconnecting any wiring, it is advisable to mark or tag the wires as a reminder of where they connect.*

Bulb

1 With the exception of AN250W to Y models and AN400X and Y models, all other models are fitted with a separate licence plate light.

2 Twist the lens anti-clockwise and remove it.

3 The bulb is of the capless type – pull it out carefully **(see illustration)**.

4 Installation is the reverse of removal. Check the operation of the light.

Removal and installation

5 On AN250K1 and K2 models and AN400K1 and K2 models, first remove the seat cowling for access (see Chapter 8). Disconnect the wiring connector from the rear of the light unit, then release the tabs securing the unit and draw it out.

6 On AN400K3 to K6 models, first follow the procedure in Chapter 8 to remove the rear panel **(see illustration 8.2a)**. Disconnect the wiring connector from the rear of the light unit **(see illustration)**. Release the tabs securing the unit and draw it out.

7 On AN400K7 models onward, first follow the procedure in Chapter 8 to remove the tail light access panel. Undo the screws securing the licence plate light and disconnect the

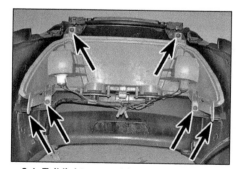

9.1 Tail light assembly screws – AN250 and AN400X to K2

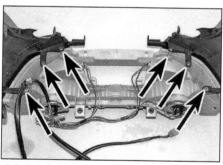

9.2 Tail light assembly screws – AN400K3 to K6 models

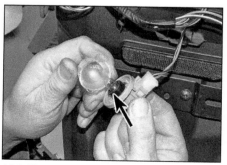

10.3 Remove the lens and pull out the bulb

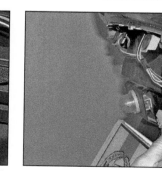

10.6 Disconnect the wiring connector

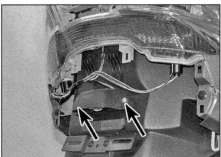

10.7a Undo the screws securing the light . . .

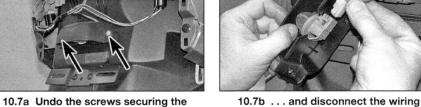

10.7b . . . and disconnect the wiring connector

10.7c Release the tab securing the bulbholder

wiring connector. Release the tab securing the bulbholder and draw it out **(see illustrations)**.
8 Installation is the reverse of removal. Check the operation of the light.

11 Turn signal circuit and relay

Circuit check

1 Most turn signal problems are the result of a burned out bulb or corroded socket. This is especially true when the turn signals function on one side (although possibly too quickly), but fail to work on the other side. If this is the case, first check the bulbs, the bulb sockets and the wiring connectors.
2 If all the turn signals fail to work, first check the signal fuse (see Section 4) and the switch (see Section 15). Refer to *Wiring Diagrams* at the end of this Chapter and check the wiring and connectors in the turn signal circuit.
3 Follow the procedure in Steps 7 to 9 to access the combined turn signal/sidestand relay.
4 Disconnect the relay from its wiring connector **(see illustration)**. On AN400K7 models onward, temporarily reconnect the instrument cluster wiring connector.
5 Using a multimeter set to the 0 to 20 dc volts range, refer to *Wiring Diagrams* at the end of this Chapter and check for voltage at the (+) wire terminal on the relay connector with the ignition ON. Battery voltage should be shown. Turn the ignition OFF when the check is complete.
6 If all other components are good it is likely the relay is faulty. No test specifications are available for the turn signal function of the relay and the only way of confirming this is to substitute the relay with a known good one.

Relay removal and installation

7 On AN250 models and some AN400X to K2 models, the relay is located centrally behind the lower windshield panel next to the fusebox – remove the panel for access (see Chapter 8). Alternatively, the relay is located on the left-hand side behind the lower windshield panel **(see illustration 11.4)**.

8 On AN400K3 to K6 models, the relay is located on the left-hand side behind the lower windshield panel **(see illustration 4.9)** – remove the panel for access (see Chapter 8).
9 On AN400K7 models onward, the relay is located below the instrument cluster **(see illustration)** – remove the instrument trim panel (part of the windshield panel removal procedure) for access (see Chapter 8).
10 Installation is the reverse of removal.

12 Turn signal bulbs

Front

Note 2: *Access to the bulbs located in the headlight unit is extremely restricted and*

11.4 Disconnect the turn signal relay from its wiring connector

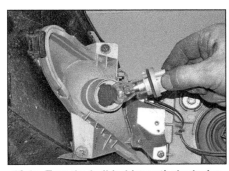

12.1a Turn the bulbholder anti-clockwise to remove it

is best undertaken after first removing the headlight panel (see Chapter 8).
1 Turn the bulbholder anti-clockwise to remove it, then push the bulb into its holder and twist it anti-clockwise to remove it **(see illustrations)**.
2 Check the socket terminals for corrosion and clean them if necessary. Line up the pins of the new bulb with the slots in the socket, then push the bulb in and turn it clockwise until it locks into place.
3 Install the bulbholder and ensure it is secure.
4 Install the remaining components in the reverse order or removal.
5 Check the operation of the turn signals.

Rear

6 On AN250W to Y models and AN400X and Y models, undo the screws securing the

11.9 Location of the turn signal relay – AN400K7-on

12.1b Push the bulb in and twist it anti-clockwise

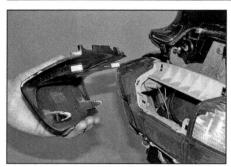

12.7a Pull the turn signals access panel off

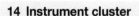

12.7b Turn the bulbholder anti-clockwise

12.7c Push the bulb in and twist it anti-clockwise

combined tail light/turn signals lens and lift it off. Push the bulb into its holder and twist it anti-clockwise to remove it.

7 On all other models, ease the turn signals access panel away from the tail light assembly to release the retaining spring clips and remove the panel **(see illustration)**. Turn the bulbholder anti-clockwise to remove it, then push the bulb into its holder and twist it anti-clockwise to remove it **(see illustrations)**.

8 Check the socket terminals for corrosion and clean them if necessary. Line up the pins of the new bulb with the slots in the socket, then push the bulb in and turn it clockwise until it locks into place.

9 Install the remaining components in the reverse order or removal.

10 Check the operation of the turn signals.

13 Turn signal assemblies

Front

1 On AN250 models and AN400X to K2 models, first remove the headlight panel (see Chapter 8), then follow the procedure in Section 7 to remove the headlight/turn signals assembly **(see illustration 7.11)**. Undo the screws securing the joining plates and separate the components.

2 On AN400K3 to K6 models, first remove the headlight panel (see Chapter 8), then follow the procedure in Section 7 to remove the headlight/turn signals assembly **(see illustration 7.13)**. Undo the screws securing the turn signals to the headlight and separate the components.

3 On AN400K7 models onward, the left and right-hand turn signals are integral with the left and right-hand headlights. First remove the headlight panel (see Chapter 8), then follow the procedure in Section 7 to remove the headlight/turn signal units **(see illustration 7.15)**.

4 Installation is the reverse of removal (see Section 7).

5 Check the operation of the turn signals.

Rear

6 The rear turn signals are integral with the tail light unit on all models (see Section 9).

14 Instrument cluster

Check

Speedometer and tachometer

1 No specifications are available for checking the speedometer and tachometer. However, if either component is though to be faulty, first check that the instrument cluster wiring connector is secure.

2 On AN250 models and AN400X to K6 models, inspect the speedometer wire and drive housing for damage (see Chapter 7, Section 18). Have the instrument checked by a Suzuki dealer.

3 On AN400K7 models onward, check the operation of the speed sensor (see Chapter 4B, Section 9). **Note:** A fault with the speed sensor should be indicated by the FI warning light (see Chapter 4B).

Temperature gauge

4 Refer to Chapter 3 to check the operation of the temperature gauge.

Fuel level gauge

5 Refer to Chapter 4A or 4B as appropriate to check the operation of the fuel level gauge.

Warning lights

6 On AN250 models and AN400X to K6 models, the warning light bulbs are located on the underside of the instrument panel, directly below the position of the relevant display. Instrument cluster illumination is provided by additional lights also located on the underside of the instrument panel.

7 To access the bulbs, follow the procedure in Step 10 or 11 as applicable to remove the instrument cluster and separate the two halves of the instrument casing.

8 To remove the relevant bulb, twist the bulbholder anti-clockwise to remove it, then pull the bulb out of the bulbholder. All bulbs are of the capless type.

9 Installation is the reverse of removal.

Removal and installation

10 On AN250 models and AN400X to K2 models, individual components are available **(see illustration)**. Follow the procedure in Chapter 8 to remove the instrument panel, then undo the screws securing the instrument cluster

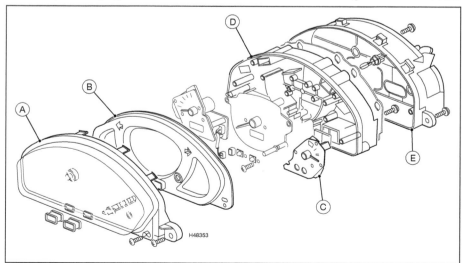

14.10a Instrument cluster components – top cover (A), display panel (B), instruments (C), casing (D) and bottom cover (E)

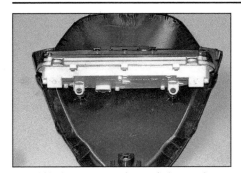

14.10b Instrument cluster is located on the underside of the instrument panel

to the underside of the panel **(see illustration)**. Undo the screws securing the top and bottom covers to the casing. Release the clips securing the top edge of the top cover and separate the top and bottom covers from the casing. Undo the screws securing the relevant component in the casing, disconnect the wiring connector and lift the component out.

11 On AN400K3 to K6 models, the speedometer, tachometer and gauges are available on a single panel. Follow the procedure in Chapter 8 to remove the instrument panel, then undo the screws securing the instrument cluster to the underside of the panel. Undo the screws securing the lower half of the instrument casing to the top half. Release the clips securing the top edge of the top half and separate the two halves. Lift off the display panel. Undo the screws securing the instrument panel and lift it out.

12 On AN400K7 models onward, check the operation of the speed sensor (see Chapter 4B, Section 9). **Note:** *A fault with the speed sensor should be indicated by the FI warning light (see Chapter 4B).* The speedometer, tachometer and gauges are available on a single panel. Follow the procedure in Chapter 8 to remove the instrument panel, then undo the screws securing the instrument cluster to the underside of the panel. Undo the screws securing the lower half of the instrument casing to the top half. Release the clips securing the top edge of the top half and separate the two halves. Lift off the display panel and lift the instrument panel out of the casing.

13 Installation is the reverse of removal.

15.8 Peg on housing locates in hole (arrowed)

15.5a Undo the screws . . .

15 Handlebar switches

Check

Note: *When disconnecting any wiring, it is advisable to mark or tag the wires as a reminder of where they connect.*

1 Generally speaking, the switches are reliable and trouble-free. Most troubles, when they do occur, are caused by dirty or corroded contacts, but wear and breakage is a possibility that should not be overlooked. If breakage does occur, the switch will have to be replaced with a new one.

2 The switches can be checked for continuity using a multimeter or a continuity tester (see Section 2). Always disconnect the battery negative (-) lead to prevent the possibility of a short circuit, before making the checks.

3 Remove the handlebar covers and appropriate body panels to access the switches and the switch wiring (see Chapter 8).

4 Trace the wiring from the switch housing to the connector and disconnect it. Check for continuity between the terminals on the switch side of the connector with the switch in various positions i.e. switch OFF – no continuity, switch ON – continuity. Use the wire colours to identify the switch terminals (see the *Wiring Diagrams* at the end of this Chapter).

5 If the test indicates a problem exists, undo the screws securing the two halves of the switch housing and separate them

16.1a Location of the horn – AN400K6

15.5b . . . and separate the housing

(see illustrations). **Note:** *To access the switches on the right-hand handlebar refer to the procedure in Chapter 4A, Section 6, and separate the two halves of the throttle twistgrip/switch housing.*

6 Inspect the wiring connections and spray the switch units with electrical contact cleaner. If any of the switch components are damaged or broken, fit a new switch housing.

Removal and installation

7 Follow the procedure in Steps 3 to 5 to remove the switch housing. Release the wiring from any clips or ties and feed it up to the housing.

8 Installation is the reverse of removal. Note how the peg in the upper half of the housing locates in the hole in the handlebar **(see illustration)**. Tighten the housing screws securely.

9 Make sure the wiring connectors are secure and test the operation of the switch before installing the body panels and handlebar coves. If applicable, check and adjust the throttle cable and twistgrip (see Chapter 4A or 4B).

16 Horn

Check

1 The horn is located at the front of the scooter next to the radiator **(see illustrations)**.

2 Refer to Chapter 8 and remove the body panels as necessary to access the horn.

16.1b Location of the horn – AN400K9

17.1 Check the bulb and switch operation

17.3 Location of the main ON-OFF switch

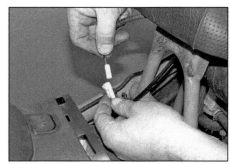

17.4 Disconnect the main wiring connector

3 Disconnect the wiring connectors from the horn. Using two jumper wires, apply battery voltage directly to the horn terminals. If the horn sounds, check the switch (see Section 15), the signal fuse (see Section 4) and the wiring between the horn, the switch and the fusebox (see the *Wiring Diagrams* at the end of this Chapter).

4 If the horn doesn't sound, renew it.

Removal and installation

5 Remove the body panels as necessary to access the horn (see Steps 1 and 2).

6 Disconnect the wiring connectors from the horn, then undo the mounting bolt and remove it.

7 Installation is the reverse or removal. Connect the wiring connectors and check the operation of the horn before installing the body panels.

17 Storage compartment light

1 If the light fails to work, first unclip the lens and check the bulb and the operation of the switch on the light unit **(see illustration)**.

2 Check the signal fuse (see Section 4).

3 If they are good the problem lies in the wiring or connectors, or the main ON-OFF switch mounted on the seat hinge bracket **(see illustration)**.

4 Remove the underseat panel (see Chapter 8). Trace the wiring from the main switch and disconnect it at the connector **(see illustration)**.

5 Using a multimeter set to the volts scale, connect the negative (-) probe to the black/white wire (earth) terminal in the loom side of the connector, and the positive (+) probe to the red wire terminal.

6 If no voltage is indicated, check for continuity between the black/white wire terminal and earth (ground). If there is no continuity, check the earth (ground) circuit for an open or poor connection.

7 If the earth circuit is good, refer to *Wiring Diagrams* at the end of this chapter and check the wiring between the connector and the instruments fuse.

8 If voltage is indicated, check for continuity between the black/white and red wire terminals on the light side of the wiring connector. Ensure the switch on the light unit is ON. With the seat raised there should be continuity, with the seat lowered there should be no continuity.

9 If the results are not as described,

disconnect the wiring from any clips or ties and renew the main ON-OFF switch **(see illustration)**.

18 Parking brake warning light

Check

1 If the light fails to work, on AN250 models and AN400X to K6 models first check the bulb in the instrument cluster (see Section 14).

2 Check the signal fuse (see Section 4).

3 If they are good, the problem lies in the wiring or connectors, or the switch mounted on the brake lever mechanism (see Chapter 7, Section 12).

4 On AN250 models and AN400X to K6 models, remove the storage compartment, seat cowling, floor panels and kick panel (see Chapter 8). On AN400K7 models onward, remove the cockpit trim panel (see Chapter 8).

5 Disconnect the wiring connectors from the switch **(see illustration)**. Using a multimeter, check for continuity between the switch terminals (see Section 2). With the brake lever at rest, there should be no continuity. Pull the

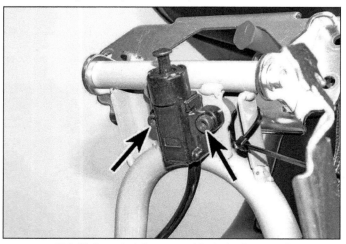

17.9 Main switch is secured by bolts (arrowed)

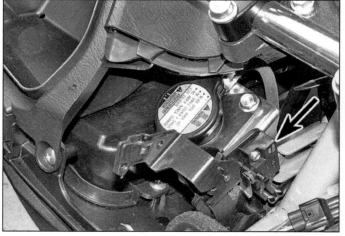

18.5 Location of the warning light switch – AN400K9 shown

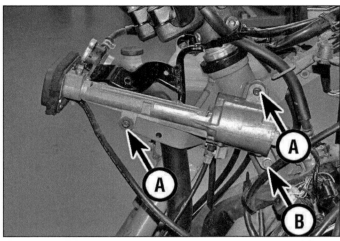

19.2 Location of the ignition switch – tamper-proof bolts (A) and nut (B)

19.4 Disconnect the wiring connector (arrowed)

brake lever in – there should now be continuity. If not, renew the switch.

6 If continuity is shown with the lever pulled in, the switch is functioning correctly and any fault must lie elsewhere in the circuit. Using a multimeter or test light connected to a good earth, check for voltage at the brake light switch wiring connectors with the ignition ON (one of them should show battery voltage). If there's no voltage present, check the wire between the switch and the fusebox (see the *Wiring Diagrams* at the end of this Chapter).

Switch renewal

7 Note the location of the warning light switch and the actuating arm on the brake lever mechanism. Disconnect the wiring connectors from the switch, then undo the screw securing the switch and lift it off.

8 Installation is the reverse of removal. Check the operation of the switch.

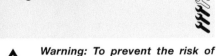

19 Ignition switch

 Warning: To prevent the risk of short circuits, disconnect the battery negative (-) lead before making any ignition switch checks.

Check

1 Disconnect the battery negative (-ve) lead (see Section 3).

2 The ignition switch is mounted on the front frame tube **(see illustration)**.

3 To check the operation of the switch, first remove the headlight panel (see Chapter 8).

4 Disconnect the wiring connector from the lower end of the switch assembly **(see illustration)**.

5 Using a multimeter, refer to the *Wiring Diagrams* at the end of this Chapter and check the continuity of the switch terminal pairs (see Section 2). Continuity should exist between

the connected terminals when the switch is in the indicated position.

6 If the switch fails any of the tests, renew it.

Removal

Special tool: *A bit suitable for undoing the tamper-proof bolts is required (see Step 11).*

Note: *If a new switch assembly is to be fitted to a scooter with an immobiliser the job should be entrusted to a Suzuki dealer who can ensure that the ECM ID signal and the new key ID signal are compatible.*

7 Follow the procedure in Chapter 8 and remove the kick panel.

8 If not already done, disconnect the switch wiring connector **(see illustration 19.4)**.

9 On AN400K5 models onward, trace the wiring from the immobiliser aerial and disconnect it at the connector **(see illustration)**.

10 On AN400K3 models onward, disconnect the seat lock cable from the lock mechanism.

11 The switch is integral with the steering lock and is secured to the frame by two tamper-proof bolts and a nut **(see illustration 19.2)**. Undo the bolts using a special bit, then undo the nut and remove the assembly.

Installation

12 Installation is the reverse of removal, noting the following:

• *Check the operation of the steering lock before fully tightening the mounting bolts.*

20 Ignition safety interlock circuit

1 The safety interlock circuit prevents the engine from starting unless the sidestand is up and one of the brake levers is pulled in. It will also cut the ignition if the sidestand is extended whilst the engine is running.

2 If, after checking the components referred to in Chapter 5 (carburettor models) or Chap-

19.9 Immobiliser aerial wiring connector

ter 4B (FI models), an ignition fault cannot be traced, check the operation of the following components as described in this Chapter.

• *Brake light switches*
• *Safety relay*
• *Sidestand switch*
• *Sidestand relay*
• *Starter relay and diode*

21 Brake light switches

Check

1 Before checking any electrical circuit, check the bulb (see Section 8) and signal fuse (see Section 4).

2 The brake light switch is secured on the underside of the brake lever bracket (see Chapter 7, Section 5). Remove the handlebar covers for access (see Chapter 8).

3 Displace the brake lever cover and disconnect the wiring connectors from the brake light switch.

4 Using a multimeter, check for continuity between the switch terminals (see Section 2). With the brake lever at rest, there should be no continuity. Pull the brake lever in – there should now be continuity. If not, renew the switch.

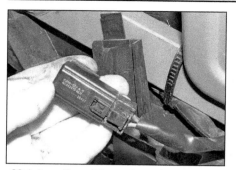

22.1 Location of the safety relay – AN250 and AN400X to K2 models

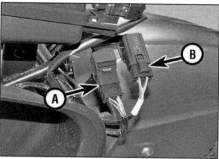

22.2 Location of the safety relay (A) and fuel pump relay (B) – AN400K3-on models

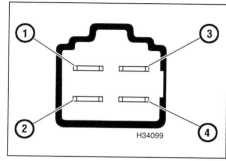

22.3 Safety relay terminal identification

5 If continuity is shown with the lever pulled in, the switch is functioning correctly and any fault must lie elsewhere in the circuit. Using a multimeter or test light connected to a good earth, check for voltage at the brake light switch wiring connectors with the ignition ON (one of them should show battery voltage). If there's no voltage present, check the wire between the switch and the fusebox (see the *Wiring Diagrams* at the end of this Chapter).

6 If both continuity and voltage are obtained the switch and its power supply are proved good. Now check the wiring between the switch and the brake light bulbs (see *Wiring Diagrams* at the end of this Chapter).

Removal and installation

7 Refer to the procedure in Chapter 7, Section 5. Note that it is not necessary to remove the brake master cylinder from the handlebar.

22 Safety relay

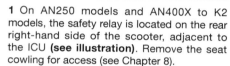

1 On AN250 models and AN400X to K2 models, the safety relay is located on the rear right-hand side of the scooter, adjacent to the ICU (see illustration). Remove the seat cowling for access (see Chapter 8).

2 On AN400K3 models onward, the safety relay is located on the fairing bracket on the front right-hand side of the scooter, adjacent to the fuel pump relay (see illustration). Refer to *Wiring Diagrams* at the end of this Chapter and check the wire colour coding to confirm the correct relay is being tested.

3 Disconnect the relay wiring connector and release the relay from its bracket. Using a multimeter, check for continuity

between terminals 1 and 2 on the relay (see illustration). There should be no continuity. Now use jumper wires to connect the positive (+) terminal of a fully charged 12 volt battery to terminal 3 on the relay and the negative (-) battery terminal to relay terminal 4. There should now be continuity between terminals 1 and 2. If the relay fails either of the checks it must be replaced with a new one.

4 On installation, ensure the relay wiring connector is secure.

23 Sidestand switch

Check

1 The switch is mounted on the sidestand bracket (see illustration). To check the operation of the switch, trace the wiring from the switch and disconnect it at the (green) connector (see illustration). Note: *The location of the wiring connector varies between models. Refer to Chapter 8 and remove the left-hand floor panel or right-hand side belly panel as appropriate.*

2 First, ensure that the switch plunger moves freely in and out of the switch body (see illustration).

3 Using a multimeter, check for continuity between the wire terminals on the switch side of the connector. There should be no continuity with the stand DOWN and continuity with the stand UP (see illustrations). If the switch

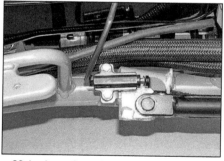

23.1a Location of the sidestand switch

23.1b Location of the sidestand switch wiring connector

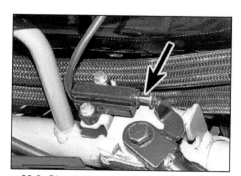

23.2 Check the operation of the switch plunger

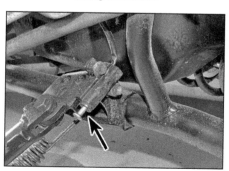

23.3a Sidestand down, switch plunger extended – no continuity

23.3b Sidestand up, switch plunger retracted – continuity

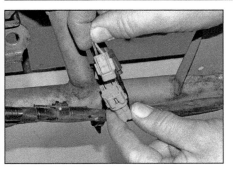

23.4 Disconnect the sidestand switch wiring connector

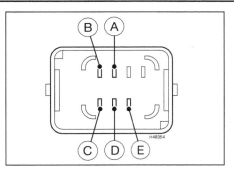

24.2 Sidestand relay terminal identification

25.3a Unclip the relay terminal cover

does not perform as described it is faulty and must be renewed.

Removal and installation

4 If not already done, trace the wiring from the switch and disconnect it at the connector **(see illustration)**. Release the wiring from any clips or ties and feed it back to the switch.

5 Undo the bolts securing the switch and remove it. If required, check the operation of the sidestand (see Chapter 6).

6 On installation, ensure the switch plunger is correctly aligned with the stand. Tighten the switch bolts securely. Check the operation of the switch (see Step 3).

7 Secure the wiring as noted on removal and ensure the connector is secure

8 Install the remaining components in the reverse order of removal.

24 Sidestand relay

1 Follow the procedure in Section 11 to access the combined turn signal/sidestand relay.

2 Disconnect the relay from its wiring connector **(see illustration 11.4)**. Using a

multimeter, check for continuity between terminals B and C on the relay **(see illustration)**. There should be no continuity. Now use jumper wires to connect the positive (+) terminal of a fully charged 12 volt battery to terminal B on the relay and the negative (-) battery terminal to relay terminal A. There should now be continuity between terminals B and C. If the relay fails either of the checks it must be replaced with a new one.

3 On installation, ensure the relay wiring connector is secure.

25 Starter relay

1 Follow the procedure in Section 4 to access the combined main fuse and starter relay.

2 First disconnect the battery negative (-) lead (see Section 3).

3 Unclip the relay terminal cover, disconnect the relay wiring connector and undo the screws securing the battery and starter motor leads to the relay **(see illustrations)**.

4 Test for continuity between the relay's A and B terminals **(see illustration)** – there should be no continuity.

5 Using two insulated jumper wires, connect a fully-charged 12 volt battery across the C and D terminals of the relay – at this point the relay should be heard to click and there should be continuity between the A and B terminals. Disconnect the battery wires.

6 Using a multimeter set to the ohms scale, measure the resistance between the relay's C and D terminals and compare the result with the specifications at the beginning of this Chapter.

7 If the test results are not as described the relay is faulty and must be renewed.

26 Starter motor removal and installation

Removal

1 The starter motor is mounted on top of the engine, behind the cylinder **(see illustration 26.3)**. Remove the air filter housing for access (see Chapter 4A or 4B as applicable).

2 Disconnect the battery negative (-) lead (see Section 3).

3 Disconnect the starter lead from the terminal on the motor **(see illustration)**.

4 Undo the two bolts securing the starter motor to the crankcase, noting the earth

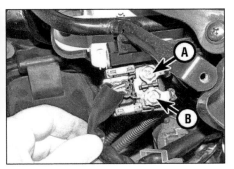

25.3b Starter motor (A) and battery (B) lead terminals

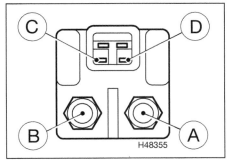

25.4 Starter relay terminal identification

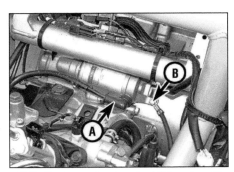

26.3 Starter motor terminal (A) and earth lead (B)

26.4a Undo the bolts (arrowed) . . .

26.4b . . . and draw the starter motor out

26.5 Remove the O-ring

27.2 Mark alignment between main housing and covers

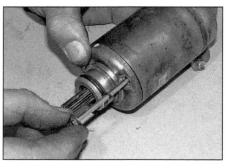

27.3 Unscrew the long bolts

lead, then draw the starter motor out of the crankcase (see illustrations).

5 Remove the O-ring on the end of the starter motor and discard it as a new one must be fitted (see illustration).

Installation

6 Installation is the reverse of removal. Fit a new O-ring on the end of the starter motor, making sure it is seated in its groove, and lubricate it with a smear of grease.

27 Starter motor overhaul

Disassembly

1 Remove the starter motor (see Section 26).
2 Note the alignment marks between the main housing and the front and rear covers, or make your own if they aren't clear (see illustration).
3 Unscrew the two long bolts, and discard the O-rings as new ones must be fitted (see illustration).
4 Draw the front cover off the motor and remove the tabbed washer from inside the cover (see illustrations). Remove the shim from the front end of the armature shaft (see illustration). Note the location of the cover O-ring (see illustration).
5 Draw off the main housing, note the location of the armature in the rear cover and brushplate assembly, then remove the rear cover (see illustration). Note the location of the cover O-ring.

27.4a Draw off the front cover . . .

27.4b . . . and remove the tabbed washer

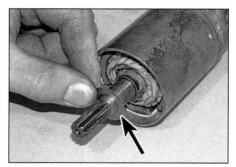

27.4c Remove the shim . . .

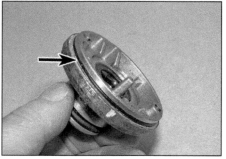

27.4d . . . and the cover O-ring

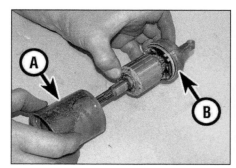

27.5 Draw off the main housing (A) and the rear cover (B)

27.6 Note location of the brushes

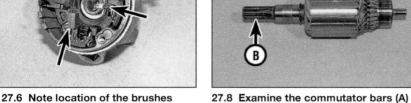

27.8 Examine the commutator bars (A) and gear teeth (B)

27.10a Check for continuity between the commutator bars

6 Note the location of the brushes in the brushplate **(see illustration)**.

Inspection

7 The parts of the starter motor that are most likely to wear and require attention are the brushes. Clean the brushplate and cover assembly carefully, then inspect the brushes for damage and excessive wear. Measure the length of the brushes and compare the results with *Specifications* at the beginning of this Chapter. If the brushes are worn or damaged, fit a new rear cover and brushplate assembly – individual components are not available.
8 Inspect the commutator bars on the armature for scoring, scratches and discoloration **(see illustration)**. The commutator can be cleaned and polished with crocus cloth - do not use sandpaper or emery paper. After cleaning, wipe away any residue with a cloth soaked in electrical system cleaner or denatured alcohol.
9 Clean the gaps between the commutator bars with a penknife or small file.
10 Using an multimeter, check for continuity between the commutator bars **(see illustration)**. Continuity (zero resistance) should exist between each bar and all of the others. Also, check for continuity between the commutator bars and the armature shaft **(see illustration)**. There should be no continuity (infinite resistance) between the commutator and the shaft. If the checks indicate otherwise, the armature is defective and must be renewed.

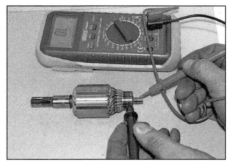

27.10b Check for no continuity between the commutator bars and the armature

11 Check for continuity between each brush and the starter motor terminal **(see illustration)**. There should be continuity (zero resistance). Check for continuity between the terminal and the housing (when assembled). There should be no continuity (infinite resistance).
12 Check the front end of the armature shaft for worn, cracked or broken teeth **(see illustration 27.8)**. If the shaft is damaged or worn, a new armature will have to be fitted.
13 Inspect the seal in the front cover – if it is worn, engine oil will enter the starter motor **(see illustration)**. Fit a new seal if necessary.

Reassembly

14 Reassemble the starter motor in the reverse order of disassembly, noting the following:

27.11 Check for continuity between each brush and the terminal (arrowed)

- *Fit new cover O-rings.*
- *Retain the brushes in their holders with small clips to facilitate installing the armature (see illustration).*
- *Align the marks on the front and rear covers and the main housing (see illustration 27.2).*
- *Fit new O-rings on the long bolts (see illustration 27.3).*
- *Check that the armature turns freely before installing the starter motor.*

28 Charging system

General information

1 If the performance of the charging system is suspect, the system as a whole should be checked first, followed by testing of the individual components. **Note:** *Before beginning the checks, make sure the battery is fully charged and that all system connections are clean and tight.*
2 Checking the output of the charging system and the performance of the various components within the charging system requires the use of a multimeter. If a multimeter is not available, the job of checking the charging system should be left to a Suzuki dealer.
3 When making the checks, follow the procedures carefully to prevent incorrect connections or short circuits resulting in irreparable damage to electrical system components.

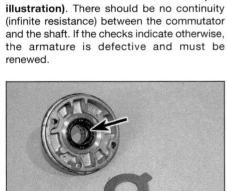

27.13 Check the condition of the seal (arrowed)

27.14 Use small clips to hold the brushes in position

Leakage test

Caution: Always connect an ammeter in series, never in parallel with the battery, otherwise it will be damaged. Do not turn the ignition ON or operate the starter motor when the ammeter is connected – a sudden surge in current will blow the meter's fuse.

4 Ensure the ignition is OFF and disconnect the lead from the battery negative (-) terminal (see Section 3).

5 Set the multimeter to the Amps function and connect its negative (-) probe to the battery negative (-) terminal, and positive (+) probe to the disconnected negative (-) lead **(see illustration)**. Always set the meter to a high amps range initially and then bring it down to the mA (milli Amps) range; if there is a high current flow in the circuit it may blow the meter's fuse.

6 Battery current leakage should not exceed the maximum limit (see *Specifications* at the beginning of this Chapter). If a higher leakage rate is shown there is a short circuit in the wiring, although if an after-market immobiliser or alarm is fitted, its current draw should be taken into account. Disconnect the meter and reconnect the battery negative (-) lead.

7 If leakage is indicated, use the *Wiring Diagrams* at the end of this Chapter to systematically disconnect individual electrical components and repeat the test until the source is identified.

Alternator tests

Regulated voltage

8 Start the engine and warm it up to normal operating temperature. Turn the engine OFF.
9 Remove the battery cover (see Section 3).
10 Start the engine, switch the headlight high beam ON, then slowly increase the engine speed to 5000 rpm.
11 Connect a multimeter set to the 0-20 volts DC scale to the terminals of the battery – positive (+) meter probe to battery positive (+) terminal and the negative (-) meter probe to

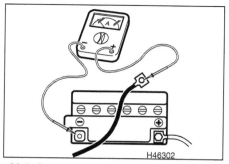

28.5 Checking the battery leakage rate – connect the meter as shown

battery negative (-) terminal **(see illustration)**. Note the reading obtained.
12 Compare the result with *Specifications* at the beginning of this Chapter. If the regulated voltage output is outside the specification, first check the alternator coil resistance and unregulated voltage output. If those results are within the specifications it is likely the regulator/rectifier is faulty – have it checked by a Suzuki dealer.

Clues to a faulty regulator are constantly blowing bulbs, with brightness varying considerably with engine speed, and battery overheating.

Alternator coil resistance

13 The alternator is located on the right-hand side of the engine. Trace the wiring (three yellow wires) from the alternator and disconnect it at the connector **(see illustrations)**. **Note:** *The location of the wiring connector varies between models. Refer to Chapter 8 and remove the seat cowling, kick panel or storage compartment as appropriate.*
14 Using a multimeter set to the ohms scale, connect the meter probes to one pair of terminals at a time on the alternator side of the

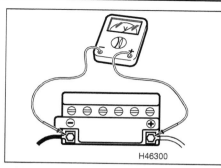

28.11 Checking the regulated voltage – connect the meter as shown

wiring connector and measure the resistance between the terminals. Note the three readings obtained. Now check for continuity between each terminal and earth (ground).
15 If the stator coil windings are in good condition the three resistance readings should be within the range shown in *Specifications* at the beginning of this Chapter and there should be no continuity (infinite resistance) between any of the terminals and earth (ground). If not, the alternator stator coil assembly is faulty and should be renewed. **Note:** *Before condemning the stator coils, check the fault is not due to damaged wiring between the connector and coils.*

Unregulated voltage

Note: *The voltage specified at the beginning of this Chapter should be recorded when the engine is cold.*
16 Trace the wiring (three yellow wires) from the alternator and disconnect it at the connector (see Step 13).
17 Start the engine, then slowly increase the engine speed to 5000 rpm.
18 Using a multimeter set to the volts AC scale, connect the meter probes to one pair of terminals at a time on the alternator side of the wiring connector. Note the three readings obtained.

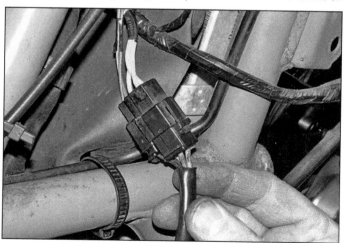

28.13a Location of the alternator wiring connector – AN400K6 shown

28.13b Location of the alternator wiring connector – AN400K9 shown

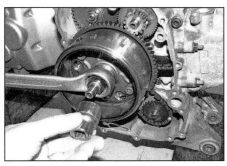

29.2a Hold the rotor with a ring spanner, then fit a socket on the rotor nut . . .

29.2b . . . and undo the rotor nut

29.3a Thread the puller onto the rotor . . .

19 Compare the result with *Specifications* at the beginning of this Chapter. If the unregulated voltage output is outside the specification the alternator stator coil assembly is faulty and should be renewed.

29 Alternator

Special tool: *A rotor puller is necessary to remove the alternator rotor from the crankshaft (see Steps 3 and 19).*
Note: *If the starter clutch is to be removed, slacken the six starter clutch bolts before removing the alternator rotor.*

AN250 models and AN400X to K6 models

Removal

1 Follow the procedure in Chapter 2A, Section 14, to remove the alternator cover.
2 Hold the rotor with a suitable ring spanner to prevent it turning, then undo the rotor nut **(see illustrations)**.
3 To remove the rotor from the crankshaft taper it is necessary to use a rotor puller. Suzuki produces service tools (Part Nos. 09930-30721 and 09930-31920) to do this. Alternatively, use a commercially available puller **(see illustration)**. Thread the puller onto the centre of the rotor, then counter-hold it using a spanner on the flats and tighten the

29.3b . . . then draw the rotor off the crankshaft taper

centre bolt until the rotor is displaced **(see illustration)**.
4 Draw the rotor off the crankshaft and remove the key from its slot in the crankshaft if it is loose **(see illustration)**.
5 If required, follow the procedure in Chapter 2A, Section 14, to separate the starter clutch housing from the alternator rotor.
6 The alternator stator is located inside the alternator cover – the stator and the ignition pulse generator/CKP sensor are an integral assembly **(see illustration)**.
7 First undo the bolts securing the pulse generator/CKP sensor and the wiring clamp **(see illustration)**, then displace the wiring grommet from the cover. Undo the bolts securing the stator **(see illustration 29.6)** and lift it out together with the wiring sub-loom.

29.4 Remove the rotor – note location of the key in the crankshaft

Installation

8 Remove all traces of old gasket and sealant from the crankcase and cover surfaces.
9 Apply a suitable sealant to the wiring grommet, then fit the stator into the cover, aligning the grommet with the slot **(see illustration)**.
10 Install the stator bolts and tighten them to the torque setting specified at the beginning of this Chapter.
11 Install the pulse generator/CKP sensor and the wiring clamp and tighten the bolts to the specified torque settings.
12 If removed, fit the key into its slot in the crankshaft.
13 Clean the tapered section of the crankshaft and inside of the alternator rotor with suitable solvent, then install the rotor – ensure the

29.6 Location of the alternator stator – note the retaining bolts

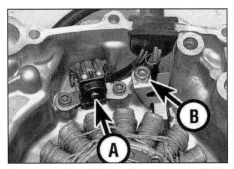

29.7 Location of the pulse generator/CKP sensor (A) and wiring clamp (B)

29.9 Align the grommet with the slot in the cover

29.13 Align the slot in the rotor (arrowed) with the crankshaft key

29.14 Tighten the alternator rotor nut to the specified torque

29.17a Remove the spacer . . .

29.17b . . . withdraw the shaft . . .

29.17c . . . and lift out the reduction gear

28.18a Hold the rotor with a ring spanner . . .

slot on the inside of the rotor aligns with the key and press the rotor all the way on **(see illustration)**.

14 Fit the alternator nut, then hold the rotor with a suitable ring spanner and tighten the nut to the torque setting specified at the beginning of this Chapter **(see illustration)**.

15 Follow the procedure in Chapter 2A, Section 14, to install the alternator cover.

AN400K7 model onward

Removal

16 Follow the procedure in Chapter 2B, Section 14, to remove the alternator cover.

17 Note the location of the spacer on the starter reduction gear shaft, then remove the spacer, withdraw the shaft and lift out the reduction gear **(see illustrations)**. Note how

the larger gear pinion engages with the starter motor pinion.

18 Hold the rotor with a suitable ring spanner to prevent it turning, then undo the rotor nut **(see illustrations)**.

19 To remove the rotor from the crankshaft taper it is necessary to use a rotor puller. Suzuki produces service tools (Part Nos. 09930-30721 and 09930-31920) to do this. Alternatively, use a commercially available puller **(see illustration 29.3a)**. Thread the puller onto the centre of the rotor, then counter-hold it using a spanner on the flats and tighten the centre bolt until the rotor is displaced **(see illustration 29.3b)**.

20 Draw the rotor off the crankshaft and remove the key from its slot in the crankshaft if it is loose **(see illustration 29.4)**.

21 If required, follow the procedure in Chapter

2B, Section 14, to separate the starter clutch housing from the alternator rotor.

22 The alternator stator is located inside the alternator cover – the stator and the CKP sensor are an integral assembly **(see illustration)**.

23 First undo the bolts securing the CKP sensor, then displace the wiring grommet from the cover **(see illustration)**. Undo the bolts securing the stator and lift it out together with the wiring sub-loom.

Installation

24 Remove all traces of old gasket and sealant from the crankcase and cover surfaces.

25 Apply a suitable sealant to the wiring grommet, then fit the stator into the cover, aligning the grommet with the slot **(see illustration 29.9)**.

29.18b . . . and undo the rotor nut

29.22 Location of the alternator stator

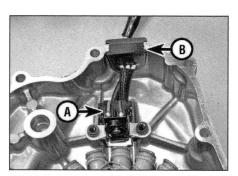

29.23 Location of the CKP sensor (A) and wiring grommet (B)

29.29 Align the slot in the rotor (arrowed) with the crankshaft key

26 Install the stator bolts and tighten them to the torque setting specified at the beginning of this Chapter.
27 Install the CKP sensor and tighten the bolts to the specified torque setting.
28 If removed, fit the key into its slot in the crankshaft.
29 Clean the tapered section of the crankshaft and inside of the alternator rotor with suitable solvent, then install the rotor – ensure the slot on the inside of the rotor aligns with the key and press the rotor all the way on **(see illustration)**.

30 Fit the alternator nut, then hold the rotor with a suitable ring spanner and tighten the nut to the torque setting specified at the beginning of this Chapter **(see illustration 29.14)**.
31 Follow the procedure in Chapter 2B, Section 14, to install the alternator cover.

30 Regulator/rectifier

1 Follow the procedure in Section 28 to test the regulated output of the alternator and compare the result with the *Specifications* at the beginning of this Chapter. If the regulated voltage is outside the specifications, yet the unregulated voltage output from the alternator is correct, a new regulator/rectifier must be fitted.

 Clues to a faulty regulator are constantly blowing bulbs, with brightness varying considerably with engine speed, and battery overheating.

2 On AN250 models and AN400X to K2 models, the regulator/rectifier is located on the right-hand side of the steering head **(see illustration)**.
3 On AN400K3 to K6 models, the regulator/rectifier is located on the fairing bracket **(see illustration)**.
4 On AN400K7 models onward, the regulator/rectifier is located on the front left-hand side **(see illustration)**.
5 Follow the procedure in Chapter 8 to remove the headlight panel for access.
6 Disconnect the battery negative (-) terminal (see Section 3).
7 On AN250 models and AN400X to K2 models, trace the wiring from the regulator/rectifier and disconnect it at the connector.
8 On AN400K3 models onward, disconnect the connector from the regulator/rectifier.
9 Undo the bolts securing the regulator/rectifier and remove it.
10 Install the new unit and tighten the bolts securely. Ensure the wiring connector is secure.
11 Install the remaining components in the reverse order of removal and reconnect the battery negative (-) terminal.

30.2 Location of the regulator/rectifier – AN250 and AN400X to K2

30.3 Location of the regulator/rectifier – AN400K3 to K6

30.4 Location of the regulator/rectifier – AN400K7-on

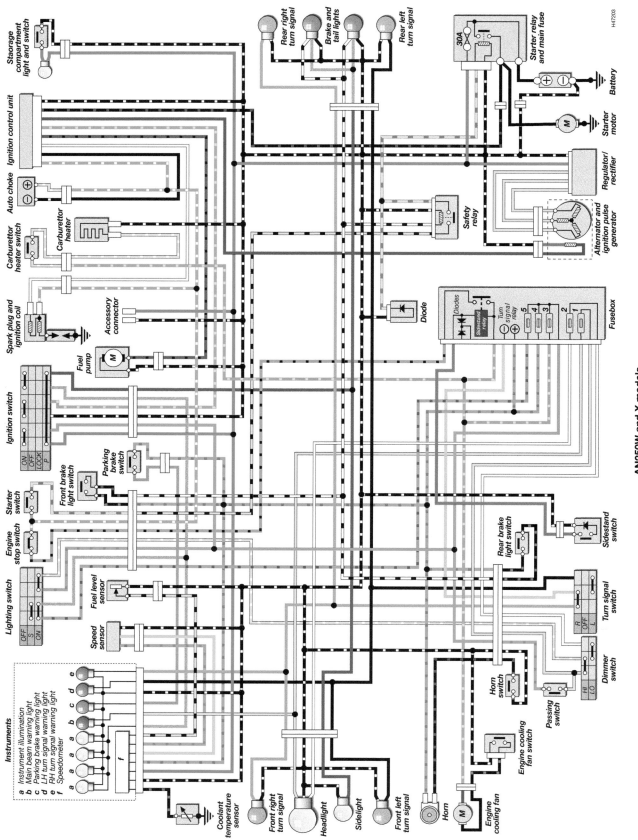

AN250W and X models
(for fuse details see Chapter 9 specifications)

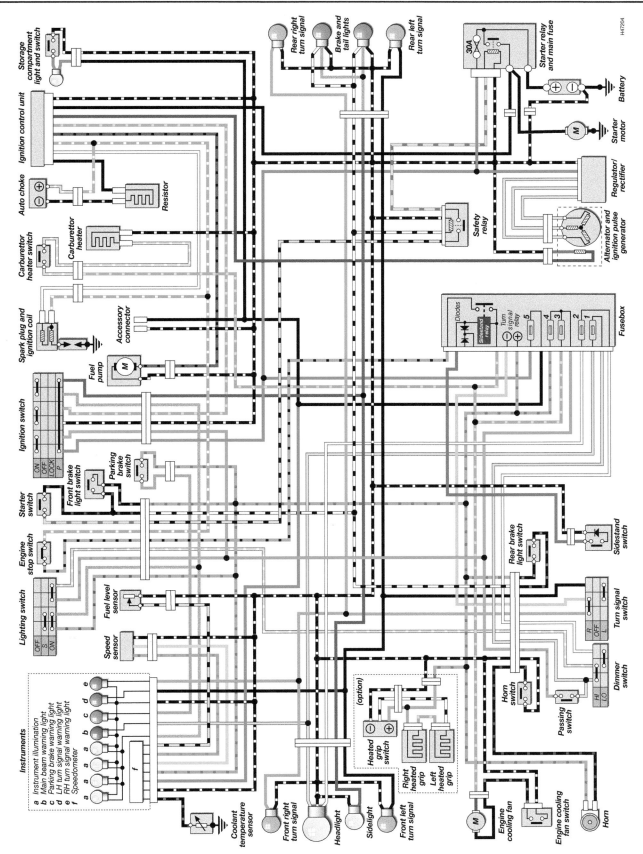

AN250Y models
(for fuse details see Chapter 9 specifications)

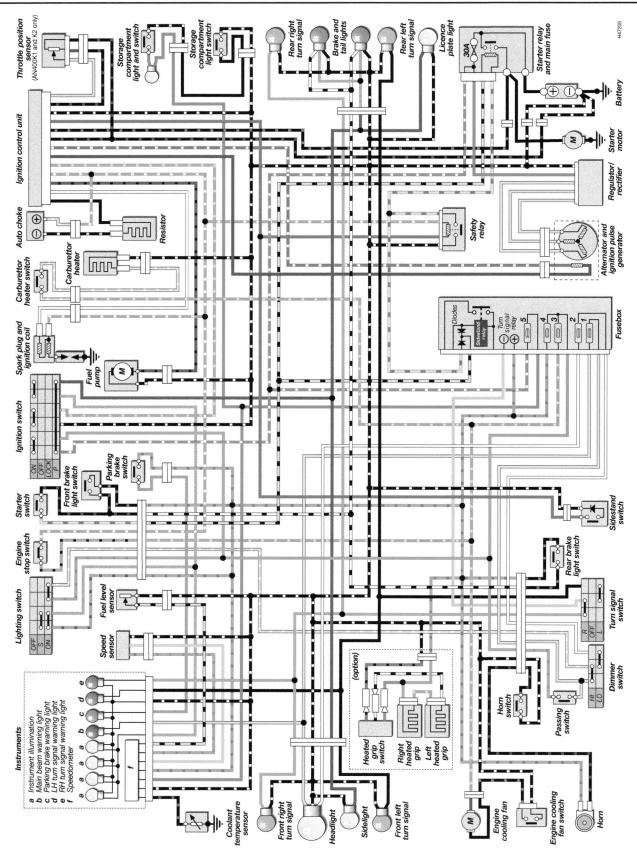

AN250/400K1 and K2 models
(for fuse details see Chapter 9 specifications)

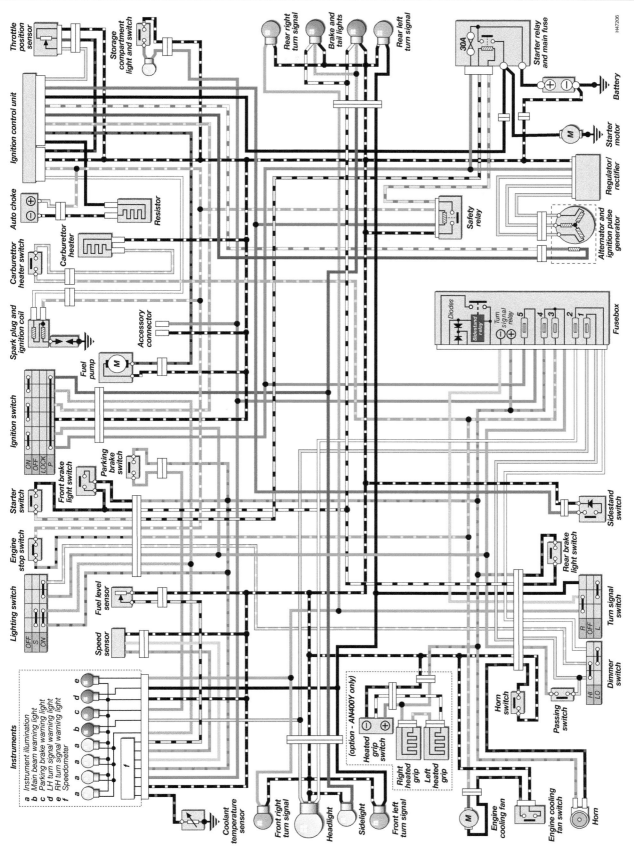

AN400X and Y models
(for fuse details see Chapter 9 specifications)

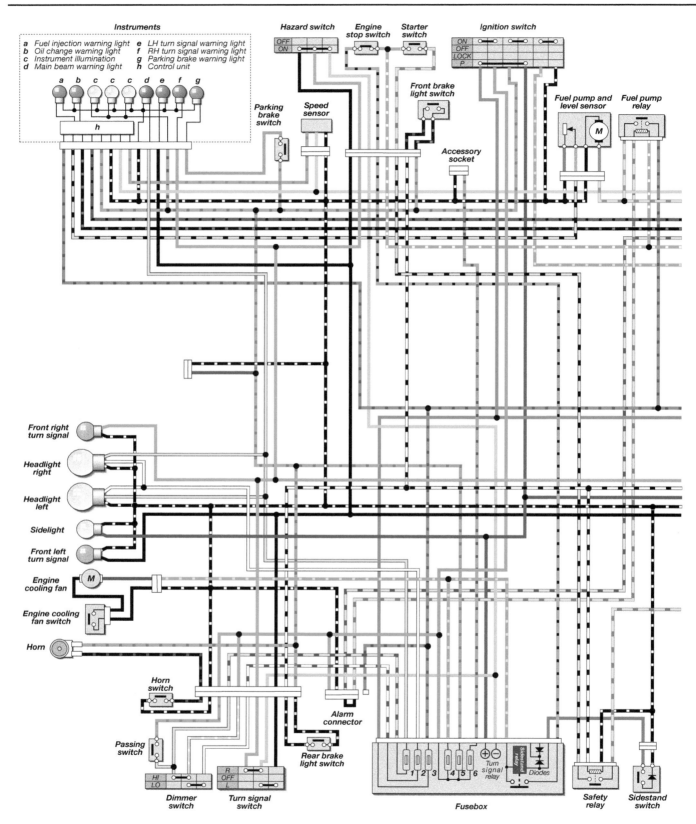

Instruments

a Fuel injection warning light
b Oil change warning light
c Instrument illumination
d Main beam warning light
e LH turn signal warning light
f RH turn signal warning light
g Parking brake warning light
h Control unit

H47207

AN400K3 and K4 (except US and Canada)
(for fuse details see Chapter 9 specifications)

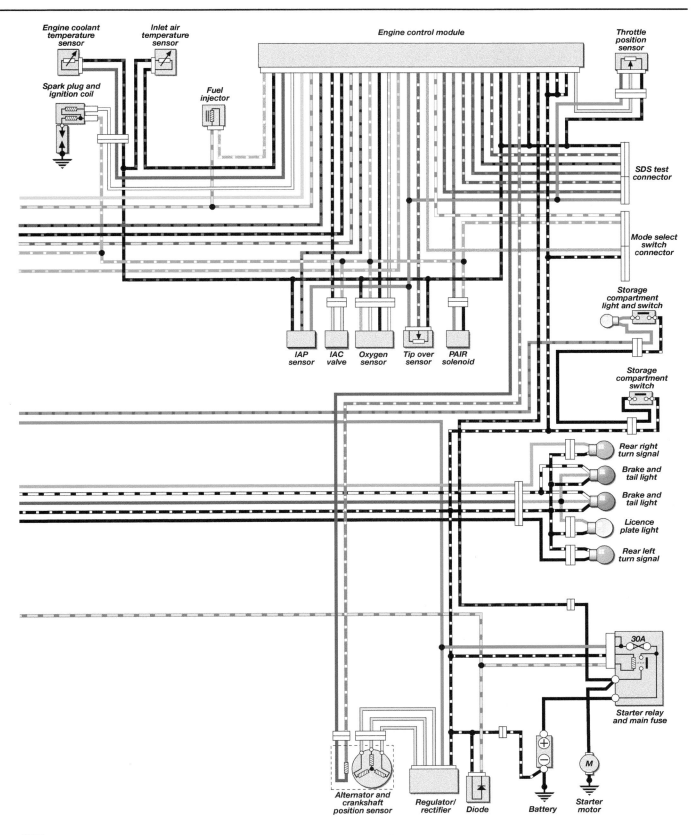

Engine coolant temperature sensor

Inlet air temperature sensor

Engine control module

Throttle position sensor

Spark plug and ignition coil

Fuel injector

SDS test connector

Mode select switch connector

Storage compartment light and switch

Storage compartment switch

IAP sensor

IAC valve

Oxygen sensor

Tip over sensor

PAIR solenoid

Rear right turn signal

Brake and tail light

Brake and tail light

Licence plate light

Rear left turn signal

30A

Starter relay and main fuse

Alternator and crankshaft position sensor

Regulator/ rectifier

Diode

Battery

Starter motor

H47208

AN400K3
(for fuse details see Chapter 9 specifications)

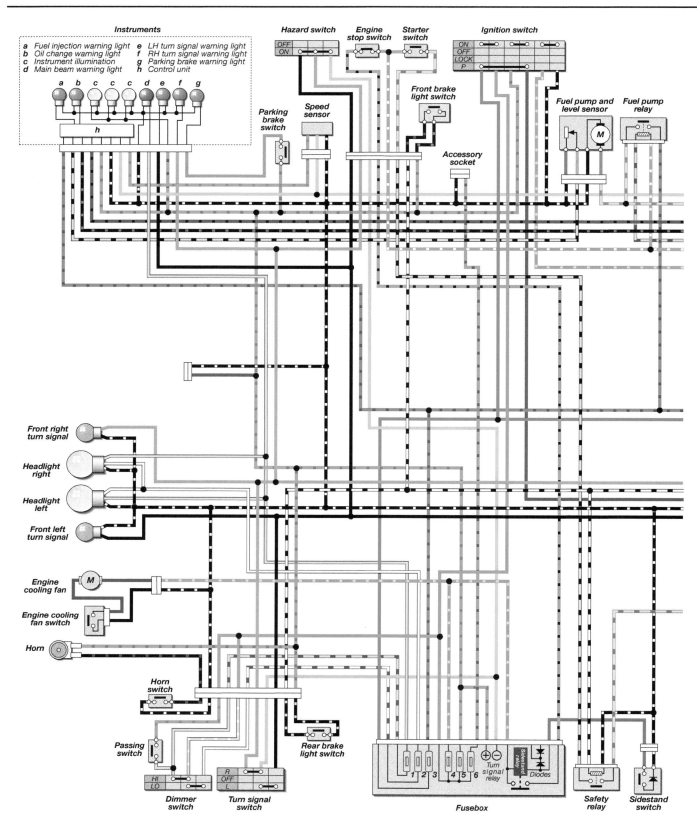

Instruments

a Fuel injection warning light
b Oil change warning light
c Instrument illumination
d Main beam warning light
e LH turn signal warning light
f RH turn signal warning light
g Parking brake warning light
h Control unit

Hazard switch

Engine stop switch

Starter switch

Ignition switch

Front brake light switch

Fuel pump and level sensor

Fuel pump relay

Parking brake switch

Speed sensor

Accessory socket

Front right turn signal

Headlight right

Headlight left

Front left turn signal

Engine cooling fan

Engine cooling fan switch

Horn

Horn switch

Passing switch

Rear brake light switch

Dimmer switch

Turn signal switch

Fusebox

Turn signal relay

Diodes

Safety relay

Sidestand switch

H47209

AN400K4 (US and Canada)
(for fuse details see Chapter 9 specifications)

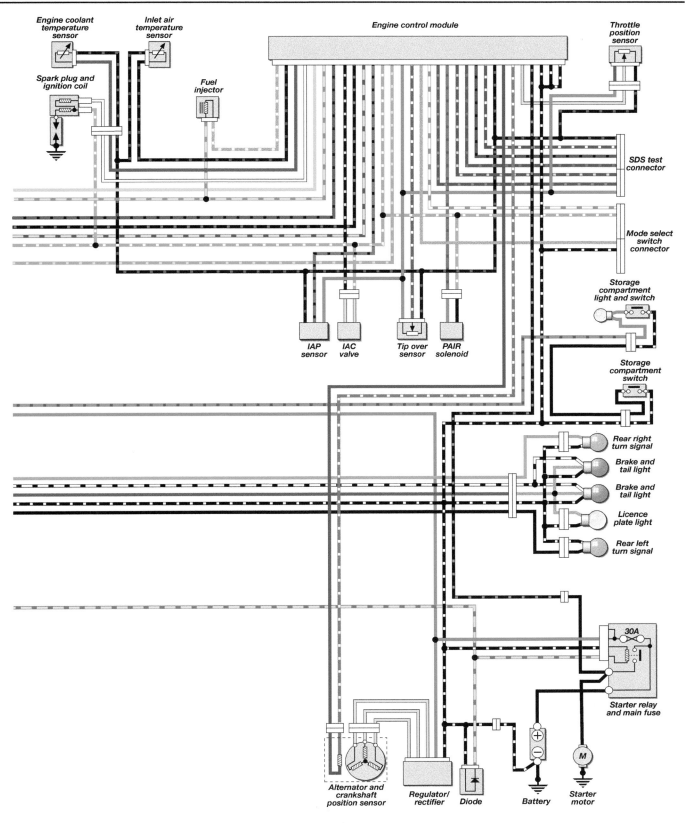

Engine coolant temperature sensor

Inlet air temperature sensor

Engine control module

Throttle position sensor

Spark plug and ignition coil

Fuel injector

SDS test connector

Mode select switch connector

Storage compartment light and switch

IAP sensor

IAC valve

Tip over sensor

PAIR solenoid

Storage compartment switch

Rear right turn signal

Brake and tail light

Brake and tail light

Licence plate light

Rear left turn signal

30A

Starter relay and main fuse

Alternator and crankshaft position sensor

Regulator/ rectifier

Diode

Battery

Starter motor

H47210

AN400K4 (US snd Canada)
(for fuse details see Chapter 9 specifications)

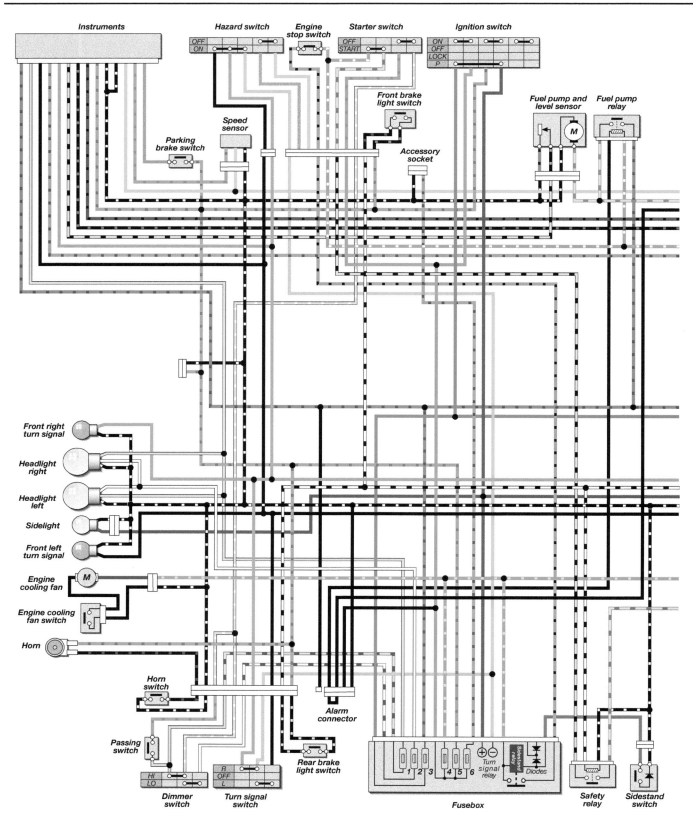

H47211

AN400K5 and K6
(for fuse details see Chapter 9 specifications)

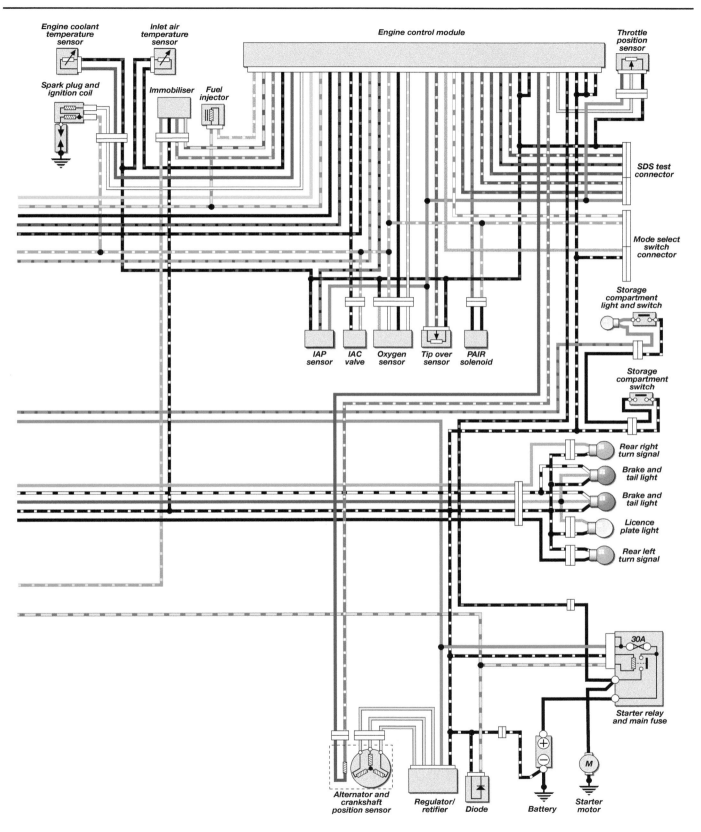

AN400K5 and K6
(for fuse details see Chapter 9 specifications)

H47212

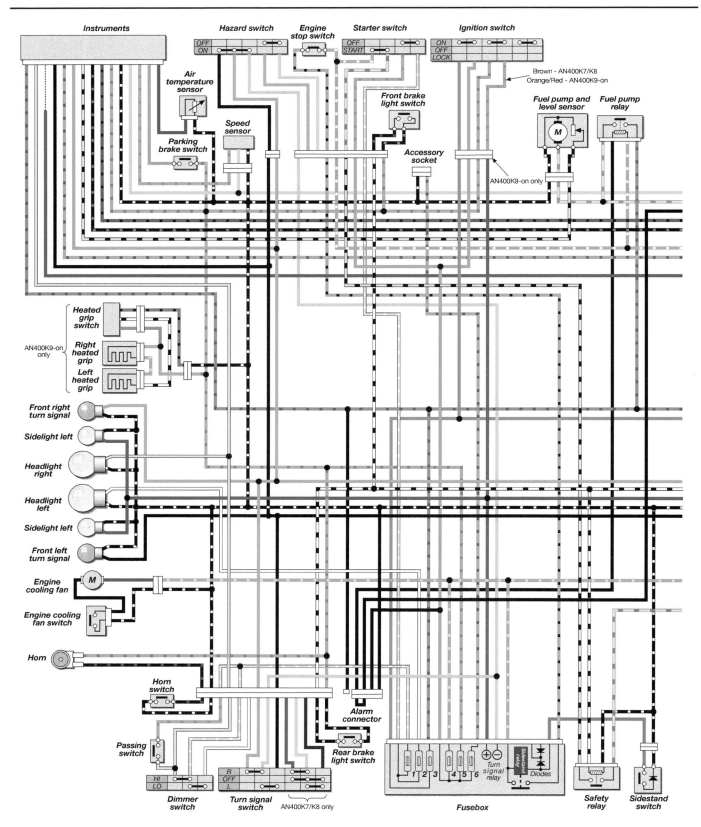

AN400K7 onward (ABS components relate to AN400ZA models)
(for fuse details see Chapter 9 specifications)

H47213

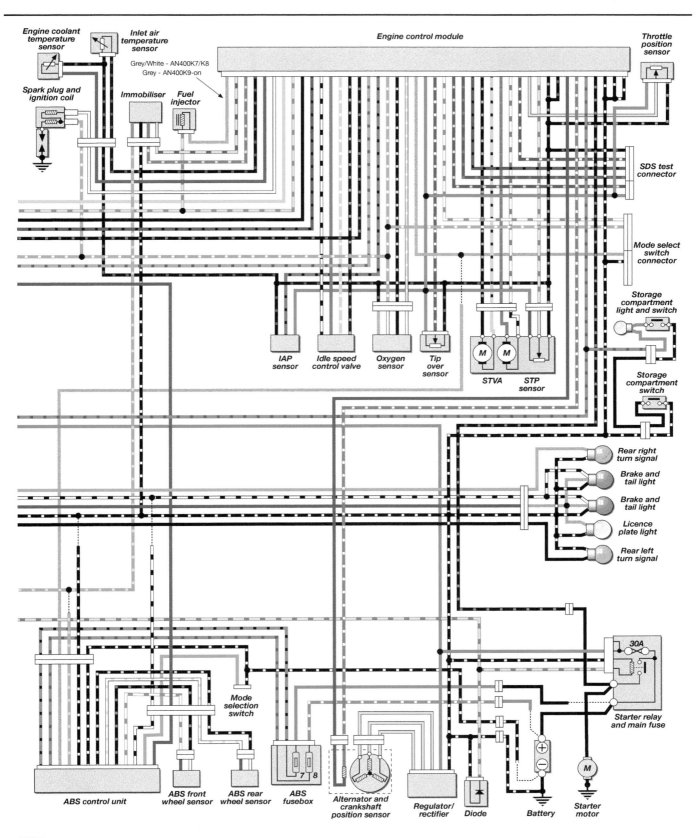

AN400K7 onward (ABS components relate to AN400ZA models)
(for fuse details see Chapter 9 specifications)

H47214

Notes

Reference

Tools and Workshop Tips

● Building up a tool kit and equipping your workshop ● Using tools ● Understanding bearing, seal, fastener and chain sizes and markings ● Repair techniques

Conversion Factors

$$34 \; N_m \times 0.738 = 25 \; lbf \, ft$$

● Formulae for conversion of the metric (SI) units used throughout the manual into Imperial measures

Security

● Locks and chains ● U-locks ● Disc locks ● Alarms and immobilisers ● Security marking systems ● Tips on how to prevent bike theft

Lubricants and fluids

● Engine oils ● Transmission (gear) oils ● Coolant/anti-freeze ● Fork oils and suspension fluids ● Brake/clutch fluids ● Spray lubes, degreasers and solvents

MOT Test Checks

● A guide to the UK MOT test ● Which items are tested ● How to prepare your motorcycle for the test and perform a pre-test check

Fault Finding

● Common faults and their likely causes ● Links to main chapters for testing or repair procedures

Technical Terms Explained

● Component names, technical terms and common abbreviations explained

Index

REF•2 Tools and Workshop Tips

Buying tools

A toolkit is a fundamental requirement for servicing and repairing a motorcycle. Although there will be an initial expense in building up enough tools for servicing, this will soon be offset by the savings made by doing the job yourself. As experience and confidence grow, additional tools can be added to enable the repair and overhaul of the motorcycle. Many of the specialist tools are expensive and not often used so it may be preferable to hire them, or for a group of friends or motorcycle club to join in the purchase.

As a rule, it is better to buy more expensive, good quality tools. Cheaper tools are likely to wear out faster and need to be renewed more often, nullifying the original saving.

Warning: To avoid the risk of a poor quality tool breaking in use, causing injury or damage to the component being worked on, always aim to purchase tools which meet the relevant national safety standards.

The following lists of tools do not represent the manufacturer's service tools, but serve as a guide to help the owner decide which tools are needed for this level of work. In addition, items such as an electric drill, hacksaw, files, soldering iron and a workbench equipped with a vice, may be needed. Although not classed as tools, a selection of bolts, screws, nuts, washers and pieces of tubing always come in useful.

For more information about tools, refer to the Haynes *Motorcycle Workshop Practice Techbook* (Bk. No. 3470).

Manufacturer's service tools

Inevitably certain tasks require the use of a service tool. Where possible an alternative tool or method of approach is recommended, but sometimes there is no option if personal injury or damage to the component is to be avoided. Where required, service tools are referred to in the relevant procedure.

Service tools can usually only be purchased from a motorcycle dealer and are identified by a part number. Some of the commonly-used tools, such as rotor pullers, are available in aftermarket form from mail-order motorcycle tool and accessory suppliers.

Maintenance and minor repair tools

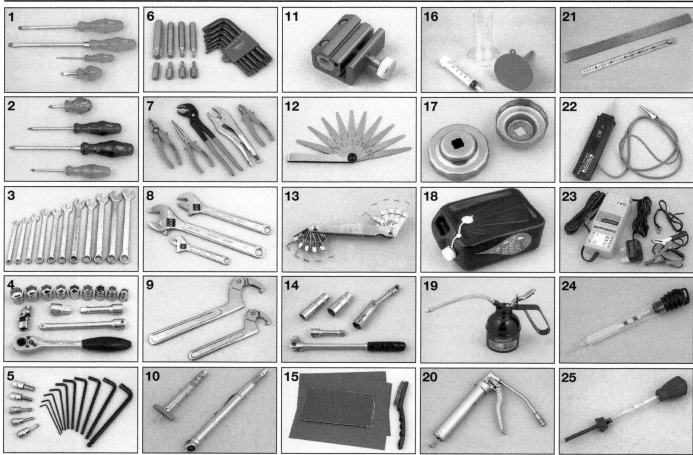

1 Set of flat-bladed screwdrivers
2 Set of Phillips head screwdrivers
3 Combination open-end and ring spanners
4 Socket set (3/8 inch or 1/2 inch drive)
5 Set of Allen keys or bits
6 Set of Torx keys or bits
7 Pliers, cutters and self-locking grips (Mole grips)
8 Adjustable spanners
9 C-spanners
10 Tread depth gauge and tyre pressure gauge
11 Cable oiler clamp
12 Feeler gauges
13 Spark plug gap measuring tool
14 Spark plug spanner or deep plug sockets
15 Wire brush and emery paper
16 Calibrated syringe, measuring vessel and funnel
17 Oil filter adapters
18 Oil drainer can or tray
19 Pump type oil can
20 Grease gun
21 Straight-edge and steel rule
22 Continuity tester
23 Battery charger
24 Hydrometer (for battery specific gravity check)
25 Anti-freeze tester (for liquid-cooled engines)

Repair and overhaul tools

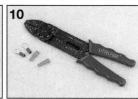

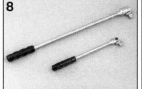

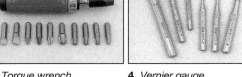
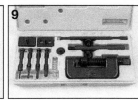

1 *Torque wrench (small and mid-ranges)*
2 *Conventional, plastic or soft-faced hammers*
3 *Impact driver set*
4 *Vernier gauge*
5 *Circlip pliers (internal and external, or combination)*
6 *Set of cold chisels and punches*
7 *Selection of pullers*
8 *Breaker bars*
9 *Chain breaking/ riveting tool set*
10 *Wire stripper and crimper tool*
11 *Multimeter (measures amps, volts and ohms)*
12 *Stroboscope (for dynamic timing checks)*
13 *Hose clamp (wingnut type shown)*
14 *Clutch holding tool*
15 *One-man brake/clutch bleeder kit*

Specialist tools

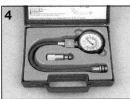

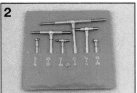
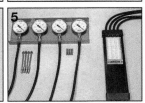
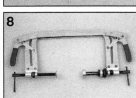
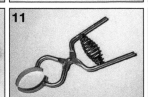

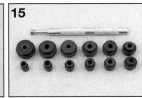

1 *Micrometers (external type)*
2 *Telescoping gauges*
3 *Dial gauge*
4 *Cylinder compression gauge*
5 *Vacuum gauges (left) or manometer (right)*
6 *Oil pressure gauge*
7 *Plastigauge kit*
8 *Valve spring compressor (4-stroke engines)*
9 *Piston pin drawbolt tool*
10 *Piston ring removal and installation tool*
11 *Piston ring clamp*
12 *Cylinder bore hone (stone type shown)*
13 *Stud extractor*
14 *Screw extractor set*
15 *Bearing driver set*

1 Workshop equipment and facilities

The workbench

● Work is made much easier by raising the bike up on a ramp - components are much more accessible if raised to waist level. The hydraulic or pneumatic types seen in the dealer's workshop are a sound investment if you undertake a lot of repairs or overhauls **(see illustration 1.1)**.

1.1 Hydraulic motorcycle ramp

● If raised off ground level, the bike must be supported on the ramp to avoid it falling. Most ramps incorporate a front wheel locating clamp which can be adjusted to suit different diameter wheels. When tightening the clamp, take care not to mark the wheel rim or damage the tyre - use wood blocks on each side to prevent this.

● Secure the bike to the ramp using tie-downs **(see illustration 1.2)**. If the bike has only a sidestand, and hence leans at a dangerous angle when raised, support the bike on an auxiliary stand.

1.2 Tie-downs are used around the passenger footrests to secure the bike

● Auxiliary (paddock) stands are widely available from mail order companies or motorcycle dealers and attach either to the wheel axle or swingarm pivot **(see illustration 1.3)**. If the motorcycle has a centrestand, you can support it under the crankcase to prevent it toppling whilst either wheel is removed **(see illustration 1.4)**.

1.3 This auxiliary stand attaches to the swingarm pivot

1.4 Always use a block of wood between the engine and jack head when supporting the engine in this way

Fumes and fire

● Refer to the Safety first! page at the beginning of the manual for full details. Make sure your workshop is equipped with a fire extinguisher suitable for fuel-related fires (Class B fire - flammable liquids) - it is not sufficient to have a water-filled extinguisher.

● Always ensure adequate ventilation is available. Unless an exhaust gas extraction system is available for use, ensure that the engine is run outside of the workshop.

● If working on the fuel system, make sure the workshop is ventilated to avoid a build-up of fumes. This applies equally to fume build-up when charging a battery. Do not smoke or allow anyone else to smoke in the workshop.

Fluids

● If you need to drain fuel from the tank, store it in an approved container marked as suitable for the storage of petrol (gasoline) **(see illustration 1.5)**. Do not store fuel in glass jars or bottles.

1.5 Use an approved can only for storing petrol (gasoline)

● Use proprietary engine degreasers or solvents which have a high flash-point, such as paraffin (kerosene), for cleaning off oil, grease and dirt - never use petrol (gasoline) for cleaning. Wear rubber gloves when handling solvent and engine degreaser. The fumes from certain solvents can be dangerous - always work in a well-ventilated area.

Dust, eye and hand protection

● Protect your lungs from inhalation of dust particles by wearing a filtering mask over the nose and mouth. Many frictional materials still contain asbestos which is dangerous to your health. Protect your eyes from spouts of liquid and sprung components by wearing a pair of protective goggles **(see illustration 1.6)**.

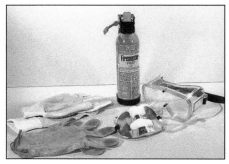

1.6 A fire extinguisher, goggles, mask and protective gloves should be at hand in the workshop

● Protect your hands from contact with solvents, fuel and oils by wearing rubber gloves. Alternatively apply a barrier cream to your hands before starting work. If handling hot components or fluids, wear suitable gloves to protect your hands from scalding and burns.

What to do with old fluids

● Old cleaning solvent, fuel, coolant and oils should not be poured down domestic drains or onto the ground. Package the fluid up in old oil containers, label it accordingly, and take it to a garage or disposal facility. Contact your local authority for location of such sites or ring the oil care hotline.

Note: It is antisocial and illegal to dump oil down the drain. To find the location of your local oil recycling bank in the UK, call 08708 506 506 or visit www.oilbankline.org.uk

2 Fasteners - screws, bolts and nuts

Fastener types and applications

Bolts and screws

● Fastener head types are either of hexagonal, Torx or splined design, with internal and external versions of each type (see illustrations 2.1 and 2.2); splined head fasteners are not in common use on motorcycles. The conventional slotted or Phillips head design is used for certain screws. Bolt or screw length is always measured from the underside of the head to the end of the item (see illustration 2.11).

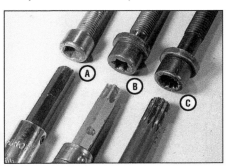

2.1 Internal hexagon/Allen (A), Torx (B) and splined (C) fasteners, with corresponding bits

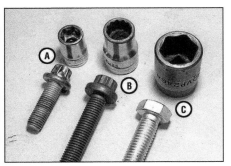

2.2 External Torx (A), splined (B) and hexagon (C) fasteners, with corresponding sockets

● Certain fasteners on the motorcycle have a tensile marking on their heads, the higher the marking the stronger the fastener. High tensile fasteners generally carry a 10 or higher marking. Never replace a high tensile fastener with one of a lower tensile strength.

Washers (see illustration 2.3)

● Plain washers are used between a fastener head and a component to prevent damage to the component or to spread the load when torque is applied. Plain washers can also be used as spacers or shims in certain assemblies. Copper or aluminium plain washers are often used as sealing washers on drain plugs.

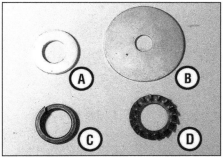

2.3 Plain washer (A), penny washer (B), spring washer (C) and serrated washer (D)

● The split-ring spring washer works by applying axial tension between the fastener head and component. If flattened, it is fatigued and must be renewed. If a plain (flat) washer is used on the fastener, position the spring washer between the fastener and the plain washer.
● Serrated star type washers dig into the fastener and component faces, preventing loosening. They are often used on electrical earth (ground) connections to the frame.
● Cone type washers (sometimes called Belleville) are conical and when tightened apply axial tension between the fastener head and component. They must be installed with the dished side against the component and often carry an OUTSIDE marking on their outer face. If flattened, they are fatigued and must be renewed.
● Tab washers are used to lock plain nuts or bolts on a shaft. A portion of the tab washer is bent up hard against one flat of the nut or bolt to prevent it loosening. Due to the tab washer being deformed in use, a new tab washer should be used every time it is disturbed.
● Wave washers are used to take up endfloat on a shaft. They provide light springing and prevent excessive side-to-side play of a component. Can be found on rocker arm shafts.

Nuts and split pins

● Conventional plain nuts are usually six-sided (see illustration 2.4). They are sized by thread diameter and pitch. High tensile nuts carry a number on one end to denote their tensile strength.

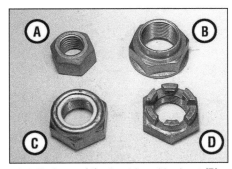

2.4 Plain nut (A), shouldered locknut (B), nylon insert nut (C) and castellated nut (D)

● Self-locking nuts either have a nylon insert, or two spring metal tabs, or a shoulder which is staked into a groove in the shaft - their advantage over conventional plain nuts is a resistance to loosening due to vibration. The nylon insert type can be used a number of times, but must be renewed when the friction of the nylon insert is reduced, ie when the nut spins freely on the shaft. The spring tab type can be reused unless the tabs are damaged. The shouldered type must be renewed every time it is disturbed.
● Split pins (cotter pins) are used to lock a castellated nut to a shaft or to prevent slackening of a plain nut. Common applications are wheel axles and brake torque arms. Because the split pin arms are deformed to lock around the nut a new split pin must always be used on installation - always fit the correct size split pin which will fit snugly in the shaft hole. Make sure the split pin arms are correctly located around the nut (see illustrations 2.5 and 2.6).

2.5 Bend split pin (cotter pin) arms as shown (arrows) to secure a castellated nut

2.6 Bend split pin (cotter pin) arms as shown to secure a plain nut

Caution: If the castellated nut slots do not align with the shaft hole after tightening to the torque setting, tighten the nut until the next slot aligns with the hole - never slacken the nut to align its slot.

● R-pins (shaped like the letter R), or slip pins as they are sometimes called, are sprung and can be reused if they are otherwise in good condition. Always install R-pins with their closed end facing forwards (see illustration 2.7).

2.7 Correct fitting of R-pin. Arrow indicates forward direction

Circlips (see illustration 2.8)

● Circlips (sometimes called snap-rings) are used to retain components on a shaft or in a housing and have corresponding external or internal ears to permit removal. Parallel-sided (machined) circlips can be installed either way round in their groove, whereas stamped circlips (which have a chamfered edge on one face) must be installed with the chamfer facing away from the direction of thrust load **(see illustration 2.9)**.

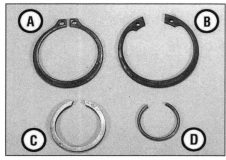

2.8 External stamped circlip (A), internal stamped circlip (B), machined circlip (C) and wire circlip (D)

● Always use circlip pliers to remove and install circlips; expand or compress them just enough to remove them. After installation, rotate the circlip in its groove to ensure it is securely seated. If installing a circlip on a splined shaft, always align its opening with a shaft channel to ensure the circlip ends are well supported and unlikely to catch **(see illustration 2.10)**.

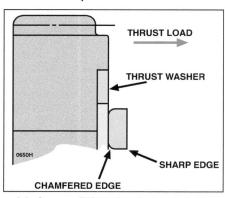

THRUST LOAD

THRUST WASHER

0650H

SHARP EDGE

CHAMFERED EDGE

2.9 Correct fitting of a stamped circlip

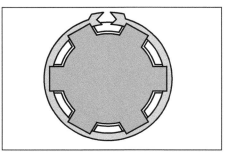

2.10 Align circlip opening with shaft channel

● Circlips can wear due to the thrust of components and become loose in their grooves, with the subsequent danger of becoming dislodged in operation. For this reason, renewal is advised every time a circlip is disturbed.
● Wire circlips are commonly used as piston pin retaining clips. If a removal tang is provided, long-nosed pliers can be used to dislodge them, otherwise careful use of a small flat-bladed screwdriver is necessary. Wire circlips should be renewed every time they are disturbed.

Thread diameter and pitch

● Diameter of a male thread (screw, bolt or stud) is the outside diameter of the threaded portion **(see illustration 2.11)**. Most motorcycle manufacturers use the ISO (International Standards Organisation) metric system expressed in millimetres, eg M6 refers to a 6 mm diameter thread. Sizing is the same for nuts, except that the thread diameter is measured across the valleys of the nut.
● Pitch is the distance between the peaks of the thread **(see illustration 2.11)**. It is expressed in millimetres, thus a common bolt size may be expressed as 6.0 x 1.0 mm (6 mm thread diameter and 1 mm pitch). Generally pitch increases in proportion to thread diameter, although there are always exceptions.
● Thread diameter and pitch are related for conventional fastener applications and the accompanying table can be used as a guide. Additionally, the AF (Across Flats), spanner or socket size dimension of the bolt or nut **(see illustration 2.11)** is linked to thread and pitch specification. Thread pitch can be measured with a thread gauge **(see illustration 2.12)**.

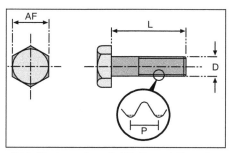

AF

L

D

P

2.11 Fastener length (L), thread diameter (D), thread pitch (P) and head size (AF)

2.12 Using a thread gauge to measure pitch

AF size	Thread diameter x pitch (mm)
8 mm	M5 x 0.8
8 mm	M6 x 1.0
10 mm	M6 x 1.0
12 mm	M8 x 1.25
14 mm	M10 x 1.25
17 mm	M12 x 1.25

● The threads of most fasteners are of the right-hand type, ie they are turned clockwise to tighten and anti-clockwise to loosen. The reverse situation applies to left-hand thread fasteners, which are turned anti-clockwise to tighten and clockwise to loosen. Left-hand threads are used where rotation of a component might loosen a conventional right-hand thread fastener.

Seized fasteners

● Corrosion of external fasteners due to water or reaction between two dissimilar metals can occur over a period of time. It will build up sooner in wet conditions or in countries where salt is used on the roads during the winter. If a fastener is severely corroded it is likely that normal methods of removal will fail and result in its head being ruined. When you attempt removal, the fastener thread should be heard to crack free and unscrew easily - if it doesn't, stop there before damaging anything.
● A smart tap on the head of the fastener will often succeed in breaking free corrosion which has occurred in the threads **(see illustration 2.13)**.
● An aerosol penetrating fluid (such as WD-40) applied the night beforehand may work its way down into the thread and ease removal. Depending on the location, you may be able to make up a Plasticine well around the fastener head and fill it with penetrating fluid.

2.13 A sharp tap on the head of a fastener will often break free a corroded thread

● If you are working on an engine internal component, corrosion will most likely not be a problem due to the well lubricated environment. However, components can be very tight and an impact driver is a useful tool in freeing them (see illustration 2.14).

2.14 Using an impact driver to free a fastener

● Where corrosion has occurred between dissimilar metals (eg steel and aluminium alloy), the application of heat to the fastener head will create a disproportionate expansion rate between the two metals and break the seizure caused by the corrosion. Whether heat can be applied depends on the location of the fastener - any surrounding components likely to be damaged must first be removed (see illustration 2.15). Heat can be applied using a paint stripper heat gun or clothes iron, or by immersing the component in boiling water - wear protective gloves to prevent scalding or burns to the hands.

2.15 Using heat to free a seized fastener

● As a last resort, it is possible to use a hammer and cold chisel to work the fastener head unscrewed (see illustration 2.16). This will damage the fastener, but more importantly extreme care must be taken not to damage the surrounding component.

Caution: Remember that the component being secured is generally of more value than the bolt, nut or screw - when the fastener is freed, do not unscrew it with force, instead work the fastener back and forth when resistance is felt to prevent thread damage.

2.16 Using a hammer and chisel to free a seized fastener

Broken fasteners and damaged heads

● If the shank of a broken bolt or screw is accessible you can grip it with self-locking grips. The knurled wheel type stud extractor tool or self-gripping stud puller tool is particularly useful for removing the long studs which screw into the cylinder mouth surface of the crankcase or bolts and screws from which the head has broken off (see illustration 2.17). Studs can also be removed by locking two nuts together on the threaded end of the stud and using a spanner on the lower nut (see illustration 2.18).

2.17 Using a stud extractor tool to remove a broken crankcase stud

2.18 Two nuts can be locked together to unscrew a stud from a component

● A bolt or screw which has broken off below or level with the casing must be extracted using a screw extractor set. Centre punch the fastener to centralise the drill bit, then drill a hole in the fastener (see illustration 2.19). Select a drill bit which is approximately half to three-quarters the diameter of the fastener

2.19 When using a screw extractor, first drill a hole in the fastener . . .

and drill to a depth which will accommodate the extractor. Use the largest size extractor possible, but avoid leaving too small a wall thickness otherwise the extractor will merely force the fastener walls outwards wedging it in the casing thread.

● If a spiral type extractor is used, thread it anti-clockwise into the fastener. As it is screwed in, it will grip the fastener and unscrew it from the casing (see illustration 2.20).

2.20 . . . then thread the extractor anti-clockwise into the fastener

● If a taper type extractor is used, tap it into the fastener so that it is firmly wedged in place. Unscrew the extractor (anti-clockwise) to draw the fastener out.

⚠️ *Warning: Stud extractors are very hard and may break off in the fastener if care is not taken - ask an engineer about spark erosion if this happens.*

● Alternatively, the broken bolt/screw can be drilled out and the hole retapped for an oversize bolt/screw or a diamond-section thread insert. It is essential that the drilling is carried out squarely and to the correct depth, otherwise the casing may be ruined - if in doubt, entrust the work to an engineer.
● Bolts and nuts with rounded corners cause the correct size spanner or socket to slip when force is applied. Of the types of spanner/socket available always use a six-point type rather than an eight or twelve-point type - better grip

2.21 Comparison of surface drive ring spanner (left) with 12-point type (right)

is obtained. Surface drive spanners grip the middle of the hex flats, rather than the corners, and are thus good in cases of damaged heads **(see illustration 2.21)**.

● Slotted-head or Phillips-head screws are often damaged by the use of the wrong size screwdriver. Allen-head and Torx-head screws are much less likely to sustain damage. If enough of the screw head is exposed you can use a hacksaw to cut a slot in its head and then use a conventional flat-bladed screwdriver to remove it. Alternatively use a hammer and cold chisel to tap the head of the fastener around to slacken it. Always replace damaged fasteners with new ones, preferably Torx or Allen-head type.

HAYNES HiNT

A dab of valve grinding compound between the screw head and screw-driver tip will often give a good grip.

Thread repair

● Threads (particularly those in aluminium alloy components) can be damaged by overtightening, being assembled with dirt in the threads, or from a component working loose and vibrating. Eventually the thread will fail completely, and it will be impossible to tighten the fastener.

● If a thread is damaged or clogged with old locking compound it can be renovated with a thread repair tool (thread chaser) **(see illustrations 2.22 and 2.23)**; special thread

2.22 A thread repair tool being used to correct an internal thread

2.23 A thread repair tool being used to correct an external thread

chasers are available for spark plug hole threads. The tool will not cut a new thread, but clean and true the original thread. Make sure that you use the correct diameter and pitch tool. Similarly, external threads can be cleaned up with a die or a thread restorer file **(see illustration 2.24)**.

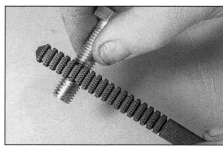

2.24 Using a thread restorer file

● It is possible to drill out the old thread and retap the component to the next thread size. This will work where there is enough surrounding material and a new bolt or screw can be obtained. Sometimes, however, this is not possible - such as where the bolt/screw passes through another component which must also be suitably modified, also in cases where a spark plug or oil drain plug cannot be obtained in a larger diameter thread size.

● The diamond-section thread insert (often known by its popular trade name of Heli-Coil) is a simple and effective method of renewing the thread and retaining the original size. A kit can be purchased which contains the tap, insert and installing tool **(see illustration 2.25)**. Drill out the damaged thread with the size drill specified **(see illustration 2.26)**. Carefully retap the thread **(see illustration 2.27)**. Install the

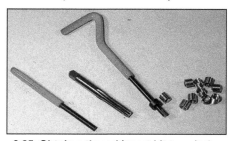

2.25 Obtain a thread insert kit to suit the thread diameter and pitch required

2.26 To install a thread insert, first drill out the original thread . . .

2.27 . . . tap a new thread . . .

2.28 . . . fit insert on the installing tool . . .

2.29 . . . and thread into the component . . .

2.30 . . . break off the tang when complete

insert on the installing tool and thread it slowly into place using a light downward pressure **(see illustrations 2.28 and 2.29)**. When positioned between a 1/4 and 1/2 turn below the surface withdraw the installing tool and use the break-off tool to press down on the tang, breaking it off **(see illustration 2.30)**.

● There are epoxy thread repair kits on the market which can rebuild stripped internal threads, although this repair should not be used on high load-bearing components.

Thread locking and sealing compounds

● Locking compounds are used in locations where the fastener is prone to loosening due to vibration or on important safety-related items which might cause loss of control of the motorcycle if they fail. It is also used where important fasteners cannot be secured by other means such as lockwashers or split pins.

● Before applying locking compound, make sure that the threads (internal and external) are clean and dry with all old compound removed. Select a compound to suit the component being secured - a non-permanent general locking and sealing type is suitable for most applications, but a high strength type is needed for permanent fixing of studs in castings. Apply a drop or two of the compound to the first few threads of the fastener, then thread it into place and tighten to the specified torque. Do not apply excessive thread locking compound otherwise the thread may be damaged on subsequent removal.

● Certain fasteners are impregnated with a dry film type coating of locking compound on their threads. Always renew this type of fastener if disturbed.

● Anti-seize compounds, such as copper-based greases, can be applied to protect threads from seizure due to extreme heat and corrosion. A common instance is spark plug threads and exhaust system fasteners.

3 Measuring tools and gauges

Feeler gauges

● Feeler gauges (or blades) are used for measuring small gaps and clearances **(see illustration 3.1)**. They can also be used to measure endfloat (sideplay) of a component on a shaft where access is not possible with a dial gauge.

● Feeler gauge sets should be treated with care and not bent or damaged. They are etched with their size on one face. Keep them clean and very lightly oiled to prevent corrosion build-up.

3.1 Feeler gauges are used for measuring small gaps and clearances - thickness is marked on one face of gauge

● When measuring a clearance, select a gauge which is a light sliding fit between the two components. You may need to use two gauges together to measure the clearance accurately.

Micrometers

● A micrometer is a precision tool capable of measuring to 0.01 or 0.001 of a millimetre. It should always be stored in its case and not in the general toolbox. It must be kept clean and never dropped, otherwise its frame or measuring anvils could be distorted resulting in inaccurate readings.

● External micrometers are used for measuring outside diameters of components and have many more applications than internal micrometers. Micrometers are available in different size ranges, eg 0 to 25 mm, 25 to 50 mm, and upwards in 25 mm steps; some large micrometers have interchangeable anvils to allow a range of measurements to be taken. Generally the largest precision measurement you are likely to take on a motorcycle is the piston diameter.

● Internal micrometers (or bore micrometers) are used for measuring inside diameters, such as valve guides and cylinder bores. Telescoping gauges and small hole gauges are used in conjunction with an external micrometer, whereas the more expensive internal micrometers have their own measuring device.

External micrometer

Note: *The conventional analogue type instrument is described. Although much easier to read, digital micrometers are considerably more expensive.*

● Always check the calibration of the micrometer before use. With the anvils closed (0 to 25 mm type) or set over a test gauge

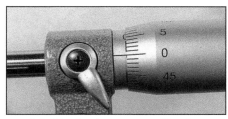

3.2 Check micrometer calibration before use

(for the larger types) the scale should read zero **(see illustration 3.2)**; make sure that the anvils (and test piece) are clean first. Any discrepancy can be adjusted by referring to the instructions supplied with the tool. Remember that the micrometer is a precision measuring tool - don't force the anvils closed, use the ratchet (4) on the end of the micrometer to close it. In this way, a measured force is always applied.

● To use, first make sure that the item being measured is clean. Place the anvil (1) of the micrometer against the item and use the thimble (2) to bring the spindle (3) lightly into contact with the other side of the item **(see illustration 3.3)**. Don't tighten the thimble down because this will damage the micrometer - instead use the ratchet (4) on the end of the micrometer. The ratchet mechanism applies a measured force preventing damage to the instrument.

● The micrometer is read by referring to the linear scale on the sleeve and the annular scale on the thimble. Read off the sleeve first to obtain the base measurement, then add the fine measurement from the thimble to obtain the overall reading. The linear scale on the sleeve represents the measuring range of the micrometer (eg 0 to 25 mm). The annular scale

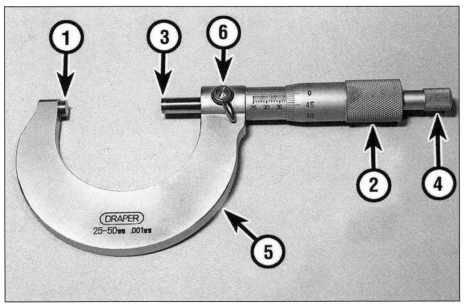

3.3 Micrometer component parts

1	Anvil	3	Spindle	5	Frame
2	Thimble	4	Ratchet	6	Locking lever

on the thimble will be in graduations of 0.01 mm (or as marked on the frame) - one full revolution of the thimble will move 0.5 mm on the linear scale. Take the reading where the datum line on the sleeve intersects the thimble's scale. Always position the eye directly above the scale otherwise an inaccurate reading will result.

In the example shown the item measures 2.95 mm **(see illustration 3.4)**:

Linear scale	2.00 mm
Linear scale	0.50 mm
Annular scale	0.45 mm
Total figure	2.95 mm

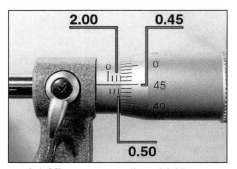

3.4 Micrometer reading of 2.95 mm

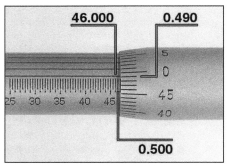

3.5 Micrometer reading of 46.99 mm on linear and annular scales . . .

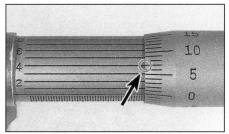

3.6 . . . and 0.004 mm on vernier scale

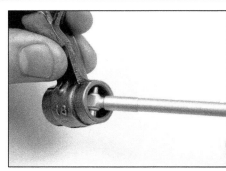

3.7 Expand the telescoping gauge in the bore, lock its position . . .

3.8 . . . then measure the gauge with a micrometer

3.9 Expand the small hole gauge in the bore, lock its position . . .

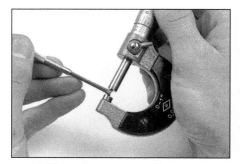

3.10 . . . then measure the gauge with a micrometer

Most micrometers have a locking lever (6) on the frame to hold the setting in place, allowing the item to be removed from the micrometer.
● Some micrometers have a vernier scale on their sleeve, providing an even finer measurement to be taken, in 0.001 increments of a millimetre. Take the sleeve and thimble measurement as described above, then check which graduation on the vernier scale aligns with that of the annular scale on the thimble **Note:** *The eye must be perpendicular to the scale when taking the vernier reading - if necessary rotate the body of the micrometer to ensure this.* Multiply the vernier scale figure by 0.001 and add it to the base and fine measurement figures.

In the example shown the item measures 46.994 mm **(see illustrations 3.5 and 3.6)**:

Linear scale (base)	46.000 mm
Linear scale (base)	00.500 mm
Annular scale (fine)	00.490 mm
Vernier scale	00.004 mm
Total figure	46.994 mm

Internal micrometer

● Internal micrometers are available for measuring bore diameters, but are expensive and unlikely to be available for home use. It is suggested that a set of telescoping gauges and small hole gauges, both of which must be used with an external micrometer, will suffice for taking internal measurements on a motorcycle.
● Telescoping gauges can be used to measure internal diameters of components. Select a gauge with the correct size range, make sure its ends are clean and insert it into the bore. Expand the gauge, then lock its position and withdraw it from the bore **(see illustration 3.7)**. Measure across the gauge ends with a micrometer **(see illustration 3.8)**.
● Very small diameter bores (such as valve guides) are measured with a small hole gauge. Once adjusted to a slip-fit inside the component, its position is locked and the gauge withdrawn for measurement with a micrometer **(see illustrations 3.9 and 3.10)**.

Vernier caliper

Note: *The conventional linear and dial gauge type instruments are described. Digital types are easier to read, but are far more expensive.*
● The vernier caliper does not provide the precision of a micrometer, but is versatile in being able to measure internal and external diameters. Some types also incorporate a depth gauge. It is ideal for measuring clutch plate friction material and spring free lengths.
● To use the conventional linear scale vernier, slacken off the vernier clamp screws (1) and set its jaws over (2), or inside (3), the item to be measured **(see illustration 3.11)**. Slide the jaw into contact, using the thumb-wheel (4) for fine movement of the sliding scale (5) then tighten the clamp screws (1). Read off the main scale (6) where the zero on the sliding scale (5) intersects it, taking the whole number to the left of the zero; this provides the base measurement. View along the sliding scale and select the division which

lines up exactly with any of the divisions on the main scale, noting that the divisions usually represents 0.02 of a millimetre. Add this fine measurement to the base measurement to obtain the total reading.

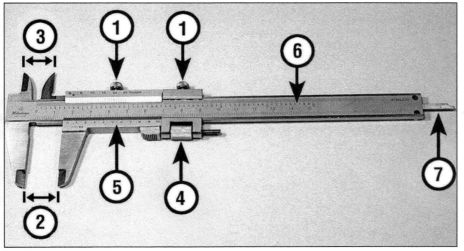

3.11 Vernier component parts (linear gauge)

1 Clamp screws   3 Internal jaws   5 Sliding scale   7 Depth gauge
2 External jaws   4 Thumbwheel   6 Main scale

In the example shown the item measures 55.92 mm **(see illustration 3.12)**:

Base measurement	55.00 mm
Fine measurement	00.92 mm
Total figure	55.92 mm

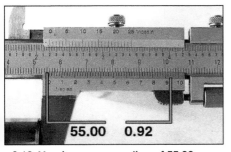

3.12 Vernier gauge reading of 55.92 mm

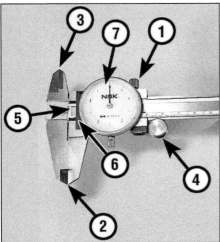

3.13 Vernier component parts (dial gauge)

1 Clamp screw   5 Main scale
2 External jaws   6 Sliding scale
3 Internal jaws   7 Dial gauge
4 Thumbwheel

● Some vernier calipers are equipped with a dial gauge for fine measurement. Before use, check that the jaws are clean, then close them fully and check that the dial gauge reads zero. If necessary adjust the gauge ring accordingly. Slacken the vernier clamp screw (1) and set its jaws over (2), or inside (3), the item to be measured **(see illustration 3.13)**. Slide the jaws into contact, using the thumbwheel (4) for fine movement. Read off the main scale (5) where the edge of the sliding scale (6) intersects it, taking the whole number to the left of the zero; this provides the base measurement. Read off the needle position on the dial gauge (7) scale to provide the fine measurement; each division represents 0.05 of a millimetre. Add this fine measurement to the base measurement to obtain the total reading.

In the example shown the item measures 55.95 mm **(see illustration 3.14)**:

Base measurement	55.00 mm
Fine measurement	00.95 mm
Total figure	55.95 mm

3.14 Vernier gauge reading of 55.95 mm

Plastigauge

● Plastigauge is a plastic material which can be compressed between two surfaces to measure the oil clearance between them. The width of the compressed Plastigauge is measured against a calibrated scale to determine the clearance.

● Common uses of Plastigauge are for measuring the clearance between crankshaft journal and main bearing inserts, between crankshaft journal and big-end bearing inserts, and between camshaft and bearing surfaces. The following example describes big-end oil clearance measurement.

● Handle the Plastigauge material carefully to prevent distortion. Using a sharp knife, cut a length which corresponds with the width of the bearing being measured and place it carefully across the journal so that it is parallel with the shaft **(see illustration 3.15)**. Carefully install both bearing shells and the connecting rod. Without rotating the rod on the journal tighten its bolts or nuts (as applicable) to the specified torque. The connecting rod and bearings are then disassembled and the crushed Plastigauge examined.

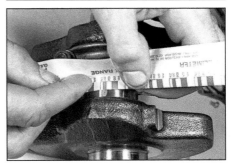

3.15 Plastigauge placed across shaft journal

● Using the scale provided in the Plastigauge kit, measure the width of the material to determine the oil clearance **(see illustration 3.16)**. Always remove all traces of Plastigauge after use using your fingernails.

Caution: Arriving at the correct clearance demands that the assembly is torqued correctly, according to the settings and sequence (where applicable) provided by the motorcycle manufacturer.

3.16 Measuring the width of the crushed Plastigauge

Dial gauge or DTI (Dial Test Indicator)

● A dial gauge can be used to accurately measure small amounts of movement. Typical uses are measuring shaft runout or shaft endfloat (sideplay) and setting piston position for ignition timing on two-strokes. A dial gauge set usually comes with a range of different probes and adapters and mounting equipment.

● The gauge needle must point to zero when at rest. Rotate the ring around its periphery to zero the gauge.

● Check that the gauge is capable of reading the extent of movement in the work. Most gauges have a small dial set in the face which records whole millimetres of movement as well as the fine scale around the face periphery which is calibrated in 0.01 mm divisions. Read off the small dial first to obtain the base measurement, then add the measurement from the fine scale to obtain the total reading.

In the example shown the gauge reads 1.48 mm (see illustration 3.17):

Base measurement	1.00 mm
Fine measurement	0.48 mm
Total figure	1.48 mm

3.17 Dial gauge reading of 1.48 mm

● If measuring shaft runout, the shaft must be supported in vee-blocks and the gauge mounted on a stand perpendicular to the shaft. Rest the tip of the gauge against the centre of the shaft and rotate the shaft slowly whilst watching the gauge reading (see illustration 3.18). Take several measurements along the length of the shaft and record the

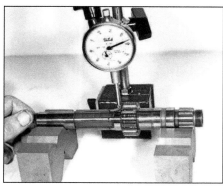

3.18 Using a dial gauge to measure shaft runout

maximum gauge reading as the amount of runout in the shaft. **Note:** *The reading obtained will be total runout at that point - some manufacturers specify that the runout figure is halved to compare with their specified runout limit.*

● Endfloat (sideplay) measurement requires that the gauge is mounted securely to the surrounding component with its probe touching the end of the shaft. Using hand pressure, push and pull on the shaft noting the maximum endfloat recorded on the gauge (see illustration 3.19).

3.19 Using a dial gauge to measure shaft endfloat

● A dial gauge with suitable adapters can be used to determine piston position BTDC on two-stroke engines for the purposes of ignition timing. The gauge, adapter and suitable length probe are installed in the place of the spark plug and the gauge zeroed at TDC. If the piston position is specified as 1.14 mm BTDC, rotate the engine back to 2.00 mm BTDC, then slowly forwards to 1.14 mm BTDC.

Cylinder compression gauges

● A compression gauge is used for measuring cylinder compression. Either the rubber-cone type or the threaded adapter type can be used. The latter is preferred to ensure a perfect seal against the cylinder head. A 0 to 300 psi (0 to 20 Bar) type gauge (for petrol/gasoline engines) will be suitable for motorcycles.

● The spark plug is removed and the gauge either held hard against the cylinder head (cone type) or the gauge adapter screwed into the cylinder head (threaded type) (see illustration 3.20). Cylinder compression is measured with the engine turning over, but not running - carry out the compression test as described in

3.20 Using a rubber-cone type cylinder compression gauge

Fault Finding Equipment. The gauge will hold the reading until manually released.

Oil pressure gauge

● An oil pressure gauge is used for measuring engine oil pressure. Most gauges come with a set of adapters to fit the thread of the take-off point (see illustration 3.21). If the take-off point specified by the motorcycle manufacturer is an external oil pipe union, make sure that the specified replacement union is used to prevent oil starvation.

3.21 Oil pressure gauge and take-off point adapter (arrow)

● Oil pressure is measured with the engine running (at a specific rpm) and often the manufacturer will specify pressure limits for a cold and hot engine.

Straight-edge and surface plate

● If checking the gasket face of a component for warpage, place a steel rule or precision straight-edge across the gasket face and measure any gap between the straight-edge and component with feeler gauges (see illustration 3.22). Check diagonally across the component and between mounting holes (see illustration 3.23).

3.22 Use a straight-edge and feeler gauges to check for warpage

3.23 Check for warpage in these directions

● Checking individual components for warpage, such as clutch plain (metal) plates, requires a perfectly flat plate or piece or plate glass and feeler gauges.

4 Torque and leverage

What is torque?

● Torque describes the twisting force about a shaft. The amount of torque applied is determined by the distance from the centre of the shaft to the end of the lever and the amount of force being applied to the end of the lever; distance multiplied by force equals torque.

● The manufacturer applies a measured torque to a bolt or nut to ensure that it will not slacken in use and to hold two components securely together without movement in the joint. The actual torque setting depends on the thread size, bolt or nut material and the composition of the components being held.

● Too little torque may cause the fastener to loosen due to vibration, whereas too much torque will distort the joint faces of the component or cause the fastener to shear off. Always stick to the specified torque setting.

Using a torque wrench

● Check the calibration of the torque wrench and make sure it has a suitable range for the job. Torque wrenches are available in Nm (Newton-metres), kgf m (kilograms-force metre), lbf ft (pounds-feet), lbf in (inch-pounds). Do not confuse lbf ft with lbf in.

● Adjust the tool to the desired torque on the scale (see illustration 4.1). If your torque wrench is not calibrated in the units specified, carefully convert the figure (see Conversion Factors). A manufacturer sometimes gives a torque setting as a range (8 to 10 Nm) rather than a single figure - in this case set the tool midway between the two settings. The same torque may be expressed as 9 Nm ± 1 Nm. Some torque wrenches have a method of locking the setting so that it isn't inadvertently altered during use.

4.1 Set the torque wrench index mark to the setting required, in this case 12 Nm

● Install the bolts/nuts in their correct location and secure them lightly. Their threads must be clean and free of any old locking compound. Unless specified the threads and flange should be dry - oiled threads are necessary in certain circumstances and the manufacturer will take this into account in the specified torque figure. Similarly, the manufacturer may also specify the application of thread-locking compound.

● Tighten the fasteners in the specified sequence until the torque wrench clicks, indicating that the torque setting has been reached. Apply the torque again to double-check the setting. Where different thread diameter fasteners secure the component, as a rule tighten the larger diameter ones first.

● When the torque wrench has been finished with, release the lock (where applicable) and fully back off its setting to zero - do not leave the torque wrench tensioned. Also, do not use a torque wrench for slackening a fastener.

Angle-tightening

● Manufacturers often specify a figure in degrees for final tightening of a fastener. This usually follows tightening to a specific torque setting.

● A degree disc can be set and attached to the socket (see illustration 4.2) or a protractor can be used to mark the angle of movement on the bolt/nut head and the surrounding casting (see illustration 4.3).

4.2 Angle tightening can be accomplished with a torque-angle gauge . . .

4.3 . . . or by marking the angle on the surrounding component

Loosening sequences

● Where more than one bolt/nut secures a component, loosen each fastener evenly a little at a time. In this way, not all the stress of the joint is held by one fastener and the components are not likely to distort.

● If a tightening sequence is provided, work in the REVERSE of this, but if not, work from the outside in, in a criss-cross sequence (see illustration 4.4).

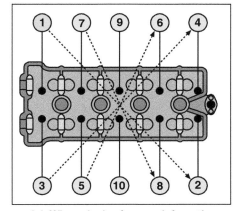

4.4 When slackening, work from the outside inwards

Tightening sequences

● If a component is held by more than one fastener it is important that the retaining bolts/nuts are tightened evenly to prevent uneven stress build-up and distortion of sealing faces. This is especially important on high-compression joints such as the cylinder head.

● A sequence is usually provided by the manufacturer, either in a diagram or actually marked in the casting. If not, always start in the centre and work outwards in a criss-cross pattern (see illustration 4.5). Start off by securing all bolts/nuts finger-tight, then set the torque wrench and tighten each fastener by a small amount in sequence until the final torque is reached. By following this practice, the joint

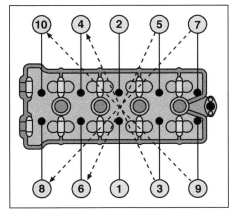

4.5 When tightening, work from the inside outwards

will be held evenly and will not be distorted. Important joints, such as the cylinder head and big-end fasteners often have two- or three-stage torque settings.

Applying leverage

● Use tools at the correct angle. Position a socket wrench or spanner on the bolt/nut so that you pull it towards you when loosening. If this can't be done, push the spanner without curling your fingers around it **(see illustration 4.6)** - the spanner may slip or the fastener loosen suddenly, resulting in your fingers being crushed against a component.

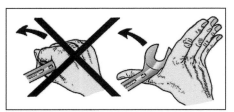

4.6 If you can't pull on the spanner to loosen a fastener, push with your hand open

● Additional leverage is gained by extending the length of the lever. The best way to do this is to use a breaker bar instead of the regular length tool, or to slip a length of tubing over the end of the spanner or socket wrench.
● If additional leverage will not work, the fastener head is either damaged or firmly corroded in place (see Fasteners).

5 Bearings

Bearing removal and installation

Drivers and sockets

● Before removing a bearing, always inspect the casing to see which way it must be driven out - some casings will have retaining plates or a cast step. Also check for any identifying markings on the bearing and if installed to a certain depth, measure this at this stage. Some roller bearings are sealed on one side - take note of the original fitted position.
● Bearings can be driven out of a casing using a bearing driver tool (with the correct size head) or a socket of the correct diameter. Select the driver head or socket so that it contacts the outer race of the bearing, not the balls/rollers or inner race. Always support the casing around the bearing housing with wood blocks, otherwise there is a risk of fracture. The bearing is driven out with a few blows on the driver or socket from a heavy mallet. Unless access is severely restricted (as with wheel bearings), a pin-punch is not recommended unless it is moved around the bearing to keep it square in its housing.

● The same equipment can be used to install bearings. Make sure the bearing housing is supported on wood blocks and line up the bearing in its housing. Fit the bearing as noted on removal - generally they are installed with their marked side facing outwards. Tap the bearing squarely into its housing using a driver or socket which bears only on the bearing's outer race - contact with the bearing balls/rollers or inner race will destroy it **(see illustrations 5.1 and 5.2)**.
● Check that the bearing inner race and balls/rollers rotate freely.

5.1 Using a bearing driver against the bearing's outer race

5.2 Using a large socket against the bearing's outer race

Pullers and slide-hammers

● Where a bearing is pressed on a shaft a puller will be required to extract it **(see illustration 5.3)**. Make sure that the puller clamp or legs fit securely behind the bearing and are unlikely to slip out. If pulling a bearing

5.3 This bearing puller clamps behind the bearing and pressure is applied to the shaft end to draw the bearing off

off a gear shaft for example, you may have to locate the puller behind a gear pinion if there is no access to the race and draw the gear pinion off the shaft as well **(see illustration 5.4)**.

> *Caution: Ensure that the puller's centre bolt locates securely against the end of the shaft and will not slip when pressure is applied. Also ensure that puller does not damage the shaft end.*

5.4 Where no access is available to the rear of the bearing, it is sometimes possible to draw off the adjacent component

● Operate the puller so that its centre bolt exerts pressure on the shaft end and draws the bearing off the shaft.
● When installing the bearing on the shaft, tap only on the bearing's inner race - contact with the balls/rollers or outer race with destroy the bearing. Use a socket or length of tubing as a drift which fits over the shaft end **(see illustration 5.5)**.

5.5 When installing a bearing on a shaft use a piece of tubing which bears only on the bearing's inner race

● Where a bearing locates in a blind hole in a casing, it cannot be driven or pulled out as described above. A slide-hammer with knife-edged bearing puller attachment will be required. The puller attachment passes through the bearing and when tightened expands to fit firmly behind the bearing **(see illustration 5.6)**. By operating the slide-hammer part of the tool the bearing is jarred out of its housing **(see illustration 5.7)**.
● It is possible, if the bearing is of reasonable weight, for it to drop out of its housing if the casing is heated as described opposite. If

5.6 Expand the bearing puller so that it locks behind the bearing . . .

5.7 . . . attach the slide hammer to the bearing puller

this method is attempted, first prepare a work surface which will enable the casing to be tapped face down to help dislodge the bearing - a wood surface is ideal since it will not damage the casing's gasket surface. Wearing protective gloves, tap the heated casing several times against the work surface to dislodge the bearing under its own weight **(see illustration 5.8)**.

5.8 Tapping a casing face down on wood blocks can often dislodge a bearing

● Bearings can be installed in blind holes using the driver or socket method described above.

Drawbolts

● Where a bearing or bush is set in the eye of a component, such as a suspension linkage arm or connecting rod small-end, removal by drift may damage the component. Furthermore, a rubber bushing in a shock absorber eye cannot successfully be driven out of position. If access is available to a engineering press, the task is straightforward. If not, a drawbolt can be fabricated to extract the bearing or bush.

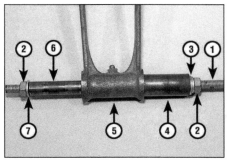

5.9 Drawbolt component parts assembled on a suspension arm

1 Bolt or length of threaded bar
2 Nuts
3 Washer (external diameter greater than tubing internal diameter)
4 Tubing (internal diameter sufficient to accommodate bearing)
5 Suspension arm with bearing
6 Tubing (external diameter slightly smaller than bearing)
7 Washer (external diameter slightly smaller than bearing)

5.10 Drawing the bearing out of the suspension arm

● To extract the bearing/bush you will need a long bolt with nut (or piece of threaded bar with two nuts), a piece of tubing which has an internal diameter larger than the bearing/bush, another piece of tubing which has an external diameter slightly smaller than the bearing/bush, and a selection of washers **(see illustrations 5.9 and 5.10)**. Note that the pieces of tubing must be of the same length, or longer, than the bearing/bush.
● The same kit (without the pieces of tubing) can be used to draw the new bearing/bush back into place **(see illustration 5.11)**.

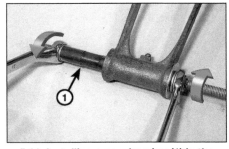

5.11 Installing a new bearing (1) in the suspension arm

Temperature change

● If the bearing's outer race is a tight fit in the casing, the aluminium casing can be heated to release its grip on the bearing. Aluminium will expand at a greater rate than the steel bearing outer race. There are several ways to do this, but avoid any localised extreme heat (such as a blow torch) - aluminium alloy has a low melting point.
● Approved methods of heating a casing are using a domestic oven (heated to 100°C) or immersing the casing in boiling water **(see illustration 5.12)**. Low temperature range localised heat sources such as a paint stripper heat gun or clothes iron can also be used **(see illustration 5.13)**. Alternatively, soak a rag in boiling water, wring it out and wrap it around the bearing housing.

> ⚠️ **Warning: All of these methods require care in use to prevent scalding and burns to the hands. Wear protective gloves when handling hot components.**

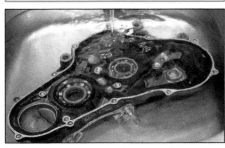

5.12 A casing can be immersed in a sink of boiling water to aid bearing removal

5.13 Using a localised heat source to aid bearing removal

● If heating the whole casing note that plastic components, such as the neutral switch, may suffer - remove them beforehand.
● After heating, remove the bearing as described above. You may find that the expansion is sufficient for the bearing to fall out of the casing under its own weight or with a light tap on the driver or socket.
● If necessary, the casing can be heated to aid bearing installation, and this is sometimes the recommended procedure if the motorcycle manufacturer has designed the housing and bearing fit with this intention.

● Installation of bearings can be eased by placing them in a freezer the night before installation. The steel bearing will contract slightly, allowing easy insertion in its housing. This is often useful when installing steering head outer races in the frame.

Bearing types and markings

● Plain shell bearings, ball bearings, needle roller bearings and tapered roller bearings will all be found on motorcycles **(see illustrations 5.14 and 5.15)**. The ball and roller types are usually caged between an inner and outer race, but uncaged variations may be found.

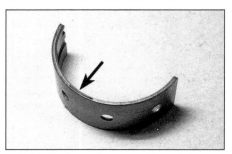

5.14 Shell bearings are either plain or grooved. They are usually identified by colour code (arrow)

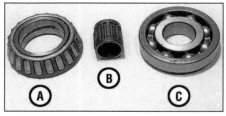

5.15 Tapered roller bearing (A), needle roller bearing (B) and ball journal bearing (C)

● Shell bearings (often called inserts) are usually found at the crankshaft main and connecting rod big-end where they are good at coping with high loads. They are made of a phosphor-bronze material and are impregnated with self-lubricating properties.
● Ball bearings and needle roller bearings consist of a steel inner and outer race with the balls or rollers between the races. They require constant lubrication by oil or grease and are good at coping with axial loads. Taper roller bearings consist of rollers set in a tapered cage set on the inner race; the outer race is separate. They are good at coping with axial loads and prevent movement along the shaft - a typical application is in the steering head.
● Bearing manufacturers produce bearings to ISO size standards and stamp one face of the bearing to indicate its internal and external diameter, load capacity and type **(see illustration 5.16)**.
● Metal bushes are usually of phosphor-bronze material. Rubber bushes are used in suspension mounting eyes. Fibre bushes have also been used in suspension pivots.

5.16 Typical bearing marking

Bearing fault finding

● If a bearing outer race has spun in its housing, the housing material will be damaged. You can use a bearing locking compound to bond the outer race in place if damage is not too severe.
● Shell bearings will fail due to damage of their working surface, as a result of lack of lubrication, corrosion or abrasive particles in the oil **(see illustration 5.17)**. Small particles of dirt in the oil may embed in the bearing material whereas larger particles will score the bearing and shaft journal. If a number of short journeys are made, insufficient heat will be generated to drive off condensation which has built up on the bearings.

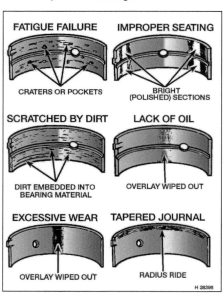

5.17 Typical bearing failures

● Ball and roller bearings will fail due to lack of lubrication or damage to the balls or rollers. Tapered-roller bearings can be damaged by overloading them. Unless the bearing is sealed on both sides, wash it in paraffin (kerosene) to remove all old grease then allow it to dry. Make a visual inspection looking to dented balls or rollers, damaged cages and worn or pitted races **(see illustration 5.18)**.
● A ball bearing can be checked for wear by listening to it when spun. Apply a film of light oil to the bearing and hold it close to the ear - hold the outer race with one hand and spin the

5.18 Example of ball journal bearing with damaged balls and cages

5.19 Hold outer race and listen to inner race when spun

inner race with the other hand **(see illustration 5.19)**. The bearing should be almost silent when spun; if it grates or rattles it is worn.

6 Oil seals

Oil seal removal and installation

● Oil seals should be renewed every time a component is dismantled. This is because the seal lips will become set to the sealing surface and will not necessarily reseal.
● Oil seals can be prised out of position using a large flat-bladed screwdriver **(see illustration 6.1)**. In the case of crankcase seals, check first that the seal is not lipped on the inside, preventing its removal with the crankcases joined.

6.1 Prise out oil seals with a large flat-bladed screwdriver

● New seals are usually installed with their marked face (containing the seal reference code) outwards and the spring side towards the fluid being retained. In certain cases, such as a two-stroke engine crankshaft seal, a double lipped seal may be used due to there being fluid or gas on each side of the joint.

● Use a bearing driver or socket which bears only on the outer hard edge of the seal to install it in the casing - tapping on the inner edge will damage the sealing lip.

Oil seal types and markings

● Oil seals are usually of the single-lipped type. Double-lipped seals are found where a liquid or gas is on both sides of the joint.

● Oil seals can harden and lose their sealing ability if the motorcycle has been in storage for a long period - renewal is the only solution.

● Oil seal manufacturers also conform to the ISO markings for seal size - these are moulded into the outer face of the seal (see illustration 6.2).

6.2 These oil seal markings indicate inside diameter, outside diameter and seal thickness

7 Gaskets and sealants

Types of gasket and sealant

● Gaskets are used to seal the mating surfaces between components and keep lubricants, fluids, vacuum or pressure contained within the assembly. Aluminium gaskets are sometimes found at the cylinder joints, but most gaskets are paper-based. If the mating surfaces of the components being joined are undamaged the gasket can be installed dry, although a dab of sealant or grease will be useful to hold it in place during assembly.

● RTV (Room Temperature Vulcanising) silicone rubber sealants cure when exposed to moisture in the atmosphere. These sealants are good at filling pits or irregular gasket faces, but will tend to be forced out of the joint under very high torque. They can be used to replace a paper gasket, but first make sure that the width of the paper gasket is not essential to the shimming of internal components. RTV sealants should not be used on components containing petrol (gasoline).

● Non-hardening, semi-hardening and hard setting liquid gasket compounds can be used with a gasket or between a metal-to-metal joint. Select the sealant to suit the application: universal non-hardening sealant can be used on virtually all joints; semi-hardening on joint faces which are rough or damaged; hard setting sealant on joints which require a permanent bond and are subjected to high temperature and pressure. Note: Check first if the paper gasket has a bead of sealant

impregnated in its surface before applying additional sealant.

● When choosing a sealant, make sure it is suitable for the application, particularly if being applied in a high-temperature area or in the vicinity of fuel. Certain manufacturers produce sealants in either clear, silver or black colours to match the finish of the engine. This has a particular application on motorcycles where much of the engine is exposed.

● Do not over-apply sealant. That which is squeezed out on the outside of the joint can be wiped off, whereas an excess of sealant on the inside can break off and clog oilways.

Breaking a sealed joint

● Age, heat, pressure and the use of hard setting sealant can cause two components to stick together so tightly that they are difficult to separate using finger pressure alone. Do not resort to using levers unless there is a pry point provided for this purpose (see illustration 7.1) or else the gasket surfaces will be damaged.

● Use a soft-faced hammer (see illustration 7.2) or a wood block and conventional hammer to strike the component near the mating surface. Avoid hammering against cast extremities since they may break off. If this method fails, try using a wood wedge between the two components.

Caution: If the joint will not separate, double-check that you have removed all the fasteners.

7.1 If a pry point is provided, apply gently pressure with a flat-bladed screwdriver

7.2 Tap around the joint with a soft-faced mallet if necessary - don't strike cooling fins

Removal of old gasket and sealant

● Paper gaskets will most likely come away complete, leaving only a few traces stuck

Most components have one or two hollow locating dowels between the two gasket faces. If a dowel cannot be removed, do not resort to gripping it with pliers - it will almost certainly be distorted. Install a close-fitting socket or Phillips screwdriver into the dowel and then grip the outer edge of the dowel to free it.

on the sealing faces of the components. It is imperative that all traces are removed to ensure correct sealing of the new gasket.

● Very carefully scrape all traces of gasket away making sure that the sealing surfaces are not gouged or scored by the scraper (see illustrations 7.3, 7.4 and 7.5). Stubborn deposits can be removed by spraying with an aerosol gasket remover. Final preparation of

7.3 Paper gaskets can be scraped off with a gasket scraper tool . . .

7.4 . . . a knife blade . . .

7.5 . . . or a household scraper

7.6 Fine abrasive paper is wrapped around a flat file to clean up the gasket face

7.7 A kitchen scourer can be used on stubborn deposits

the gasket surface can be made with very fine abrasive paper or a plastic kitchen scourer **(see illustrations 7.6 and 7.7)**.

● Old sealant can be scraped or peeled off components, depending on the type originally used. Note that gasket removal compounds are available to avoid scraping the components clean; make sure the gasket remover suits the type of sealant used.

8 Hoses

Clamping to prevent flow

● Small-bore flexible hoses can be clamped to prevent fluid flow whilst a component is worked on. Whichever method is used, ensure that the hose material is not permanently distorted or damaged by the clamp.

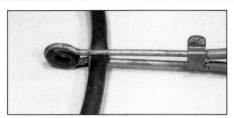

8.1 Hoses can be clamped with an automotive brake hose clamp . . .

8.2 . . . a wingnut type hose clamp . . .

a) A brake hose clamp available from auto accessory shops **(see illustration 8.1)**.
b) A wingnut type hose clamp **(see illustration 8.2)**.
c) Two sockets placed each side of the hose and held with straight-jawed self-locking grips **(see illustration 8.3)**.

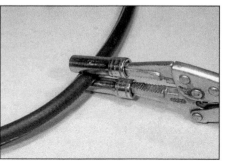

8.3 . . . two sockets and a pair of self-locking grips . . .

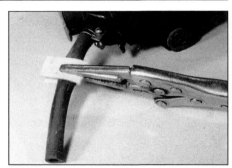

8.4 . . . or thick card and self-locking grips

d) Thick card each side of the hose held between straight-jawed self-locking grips **(see illustration 8.4)**.

Freeing and fitting hoses

● Always make sure the hose clamp is moved well clear of the hose end. Grip the hose with your hand and rotate it whilst pulling it off the union. If the hose has hardened due to age and will not move, slit it with a sharp knife and peel its ends off the union **(see illustration 8.5)**.

● Resist the temptation to use grease or soap on the unions to aid installation; although it helps the hose slip over the union it will equally aid the escape of fluid from the joint. It is preferable to soften the hose ends in hot water and wet the inside surface of the hose with water or a fluid which will evaporate.

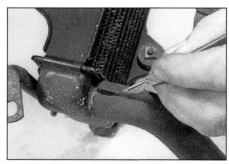

8.5 Cutting a coolant hose free with a sharp knife

Length (distance)

Inches (in)	x 25.4	= Millimetres (mm)	x 0.0394	=	Inches (in)
Feet (ft)	x 0.305	= Metres (m)	x 3.281	=	Feet (ft)
Miles	x 1.609	= Kilometres (km)	x 0.621	=	Miles

Volume (capacity)

Cubic inches (cu in; in³)	x 16.387	= Cubic centimetres (cc; cm³)	x 0.061	=	Cubic inches (cu in; in³)
Imperial pints (Imp pt)	x 0.568	= Litres (l)	x 1.76	=	Imperial pints (Imp pt)
Imperial quarts (Imp qt)	x 1.137	= Litres (l)	x 0.88	=	Imperial quarts (Imp qt)
Imperial quarts (Imp qt)	x 1.201	= US quarts (US qt)	x 0.833	=	Imperial quarts (Imp qt)
US quarts (US qt)	x 0.946	= Litres (l)	x 1.057	=	US quarts (US qt)
Imperial gallons (Imp gal)	x 4.546	= Litres (l)	x 0.22	=	Imperial gallons (Imp gal)
Imperial gallons (Imp gal)	x 1.201	= US gallons (US gal)	x 0.833	=	Imperial gallons (Imp gal)
US gallons (US gal)	x 3.785	= Litres (l)	x 0.264	=	US gallons (US gal)

Mass (weight)

Ounces (oz)	x 28.35	= Grams (g)	x 0.035	=	Ounces (oz)
Pounds (lb)	x 0.454	= Kilograms (kg)	x 2.205	=	Pounds (lb)

Force

Ounces-force (ozf; oz)	x 0.278	= Newtons (N)	x 3.6	=	Ounces-force (ozf; oz)
Pounds-force (lbf; lb)	x 4.448	= Newtons (N)	x 0.225	=	Pounds-force (lbf; lb)
Newtons (N)	x 0.1	= Kilograms-force (kgf; kg)	x 9.81	=	Newtons (N)

Pressure

Pounds-force per square inch (psi; lbf/in²; lb/in²)	x 0.070	= Kilograms-force per square centimetre (kgf/cm²; kg/cm²)	x 14.223	=	Pounds-force per square inch (psi; lbf/in²; lb/in²)
Pounds-force per square inch (psi; lbf/in²; lb/in²)	x 0.068	= Atmospheres (atm)	x 14.696	=	Pounds-force per square inch (psi; lbf/in²; lb/in²)
Pounds-force per square inch (psi; lbf/in²; lb/in²)	x 0.069	= Bars	x 14.5	=	Pounds-force per square inch (psi; lbf/in²; lb/in²)
Pounds-force per square inch (psi; lbf/in²; lb/in²)	x 6.895	= Kilopascals (kPa)	x 0.145	=	Pounds-force per square inch (psi; lbf/in²; lb/in²)
Kilopascals (kPa)	x 0.01	= Kilograms-force per square centimetre (kgf/cm²; kg/cm²)	x 98.1	=	Kilopascals (kPa)
Millibar (mbar)	x 100	= Pascals (Pa)	x 0.01	=	Millibar (mbar)
Millibar (mbar)	x 0.0145	= Pounds-force per square inch (psi; lbf/in²; lb/in²)	x 68.947	=	Millibar (mbar)
Millibar (mbar)	x 0.75	= Millimetres of mercury (mmHg)	x 1.333	=	Millibar (mbar)
Millibar (mbar)	x 0.401	= Inches of water (inH₂O)	x 2.491	=	Millibar (mbar)
Millimetres of mercury (mmHg)	x 0.535	= Inches of water (inH₂O)	x 1.868	=	Millimetres of mercury (mmHg)
Inches of water (inH₂O)	x 0.036	= Pounds-force per square inch (psi; lbf/in²; lb/in²)	x 27.68	=	Inches of water (inH₂O)

Torque (moment of force)

Pounds-force inches (lbf in; lb in)	x 1.152	= Kilograms-force centimetre (kgf cm; kg cm)	x 0.868	=	Pounds-force inches (lbf in; lb in)
Pounds-force inches (lbf in; lb in)	x 0.113	= Newton metres (Nm)	x 8.85	=	Pounds-force inches (lbf in; lb in)
Pounds-force inches (lbf in; lb in)	x 0.083	= Pounds-force feet (lbf ft; lb ft)	x 12	=	Pounds-force inches (lbf in; lb in)
Pounds-force feet (lbf ft; lb ft)	x 0.138	= Kilograms-force metres (kgf m; kg m)	x 7.233	=	Pounds-force feet (lbf ft; lb ft)
Pounds-force feet (lbf ft; lb ft)	x 1.356	= Newton metres (Nm)	x 0.738	=	Pounds-force feet (lbf ft; lb ft)
Newton metres (Nm)	x 0.102	= Kilograms-force metres (kgf m; kg m)	x 9.804	=	Newton metres (Nm)

Power

Horsepower (hp)	x 745.7	= Watts (W)	x 0.0013	=	Horsepower (hp)

Velocity (speed)

Miles per hour (miles/hr; mph)	x 1.609	= Kilometres per hour (km/hr; kph)	x 0.621	=	Miles per hour (miles/hr; mph)

Fuel consumption*

Miles per gallon (mpg)	x 0.354	= Kilometres per litre (km/l)	x 2.825	=	Miles per gallon (mpg)

Temperature

Degrees Fahrenheit = (°C x 1.8) + 32   Degrees Celsius (Degrees Centigrade; °C) = (°F - 32) x 0.56

It is common practice to convert from miles per gallon (mpg) to litres/100 kilometres (l/100km), where mpg x l/100 km = 282

Introduction

In less time than it takes to read this introduction, a thief could steal your motorcycle. Returning only to find your bike has gone is one of the worst feelings in the world. Even if the motorcycle is insured against theft, once you've got over the initial shock, you will have the inconvenience of dealing with the police and your insurance company.

The motorcycle is an easy target for the professional thief and the joyrider alike and the official figures on motorcycle theft make for depressing reading; on average a motorcycle is stolen every 16 minutes in the UK!

Motorcycle thefts fall into two categories, those stolen 'to order' and those taken by opportunists. The thief stealing to order will be on the look out for a specific make and model and will go to extraordinary lengths to obtain that motorcycle. The opportunist thief on the other hand will look for easy targets which can be stolen with the minimum of effort and risk.

Whilst it is never going to be possible to make your machine 100% secure, it is estimated that around half of all stolen motorcycles are taken by opportunist thieves. Remember that the opportunist thief is always on the look out for the easy option: if there are two similar motorcycles parked side-by-side, they will target the one with the lowest level of security. By taking a few precautions, you can reduce the chances of your motorcycle being stolen.

Security equipment

There are many specialised motorcycle security devices available and the following text summarises their applications and their good and bad points.

Once you have decided on the type of security equipment which best suits your needs, we recommended that you read one of the many equipment tests regularly carried

Ensure the lock and chain you buy is of good quality and long enough to shackle your bike to a solid object

out by the motorcycle press. These tests compare the products from all the major manufacturers and give impartial ratings on their effectiveness, value-for-money and ease of use.

No one item of security equipment can provide complete protection. It is highly recommended that two or more of the items described below are combined to increase the security of your motorcycle (a lock and chain plus an alarm system is just about ideal). The more security measures fitted to the bike, the less likely it is to be stolen.

Lock and chain

Pros: *Very flexible to use; can be used to secure the motorcycle to almost any immovable object. On some locks and chains, the lock can be used on its own as a disc lock (see below).*

Cons: *Can be very heavy and awkward to carry on the motorcycle, although some types*

will be supplied with a carry bag which can be strapped to the pillion seat.

● Heavy-duty chains and locks are an excellent security measure **(see illustration 1)**. Whenever the motorcycle is parked, use the lock and chain to secure the machine to a solid, immovable object such as a post or railings. This will prevent the machine from being ridden away or being lifted into the back of a van.

● When fitting the chain, always ensure the chain is routed around the motorcycle frame or swingarm **(see illustrations 2 and 3)**. Never merely pass the chain around one of the wheel rims; a thief may unbolt the wheel and lift the rest of the machine into a van, leaving you with just the wheel! Try to avoid having excess chain free, thus making it difficult to use cutting tools, and keep the chain and lock off the ground to prevent thieves attacking it with a cold chisel. Position the lock so that its lock barrel is facing downwards; this will make it harder for the thief to attack the lock mechanism.

Pass the chain through the bike's frame, rather than just through a wheel . . .

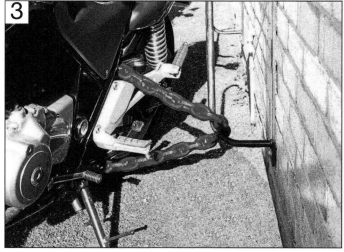

. . . and loop it around a solid object

U-locks

Pros: Highly effective deterrent which can be used to secure the bike to a post or railings. Most U-locks come with a carrier which allows the lock to be easily carried on the bike.

Cons: Not as flexible to use as a lock and chain.

● These are solid locks which are similar in use to a lock and chain. U-locks are lighter than a lock and chain but not so flexible to use. The length and shape of the lock shackle limit the objects to which the bike can be secured **(see illustration 4)**.

Disc locks

Pros: Small, light and very easy to carry; most can be stored underneath the seat.

Cons: Does not prevent the motorcycle being lifted into a van. Can be very embarrassing if you

U-locks can be used to secure the bike to a solid object – ensure you purchase one which is long enough

forget to remove the lock before attempting to ride off!

● Disc locks are designed to be attached to the front brake disc. The lock passes through one of the holes in the disc and prevents the wheel rotating by jamming against the fork/brake caliper **(see illustration 5)**. Some are equipped with an alarm siren which sounds if the disc lock is moved; this not only acts as a theft deterrent but also as a handy reminder if you try to move the bike with the lock still fitted.

● Combining the disc lock with a length of cable which can be looped around a post or railings provides an additional measure of security **(see illustration 6)**.

Alarms and immobilisers

Pros: Once installed it is completely hassle-free to use. If the system is 'Thatcham' or 'Sold Secure-approved', insurance companies may give you a discount.

Cons: Can be expensive to buy and complex to install. No system will prevent the motorcycle from being lifted into a van and taken away.

● Electronic alarms and immobilisers are available to suit a variety of budgets. There are three different types of system available: pure alarms, pure immobilisers, and the more expensive systems which are combined alarm/immobilisers **(see illustration 7)**.

● An alarm system is designed to emit an audible warning if the motorcycle is being tampered with.

● An immobiliser prevents the motorcycle being started and ridden away by disabling its electrical systems.

● When purchasing an alarm/immobiliser system, check the cost of installing the system unless you are able to do it yourself. If the motorcycle is not used regularly, another consideration is the current drain of the system. All alarm/immobiliser systems are powered by the motorcycle's battery; purchasing a system with a very low current drain could prevent the battery losing its charge whilst the motorcycle is not being used.

A typical disc lock attached through one of the holes in the disc

A disc lock combined with a security cable provides additional protection

A typical alarm/immobiliser system

Indelible markings can be applied to most areas of the bike – always apply the manufacturer's sticker to warn off thieves

Chemically-etched code numbers can be applied to main body panels . . .

. . . again, always ensure that the kit manufacturer's sticker is applied in a prominent position

Security marking kits

Pros: *Very cheap and effective deterrent. Many insurance companies will give you a discount on your insurance premium if a recognised security marking kit is used on your motorcycle.*

Cons: *Does not prevent the motorcycle being stolen by joyriders.*

● There are many different types of security marking kits available. The idea is to mark as many parts of the motorcycle as possible with a unique security number (see illustrations 8, 9 and 10). A form will be included with the kit to register your personal details and those of the motorcycle with the kit manufacturer. This register is made available to the police to help them trace the rightful owner of any motorcycle or components which they recover should all other forms of identification have been removed. Always apply the warning stickers provided with the kit to deter thieves.

Ground anchors, wheel clamps and security posts

Pros: *An excellent form of security which will deter all but the most determined of thieves.*

Cons: *Awkward to install and can be expensive.*

● Whilst the motorcycle is at home, it is a good idea to attach it securely to the floor or a solid wall, even if it is kept in a securely locked garage. Various types of ground anchors, security posts and wheel clamps are available for this purpose (see illustration 11). These security devices are either bolted to a solid concrete or brick structure or can be cemented into the ground.

Permanent ground anchors provide an excellent level of security when the bike is at home

Security at home

A high percentage of motorcycle thefts are from the owner's home. Here are some things to consider whenever your motorcycle is at home:

✔ Where possible, always keep the motorcycle in a securely locked garage. Never rely solely on the standard lock on the garage door, these are usual hopelessly inadequate. Fit an additional locking mechanism to the door and consider having the garage alarmed. A security light, activated by a movement sensor, is also a good investment.

✔ Always secure the motorcycle to the ground or a wall, even if it is inside a securely locked garage.

✔ Do not regularly leave the motorcycle outside your home, try to keep it out of sight wherever possible. If a garage is not available, fit a motorcycle cover over the bike to disguise its true identity.

✔ It is not uncommon for thieves to follow a motorcyclist home to find out where the bike is kept. They will then return at a later date. Be aware of this whenever you are returning

home on your motorcycle. If you suspect you are being followed, do not return home, instead ride to a garage or shop and stop as a precaution.

✔ When selling a motorcycle, do not provide your home address or the location where the bike is normally kept. Arrange to meet the buyer at a location away from your home. Thieves have been known to pose as potential buyers to find out where motorcycles are kept and then return later to steal them.

Security away from the home

As well as fitting security equipment to your motorcycle here are a few general rules to follow whenever you park your motorcycle.

✔ Park in a busy, public place.

✔ Use car parks which incorporate security features, such as CCTV.

✔ At night, park in a well-lit area, preferably directly underneath a street light.

✔ Engage the steering lock.

✔ Secure the motorcycle to a solid, immovable object such as a post or railings with an additional lock. If this is not possible,

secure the bike to a friend's motorcycle. Some public parking places provide security loops for motorcycles.

✔ Never leave your helmet or luggage attached to the motorcycle. Take them with you at all times.

Lubricants and fluids

A wide range of lubricants, fluids and cleaning agents is available for motor-cycles. This is a guide as to what is available, its applications and properties.

Four-stroke engine oil

● Engine oil is without doubt the most important component of any four-stroke engine. Modern motorcycle engines place a lot of demands on their oil and choosing the right type is essential. Using an unsuitable oil will lead to an increased rate of engine wear and could result in serious engine damage. Before purchasing oil, always check the recommended oil specification given by the manufacturer. The manufacturer will state a recommended 'type or classification' and also a specific 'viscosity' range for engine oil.

● The oil 'type or classification' is identified by its API (American Petroleum Institute) rating. The API rating will be in the form of two letters, e.g. SG. The S identifies the oil as being suitable for use in a petrol (gasoline) engine (S stands for spark ignition) and the second letter, ranging from A to J, identifies the oil's performance rating. The later this letter, the higher the specification of the oil; for example API SG oil exceeds the requirements of API SF oil. **Note:** *On some oils there may also be a second rating consisting of another two letters, the first letter being C, e.g. API SF/CD. This rating indicates the oil is also suitable for use in a diesel engines (the C stands for compression ignition) and is thus of no relevance for motorcycle use.*

● The 'viscosity' of the oil is identified by its SAE (Society of Automotive Engineers) rating. All modern engines require multigrade oils and the SAE rating will consist of two numbers, the first followed by a W, e.g.

10W/40. The first number indicates the viscosity rating of the oil at low temperatures (W stands for winter – tested at –20°C) and the second number represents the viscosity of the oil at high temperatures (tested at 100°C). The lower the number, the thinner the oil. For example an oil with an SAE 10W/40 rating will give better cold starting and running than an SAE 15W/40 oil.

● As well as ensuring the 'type' and 'viscosity' of the oil match the recommendations, another consideration to make when buying engine oil is whether to purchase a standard mineral-based oil, a semi-synthetic oil (also known as a synthetic blend or synthetic-based oil) or a fully-synthetic oil. Although all oils will have a similar rating and viscosity, their cost will vary considerably; mineral-based oils are the cheapest, the fully-synthetic oils the most expensive with the semi-synthetic oils falling somewhere in-between. This decision is very much up to the owner, but it should be noted that modern synthetic oils have far better lubricating and cleaning qualities than traditional mineral-based oils and tend to retain these properties for far longer. Bearing in mind the operating conditions inside a modern, high-revving motorcycle engine it is highly recommended that a fully synthetic oil is used. The extra expense at each service could save you money in the long term by preventing premature engine wear.

● As a final note always ensure that the oil is specifically designed for use in motorcycle engines. Engine oils designed primarily for use in car engines sometimes contain additives or friction modifiers which could cause clutch slip on a motorcycle fitted with a wet-clutch.

Two-stroke engine oil

● Modern two-stroke engines, with their high power outputs, place high demands on their oil. If engine seizure is to be avoided it is essential that a high-quality oil is used. Two-stroke oils differ hugely from four-stroke oils. The oil lubricates only the crankshaft and piston(s) (the transmission has its own lubricating oil) and is used on a total-loss basis where it is burnt completely during the combustion process.

● The Japanese have recently introduced a classification system for two-strokes oils, the JASO rating. This rating is in the form of two letters, either FA, FB or FC – FA is the lowest classification and FC the highest. Ensure the oil being used meets or exceeds the recommended rating specified by the manufacturer.

● As well as ensuring the oil rating matches the recommendation, another consideration to make when buying engine oil is whether to purchase a standard mineral-based oil, a semi-synthetic oil (also known as a synthetic blend or synthetic-based oil) or a fully-synthetic oil. The cost of each type of oil varies considerably; mineral-based oils are the cheapest, the fully-synthetic oils the most expensive with the semi-synthetic oils falling somewhere in-between. This decision is very much up to the owner, but it should be noted that modern synthetic oils have far better lubricating properties and burn cleaner than traditional mineral-based oils. It is therefore recommended that a fully synthetic oil is used. The extra expense could save you money in the long term by preventing premature engine wear, engine performance will be improved, carbon deposits and exhaust smoke will be reduced.

● Always ensure that the oil is specifically designed for use in an injector system. Many high quality two-stroke oils are designed for competition use and need to be pre-mixed with fuel. These oils are of a much higher viscosity and are not designed to flow through the injector pumps used on road-going two-stroke motorcycles.

Transmission (gear) oil

● On a two-stroke engine, the transmission and clutch are lubricated by their own separate oil bath which must be changed in accordance with the Maintenance Schedule.
● Although the engine and transmission units of most four-strokes use a common lubrication supply, there are some exceptions where the engine and gearbox have separate oil reservoirs and a dry clutch is used.
● Motorcycle manufacturers will either recommend a monograde transmission oil or a four-stroke multigrade engine oil to lubricate the transmission.
● Transmission oils, or gear oils as they are often called, are designed specifically for use in transmission systems. The viscosity of these oils is represented by an SAE number, but the scale of measurement applied is different to that used to grade engine oils. As a rough guide a SAE90 gear oil will be of the same viscosity as an SAE50 engine oil.

Shaft drive oil

● On models equipped with shaft final drive, the shaft drive gears are will have their own oil supply. The manufacturer will state a recommended 'type or classification' and also a specific 'viscosity' range in the same manner as for four-stroke engine oil.
● Gear oil classification is given by the number which follows the API GL (GL standing for gear lubricant) rating, the higher the number, the higher the specification of the oil, e.g. API GL5 oil is a higher specification than API GL4 oil. Ensure the oil meets or

exceeds the classification specified and is of the correct viscosity. The viscosity of gear oils is also represented by an SAE number but the scale of measurement used is different to that used to grade engine oils. As a rough guide an SAE90 gear oil will be of the same viscosity as an SAE50 engine oil.
● If the use of an EP (Extreme Pressure) gear oil is specified, ensure the oil purchased is suitable.

Fork oil and suspension fluid

● Conventional telescopic front forks are hydraulic and require fork oil to work. To ensure the forks function correctly, the fork oil must be changed in accordance with the Maintenance Schedule.
● Fork oil is available in a variety of viscosities, identified by their SAE rating; fork oil ratings vary from light (SAE 5) to heavy (SAE 30). When purchasing fork oil, ensure the viscosity rating matches that specified by the manufacturer.
● Some lubricant manufacturers also produce a range of high-quality suspension fluids which are very similar to fork oil but are designed mainly for competition use. These fluids may have a different viscosity rating system which is not to be confused with the SAE rating of normal fork oil. Refer to the manufacturer's instructions if in any doubt.

Brake and clutch fluid

● All disc brake systems and some clutch systems are hydraulically operated. To ensure correct operation, the hydraulic fluid must be changed in accordance with the Maintenance Schedule.
● Brake and clutch fluid is classified by its DOT rating with most motorcycle manufacturers specifying DOT 3 or 4 fluid. Both fluid types are glycol-based and can be mixed together without adverse effect; DOT 4 fluid exceeds the requirements of DOT 3

fluid. Although it is safe to use DOT 4 fluid in a system designed for use with DOT 3 fluid, never use DOT 3 fluid in a system which specifies the use of DOT 4 as this will adversely affect the system's performance. The type required for the system will be marked on the fluid reservoir cap.
● Some manufacturers also produce a DOT 5 hydraulic fluid. DOT 5 hydraulic fluid is silicone-based and is not compatible with the glycol-based DOT 3 and 4 fluids. Never mix DOT 5 fluid with DOT 3 or 4 fluid as this will seriously affect the performance of the hydraulic system.

Coolant/antifreeze

● When purchasing coolant/antifreeze, always ensure it is suitable for use in an aluminium engine and contains corrosion inhibitors to prevent possible blockages of the internal coolant passages of the system. As a general rule, most coolants are designed to be used neat and should not be diluted whereas antifreeze can be mixed with distilled water to provide a coolant solution of the required strength. Refer to the manufacturer's instructions on the bottle.
● Ensure the coolant is changed in accordance with the Maintenance Schedule.

Chain lube

● Chain lube is an aerosol-type spray lubricant specifically designed for use on motorcycle final drive chains. Chain lube has two functions, to minimise friction between the final drive chain and sprockets and to prevent corrosion of the chain. Regular use of a good-quality chain lube will extend the life of the drive chain and sprockets and thus maximise the power being transmitted from the transmission to the rear wheel.
● When using chain lube, always allow some time for the solvents in the lube to evaporate before riding the motorcycle. This will minimise the amount of lube which will

'fling' off from the chain when the motorcycle is used. If the motorcycle is equipped with an 'O-ring' chain, ensure the chain lube is labelled as being suitable for use on 'O-ring' chains.

Degreasers and solvents

● There are many different types of solvents and degreasers available to remove the grime and grease which accumulate around the motorcycle during normal use. Degreasers and solvents are usually available as an aerosol-type spray or as a liquid which you apply with a brush. Always closely follow the manufacturer's instructions and wear eye protection during use. Be aware that many solvents are flammable and may give off noxious fumes; take adequate precautions when using them (see Safety First!).

● For general cleaning, use one of the many solvents or degreasers available from most motorcycle accessory shops. These solvents are usually applied then left for a certain time before being washed off with water.

Brake cleaner is a solvent specifically designed to remove all traces of oil, grease and dust from braking system components. Brake cleaner is designed to evaporate quickly and leaves behind no residue.

Carburettor cleaner is an aerosol-type solvent specifically designed to clear carburettor blockages and break down the hard deposits and gum often found inside carburettors during overhaul.

Contact cleaner is an aerosol-type solvent designed for cleaning electrical components. The cleaner will remove all traces of oil and dirt from components such as switch contacts or fouled spark plugs and then dry, leaving behind no residue.

Gasket remover is an aerosol-type solvent designed for removing stubborn gaskets from engine components during overhaul. Gasket remover will minimise the amount of scraping required to remove the gasket and therefore reduce the risk of damage to the mating surface.

Spray lubricants

● Aerosol-based spray lubricants are widely available and are excellent for lubricating lever pivots and exposed cables and switches. Try to use a lubricant which is of the dry-film type as the fluid evaporates, leaving behind a dry-film of lubricant. Lubricants which leave behind an oily residue will attract dust and dirt which will increase the rate of wear of the cable/lever.

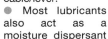

● Most lubricants also act as a moisture dispersant and a penetrating fluid. This means they can also be used to 'dry out' electrical components such as wiring connectors or switches as well as helping to free seized fasteners.

Greases

● Grease is used to lubricate many of the pivot-points. A good-quality multi-purpose grease is suitable for most applications but some manufacturers will specify the use of specialist greases for use on components such as swingarm and suspension linkage bushes. These specialist greases can be purchased from most motorcycle (or car) accessory shops; commonly specified types include molybdenum disulphide grease, lithium-based grease, graphite-based grease, silicone-based grease and high-temperature copper-based grease.

Gasket sealing compounds

● Gasket sealing compounds can be used in conjunction with gaskets, to improve their sealing capabilities, or on their own to seal metal-to-metal joints. Depending on their type, sealing compounds either set hard or stay relatively soft and pliable.

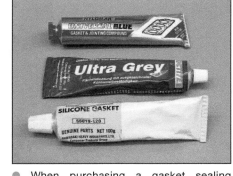

● When purchasing a gasket sealing compound, ensure that it is designed specifically for use on an internal combustion engine. General multi-purpose sealants available from DIY stores may appear visibly similar but they are not designed to withstand the extreme heat or contact with fuel and oil encountered when used on an engine (see 'Tools and Workshop Tips' for further information).

Thread locking compound

● Thread locking compounds are used to secure certain threaded fasteners in position to prevent them from loosening due to vibration. Thread locking compounds can be purchased from most motorcycle (and car) accessory shops. Ensure the threads of the both components are completely clean and dry before sparingly applying the locking compound (see 'Tools and Workshop Tips' for further information).

Fuel additives

● Fuel additives which protect and clean the fuel system components are widely available. These additives are designed to remove all traces of deposits that build up on the carburettors/injectors and prevent wear, helping the fuel system to operate more efficiently. If a fuel additive is being used, check that it is suitable for use with your motorcycle, especially if your motorcycle is equipped with a catalytic converter.

● Octane boosters are also available. These additives are designed to improve the performance of highly-tuned engines being run on normal pump-fuel and are of no real use on standard motorcycles.

About the MOT Test

In the UK, all vehicles more than three years old are subject to an annual test to ensure that they meet minimum safety requirements. A current test certificate must be issued before a machine can be used on public roads, and is required before a road fund licence can be issued. Riding without a current test certificate will also invalidate your insurance.

For most owners, the MOT test is an annual cause for anxiety, and this is largely due to owners not being sure what needs to be checked prior to submitting the scooter for testing. The simple answer is that a fully roadworthy scooter will have no difficulty in passing the test.

This is a guide to getting your scooter through the MOT test. Obviously it will not be possible to examine the scooter to the same standard as the professional MOT tester, particularly in view of the equipment required for some of the checks. However, working through the following procedures will enable you to identify any problem areas before submitting the scooter for the test.

It has only been possible to summarise the test requirements here, based on the regulations in force at the time of printing. Test standards are becoming increasingly stringent, although there are some exemptions for older vehicles. More information about the MOT test can be obtained from the TSO publications, *How Safe is your Motorcycle* and *The MOT Inspection Manual for Motorcycle Testing*.

Many of the checks require that one of the wheels is raised off the ground. Additionally, the help of an assistant may prove useful.

Check that the frame number is clearly visible.

Electrical System

Lights, turn signals, horn and reflector

☐ With the ignition on, check the operation of the following electrical components. **Note:** *The electrical components on certain small-capacity machines are powered by the generator, requiring that the engine is run for this check.*

a) *Headlight and tail light. Check that both illuminate in the low and high beam switch positions.*
b) *Position lights. Check that the front position (or sidelight) and tail light illuminate in this switch position.*
c) *Turn signals. Check that all flash at the correct rate, and that the warning light(s) function correctly. Check that the turn signal switch works correctly.*
d) *Hazard warning system (where fitted). Check that all four turn signals flash in this switch position.*

e) *Brake stop light. Check that the light comes on when the front and rear brakes are independently applied. Models first used on or after 1st April 1986 must have a brake light switch on each brake.*
f) *Horn. Check that the sound is continuous and of reasonable volume.*

☐ Check that there is a red reflector on the rear of the machine, either mounted separately or as part of the tail light lens.
☐ Check the condition of the headlight, tail light and turn signal lenses.

Headlight beam height

☐ The MOT tester will perform a headlight beam height check using specialised beam setting equipment **(see illustration 1)**. This equipment will not be available to the home mechanic, but if you suspect that the headlight is incorrectly set or may have been maladjusted in the past, you can perform a rough test as follows.

☐ Position the scooter in a straight line facing a brick wall. The scooter must be off its stand, upright and with a rider seated. Measure the height from the ground to the centre of the headlight and mark a horizontal line on the wall at this height. Position the scooter 3.8 metres from the wall and draw a vertical line up the wall central to the centreline of the scooter. Switch to dipped beam and check that the beam pattern falls slightly lower than the horizontal line and to the left of the vertical line **(see illustration 2)**.

Headlight beam height checking equipment

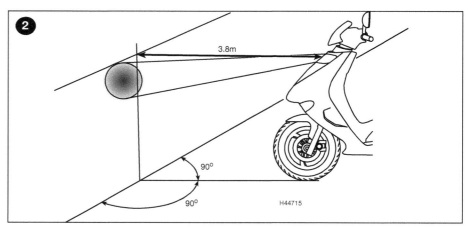

Home workshop beam alignment check

Exhaust System

Exhaust

☐ Check that the exhaust mountings are secure and that the system does not foul any of the rear suspension components.

☐ Start the scooter. When the revs are increased, check that the exhaust is neither holed nor leaking from any of its joints. On a linked system, check that the collector box is not leaking due to corrosion.

☐ Note that the exhaust decibel level ("loudness") of the exhaust) is assessed at the discretion of the tester. If the scooter was first used on or after 1st January 1985 the silencer must carry the BSAU 193 stamp, or a marking relating to its make and model, or be of OE (original equipment) manufacture. If the silencer is marked NOT FOR ROAD USE, RACING USE ONLY or similar, it will fail the MOT.

Steering and Suspension

Steering

☐ With the front wheel raised off the ground, rotate the steering from lock to lock. The handlebar or switches must not contact anything. Problems can be caused by damaged lock stops on the lower yoke and frame, or by the fitting of non-standard handlebars.

☐ When performing the lock to lock check, also ensure that the steering moves freely without drag or notchiness. Steering movement can be impaired by poorly routed cables, or by overtight head bearings or worn bearings. The tester will perform a check of the steering head bearing lower race by mounting the front wheel on a surface plate, then performing a lock to lock check with the weight of the machine on the lower bearing **(see illustration 3)**.

☐ Grasp the fork sliders (lower legs) and attempt to push and pull on the forks **(see illustration 4)**. Any play in the steering head bearings will be felt. Note that in extreme cases, wear of the front fork bushes can be misinterpreted for head bearing play.

☐ Check that the handlebars are securely mounted.

☐ Check that the handlebar grip rubbers are secure. They should by bonded to the bar left end and to the throttle twistgrip on the right end.

Front suspension

☐ With the scooter off the stand, hold the front brake on and pump the front suspension up and down **(see illustration 5)**. Check that the movement is adequately damped.

☐ Inspect the area above and around the front fork oil seals **(see illustration 6)**. There should be no sign of oil on the fork tube (stanchion) nor leaking down the slider (lower leg).

☐ On models with leading or trailing link front suspension, check that there is no freeplay in the linkage when moved from side to side.

Front wheel mounted on a surface plate for steering head bearing lower race check

Checking the steering head bearings for freeplay

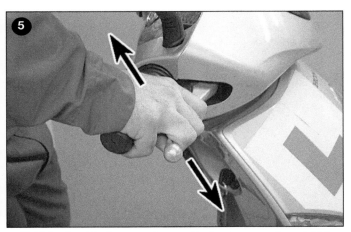

Hold the front brake on and pump the front suspension up and down to check operation

Inspect the area around the fork dust seal for oil leakage

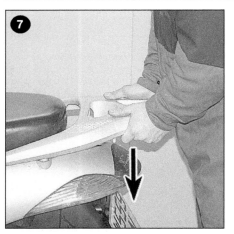

Bounce the rear of the scooter to check rear suspension operation

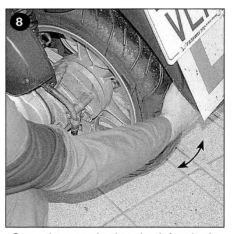

Grasp the rear wheel to check for play in the engine-to-frame mountings

Rear suspension

☐ With the scooter off the stand and an assistant supporting the scooter by its handlebars, bounce the rear suspension (see illustration 7). Check that the suspension components do not foul the bodywork and check that the shock absorber(s) provide adequate damping.

☐ Visually inspect the shock absorber(s) and check that there is no sign of oil leakage from its damper.

☐ With the rear wheel raised off the ground, grasp the wheel as shown and attempt to move it from side to side (see illustration 8). Any play in the engine-to-frame mountings will be felt as movement.

Brakes, Wheels and Tyres

Brakes

☐ With the wheel raised off the ground, apply the brake then free it off, and check that the wheel is about to revolve freely without brake drag.

Brake pad wear can usually be viewed without removing the caliper. Some pads have wear indicator grooves (arrow)

Check for wheel bearing play by trying to move the wheel about the axle (spindle)

☐ On disc brakes, examine the disc itself. Check that it is securely mounted and not cracked.

☐ On disc brakes, view the pad material through the caliper mouth and check that the pads are not worn down beyond the limit (see illustration 9).

☐ On drum brakes, check that when the brake is applied the angle between the operating

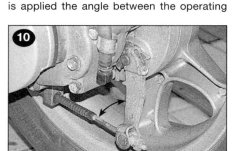

On drum brakes, check the angle of the operating lever with the brake fully applied. Most drum brakes have a wear indicator pointer and scale

Checking the tyre tread depth

lever and cable or rod is not too great (see illustration 10). Check also that the operating lever doesn't foul any other components.

☐ On disc brakes, examine the flexible hoses from top to bottom. Have an assistant hold the brake on so that the fluid in the hose is under pressure, and check that there is no sign of fluid leakage, bulges or cracking. If there are any metal brake pipes or unions, check that these are free from corrosion and damage.

☐ The MOT tester will perform a test of the scooter's braking efficiency based on a calculation of rider and scooter weight. Although this cannot be carried out at home, you can at least ensure that the braking systems are properly maintained. For hydraulic disc brakes, check the fluid level, lever/pedal feel (bleed of air if its spongy) and pad material. For drum brakes, check adjustment, cable or rod operation and shoe lining thickness.

Wheels and tyres

☐ Check the wheel condition. Cast wheels should be free from cracks and if of the built-up design, all fasteners should be secure.

☐ With the wheel raised off the ground, spin the wheel and visually check that the tyre and wheel run true. Check that the tyre does not foul the suspension or mudguards.

☐ With the wheel raised off the ground, grasp the wheel and attempt to move it about the axle (see illustration 11). Any play felt here indicates wheel bearing failure.

☐ Check the tyre tread depth, tread condition and sidewall condition (see illustration 12).

☐ Check the tyre type. Front and rear tyre types must be compatible and be suitable for

Tyre direction of rotation arrow can be found on tyre sidewall

Two straight-edges are used to check wheel alignment

road use. Tyres marked NOT FOR ROAD USE, COMPETITION USE ONLY or similar, will fail the MOT.

☐ If the tyre sidewall carries a direction of rotation arrow, this must be pointing in the direction of normal wheel rotation **(see illustration 13)**.

☐ Check that the wheel axle nuts (where applicable) are properly secured. A self-locking nut or castellated nut with a split-pin or R-pin can be used.

☐ Wheel alignment is checked with the scooter off the stand and a rider seated. With the front wheel pointing straight ahead, two

perfectly straight lengths of metal or wood and placed against the sidewalls of both tyres **(see illustration 14)**. The gap each side of the front tyre must be equidistant on both sides. Incorrect wheel alignment may be due to a cocked rear wheel or in extreme cases, a bent frame.

General checks and condition

☐ Check the security of all major fasteners, bodypanels, seat and mudguards.

☐ Check that the pillion footrests, handlebar levers and stand are securely mounted.

☐ Check for corrosion on the frame or any load-bearing components. If severe, this may affect the structure, particularly under stress.

This Section provides an easy reference-guide to the more common faults that are likely to afflict your machine. Obviously, the opportunities are almost limitless for faults to occur as a result of obscure failures, and to try and cover all eventualities would require a book. Indeed, a number have been written on the subject.

Successful troubleshooting is not a mysterious 'black art' but the application of a bit of knowledge combined with a systematic and logical approach to the problem. Approach any troubleshooting by first accurately identifying the symptom and then checking through the list of possible causes, starting with the simplest or most obvious and progressing in stages to the most complex.

Take nothing for granted, but above all apply liberal quantities of common sense.

The main symptom of a fault is given in the text as a major heading below which are listed the various systems or areas which may contain the fault. Details of each possible cause for a fault and the remedial action to be taken are given, in brief, in the paragraphs below each heading. Further information should be sought in the relevant Chapter.

1 Engine doesn't start or is difficult to start

☐ Starter motor doesn't rotate
☐ Starter motor rotates but engine does not turn over
☐ Starter works but engine won't turn over (seized)
☐ No fuel flow
☐ Engine flooded
☐ No spark or weak spark
☐ Compression low
☐ Stalls after starting
☐ Rough idle

2 Poor running at low speed

☐ Spark weak
☐ Fuel/air mixture incorrect
☐ Compression low
☐ Poor acceleration

3 Poor running or no power at high speed

☐ Firing incorrect
☐ Fuel/air mixture incorrect
☐ Compression low
☐ Knocking or pinking
☐ Miscellaneous causes

4 Overheating

☐ Engine overheats
☐ Firing incorrect
☐ Fuel/air mixture incorrect
☐ Compression too high
☐ Engine load excessive
☐ Lubrication inadequate

5 Transmission problems

☐ No drive to rear wheel
☐ Vibration
☐ Poor performance
☐ Clutch not disengaging completely

6 Abnormal engine noise

☐ Knocking or pinking
☐ Piston slap or rattling
☐ Valve noise
☐ Other noise

7 Abnormal frame and suspension noise

☐ Front end noise
☐ Shock absorber noise
☐ Brake noise

8 Excessive exhaust smoke

☐ White smoke
☐ Black smoke
☐ Brown smoke

9 Poor handling or stability

☐ Handlebar hard to turn
☐ Handlebar shakes or vibrates excessively
☐ Handlebar pulls to one side
☐ Poor shock absorbing qualities

10 Braking problems

☐ Brakes are ineffective
☐ Brake lever pulsates
☐ Brakes drag

11 Electrical problems

☐ Battery dead or weak
☐ Battery overcharged

1 Engine doesn't start or is difficult to start

Starter motor doesn't rotate

☐ Fuse blown. Check fuse and starter circuit (Chapter 9).
☐ Battery voltage low. Check and recharge battery (Chapter 9).
☐ Starter motor defective. Make sure the wiring to the starter is secure. Make sure the starter relay clicks when the start button is pushed. If the relay clicks, then the fault is in the wiring or motor.
☐ Starter relay faulty. Check it (Chapter 9).
☐ Starter button on handlebar not contacting. The contacts could be wet, corroded or dirty. Disassemble and clean the switch (Chapter 9).
☐ Wiring open or shorted. Check all wiring connections and harnesses to make sure that they are dry, tight and not corroded. Also check for broken or frayed wires that can cause a short to earth.
☐ Ignition switch defective. Check the switch according to the procedure in Chapter 9. Renew the switch if it is defective.
☐ Starter safety circuit fault. Check circuit components and wiring (Chapter 9).

Starter motor rotates but engine does not turn over

☐ Starter clutch defective. Inspect and repair or renew (Chapter 2A or 2B).
☐ Damaged starter gears. Inspect and renew the damaged parts (Chapter 2A or 2B).

Starter works but engine won't turn over (seized)

☐ Seized engine caused by one or more internally damaged components. Failure due to wear, abuse or lack of lubrication. Damage can include piston, cylinder, connecting rod, crankshaft and bearings (Chapter 2A or 2B).

No fuel flow – carburettor models

☐ No fuel in tank.
☐ Fuel hose pinched – check the hose and its routing (Chapter 4A).
☐ Fuel hose clogged. Remove the fuel hose and carefully blow through it.
☐ Fuel tank vent blocked. Clean and blow through or replace with a new one (Chapter 4A).
☐ Fuel filter clogged. Renew the filter (Chapter 4A).
☐ Fuel pump faulty. Check the pump (Chapter 4A).
☐ Float needle valve or carburettor jets clogged. The carburettor should be removed and overhauled if draining the float chamber doesn't solve the problem (Chapter 4A).

No fuel flow – fuel injection models

☐ No fuel in tank.
☐ Fuel hose pinched – check the hose and its routing (Chapter 4B).
☐ Fuel hose clogged. Remove the fuel hose and carefully blow through it.
☐ Fuel tank vent in blocked. Clean and blow through or replace with a new one (Chapter 4B).
☐ Fuel pump circuit fault – check all components in the circuit (Chapter 4B).
☐ Fuel pump defective – problems could include a faulty pump motor, faulty pressure regulator or blocked filter (Chapter 4B).
☐ Fuel injection system fault (Chapter 4B).

Engine flooded

☐ On carburettor models the float needle valve could be worn or stuck open. A piece of dirt, rust or other debris can cause the valve to seat improperly, causing excess fuel to be admitted to the float chamber. In this case, the float chamber should be cleaned and the needle valve and seat inspected. If the needle and seat are worn, then the leaking will persist and the parts should be renewed (Chapter 4A).
☐ On fuel injection models the injector could be stuck open, or there could be too much pressure in the system. Check the injector first, then check fuel pressure (Chapter 4B).
☐ Starting technique incorrect. Under normal circumstances the machine should start with no throttle, whatever the temperature.

No spark or weak spark

☐ Battery voltage low. Check and recharge the battery as necessary (Chapter 9).
☐ Spark plug dirty, defective or worn out. Locate reason for fouled plug using spark plug condition chart at the end of this manual and follow the plug maintenance procedures (Chapter 1).
☐ Spark plug cap or lead faulty. Check condition (Chapter 4B or 5).
☐ Spark plug cap not making good contact. Make sure that the plug cap fits snugly over the plug end.
☐ Electronic control unit (ICU/ECM) defective. Check the unit, referring to Chapter 4B or 5 for details.
☐ Pulse generator coil defective. Check it, referring to Chapter 4B or 5 for details.
☐ Ignition coil defective. Check the coil, referring to Chapter 4B or 5.
☐ Wiring shorted or broken. Make sure that all wiring connections are clean, dry and tight. Check for chafed and broken wires (Chapter 9).

Compression low

☐ Spark plug loose (Chapter 1).
☐ Cylinder head not sufficiently tightened down. If the cylinder head is suspected of being loose (Chapter 2A or 2B).
☐ Cylinder and/or piston worn. Excessive wear will cause compression pressure to leak past the rings. This is usually accompanied by worn rings as well. A top-end overhaul is necessary (Chapter 2A or 2B).
☐ Piston rings worn, weak, broken, or sticking. Broken or sticking piston rings usually indicate a lubrication or fuelling problem that causes excess carbon deposits to form on the pistons and rings. Top-end overhaul is necessary (Chapter 2A or 2B).
☐ Piston ring-to-groove clearance excessive. This is caused by excessive wear of the piston ring lands. Piston renewal is necessary (Chapter 2A or 2B).
☐ Cylinder head gasket damaged. If the head is allowed to become loose, or if excessive carbon build-up on the piston crown and combustion chamber causes extremely high compression, the head gasket may leak. Retorquing the head is not always sufficient to restore the seal, so gasket renewal is necessary (Chapter 2A or 2B).
☐ Cylinder head warped. This is caused by overheating or improperly tightened camshaft holder nuts. Machine shop resurfacing or head renewal is necessary (Chapter 2A or 2B).
☐ Incorrect valve clearance. If a valve is not closing completely then engine pressure will leak past the valve. Check and adjust the valve clearances (Chapter 1).
☐ Valve not seating properly. This is caused by a bent valve (from over-revving or improper valve adjustment), burned valve or seat (improper combustion) or an accumulation of carbon deposits on the seat (from combustion or lubrication problems). The valves must be cleaned and/or renewed and the seats serviced if possible (Chapter 2A or 2B).
☐ Valve spring broken or weak. Caused by component failure or wear; the springs must be renewed (Chapter 2A or 2B).

1 Engine doesn't start or is difficult to start (continued)

Stalls after starting – carburettor models
- [ ] Faulty automatic choke unit (Chapter 4A).
- [ ] Faulty idle air control valve (Chapter 4A).
- [ ] Carburettor fault (Chapter 4A).
- [ ] Ignition system fault (Chapter 5).
- [ ] Fuel contaminated. The fuel can be contaminated with either dirt or water, or can change chemically if the machine is allowed to sit for several months or more. Drain the tank and carburettor (Chapter 4A).
- [ ] Intake air leak. Check for loose carburettor-to-intake manifold connection, loose carburettor top (Chapter 4A).

Stalls after starting – fuel injection models
- [ ] Faulty idle air control valve – the valve is part of the throttle body (Chapter 4B).
- [ ] Ignition malfunction (Chapter 4B).
- [ ] Fuel injection system fault (Chapter 4B).

- [ ] Fuel contaminated. The fuel can be contaminated with either dirt or water, or can change chemically if the machine is allowed to sit for several months or more. Drain the tank (Chapter 4B).
- [ ] Intake air leak. Check for loose throttle body-to-intake manifold connection (Chapter 4B).

Rough idle
- [ ] Ignition malfunction (Chapter 4B or 5).
- [ ] Idle speed incorrect (Chapter 1).
- [ ] Carburettor or fuel injection system fault (Chapter 4A or 4B).
- [ ] Fuel contaminated. The fuel can be contaminated with either dirt or water, or can change chemically if the machine is allowed to sit for several months or more. Drain the tank and fuel system components (Chapter 4A or 4B).
- [ ] Intake air leak. Check for loose intake manifold connection (Chapter 4A or 4B).
- [ ] Air filter clogged. Clean or renew the air filter element (Chapter 1).

2 Poor running at low speeds

Spark weak
- [ ] Battery voltage low. Check and recharge battery (Chapter 9).
- [ ] Spark plug fouled, defective or worn out. Refer to Chapter 1 for spark plug maintenance.
- [ ] Spark plug cap or HT wiring defective. Refer to Chapter 4B or 5 for details on the ignition system.
- [ ] Spark plug cap not making contact.
- [ ] Incorrect spark plug. Wrong type, heat range or cap configuration. Check and install correct plug listed in Chapter 1.
- [ ] Electronic control unit (ICU/ECM) defective (Chapter 4B or 5).
- [ ] Pulse generator coil defective (Chapter 4B or 5).
- [ ] Ignition coil defective (Chapter 4B or 5).

Fuel/air mixture incorrect – carburettor models
- [ ] Faulty automatic choke unit (Chapter 4A).
- [ ] Faulty idle air control valve (Chapter 4A).
- [ ] Pilot screw out of adjustment (Chapter 4A).
- [ ] Pilot jet or air passage clogged. Remove and clean the carburettor (Chapter 4A).
- [ ] Air hole clogged. Remove carburettor and blow out all passages (Chapter 4A).
- [ ] Air filter clogged, poorly sealed or missing (Chapter 1).
- [ ] Air filter housing poorly sealed. Look for cracks, holes or loose screws and renew or repair defective parts.
- [ ] Carburettor intake duct loose. Check for cracks, breaks, tears or loose fixings.
- [ ] Fuel tank vent blocked. Clean and blow through or replace with a new one (Chapter 4A).

Fuel/air mixture incorrect – fuel injection models
- [ ] Fuel injector clogged or fuel injection system fault (see Chapter 4B).
- [ ] Air filter clogged, poorly sealed or missing (Chapter 1).
- [ ] Air filter housing poorly sealed. Look for cracks, holes or loose clamps and renew or repair defective parts.
- [ ] Intake air leak. Check for loose throttle body-to-intake manifold connections or a leaking gasket (Chapter 4B).
- [ ] Faulty idle air control valve (Chapter 4B).
- [ ] Fuel tank vent blocked. Clean and blow through or replace with a new one (Chapter 4B).

Compression low
- [ ] Spark plug loose (Chapter 1).
- [ ] Cylinder head not sufficiently tightened down. If the cylinder head is suspected of being loose, then there's a chance that the gasket

or head is damaged if the problem has persisted for any length of time (Chapter 2A or 2B).
- [ ] Cylinder and/or piston worn. Excessive wear will cause compression pressure to leak past the rings. This is usually accompanied by worn rings as well. A top-end overhaul is necessary (Chapter 2A or 2B).
- [ ] Piston rings worn, weak, broken, or sticking. Broken or sticking piston rings usually indicate a lubrication or fuelling problem that causes excess carbon deposits to form on the pistons and rings. Top-end overhaul is necessary (Chapter 2A or 2B).
- [ ] Piston ring-to-groove clearance excessive. This is caused by excessive wear of the piston ring lands. Piston renewal is necessary (Chapter 2A or 2B).
- [ ] Cylinder head gasket damaged. If the head is allowed to become loose, or if excessive carbon build-up on the piston crown and combustion chamber causes extremely high compression, the head gasket may leak. Retorquing the head is not always sufficient to restore the seal, so gasket renewal is necessary (Chapter 2A or 2B).
- [ ] Cylinder head warped. This is caused by overheating or improperly tightened camshaft holder nuts. Machine shop resurfacing or head renewal is necessary (Chapter 2A or 2B).
- [ ] Incorrect valve clearance. If a valve is not closing completely then engine pressure will leak past the valve. Check and adjust the valve clearances (Chapter 1).
- [ ] Valve not seating properly. This is caused by a bent valve (from over-revving or improper valve adjustment), burned valve or seat (improper combustion) or an accumulation of carbon deposits on the seat (from combustion or lubrication problems). The valves must be cleaned and/or renewed and the seats serviced if possible (Chapter 2A or 2B).
- [ ] Valve spring broken or weak. Caused by component failure or wear; the springs must be renewed (Chapter 2A or 2B).

Poor acceleration
- [ ] Carburettor leaking or dirty. Overhaul the carburettor (Chapter 4A).
- [ ] Faulty automatic choke unit or idle air control valve (Chapter 4A or 4B).
- [ ] Fuel injection system fault (Chapter 4B).
- [ ] Timing not advancing. The pulse generator coil or the ignition control unit (ECU) may be defective (Chapter 5).
- [ ] Brakes dragging. Caused by debris which has entered the brake piston seals, or from a warped disc or bent axle.
- [ ] Clutch slipping, drive belt worn, or variator faulty (Chapter 2C).

3 Poor running or no power at high speed

Firing incorrect

- [ ] Air filter clogged. Clean or renew filter (Chapter 1).
- [ ] Spark plug fouled, defective or worn out (Chapter 1).
- [ ] Spark plug cap or HT lead defective. See Chapter 4B or 5 for details of the ignition system.
- [ ] Spark plug cap not in good contact (Chapter 4B or 5).
- [ ] Incorrect spark plug. Wrong type, heat range or cap configuration. Check and install correct plug listed in Chapter 1.
- [ ] Ignition control unit (ICU/ECM) or ignition coil defective (Chapter 4B or 5).

Fuel/air mixture incorrect – carburettor models

- [ ] Faulty automatic choke unit (Chapter 4A).
- [ ] Faulty idle air control valve (Chapter 4A).
- [ ] Pilot screw out of adjustment (Chapter 4A).
- [ ] Pilot jet or air passage clogged. Remove and clean the carburettor (Chapter 4A).
- [ ] Air hole clogged. Remove carburettor and blow out all passages (Chapter 4A).
- [ ] Air filter clogged, poorly sealed or missing (Chapter 1).
- [ ] Air filter housing poorly sealed. Look for cracks, holes or loose screws and renew or repair defective parts.
- [ ] Carburettor intake duct loose. Check for cracks, breaks, tears or loose fixings.
- [ ] Fuel tank vent blocked. Clean and blow through or replace with a new one (Chapter 4A).

Fuel/air mixture incorrect – fuel injection models

- [ ] Fuel injector clogged or fuel injection system fault (see Chapter 4B).
- [ ] Air filter clogged, poorly sealed or missing (Chapter 1).
- [ ] Air filter housing poorly sealed. Look for cracks, holes or loose clamps and renew or repair defective parts.
- [ ] Intake air leak. Check for loose throttle body-to-intake manifold connections or a leaking gasket (Chapter 4B).
- [ ] Faulty idle air control valve (Chapter 4B).
- [ ] Fuel tank vent blocked. Clean and blow through or replace with a new one (Chapter 4B).

Compression low

- [ ] Spark plug loose (Chapter 1).
- [ ] Cylinder head not sufficiently tightened down. If the cylinder head is suspected of being loose, then there's a chance that the gasket or head is damaged if the problem has persisted for any length of time (Chapter 2A or 2B).
- [ ] Cylinder and/or piston worn. Excessive wear will cause compression pressure to leak past the rings. This is usually accompanied by worn rings as well. A top-end overhaul is necessary (Chapter 2A or 2B).
- [ ] Piston rings worn, weak, broken, or sticking. Broken or sticking piston rings usually indicate a lubrication or fuelling problem that causes excess carbon deposits to form on the pistons and rings.

- [ ] Top-end overhaul is necessary (Chapter 2A or 2B).
- [ ] Piston ring-to-groove clearance excessive. This is caused by excessive wear of the piston ring lands. Piston renewal is necessary (Chapter 2A or 2B).
- [ ] Cylinder head gasket damaged. If the head is allowed to become loose, or if excessive carbon build-up on the piston crown and combustion chamber causes extremely high compression, the head gasket may leak. Retorquing the head is not always sufficient to restore the seal, so gasket renewal is necessary (Chapter 2A or 2B).
- [ ] Cylinder head warped. This is caused by overheating or improperly tightened camshaft holder nuts. Machine shop resurfacing or head renewal is necessary (Chapter 2A or 2B).
- [ ] Incorrect valve clearance. If a valve is not closing completely then engine pressure will leak past the valve. Check and adjust the valve clearances (Chapter 1).
- [ ] Valve not seating properly. This is caused by a bent valve (from over-revving or improper valve adjustment), burned valve or seat (improper combustion) or an accumulation of carbon deposits on the seat (from combustion or lubrication problems). The valves must be cleaned and/or renewed and the seats serviced if possible (Chapter 2A or 2B).
- [ ] Valve spring broken or weak. Caused by component failure or wear; the springs must be renewed (Chapter 2A or 2B).

Knocking or pinking

- [ ] Carbon build-up in combustion chamber. Use of a fuel additive that will dissolve the adhesive bonding the carbon particles to the crown and chamber is the easiest way to remove the build-up. Otherwise, the cylinder head will have to be removed and decarbonised (Chapter 2A or 2B).
- [ ] Incorrect or poor quality fuel. Old or improper grades of fuel can cause detonation. This causes the piston to rattle, thus the knocking or pinking sound. Drain old fuel and always use the recommended fuel grade (Chapter 4A or 4B).
- [ ] Spark plug heat range incorrect. Uncontrolled detonation indicates the plug heat range is too hot. The plug in effect becomes a glow plug, raising cylinder temperatures. Install the proper heat range plug (Chapter 1).
- [ ] Improper air/fuel mixture. This will cause the cylinder to run hot, which leads to detonation. Clogged carburettor jets, a fuel injection system fault or an air leak can cause this imbalance (Chapter 4A or 4B).

Miscellaneous causes

- [ ] Throttle valve doesn't open fully. Check the action of the twistgrip, and check the cable for kinks and incorrect routing. Adjust the throttle twistgrip freeplay (Chapter 1).
- [ ] Clutch slipping, drive belt worn, or variator faulty (Chapter 2C).
- [ ] Brakes dragging. Usually caused by debris which has entered the brake piston seals, or from a warped disc or bent axle. Repair as necessary (Chapter 7).

4   Overheating

Cooling system fault

- ☐ Coolant level low. Check and add coolant (*Pre-ride checks*).
- ☐ Leak in cooling system. Check cooling system hoses and radiator for leaks and other damage. Repair or renew parts as necessary (Chapter 3).
- ☐ Thermostat sticking open or closed (Chapter 3).
- ☐ Coolant passages clogged. Drain and flush the entire system, then refill with fresh coolant (Chapter 3).
- ☐ Air lock in system – usually follows draining and refilling of the system. If less than the specified amount of coolant could be added when filling, drain the system again, then refill adding the coolant slowly, and tip the scooter from side to side to dislodge any trapped air (Chapter 3).
- ☐ Water pump defective. Remove the pump and check the components (Chapter 3).
- ☐ Clogged radiator fins. Clean them by blowing compressed air through the fins from the back of the radiator.

Firing incorrect

- ☐ Air filter clogged. Clean or renew filter (Chapter 1).
- ☐ Spark plug fouled, defective or worn out (Chapter 1).
- ☐ Spark plug cap or HT lead defective. See Chapter 4B or 5 for details of the ignition system.
- ☐ Spark plug cap not in good contact.
- ☐ Incorrect spark plug. Wrong type, heat range or cap configuration. Check and install correct plug listed in Chapter 1.
- ☐ Ignition control unit (ICU/ECM) or ignition coil defective (Chapter 4B or 5).

Fuel/air mixture incorrect – carburettor models

- ☐ Faulty automatic choke unit (Chapter 4A).
- ☐ Faulty idle air control valve (Chapter 4A).
- ☐ Pilot screw out of adjustment (Chapter 4A).
- ☐ Pilot jet or air passage clogged. Remove and clean the carburettor (Chapter 4A).
- ☐ Air hole clogged. Remove carburettor and blow out all passages (Chapter 4A).
- ☐ Air filter clogged, poorly sealed or missing (Chapter 1).
- ☐ Air filter housing poorly sealed. Look for cracks, holes or loose screws and renew or repair defective parts.

- ☐ Carburettor intake duct loose. Check for cracks, breaks, tears or loose fixings.
- ☐ Fuel tank vent blocked. Clean and blow through or replace with a new one (Chapter 4A).

Fuel/air mixture incorrect – fuel injection models

- ☐ Fuel injector clogged or fuel injection system fault (see Chapter 4B).
- ☐ Air filter clogged, poorly sealed or missing (Chapter 1).
- ☐ Air filter housing poorly sealed. Look for cracks, holes or loose clamps and renew or repair defective parts.
- ☐ Intake air leak. Check for loose throttle body-to-intake manifold connections or a leaking gasket (Chapter 4B).
- ☐ Faulty idle air control valve (Chapter 4B).
- ☐ Fuel tank vent blocked. Clean and blow through or replace with a new one (Chapter 4B).

Compression too high

- ☐ Carbon build-up in combustion chamber. Use of a fuel additive that will dissolve the adhesive bonding the carbon particles to the piston crown and chamber is the easiest way to remove the build-up. Otherwise, the cylinder head will have to be removed and cleaned (Chapter 2A or 2B).

Engine load excessive

- ☐ Clutch slipping, drive belt worn, or variator faulty (Chapter 2C).
- ☐ Brakes dragging. Usually caused by debris which has entered the brake piston seals, or from a warped disc or bent axle. Repair as necessary (Chapter 7).

Lubrication inadequate

- ☐ Engine oil level too low. Friction caused by intermittent lack of lubrication or from oil that is overworked can cause overheating. The oil provides a definite cooling function in the engine. Check the oil level (*Pre-ride checks*).
- ☐ Poor quality engine oil or incorrect viscosity or type. Oil is rated not only according to viscosity but also according to type. Some oils are not rated high enough for use in this engine. Check the Specifications section and change to the correct oil (*Pre-ride checks*).

5 Transmission problems

No drive to rear wheel

- ☐ Drive belt broken (Chapter 2C).
- ☐ Clutch not engaging (Chapter 2C).
- ☐ Clutch shoes or drum excessively worn (Chapter 2C).

Transmission noise or vibration

- ☐ Bearings worn. Also includes the possibility that the shafts are worn. Overhaul the gearbox (Chapter 2C).
- ☐ Gears worn or chipped (Chapter 2C).
- ☐ Clutch drum worn unevenly (Chapter 2C).
- ☐ Worn bearings or bent shaft (Chapter 2C).
- ☐ Loose clutch assembly nut or drum nut (Chapter 2C).

Poor performance

- ☐ Variator worn or damaged (Chapter 2C).
- ☐ Weak or broken clutch spring (Chapter 2C).
- ☐ Clutch shoes or drum excessively worn (Chapter 2C).
- ☐ Grease, oil or dust on clutch friction material (Chapter 2C).
- ☐ Drive belt excessively worn (Chapter 2C).

Clutch not disengaging completely

- ☐ Weak or broken clutch shoe springs (Chapter 2C).
- ☐ Engine idle speed too high (Chapter 1).

6 Abnormal engine noise

Knocking or pinking

- ☐ Carbon build-up in combustion chamber. Use of a fuel additive that will dissolve the adhesive bonding the carbon particles to the piston crown and chamber is the easiest way to remove the build-up. Otherwise, the cylinder head will have to be removed and decarbonised (Chapter 2A or 2B).
- ☐ Incorrect or poor quality fuel. Old or improper fuel can cause detonation. This causes the piston to rattle, thus the knocking or pinking sound. Drain the old fuel and always use the recommended grade fuel (Chapter 4A or 4B).
- ☐ Spark plug type incorrect. Uncontrolled detonation indicates that the plug heat range is too hot. The plug in effect becomes a glow plug, raising cylinder temperatures. Install the proper plug (Chapter 1).
- ☐ Improper air/fuel mixture. This will cause the cylinder to run hot and lead to detonation. Clogged carburettor jets, a fuel injection system fault or an air leak can cause this imbalance (Chapter 4A or 4B).

Piston slap or rattling

- ☐ Cylinder-to-piston clearance excessive. Caused by improper assembly. Inspect and overhaul top-end parts (Chapter 2A or 2B).
- ☐ Connecting rod bent. Caused by over-revving, trying to start a badly flooded engine or from ingesting a foreign object into the combustion chamber. Renew the damaged parts (Chapter 2A or 2B).
- ☐ Piston pin or piston pin bore worn or seized from wear or lack of lubrication. Renew damaged parts (Chapter 2A or 2B).
- ☐ Piston ring(s) worn, broken or sticking. Overhaul the top-end (Chapter 2A or 2B).
- ☐ Piston seizure damage. Usually from lack of lubrication or overheating. First find and cure the cause of the problem (Chapters 2A, 2B or 3). A new cylinder, piston and piston ring set will have to be fitted.
- ☐ Connecting rod small- or big-end clearance excessive. Caused by excessive wear or lack of lubrication. Renew worn parts (Chapter 2A or 2B).

Other noise

- ☐ Exhaust pipe leaking at cylinder head connection. Caused by improper fit of pipe or damaged gasket. All exhaust fasteners should be tightened evenly and carefully (Chapter 1).
- ☐ Crankshaft runout excessive. Caused by a bent crankshaft (from over-revving) or damage from an upper cylinder component failure (Chapter 2A or 2B).
- ☐ Engine mounting bolts loose. Tighten all engine mounting bolts (Chapter 2A or 2B).
- ☐ Crankshaft bearings worn (Chapter 2A or 2B).

7 Abnormal frame and suspension noise

Front end noise

- [ ] Steering head bearings loose or damaged. Clicks when braking. Check and adjust or replace as necessary (Chapters 1 and 6).
- [ ] Bolts loose. Make sure all bolts are tightened to the specified torque (Chapter 6).
- [ ] Fork tube bent. Good possibility if machine has been in a collision. Renew the tube or the fork assembly (Chapter 6).
- [ ] Front axle or pinch bolt loose. Tighten to the specified torque (Chapter 7).
- [ ] Loose or worn wheel bearings. Check and renew as needed (Chapter 7).

Shock absorber noise

- [ ] Fluid level low due to leakage from defective seal. Shock will be covered with oil. Renew the shock (Chapter 6).
- [ ] Defective shock absorber with internal damage. Renew the shock (Chapter 6).
- [ ] Bent or damaged shock body. Renew the shock (Chapter 6).
- [ ] Loose or worn rear suspension swingarm components. Check and renew as necessary (Chapter 6).

Brake noise

- [ ] Squeal caused by dust on brake pads. Usually found in combination with glazed pads. Renew the pads (Chapter 7).
- [ ] Contamination of brake pads. Oil or brake fluid causing pads chatter or squeal. Renew the pads (Chapter 7).
- [ ] Pads glazed. Caused by excessive heat from prolonged use or from contamination. Do not use sandpaper, emery cloth, carborundum cloth or any other abrasive to roughen the pad surfaces as abrasives will stay in the pad material and damage the disc. A very fine flat file can be used, but pad renewal is advised (Chapter 7).
- [ ] Disc warped. Can cause a chattering, clicking or intermittent squeal. Usually accompanied by a pulsating lever and uneven braking. Check the disc runout (Chapter 7).
- [ ] Loose or worn wheel (front) or transmission (rear) bearings. Check and renew as needed (Chapter 7).

8 Excessive exhaust smoke

White smoke

- [ ] Piston oil ring worn. The ring may be broken or damaged, causing oil from the crankcase to be pulled past the piston into the combustion chamber. Replace the rings with new ones (Chapter 2A or 2B).
- [ ] Cylinder worn, cracked, or scored. Caused by overheating or oil starvation. First find and cure the cause of the problem (Chapters 2A 2B or 3). A new cylinder, piston and piston ring set will have to be fitted.
- [ ] Valve stem seal damaged or worn. Remove valves and replace seals with new ones (Chapter 2A or 2B).
- [ ] Valve guide worn. Perform a complete valve job (Chapter 2A or 2B).
- [ ] Engine oil level too high, which causes the oil to be forced past the rings. Drain oil to the proper level (Chapter 1 and *Pre-ride checks*).
- [ ] Head gasket broken between oil return and cylinder. Causes oil to be pulled into the combustion chamber. Renew the head gasket and check the head for warpage (Chapter 2A or 2B).
- [ ] Abnormal crankcase pressurisation, which forces oil past the rings. Clogged crankcase breather or kinked breather hose is usually the cause.

Black smoke (rich mixture) – carburettor models

- [ ] Air filter clogged. Clean or renew the element (Chapter 1).
- [ ] Main jet too large or loose. Compare the jet size to the Specifications (Chapter 4A).

- [ ] Automatic choke unit or idle air control valve faulty (Chapter 4A).
- [ ] Float needle valve held off needle seat. Clean the float chamber and fuel line and renew the needle if necessary (Chapter 4A).

Black smoke (rich mixture) – fuel injection models

- [ ] Air filter clogged. Clean or renew the element (Chapter 1).
- [ ] Fuel injection system or idle air control valve malfunction (Chapter 4B).
- [ ] Fuel pressure too high. Check the fuel pressure (Chapter 4B).

Brown smoke (lean mixture) – carburettor models

- [ ] Main jet too small or clogged. Lean condition caused by wrong size main jet or by a restricted orifice. Clean float chamber and jets and compare jet size to specifications (Chapter 4A).
- [ ] Fuel flow insufficient. Float needle valve stuck closed due to chemical reaction with old fuel. Restricted fuel hose. Clean hose and float chamber (Chapter 4A).
- [ ] Carburettor clamp or intake manifold bolts loose (Chapter 4A).
- [ ] Air filter poorly sealed or not installed (Chapter 1).

Brown smoke (lean mixture) – fuel injection models

- [ ] Fuel pump faulty or pressure regulator stuck open (Chapter 4B).
- [ ] Throttle body clamp or intake manifold bolts loose (Chapter 4B).
- [ ] Air filter poorly sealed or not installed (Chapter 1).
- [ ] Fuel injection system malfunction (Chapter 4B).

9   Poor handling or stability

Handlebar hard to turn

- [ ] Front tyre air pressure too low (*Pre-ride checks*).
- [ ] Steering head bearing adjuster nut too tight. Check adjustment as described in Chapter 1.
- [ ] Bearings damaged. Roughness can be felt as the bars are turned from side-to-side. Replace bearings and races (Chapter 6).
- [ ] Races dented or worn. Denting results from wear in only one position (e.g. straight ahead), from a collision or hitting a pothole or from dropping the machine. Renew races and bearings (Chapter 6).
- [ ] Steering stem lubrication inadequate. Causes are grease getting hard from age or being washed out by high pressure car washes. Disassemble steering head and repack bearings (Chapter 6).
- [ ] Steering stem bent. Caused by a collision, hitting a pothole or by dropping the machine. Renew damaged part. Don't try to straighten the steering stem (Chapter 6).

Handlebar shakes or vibrates excessively

- [ ] Tyres worn (*Pre-ride checks*).
- [ ] Suspension worn. Renew worn components (Chapter 6).
- [ ] Wheel rim(s) warped or damaged. Inspect wheels for runout (Chapter 7).
- [ ] Wheel bearings worn. Worn wheel bearings (front) or transmission bearings (rear) can cause poor tracking. Worn front bearings will cause wobble (Chapter 7).
- [ ] Handlebar mounting loose (Chapter 6).
- [ ] Front suspension bolts loose. Tighten them to the specified torque (Chapter 6).

- [ ] Engine mounting bolts loose. Will cause excessive vibration with increased engine rpm (Chapter 2A or 2B).

Handlebar pulls to one side

- [ ] Frame bent. Definitely suspect this if the machine has been in a collision. May or may not be accompanied by cracking near the bend. Renew the frame (Chapter 6).
- [ ] Wheels out of alignment. Caused by improper location of axle spacers or from bent steering stem or frame (Chapter 7).
- [ ] Steering stem bent. Caused by impact damage or by dropping the machine. Renew the steering stem (Chapter 6).
- [ ] Fork tube bent. Disassemble the forks and renew the damaged parts (Chapter 6).

Poor shock absorbing qualities

Too hard:
a) *Fork oil quantity excessive (Chapter 6).*
b) *Fork oil viscosity too high (Chapter 6).*
c) *Suspension bent. Causes a harsh, sticking feeling (Chapter 6).*
d) *Fork internal damage (Chapter 6).*
e) *Rear shock internal damage (Chapter 6).*
f) *Tyre pressure too high (Pre-ride checks).*

Too soft:
a) *Fork oil viscosity too light (Chapter 6).*
b) *Fork or shock spring(s) weak or broken (Chapter 6).*
c) *Fork or shock internal damage or leakage (Chapter 6).*

10 Braking problems

Brake is ineffective

- [ ] Air in brake system. Caused by inattention to master cylinder fluid level (*Pre-ride checks*) or by leakage. Locate problem and bleed brake (Chapter 7).
- [ ] Pads or disc worn (Chapters 1 and 7).
- [ ] Brake fluid leak. Locate problem and rectify (Chapter 7).
- [ ] Contaminated pads. Caused by contamination with oil, grease, brake fluid, etc. Renew pads. Clean disc thoroughly with brake cleaner (Chapter 7).
- [ ] Brake fluid deteriorated. Fluid is old or contaminated. Drain system, replenish with new fluid and bleed the system (Chapter 7).
- [ ] Master cylinder internal parts worn or damaged causing fluid to bypass the piston (Chapter 7).
- [ ] Master cylinder bore scratched by foreign material or broken spring. Repair or renew master cylinder (Chapter 7).
- [ ] Disc warped. Renew disc (Chapter 7).

Brake lever pulsates

- [ ] Disc warped. Renew disc (Chapter 7).
- [ ] Axle bent. Renew axle (Chapter 7).
- [ ] Brake caliper bolts loose (Chapter 7).
- [ ] Wheel warped or otherwise damaged (Chapter 7).
- [ ] Wheel or transmission bearings damaged or worn (Chapter 7).

Brake drags

- [ ] Master cylinder piston seized. Caused by wear or damage to piston or cylinder bore (Chapter 7).
- [ ] Lever balky or stuck. Check pivot and lubricate (Chapter 7).
- [ ] Brake caliper piston seized in bore. Caused by wear or ingestion of dirt past deteriorated seal (Chapter 7).
- [ ] Brake pads damaged. Pad material separated from backing plate. Usually caused by faulty manufacturing process or from contact with chemicals. Renew pads (Chapter 7).
- [ ] Caliper slider pins sticking (sliding caliper). Clean the slider pins and apply a smear of silicone grease (Chapter 7).
- [ ] Pads improperly installed (Chapter 7).

11 Electrical problems

Battery dead or weak

- [ ] Battery faulty. Caused by sulphated plates which are shorted through sedimentation. Also, broken battery terminal making only occasional contact (Chapter 9).
- [ ] Battery leads making poor electrical contact (Chapter 9).
- [ ] Load excessive. Caused by addition of high wattage lights or other electrical accessories.
- [ ] Ignition switch defective. Switch either earths internally or fails to shut off system. Renew the switch (Chapter 9).
- [ ] Regulator/rectifier defective (Chapter 9).
- [ ] Alternator stator coil open or shorted (Chapter 9).

- [ ] Wiring faulty. Wiring either shorted to earth or connections loose in ignition, charging or lighting circuits (Chapter 9).

Battery overcharged

- [ ] Regulator/rectifier defective. Overcharging is noticed when battery gets excessively warm (Chapter 9).
- [ ] Battery defective. Renew battery (Chapter 9).
- [ ] Battery amperage too low, wrong type or size. Install manufacturer's specified amp-hour battery to handle charging load (Chapter 9).

A

ABS (Anti-lock braking system) A system, usually electronically controlled, that senses incipient wheel lockup during braking and relieves hydraulic pressure at wheel which is about to skid.
Aftermarket Components suitable for the motorcycle, but not produced by the motorcycle manufacturer.
Allen key A hexagonal wrench which fits into a recessed hexagonal hole.
Alternating current (ac) Current produced by an alternator. Requires converting to direct current by a rectifier for charging purposes.
Alternator Converts mechanical energy from the engine into electrical energy to charge the battery and power the electrical system.
Ampere (amp) A unit of measurement for the flow of electrical current. Current = Volts ÷ Ohms.
Ampere-hour (Ah) Measure of battery capacity.
Angle-tightening A torque expressed in degrees. Often follows a conventional tightening torque for cylinder head or main bearing fasteners **(see illustration)**.

Angle-tightening cylinder head bolts

Antifreeze A substance (usually ethylene glycol) mixed with water, and added to the cooling system, to prevent freezing of the coolant in winter. Antifreeze also contains chemicals to inhibit corrosion and the formation of rust and other deposits that would tend to clog the radiator and coolant passages and reduce cooling efficiency.
Anti-dive System attached to the fork lower leg (slider) to prevent fork dive when braking hard.
Anti-seize compound A coating that reduces the risk of seizing on fasteners that are subjected to high temperatures, such as exhaust clamp bolts and nuts.
API American Petroleum Institute. A quality standard for 4-stroke motor oils.
Asbestos A natural fibrous mineral with great heat resistance, commonly used in the composition of brake friction materials. Asbestos is a health hazard and the dust created by brake systems should never be inhaled or ingested.
ATF Automatic Transmission Fluid. Often used in front forks.
ATU Automatic Timing Unit. Mechanical device for advancing the ignition timing on early engines.
ATV All Terrain Vehicle. Often called a Quad.
Axial play Side-to-side movement.
Axle A shaft on which a wheel revolves. Also known as a spindle.

B

Backlash The amount of movement between meshed components when one component is held still. Usually applies to gear teeth.
Ball bearing A bearing consisting of a hardened inner and outer race with hardened steel balls between the two races.
Bearings Used between two working surfaces to prevent wear of the components and a build-up of heat. Four types of bearing are commonly used on motorcycles: plain shell bearings, ball bearings, tapered roller bearings and needle roller bearings.
Bevel gears Used to turn the drive through 90°. Typical applications are shaft final drive and camshaft drive **(see illustration)**.

Bevel gears are used to turn the drive through 90°

BHP Brake Horsepower. The British measurement for engine power output. Power output is now usually expressed in kilowatts (kW).
Bias-belted tyre Similar construction to radial tyre, but with outer belt running at an angle to the wheel rim.
Big-end bearing The bearing in the end of the connecting rod that's attached to the crankshaft.
Bleeding The process of removing air from an hydraulic system via a bleed nipple or bleed screw.
Bottom-end A description of an engine's crankcase components and all components contained there-in.
BTDC Before Top Dead Centre in terms of piston position. Ignition timing is often expressed in terms of degrees or millimetres BTDC.
Bush A cylindrical metal or rubber component used between two moving parts.
Burr Rough edge left on a component after machining or as a result of excessive wear.

C

Cam chain The chain which takes drive from the crankshaft to the camshaft(s).
Canister The main component in an evaporative emission control system (California market only); contains activated charcoal granules to trap vapours from the fuel system rather than allowing them to vent to the atmosphere.
Castellated Resembling the parapets along the top of a castle wall. For example, a castellated wheel axle or spindle nut.
Catalytic converter A device in the exhaust system of some machines which converts certain pollutants in the exhaust gases into less harmful substances.
Charging system Description of the components which charge the battery, ie the alternator, rectifier and regulator.
Circlip A ring-shaped clip used to prevent endwise movement of cylindrical parts and shafts. An internal circlip is installed in a groove in a housing; an external circlip fits into a groove on the outside of a cylindrical piece such as a shaft. Also known as a snap-ring.
Clearance The amount of space between two parts. For example, between a piston and a cylinder, between a bearing and a journal, etc.
Coil spring A spiral of elastic steel found in various sizes throughout a vehicle, for example as a springing medium in the suspension and in the valve train.
Compression Reduction in volume, and increase in pressure and temperature, of a gas, caused by squeezing it into a smaller space.
Compression damping Controls the speed the suspension compresses when hitting a bump.
Compression ratio The relationship between cylinder volume when the piston is at top dead centre and cylinder volume when the piston is at bottom dead centre.
Continuity The uninterrupted path in the flow of electricity. Little or no measurable resistance.
Continuity tester Self-powered bleeper or test light which indicates continuity.
Cp Candlepower. Bulb rating commonly found on US motorcycles.
Crossply tyre Tyre plies arranged in a criss-cross pattern. Usually four or six plies used, hence 4PR or 6PR in tyre size codes.
Cush drive Rubber damper segments fitted between the rear wheel and final drive sprocket to absorb transmission shocks **(see illustration)**.

Cush drive rubbers dampen out transmission shocks

D

Degree disc Calibrated disc for measuring piston position. Expressed in degrees.
Dial gauge Clock-type gauge with adapters for measuring runout and piston position. Expressed in mm or inches.
Diaphragm The rubber membrane in a master cylinder or carburettor which seals the upper chamber.
Diaphragm spring A single sprung plate often used in clutches.
Direct current (dc) Current produced by a dc generator.

Technical Terms Explained REF•39

Decarbonisation The process of removing carbon deposits - typically from the combustion chamber, valves and exhaust port/system.

Detonation Destructive and damaging explosion of fuel/air mixture in combustion chamber instead of controlled burning.

Diode An electrical valve which only allows current to flow in one direction. Commonly used in rectifiers and starter interlock systems.

Disc valve (or rotary valve) A induction system used on some two-stroke engines.

Double-overhead camshaft (DOHC) An engine that uses two overhead camshafts, one for the intake valves and one for the exhaust valves.

Drivebelt A toothed belt used to transmit drive to the rear wheel on some motorcycles. A drivebelt has also been used to drive the camshafts. Drivebelts are usually made of Kevlar.

Driveshaft Any shaft used to transmit motion. Commonly used when referring to the final driveshaft on shaft drive motorcycles.

E

Earth return The return path of an electrical circuit, utilising the motorcycle's frame.

ECU (Electronic Control Unit) A computer which controls (for instance) an ignition system, or an anti-lock braking system.

EGO Exhaust Gas Oxygen sensor. Sometimes called a Lambda sensor.

Electrolyte The fluid in a lead-acid battery.

EMS (Engine Management System) A computer controlled system which manages the fuel injection and the ignition systems in an integrated fashion.

Endfloat The amount of lengthways movement between two parts. As applied to a crankshaft, the distance that the crankshaft can move side-to-side in the crankcase.

Endless chain A chain having no joining link. Common use for cam chains and final drive chains.

EP (Extreme Pressure) Oil type used in locations where high loads are applied, such as between gear teeth.

Evaporative emission control system Describes a charcoal filled canister which stores fuel vapours from the tank rather than allowing them to vent to the atmosphere. Usually only fitted to California models and referred to as an EVAP system.

Expansion chamber Section of two-stroke engine exhaust system so designed to improve engine efficiency and boost power.

F

Feeler blade or gauge A thin strip or blade of hardened steel, ground to an exact thickness, used to check or measure clearances between parts.

Final drive Description of the drive from the transmission to the rear wheel. Usually by chain or shaft, but sometimes by belt.

Firing order The order in which the engine cylinders fire, or deliver their power strokes, beginning with the number one cylinder.

Flooding Term used to describe a high fuel level in the carburettor float chambers, leading to fuel overflow. Also refers to excess fuel in the combustion chamber due to incorrect starting technique.

Free length The no-load state of a component when measured. Clutch, valve and fork spring lengths are measured at rest, without any preload.

Freeplay The amount of travel before any action takes place. The looseness in a linkage, or an assembly of parts, between the initial application of force and actual movement. For example, the distance the rear brake pedal moves before the rear brake is actuated.

Fuel injection The fuel/air mixture is metered electronically and directed into the engine intake ports (indirect injection) or into the cylinders (direct injection). Sensors supply information on engine speed and conditions.

Fuel/air mixture The charge of fuel and air going into the engine. See **Stoichiometric ratio**.

Fuse An electrical device which protects a circuit against accidental overload. The typical fuse contains a soft piece of metal which is calibrated to melt at a predetermined current flow (expressed as amps) and break the circuit.

G

Gap The distance the spark must travel in jumping from the centre electrode to the side electrode in a spark plug. Also refers to the distance between the ignition rotor and the pickup coil in an electronic ignition system.

Gasket Any thin, soft material - usually cork, cardboard, asbestos or soft metal - installed between two metal surfaces to ensure a good seal. For instance, the cylinder head gasket seals the joint between the block and the cylinder head.

Gauge An instrument panel display used to monitor engine conditions. A gauge with a movable pointer on a dial or a fixed scale is an analogue gauge. A gauge with a numerical readout is called a digital gauge.

Gear ratios The drive ratio of a pair of gears in a gearbox, calculated on their number of teeth.

Glaze-busting see **Honing**

Grinding Process for renovating the valve face and valve seat contact area in the cylinder head.

Gudgeon pin The shaft which connects the connecting rod small-end with the piston. Often called a piston pin or wrist pin.

H

Helical gears Gear teeth are slightly curved and produce less gear noise that straight-cut gears. Often used for primary drives.

Installing a Helicoil thread insert in a cylinder head

Helicoil A thread insert repair system. Commonly used as a repair for stripped spark plug threads **(see illustration)**.

Honing A process used to break down the glaze on a cylinder bore (also called glaze-busting). Can also be carried out to roughen a rebored cylinder to aid ring bedding-in.

HT (High Tension) Description of the electrical circuit from the secondary winding of the ignition coil to the spark plug.

Hydraulic A liquid filled system used to transmit pressure from one component to another. Common uses on motorcycles are brakes and clutches.

Hydrometer An instrument for measuring the specific gravity of a lead-acid battery.

Hygroscopic Water absorbing. In motorcycle applications, braking efficiency will be reduced if DOT 3 or 4 hydraulic fluid absorbs water from the air - care must be taken to keep new brake fluid in tightly sealed containers.

I

lbf ft Pounds-force feet. An imperial unit of torque. Sometimes written as ft-lbs.

lbf in Pound-force inch. An imperial unit of torque, applied to components where a very low torque is required. Sometimes written as in-lbs.

IC Abbreviation for Integrated Circuit.

Ignition advance Means of increasing the timing of the spark at higher engine speeds. Done by mechanical means (ATU) on early engines or electronically by the ignition control unit on later engines.

Ignition timing The moment at which the spark plug fires, expressed in the number of crankshaft degrees before the piston reaches the top of its stroke, or in the number of millimetres before the piston reaches the top of its stroke.

Infinity (∞) Description of an open-circuit electrical state, where no continuity exists.

Inverted forks (upside down forks) The sliders or lower legs are held in the yokes and the fork tubes or stanchions are connected to the wheel axle (spindle). Less unsprung weight and stiffer construction than conventional forks.

J

JASO Quality standard for 2-stroke oils.

Joule The unit of electrical energy.

Journal The bearing surface of a shaft.

K

Kickstart Mechanical means of turning the engine over for starting purposes. Only usually fitted to mopeds, small capacity motorcycles and off-road motorcycles.

Kill switch Handebar-mounted switch for emergency ignition cut-out. Cuts the ignition circuit on all models, and additionally prevent starter motor operation on others.

km Symbol for kilometre.

kmh Abbreviation for kilometres per hour.

L

Lambda (λ) sensor A sensor fitted in the exhaust system to measure the exhaust gas oxygen content (excess air factor).

Lapping see **Grinding**.
LCD Abbreviation for Liquid Crystal Display.
LED Abbreviation for Light Emitting Diode.
Liner A steel cylinder liner inserted in a aluminium alloy cylinder block.
Locknut A nut used to lock an adjustment nut, or other threaded component, in place.
Lockstops The lugs on the lower triple clamp (yoke) which abut those on the frame, preventing handlebar-to-fuel tank contact.
Lockwasher A form of washer designed to prevent an attaching nut from working loose.
LT Low Tension Description of the electrical circuit from the power supply to the primary winding of the ignition coil.

M

Main bearings The bearings between the crankshaft and crankcase.
Maintenance-free (MF) battery A sealed battery which cannot be topped up.
Manometer Mercury-filled calibrated tubes used to measure intake tract vacuum. Used to synchronise carburettors on multi-cylinder engines.
Micrometer A precision measuring instrument that measures component outside diameters **(see illustration)**.

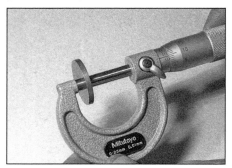

Tappet shims are measured with a micrometer

MON (Motor Octane Number) A measure of a fuel's resistance to knock.
Monograde oil An oil with a single viscosity, eg SAE80W.
Monoshock A single suspension unit linking the swingarm or suspension linkage to the frame.
mph Abbreviation for miles per hour.
Multigrade oil Having a wide viscosity range (eg 10W40). The W stands for Winter, thus the viscosity ranges from SAE10 when cold to SAE40 when hot.
Multimeter An electrical test instrument with the capability to measure voltage, current and resistance. Some meters also incorporate a continuity tester and buzzer.

N

Needle roller bearing Inner race of caged needle rollers and hardened outer race. Examples of uncaged needle rollers can be found on some engines. Commonly used in rear suspension applications and in two-stroke engines.
Nm Newton metres.
NOx Oxides of Nitrogen. A common toxic pollutant emitted by petrol engines at higher temperatures.

O

Octane The measure of a fuel's resistance to knock.
OE (Original Equipment) Relates to components fitted to a motorcycle as standard or replacement parts supplied by the motorcycle manufacturer.
Ohm The unit of electrical resistance. Ohms = Volts ÷ Current.
Ohmmeter An instrument for measuring electrical resistance.
Oil cooler System for diverting engine oil outside of the engine to a radiator for cooling purposes.
Oil injection A system of two-stroke engine lubrication where oil is pump-fed to the engine in accordance with throttle position.
Open-circuit An electrical condition where there is a break in the flow of electricity - no continuity (high resistance).
O-ring A type of sealing ring made of a special rubber-like material; in use, the O-ring is compressed into a groove to provide the sealing action.
Oversize (OS) Term used for piston and ring size options fitted to a rebored cylinder.
Overhead cam (sohc) engine An engine with single camshaft located on top of the cylinder head.
Overhead valve (ohv) engine An engine with the valves located in the cylinder head, but with the camshaft located in the engine block or crankcase.
Oxygen sensor A device installed in the exhaust system which senses the oxygen content in the exhaust and converts this information into an electric current. Also called a Lambda sensor.

P

Plastigauge A thin strip of plastic thread, available in different sizes, used for measuring clearances. For example, a strip of Plastigauge is laid across a bearing journal. The parts are assembled and dismantled; the width of the crushed strip indicates the clearance between journal and bearing.
Polarity Either negative or positive earth (ground), determined by which battery lead is connected to the frame (earth return). Modern motorcycles are usually negative earth.
Pre-ignition A situation where the fuel/air mixture ignites before the spark plug fires. Often due to a hot spot in the combustion chamber caused by carbon build-up. Engine has a tendency to 'run-on'.
Pre-load (suspension) The amount a spring is compressed when in the unloaded state. Preload can be applied by gas, spacer or mechanical adjuster.
Premix The method of engine lubrication on older two-stroke engines. Engine oil is mixed with the petrol in the fuel tank in a specific ratio. The fuel/oil mix is sometimes referred to as "petroil".
Primary drive Description of the drive from the crankshaft to the clutch. Usually by gear or chain.
PS Pfedestärke - a German interpretation of BHP.
PSI Pounds-force per square inch. Imperial measurement of tyre pressure and cylinder pressure measurement.
PTFE Polytetrafluroethylene. A low friction substance.

Pulse secondary air injection system A process of promoting the burning of excess fuel present in the exhaust gases by routing fresh air into the exhaust ports.

Q

Quartz halogen bulb Tungsten filament surrounded by a halogen gas. Typically used for the headlight **(see illustration)**.

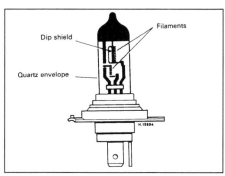

Quartz halogen headlight bulb construction

R

Rack-and-pinion A pinion gear on the end of a shaft that mates with a rack (think of a geared wheel opened up and laid flat). Sometimes used in clutch operating systems.
Radial play Up and down movement about a shaft.
Radial ply tyres Tyre plies run across the tyre (from bead to bead) and around the circumference of the tyre. Less resistant to tread distortion than other tyre types.
Radiator A liquid-to-air heat transfer device designed to reduce the temperature of the coolant in a liquid cooled engine.
Rake A feature of steering geometry - the angle of the steering head in relation to the vertical **(see illustration)**.

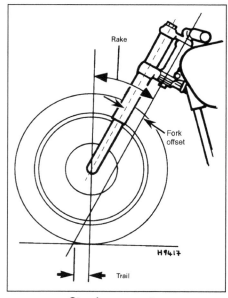

Steering geometry

Rebore Providing a new working surface to the cylinder bore by boring out the old surface. Necessitates the use of oversize piston and rings.

Rebound damping A means of controlling the oscillation of a suspension unit spring after it has been compressed. Resists the spring's natural tendency to bounce back after being compressed.

Rectifier Device for converting the ac output of an alternator into dc for battery charging.

Reed valve An induction system commonly used on two-stroke engines.

Regulator Device for maintaining the charging voltage from the generator or alternator within a specified range.

Relay A electrical device used to switch heavy current on and off by using a low current auxiliary circuit.

Resistance Measured in ohms. An electrical component's ability to pass electrical current.

RON (Research Octane Number) A measure of a fuel's resistance to knock.

rpm revolutions per minute.

Runout The amount of wobble (in-and-out movement) of a wheel or shaft as it's rotated. The amount a shaft rotates 'out-of-true'. The out-of-round condition of a rotating part.

S

SAE (Society of Automotive Engineers) A standard for the viscosity of a fluid.

Sealant A liquid or paste used to prevent leakage at a joint. Sometimes used in conjunction with a gasket.

Service limit Term for the point where a component is no longer useable and must be renewed.

Shaft drive A method of transmitting drive from the transmission to the rear wheel.

Shell bearings Plain bearings consisting of two shell halves. Most often used as big-end and main bearings in a four-stroke engine. Often called bearing inserts.

Shim Thin spacer, commonly used to adjust the clearance or relative positions between two parts. For example, shims inserted into or under tappets or followers to control valve clearances. Clearance is adjusted by changing the thickness of the shim.

Short-circuit An electrical condition where current shorts to earth (ground) bypassing the circuit components.

Skimming Process to correct warpage or repair a damaged surface, eg on brake discs or drums.

Slide-hammer A special puller that screws into or hooks onto a component such as a shaft or bearing; a heavy sliding handle on the shaft bottoms against the end of the shaft to knock the component free.

Small-end bearing The bearing in the upper end of the connecting rod at its joint with the gudgeon pin.

Spalling Damage to camshaft lobes or bearing journals shown as pitting of the working surface.

Specific gravity (SG) The state of charge of the electrolyte in a lead-acid battery. A measure of the electrolyte's density compared with water.

Straight-cut gears Common type gear used on gearbox shafts and for oil pump and water pump drives.

Stanchion The inner sliding part of the front forks, held by the yokes. Often called a fork tube.

Stoichiometric ratio The optimum chemical air/fuel ratio for a petrol engine, said to be 14.7 parts of air to 1 part of fuel.

Sulphuric acid The liquid (electrolyte) used in a lead-acid battery. Poisonous and extremely corrosive.

Surface grinding (lapping) Process to correct a warped gasket face, commonly used on cylinder heads.

T

Tapered-roller bearing Tapered inner race of caged needle rollers and separate tapered outer race. Examples of taper roller bearings can be found on steering heads.

Tappet A cylindrical component which transmits motion from the cam to the valve stem, either directly or via a pushrod and rocker arm. Also called a cam follower.

TCS Traction Control System. An electronically-controlled system which senses wheel spin and reduces engine speed accordingly.

TDC Top Dead Centre denotes that the piston is at its highest point in the cylinder.

Thread-locking compound Solution applied to fastener threads to prevent slackening. Select type to suit application.

Thrust washer A washer positioned between two moving components on a shaft. For example, between gear pinions on gearshaft.

Timing chain See **Cam Chain.**

Timing light Stroboscopic lamp for carrying out ignition timing checks with the engine running.

Top-end A description of an engine's cylinder block, head and valve gear components.

Torque Turning or twisting force about a shaft.

Torque setting A prescribed tightness specified by the motorcycle manufacturer to ensure that the bolt or nut is secured correctly. Undertightening can result in the bolt or nut coming loose or a surface not being sealed. Overtightening can result in stripped threads, distortion or damage to the component being retained.

Torx key A six-point wrench.

Tracer A stripe of a second colour applied to a wire insulator to distinguish that wire from another one with the same colour insulator. For example, Br/W is often used to denote a brown insulator with a white tracer.

Trail A feature of steering geometry. Distance from the steering head axis to the tyre's central contact point.

Triple clamps The cast components which extend from the steering head and support the fork stanchions or tubes. Often called fork yokes.

Turbocharger A centrifugal device, driven by exhaust gases, that pressurises the intake air. Normally used to increase the power output from a given engine displacement.

TWI Abbreviation for Tyre Wear Indicator. Indicates the location of the tread depth indicator bars on tyres.

U

Universal joint or U-joint (UJ) A double-pivoted connection for transmitting power from a driving to a driven shaft through an angle. Typically found in shaft drive assemblies.

Unsprung weight Anything not supported by the bike's suspension (ie the wheel, tyres, brakes, final drive and bottom (moving) part of the suspension).

V

Vacuum gauges Clock-type gauges for measuring intake tract vacuum. Used for carburettor synchronisation on multi-cylinder engines.

Valve A device through which the flow of liquid, gas or vacuum may be stopped, started or regulated by a moveable part that opens, shuts or partially obstructs one or more ports or passageways. The intake and exhaust valves in the cylinder head are of the poppet type.

Valve clearance The clearance between the valve tip (the end of the valve stem) and the rocker arm or tappet/follower. The valve clearance is measured when the valve is closed. The correct clearance is important - if too small the valve won't close fully and will burn out, whereas if too large noisy operation will result.

Valve lift The amount a valve is lifted off its seat by the camshaft lobe.

Valve timing The exact setting for the opening and closing of the valves in relation to piston position.

Vernier caliper A precision measuring instrument that measures inside and outside dimensions. Not quite as accurate as a micrometer, but more convenient.

VIN Vehicle Identification Number. Term for the bike's engine and frame numbers.

Viscosity The thickness of a liquid or its resistance to flow.

Volt A unit for expressing electrical "pressure" in a circuit. Volts = current x ohms.

W

Water pump A mechanically-driven device for moving coolant around the engine.

Watt A unit for expressing electrical power. Watts = volts x current.

Wear limit see **Service limit**

Wet liner A liquid-cooled engine design where the pistons run in liners which are directly surrounded by coolant **(see illustration).**

Wet liner arrangement

Wheelbase Distance from the centre of the front wheel to the centre of the rear wheel.

Wiring harness or loom Describes the electrical wires running the length of the motorcycle and enclosed in tape or plastic sheathing. Wiring coming off the main harness is usually referred to as a sub harness.

Woodruff key A key of semi-circular or square section used to locate a gear to a shaft. Often used to locate the alternator rotor on the crankshaft.

Wrist pin Another name for gudgeon or piston pin.

Note: *References throughout this index are in the form - "Chapter number" • "Page number"*

REF•48 Notes

Preserving Our Motoring Heritage

<
The Model J Duesenberg
Derham Tourster.
Only eight of these
magnificent cars were
ever built – this is the
only example to be found
outside the United States
of America

Almost every car you've ever loved, loathed or desired is gathered under one roof at the Haynes Motor
Museum. Over 300 immaculately presented cars and motorbikes represent every aspect of our motoring
heritage, from elegant reminders of bygone days, such as the superb Model J Duesenberg to curiosities like the
bug-eyed BMW Isetta. There are also many old friends and flames. Perhaps you remember the 1959 Ford
Popular that you did your courting in? The magnificent 'Red Collection' is a spectacle of classic sports cars
including AC, Alfa Romeo, Austin Healey, Ferrari, Lamborghini, Maserati, MG, Riley, Porsche and Triumph.

A Perfect Day Out

Each and every vehicle at the Haynes Motor Museum has played its part in the history and culture of Motoring.
Today, they make a wonderful spectacle and a great day out for all the family. Bring the kids, bring Mum and
Dad, but above all bring your camera to capture those golden memories for ever. You will also find an
impressive array of motoring memorabilia, a comfortable 70 seat video cinema and one of the most extensive
transport book shops in Britain. The Pit Stop Cafe serves everything from a cup of tea to wholesome, home-
made meals or, if you prefer, you can enjoy the large picnic area nestled in the beautiful rural surroundings of
Somerset.

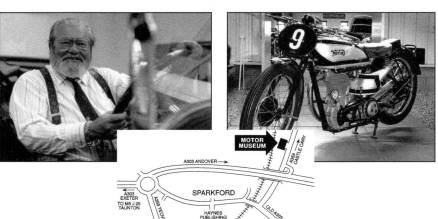

>
John Haynes O.B.E.,
Founder and
Chairman of the
museum at the wheel
of a Haynes Light 12.

<
The 1936 490cc
sohc-engined
International
Norton – well known
for its racing success

The Museum is situated on the A359 Yeovil to Frome road at Sparkford, just off the A303 in Somerset. It is about 40 miles south of Bristol, and
25 minutes drive from the M5 intersection at Taunton.
Open 9.30am - 5.30pm (10.00am - 4.00pm Winter) 7 days a week, *except Christmas Day, Boxing Day and New Years Day*
Special rates available for schools, coach parties and outings Charitable Trust No. 292048